America and the Cold War, 1941–1991

America and the Cold War, 1941–1991

A REALIST INTERPRETATION

Volume 2

Norman A. Graebner, Richard Dean Burns, and Joseph M. Siracusa

Praeger Security International

 PRAEGER

AN IMPRINT OF ABC-CLIO, LLC
Santa Barbara, California • Denver, Colorado • Oxford, England

Library of Congress Cataloging-in-Publication Data

Graebner, Norman A.
  America and the Cold War, 1941-1991 : a realist interpretation / Norman A. Graebner, Richard Dean Burns, Joseph M. Siracusa.
    p. cm.
  Includes bibliographical references and index.
    ISBN 978–0–313–38525–4 (hard copy : alk. paper) — ISBN 978–0–313–38526–1 (ebook)
1. United States—Foreign relations—1945–1989. 2. United States—Politics and government —1945–1989. 3. United States—Foreign relations—Soviet Union. 4. Soviet Union—Foreign relations—United States. 5. Cold War. I. Burns, Richard Dean. II. Siracusa, Joseph M. III. Title.
E744.G683   2010
327.73009′04—dc22   2010000523

ISBN: 978–0–313–38525–4
EISBN: 978–0–313–38526–1

14 13 12 11 10   1 2 3 4 5

This book is also available on the World Wide Web as an eBook.
Visit www.abc-clio.com for details.

Praeger
An Imprint of ABC-CLIO, LLC

ABC-CLIO, LLC
130 Cremona Drive, P.O. Box 1911
Santa Barbara, California 93116-1911

This book is printed on acid-free paper (∞)

Manufactured in the United States of America

Contents

Volume 1

Preface   vii

Introduction   1

Chapter 1   The Grand Alliance   17

Chapter 2   The Road to Yalta   37

Chapter 3   A Troubled World at Peace: 1945   65

Chapter 4   End of the Grand Alliance   97

Chapter 5   The Stabilization of Europe   115

Chapter 6   The Cold War in East Asia   153

Chapter 7   The National Security State   181

Chapter 8   High Tide: The Eisenhower Years   211

Chapter 9   The Kennedy Years   251

Volume 2

Chapter 10 The Cold War at Mid-1960s: The Johnson Years   283

Chapter 11 Watershed: The War in Vietnam   313

Chapter 12 The Search for Détente: Nixon, Kissinger,   343
            and Ford

Chapter 13 The Carter Years   393

Chapter 14 Rise and Fall of the Second Cold War: 441
            Reagan and Gorbachev

Chapter 15 The Final Days of the Cold War   487

Chapter 16 Reflections   513

Notes   527

Selected Bibliography   625

Index   645

CHAPTER 10

The Cold War at Mid-1960s: The Johnson Years

For much of the nation's Cold War elite, for whom the Kennedy and Johnson administrations spoke, the world remained largely bipolar, with Kennedy's final speeches still portraying the United States as freedom's lone defender against an insatiable Communist threat. During April 1963, Kennedy, in characteristic phraseology, observed, "two irreconcilable views of the value, the rights and the role of the individual human being confront the peoples of the world." Dean Rusk, who continued as secretary of state under Johnson, declared as late as September: "There can be no assured and lasting peace until Communist leaders abandon their goal of world revolution."[1]

For America's Cold Warriors, consequently, Moscow could only be dealt with from a position of strength. Expression of this notion began early in the Cold War. "The only way to deal with the Soviet Union, we have found from hard experience," Secretary of State Dean Acheson told a press conference in February 1950, "is to create situations of strength.... When we have reached unity and determination on the part of free nations ... we will be able to evolve working agreements with the Russians." President Kennedy declared characteristically, "It is only when we have military force strong enough to convince the Russians that they will never be able to gain any advantage through military strength that we can hope for fruitful negotiations." Similarly, Secretary Rusk assured the country in 1961: "We are not dealing in the world these days from a position of weakness.... I have no doubt the Soviet government knows a good deal about our strength and has an accurate assessment of it." In defending the nation's decision to construct an antiballistic system, Robert McNamara's successor, Clark Clifford, asserted,

"You deal much better with the Soviet Union when you deal from strength."[2]

That the United States had long possessed sufficient strength for successful negotiation seemed clear enough. Indeed, U.S. diplomats enjoyed the backing of a universally recognized national capacity to reduce much of the earth's surface to rubble in a period of hours. Still there were no fruitful negotiations. Fortunately for Europe, the absence of genuine negotiations was a matter of limited consequence. After mid-century, the actual policies of both the United States and the U.S.S.R., whatever the rhetoric both countries employed, were designed primarily to stabilize a Europe already divided.

Whatever the failures of any serious attempts at diplomacy, those failures resulted less from the elusiveness of power than from the objectives pursued. Whereas the United States and the Soviet Union, in their day-to-day decisions, accepted the European *status quo* as a necessity, their official purposes eliminated, as politically and ideologically unacceptable, the only world available to them. What the United States sought officially was not hegemony, but a compatible world in which all countries would accept the liberal principles of self-determination, peaceful cooperation, and the rule of law. Secretary Rusk, employing standard American rhetoric, reminded a television audience on September 24, 1962, that the United States desired "a peaceful world community of free and independent states, free to choose their own future and their own system so long as it does not threaten the freedom of others." Rusk explained why the United States continued to avoid serious negotiations with the Kremlin. "Our goal, the goal of all free men," he said, "is incompatible with the communist goal. This contest between two incompatible systems and concepts will continue until freedom triumphs. Our objective is a worldwide victory not of one people or one nation over another, but a worldwide victory for all mankind, for freedom and a decent world order."[3] Such goals exceeded the possibilities of negotiation, even of war.

As a stabilizing force, NATO's contribution to postwar Europe, through 20 years of Cold War, was profound. Western policies of containment underwrote the continent's astonishing political and economic achievements. But they failed to eliminate the unforeseen and unwanted consequences of the Allied victory over Germany; they did not unify Germany or erase the Soviet hegemony in Eastern Europe. In the absence of major Cold War victories or defeats for either side, time merely confirmed Europe's de facto postwar boundaries. For most Western Europeans, Soviet policies did not infringe on their prosperity or welfare. What NATO lacked from its initial formulation was not the power, backed by the American nuclear arsenal, to stabilize Europe, but a set of clearly defined goals, achievable within the constraints placed on power by the irrationality of another European war. Nothing would demonstrate so effectively the limited choices confronting the West as the outbreak of a conventional war that involved the forces of the United States and the U.S.S.R., for military conflicts in the 1960s could be limited only by an unequivocal acceptance of the *status quo* as the object of policy.

In nearly two decades of Cold War the U.S.S.R. had achieved no genuine ideological advances in Europe. By the mid-1960s it became apparent to Soviet experts that the earlier assumptions of unity in world Communism, sustaining images of the Kremlin's commanding ideological power, had never been particularly accurate. Rather, the Communist bloc had suffered deep and debilitating divisions, cutting deeply into the discipline that seemed to characterize the early postwar Communist movement. The loss of Yugoslavia in 1948 and the repressions in Poland and Hungary in 1956 demonstrated that the Kremlin's authority extended as far as the reach of its tanks. Outside the Soviet hegemony, the Soviets had some influence in a number of Europe's Communist parties, but the degree of control was inversely proportional to the importance of those parties in the life of their countries. Only extensive concessions, observed George F. Kennan, enabled the Kremlin to maintain some semblance of solidarity with Communist movements beyond the area of military occupation. The conflicting purposes among Communist leaders on matters of foreign policy, national interests, and strategy suggest that little remained of a cohesive international Communist movement. Indeed, for many Soviet experts world Communism no longer existed. That the Soviets could sustain a Communist monolith on free consent was always an illusion.

Nowhere in Asia, Africa, or Latin America could the Kremlin's ideological expansionism overcome the power of nationalism. The political evolution of the Third World mocked the prediction that it would become the decisive battleground in the ideological struggle for the world. Not even Khrushchev's proclaimed support for wars of national liberation offered opportunities for successful Soviet involvement. Where the Soviets managed to maintain some special affinity with Third World regimes, as in Cuba or the United Arab Republic, this was on the basis of mutual interests, not Communist ideology. In the Middle East, Soviet influence was always precarious and limited. The historic Sino-Soviet split did not necessarily weaken China or the

U.S.S.R. militarily, but it created for both a new, powerful, bordering antagonist, and thereby reduced the image and the reality of both Communist giants as dangers to Western interests.

Bipolarism, whether viewed as military, political, or moral, began to disintegrate in the 1950s; by the mid-1960s it had ceased to exist. In his noted address of March 1964, Senator J. William Fulbright of Arkansas, chairman of the Senate Foreign Relations Committee, declared any policy unrealistic that failed to recognize the infinite variety of interests and objectives among nations.[4] For him, the chief myth of the Cold War had been the assumption that the Communist bloc was monolithic, and that the Communist states, as a body, were hostile to the United States. Indeed, most citizens of Communist-led countries were enemies of the Soviet Union. Moscow remained a complicating factor in the life of nations. Still, the world's troubles remained indigenous, unique, historic, and largely domestic. In July 1964, Thomas L. Hughes, State Department director of intelligence and research, suggested a necessary policy reexamination that recognized the complex origins of human conflict: "Let us beware of thinking that all internal violence can be charged off to Communist influence, when that influence may often be merely one element among others. . . . In each situation we confront we must try to identify clearly the real problem, the real enemy, and the real opportunity."

Washington no more than Moscow could hurdle the nationalist barriers that circumscribed their global influence. Western Europe had recovered an identity of its own, its security no longer anchored to U.S. power alone. Its economies had outstripped those of the Communist world. With confidence born of superior economic power, as well as the Kremlin's declining influence and prestige, Western Europe's once-leading nations became increasingly independent in their behavior. Facing profound disagreements in Western capitals on basic definitions of the Soviet problem and Third World upheavals, Washington less and less sought or received European support for its global decisions. Third World countries were equally exempt from any pervading Western influence. Asia existed as a world of its own, following the dictates of its indigenous socialist and nationalist proclivities. Nations inside and outside Europe pursued their own interests and dealt with others largely on their own terms. With each passing year, the United States and the U.S.S.R. faced a growing diffusion of world power, marked by the determination of states to stand against the pretensions of others. Such nations, whether acting independently or in combination, were powerful factors in international stability.

Experience suggested that the real world of sovereign nations was tougher, more resilient, and more resistant to unwanted pressures than that portrayed by the image of a vulnerable world, subject to the bipolar antagonism of two superpowers.

* * *

By the mid-1960s, many leading analysts were questioning the accepted notion of a continuing bipolar East-West arms buildup driven by two conflicting ideologies. The world they perceived had little relationship to that envisioned in official U.S. policies and attitudes. For them many fundamental aspects of world politics never conformed to the Cold War stereotypes. Equally troubling were the powerful, often dramatic, changes in global politics after mid-century that seemed to undermine the foundations of Cold War relationships without producing much official reevaluation. Indeed, for countless Americans and Europeans, the Soviet-American rivalry and the unprecedented arms race that it spawned seemed irrelevant to the main currents of international life.

To its critics, Washington's full spectrum of inflexible positions on questions that mattered, however acceptable to the American public, denied the certainty that the only long-term alternative to cold war was the acceptance of agreements that reflected the realities of global power and the known interests of the country's antagonists. Despite the sword of Damocles suspended over them, the great powers had managed to negotiate away no major issue in dispute throughout the period of the Cold War. That the West had moved through crisis after crisis, neither compromising its established diplomatic posture nor experiencing attack, reflected, for many observers, the existence of mitigating factors in world politics that challenged the concept of a protracted, dangerous confrontation with an international Communist enemy. Not the least of these moderating elements was a general appreciation of the ultimate costs that a nuclear exchange would impose on the warring powers.

By the mid-1960s few writers and scientists regarded nuclear war a reasonable alternative to the perpetuation of the highly satisfactory peace that had become remarkably stabilized through 20 years of Cold War. English philosopher Bertrand Russell had warned that there was no escape from the simple choice that faced humanity: there would be peace or the annihilation of the species. Indeed, officials of both the United States and the U.S.S.R. repeatedly acknowledged this simple reality. Together they sought to encourage caution among defiant, over-demanding elements, at home and abroad, by citing the threat to civilization inherent in the nuclear arms race. "A full-scale nuclear exchange, lasting less than 60 minutes, with the weapons now in existence," President Kennedy warned the nation on July 26, 1963, "could wipe out more than 300 million Americans, Europeans, and Russians, as well as untold numbers elsewhere." Such an exchange, added Secretary Rusk a month later, "could erase all that man has built over the centuries."

Similarly, Chairman Nikita Khrushchev warned the Soviet populace that over a half billion people would be killed in the initial stages of a nuclear war. There would be no escape. Writing in October 1959, the Soviet leader observed that "with military techniques what they are today, there are no inaccessible place in the world. Should a war break out, no country will be able to shut itself off from a crushing blow." Those that survived, Khrushchev added, would envy the dead; the world that they inherited would be so devastated by explosions, poison, and fire that one could hardly conceive the horrors. Nor would the survivors have any assurance that they had experienced the last of such catastrophes. That such predictions of disaster—added to those of writers, statesmen, and scientists—were a force for peace seemed undeniable.[5]

Unfortunately, the inadmissibility of nuclear war was no impediment to the continued proliferation of nuclear weapons. In a nuclear world, the maintenance of an adequate nuclear deterrent remained rational policy, but the design for optimum nuclear preparation, sufficient to deter nuclear attack, remained elusive. Despite the mutual agreement on the irrationality of war, both the United States and the U.S.S.R. perpetuated an unrestricted arms race, largely to guarantee that neither side would use such weapons. For George Kennan, the entire Soviet-American conflict had been reduced largely to "the fantasy world of nuclear weaponry." The arms race, he wrote, was caught up in a momentum without any discernible objective that required the constant preparation for an ever more destructive nuclear war. Indeed, he argued, if the two powers would roll back their nuclear armaments to some reasonable level, the U.S.S.R. would cease to be a threat to American security. No quarrel with the Kremlin would tolerate a resolution at the price of such a war.[6] To Columbia's Marshall D. Shulman and Chicago's Hans J. Morgenthau, it seemed essential that the United States and the U.S.S.R. curtail their nuclear programs, long redundant, and demonstrate more restraint in their military competition. For them, as for Kennan and many scientists, the nuclear arms race, fed by mutual fears that left the rest of the world behind, was the last remaining evidence of a direct Soviet-American clash in world politics.[7]

No wall of power, whatever its magnitude, ever prevented war over long periods of time without the restoration of conditions that rendered it pointless. Europe's peace and stability reflected not merely the mutual fear of nuclear destruction, but, even more, the realization that the unresolved issues between East and West were considerably less than vital for one side or the other. As James Reston observed in the *New York Times*, "At no period of history have enemies faced each other for so long over so vast an area and yet shown more restraint than the Western powers and the Communists." There had been incidents and provocations, but no nation possessing nuclear striking power had passed, or perhaps even approached, the point of no return. Few lines of demarcation could experience tampering without setting off a war. With good reason, the Kremlin had refused repeatedly to follow with action its unsuccessful quests for change in the status of West Berlin. The resolution of no European conflict dictated the necessity or wisdom of another Armageddon.[8] Already the Western powers had coexisted with the Soviet empire in Europe for almost two decades with remarkable success. The United States had demonstrated the capacity and will to maintain the European *status quo* where it mattered; it had demonstrated no power to alter it peacefully. Liberation had been an illusion. To avoid unwanted military confrontation across Europe, the West chose to coexist with the political realities of Soviet-occupied Europe as a matter of necessity. With the Western acceptance of Soviet domination of Eastern Europe, the United States no longer had any serious territorial-political conflict with the U.S.S.R.[9]

Outside the areas of Soviet occupation, policies justified in terms of international Communism seemed equally divorced from reality. For orthodox Marxists, who discounted the power of nationalism, international quarrels among Communists were unthinkable. Stalin and his associates might have assumed that any Communist movement would accept Moscow's direction. In practice, however, the Kremlin quickly abandoned its antinationalism and concomitant hope for a united Communist world. Stalin himself grounded Soviet foreign policy in national interests. Communist dogma emerged neither as a serious guide to Soviet policy or a source of unique expansive power. In Eastern Europe, Stalin merely exploited the instruments of Communism, anchored to Soviet military dominance, to establish and maintain puppet regimes. "It may be," wrote Louis J. Halle, formerly a key member of the Policy Planning Staff, as late as 1959, "that Marx's vision of Utopia is still entertained as a daydream by some Russian Communists. But the men who run things in Moscow are tough, practical operators.... [T]heir working objectives are surely of quite a different order. They are the familiar objectives of a great power, to realize its interests and ambitions as one state in a world of rival states."[10] In the world of power politics, what mattered for the United States was the Kremlin's definition of its territorial and political interests and the strength and will of the external world to resist unwanted Soviet encroachments. Soviet expansion would flow from military conquest, with all the risks that such policy assumed, or it would not occur at all.[11]

* * *

With President Kennedy's assassination in Dallas on November 22, 1963, Vice President Lyndon B. Johnson inherited not only the Kennedy policies, carrying major responsibility for defending Western society in a presumably dangerous world, but also a body of advisers whom he had learned to know and respect—indeed, to hold in awe as members of the country's so-called "best and brightest." His membership in the Kennedy administration, added to the nature of his dramatic, unanticipated succession to the White House, appeared to assure continuity in policy. His foreign policy convictions varied little from those held by the administration's key interpreters of world events.

Contrary to widely held contemporary (and historical) views, Johnson would be more fully involved than Kennedy in directing his administration's foreign policy, tending on occasions toward micromanaging. To a much greater extent than his predecessor, Johnson's decisions emphasized the relationship between domestic and foreign policy. As historian Thomas A. Schwartz has emphasized, he "thoroughly understood that American domestic politics constrained or limited U.S. foreign policy." Johnson also understood that domestic politics of other nations, both allies and adversaries, conditioned their response to Washington's initiatives. Recognizing the issues and limits confronting Allied leaders allowed him to skillfully manage the politics of NATO.

Johnson never allowed his staunchly held anti-Communist views to question "the legitimacy of the Soviet Union." Rather, he was determined to reduce tensions between Washington and Moscow, and as an initial step avoided the use of such terms as "total victory," "captive nations" and "ruthless totalitarians." He only tentatively, however, adapted policies to reshape the profound restraints that the world imposed on its two superpowers. If the new president failed to deal with the core issues—for example, the unification of Germany, removing the threat of nuclear war, and formal recognition of Soviet domination of Eastern Europe—he and his advisers did understand that the Cold War was centered in Europe. "Europeans were not innocent bystanders in the Cold War," as Secretary of State Dean Rusk often noted. "They were the issue."[12]

Johnson's awareness of the dangers posed by nuclear weapons led him to rule out any idea of a "limited nuclear war" or, as Barry Goldwater urged, vesting authority in the supreme commander of NATO to employ nuclear weaponry. At Detroit in September 1964, the president declared: "Modern weapons are not like any other. In the first nuclear exchange, 100 million Americans and more than 100 million Russians would all be dead. And when it was all over, our great cities would be in ashes, our fields would be barren, our industry would be destroyed, and our American dreams would have vanished. As long as I am president, I will bend every effort to make sure that day never comes."[13]

If Johnson was, as biographer Robert Dallek discerned, "a forceful foreign policy leader," he often disguised his intentions behind a bewildering mixture of "rhetorical bombast, jokes, role playing, and folksy sentimentalism." Consequently, H. W. Brands has suggested: "Johnson could be wise, and he could be foolish; his efforts to secure American interest in various parts of the world sometimes succeeded, and sometimes failed. Vietnam was an important influence on American foreign policy, but it wasn't always determinative."[14]

* * *

Kennedy's assassination was a devastating blow to many people throughout Latin America. "The young, dashing president with . . . the beautiful wife who spoke Spanish . . . during their visits to countries in the region," as a noted historian has written, "had captured the imagination and the heart of people rich and poor, old and young, from Mexico to the Southern Cone." Kennedy's Alliance for Progress program, which projected billions of U.S. dollars available in economic development assistance, was greeted rather passively in the United States. But it had created widespread anticipation south of the border, especially among those who saw it as sparking a shift from authoritarian to democratic governments. Many hoped the Alliance would see "the twilight of the tyrants."[15] In Washington, Kennedy saw his program as a counterweight to Communist Cuba and its fiery leader; he hoped it would neutralize Fidel Castro's support for revolution throughout the region.

The Johnson administration, however, took a different, more pragmatic and technical, view of the Alliance for Progress. The new approach prompted Johnson to remove key Kennedy appointees, Edwin M. Martin and Teodoro Moscoso, and combined State Department and AID activities under Thomas C. Mann, former ambassador to Mexico, a trusted fellow Texan and staunch supporter of U.S. business interests. As the new assistant secretary for Inter-American Affairs, Mann argued that any progress toward social and political democracy needed to be evolutionary; revolutionaries, he complained, tended to be Marxist and anti-American. Mann assumed that Castro, as the hemisphere's leading purveyor of revolution, was linked to any Latin American political disturbance. In March 1964, he instituted what became "the Mann doctrine" that redefined the Alliance's essential objectives: "(1) to foster economic growth and be neutral on internal social reforms; (2) to protect U.S. private investments in the hemisphere; (3) to show no preference, through aid or otherwise, for representative democratic institutions; and (4) to oppose communism." Cooperation with authoritarian or military governments was fine as long they were not Communist controlled. In a December 30, 1964 *U.S. News and World Report* article, Mann emphasized the administration's anti-Castro line by calling Cuba a "cancer" that the United States "needed to isolate," while warning that some social reforms had frightened private investment.[16]

Both the Kennedy and Johnson administrations worried about possible Communist influence or domination of other Latin American governments. In January 1963, the Standing Group on Cuba within Kennedy's National Security Council had concluded that the Alliance for Progress was "not strong enough to serve as the first line of defense against subversion" by radicals in the region. Johnson and his advisers, who put much time and energy into the Alliance, were constantly concerned that some political instability, in what they referred to as the Caribbean Danger Zone, might result in "another Cuba." This fear resulted in U.S. policies "driven by spasmodic reactions to crises," according to historian Joseph S. Tulchin, and frequently led to a "style of crisis management through damage control" that slowly reduced options Johnson would consider.[17]

The 1964 Panamanian incident demonstrated the administration's new rigidity. Earlier the Kennedy administration agreed that both the U.S. and Panamanian flags could fly together at certain locations while legitimate Panamanian complaints were examined. A violent confrontation erupted in January 1964 between Panamanian nationals and Canal Zone residents over flying the Panama flag. The clash ultimately resulted in the death of some 20 individuals. After U.S. embassy personnel were evacuated, the rioters destroyed files and office machines, prompting McGeorge Bundy to surmise that "left wing agitators" were attempting to create as much chaos as possible. When President Roberto Chiari insisted that the original treaties governing control of the canal must be renegotiated, Johnson refused. Mann was told that under no circumstances would Washington be pressured to negotiate, for as Bundy put it, "we cannot let our foreign policy be governed by Molotov cocktails." A longtime friend and former colleague, Senator Mike Mansfield, wrote Johnson a short time later urging him to allow negotiations to resolve the minor disputes that confronted the two nations. Local problems that created pressure for social change, he noted, came primarily from the inside.

The Department of State actually drafted an agreement that abrogated existing treaties and provided for negotiation of new ones that recognized Panamanian sovereignty and stipulated a termination date, that essentially eliminated the Canal Zone while providing for the safety of its inhabitants. Discussions extended into 1967 when the new treaties were completed. They would, however, remain in limbo for a decade until President Jimmy Carter acted on them. Nonetheless, the 1964 Panamanian challenge prompted the Johnson administration to make hemispheric stability its top priority to neutralize subversive elements. Long after rioting had ended in Panama, Mann and Johnson insisted that Panama faced a Castro-backed Communist revolution. Promotion of democracy no longer possessed the same priority as supporting stability.[18]

Santo Domingo presented the ultimate test of the Johnson administration's anti-Castro policy in Latin America. That Caribbean country's immediate troubles began in December 1962 when Juan Bosch, a reformist intellectual, overwhelming won election as president. American officials who met him were not impressed. Diplomat George Ball thought him unfit to run a social club, much less a country. Predictably, in September 1963 a military coup overthrew and exiled Bosch. The new regime was scarcely more effective. On April 24, 1965, a few Dominican army units, whose officers favored Bosch, initiated an armed uprising. Communists and other radicals entered the fray leading to general chaos.[19]

President Johnson, on April 28, landed marines and naval personnel ostensibly to protect American lives and restore order, but actually to quash the Communists and Bosch supporters. Mann had concluded that the rebel cause was Communist-dominated; only its defeat, he warned, would prevent another Communist encroachment in the Caribbean. The administration produced lists of Communists involved in the revolt. On April 30, Jack Valenti of the White House staff advised the president that he faced the choice of U.S. intervention or another Castroist triumph. Valenti commented: "One thing is clear: A Castro victor in D.R. [the Dominican Republic] would be the worst domestic political disaster we could possibly suffer."[20] The administration did not want "another Cuba." On May 3, the president told the Building Trades Council that he "didn't propose to sit here" in his rocking chair and "let the Communists set up any government in the Western Hemisphere." This bald declaration of Latin America as the United States' dominate sphere of interest has been referred to as Johnson's "rocking chair doctrine."

The president claimed that the U.S. ambassador to Santo Domingo, W. Tapley Bennett, insisted that he "must land troops immediately or ... American blood will run in the streets." Shortly, however, the administration's hemispheric anti-Communist program began to unravel. Correspondents in Santo Domingo discovered that the lists of alleged Communists released by the U.S. embassy were largely incorrect. Meanwhile, American observers learned that the military junta the administration supported was too narrowly based to survive the assaults of the pro-Bosch forces. The president dispatched Ellsworth Bunker, ambassador to the Organization of American States (OAS), to the Dominican Republic where, with infinite patience, skill, and OAS support, he negotiated an interim government under Hector Garcia Godoy. Godoy arranged an election for mid-1966 that Bosch lost to Joaquin Balaguer.[21]

By the end of the decade, the objectives announced in eloquent fashion at Punta del Este in 1961 were on the wane. The ongoing contributions of the Agency for International Development and the expansion of the Inter-American Development Bank allowed the Alliance for Progress to leave a permanent legacy; but hemispheric relations continue to be diminished by the fear of Cuban subversion. The persistent, knee-jerk rejection of all Cuban proposals, often for domestic political reasons, carried a penalty that neither Kennedy nor

Johnson likely grasped. It was the ultimate irony that the United States came to be increasingly perceived in Latin America "not as a force for change, reform, and democracy," Tulchin argues, "but as a counter-revolutionary power, a reactionary force in hemispheric affairs." Washington had presented an almost compulsive opposition to reformist governments and a poorly managed endorsement of authoritarian and military ones "whose only claim to legitimacy was fervent anticommunism and the violent suppression of dissidents."[22]

Had not Johnson been caught up in Asian affairs after 1964, perhaps he would have been able to harness his political energy to an improvement of hemispheric relations. But East Asian events came to consume his attention.

* * *

Johnson inherited Washington's potentially dangerous, noncompromising U.S. posture toward China. The State Department, recognizing the deepening Sino-Soviet schism, initially hoped that the People's Republic somehow might be brought into a new alignment with Washington against Moscow. In an address to the Commonwealth Club of San Francisco on December 13, 1963, Assistant Secretary of State Roger Hilsman suggested that the new administration might be prepared to undertake a more pragmatic approach to the China question. While acknowledging that Taiwan would continue to enjoy U.S. protection, he offered the possibility of a "two China" policy because the People's Republic was unlikely to collapse. While Hilsman offered little that was new, his speech caused a sensation, eliciting favorable comments from individuals at home and abroad who surmised that the administration was adopting a more constructive approach. Surprisingly, there was little domestic opposition to the notion.

As it became evident that China was determined to join the nuclear weapons club, Washington launched futile efforts to engage Beijing in discussions aimed at limiting its nuclear programs. Ignoring calls to participate in conferences at Geneva, Beijing officials refused to sign the nuclear test ban and nonproliferation pacts insisting that they were designed to guarantee a Soviet-American monopoly. With China refusing to curb its nuclear intentions, Johnson, Rusk, McNamara, and CIA director John McCone explored the possibility of approaching Moscow for a "preventive military action." Nothing came of the discussion and the administration accepted a nuclear China, while hastening to inform its Asian friends that China's primitive devices did not alter the balance of power.

With the explosion of its nuclear device in October 1964, and its call for global revolution, China was seen in Washington as the world's gravest danger to peace and security, surpassing the U.S.S.R. In December 1965, McNamara warned the NATO ministers that soon China, possessing nuclear weapons and an adequate delivery system, would pose a threat to Europe itself. In the United Nations, Secretary Rusk, supported by Ambassador Arthur Goldberg, insisted that the United States would never revise its commitment to the Republic of China or accept mainland Chinese membership in the United Nations. "The admission of Peiping," warned Goldberg, "would bring into our midst a force determined to destroy the orderly and progressive world which the United Nations has been helping to build over the past 20 years."[23] Recognition of the Beijing regime would only encourage its violence nature, reward its international misbehavior, and strengthen its belief in the righteousness of its ideology.

What confirmed Washington's perception of a dangerous and aggressive China was Marshal Lin Piao's doctrinal article that appeared in the Beijing press on September 3, 1965. This manifesto by the Chinese Defense Minister proclaimed a worldwide people's war against the West thus reaffirming Beijing's commitment to global revolution. For Lin Piao, the countryside, the underdeveloped regions of Asia, Africa, and Latin America, would provide the revolutionary bases from which the revolutionaries would achieve a final victory over the cities—the industrial regions of North America and Western Europe. This revolution, he admitted, would be long and costly, but it would triumph.[24] Washington measured Lin Piao's call for revolutionary action with Indonesian President Sukarno's decision in early 1965 to withdraw from the United Nations and embrace Beijing. The Indonesian president's endorsement of Communist policies and the repeated anti-Americanism demonstrations at the U.S. embassy were seen as a product of China's new belligerency. Even though a coup by General Suharto a month later returned a more tractable Indonesian government, U.S. officials and friends of Chiang Kai-shek responded to Lin Piao's call for revolution with renewed fears of Beijing.

Rusk advised the nation in April 1966, "Peking is prepared to train and indoctrinate the leaders of these revolutions and to support them with funds, arms, and propaganda, as well as politically. It is even prepared to manufacture these revolutionary movements out of whole cloth." China's alleged support for global revolution provided the ultimate rationale for a policy of universal opposition to China; Lin Piao had announced to the world both the ends and the means of

Chinese expansionism. Beijing's new challenge, warned Rusk, would lead to catastrophe if not met by a timely, if indefinable, response.[25]

Nevertheless, a somewhat greater flexibility in policy slowly emerged in Washington. In contrast to the earlier Eisenhower and Kennedy hard-line condemnation of mainland China, the United States now offered some limited initiatives. In 1965–1966, Washington eased travel restrictions for certain classes of professionals; in 1967 it lifted prohibitions on the sale of pharmaceuticals for several extremely contagious diseases; and in 1968 it invited Chinese journalists to witness and report on the presidential campaign. If the opportunity arose, American officials abroad were permitted to engage in informal social contract with Communist Chinese; however, they were to avoid "conveying the public impression of a change in US policy of nonrecognition." Beijing rebuffed these American initiatives, insisting improvement of relations depended upon recognizing Taiwan as part of Communist China.

Official efforts to sustain the perennial anti-Chinese consensus at home were doomed to failure. That behavior toward mainland China, with rationales that had little relation to reality, had long faced a telling

Figure 10.1
(L to R) Secretary of State Rusk, President Johnson, and Secretary of Defense McNamara at a Cabinet Meeting, February 9, 1968 (Courtesy: Lyndon B. Johnson Library)

criticism from those, in Washington and out, who denied the United States had any genuine interests or objectives in Asia demanding the endless, ineffectual crusade. As late as 1965, the Committee of One Million, Nationalist China's powerful American lobby, could still muster majorities in both houses of Congress, but it could no longer wield much influence outside government or in the United Nations. In December 1966, several senators, including staunch Nationalist Chinese supporter Paul Douglas of Illinois, formally severed their ties with the committee. By 1968, the committee had fewer than one hundred supporters in the House and failed that year to extract a hard anti-Beijing statement from Republican candidate Richard Nixon. Indeed, much of the Congress and the country's intellectual community demanded a new approach to China.[26]

* * *

In Europe, Johnson faced a series of significant challenges ranging from preventing West Germany from gaining nuclear arms, to Charles de Gaulle's challenge of Washington's Southeast Asia policy, and to France's withdrawal from NATO. However, as Thomas Schwartz concludes, Johnson's ability to deal with them and hold the alliance together was "impressive."

By June 1963, Kennedy administration's tepid interest for the Multilateral Defense Force (MLF), concocted in an effort to provide NATO with a voice in decision-making regarding use of nuclear weapons, had waned. Their original interest in MLF stemmed in part from the need to sooth British sensitivities following cancellation of Skybolt, an air-to-ground missile, when the improved Polaris submarine-launched missile proved more effective. Kennedy's national security adviser, McGeorge Bundy, noted three strike against MLF: it had gained little Western European support, France's de Gaulle had failed to obtain German support for his nuclear force, and the Soviets—who were prepared to sign a nuclear test ban—were opposed to it. Many of its critics labeled the MLF the "multifarce." Nonetheless, in April 1964, Johnson renewed interest in nuclear sharing within NATO, determined to obtain NATO approval of MLF by year's end, for he viewed MLF as a means of curbing West Germany's interest in nuclear weaponry and diminishing the significance of de Gaulle's *force de frappe*. His decision pitted MLF advocates in the State Department, who saw it as a means of European integration under U.S. management, against the U.S. Arms Control and Disarmament Agency seeking to halt nuclear proliferation. MLF stalwarts in

State hoped the "shared decision-making" would eventually lead London and Paris to phase out their nuclear weapons systems and assume the costs of U.S. forces stationed in Europe. But Washington was not prepared to give up its veto over nuclear weapons usage. In a restatement of the standard assurances that the United States was "prepared to make nuclear decisions jointly with Europe," Secretary Rusk laid out for the Italian ambassador, perhaps unintentionally, what "jointly" actually meant. Europe must make the choices the United States wanted. "We do not want separate European and U.S. decisions", he continued. "We will not accept a situation in which Europe can in fact decide for us on the use of nuclear weapons, while we have 95% of the total alliance power." Only the West German government expressed interest in the MLF program in hopes of tying the United States ever closer to Germany's defense and, at the same time, employing it as a bargaining chip in reunification negotiations. Britain, France, and the Soviet Union were outspoken in their opposition, the Soviet Union urging instead a focus on nonproliferation. With Congress also opposed to the idea of nuclear sharing, the Johnson administration finally decided to "arrange to let MLF sink out of sight."[27]

Late in January 1964, in a dramatic press conference, de Gaulle openly defied U.S. Far Eastern policy by announcing the French recognition of mainland China and stressing again the need for the neutralization of Southeast Asia.[28] Never before had French policies clashed so directly and universally with those of the United States. Then in the summer of 1965, de Gaulle proclaimed that France would no longer tolerate its subordinate position in the Atlantic Alliance. Not without reason. Throughout NATO's history, U.S. officers had always held the two supreme command posts. Of the ten principal subordinate commands, British officers always held six, the United States three, and France never more than one. In September, de Gaulle declared that France would terminate that subordination no later than 1969. But on February 11, 1966, the French leader informed a press conference that France would withdraw all French officers and troops from NATO's integrated command and remove all military installations not under exclusive French control. French independence, he said, would permit nothing less. Premier Georges Pompidou explained to the French Assembly that France would continue to favor nuclear deterrence above flexible response—a device, he noted, to limit a future war to European battlefields and spare the territories of the United States. France ran no risks. As de Gaulle pointed out, the United States could not defend Europe without defending France.[29]

American reaction to de Gaulle's repeated assertions of French independence was not unanimous. If Johnson personally downplayed de Gaulle's actions, other in Washington denounced the French leader as rude and malicious. Those who placed faith in Western power and unity believed de Gaulle's policies both dishonest and disastrous. Acheson, key architect of the NATO alliance, termed the French leader's behavior "an erosion on one side of the Grand Alliance." French policy, he added, "increases the difficulty of action within the alliance by opposition to joint and integrated measures designed to advance common interests and solve common problems."[30] To other American analysts, conscious of the changes the past two decades had wrought in Europe's economic and military progress, de Gaulle's challenge to American policies was both rational and predictable.

The Atlantic Alliance remained what President Truman described as a "shield against aggression." But even this continuing common interest in mutual defense did not, in itself, create a body of policy. Indeed, after 15 years of NATO the common policies required to implement the alliance remained elusive. There was not one European issue, political or military, on which all members agreed. On questions outside Europe, the United States stood almost alone, pursuing unilateral policies or none at all. Ultimately the challenge to allied unity rested on the sheer quality of U.S. foreign policy, for no country would willingly follow another to its destruction.

* * *

Caught up with the continuing crises unfolding in Southeast Asia, Johnson initially ignored the Middle East. Nevertheless, U.S. interests were at stake in the region. There was the problem of how to contain Moscow's expanding influence, especially its issuing credits and offering weapons to Arab states. Closely connected to this dilemma was Israel's survival, a significant factor in American domestic politics and well as a key to maintaining a balance of power in the Middle East. Finally, there was the matter vital to the economic health of U.S. allies—maintaining the flow of oil to industries in Europe and Japan. The National Security Council (NSC) Planning Board crystallized the growing feeling within the Eisenhower White House and the State Department. "If we choose to combat radical Arab nationalism and to hold Persian Gulf oil by force if necessary," the planning board reasoned, "a logical corollary would be to support Israel as the only strong pro-West power left in the Near East."[31]

During the Kennedy administration's brief tenure a "special relationship" between the United States and Israel evolved. Increased military support of Israel was the by-product of the informal alliance, cemented in Kennedy's meeting with Foreign Minister Golda Meir on December 27, 1962. There was a caveat however, as Kennedy explained, "for us to play properly the role we are called to play, we cannot afford the luxury of identifying Israel . . . as our exclusive friend . . . and letting other countries go. If we pulled out of the Arab Middle East and maintained our ties only with Israel this would not be in Israel's best interests."[32] In preparation for the meeting with Meir, State submitted briefing material to the White House. Much of Washington was more concerned with the fate of Palestinian refugees, Israel's nuclear facilities, and military aid.[33]

Affairs in the Middle East were relatively stable during 1963 when Johnson assumed the presidency and set about preparing for the 1964 presidential campaign. Focusing on domestic reforms and Vietnam, he handed over Middle Eastern matters to his secretary of state and national security adviser who were largely successful in guiding policy. Johnson reassured Israeli President Zalman Shazar that "there would be no diminution in U.S. support of Israel as a result of President Kennedy's death." Indeed, Washington's support might even be greater.[34] American policy was further influenced by Johnson's sympathies toward Israel. His own National Security Advisor, Walt Rostow, described Johnson as "the most pro-Semitic man" he had ever met.[35] Yet, a National Security Council staff member, Robert W. Komer, worried about the Israeli-American embrace. He suggested to Johnson that while he could assure Israeli Prime Minister Levi Eshkol of U.S. support, he should inform the prime minister, "The one thing we ask of Israel is not to keep trying to force us to an all-out pro-Israel policy." The United States needed to maintain at least the public image of a balance between the Arabs and Israel to prevent the Soviet getting a foothold in the Middle East.[36]

Meanwhile Washington's relations with its Arab counterparts grew worse as Arab moderates' sense of isolation and fear that their positions grew increasingly tenuous. The Palestine Liberation Organization (PLO) was established in May 1964. Both the PLO and its military wing, the Palestinian Liberation Army, were formally recognized by the Arab world later that year. The Arab Middle East was undergoing radical transformation in what has been termed the Arab Cold War. Not surprisingly, the bilateral relationship between Israel and the United States strengthened as a result. Moscow's ever-present strategic alliances with radical Arab regimes, such as Gamal Abdel Nasser's Egypt, gradually fed the mounting hostility between the United States and the Arab world. The charismatic Nasser was a major player in Middle Eastern affairs from November 1963 to January 1969. "Virtually every event of consequence bore his imprint as he rallied Arab masses, manipulated American presidents and Soviet premiers, terrified local potentates, and ranted against Israel," Warren Cohen has written. "Only in the crisis in Cyprus was he peripheral— and even there his existence increased American anxiety. Important supporting roles were played by Johnson, Archbishop Makarios in Cyprus, King Faisal of Saudi Arabia, Levi Eshkol, prime minister of Israel, the shah of Iran, and the men in the Kremlin."[37] If Kennedy thought Nasser to be an interesting figure, Johnson did not.

The Johnson White House was continually frustrated by the Arab world, particularly by Nasser.[38] Differences emerged between Cairo and Washington over Nasser's role in the chaotic affairs of Yemen that brought Egypt and Saudi Arabia into conflict. Both the Israelis and Saudis opposed Egypt's armed intervention, while both the United States and the U.S.S.R. jockeyed for influence. In Washington, officials had learned from their Vietnam experience; they avoided becoming enmeshed in Yemeni affairs. Moscow officials were not as fortunate for they invested considerable for little gain. American-Egyptian relations suffered a setback as Congress cancelled U.S. economic assistance to Cairo.[39]

Meanwhile, a serious crisis was developing on the island of Cyprus in the eastern Mediterranean that could result in armed hostilities between two NATO allies, Greece and Turkey. In December 1963, the Greek-Cypriot president of Cyprus, Archbishop Makarios, declared that he would no longer recognize the constitutional protections accorded to the minority Turkish Cypriots. Before the month was over, Greek Cypriots in Nicosia had massacred some 300 Turkish Cypriots. A succession of officials, including Under Secretary of State George Ball, UN diplomat Ralph Bunche, former secretary of state Dean Acheson, and Senator J. William Fulbright, traveled to Nicosia in 1964, but failed to persuade Makarios to halt the attacks on Turkish-Cypriot villagers. The Archbishop, instead, sought Soviet and Egyptian support. All he received was verbal endorsements. In 1967, infuriated Turkish officials were preparing to invade the island but were dissuaded by the U.S. officials who succeeded in negotiating a temporary settlement that lasted until the mid-1970s. Johnson had escaped a crisis, perhaps losing some unneeded Greek votes in 1964. Nikita Khrushchev had refused to intervene, playing both sides of the dispute, yet Moscow did benefit from the strife created by Makarios. Washington's relations with both Greece and Turkey remained strained and NATO's southern flank was weakened.[40]

Yet Johnson's real frustration lay with the Soviet Union, which since 1955 had been involved in Egyptian affairs. He maintained that Moscow's tactics were designed to expand its influence throughout the Mediterranean by employing "Arab hostility toward Israel to inflame Arab politics to the boiling point."[41] While the administration's special relationship with Israel was useful in one sense—providing a bastion of Western influence in the Middle East—the informal alliance was also burdensome as it undermined the stability of the Arab conservatives, whose informal strategic alliances with Washington threatened their own regimes. In time, Johnson's strategy towards the Arab-Israeli conflict only increased the Arab moderates' sense of isolation and fear that their positions were increasingly tenuous.[42] The president, however, was greatly irritated that the Israeli government refused to support formally his Vietnam policies, despite considerable past aid and assistance extended by Washington. The Israelis consistently ignored Johnson's requests, because they were confident that their U.S. supporters could deflect any possible fallout.

This situation changed dramatically in May and June 1967. In mid-May, Nasser ordered mobilization of Egyptian forces in the Sinai and proceeded to demand the eviction of the UN Emergency Forces and on May 22 declared a blockade in the Straits of Tiran.[43] As was the case in 1956, these events precipitated a crisis that caught Washington largely unaware. Walt Rostow held Moscow chiefly responsible, maintaining that the Soviet Union "set the pot boiling" when its leadership claimed that Israel was massing on the Syrian frontier. President Johnson immediately declared that the United States was "firmly committed to the political independence and territorial integrity of all the nations of the area." Frenzied diplomatic efforts in Washington now focused on two points: to ensure the Israeli right of passage through the Straits and to persuade Israel to hold off launching a preemptive military strike. Clarifying Eisenhower's commitment to Israel in 1957, the Johnson administration stood firm in its appraisal that Israel did indeed possess clear rights against Nasser's belligerency. Moscow's response to the growing threat was also monitored. At a meeting of the NSC in late May, Secretary of State Rusk claimed that Moscow was "playing a generally moderate game." While endorsing the Arab position and blaming Israel and the United States for the increased tension, State concluded that Moscow had "stopped short of endorsing Nasser's position" with regards to the Straits and appeared to prefer a "freezing" of the current situation.[44]

President Johnson and State Department officials sought to convince the Israelis that they needed time to find a diplomatic solution, while at the same time they refused to offer a firm, unequivocal commitment to come to Israel's aid in case of an Egyptian attack. The president insisted on lining up congressional approval and public support for any action that might be required to open the straits. All indications suggested that American opinion, no doubt influenced in part by the well-organized campaign of American Jews, was overwhelmingly supportive of the Israeli position.

When approached, the Pentagon showed no interest in undertaking any type of military action in the Middle East; Vietnam had their full attention. The Defense Department, including McNamara, General Wheeler, and intelligence analysts were convinced that Israeli forces, although facing foes on three fronts, would be able to defeat the Arabs. On May 25, the Israeli foreign minister, who had just arrived in Washington, was instructed to warn the White House that an Egyptian attack was imminent and that a formal U.S. commitment was needed. After an all-night review, American intelligence experts concluded Tel Aviv's fears were unwarranted. Johnson became suspicious he was being crowded and resented the notion he must accept Israel's analysis of the crisis. Meeting with Abba Eban late the following day, Johnson handed the foreign minister a memorandum that pointed out he had "already publicly stated this week our views on the safety of Israel and on the Strait of Tiran." The United States planned "to pursue vigorously" measures to assure that the Strait and Gulf would "remain open to free and innocent passage" of all ships. "I must emphasize," the president concluded, "the necessity for Israel not to make itself responsible for the initiation of hostilities. Israel will not be alone unless it decides to go alone."[45]

If the president did not formally indicate approval of the impending Israeli preemptive strike, the Israelis believed that Washington would accept actions that they felt necessary to meet the Arab threat to their security. Although Johnson had received virtually a promise that preemptive action would not take place before June 11, the Israelis had run out of time. On June 4, without informing Washington, Israel launched their attack the next day—the 1967 war was underway. There was concern in Washington that the United States not be drawn into the conflict.

Shortly after hostilities began, Secretary of State Rush cabled Moscow, indicating Washington's surprise at the outbreak of fighting and its hope for an early termination of the war. A short time later, Premier Kosygin responded (in the initial use of the crisis "hot line" communication system) that the situation called for U.S.-Soviet cooperation to achieve a cease-fire. The White House concurred with the need for a cease-fire and urged both superpowers to remain neutral. Johnson's behavior belied the administration's leaning toward Tel Aviv. Israel's deliberate attack on the American intelligence gathering vessel, the *Liberty*, resulting in 34 crew member killed and 171 wounded, was quickly covered up by the administration. Washington never condemned Israeli for firing the first shot or for its obvious intent of gaining additional territory. To Johnson, Egypt's closing the Strait of Tiran was an "act of folly."

In an effort to boost its sagging influence in Arab circles, Moscow severed its diplomatic relations with Israel and called upon the United Nations to force Israel back to its prewar frontiers. Sidestepping a determined peacemaking effort, Washington would not—in direct contrast to Eisenhower's action in 1956 prompting an Israeli withdrawal—press the Israelis to withdraw from occupied territories without a peace agreement. The five principles for such a peace were acknowledgment of Israel's existence, fair treatment of refugees, limits on armaments, mutual right of maritime passage, and mutual recognition of the political sovereignty and territorial integrity of all parties. The administration hoped that all previous outstanding differences would be resolved; it did not expect Israel's territorial gains to be permanent. This was not, however, what Tel Aviv officials had in mind.

Washington's efforts focused on obtaining a UN Security Council resolution that would incorporate its five-point program. The debates found Moscow generally supporting the radical Arab demands for the immediate withdrawal of Israeli occupation forces, while Washington agreed with Tel Aviv's insistence on a political settlement then withdrawal of its forces. Eventually, on November 22, 1967, the Council approved UN Resolution 242 that attempted to balance the demands of both sides and, later, appointed a UN representative, Swedish diplomat Gunnar Jarring, to bring the hostile parties together. Preoccupied with the Vietnam conflict, the president did not become actively engaged with Middle Eastern affairs and, even though the United States continued to supply Israel with arms, the relationship between the two nations cooled considerably. It would fall to the Nixon administration to focus on the unresolved issues.[46]

* * *

Despite Moscow's major expansion of its nuclear arms program, by the mid-1960s the prospects of a Soviet military assault upon Western Europe or launching their nuclear-tipped ICBMs toward U.S. targets appeared increasingly remote. Even the monolithic nature of the competing alliances gave signs of decay as nationalist forces emerged in Rumania, Hungary, and Czechoslovakia, on the one hand, and in France and West Germany on the other. If some Eastern bloc countries began looking westward, some members of Western bloc looked eastward. In June 1966, de Gaulle visited Moscow in hope of reaching an understanding that would contain the Germans and sustain for France a predominate role in the West and the Soviet Union in the East. Earlier, West German Foreign Minister Gerhard Schroeder had initiated contact with the Soviets aimed at improving relations with East Germany and the other Eastern bloc nations. Seeking to catch up with the changing European scene, officials in Washington sought to expand contacts with the Eastern European Communist governments.[47]

The spring of 1966 witnessed the emergence of the Johnson administration's "bridge building" policy toward the U.S.S.R. and Eastern European states consisting of political, economic, and cultural contacts. While the president was often frustrated by the actions of America's allies and strategic competition in regions beyond Europe, he reached out to Moscow in search of an "understanding" that would later be called détente. As an administration staff member saw it, Johnson's efforts to engage Soviet leadership had provided "the most productive period in the history of our relations, despite Vietnam." This was not at all what many hard-line American anti-Communists, such as the American Security Council, had in mind. In August 1964, the Council's policy-making arm, known as the National Strategy Committee, unveiled its own strategic agenda in a booklet entitled *Guidelines for a Cold War Victory*. This committee, chaired by Robert Galvin, the head of Motorola, included prominent retired generals such as Mark Clark, the former head of the UN forces in Korea, and physicist Edward Teller, father of the H-bomb and a strident foe of Moscow.

Put briefly, the *Guidelines* called on the U.S. government to eschew its failed policy of accommodation with Russia and actively pursue a Cold War victory that could be achieved primarily by putting pressure on the enemy just "short of [nuclear] war." Inherent in this plan was the recognition that the Soviets currently held a position of strategic inferiority, and were thus unable to launch a decisive strike on the

United States. Beyond this point, however, *Guidelines* cautioned that the United States might not retain its advantage, because Russia "had approached the problem [of missile defense] in a positive manner," perhaps enabling it eventually to alter the strategic balance. As a result, it claimed that there was an "urgent need" for the United States to develop an "effective" system of missile defense, including a fallout shelter system. Although not minimizing the technical difficulties involved, *Guidelines* nonetheless echoed Teller's confident forecast: if a Soviet strike occurred, active and passive defense together could lead to a survival rate of 90 percent.[48] The Soviet missile defense system, which was ineffective against the massive U.S. fleet of ground- and submarine-based missiles, would long remain a contentious issue with Cold War hawks.

Choosing to ignore this advice, Johnson launched a significant effort at bridge building, involving initiatives aimed at slowing down or placing limitations on the arms race. A major result of the discussions over Washington's many proposals for new arms control agreements— some resulted in useful treaties, others were nonstarters—was the gradual development of a more relaxed superpower relationship. Only six weeks in office, President Johnson had optimistically submitted a 14-point arms control program to the Eighteen Nation Disarmament Conference (ENDC) meeting at Geneva. Such a comprehensive initiative, however, had little hope of gaining much attention. Consequently, National Security Adviser McGeorge Bundy suggested the best approach for the administration to take would be small steps seeking to encourage American-Soviet cooperation.

In early 1964, officials in the Atomic Energy Agency and the Arms Control and Disarmament Agency revived a Kennedy administration proposal to cut back the production of weapons-grade uranium (U-235). Kennedy hesitated to press the idea until after the 1964 election, but Johnson promptly moved ahead. In his 1964 State of the Union message, the president announced that the United States was unilaterally cutting back production of U-235 by 25 percent and urged the Soviets to do the same. After an exchange of favorable messages, Moscow agreed to close down two facilities and Washington four. The result was strategically insignificant but important symbolically. "It was not a big step," Johnson wrote in his memoirs, "but it was a movement." Other immediate small steps met with mixed results. In 1963–1964, Washington and Moscow each unilaterally announced military budget cuts; but in 1965 the United States began increasing its spending because of the Vietnam conflict. The Soviets were upset over this turn of events and the unilateral effort to reduce military budgets collapsed. In January 1964, the United States proposed a "Strategic Nuclear Delivery Vehicle Freeze" that called for both superpowers to halt production of ballistic missiles capable of carrying nuclear warheads and to maintain each force at its current level. This was a nonstarter because it would have frozen the U.S.S.R. in a strategic inferiority.[49]

Subsequent American initiatives, focusing on banning nuclear weapons in outer space, halting the proliferation of nuclear weaponry, and limiting defensive and offensive missiles, gained a more productive response. Because of his earlier involvement in the U.S. space program, Johnson was determined to expand the 1962 UN resolution prohibiting deployment of nuclear weapons in outer space into a binding international agreement. The Joint Chiefs of Staff, opposed to any formal treaty, delayed final negotiations for nearly two years. On May 7, 1966, the president overruled the Joint Chiefs and publicly declared, "no country should be permitted to station weapons of mass destruction on a celestial body; weapons test and military maneuvers should be forbidden." The Soviets entered into negotiations, despite Communist Chinese propaganda condemning Moscow for dealing with the Western nations. The Outer Space Treaty emerged in August 1966.[50]

The troubling prospect of nuclear proliferation, with possibly West Germany, the Peoples Republic of China, and other nations seeking nuclear weapons, was another inheritance from the Kennedy administration. That Communist China would soon join the nuclear club was particularly upsetting to the Johnson administration. When exploration of American "covert activities" or joint U.S.-Soviet preventive military action to stop testing of China's initial bomb proved unfeasible, Washington focused its attention on a nonproliferation pact. Between November 1964 and January 1965, the Gilpatric Committee reviewed U.S. options, including abandonment of the MLF proposal, to gain Soviet support. "For a U.S. non-proliferation policy to be effective," argued Roswell Gilpatric, McNamara's deputy at the Defense Department, "Soviet cooperation, either implicit or explicit, would be essential." Brushing aside the State Department's hopes for the MLF, Johnson authorized the Arms Control and Disarmament Agency to draft a formal proposal. When the new Moscow team of Leonid Brezhnev and Alexei Kosygin learned of the demise of MLF, they concurred that a nonproliferation agreement would be in their best interest as well. Negotiations between 1966 and 1968 narrowed the superpowers' differences; their influence and coercion of other nations resulted in the signing of the Nuclear Non-Proliferation Treaty on July 1, 1968. At the signing, Johnson declared that the treaty was "the most important international agreement since the beginning of the nuclear age." He was not far off the mark.[51]

The increasing sophistication of strategic weaponry—intercontinental ballistic missiles (ICBMs), antiballistic missiles (ABMs), and multiple independently targeted reentry vehicles (MIRVs) carrying nuclear warheads—prompted Defense Secretary McNamara and Johnson to seek ways to dampen the arms competition. As early as March 1963, McNamara advised an audience of advertising executives, "The increasing numbers of survivable missiles in the hands of both the United States and the Soviet Union are a fact of life. Neither side today possesses a force which can save its country from severe damage in a nuclear exchange. Neither side can realistically expect to achieve such a force in the foreseeable future." Despite bitter complaints, the secretary launched a prolonged campaign to convince the public and military that existing nuclear weaponry, which "assured" the destruction of one's adversary, was a deterrent—the best defense against their use.[52]

As early as 1961, McNamara together with other defense scientists had concluded that expanding ABM programs would only greatly drive up the cost of the arms race, for it was cheaper to build offensive missiles. By 1967, he was convinced that ABMs were becoming a destabilizing factor, endangering the existing nuclear parity. He offered two cost-effective alternatives: improve U.S. offensive systems and seek with Moscow ABM limitations. Between June 23 and 25, Johnson and McNamara unsuccessfully presented the idea of limiting ABMs and offensive strategic weaponry to an unprepared Premier Kosygin during a hastily arranged summit at Glassboro, New Jersey. Subsequently, pointing to the Soviet ABM system (named by Americans "Galosh"), the Joint Chiefs of Staff and Congress pressed the reluctant defense secretary in 1968 to authorize deployment of a "thin-line" ABM system, which they acknowledged could not protect the United States from Soviet ICBMs.

Overlooked or ignored by the public, Congress, and the military was the fact that existing anti-missile technology, both American and Soviet, was inadequate. At a White House meeting, a distinguished group of defense scientists were unanimous in opposing deployment of an ABM system simply because it would not be effective. Meanwhile Soviet leaders, who initially resisted the idea of placing limits on missile defenses, found some members of the Russian scientific community arguing that "an effective ABM system was technically infeasible given existing technologies." Nevertheless, the Nixon administration would deploy an ABM system designed to defend U.S. ICBM sites. Eventually the ineffectiveness of ABMs, however, would result in their being significantly restricted in 1972.[53]

The road to détente began with Johnson's efforts to secure a Soviet commitment to seek limits on strategic nuclear weapons and their delivery systems. In his January 1967 State of the Union message, the president declared, "Our objective is not to continue the cold war, but to end it. . . . We have a solemn duty to slow down the arms race." Following a number of frustrating attempts to extract a commitment from the Soviets, Johnson was able to announce in July 1968 that discussions on limiting strategic weapons would begin the near future. The Politburo's annoyance with the U.S. intervention in Vietnam, off-set by their disagreements with China, would not halt Moscow efforts to reach an accommodation with Washington.[54]

* * *

Johnson's planned visit, in 1968, to Moscow to launch the strategic arms limitation talks was abruptly derailed. Earlier that year, Antonin Novotny, the arbitrary Communist dictator who had rule Czechoslovakia with an iron fist since 1953, was forced out of office. His successor, the reform-minded Alexander Dubcek, began instituting changes designed to create a form of "democratic socialism." The "Prague Spring," as it was known, expanded civil rights, extended the freedom of the press, and initiated steps toward a democratic political process. Unable to tolerate these actions, in August Brezhnev ordered Soviet troops and tanks into Czechoslovakia to remove Dubcek from office and replace him with a hard-line Moscow loyalist, Gustav Husak. This heavy-handed intervention prompted international condemnation, even outcries of indignation from foreign Communist party leaders and other Communist-led nations.

Subsequently, a *Pravda* article laid out the official justification of Moscow's decision: heads of Communist nations "must damage neither socialism in their own country nor the fundamental interests of the other socialist countries." Brezhnev later added that "when . . . forces hostile to socialism seek to reverse the development of any socialist country," this action poses "a common problem and concern of all socialist countries." Thus emerged the "Brezhnev Doctrine." Critics of U.S. interventionist policies did not hesitate to compare President Johnson's justification for intervening in the Dominican

Republic to that of the Soviet leader. Johnson had, in his "rocking chair doctrine," made it plain that the United States was not going "to let the Communists set up any [new] government Western Hemisphere."

The Nixon administration would have to put the preliminary Johnson-Brezhnev discussions regarding strategic arms limitation, and the notion of détente, back on track.[55]

CHAPTER 11

Watershed: The War in Vietnam

John F. Kennedy inherited a deepening U.S. commitment to Ngo Dinh Diem's faltering regime in South Vietnam, one key element in the country's program of global containment. Viet Cong guerrillas, with Hanoi's encouragement, had gained control of much of the countryside, putting the rhetoric of falling dominoes to the test. Kennedy's previous stand on Vietnam was hardly consistent. In April 1954, he warned the nation, in words both eloquent and perceptive, to avoid any involvement in Vietnam. "To pour money, material, and men into the jungles of Vietnam without at least a remote prospect of victory," he warned, "would be dangerously futile. . . . I am frankly of the belief that no amount of American assistance in Indochina can conquer an enemy which is everywhere and at the same time nowhere." But in June 1956, having accepted the domino theory, he declared Vietnam "the cornerstone of the free world in Southeast Asia, the keystone in the arch, the finger in the dike. Burma, Thailand, India, Japan, the Philippines and obviously Laos and Cambodia . . . would be threatened if the red tide of Communism overflowed into Vietnam."[1]

Such shopworn metaphors did not of course close out the president's options in Southeast Asia, but, in reflecting his firm adherence to global containment, they ruled out any critical review of past commitments. Persuaded that Congress, the public, and the press would not tolerate another Bay of Pigs, Kennedy confided to John Kenneth Galbraith, "There are just so many concessions that one can make to the Communists in one year and survive politically." With his credibility thoroughly challenged, it required only his unsettling exchange with Khrushchev in June to send him in search of some promising area of confrontation. "Vietnam," he concluded, "looks like the place."[2]

For the moment, however, Laos appeared the more explosive threat. By early 1961, a coalition of Prince Souvanna Phouma's neutralist forces and the Communist Pathet Lao guerrillas, supported by the U.S.S.R., threatened to overwhelm the unpromising U.S.-backed regime of Prince Boun Oum. During the presidential transition, President Eisenhower argued that Laos was the real key to the future of Southeast Asia. Once in possession of Laos, the Communists, he warned, would bring extreme pressure on Thailand, Cambodia, and South Vietnam. Thailand, bordering on Laos, appeared uniquely vulnerable to Communist encroachment. For Bangkok, the containment of Communism in Laos loomed as both a necessity and the ultimate test of SEATO's effectiveness.

* * *

Washington shared Thailand's fears of the Communist challenge to Laos no less than SEATO itself. One high-level State Department official observed, as early as January 18, "the attitude of Thailand can well be imagined under present circumstances when Laos is actually under communist aggression. . . . If SEATO fails to act in any helpful capacity . . . , we may well be faced within the next few months either with its dissolution or at least with the threat to withdraw by Thailand."[3] The National Intelligence Estimate of March 28, 1961, warned that Laos posed an inescapable challenge to the United States as well. "The governments of [Southeast Asia]," ran the report, "tend to regard the Laotian crisis as a symbolic test of intentions, wills and strengths between the major powers of the West and the Communist Bloc. . . . In short, the loss of Laos would severely damage the US position and its influence in Thailand and South Vietnam."[4]

For Washington and Bangkok, the SEATO protocols appeared sufficient to defend Laos, Cambodia, and South Vietnam against any identifiable external aggression. Allied action, however, faced SEATO's well-established principle of unanimity. Australia, Pakistan, and the Philippines readily supported the Thai-American determination to prevent any further Communist expansion in Southeast Asia. But Britain, France, and New Zealand had no intention of fighting in Southeast Asia; they even denied the presence of aggression in the ongoing struggle for Laos. With SEATO unable to act, Rusk informed Kennedy that Field Marshal Sarit Thanarat, Thailand's prime minister, was "gravely concerned over the threat to Thailand's security posed by the troubled situation in Laos and the resulting prospect of a southward thrust of Communist power in Southeast Asia." With Kennedy's approval, the secretary assured Sarit that the United States intended to honor fully its obligations under the SEATO pact, including full military support against any Communist attack.[5] Rusk cautioned Sarit that an exchange between heads of state on matters of such delicacy must remain confidential. Soon the Joint Chiefs advocated the stationing of U.S. troops in Thailand to demonstrate America's deep commitment to that country's territorial integrity, to discourage Communist infiltration across the Mekong frontier, and to establish the necessary facilities for any subsequent SEATO operations. No U.S. forces would participate in antiguerrilla activities.[6]

Still, landlocked Laos, despite the heavy official American commitment to its political independence, was not a matter of major public or congressional concern. Afforded room to maneuver, in April, the president followed the British and Soviet lead in calling a 14-nation conference in Geneva to resolve the Laotian question. For the troubled Asian allies, Washington and London's commitment to the establishment of a "neutral and independent" Laos left SEATO's Asian members fearing that Asian neutrals would lean strongly toward the U.S.S.R.[7] Kennedy, determined to avoid U.S. military involvement in Laos, had no choice but to entrust Southeast Asia's future to the Geneva negotiations.[8]

In early October, President Kennedy assured Thai foreign minister Thanat Khoman, in Washington, that the U.S. government remained deeply concerned over the security of Southeast Asia but continued to favor a peaceful solution in Laos that would eliminate the need for military intervention. "Military action at best," he said, "would be uncertain in its result, and hazardous. The lines of communication would be very long and overland routes would be difficult."[9] Thanat was worried that SEATO would never fulfill its responsibilities; but Kennedy emphasized that the refusal of some allies to act was no threat to Thailand's security. "The unanimity interpretation," he said, "does not limit our action or remove our obligation under the Treaty. We would not be inhibited even if the action could not be under the SEATO flag."[10]

Washington faced the difficult task, then, of preserving its interests in SEATO against the widespread conviction that the alliance, as constituted, would never function. Privately, U.S. officials recognized the need to reduce SEATO's political and economic role, leaving the treaty intact as a vehicle for American action while scaling down the headquarters activity in Bangkok.[11] By February 1962, U.S. officials had resolved to satisfy Bangkok's security requirements, not by changing the voting procedure or negotiating a bilateral defense pact, but by providing security guarantees within the SEATO framework. This program would sustain the SEATO alliance while recognizing its limitations.[12] The Thais had long sought a formal U.S. defense commitment; however, the administration had resisted because it required consultation with Congress.[13] But on February 13, Washington agreed to embody its bilateral guarantee to Thailand in a public document.[14] The Rusk-Thanat communiqué of March 1962 formalized the U.S. commitment to Thailand's defense.[15] The subsequent movement of U.S. Marines, as well as token SEATO forces, into Thailand, added to the program for improved logistics, resolved Bangkok's serious doubts regarding Washington's reliability.[16] In March 1963, Rusk boasted that U.S. efforts to keep SEATO intact through two challenging years had protected the country's two essential interests in the alliance's continuance. SEATO still provided the legal instrument for the creation and pursuit of U.S. security commitments in Southeast Asia; in addition, it underwrote the country's critical strategic relationship with Thailand.[17]

The SEATO alliance was scarcely an exercise in collective security because it never possessed any effective military presence in Asia beyond the mobile striking power of the United States. Yet spokesmen for the alliance never questioned its adequacy as a barrier to Communist expansion in Southeast Asia. From the moment of its inception, SEATO embarked on a program of self-adulation that continued, with diminishing restraint, into the 1960s. Although the alliance had never functioned as a unit, Secretary of Defense Robert McNamara, as late as 1962, assured a congressional committee that SEATO's evolution into a sound military organization had eliminated the need for U.S. ground forces in any foreseeable Asian conflict.

As early as October 1961, after weeks of wrangling, the Geneva Conference agreed to neutralize Laos, instructing Souvanna Phouma to form a coalition government that included representatives of the right, center, and left in Laotian politics. Thai officials were not reassured. Prime Minister Sarit and his generals condemned Washington for its refusal to send troops into Laos and thereby guarantee the triumph of the country's anti-Communist elements, gain control of the vital supply routes from Laos into South Vietnam, and save all Southeast Asia, including Thailand, from Communist domination.[18] When Souvanna's neutral regime took office in June 1962, Thai officials complained that Thailand was bearing the brunt of the West's Laotian "experiment."[19] W. Averell Harriman, assistant secretary of state for Far Eastern Affairs, who had confidence in the Geneva decisions, advised Washington that Sarit's warnings of disaster in Laos were "intended to frighten us into increasing our military assistance to him and modifying our policy toward Cambodia and Laos."[20]

By the spring of 1963 the Pathet Lao had deserted the government, driving the center toward the right and subjecting the country to a renewal of the Laotian civil war. Thereafter the Pathet Lao, with North Vietnamese help, solidified their control over much of the country, especially its eastern fringes. Simultaneous Communist-led threats of subversion across the Mekong created a new sense of urgency in Bangkok. Ambassador Kenneth T. Young warned Washington on March 29: "Thailand could become another Vietnam. We hope public pressures at home will not force penny-wise and pound-foolish reductions in our aid effort here while Communists make continuing headway in spreading their influence in the countryside."[21] At the end, U.S. officials reminded the Bangkok government that it carried the major responsibility for its country's defense.

⋆ ⋆ ⋆

Kennedy escaped a military confrontation in Laos; he would not do so in Vietnam. That this recently established Asian country would, in time, dominate the nation's external relations longer and more divisively than any other conflict in its history suggests a profound dilemma. Why should the United States have concerned itself for so long and at such heavy cost with the internal affairs of a new Asian state, over 10,000 miles away, without a navy or air force, and with exceedingly limited ground forces when contrasted to those that existed elsewhere even in Asia? On the other hand, why should a small, backward, jungle-ridden country embarrass the U.S. militarily when this country possessed more destructive power than any nation in history? Only a cursory examination is sufficient to answer the first question; the answers demanded by the second would become apparent only with the passage of time.

Kennedy never considered a political settlement for Vietnam. After coming under fire for agreeing to do so in Laos, he was even more determined to avoid it. Indeed, key officials in the Kennedy administration refused to consider any serious reevaluation of the Southeast Asian policies they had inherited.[22] Perhaps they no longer believed that the earlier perceptions of a Moscow-based monolith were accurate, but they defined U.S. interests in Southeast Asia in no other terms. President Eisenhower's repeated assertions of an American interest in Vietnam, Kennedy's apologists argued, created a vital American interest that the new president could not ignore. Whether or not the domino theory was valid in 1954, wrote Arthur Schlesinger, Jr., "it had acquired validity seven years after neighboring governments had staked their own security on the ability of the United States to live up to its pledges to Saigon."[23]

Kennedy's determination to avoid any retreat in Vietnam reflected his desire to protect his administration from charges of weakness in confronting the Communist enemy abroad. Indeed, the president seemed to be troubled far less by Communists in Vietnam, whose containment, he believed, would scarcely tax the country's resources or patience, than by anti-Communists in Congress and the press.[24] No longer, Kennedy ruefully told his aides, could he afford to accept a defeat in Southeast Asia as Eisenhower had done in 1954. If the United States had invented South Vietnam, by 1961, as journalist David Halberstam wrote, Americans "believed firmly in Diem, believed in his legitimacy; they saw South Vietnam as a real country, with a real flag."[25]

Kennedy's involvement began early. On January 28, 1961, he called a top-level meeting to discuss General Edward C. Lansdale's report on Vietnam that advocated a strong economic, political, and military program to help Diem establish his control of the country. Unfortunately, Diem was rapidly losing command of the South Vietnamese countryside as he faced skillful guerrilla warfare and effective Vietminh recruitment. Lansdale, the leading U.S. expert on counterinsurgency, recommended the replacement of Elbridge Durbrow with an ambassador more sympathetic to Diem's problems. Unless conditions improved, Lansdale predicted, the Saigon regime faced certain defeat. Lansdale's memorandum, the president acknowledged, made him aware, for the first time, of the seriousness and urgency of affairs in Vietnam.[26] The National Intelligence Estimate of March 28 corroborated Lansdale's findings, observing that Saigon's situation "seems likely to become increasingly difficult because of rising Communist guerrilla strength and of widening dissatisfaction with Diem's government."[27]

Walt Rostow's memorandum of April, followed later that month by the long report of his special task force, reinforced Kennedy's conviction that the United States must prevent the Communist domination of South Vietnam. Vice President Lyndon Johnson, on May 23, submitted to Kennedy a report on his trip to Southeast Asia. In what became standard phraseology, he advised the president:

The battle against Communism must be joined in Southeast Asia with strength and determination to achieve success there—or the United States, inevitably, must surrender the Pacific and take up our defenses in our own shores. Asian Communism is comprised and contained by the maintenance of free nations on the sub-continent. Without this inhibitory influence, the island outposts—Philippines, Japan, Taiwan—have no security and the vast Pacific becomes a Red Sea. . . . The basic decision in Southeast Asia is here. We must decide whether to help these countries to the best of our ability or throw in the towel in the area and pull back our defenses to San Francisco and a "Fortress America" concept. More important, we would say to the world in this case that we don't live up to the treaties and don't stand by our friends.[28]

Still, for Johnson, the defense, not only of South Vietnam but of the entire Pacific basin, demanded little. In each country, he assured the president, the United States could build "a sound structure capable of withstanding and turning the Communist surge." Asian leaders, he assured Washington, did not want American troops other than on training missions. Economic aid would remain a mutual effort, because ultimately the Asian states would save themselves.

As Saigon's authority continued to deteriorate, Kennedy, in October 1961, dispatched General Maxwell E. Taylor, his personal military adviser, and Walt Rostow to Vietnam to gather information for a major reassessment of the American position in Southeast Asia. The absence of State Department personnel on the mission revealed the president's growing acceptance of a military solution.[29] Ambassador Young, on October 17, reminded Taylor from Bangkok that in defending South Vietnam the United States was defending much of the globe:

Southeast Asia is the critical bottleneck stopping Sino-Soviet territorial and ideological expansion. . . . Southeast Asia is somewhat like the hub of a wheel; lose the hub and the wheel collapses. And Laos, plus South Vietnam, is the cotter-pin holding the hub. If we let Laos-South Vietnam go, the Viet Cong and Chinese Communists will soon dominate all of Southeast Asia, including Indonesia. The United States will be forced off the mainland of Asia, Australia will be surrounded and actually flanked, while India and Japan will be permanently separated. All of this is what the Communists are trying to do in Asia. Their success there will intensify their impact in Africa and South America.[30]

Taylor, in his report of November 4, accused North Vietnam of aggression and attributed Saigon's military failures to favoritism, inefficiency, and corruption. Nevertheless, to defend South Vietnam's northern frontier against infiltration, he recommended an initial deployment of 10,000 American troops. His report offered Washington the choice of defeat, reform, or direct U.S. military involvement. Kennedy rejected the first alternative, but would not, as yet, embrace the third; reform remained the least expensive and most promising solution. "Let me assure you again," he addressed Diem, "that the United States is determined to help Vietnam preserve its independence, protect its people against Communist assassins and build a better life through economic growth."[31]

From the beginning, Secretary of Defense Robert McNamara reminded him that no reasonable U.S. involvement would tip the military scales in Southeast Asia; the United States might become mired in a land war that it could not win. Kennedy shared that pessimism and wondered whether the United States would be more successful than the French in securing the support of the villagers, so essential for success against guerrilla forces.[32] Responding to Taylor's request for troops, Kennedy complained: "They want a force of American troops. . . . They say it's necessary in order to restore confidence and maintain morale. But it will be just like Berlin. The troops will march in; the bands will play; the crowds will cheer; and in four days everyone will have forgotten. Then we will be told we have to send in more troops. It's like taking a drink. The effect wears off, and you take another."[33] Kennedy, in time, offered the nation a small drink himself.

The president had genuine policy choices available; he chose not to exercise them. Politically, it was more feasible to entangle the United States gradually, promising with each additional increment the gains that each preceding increment has assured but failed to deliver. "In retrospect," Schlesinger concluded, "Vietnam is a triumph of the politics of inadvertence. We have achieved our present entanglement, not after due and deliberate consideration, but through a series of small decisions. . . . Each step in the deepening of the American commitment was reasonably regarded at the time as the last that would be necessary."[34]

Schlesinger's defense of inadvertence faced a serious challenge in the writings of Daniel Ellsberg, who understood from the Pentagon Papers what unending presumptions drove the country's continuing escalation in Vietnam. What defines an external policy are its ends, and in Vietnam the persistent quest for victory permitted only escalation. McNamara and the Joint Chiefs accepted without question the basic uncompromisable proposition: "The fall of South Vietnam to Communism would lead to the fairly rapid extension of Communist control . . . in the rest of mainland Southeast Asia. . . . The strategic implications worldwide, particularly in the Orient, would be extremely serious."[35] On January 27, 1962, McNamara sent to the president a memorandum, prepared by the Joint Chiefs, suggesting that the loss of South Vietnam "would have a widespread and disastrous effect on U.S. policy in the rest of Southeast Asia."[36] What mattered thereafter was not the nature of the escalation, but its unending purpose: to protect the Saigon regime and the credibility of U.S. commitments elsewhere. At no time could the administration regard any escalation the last, but only the next step in the pursuit of the constant goal of denying victory to Vietnam's Communist forces.[37]

During 1962 the president gradually increased the military aid to South Vietnam from 4,000 military advisers in January to 10,000 by October, while the secretary of defense assured the American people that the government had no policy for introducing combat forces into South Vietnam. Thus the Kennedy administration trapped itself in a struggle that it dared not lose but could not win. Neither the acceptance of failure nor the pursuit of a decisive victory on Asian soil appeared politically and emotionally bearable. Halfway measures would not bring success, but they would buy time, keep Washington's options open and, over the short run, enable the administration to avoid painful decisions. The Kennedy administration, with all its apparent brilliance, lived in the unreal world of its predecessors.

* * *

Kennedy required a strategy that would bridge the gap between the goal of victory and the reality of a limited U.S. involvement. He found it in the political-military program of counterinsurgency. During the spring of 1961, the president prepared to increase the effectiveness of the antiguerrilla activities in South Vietnam. On March 28, he reminded Congress that since 1945 the "most active and constant threat to Free World security" had been guerrilla warfare. To meet that challenge, the United States, he warned, must organize "strong, highly mobile forces trained in this type of warfare, some of which must be deployed in forward areas."[38] The United States required forces that could deal successfully with small, externally equipped guerrilla bands. Reflecting the activist spirit of the New Frontier, counterinsurgency became fashionable, even faddish. Skilled, finely trained American units would be more than a match for any competing force, even in the jungles of Asia. Yet when U.S. forces later assumed responsibility for South Vietnam's defense, they reverted to traditional modes of warfare.

In practice, counterinsurgency assumed the form of the strategic hamlet program, instituted in March 1962 to insulate the peasants and deprive the Viet Cong guerrillas of a necessary source of supplies. In April, Ngo Dinh Nhu, Diem's brother and political adviser, adopted the successful Malayan model of counterinsurgency, along with the

British officers who devised it. Unfortunately, South Vietnam possessed none of the sociological, political, and ethnic factors that had been crucial to Malaya's apparent triumph over its guerrilla movement. Malaya, unlike South Vietnam, had no common border with another Communist-led country. All of its guerrillas were Chinese, and their support came from a small minority of Chinese squatters who had nothing to lose but their illicitly acquired rice fields. South Vietnam's guerillas were ethnically indistinguishable from their countrymen. Vietnamese peasants, closely tied to the land, deeply resented the effort to move them to more secure locations. The tight security measures required to render the strategic hamlets effective managed to turn them into prison camps without stopping Viet Cong infiltration or preventing their occasional destruction by guerrilla forces.[39]

Kennedy's critics wondered why he continued to commit the United States so deeply to a Vietnam involvement that never promised success—and all without any serious public or congressional debate. In June 1963, Chester Bowles, Kennedy's special adviser on Africa, Asia, and Latin America, addressed the president directly: "As matters now stand, we may find ourselves forced to choose between an escalating war or a humiliating retreat in an area where the strategic conditions are disadvantageous to us." The administration's failure to explain U.S. objectives in Southeast Asia except in terms of "falling dominoes," he warned, would leave it "the captive of events with unpredictable results both at home and abroad."[40] Similarly Galbraith queried the president on March 2, 1962, "[W]ho is the man in your administration who decided what countries are strategic? I would like to ... ask him what is so important about this real estate in the space age."[41] France's Charles de Gaulle, recalling the French disaster in Southeast Asia, warned the president that Vietnam was totally unsuitable for Western tanks and politics. On one occasion in 1961 he told Kennedy that "he would be a damned fool if he got drawn into the Asian morass." In July 1962, Nikita Khrushchev observed that the United States had "stumbled into a bog in which it would be mired for a long time."[42]

What encouraged the Kennedy and his White House advisers to ignore such advice was their common assumption that they could sustain the military operation in Vietnam indefinitely and thereby push a national decision into a more propitious future.

* * *

In the absence of any direct U.S. military involvement in the war, the means for victory lay essentially in Saigon's capacity to organize, staff, and direct a successful counterinsurgency campaign. By January 1962, noted correspondent Robert Shaplen reported, the United States had given Diem everything he wanted without achieving any measurable influence in Saigon's administration of public policy.[43] It became clear throughout the succeeding months that the Diem regime was the weakest component in the struggle for Vietnam. Kennedy soon discovered that the American program for Vietnam, tied overwhelmingly to Diem's political survival, granted the Vietnamese leader incredible leverage in dealing with Washington. Powerless to desert the Saigon regime or to reform it, Washington could only encourage U.S. commander General Paul Harkins and Ambassador Frederick E. Nolting, Jr., to assure Diem of the continuing U.S. commitment to his success and to repress any evidence of failure in the performance of the South Vietnamese government and military forces.

Whenever Saigon's progress appeared substantial, official expectations knew no bounds. Visiting U.S. officials, usually briefed by Harkins and Nolting, reflected Saigon's mood of optimism in their official reports.[44] Following his first trip to Saigon that year, McNamara reported, "Every quantitative measure we have shows we're winning this war." Halberstam recalled that McNamara "scurried around Vietnam, looking for what he wanted to see; and he never saw or smelled nor felt what was really there, right in front of him." In a sense, Halberstam concluded, McNamara acted on knowledge that he himself created.[45] The president summed up the year's successes in his State of the Union message of January 1963, "The spearhead of aggression has been blunted in South Vietnam."[46] With the economic and military increments of early 1963, official optimism became even more pronounced. During March, Secretary of State Dean Rusk declared, "government forces clearly have the initiative in most areas of the country." Not long thereafter the Defense Department announced that "the corner has definitely been turned toward victory in Vietnam."[47]

Washington's official optimism had long ignored the flow of countering evidence from the writings of foreign correspondents in Vietnam. The effort to sustain Diem's favorable image faced a major challenge in early January 1963 when, at Ap Bac in the Mekong Delta, a South Vietnamese (ARVN) force, supported by American planes and helicopters, surrounded a Viet Cong battalion one-fourth its size. After Saigon's forces had suffered heavy casualties, with five U.S. helicopters shot down and nine more damaged, they withdrew and permitted the Viet Cong to escape.[48] Such correspondents as Halberstam of the *New York Times* and Neil Sheehan of United Press International, had become persuaded that Diem's regime was politically and militarily defective.[49] Their reporting had become a matter of deep concern to both Harkins and Diem. What destroyed their confidence in Harkins irreparably was his announcement that Ap Bac was a victory for Saigon.

Lieutenant Colonel John Paul Vann, who had observed the battle of Ap Bac, wrote a scathing report to Harkins on Saigon's forces' persistent refusal to engage the enemy. A Joint Chiefs commission, headed by General Victor Krulac and sent to examine the war's status, heard the negative evaluations of American field officers; but its report praised ARVN. Krulac accused Vann and his field staff of being unduly harsh. Subsequently, Vann revealed to Halberstam privately what he knew about the Viet Cong—their strength and locations, the refusal of ARVN to face them, and Harkins's reluctance to confront Diem on the failures of his army. Early in March, this information began to appear on the pages of the *New York Times* and led, finally, to Halberstam's book, *The Making of a Quagmire* (1965), which won the Pulitzer Prize.[50] For Harkens, McNamara, and Rusk, Ap Bac was only an embarrassing dip in the upward-moving curve of progress in Vietnam.[51]

In the summer of 1963, the South Vietnamese leader, with his brother, Ngo Dinh Nhu, instituted a drastic repression of the Buddhists and, amid the rioting and public self-immolations of dissenting Buddhists, the Diem regime began to disintegrate. Henry Cabot Lodge, Jr., who succeeded Nolting as ambassador in August, as well as the White House, found Diem's behavior toward the Buddhists embarrassing. In Washington, the president admitted: "[I]n the final analysis it is the people and the Government itself who have to win or lose this struggle. All we can do is help, and we are making it very clear. But I don't agree with those who say we should withdraw. That would be a great mistake."[52] Lodge soon discovered a plot among South Vietnam's leading officers to overthrow the Diem regime. Supported by Kennedy and his top advisers, Lodge encouraged Diem's opponents by assuring them that the United States would do nothing to prevent a coup; but Vietnamese officers alone planned and executed the coup on November 1. Washington officials anticipated the coup, but not the assassination of Diem and his brother.[53] Nolting, in Washington, defended Diem to the end.[54] Kennedy's own assassination followed three weeks later. At that moment the United States had 16,000 troops in Vietnam, with a continuing commitment to victory and no exit strategy.

As the American effort in Vietnam continued to falter, Kennedy, according to staffer Kenneth O'Donnell, had responded favorably to Senator Mike Mansfield's many admonitions that the United States should withdraw totally from Vietnam's civil conflict. "But I can't do it until 1965—after I'm reelected," Kennedy observed. He explained: " [I]n 1965, I'll be damned everywhere as a Communist appeaser. But I don't care. If I tried to pull out completely now, we would have another Joe McCarthy red scare on our hands, but I can do it after I'm reelected. So we had better make damned sure that I am reelected."[55] For Ellsberg, the president's supposition that it was acceptable to leave South Vietnam to its fate in 1965, but not in 1963, suggested that the president regarded his own political career more important than the lives of the thousands who would die before the election.[56] Kennedy had, wrote Sheehan, "raised the Stars and Stripes and shed blood and enveloped the protection and self-esteem of the United States."[57] Thus Kennedy bequeathed to Lyndon Johnson a commitment to Southeast Asia far more pervading and dangerous than the one he had inherited from Eisenhower.

* * *

Johnson entered the presidency no less determined than Kennedy to avoid defeat in Southeast Asia. Unfortunately, he faced a new crisis. After Ap Bac the Viet Cong had spent 10 months preparing for the unremitting offensive they launched in November. Outposts fell by the dozens. The strategic hamlet program, lauded by Harkins, Nolting, and top officials in Washington, ceased to exist. Saigon's forces entered the countryside only at a heavy price.[58] At a conference on November 20, McNamara endorsed a program, proposed by General Krulac, designed to control the guerrilla activity in the South by exerting military and psychological pressure on the North. By attacking North Vietnamese targets directly, U.S. officials hoped to frighten Hanoi into abandoning the Viet Cong and terminating its persistent infiltration of the South. Johnson was no more willing than Kennedy to become the first American president to lose a war.[59] He accepted the conference's recommendation to inaugurate a clandestine war against North Vietnam. That program, Operation Plan 34A, went into effect on February 1, 1964, with the bombardment and destruction of radar sites, coastal installations, and rail and highway bridges. Critics could discover no justification for the notion that the new offensive would stabilize the Saigon government or increase its prospects for survival.[60] Nor would it, they agreed, intimidate the North.

Washington readily accepted the government of General Duong Van Minh as a necessity; but in January 1964 a military junta headed by General Nguyen Khanh overthrew the Minh government. On March 26,

McNamara declared that General Khanh, with his grasp of the problems facing his country, would in time dispose of the South Vietnamese guerrillas. Still, there existed in Washington a growing conviction, spanning many months, that the fundamental challenge facing Saigon lay not in the Viet Cong guerrillas, but in the pressures exerted by North infiltration.[61] As early as May 1964, Ambassador Lodge, National Security Adviser McGeorge Bundy, and the Joint Chiefs of Staff advocated, beyond the program of harassment, a major bombing campaign against North Vietnamese targets to strengthen the Saigon government.

On June 10, a group of senior advisers, led by McGeorge Bundy and his brother, William, assistant secretary of state for Far Eastern Affairs, prepared the draft of a congressional resolution seeking support for an American air and ground war in Asia.[62] Operation Plan 34A created the occasion for such a resolution in early August when it provoked the Gulf of Tonkin incident. On August 4, the president ordered retaliatory air strikes on North Vietnamese torpedo-boat bases and storage tank depots. He then submitted a resolution to Congress designed to commit that body to any future executive action required to defend the Saigon government. The resolution, adopted by the Senate 88 to 2, declared that inasmuch as the security of Southeast Asia was vital, the United States was "prepared as the president determines, to take all necessary steps, including the use of armed forces, to assist any protocol state of the Southeast Asia Collective Defense Treaty requesting assistance in the defense of its freedom."[63] Congress unwittingly gave the president enormous latitude in responding to enemy action in Southeast Asia.

Whatever the troubling concerns of many citizens regarding U.S. intentions in Southeast Asia, throughout the 1964 presidential campaign, the president promised to keep the nation out of a land war in Asia. "I have not thought," he said, "that we were ready for American boys to do the fighting for Asian boys." On August 12, he declared in New York: "Some others are eager to enlarge the conflict. They call upon us to supply American boys to do the job that Asian boys should do. They ask us to take reckless action which might risk the lives of millions. . . . [S]uch action would offer no solution at all to the real problem of Vietnam." Still, in a major campaign speech of late September in Manchester, New Hampshire, the president reminded the nation that American goals in Southeast Asia had not changed and that the United States could not leave until the North Vietnamese and Chinese had been taught to leave their neighbors alone.[64]

Yet already talk of intervention was in the air. During the summer of 1964, when General Khanh called for U.S. bombing of the North, the new American ambassador, Maxwell Taylor, reminded him that the United States could not embrace such a program during the presidential campaign. However, on August 15, William Bundy acknowledged that the United States might find it necessary to broaden the war if North Vietnam did not stop its attacks on the South.[65] As the CIA continued to issue pessimistic reports on the absence of leadership and motivation in the South Vietnamese army, the pressures for bombing continued to mount. Relying on his World War II experiences, Walt Rostow, head of the state department's policy planning staff, argued that North Vietnam was vulnerable to air attacks. Indeed, in late August the president, using the Tonkin Gulf Resolution as a pretext, ordered a series of bombing raids against the North Vietnamese to demonstrate the costs should Hanoi persist in its efforts to undermine the Saigon government. Then on September 29, William Bundy told a Tokyo audience: "Expansion of the war outside South Vietnam, while not a course we want to seek, could be forced upon us by the increased pressures of the Communists, including the rising scale of infiltration." Several days later, James Reston noted in the *New York Times* that the administration was merely seeking an excuse to launch a bombing campaign against the North. On December 1, during one of Taylor's visits to Washington, a top-level meeting at the White House adopted a bombing strategy to persuade Hanoi to stop its support of Saigon's enemies.[66]

Following his inaugural in January 1965, the president faced ever-narrowing choices in Vietnam. Reluctant to order the bombing, he was even more reluctant to accept the collapse of the Saigon government. As Johnson himself explained, "[T]here would follow in this country an endless national debate—a mean and destructive debate—that would shatter my Presidency, kill my administration, and damage our democracy."[67] Nowhere was it apparent that the administration could achieve the necessary public support for an escalating intervention. McNamara and McGeorge Bundy met the challenge by advocating sustained bombing of the North as the necessary prelude to the establishment of a viable government in Saigon. Under Secretary George Ball, long a critic of U.S. involvement in Southeast Asia, examined the new rationale for bombing the North:

I have always marveled at the way ingenious men can, when they wish, turn logic upside down, and I was not surprised when my colleagues interpreted the crumbling of the South Vietnamese government . . . not as proving that we should cut our losses and get out, but rather that we must promptly begin bombing to stiffen the resolve of the corrupt South Vietnamese government. It was classic bureaucratic casuistry. A faulty rationalization was improvised to obscure the painful reality that America could arrest the galloping deterioration of its position only by the surgery of extrication.[68]

Armed with a rationale for bombing, the president still hesitated to order it. However, Viet Cong elements, on February 7, 1965, attacked a U.S. helicopter base at Pleiku in the Central Highlands, killing eight Americans and wounding 126. Even as the president retaliated with a limited bombing campaign, he assured the nation that "we seek no wider war." At a meeting on February 8, McGeorge Bundy, returning from Saigon, presented the final rationale for an air war against the North: "The situation in Vietnam is deteriorating, and without new U.S. action defeat appears inevitable. . . . The stakes in Vietnam are extremely high. The American investment is very large, the American responsibility is a fact of life. . . . The international prestige of the United States, and a substantial part of our influence, are directly at risk in Vietnam." Bundy argued that sustained reprisal through air and naval action would improve the climate in Saigon by affecting "a sharp immediate increase in optimism in the South among all articulate groups. . . . This favorable action should offer opportunity for increased American influence in pressing for a more effective government."[69] Bombing, apparently, would leave no problem unresolved.

On February 13, the president, accepting Bundy's rationale, authorized Rolling Thunder, a program of sustained bombing. According to official dogma in Washington, the bombing would bring Ho Chi Minh to the negotiating table in six weeks, at most ten.[70] Victory would now be swift and inexpensive. Whether the bombing would strengthen the South Vietnamese government and broaden is political base depended on the quality of leadership. Taylor assured the Vietnamese officers who favored Rolling Thunder, especially the trio of Nguyen Cao Ky, Nguyen Van Thieu, and Nguyen Bao Tri, that the United States no longer favored Khanh. With the backing of Taylor and General William Westmoreland, who had succeeded Harkins, Ky prevailed upon the Armed Forces Council to remove Khanh as commander in chief.

Thieu and Ky now emerged as South Vietnam's most powerful public figures. On March 1, the South Vietnamese government announced its approval of the air war against the North; one day later American planes launched their first sustained attack. In June, Thieu and Ky assumed command of Saigon's new military government, with Thieu as chief of state and Ky as prime minister. Senator Mansfield reminded the president that the United States no longer dealt in Vietnam "with anyone who represents anybody in a political sense." Within days it became clear that Rolling Thunder, largely an act of desperation, would achieve none of its objectives.[71]

Washington's decision to enter an open war against North Vietnam, at a price that defied measurement, required stronger justification. During the autumn of 1964, spokesmen of the Johnson administration defined the challenge of Southeast Asia, like that of Korea, as one of Northern aggression against an independent South Vietnam. The president proclaimed that view in an address on October 14, "With our help, the people of South Vietnam can defeat Communist aggression."[72] To prove the supposition of international aggression, the administration, on February 27, 1965, published a White Paper entitled *Aggression from the North: The Record of North Viet-Nam's Campaign to Conquer South Vietnam*. Secretary Rusk took up the theme, asserting that "small and large nations have a right to live without being molested by their neighbors." The United States would leave Southeast Asia, he concluded, when North Vietnam stopped its aggression.[73] Scholars agree that North Vietnamese units moved into South Vietnam in late 1963, and that regular units arrived by October 1964—well before the U.S. bombing decision.[74] Whether the presence of North Vietnamese forces in South Vietnam constituted international aggression depended on countering perceptions of the historic legitimacy of the state of South Vietnam. For officials and scholars who accepted the supposition that the single Vietnam of the Geneva Accords had evolved into two countries, the United States had ample justification to repel the aggression and thereby defend the principle of collective security and the rule of law.[75] For its critics, however, the White Paper was designed less to present evidence of Northern aggression than to justify the bombing.[76]

Even before Rolling Thunder, Westmoreland had requested troops to provide security for U.S. facilities and installations in South Vietnam. Amid a debate within the administration, on March 8, two Marine battalions landed at Danang. Convinced now that Rolling Thunder would not cripple North Vietnam's fighting capacity or stop the infiltration Communist infiltration into the South, the Joint Chiefs, supported by Westmoreland, asked for two divisions for operations against the Viet Cong.[77] Taylor argued for an expanded air war; CIA Director John McCone warned against all military escalation. McNamara, while acknowledging the risks, advocated greater U.S. military involvement. On July 1, he assured the president that the American public would support such a course action because it promised a favorable solution of the Vietnam problem.[78] John T. McNaughton, assistant secretary of defense, reminded the administration that its most important objective in Vietnam was the avoidance of a humiliating defeat and, with it, the destruction of the American reputation as the guarantor against Communist aggression. Johnson, still unconvinced, created an outside Vietnam panel consisting of General Omar Bradley, Roswell Gilpatric, Dr. George Kistiakowsky, Arthur Larson, and John J. McCloy. Except for Larson, Bundy wrote, the panel members agreed with him that the stakes in Vietnam were high and that Vietnam was a test case for Soviet-backed wars of national liberation.[79]

Throughout the critical weeks of decision, George Ball challenged the assumptions of U.S. Vietnamese policy, troubled by the persistent refusal of official Washington to reexamine the bases of that policy. "What we charitably referred to as a government in Saigon was falling apart," Ball recorded, "yet we had to bomb the North as a form of political therapy. . . . Such a tortuous argument was . . . the last resort of those who believed we could not with withdraw from Vietnam without humiliation." The fear of humiliation, wrote Ball, gave Saigon its incredible power over Washington, placing the United States on the verge of becoming a "puppet of our puppet." On July 1, Ball presented the president with his argument for a negotiated settlement and an American withdrawal:

The South Vietnamese are losing the war to the Viet Cong. No one can assure you that we can beat the Viet Cong or even force them to the conference table on our terms no matter how many hundred thousand *white foreign* (US) troops we deploy. . . . The decision you face now, therefore, is crucial. Once large numbers of US troops are committed to direct combat they will begin to take heavy casualties in a war they are ill-equipped to fight in a non-cooperative if not downright hostile countryside. Once we suffer large casualties we will have started a well-nigh irreversible process. Our involvement will be so great that we cannot—without national humiliation— stop short of achieving our complete objectives. *Of the two possibilities I think humiliation would be more likely than the achievement of our objectives—even after we had paid terrible costs.*[80]

Troubled by the continuing pleas for escalation, Johnson, in mid-July, sent McNamara to confer with Taylor, Westmoreland, Thieu, and Ky in Saigon. Thieu, dwelling on his country's profound weakness, asked for 200,000 U.S. troops. Backed by the nation's military leaders in the Pacific theater, McNamara now advocated heavy increases in U.S. personnel, helicopters, air squadrons, and advisory units to assure the final success of the Saigon government.[81] The president, on July 21 and for the following week, met with all of his senior civilian and military advisers in Washington and Camp David to resolve the issue of military escalation. Ball argued that a long, protracted war in Vietnam would demonstrate the weakness, not the strength, of the United States. American prudence, not American power, was being tested in Vietnam. Clark Clifford, noted Democratic adviser to presidents, shared Ball's opposition to an American war in Southeast Asia. What he faced, he recalled, was "a solid phalanx of advice from the main advisers" who accepted the domino theory without question and, with it, the mission to help the South Vietnamese save themselves from "Communist aggression."[82]

At Camp David, on July 25, the final and most critical meeting of Johnson's top advisers, Clifford again warned against escalation and advised the administration to probe for a way to leave Vietnam. The president produced a letter from Mansfield that insisted Vietnam involved no high principle, and that the task of the United States was to avoid being thrown out of Vietnam under fire.[83] Nonetheless, at a press conference on July 28, the president announced an immediate increase in U.S. fighting strength in Vietnam from 75,000 to 125,000, with additional forces as required. Should the United States be driven from the field in Vietnam, he warned, no nation again would ever trust its promises. But he added, "We do not want an expanding struggle with consequences that no one can perceive."[84] What troubled the critics was the willingness of the president and his close advisers to make such a fateful decision without reference to Congress or the public.[85]

* * *

Washington ventured into its program of military escalation with the firm conviction that Hanoi would quickly comply with its demands. In setting its course of escalation, the administration overlooked two inescapable factors: What was it asking of Hanoi? And what were the relative economic and strategic interests of the United States and North Vietnam in Southeast Asia?[86] What the United States expected of Hanoi was precise and nonnegotiable. It rested on deeply held suppositions of danger that conformed to the imagery of falling dominoes, rendering the conflict in Southeast Asia one element in a wider pattern of aggression. The president restated the requirements of containment in Asia in his Baltimore address of April 7, 1965, "Our objective is the independence of South Vietnam, and its freedom from attack. We want nothing for ourselves—only that the people of South Vietnam be allowed to guide their country in their own way."[87] The president did not offer negotiations; there was nothing to negotiate. In subsequent statements, members of the administration repeated these minimum demands, inviting Hanoi to stop its aggression and accept the independence of South Vietnam.[88] Realist critics inside and outside the government warned that such inflexible demands would lead to interminable war.

James C. Thomson, Jr., complained to Bundy that the administration had "failed to do any significant exploration of Hanoi's actual private terms for a settlement." Nor had Washington offered any negotiable terms of its own. Ball reminded his colleagues that their definition of American success required Hanoi's unconditional surrender. There would be no settlement, he declared, until the administration was prepared to negotiate a tactical withdrawal, even one that might enable Hanoi to prevail in the end. After reading the president's April 7 speech, Walter Lippmann told Bundy: "It's just a disguised demand for capitulation. You've got to give the communists some incentive to negotiate."[89]

Washington had failed to recognize the infinite resiliency and determination of North Vietnam's leadership. Ho Chi Minh and others who defined Hanoi's objectives had invested a full quarter century or more in their struggle for the independence and unification of Vietnam.[90] North Vietnamese Premier Pham Van Dong proclaimed his country's minimum goals in April 1965 as "The peaceful reunification of Vietnam is to be settled by the Vietnamese people in both zones, without any foreign interference."[91] No one in Washington could estimate what level of destruction would prompt Hanoi to accept a settlement that failed to ratify that purpose. From the beginning Hanoi understood its ultimate advantage—that the United States, whatever its official, terror-ridden rhetoric of potential disaster, never had more than a limited interest in the war.[92] This enabled the North Vietnamese to dwell less on objectives than on the nature and timing of their counter-strategies.

Even as Washington unleashed the American war in Southeast Asia, it accepted constraints in the use of force that denied the seriousness of its intentions. From the outset, the Johnson administration adopted a strategy, not for military victory, but for the avoidance of defeat.

The president wanted from the public the requisite support to underwrite the war effort, but not enough to endanger his determination to fight a limited war. As Congress passed measure after measure of his Great Society program during the spring of 1965, Johnson did not wish to see that program die in the jungles of Southeast Asia. Nor did he desire to invite direct Soviet or Chinese involvement. His decision to defend South Vietnam with minimal demands on the American people—a guns and butter program—sustained the necessary public and congressional support, but it compelled financing the expanding war with increasing federal borrowing.[93]

Johnson's domestic strategy initially worked. Fighting the war at minimum cost—amid unending promises of victory—won the support of Congress, as well as the American public.[94] Backed by the computers in the department of defense, the administration, following the critical decision of July 27 to launch a ground war, reassured the country that success lay just beyond each accretion of allied power in Vietnam. The U.S. troop buildup reached 200,000 in 1966 and continued upward until it exceeded a half-million in 1967. The bomb tonnage dropped on Vietnam gradually surpassed by fifty percent that dropped on both Germany and Japan during World War II. By 1968 the price of war reached 200,000 American casualties, with 30,000 dead, and $30 billion a year. Despite that vast expenditure of effort the administration could devise no strategy to break Hanoi's resistance.[95]

The U.S. effort in Vietnam was designed to achieve capitulation, not negotiation. Hanoi's resistance continued to puzzle American officials. General Taylor complained that "one likes to feel able to count on the rationality and good sense of a dangerous opponent." When it became clear that bombing alone would not produce Hanoi's capitulation, General Westmoreland formulated a plan of operations designed to avert defeat and then assume the offensive en route to victory. The strategy anticipated an end to the fighting sometime after 1968 as the United States achieved total military predominance on the battlefield. Westmoreland assigned the major burden of the fighting to American troops. Except in the Delta, he employed the South Vietnamese forces largely for pacification—the occupation and organization of areas presumably freed of Viet Cong control. Without battle lines or territorial objectives, American officers resorted to body counts to measure the success of allied military operations. Yet the war continued unabated, with Hanoi, now fully committed to the struggle for the South, matching each new U.S. increment with a continuing escalation of its own. As the war dragged on with mounting casualties, the freedom of the enemy to strike anywhere and everywhere suggested that the struggle remained generally a civil war in which political as well as military effectiveness was the ultimate measure of success.

To stabilize the political environment, McNamara advocated a more effective pacification effort throughout the countryside. In 1967, President Johnson gave Westmoreland the responsibility for pacification, civil as well as military, and sent Robert Komer to Saigon as the general's deputy for pacification. Ellsworth Bunker, who replaced Taylor as ambassador in May 1967, refused to distinguish between military and civil pacification. "To me," he declared, "this is all one war. Everything we do is an aspect of the total effort to achieve our objective here." At the same time, the president sent General Creighton Abrams to South Vietnam to improve the performance of the country's military forces. Ultimately, an independent South Vietnam required an effective military and political structure no less than the elimination of all Viet Cong and North Vietnamese authority from the country.[96]

As the war raged on, U.S. officials made little effort to encourage the development of a viable democratic order in South Vietnam. Between 1965 and 1967, the South Vietnamese drafted and adopted a constitution, elected a president, vice president, and legislature. Despite the ubiquitous trials of war, they successfully held many local elections. But such evidences of democratic progress were not of primary American concern. For the conduct of the American war, Vietnamese political activity was fundamentally irrelevant.[97]

* * *

Even as the United States embarked on its massive escalation of the war in 1965, some Washington officials suspected that the effort would not succeed. John T. McNaughton began his famed memorandum of January 17, 1966, "We have in Vietnam the ingredients of an enormous miscalculation. . . . The ARVN is tired, passive and accommodation prone. . . . The bombing of the North may or may not be able effectively to interdict infiltration. . . . South Vietnam is near the edge of serious inflation and economic chaos. We are in an escalating military stalemate."[98] For McNaughton, the only realistic U.S. purpose remaining in Vietnam was the avoidance of humiliation, but he understood that in the absence of a national decision, it would never bring enough power to bear on Vietnam to successfully terminate the war. Perhaps the country's reputation required the prevention of Saigon's fall, but not necessarily the prevention of a coalition government or a neutralized South Vietnam.[99] For the more optimistic, McNaughton's goal of reputation-saving was scarcely adequate, although even that limited objective could become frightfully expensive.

To explain the incipient global aggression of an expansive Communism in Vietnam, the administration dwelled on the so-called lessons of Munich. Secretary Rusk instructed the American Society of International Law in April 1965 that Western inaction in Manchuria and Ethiopia had demanded the terrible price of World War II. He asserted: "surely we have learned over the past decades that the acceptance of aggression leads only to a sure catastrophe. Surely, we have learned that the aggressor must face the consequences of his action and be saved from the frightful miscalculation that brings all to ruin."[100] "In Vietnam today," warned Senator Thomas J. Dodd of Connecticut, "we are confronted by an incorrigible aggressor, fanatically committed to the destruction of the free world, whose agreements are as worthless as Hitler's. . . . If we fail to draw the line in Viet-Nam, in short, we may find ourselves compelled to draw a defense line as far back as Seattle." Senator Henry M. Jackson of Washington reminded NATO officials in 1966 that "the world might have been spared enormous misfortune if Japan had not been permitted to succeed in Manchuria, or Mussolini in Ethiopia, or Hitler in Czechoslovakia or in the Rhineland. And we think that our sacrifices in this dirty war in little Vietnam will make a dirtier and bigger war less likely." President Johnson told a New Hampshire audience, in August 1966, that men regrettably had to fight limited wars to avoid the need to fight larger ones.[101] The concept of falling dominoes, placed in the context of Munich, became the most powerful of all governmental appeals for public support during the critical years of military escalation in Southeast Asia.

* * *

Criticism of the war kept pace with official efforts to escalate both the costs and the importance of the struggle. Most critics were not pacifists and agreed readily that the country had the right to war against those who threatened its welfare or existence. Those who challenged the U.S. military escalation in Southeast Asia agreed generally that the struggle for Vietnam was chiefly an indigenous contest to be resolved by the Vietnamese people themselves. Such argumentation reduced the U.S. effort to a largely illegitimate intervention in the internal affairs of another country. The critics thus demanded a cessation of the bombing of the North, the segregation of American forces from the fighting to reduce casualties, the acceptance of a coalition government for Saigon that included all elements involved in that country's struggle for power, and, finally, a measured withdrawal of U.S. forces from Vietnam. Among the war's active critics after 1965 were not only many students, scholars, and writers, but also retired generals of major distinction and both Democratic and Republican members of Congress. Many critics in government and the press had supported the initial U.S. intervention; they entered the opposition when it became clear that the United States could not win the war in any traditional sense.

During 1967, consequently, Johnson's escalating war in Vietnam collided with the equally burgeoning antiwar movement. By then the soaring cost of the war in death and destruction, without evidence of progress in creating a viable South Vietnamese state or winning the war, had begun to fracture the consensus that underwrote the initial U.S. involvement. Much of the media, both press and television, had turned against the war, and such critics as Galbraith and George F. Kennan denied that the United States had any vital interests in Southeast Asia and should withdraw as quickly as possible.[102] President Johnson, his advisers, and members of his cabinet launched a vigorous counterattack. They not only re-explained the war but also challenged the reports pouring out of Saigon that denied any military progress.[103] Vice President Hubert Humphrey, returning from a tour of the western Pacific, announced that U.S. policy was achieving gains on all fronts. Soon Ambassador Bunker, on a reporting trip to Washington, assured the nation that the allies in Vietnam were making steady progress on every front. General Westmoreland assured the National Press Club in November, "whereas in 1965 the enemy was winning, today he is certainly losing." With U.S. forces numbering a half-million, he said, "we have reached the important point where the end begins to come into view."[104]

Still, the national consensus on the war continued to disintegrate. A secret White House survey of September 1967 revealed the administration's continuing loss of public and congressional support. McNamara and many of his Pentagon associates had become privately disillusioned with the war, persuaded that the bombing would not stop Hanoi even as the destruction created lasting enemies for the United States.[105] National Security Adviser Rostow had become the administration's chief dispenser of optimism. In his White House office his aides culled the reports from Saigon, segregating the favorable ones to prove that the war was going well—indeed, about to be won.[106] In late January 1968, Rostow informed newsmen that captured documents foretold the impending collapse of the enemy in Vietnam.

Even as he spoke, the Tet Offensive burst like a bombshell over South Vietnam. U.S. and ARVN casualties were considerable; those of the Viet Cong and North Vietnamese far more so—almost eliminating the Viet Cong as an independent fighting force. Officials and pro-administration members of the press agreed that the Communist offensive had been a military disaster; Westmoreland proclaimed Tet a major enemy defeat.[107] Reports of death and destruction on television and in the press revealed the horrors of war and destroyed any illusion that the United States had the contest well in hand. Walter Cronkite of CBS exemplified this conclusion when he declared: "It is increasingly clear to this reporter that the only rational way out ... would be to negotiate, not as victors, but as an honorable people."[108]

The contrast between its promises of victory and the violence of Tet exaggerated the perception of disaster. Townsend Hoopes explained the adverse reaction of many top Pentagon officials, "One thing was clear to us all: the Tet offensive was the eloquent counterpoint to the effusive optimism of November. It showed conclusively that ... the enemy retained enormous strength and vitality—certainly enough to extinguish the notion of a clear-cut allied victory in the minds of all objective men."[109]

President Johnson responded to Tet by summoning key members of the country's Cold War elite, the Wise Men, to the White House. Westmoreland argued that victory was in sight and requested an additional 200,000 troops. But the president discovered that a majority of his special advisory group, including Dean Acheson and W. Averell Harriman, favored disengagement from Vietnam. So did Clark Clifford, who had succeeded the departed McNamara as Secretary of Defense. Vietnam, at last, had shattered the Cold War consensus that had underwritten every phase of the Cold War since the Truman Doctrine.

It also became clear that the widespread loss of confidence in national policy focused chiefly on the president. On the evening of March 31, Johnson informed a dismayed public that under no circumstance would he campaign further for the presidency. He preferred, he said, to curtail the growing divisiveness in the country by focusing on the problem of ending the war in Vietnam. With that decision the United States began its long, slow retreat from Southeast Asia. To facilitate the opening of negotiations with Hanoi, the president proclaimed a partial bombing halt. So thorough had been the repudiation of his

Figure 11.1
**Johnson's advisers, (R to L, clockwise): President Johnson, Sec. Robert
McNamara, Sec. Henry Fowler, McGeorge Bundy, Dean Acheson, John
Cowles, Arthur Dean, Gen. Omar Bradley, John J. McCloy, Robert Lovett, Bill
Bundy, George Ball, Sec. Dean Rusk (Yoichi Okamoto; Courtesy: Lyndon B.
Johnson Library)**

policies that neither he nor Rusk dared any longer to travel freely and
openly around the country.

* * *

Late in April, the president announced that talks with Hanoi would
soon open in Paris, with Harriman acting as chief U.S. negotiator.
Washington heralded the forthcoming exchange as a major breakthrough for peace, but its mood was not compromising. Even as it
embarked on its widely heralded peace venture, Washington would
agree to no less than a fully independent South Vietnam. When the
Paris talks opened on May 13, Xuan Thuy, the North Vietnamese
negotiator, made clear to Harriman that Hanoi would be no less
demanding. He accused the United States of intruding into the affairs
of the Vietnamese people and undermining the principle of self-
determination by placing its massive military power at the disposition
of the Saigon minority. Xuan Thuy emphasized Hanoi's oft-repeated
insistence that successful negotiations could proceed only after the
United States had halted the bombing of all North Vietnam. The
search for peace had scarcely begun.[110]

Recognizing that any political settlement would endanger its existence, the Saigon regime anticipated the Paris talks with considerable anxiety. South Vietnamese Foreign Minister Tran Van Do declared in an interview of April 12, "I feel no qualms [about the future] as long as the fighting continues, [but] I look forward to negotiations with serious misgivings." Thieu, president of the Republic of South Vietnam, reminded Washington that he opposed any withdrawal of U.S. forces from his country. Saigon assured Washington that it would never agree to the recognition of the National Liberation Front as an independent political force in South Vietnam or any halt in the bombing short of absolute guarantees from Hanoi.[111] Washington promised Thieu that the United States would never accept a political settlement for South Vietnam that defied the principle of self-determination. Clearly the only escape for the United States lay in Thieu's success in building an effective military and political structure in Saigon. The administration now made the decision to begin the transfer of responsibility for the war to the Thieu regime. To that end, Secretary of Defense Clifford promised Thieu larger quantities of the best U.S. equipment. During July, Thieu announced that the United States could begin to phase out its forces in 1969, but few American commanders in Washington or Saigon took such expressions of optimism seriously.[112]

President Johnson's decision to limit the bombing scarcely slowed the pace of war, but it created a mood of euphoria in the United States that all but eliminated the conflict as a subject of political debate, especially after the Democratic Convention in Chicago disposed of the war critics and nominated Humphrey for the presidency. Both Humphrey and Republican nominee Richard Nixon promised peace in Vietnam, but both refused to dwell on the means for achieving it. Peace required either political concessions or a vastly enlarged war that no politician dared to advocate. For his part, Nixon intimated to a reporter that he had a "secret plan" to end the war.

Meanwhile, the Paris talks, whatever hopes they generated, did not move the war any closer to a solution. Hanoi refused to compromise its demands for a total cessation of the bombing. Washington, in turn, required of Hanoi some promise of a de-escalation of the war effort.[113] Suddenly, on November 1, the president announced that new developments, which he failed to explain, had permitted him to stop the bombing of North Vietnam. Simultaneously, he declared that within a week the conversations in Paris would be broadened to include the Saigon government as well as the National Liberation Front (NLF).[114]

Washington quickly discovered again that Saigon was no less a barrier to a settlement than Hanoi. Thieu averred that under no circumstance would his government send representatives to a meeting in which the NLF appeared as a separate and equal bargaining agent. As he explained to Catholic leaders in Saigon, "[The NLF] will become the winners. . . . Our existence is at stake." Meanwhile, Nixon had moved secretly to sabotage any faint hope that Johnson's peace endeavor might have of succeeding. He sent word, primarily via Anna Chennault, widow of the famous World War II air force general, to Thieu suggesting he boycott the ongoing negotiations until after Nixon entered the White House. The South Vietnamese would then find a more supportive advocate.[115]

Xuan Thuy in Paris insisted that the NLF was the only authentic voice of the South Vietnamese people, but he informed the press that he welcomed a meeting that included a Saigon delegation. Mrs. Nguyen Thi Binh, heading the Viet Cong negotiating team, arrived in Paris on November 3, warning the Americans that the "Vietnamese people will continue their struggle until final victory."[116] The central issue of the war remained unchanged: Who would control Saigon? For the moment, at least, Hanoi and the NLF would accept a coalition government. To Saigon, however, any acceptance of the NLF as equals would lead to political compromise, and compromise would terminate in disaster.

This deadlock over purpose reduced the Paris negotiations to matters of form, not of substance. In reality, the competing intentions for Saigon were so contradictory and uncompromisable that no peaceful settlement was possible. Thus American negotiators rejected Hanoi's suggestion of a single, four-party conference around a single table, whether square, round, or doughnut-shaped. The United States countered with a seating arrangement that suggested a two-sided conference, with a green baize barrier taped diametrically across a circular table. The order of speaking, once begun, would rotate around the table. Saigon accepted this proposal, but Hanoi, recognizing in the U.S. design an effort to bury the NLF in a single Communist team, rejected it. When, late in November, Saigon, under intense U.S. pressure, agreed to enter the Paris negotiations directly, a European journalist quipped that the decision would produce "one conference with two sides, three delegations, and four chairs." Vice President Ky, heading the Saigon delegation, arrived in Paris to make clear his refusal to compromise on procedure or protocol.[117]

Finally, in January 1969, the North Vietnamese and U.S. negotiators in Paris agreed on a seating arrangement for the conference.

Their formula provided for an unmarked table, flanked by two rectangular tables for secretaries. There would be no flags or other identifying symbols. The four delegations would sit as two opposing groups, each to be followed in speaking by the other on its side. This seating arrangement permitted Hanoi to claim the presence of four delegations whereas the "AA, BB" speaking sequence enabled Saigon and Washington to claim a two-sided conference.[118]

Even as the Paris confrontation took form, neither side revealed the slightest intention to accept a compromise on the critical question of Saigon's future government. The long and costly U.S. involvement had, in no manner, created the occasion for an agreement by convincing either Hanoi or Saigon that it could not ultimately have what it wanted. Essentially it was the chasm between the ends and means of policy that rendered the entire American effort illusionary. The ends of policy upheld the rights and expectations of Saigon; the means, destructive as they were, failed to diminish the goals or expectations of Hanoi. "The Vietnam story," Adam B. Ulam concluded, "thus brings into full relief the immorality of unrealism in international politics. . . . Much could have been saved in human lives, in human freedom and contentment through the world, if only U.S. policies had been guided by less elevated and more practical goals."[119]

Within the United States, the needed national consensus, favoring either compromise or victory, remained tantalizing elusive. Ultimately, President Johnson's policies resulted in far more division at home than victory in Asia. The reason is clear: those policies were anchored to words and emotions, to high promises of success and dire warnings of the consequences of failure, and not to a body of easily recognizable circumstances that carried their own conviction and recommended their own responses. To transform the struggle of Vietnam into a momentous threat to vast areas of the globe that encompassed, ultimately, the security interests of the United States, the administration employed the rhetoric of falling dominoes and the disastrous consequences of Munich. But somehow the sound of falling dominoes and the fears of another Munich were audible only to those who defended the war. It was not strange that the country divided sharply between those who took the words and admonitions seriously and those who did not. To defend his direct military involvement with a half-million men, the president, vigorously supported by members of his administration, Congress, and the press, was compelled to exaggerate the importance of that region until he had expended more in cost and destruction than the results could justify. And even then, the end of the conflict was nowhere in sight.

CHAPTER 12

The Search for Détente: Nixon, Kissinger, and Ford

Richard M. Nixon, in assuming the presidency in January 1969, inherited a body of Cold War policies that had changed little since mid-century. To discourage feared Soviet expansionism in Europe, successive administrations, with variations in language and style, had sustained the precepts of containment as they proclaimed the country's adherence to NATO. To protect the non-European world against Communist encroachment, U.S. officials sustained the nation's undying opposition to Communist-led governments and movements everywhere, as manifestations of the Kremlin's expansive power. In Asia, containment centered on the nonrecognition of China's Beijing regime and the war against falling dominoes in Southeast Asia. Together these exercises in containment defined the U.S. contribution to the defense of diversity in the non-Soviet world. For Nixon, however, the assumptions of Communist unity and power ignored the accumulating evidence of national self-assertion and its impact on global politics. Likewise, Henry A. Kissinger, the distinguished Harvard scholar who entered the Nixon administration as presidential assistant for national security affairs, recognized the demands of a changing global environment. "When I came into office," he recalled, "we were really at the end of a period of American foreign policy in which a redesign would have been necessary to do no matter who took over."[1]

Long before the Nixon administration, the unalterable trends in international life had challenged a full spectrum of Cold War assumptions. Soviet relations with the Communist states had eroded badly, creating problems for the Kremlin that transcended its relations with the Western powers. That the Soviets could sustain a Communist monolith on free consent continued to be an expensive illusion. The decision of

Leonid Brezhnev, Khrushchev's successor, to suppress the Czech government in 1968 verified the will of the Kremlin to impose some measure of conformity across Eastern Europe with force. But if that region remained the Kremlin's private preserve, it was not monolithic. Hungary, Rumania, and Poland—as well as Finland in the north—were careful not to threaten Soviet security with anti-Soviet policies and ideologies and had long enjoyed varying degrees of independence. For Moscow, the experience of maintaining its hegemony over reluctant and highly nationalistic states had become both costly and unpromising. In China the Soviets never exercised control and, after the mid-1950s, very little influence. The Beijing regime was fiercely independent in its ideological assertions, its policies, and its behavior. It was not strange that Moscow's troubles in Eastern Europe and its troubling preoccupation with China encouraged a search for better relations with the United States and Western Europe.[2]

In the United States, as well, the costs of the Cold War had spiraled beyond any possible returns from the vast expenditure of money and effort. The heavy consumption of resources had purchased neither peace nor security—at least not on American terms. Nor was the end of the expenditure in sight. The search for absolute guarantees in a world perceived to be profoundly dangerous had produced military systems of astonishing destructiveness and sophistication. But they had eliminated neither Soviet power nor the Soviet hegemony from Eastern Europe. That failure demonstrated that the unprecedented levels of personal and national wellbeing, both in the United States and most Western countries, did not require the restoration of the Versailles order in Europe after all. Across Europe containment had won. As an end it had stabilized the division of the continent with a vengeance. As a means to an end—the negotiation of a European order based on self-determination—it had failed simply because no Western military structure could, without war, undo the Soviet political and territorial gains that flowed from Hitler's collapse. That the United States had coexisted with a world that did not measure up to its precepts of self-determination—with such perennial success and no little security—created doubts regarding the wisdom of the search for some more perfect, democratic international order.

Such doubts lay at the heart of the Nixon-Kissinger approach to the Soviet Union. Nixon understood that the postwar *Pax Americana* was exhausted, that the country had reached the outer limits of its capacity to influence the world of nations, and that it had neither the power nor the interests to push back the frontiers of the Communist world.

He expressed this sense of limits in his address to the U.S. Naval Academy in June 1974. "America is no longer a giant," he reminded his audience, "towering over the rest of the world with seemingly inexhaustible resources and a nuclear monopoly." The time had come for the country to reassess its responsibilities. Still any search for accommodation with the changing world relationships required greater pragmatism than Washington had displayed in the past. As Nixon explained, "We have to remember . . . that unrealistic idealism could be impractical and potentially dangerous. It could tempt us to forgo results that were good because we insisted on results that were perfect."

In his first annual report to Congress, prepared during his opening months in office, Nixon acknowledged the essential changes in international relations that required a new approach to foreign policy. Western Europe and Japan, he noted, "have recovered their economic strength, their political vitality, and their national self-confidence." No longer were Third World nations dependent on the United States for their security. "Once many feared," he continued, "that they would become simply a battleground of cold war rivalry and fertile ground for Communist penetration. But this fear misjudged their pride in their national identities and their determination to preserve

Figure 12.1
President Richard M. Nixon and National Security Advisor Henry Kissinger, March 14, 1969 (Courtesy: National Archives)

their newly won sovereignty." Nationalism, the new president admitted, had shattered the unity of international Communism. Finally, the revolution in military technology had eliminated the possibility of gain in a nuclear exchange, even for those who launched the first strike.[3] Such notions regarding the global impositions on the Cold War, long in circulation, now commanded Washington's attention.

For Nixon, the United States, coexisting with undesirable conditions beyond its control, had no choice but to act pragmatically, relinquishing objectives that were ideal in pursuit of results that were merely satisfactory. For him the necessary pragmatism required policies that reflected a balance between containment—protecting peaceful nations against aggression—and a coexistence that placed allied cohesion and national self-confidence above ideological confrontation. Kissinger recalled that the Nixon administration "sought a foreign policy that eschewed both moralistic crusading and escapist isolationism, submerging them in a careful analysis of the national interest. America's aim was to maintain the balance of power and seek to build upon it a more constructive future." To achieve their goals, Nixon and Kissinger adopted a geopolitical approach, anchored ostensibly to manipulative tactics, with highly calculated maneuvers designed to play both sides of the balancing equation while pursuing arrangements in one part of the world that would influence behavior and attitudes elsewhere. At the outset, they refused to discount the Soviet danger. Both men wondered whether the United States, with its long-standing Cold War consensus disintegrating under the impact of Vietnam, was still sufficiently united to lead the Western world in its continuing confrontation with the Soviet Union. "Our interests belong with Western Europe and Japan," declared Morton Halperin, former deputy assistant secretary of defense. "But less out of concern for defense against the Soviet threat to them than out of concern for our relations with them and their openness to the world for trade." In a somewhat similar vein Nixon later wrote, "I had to put Europe at the top of list" in order to secure the Western alliance.

For Nixon and Kissinger, the recovery of Washington's effective and necessary management of the international arena required an honorable peace in Vietnam that reunited the country and reassured the world that the United States remained committed to the defense of its security. Meanwhile, the president and his national security adviser regarded Soviet-American relations promising enough to pursue a program of détente.[4] It was essential, however, that the Soviets not exploit the possible gains of détente in Europe by challenging known American commitments in the Third World. The existing global balance demanded that the United States maintain its allegiance to anti-Communist elements in Asia, Africa, the Middle East, and Latin America.

In their memoirs, Nixon and Kissinger stressed the importance of *linkage*. "We insisted," Kissinger recalled:

that progress in superpower relations, to be real, had to be made on a broad front. Events in different parts of the world, in our view, were related to each other. . . . We proceeded from the premise that to separate issues . . . would encourage the Soviet leaders to believe that they could use cooperation in one area as a safety valve while striving for unilateral advantage elsewhere. This was unacceptable.[5]

Détente required reasonable Soviet behavior everywhere. As Kissinger warned in his *Pacem in Terris* address of October 8, 1973, "We will oppose the attempt by any country to achieve a position of predominance either globally or regionally. We will resist any attempt to exploit a policy of détente to weaken our alliance. We will react if relaxation of tensions is used as a cover to exacerbate conflict in international trouble spots."[6] In no area of the world, he added, could the U.S.S.R. ignore this imperative without imperiling its entire relationship with the United States.

The Nixon-Kissinger "partnership" sparked observers' curiosity as to which one held the dominate role. William Safire, writing in *Harper's*, asserted that Nixon was the creator and manager of U.S. policy in the critical years of 1971 and 1972. Nixon, he believed, used Kissinger artfully, sometimes thrusting him into the limelight, sometimes letting him down cruelly. Nixon, wrote Safire, was always the creative force. Kissinger's chief role, for example, was that of conducting the laborious preparations before the Beijing and Moscow summits. In their book on Kissinger, Marvin and Bernard Kalb agreed. However, Henry Brandon suggests that from the beginning Kissinger had a major influence on Nixon. It seems clear that the underlying precepts of national policy belonged to Kissinger as well as to Nixon.

Kissinger's historical contribution to the rules of détente flowed from the notion that the foundation of international stability lay in a generally acceptable definition of legitimacy. Kissinger observed in his study of Prince Metternich, *A World Restored*, " 'Legitimacy' . . . means no more than an international agreement about the nature of workable arrangements and about the permissible aims and methods of foreign policy. It implies the acceptance of the framework of the international order by all major powers."[7] An acceptable legitimacy did not eliminate conflict, but only its scope, with the nations in conflict always acknowledging a mutual interest in the perpetuation of the existing international order. Conflicts would be fought, if at all, within the constraints imposed by the existing order, with all measures aimed at the preservation, not the destruction, of that order. Agreements could achieve a lasting harmonization of interests only if nations adhered to such limited objectives.

Politically, the Kremlin desired Western recognition of the Soviet hegemony in Eastern Europe. For a full generation the Western adherence to the principle of self-determination had ruled out any basic Cold War settlements across Europe. Nixon's ultimate decision to discard both traditional Western revisionism toward the Soviet bloc and the American mission to rid the world of Communist influence was the key to the new age of détente. Whatever its ramifications for peace and security, détente essentially reflected a tardy U.S. recognition that the Europe wrought by Hitler's defeat had become a permanent feature of international life.

Western revisionism received its first inescapable challenge in West German Chancellor Willy Brandt's *Ostpolitik*.[8] During 1970, after months of negotiations, Brandt signed treaties with both Moscow and Warsaw that recognized the postwar frontiers of Central Europe. By accepting the existing borders, Brandt acknowledged formally that the U.S.S.R., not Germany, had won the Second World War. By autumn of that year, the corresponding Soviet aim of increased cooperation with the West became apparent in Washington. Before the president could respond, a sharp crisis in the Middle East, with Syrian forces invading Jordan with Soviet tanks, threatened the fragile Middle East cease-fire of August 1970. Almost simultaneously, the Soviets moved submarines into Cuban waters. Privately Kissinger reminded the Soviet ambassador that the Kremlin was violating the Khrushchev-Kennedy understanding of 1962 regarding Soviet bases in Cuba. Quickly the Soviets withdrew the submarines to end the crisis.[9]

Limited U.S. initiatives produced the critical gains of 1971. In March, Soviet leader Leonid Brezhnev outlined the new directions of Soviet policy before the Communist Party Congress in Moscow. Nixon responded cautiously, determined to protect the principle of linkage by seeking agreement on the broadest possible range of issues to relax tensions on all fronts. In September the Big Four, after long and tedious negotiations, reached an agreement on West Berlin. In November the American secretary of commerce began conversations in Moscow on the normalization of economic relations. In his February 1972 Foreign Policy Report to Congress, Nixon reminded the nation that the issues that divided the United States and the U.S.S.R. were still both genuine and serious.[10]

Weapons of mass destruction—biological, chemical, and nuclear—also figured prominently in Washington's early diplomatic maneuvering. The United States and its Western allies found abolishing chemical weapons a difficult challenge, in part because they did not wish to give up the option of these weapons, which, unlike biological weapons, were viewed as having military utility. However, on November 25, 1969, President Nixon reaffirmed the United States' chemical warfare "no-first-use" policy that dated from World War II. At the same time, he unilaterally renounced the United States' use of bacteriological or biological weapons, closed all facilities producing these offensive weapons, and ordered existing stockpiles of biological weapons and agents destroyed. At Geneva the Conference of the Committee on Disarmament had been preparing a convention that would ban production, acquisition, or stockpiling of biological weapons and would required destruction of stocks. In April 1972 the United States and the Soviet Union joined other nations in signing the Biological Convention.[11]

Meanwhile Nixon had informed the nation, "In light of the recent advances in bilateral and multilateral negotiations involving the two countries, it has been agreed that a meeting [between the leaders of the United States and the Soviet Union] will take place in Moscow in the latter part of May 1972." A new era of arms control had begun, one that focused on attempts to limit, and eventually, to reduce strategic nuclear weapons systems—one that lasted until the end of the Cold War. While he agreed that these talks were quite useful, former Secretary of State Dean Rusk later depicted the negotiations that would span decades as "history's longest permanent floating crap game."[12]

* * *

In the late 1950s, some individuals in Washington were beginning to recognize the need to institutionalize the strategic balance. "For all practical purposes we have in terms of nuclear capabilities reached a point which may be called 'parity'," Atomic Energy Commission Chairman Gordon Dean wrote in a preface to Henry Kissinger's 1957 book *Nuclear Weapons and Foreign Policy*. "We have long known that such a time would come. It is now upon us. I do not mean necessarily parity in numbers of large bombs. Numbers become less important when the point is reached where both sides have the capability to annihilate each other."[13] However, it was President Johnson who, in November 1966, formally invited Moscow to join in arms limitation negotiations. Even though they had greatly expanded their strategic forces, the Soviet were concerned about U.S. technological advances in strategic arms systems and wondered when Washington's deployment of new nuclear weaponry would halt. In late June 1968, Foreign Minister Andrei Gromyko suggested that discussions on limiting both offensive and defensive weapons begin on September 30, hoping to link the talks to America's withdrawal from Vietnam. Soviet and Warsaw pact forces' intervention in Czechoslovakia on August 21, caused Johnson to postpone the talks.

Soviet leaders were not opposed to enhancing their security through arms limitation negotiations because they believed that this was one way to slow the arms race and reduce the costly burden of improving their security through a continuing nuclear arms buildup. Moreover, the Politburo realized that with the election of Richard Nixon they could not link such talks with Vietnam. On the day of his inauguration, January 20, 1969, Moscow indicated to President Nixon that they were prepared to begin discussions on strategic weaponry. During the 1968 campaign Richard Nixon had insisted he would restore U.S. "military superiority"; shortly after his inauguration, however, he stated that his administration would seek strategic nuclear "sufficiency."[14] Accepting the Soviet invitation, the two delegations launched the Strategic Arms Limitation Talks (SALT) on November 17, 1969. However, the two nuclear arsenals differed significantly. The United States had developed technologically sophisticated, accurate missiles with relatively small warheads of one to two megatons, while the Soviets had deployed a number of different types of weapons. Some were similar to American weapons, but others were larger and had a greater "throw-weight"— the total weight that a missile was capable of lifting into a trajectory— that caused difficulties in negotiations for many years.

The protracted negotiations had their peculiar, even humorous, sidelights. The Soviet civilian delegates arrived knowing very little about the military capabilities of their own weapons. When a U.S. delegate sought to enlighten them, the senior Soviet general asked him to stop discussing Soviet arms; such matters, the general insisted were not the concern of Soviet civilians, even delegates. Moscow did have rather clearly defined goals that included slowing down the arms race, gaining recognition of Soviet nuclear parity, and attempting to retain some military advantages the Soviets believed they had obtained.[15] In May 1972,

Nixon and Kissinger flew to Moscow for the signing of the agreements produced by the Strategic Arms Limitation Talks with Chairman Brezhnev.

According the Thomas Graham, when the American leaders arrived:

we had a well-drafted complete treaty limiting ABM systems, and a loosely drafted and incomplete agreement limiting strategic offensive systems. . . . Adding to the confusion [was] that in working out the final deals on the Interim Agreement, Nixon and Kissinger often met alone with Brezhnev and his aides, not even accompanied by a United States interpreter who could have verified translations and made notes.[16]

Nevertheless, at the Moscow Summit three pacts were signed: an Interim Agreement (SALT I, 1972–1977) on some strategic systems, the Anti-Ballistic Missile (ABM) Treaty, and a political "Basic Principles" accord. SALT I's limits on strategic systems were actually higher than each party currently possessed; but ceilings restricted some future deployments. The ABM Treaty limited each nation to two defensive missile sites, subsequently reduced to a single location. Under development by the United States since 1967, but ignored in the discussions were multiple independently reentry vehicles (MIRVs). A single missile (or "bus") could carry aloft two or more of these "vehicles" with each of them containing warheads and each capable of striking different targets. Delegates might have halted programs during these SALT I negotiations, but the Pentagon and congressional critics warned Kissinger "don't come back with a MIRV ban."[17] Three years later, when Moscow deployed their MIRVs, the Pentagon's shortsighted insistence on a temporary advantage resulted in the greatly impaired strategic stability as each side's ICBMs had become vulnerable. The MIRVed intercontinental ballistic missiles (ICBMs) made preemptive strikes appear a more promising choice in a crisis situation.

The "Basic Principles of Relations" agreement, initiated by the Kremlin and largely ignored by American leadership, might have substantially reduced tensions between the superpowers if the pact had been better defined and realistically explained to the American public. While Nixon and Kissinger sought a "linkage" between arms control and the resolution of Third World issues, Moscow thought that this pact could provide the basis for superpower cooperation in resolving basic differences. Thus Soviet officials considered it "an important political declaration" that they wished, as Ambassador Dobrynin recalled, would be the basis of a "new political process of détente in our relations." Moscow hoped the agreement would recognize the

Figure 12.2
President Nixon and Premier Leonid Brezhnev, June 16, 1973 (Courtesy: National Archives)

Soviet doctrine of peaceful coexistence (or détente) and acknowledge the "principle of equality as a basis for the security of both countries." Failure to develop détente's boundaries and to gain public acceptance for it would doom the idea.[18]

That the two powers shared a mutuality of interests at the Moscow summit received affirmation, at least in part, in the cordiality that characterized both the private and the formal exchanges between Nixon and Brezhnev. Statesmen and journalists alike heralded the meeting as a milestone in the history of postwar American-Soviet relations. If Nixon and Kissinger viewed the pacts as significant accomplishments, however, the Defense Department and Joint Chiefs of Staff insisted on pursuing new strategic weapons systems—including the Trident submarine, ABM deployments, a submarine-launched cruise missile, and multiple independently targeted warheads—before granting their approval. Senator Henry Jackson of Washington, along with a former delegate to the talks, Paul Nitze, worried about the Soviet's retention of 308 heavy ICBMs, which conceivably could be fitted to carry forty MIRVed warheads each. Jackson insisted on an amendment that any future treaty "not limit the U.S. to levels of intercontinental strategic forces inferior to the limits for the Soviet Union," thereby launching a search for a new "yardstick" that would have a dampening effect on subsequent negotiations.

Nixon and Brezhnev opened the Washington summit in June 1973 with additional pledges to build world peace. During two days in Washington, they signed four agreements for cooperation in oceanography, transportation, cultural exchange, and agriculture. Then the two men retired to Camp David, Maryland, to focus on nuclear disarmament and troop reductions in Central Europe. Back in Washington, they signed additional pacts. One required the two countries to work together when any third country endangered the peace. They regarded their subsequent agreement to avoid nuclear war as the key to their achievements. Later the two leaders flew to the Nixon home at San Clemente, California. They terminated their working sessions by completing a 20-page communiqué calling for further détente between their two countries.[19] Despite such gains, the 1973 summit exposed the ambiguities in East-West relations. Both Washington and Moscow understood the risks and costs of their perennial disagreements and the advantages of a stable relationship. But the Soviets could not escape their ideological past and the limits it placed on their diplomacy. Nor could the Nixon administration satisfy those inside and outside the beltway who believed the Soviet threat too immediate and pervasive to permit any lasting agreements or relaxation of tension.

* * *

Having focused on U.S.-Soviet relations during his first two years in office, Nixon recognized the imperative to reaffirm American ties with its European allies. Changed conditions seemed to require a new blueprint for North Atlantic relations. Western Europe's prodigious economic revival, as well as the movement toward European unification, had eliminated Atlantic cooperation as an American enterprise. Europe had long pursued policies divorced from, and often at odds with, those of the United States. France's Charles de Gaulle had asserted repeatedly that Europe should pursue its own interests, which assuredly would diverge more and more from those of the United States.

By 1972, the Soviet extensive military buildup following the Cuban missile crisis had shifted the East-West strategic balance from U.S. preponderance to near equality. For Kissinger, this change reduced the credibility of the American deterrent and required some redefinition of Western Europe's security needs. He argued that the more reassuring international environment, in diminishing the danger of nuclear attack, placed a premium on flexible response with its greater demands on conventional preparedness. Still, Kissinger complained that these new strategic requirements prompted no response in Europe at all.[20] Even in economic matters, Europe seemed disinterested in American concerns, especially when the Common Market adopted trade policies disadvantageous to the United States. The growing network of commercial ties between the European Community and other nations of Europe and the Mediterranean seemed to endanger U.S. markets even further.[21]

To meet these political, military, and economic challenges, Nixon declared 1973 "The Year of Europe." Trouble began early. In February, British Prime Minister Edward Heath informed U.S. officials at Camp David that Britain had no interest in revitalizing the Atlantic relationship. He dismissed Nixon's appeal for British-American study groups to address the problems of defense and trans-Atlantic economic ties.[22] West Germany's Willy Brandt saw Europe's improving future less in stronger allied relations than in German reunification and better associations with Eastern Europe and the U.S.S.R. Brandt's chief aide, Egan Barr, agreed that West Germany's safety lay, not in stronger defenses, but in détente with the Soviet Union.[23] Kissinger met these continuing broadsides from Europe with his "Year of Europe" speech at New York's Waldorf-Astoria Hotel on April 23. He recounted the adverse impact of changes in Europe and other areas of the world on Atlantic unity. He assured Europe of the U.S. commitment to its defense, asking in exchange that each ally share fairly "the common effort for the common defense." Europe's response to the speech was predictably ambiguous and not reassuring. Europeans ignored Nixon's appeal for a revitalized trans-Atlantic partnership in his Foreign Policy Report of May 1973.[24] By year's end Nixon had failed totally in his approach to France. Kissinger passed final judgment on the Year of Europe in his address of December 12, before the Society of Pilgrims in London. "On both sides of the Atlantic," he declared, "we are faced with the anomalous—and dangerous—situation in which the public mind identifies foreign policy success increasingly with relations with adversaries while relations with allies seem to be characterized by bickering and drift."[25]

* * *

Despite the universal evidence of the Sino-Soviet rift after 1960, the Kennedy and Johnson administrations had accepted the previous assumptions and postures regarding China with little attempt at reexamination. To official Washington the Moscow-Beijing axis remained united on essentials and therefore dangerous. In practice, American anti-Chinese attitudes revealed themselves in ubiquitous charges of misbehavior, nonrecognition, and trade restrictions. Nixon, however, quickly adopted the argument of the China critics that the faltering U.S. effort to isolate 700 million Chinese diplomatically and economically served no useful purpose and antagonized much of the world. Indeed, Nixon wrote in the October 1967 issue of *Foreign Affairs*, "any American policy toward Asia must come urgently to grips with the reality of China."[26] As president, Nixon recognized the need for improved relations with China as one essential component of a new American foreign policy. "I was fully aware," he recalled, "of the profound ideological and political differences between our countries. . . . But I believed also that in this era we could not afford to be cut off from a quarter of the world's population. We had an obligation to try to establish contact . . . and perhaps move on to greater understanding."[27] Nixon understood that the United States and China shared many historic interests and that the two decades of animosity had been a tragic, perhaps avoidable, aberration. To him China posed a lesser danger than two decades of apocalyptic rhetoric had suggested.

As early as 1969, the Nixon administration, working cautiously through third countries, moved to establish some communication with Beijing. Its initial efforts were largely unilateral—the granting of Americans the right to purchase Chinese goods without special permission; the validating of passports after March 1970 for travel in China;

and the licensing, after April 1970, of certain nonstrategic American goods for export to China.[28] During his stop in Rumania during October 1970, Nixon, for the first time, deliberately used Beijing's official title, the Peoples Republic of China. Still, if the normalization of U.S.-Chinese relations demanded new attitudes and perceptions in Washington, it required as well conditions elsewhere that would encourage China to identify its deepest interests with that normalization.

No American initiatives toward China would have succeeded without the knowledge that they would be received with some graciousness. The president hoped to establish direct and promising contact with Beijing through President Yahya Khan of Pakistan. When, in October 1970, Yahya Khan carried Nixon's overture to Beijing, the Chinese responded: "We welcome the proposal from Washington for face-to-face discussions. We would be glad to receive a high-level person for this purpose, to discuss withdrawal of American forces from Taiwan (Formosa)." Nixon welcomed the invitation, not the Chinese objective. Shortly thereafter, Yahya Khan informed Beijing of Nixon's favorable response. During April 1971, in Nagoya, Japan, the Chinese ping-pong team invited the American team, competing for the world championships, to visit the Chinese mainland. Prime Minister Chou En-lai addressed the American team: "[W]ith your acceptance of our invitation, you have opened a new page in the relations of the Chinese and American people." Then, on July 15, the president announced to the press that several days earlier Kissinger and Chou had held private talks in Beijing.[29] The premier had invited the president to visit China at some appropriate time before May 1972 and Nixon had accepted the invitation. What lay behind the ping-pong diplomacy of 1971 was Beijing's admission that past antagonism, unless terminated, would prevent any beneficial response to the new, more promising international environment.

Washington's new opening to China culminated in the president's trip to Beijing in February 1972. Minutely prepared, the venture became one of the greatest media events of the decade. By acknowledging the legitimacy of the Chinese government—which four preceding administrations had refused to do—Nixon expected Beijing to accept the legitimacy of the existing international order and the limits of proper political and diplomatic conduct. Late in 1971 the Beijing government, facing only an adverse vote from the United States, replaced the Republic of China in the United Nations. Its admission produced none of the predicted distress among the American people; it brought no disaster to either the United Nations or the free countries of Asia.

Figure 12.3
On his visit to China, Nixon dines with Chou En-lai, seated on the left
(Courtesy: National Archives)

In 1973 the United States established a permanent liaison office in Beijing. Fortunately, the earlier tensions, extending through almost a quarter century, never disintegrated into open conflict. Yet the perennial posture of nonrecognition and the language that underwrote it were not without their price. As Walter Lippmann observed, they made China the enemy and propelled the country into a wide variety of treaties and guarantees around the eastern fringes of Asia with consequences difficult to measure.

That the president's informal recognition of the Beijing regime enjoyed almost universal approval of the American people was not strange. For many the older attitudes and intentions toward mainland China, defended with such flamboyant phraseology, never made much sense. Indeed, that language belonged largely to a small minority that had a direct political and emotional stake in this country's special attachment to the Republic of China. Long before the 1970s the charges of Chinese aggression ceased to carry much conviction. William Pfaff argued in the *New Yorker* of June 3, 1972, that Nixon's initiative merely capitalized on a suppressed popular impulse for change. "It reversed," he wrote:

an American China policy that under a succession of previous Administrations had delivered blows, bluster, and grand denunciations in the name of democracy and liberty. That way of conducting ourselves before the world ... had become so corrupt in recent years, so sterile and thick with hypocrisy, that the country was ready for some Metternichian realism.[30]

Clearly, the Asia of the seventies scarcely resembled the vision of a continent engulfed by a dangerous and revolutionary bipolar contest. Everywhere the lines of East-West tension in Asia were receding before a realignment of world power. Washington's initiatives toward Moscow and Beijing encouraged Japan to establish closer relations with both Communist powers. Japan's influence in Asia expanded with that country's trade and investment around the continent's eastern and southern rim. For hard economic reasons, the powerful bonds between the United States and Japan revealed signs of strain. China and the U.S.S.R. were in direct confrontation everywhere across Asia. As early as 1969 Moscow offered defense pacts to the countries of Southeast Asia against an allegedly aggressive China. Beijing retaliated in 1972 by inviting the United States to maintain its bases in Southeast Asia as a guarantee against Soviet encroachment. Much of the president's new pentagonal world embraced Asia where four powers competed in a fluid relationship. Nothing dramatized more effectively the revolution in the U.S. perception of Asia than the president's recognition of a new regional balance of power. "We must remember," he declared in early 1972, "the only time in the history of the world that we have had any extended period of peace is when there has been a balance of power. . . . I think it will be a safer world and a better world if we have a strong, healthy United States, Europe, Soviet Union, China, Japan— each balancing the other."[31] Thereafter the new American outlook toward Asia set the stage for a limited, ordered relationship with China.

* * *

In Vietnam, Nixon inherited a disastrous policy without a guiding strategy for victory or withdrawal. "Victory for the Vietcong," Nixon wrote as a private citizen in 1965, "would mean ultimately the destruction of freedom of speech for all men for all time, not only in Asia, but in the United States as well." He again addressed the "great stakes involved in Vietnam" during a speech on November 3, 1969, insisting that they sustained the peace "in the Middle East, in Berlin, eventually even in the Western hemisphere." He and Kissinger understood well the war's death and anguish, as well as the public dismay over an engagement that mocked every strategy to end it. No less than others, they regarded the American escalation of the Johnson years a tragic blunder.

Still, they believed that a great nation had no choice but to maintain even a mistaken commitment. "However we got into Vietnam, whatever the judgment of our actions," Kissinger warned, "ending the war honorably is essential for the peace of the world. Any other solution may unloose forces that would complicate prospects for international order." He explained further in his memoir, *White House Years*, "[W]e had to remember that scores of countries and millions of people relied for their security on our willingness to stand by allies." The United States could not morally abandon a small ally merely to obtain respite for itself. "It seemed to me important," he concluded, "for America not to be humiliated, not to be shattered, but to leave [the war] ... with dignity and self-respect."[32]

Nixon was determined to succeed where previous administrations had failed. Kissinger had outlined a plan for disengagement without defeat in the January 1969 issue of *Foreign Affairs*. His proposal began with a two-track formula, one seeking a military truce, the other a political settlement for South Vietnam. The former required success on the battlefield; the second, Saigon's willingness to broaden its base so that it might meet the Communist political challenge more effectively.[33] For Kissinger, the dual approach presaged a rapid and honorable American withdrawal. Why his approach to a Vietnam solution would never succeed was obvious as early as January 1969 when Nixon dispatched Henry Cabot Lodge to Paris and instructed him to call for a military withdrawal of all U.S. and North Vietnamese forces from South Vietnam. Washington hoped thereby to enable the Vietnamese to negotiate a political settlement. But Saigon denied that the negotiators in Paris had any right even to discuss South Vietnam's political future. Apparently South Vietnamese officials believed that if they conceded nothing to their enemies, whom they could not defeat, Hanoi and its allies in the South would be left with no choice but to either accept a settlement dictated by Saigon or continue the struggle. Hanoi warned Washington, however, that it would never recognize the Saigon government or U.S. military superiority on the battlefield.

During February 1969, Kissinger received a massive bureaucratic report on Vietnam that revealed almost total disagreement and confusion within the U.S. government on every aspect of the American involvement.[34] The war was a sinking tragedy, but U.S. officials were still determined to find some escape without capitulating. What changed under Nixon was the means whereby the United States would achieve the necessary success. The Nixon-Kissinger strategy to end the war honorably began with plans for a broader, more ruthless bombing

of enemy targets. As early as March 18, the president launched Operation Breakfast, a massive secret bombing of North Vietnamese supply
lines and sanctuaries in Cambodia.[35] The second innovation in the
Nixon strategy took form in March when Defense Secretary Melvin
Laird informed Congress that the United States would soon increase
the fighting capacity of the South Vietnamese armed forces beyond
the levels contemplated by the previous administration. Whereas
Johnson had sought to prepare Saigon to cope with internal insurgency
after the achievement of peace, Nixon ordered the creation of South
Vietnamese combat forces capable of replacing Americans in the
continuing war itself. As the South Vietnamese army approached
self-sufficiency, American forces would be withdrawn.

By promising both victory and the eventual de-Americanization of
the war, Nixon created the foundation of a salable Vietnam policy. For
George Ball, Nixon and Kissinger, apparently unmindful of either the
limits of bombing or the nature of the enemy, were doomed to repeat
Johnson's mistakes. "Kissinger's initial assessment of our Vietnam
prospects," Ball recalled, "sounded as though he had been absent on
Mars during the preceding three years. . . . By dealing North Vietnam
some 'brutal blows' we could, he was confident, force it to make the
kinds of concessions that would secure peace. . . . It was the McNamara
quantitative approach all over again."[36]

Nixon's program of gradual withdrawal ruled out any strategy for
victory, but in no way did it diminish the administration's objectives in
Southeast Asia. Thus Nixon and Kissinger widened, rather than
narrowed, the chasm between the ends and the means of U.S. policy
in Vietnam, assuring ultimate disaster. Still, Nixon embarked on his
Vietnam policy with the conviction that he could protect the interests
and survival of the Saigon regime. In June, he assured South Vietnamese
President Nguyen Van Thieu on Guam that the United States would
never negotiate away his country's right to self-determination. There
the president announced his decision to withdraw an initial 25,000 men
from Vietnam in August. In September he announced a second troop
withdrawal. The withdrawal policy, he believed, would advance negotiations by demonstrating to Hanoi that the United States was serious
about a diplomatic settlement. At a press conference on September 26,
Nixon advised newsmen: "Once the enemy recognizes that it is not
going to win its objectives . . . , then the enemy will negotiate and we will
end this war before the end of 1970." On October 10, Nixon told
Republicans: "I am not going to be the first American President who
loses a war."[37]

Kissinger, in his initial encounter in late 1969 with Xuan Thuy, then North Vietnamese negotiator, quickly discovered the limits of diplomacy. Thuy demanded a new coalition government in Saigon, without Thieu and Nguyen Cao Ky, and composed of Communist elements as well as remnants of the old Saigon regime. He demanded as well the withdrawal of all U.S. and allied forces. Kissinger explained at the outset why the United States would never achieve victory or even a graceful escape from Vietnam:

Hanoi ... continued to insist that the United States establish a new government [in Saigon] under conditions in which the non-Communist side would be made impotent by the withdrawal of the American forces and demoralized by the removal of its leadership. If the United States had the effrontery to withdraw without bringing about such a political upheaval, the war would go on and our prisoners would remain. Over the years we moved from position to position, from mutual to unilateral withdrawal, from residual forces to complete departure. But Hanoi never budged. We could have neither peace nor our prisoners until we achieved what Hanoi apparently no longer trusted itself to accomplish: the overthrow of our ally, ... This seemed to us an act of dishonor that would mortgage America's international position for a long time to come.[38]

Critics, conscious of North Vietnamese determination, charged that "Vietnamization" would never succeed militarily, and that no amount of military pressure would modify Hanoi's demands.

Throughout the autumn of 1969, the antiwar movement centered on university campuses where student activists organized the nationwide moratorium on October 15, an unprecedented outpouring of opposition to the war. The organizers now planned the giant mobilization on Washington a month later. Nixon met the student challenge head-on with a remarkably effective television address on November 3. In this massive effort to win popular support, the president argued that the country had two choices if it would end the war, either "a precipitate withdrawal of all Americans from Vietnam without regard to the effects of that action," or a "search for a just peace through a negotiated settlement if possible, or through continued implementation of our plan for Vietnamization if necessary." The president quickly disposed of the first alternative; certainly the American people would never accept disaster for South Vietnam in the cause of peace. The American stakes in Vietnam continued to demand victory. But Vietnamization combined with the gradual withdrawal of American forces, Nixon promised, would bring the war to a successful conclusion whether the peace negotiations in Paris succeeded or not. By posing two alternatives, one promising victory and peace, the other presaging humiliation and disaster, the president aroused the overwhelming support of the nation's silent majority. Again he managed to skirt the alternatives posed by the war's critics: a modification of the Saigon regime or a war without foreseeable end. Not without reason, South Vietnam's president declared the speech "the greatest and most brilliant I have known a United States President to make."[39]

Nixon's astonishingly effective appeal to the country's silent majority placed the antiwar movement in abeyance, but it did not assure any favorable settlement with Hanoi. His apparent command of public and congressional opinion could not hide the war's futility. In launching the Cambodian incursion in May 1970, the president declared the action indispensable for the success of Vietnamization. The movement of North Vietnamese men and supplies into Cambodia, he declared, gave the United States no choice but to clean out the sanctuaries and stop the border raids on American and South Vietnamese forces. The action, the president added, would strengthen negotiations for a just peace and protect American prestige. "It is not our power," he said, "but our will and character that is being tested tonight. . . . If we fail to meet this challenge all other nations will be on notice that despite its overwhelming power the United States, when a real crisis comes, will be found wanting."[40] Beyond the destruction of food and munitions, the gains from the Cambodian operation were uncertain. Within the United States it unleashed a pervasive, violent antiwar movement. In Cambodia the North Vietnamese quickly returned to their sanctuaries, expanded their areas of control, and transformed that country into an additional battleground of the war in Southeast Asia. It brought no victories for Vietnamization.

During July 1970 the president opened his promised peace offensive by naming former ambassador to England, David K. E. Bruce, as chief U.S. negotiator in Paris. Unfortunately, successful negotiations with Hanoi required a new formula far more than a new negotiator. To break the deadlock, Nixon offered a cease-fire in place, but insisted that Saigon remain in control of all political negotiations. Predictably, the Communist negotiators in Paris, determined to guarantee the desired political settlement first, rejected the proposal outright. They insisted that Saigon accept its enemies in the south politically before they would accept a cease-fire and a mutual troop withdrawal. The basic conflict over military and political priorities had not changed. Nor would it in the future. As late as June 3, 1971, Bruce complained to the North

Vietnamese negotiators in Paris: "We seek an end to the killing now, even before the other military and political issues are resolved. You insist that the fighting and killing go on unless and until the political and military issues are resolved entirely in your favor."[41]

Even as the morale of U.S. forces, trapped in a war without visible purpose, continued to disintegrate, Washington claimed ever greater triumphs for Vietnamization. Not even the disastrous South Vietnamese retreat from Laos in early 1971, following a failed effort to close the Ho Chi Minh Trail, placed any curbs on official American assurances. In February, Ambassador Ellsworth Bunker assured the American Chamber of Commerce at Saigon: "The Vietnamese armed forces have grown in strength and effectiveness. . . . In pacification, the emphasis has shifted from expansion to consolidation. Constitutional government has been strengthened." On April 7, President Nixon informed the nation via television that the South Vietnamese incursion into Laos had been more damaging to the North Vietnamese than the 1970 operations in Cambodia. "Consequently," he concluded, "tonight I can report that Vietnamization has succeeded." In his annual Foreign Policy Report of February 1972, the president again boasted, "As our role has diminished, South Vietnam has been able increasingly to meet its own defense needs and provide growing security to its people."[42]

Long before his reelection campaign of 1972 Nixon had eliminated Vietnam as a troublesome political issue. The war raged on, but the administration's Vietnamization program had successfully shifted American involvement from the ground to the air. Beginning in early 1971, Washington had unleashed on Vietnam the heaviest air war in history. This permitted extensive troop withdrawals and a precipitous reduction in U.S. casualties. By early 1972, the United States had fewer than 200,000 troops in Vietnam—a decrease of almost 400,000 from the Johnson years. The president anticipated further reductions until the United States had a residual force of some 30,000 in Vietnam. Assessing the Vietnamization strategy, Ambassador Ellsworth Bunker reported, "The Vietnamese armed forces have grown in strength and effectiveness. . . . All of these forces continue to increase in combat effectiveness and in the quality of leadership." Relying on the proclaimed successes of Vietnamization, Nixon was prepared to terminate all U.S. war activity in Southeast Asia if Hanoi would accept an internationally supervised cease-fire and release all American prisoners. Nixon's strategy rendered the opposing Democratic leadership vulnerable on the war issue. Assured of victory, Americans rejected any compromise that would threaten the existence of the Saigon government.

Columnist Stewart Alsop condemned the bipartisan maneuver in Congress to cut aid to South Vietnam. "To force those who have fought on our side to surrender," he wrote, "would be a terrible betrayal, an act of gross immorality." When Democratic frontrunner in the U.S. presidential campaign, Edmund Muskie, in February, unveiled his peace plan for Vietnam, the administration accused him of undermining the government's peace strategy and accepting defeat in Southeast Asia. Clearly the president had acquired full command of the Vietnam issue. Then came the enemy's devastating 1972 Easter offensive.[43]

Measured by the assumptions of détente—that the U.S.S.R. and China were essentially *status quo* powers—the continuing Nixon war in Vietnam appeared illogical. Détente had meaning outside Europe only if the Moscow-based Communist monolith no longer existed. But for Nixon and Kissinger, the American military initiatives in Cambodia and Laos, the mining of Haiphong harbor, and the acceleration of the air offensive underwrote the pursuit of détente with the Soviet Union. Nixon was convinced, wrote White House adviser William Safire, the negotiations with the Kremlin would achieve little unless the United States could convince the world that it was willing to use power to gain its objectives. The president explained his decision to mine Haiphong Harbor in May 1972, "If ... when I went to Moscow, late in May, at that time we had had Soviet tanks run by North Vietnamese rumbling through the streets of Hue, and Saigon being shelled, we would not have been able to deal with the Soviets on the basis of equal respect. We wouldn't have been worth talking to ... in a sense, and they would have known it."[44] Nixon wanted a "reputation for fierceness" which required the exercise of will. It was Kissinger's role in Moscow to convince Soviet leaders that the president's reputation for fierceness was thoroughly merited. The ruthless employment of force, moreover, might direct Kremlin pressure on Hanoi to end the war. For Kissinger as well, the essence of the country's capacity to limit and, ultimately, eliminate international conflict lay in the credibility of its power. It was to protect this credibility everywhere that both Kissinger and Nixon argued against any precipitous withdrawal from Vietnam. Still, the United States could not maintain its global credibility by fighting in Vietnam forever.

Nixon's long balancing act between offering assurances at home and maintaining pressure on Hanoi seemed to pay off when Linebacker I, the heavy bombing campaign to counter the North Vietnamese spring offensive, brought a breakthrough in the negotiations. On October 8,

Kissinger presented his final peace plan to Hanoi's negotiator Le Duc Tho in Paris. The United States would withdraw its troops from Vietnam, but would continue to supply the South Vietnamese army. Hanoi, in exchange, would release all American prisoners of war. There would be a National Council of Reconciliation with Communist representation, but the Thieu regime would remain in place. So would the North Vietnamese armed forces. Le Duc Tho accepted the formula. Because Hanoi had apparently dropped its perennial demand for a coalition government in Saigon, Kissinger and Nixon claimed a key diplomatic victory.[45] But Thieu saw clearly that the truce agreement threatened his country's very existence. It gave North Vietnam the right to keep 150,000 troops in the South. Moreover, Communist membership in the National Council meant, in effect, a coalition government. Thieu had the power of veto over the settlement and was determined to use it. He demanded the total withdrawal of North Vietnamese forces and the elimination of the National Council. Kissinger saw accurately that, for Thieu, any compromise was tantamount to total surrender.[46] Unwilling to reject what Hanoi had accepted, Nixon addressed Thieu on November 14, "You have my absolute assurance that if Hanoi fails to abide by the terms of the agreement, it is my intention to take swift and severe retaliatory action."[47]

Still Thieu demanded so many modifications in the October draft that the North Vietnamese broke off the negotiations. In one final effort to bring Hanoi to terms, Nixon, on December 18, launched Linebacker II, the most devastating air attack of the war. Following the bombing halt of December 29, Kissinger resumed his negotiations with the North Vietnamese while Nixon, on January 5, repeated his earlier guarantee to Thieu: "Should you decide, and I trust you will, to go with us, you have my assurance . . . that we will respond with full force should the settlement be violated by North Vietnam."[48] The revised draft of January 13, 1973, granted the United States greater freedom in supporting Saigon, restricted the power of the National Council, and reaffirmed the creation of a demilitarized zone. Kissinger believed that the changes offered the necessary guarantees to Saigon. Others wondered why the president would cause so much death and destruction merely to improve some phraseology in an empty document. Nixon warned Thieu that he had no choice but to accept the new Kissinger draft; the American war in Vietnam was over. Thieu accepted Nixon's promises and acceded to U.S. pressure. On January 27, the four Vietnam belligerents signed the cease-fire agreement in Paris. Nixon could scarcely conceal his resentment toward editors and congressmen who refused to praise his "peace with honor."[49] But the critics could see little honor in the ten-year U.S. involvement; nor would they agree with the president that the American withdrawal from the war was synonymous with peace. The war, they knew, would continue.

Kissinger's cease-fire, for which he received the Nobel Peace Prize, in large measure left the struggle for Vietnam where Americans had found it 12 years earlier. During those years the United States had sent two million men to Vietnam where some 58,000 died and 300,000 were wounded—74,000 being quadriplegics or multiple amputees. Additionally, in its long defense of Saigon America had spent some $141 billion. Now it retreated from the war with no more than its returned prisoners. Again North and South Vietnam faced each other in an unresolved conflict that knew no political or territorial bounds. There had been change; the Vietnam of 1973 was not that of 1961. Combatants could not fight a war of such magnitude, tearing apart so much of the countryside, killing hundreds of thousands of people, and creating millions of refugees, without effecting some transfer of power. But nothing that the United States had done diminished the goals of either Saigon or Hanoi. For a dozen years the United States had fought in Vietnam without coming to grips with the Vietnamese challenge at all.

After January 1973, Nixon turned to Cambodia to obtain a cease-fire between the Lon Nol government in Phnom Penh and its Communist-led Khmer Rouge enemies. By April, the cease-fire was still nonexistent and the level of fighting around the Cambodian capital had increased. The president responded to the continued insurgency with another massive air offensive. Convinced that the administration's war in Cambodia had no constitutional support, Senate leaders introduced measures to cut off funds for any U.S. military action in Cambodia not specifically approved by Congress. Republican leaders in the House hoped to head off a vote that would challenge the president's authority, but in mid-May the House voted 219 to 188 to prevent the Pentagon from using appropriated funds to carry on the bombing. Then by a vote of 234 to 172, it forbade the use of money in a $2.9 billion supplemental appropriation bill in the vicinity of Cambodia.[50] As the House continued to vote such restrictions, Nixon complained that Congress was damaging his efforts to obtain an honorable peace in Cambodia. "We are now involved," he warned, "in concluding the last element of that settlement. It would be nothing short of tragic if this great accomplishment, bought with the blood of so many Asians and Americans, were to be undone by Congressional action." Such appeals had sustained Executive control of Congress throughout the Vietnam War.

This time they failed. Congress, giving the president the choice between ending the war or seeing the government grind to a halt, moved rapidly toward a showdown with the White House. Finally, the House and Senate accepted the president's proposal of a cutoff on August 15. That day the long American war in Southeast Asia came to an end.[51]

* * *

Analysts anticipated Kissinger's appointment as Secretary of State, in August 1973, with considerable pleasure. His professional competence, they believed, would enhance the nation's opportunities for world leadership. His appointment would make him more accessible to Congress and the people, thereby subjecting his views and actions to the country's democratic processes.[52] Some state department officials lauded the shift from William P. Rogers, under whom the department had been totally neglected, to Kissinger, convinced that he would restore State to its traditional role in the creation of policy. At the time of his appointment, Kissinger was reassuring: "Durability in foreign policy is achieved in the final analysis through the deep and continuing involvement of the dedicated professionals of the State Department ... who will manage our foreign affairs long after this Administration has ended."[53] Kissinger reminded the nation that the necessary institutionalization of foreign policy would require as well a closer partnership with Congress in the planning and execution of foreign policy. Kissinger's nomination faced little opposition in the Senate. Abroad, observed columnist Joseph Kraft, the response was "positively lyrical."[54]

Many feared that Kissinger, as secretary, could not sustain his past record that had brought such effusive praise. His move to the State Department might well establish his influence there, but his departure from the White House could diminish his power, exerted through the presidential office, within the departments of Defense, Treasury, Commerce, and Agriculture. These departments had strong constituencies and, whereas they were subject to the National Security Council (still chaired by Kissinger), there was no coordinating machinery to bring them under State Department control.[55]

It required no more than the Arab-Israeli Yom Kippur War of October 1973 for Kissinger to reaffirm his predominance in the Nixon administration. Israel, never existing within accepted borders, continued to hold large areas captured in the Six Day War of June 1967. These areas comprised Egypt's Sinai region east of the Suez Canal, Syria's Golan Heights, and the West Bank of the Jordan River.

In November 1967, UN Security Council Resolution 242 favored a settlement based on "secure and recognized boundaries," but it could not define them. Arab leaders demanded Israel's withdrawal to lands held before June 1967. Gold Meir's Israeli government was equally determined to hold all occupied lands in the name of security. Suddenly on October 6, 1973, Egypt broke the uneasy peace by invading the Sinai; Syria followed by driving into the Golan Heights. Despite its heavy losses, Israel quickly gained the offensive, eventually sending its forces across the Suez into Egypt and through the Golan Heights into Syria. Egypt's President Anwar el-Sadat, in late October, invited the U.S.S.R. to send its forces into Egypt.

When Nixon learned that Soviet transports were being prepared to fly from Budapest to Egypt, he ordered a worldwide American alert. When Kissinger argued that the Israelis required additional equipment to establish stronger bases from which to negotiate a cease-fire, he faced the determined opposition of the Pentagon, where Secretary of Defense James R. Schlesinger feared that the Arabs, if pressed by Israel, would cut off oil to the Western nations. When Kissinger accused the Pentagon of defying the president's orders, it retorted that the secretary was attempting to run the war without reference to the U.S. military. With Nixon's backing, Kissinger won the argument; the huge airlift of supplies that Kissinger advocated was soon on its way to Israel.[56] The crisis passed quickly.

It was Kissinger's diplomatic agility in search of a Middle Eastern peace that sent his prestige skyrocketing toward its zenith of 1974. To arrange an Arab-Israeli peace conference in Geneva, Kissinger, early in December, set out on a 15-day diplomatic venture that carried him to 13 countries in Europe and the Middle East. After hard negotiations, Israel agreed to attend such a meeting if the Palestine Liberation Organization (PLO) did not. Syria refused to attend at all. Shortly before Christmas, the United States, the U.S.S.R., Egypt, Jordan, and Israel sent high-level representatives to Geneva—the first time that Arabs and Israelis faced each other directly in 25 years. Twice during January 1974, Kissinger undertook a tedious shuttle diplomacy between Aswan, Egypt, and Jerusalem to arrange a mutual Arab-Israeli withdrawal from the Sinai. Both countries accepted, by formal agreement on January 18, a UN buffer zone separating limited Egyptian and Israeli forces in the region. Then in May, Kissinger capped one of the greatest displays of personal diplomacy on record in securing an agreement between Syria and Israel over the disputed Golan Heights. For 28 days he flew back and forth between Jerusalem and Damascus to arrange the Israeli withdrawal from Syrian territory and the return of Israeli prisoners of war. The breakthrough came in late May when Israel dropped its insistence on a Syrian guarantee against Arab guerrilla infiltration from the north. The United States, Kissinger promised, would support Israel politically should it be compelled to retaliate against Arab attacks. During June, the United States reopened its embassy in Damascus, closed for seven years. Kissinger had brought at least momentary peace to the Middle East.[57]

Throughout the early summer of 1974 the Nixon administration was unraveling under the impact of the Watergate scandal that resulted from illegal activities during the president's election campaign, which would send many key members of his administration to prison. The president himself managed to hold on against increasingly condemnatory impeachment hearings until evidence of lying forced his resignation on August 8. With Watergate hanging over his head, Nixon, in June, ratified Kissinger's Middle Eastern achievements with a tour of Egypt, Saudi Arabia, Syria, Israel, and Jordan. For Nixon, the trip was a triumphal venture in which the very magnitude of triumph became a measure of personal disaster. As Kissinger recalled, "He was being vouchsafed a glimpse of the Promised Land that he would never be able to enter."[58] Millions of Arabs turned out to cheer the American president. King Faisal's farewell remarks in Jiddah on June 15 marked the contrast between Nixon, the world leader, and Nixon, the coming victim of Watergate. "What is very important," said the king, "is that our friends in the United States of America be themselves wise enough to stand behind you . . . in your noble efforts, almost unprecedented in the history of mankind, the efforts aiming at securing peace and justice in the world."[59]

* * *

Even as Nixon's presidency disintegrated in the summer of 1974, Kissinger's popularity reached an almost unchallengeable position. Miss Universe named him "the greatest person in the world today." Polls made him overwhelmingly the most popular personality in the United States. Noted Vietnam critic Richard A. Falk of Princeton University admitted, "Kissinger had realized the dream of every political figure—to become so valuable a public servant that it seems irresponsible to criticize him." One analyst named him "the most remarkable Secretary of State in American history."[60] For many, his record on the Soviet, Chinese, and Middle Eastern fronts established his primacy among the secretaries of the twentieth century. Kissinger was brilliant in maintaining his base of support. During the very months in which Nixon and the White House staff termed the press the enemy, Kissinger sustained a remarkably good relationship with reporters, largely because he regarded the relationship essential.

Even in Congress his power seemed complete. Few members cared to challenge him. When members of Congress and the press threatened to make an issue of Kissinger's request for FBI surveillance of several associates, Kissinger set the price that his detractors would pay for the luxury of attacking him. At his Senate confirmation hearings Kissinger had denied that he had initiated any wiretap program in his office. But at Salzburg, Austria, in June, he acknowledged that "in submitting these names, we knew that an investigation was certain." The government, he declared, had a right to defend itself against leaks. Then the secretary, knowing that the Senate Foreign Relations Committee would succumb to pressure, threatened to resign if Congress did not resolve the charges against him. During August, the committee agreed unanimously that the secretary had not misled it.[61] Eventually Kissinger was the only high-ranking member of the Nixon team to survive Watergate.

With Nixon's resignation on August 8, 1974, Kissinger readily transferred his allegiance to President Gerald Ford, retaining his dominant position in the Washington foreign policy establishment. No one, it seemed, could better lace together the strands of past decisions. Nixon's parting advice to Ford regarding the role Kissinger could play in the new administration was brief and succinct: "Henry is a genius, but you don't have to accept everything he recommends. He can be invaluable, and he'll be very loyal, but you can't let him have a totally free hand." To what extent Ford sought to rein in Kissinger is difficult to assess, for immediately after he left his meeting with Nixon in the Oval Office, he telephoned the secretary of state. In his memoirs, Ford wrote that he told Kissinger: "I need you. The country needs you. I want you to stay. I'll do everything I can to work with you." To this, Kissinger responded graciously: "Sir, it is my job to get along with you and not yours to get along with me." The decision was then reached that Kissinger would stay on as secretary of state and national security adviser to the new president.[62]

Despite his high prestige, Kissinger's leadership style already revealed serious flaws. Critics inside and outside the State Department noted his penchant for secrecy and surprise in the formulation of policy. The secrecy, moreover, seemed to flow more from habit and style than from necessity. State Department officers criticized Kissinger for isolating himself on the Seventh Floor and surrounding himself with old White House confidants. The secretary's distrust of bureaucracy was well known. As he once explained, "[I]t is no accident that most great statesmen were opposed by the 'experts' in their Foreign Offices, for the very greatness of the statesman's conception tends to make it inaccessible to those whose primary concern is with safety and minimum risk."[63] Such an approach to decision-making presumed a monopoly of wisdom that did not exist. Decisions arrived at alone or with a few trusted assistants often lack the necessary infusion of new ideas and warnings of potential failure that can come only from exposure to direct challenge. Kissinger's policies, like those of his predecessors, suffered often enough from the narrowness of views within government that came from the elimination from the advisory process of all who were not committed to established policy assumptions and goals.

During his White House years, Kissinger's personal diplomacy scarcely involved the State Department—essentially, it eliminated the agency from its traditional role in policy formulation. By late 1974 it was apparent that his habit of undertaking so much himself had prevented the State Department's recovery from the collapse of morale it experienced under Kissinger's predecessor, William P. Rogers. Kissinger's style convinced other governments that they dealt with the United States only when they were dealing with him. His presence alone could assure other countries that Washington was not actually ignoring them. Officials in the State Department complained that the secretary never bothered to explain American policy to them, leaving no one to deal with questions outside the scope of his immediate concern. James Reston observed as early as February 1974, "[Kissinger] is trying to toss too many continents around. He is not organizing the State Department to handle all the problems that need to be handled at the same time, but is almost replacing the State Department with his personal concentration on crisis situations."[64]

State Department critics and writers noted that Kissinger's successes were often tentative, evaporating quickly when basically unresolved tensions began to reassert themselves. To them, Kissinger's triumphs responded to unique circumstances that made them appear more innovative and pervasive than they actually were. First, in large measure, the initiatives for détente came from Beijing and Moscow. Building on the clearly-expressed desires of both the U.S.S.R. and China to improve their relations with the United States, Kissinger had merely to remind them that their interests were limited. Second, in both China and the Soviet Union he dealt with regimes that operated from the top down, permitting him to engage in secret negotiations that could bind those governments more readily than his own. Third, the previous relations between the United States and the two Communist powers were so thin or nonexistent that it required no more than the summits of 1972 and 1973 to create what seemed to be a massive diplomatic achievement. Thus there was always a chasm between the appearance and the reality of success. Kissinger, moreover, focused on immediate arrangements, not long-term goals. His diplomatic openings toward Beijing and Moscow, even his cease-fire agreement with Hanoi, emphasized tactics and not strategy.[65] The initial Nixon summits at Moscow and Beijing established the foundation for additional agreements, but succeeding meetings could never match the first in drama, significance, and genuine gains. Somehow Kissinger's policies, despite their heralded triumphs, produced little diminution in the demands that the Cold War imposed on the United States.

President Ford, no less than Nixon, relied on Kissinger to control Congress on matters of foreign policy. In general, the technique worked, especially because Kissinger had the full support of J. William Fulbright of Arkansas, chairman of the Senate Foreign Relations Committee. Kissinger, at the time of his appointment, assured Congress that the necessary institutionalization of foreign policy would require not only greater use of the professionals in the State Department, but also a closer partnership with Congress in the planning and execution of future policy. As secretary, Kissinger informed Congress that he planned to broaden the base of decision-making. Senators wanted to believe him, but suspected quite correctly that nothing would change.[66]

After a year of growing frustration, Congress found the occasion to defy Kissinger directly when, in October 1974, it moved to cut off military aid to Turkey, which the secretary regarded essential to maintain NATO's eastern flank. The trouble began with the Greek coup of 1967, which placed the country under military rule and exposed a powerful undercurrent of anti-American sentiment. For Washington, Greek stability and support of NATO was more essential than democracy; it backed the hated Greek colonels' seizure of power. Until 1960, Britain had held Cyprus as a NATO outpost in the eastern Mediterranean. With the island's independence, the Greek and Turkish Cypriots, under the leadership of Archbishop Makarios, established a coalition government—which Makarios and his Greek ministers overthrew in 1964. The Turkish Cypriots, denied power, enjoyed security and prosperity in isolated enclaves. Suddenly, in July 1974, the National Guard of Cyprus, led by Greek officers, overthrew the Cypriot government. The action broke the power of the Greek colonels. Turkey, to protect its interests on the island, responded to the July coup by landing troops. On August 17, the Turks broke the temporary cease-fire and took control of the northern third of the island, with its predominant agricultural and mineral wealth. The Nixon administration, regarding Turkey of prime importance to NATO, supported the Turkish demands. The Greek press condemned the United States for supporting both Greece's former dictatorial regime and Turkey's conquests on Cyprus.

Congress had long forbidden the use of American weapons for aggressive purposes, and Turkey had employed such weapons in its successful seizure of Cypriot territory. Congress's pro-Greek majority accused Turkey of aggression with U.S. weaponry. What mattered to Congress was not Turkish policy, which in large measure was justifiable, but rather its growing disillusionment with Kissinger's operating style. Among congressional frustrations was his approval of the Central Intelligence Agency's operation against the duly elected Salvador Allende government in Chile. The congressional assault on Kissinger, when it came, was bitter. Congressman Benjamin S. Rosenthal, Democrat of New York, declared: "There is a two-tiered Kissinger. The one who is public and eloquent and says the right things, and the one who deals from within the corridors of power." Similarly, Senator Thomas F. Eagleton of Missouri accused Kissinger of double-talk, "Our distinguished Secretary of State is famous for his tilts. He tilts toward the junta in Chile. He tilts toward Thieu in Vietnam.... His current tilt, his pro-Turkey tilt, is no wiser than the others." Kissinger's troubles were not unexpected. What disturbed his supporters was the vehemence of the congressional attack. As one State Department spokesman expressed it, "I'm not surprised that Congress is beginning to assert itself more. The only thing that troubles me is that it has gotten off to such a raucous beginning—which has such a vindictive air about it."[67]

Kissinger's critics in Congress and the press accused him of abusing the powers of government, as well as employing public relations, deviousness, and outright dishonesty to sustain his control of external policy.[68] Criticizing Congress for meddling, Kissinger explained to Reston that "there is an almost instinctive rebellion in America against the pragmatic aspect of diplomacy . . . that seeks to settle for the best attainable, rather than for the best."[69] At Los Angeles, on January 24, 1975, the secretary called for a "new national partnership" to avoid further domestic confrontation on foreign affairs. He promised that the administration would seek the advice and consent of Congress in the broadest sense.[70] Such promises mattered little.

In December 1974, Congress voted to discontinue all military aid to Turkey unless the negotiations between Greece and Turkey over the future of Cyprus made substantial progress. Despite Kissinger's reminder that any cutoff of military aid to Turkey would be a disaster for U.S. policy, Congress, in February 1975, responded to the absence of progress in the negotiations by putting the cutoff into effect. Late in July, the House upheld the arms embargo by a vote of 223 to 206. Kissinger could not establish the necessary consensus. As G. Warren Nutter, former assistant secretary of defense, complained, "confusion reigns in Congress and the public, and it cannot be dispelled by consensus because diplomacy has become personalized. There is no way for the legitimate organs of government to guide the direction of American foreign policy as long as it conforms to Kissinger's grand design."[71]

* * *

Unfortunately, by 1975 the European alliance was troubled along the entire Mediterranean basin. Turkey answered Congress's decision to cut off military aid by taking command of all U.S. bases on Turkish territory. The move did not affect the actual operation of the bases, or imply Turkey's withdrawal from NATO. Few Turkish leaders, conscious of their country's common border with the Soviet Union, cared to see the United States dismantle the large Incirlik Air Base near Adana or its four key monitoring stations. Only in the Aegean, where Turkey remained at odds with Greece, did Turkish policy endanger NATO's effectiveness. If Washington antagonized Turkey, it failed equally to establish better relations with Greece.

Certainly the Greek-Turkish confrontation over Cyprus, as well as Communist challenges to Italy, France, and Portugal, weakened NATO's Mediterranean front. Yet the significance of that erosion remained unclear. These unwanted developments offered no clear advantages to the U.S.S.R., and, to the extent that they lay outside U.S. control, exposed Kissinger to little criticism, either in Europe or in the United States. What the Mediterranean allies contributed to Europe's defense or to U.S. policy in the Middle East was never definable. American relations with Greece and Turkey raised serious questions about the meaning of an alliance among countries of vastly unequal power. Greece no longer participated in allied military planning. Turkey, like Greece, could scarcely impede a Soviet advance. Their importance for Western defense lay in their geographic location as an outpost for intelligence operations and their power to sustain an American commitment to the defense of the eastern Mediterranean. Against what danger was not clear; it was basically the absence of any perceived threat that enabled Greece and Turkey to indulge their historic grudges against each other.

Elsewhere NATO's southern flank was in trouble. Spain's noted dictator, Francisco Franco, failed to negotiate membership in the Atlantic alliance because of the resistance of the European partners. But the United States, to perfect southern Europe's defenses, established a number of major air and naval bases on Spanish soil through special bilateral agreements. In addition, the United States assigned the Sixth Fleet to patrol the Mediterranean. But Italy's economic disintegration suggested the collapse of that country's active role in the European alliance. Italy's Communist Party, the largest outside the Communist bloc, posed an additional challenge. To enhance the party's political chances, its leader, Enrico Berlinguer, issued strong public claims to independence from Moscow and his preference for Western-style democracy. The Italian Communist Party, the country's second largest, gained 33 percent of the national vote in 1975. Locally Italy's Communists governed about 48 percent of the population. Clearly Berlinguer's moderation paid rich dividends.

French politics taught the French Communists a similar lesson. After the Communist failure to make progress in alliance with Francois Mitterand's powerful Socialist Party, the French Communist leader, Georges Marchais, joined Berlinguer in a joint statement that pledged their two parties to respect the right of opposition parties. Such statements were reassuring, but many Europeans viewed the growing Communist influence in Italy and France with misgivings. In France, Mitterand accepted the Communist claim to moderation at face value; other Frenchmen did not.[72]

Ford and Kissinger viewed the presence of Eurocommunism in French and Italian politics as an unacceptable threat to NATO's continued existence. The president warned Italian Prime Minister Aldo Moro in Helsinki against a proposed coalition government with Italy's Communist party. "We do not see how it is possible to tolerate a Marxist government in NATO. . . . With the liberal, leftist leanings of these people, you are sure to end up with a Communist government, and such a situation would be completely unacceptable to us if they were in NATO."

Kissinger instructed Italian and French leaders that NATO would not tolerate the participation of Communists in their governments.

In a private and confidential presentation in December 1975 to U.S. ambassadors assigned to European capitals, Kissinger warned that the inclusion of Italy's Communists in a coalition government would lead to the destruction of NATO and the American withdrawal from Europe. "One thing is clear," he continued, "the dominance of Communist parties in the West is unacceptable. This has nothing to do with the reasonableness of these parties or with the degree of their independence from Russia." Consequently, "We cannot encourage dialogue with Communist Parties within NATO nations." In ten years, he predicted, all Europe would be Communist dominated. To keep Communists out of the Italian government, Washington prepared to distribute some $6 million to Italy's governing coalition, dominated by Italy's largest— but declining—party, the Christian Democrats. So vehement was the Kissinger's opposition to Berlinguer that it bewildered many Europeans. Washington's war on Eurocommunism demonstrated how little the evidence of national self-assertion diminished official U.S. fears of Communists everywhere. Berlinguer accused Washington of interfering in Italy's internal affairs. The task of reviving the Christian Democrats belonged to Italians alone. But to Kissinger, should Western Europe's Communist parties achieve power, it would surely create "a shocking change in the established patterns of American policy."[73]

Meanwhile, in April 1974, Portugal experienced a revolution that toppled a dictatorship that had lasted 50 years. The Communists, as a major political force, were influential in the armed forces, labor unions, press, schools, and public administration. Then, in March 1975, the radical Armed Forces Movement (AFM) took control of the government and moved toward a dictatorship of the left. The military rulers quickly imposed a program for the nationalization of banking, insurance, electric power, transportation, petroleum, as well as sweeping land reform. The Communist Party, Moscow-financed and closely allied with the AFM, emerged as the country's most disciplined and determined political force. Portugal's Communist leader, Alvaro Cunhal, who had spent 14 years of exile in Moscow and Prague, was a hard-line Stalinist and bitter opponent of political compromise. For many American and European officials, Cunhal, not Berlinguer, represented the true character of West European Communism.[74]

Washington, deeply fearful of all evidences of Eurocommunism, viewed Portugal's political turmoil with alarm. With Communists in the Portuguese government, NATO's relations with Lisbon, especially those of a confidential nature, were no longer open. During August 1975, President Ford voiced his concern, "I don't see how you can have a Communist element significant in an organization ... put together and formed for the purpose of meeting a challenge by Communist elements from the East." Pressed by events in Portugal, the United States pursued negotiations in Madrid for a renewal of its base agreement. To overcome the Spanish demand that the United States give up its use of the large Torrejon base outside Madrid and the standby Moron Air Base in southern Spain, the president offered additional aid and assured Madrid officials that Spain belonged to the Atlantic community, whatever the opposition it faced from NATO members. Kissinger signed the renewal treaty in January 1976. With its Portuguese bases endangered, the United States sustained its access to those in Spain.[75]

Perhaps the Portuguese challenge had been exaggerated. That Portugal would come under Communist rule was always doubtful; the country was predominantly rural and Catholic. In 1975 the Communist Party controlled only one-eighth of the electorate. The party's support among the populace was marginal, and the army leadership, if dominated by radicals, was not itself Communist. The army represented the Portuguese people politically, socially, and economically. By January 1976, Lisbon's non-Communist parties had made clear their opposition to further military rule and demanded a return to civilian government. For Washington, the crisis had passed.

Meanwhile, since the late 1960s Moscow had been dealing with its own Eurocommunism problems in Eastern Europe prompted by two serious developments. The first was Moscow's introduction of the Brezhnev Doctrine in 1968–1969, to justify the Soviet-led military suppression of Alexander Dubcek's liberal Communist Czechoslovakia. Subsequently, the movement toward détente in Europe prompted Soviet efforts to enforce internal ideological orthodoxy and discipline throughout the Soviet Union, the Communist parties in Eastern Europe, and international Communist parties generally. As early as the Twenty-fourth Party Congress, general secretary Leonid Brezhnev had chastised those Communists who sought to demonstrate their nationalism and independence of Moscow's leadership, labeling them "so-called Marxists" and revisionists.

The result was that while Washington felt threatened by Eurocommunism in Western Europe, Moscow perceived Eurocommunism to be a threat to its dominant role in the Eastern Europe. This led occasionally to "an odd congruence of American and Soviet positions." Raymond Garthoff has noted, "both opposed the legalization of the Communist Party of Spain in 1976–1977; both feared the rising influence of the Communist Party of Italy in 1976; and both preferred center-right governments in France." Apparently neither Washington nor Moscow wished to see a growing nationalism lead to pan-European independence.[76]

* * *

Unfortunately, by 1974 the heralded successes of the Nixon years were already unraveling. The truce of January 1973 left South Vietnam's future precarious. Kissinger acknowledged in his memoirs that the years of war had not improved Saigon's power to survive in its continuing struggle with Hanoi. South Vietnam, he knew, was not psychologically prepared to confront the North Vietnamese alone. George Ball suggested that Kissinger "never concealed his belief that Hanoi would probably prevail at the end of the road."[77] Both sides quickly violated the truce agreement as Thieu, in a defensive maneuver, launched a campaign to drive the North Vietnam forces back to their sanctuaries. Without congressional approval, Nixon could not fulfill his private commitments of aid to Saigon. Kissinger reminded Congress that the long U.S. involvement in Vietnam bound the country, politically and morally. The Ford administration reacted bitterly when Congress, in May 1974, reduced the Vietnam appropriation from $2.4 to $1.1 billion. Such action, one Washington official complained, called the reliability of the United States into question.[78]

Throughout the spring of 1975, the inexorable disasters in South Vietnam created a profound moral and intellectual crisis in Washington. In its retreat from Hue, the South Vietnamese army abandoned or destroyed hundreds of millions of dollars worth of supplies and equipment. In robbing and killing their own people, these forces revealed a lack of will and discipline scarcely matched in modern times. A decade of official U.S. policy was reaching the end long predicted. Throughout that period, Washington had entrusted the country's international standing to governments and military forces in Southeast Asia that had little chance of success. Still, Kissinger and the Ford administration battled Congress into March and April for military aid appropriations to save the South Vietnamese and Cambodian regimes. Vice President Nelson A. Rockefeller predicted the extermination of a million Vietnamese in a Communist takeover. If that were true, only a genuine, permanent victory for Saigon would prevent it. The time had long passed when Washington would entertain an obligation of that magnitude.

Kissinger led the attack on Congress for its refusal to appropriate the requested $722 million in military aid for Cambodia and South

Vietnam. What kind of people, he asked, would deliberately destroy an ally? Arguing against the principle of "selective reliability," he warned that peace was indivisible. Any break in the American effort to save Saigon would cause the whole international order to collapse.[79] As late as April, Kissinger reminded the Senate that the United States had moral obligations to the South Vietnamese that it could not ignore. " [O]ur failure to act in accordance with that obligation," he said, "would inevitably influence other nations' perceptions of our constancy and our determination. American credibility would not collapse, and American honor would not be destroyed. But both would be weakened, to the detriment of this Nation and the peaceful world order we have sought to build."[80] Still, he refused to recommend the commitment of single American soldier to rescue South Vietnam. Throughout the crisis it was clear that the administration hoped less to save Saigon than to affect a graceful escape from its self-imposed dilemma. The overriding task of 1975 was that of assuring the world that the coming fall of South Vietnam would not be the fault of the United States. As one U.S. official in Cambodia explained, "Sometimes you have to go through the motions. Sometimes the motions are more important than the substance."[81]

As North Vietnamese forces poured into Saigon late in April, Ambassador Graham Martin and his staff, in a final demonstration of the American failure, left the embassy roof aboard a helicopter. U.S. soldiers prevented fleeing Vietnamese employees from boarding. Analysts and writers, who had predicted such an ending for a full decade, reminded the American people that the evidence of continuing disaster had been available to those in Washington who had carried the nation into Vietnam. Still the administration assumed no responsibility for what it and previous administrations had done. Kissinger explained why the long Vietnam experience would sink into history without compensation even in the form of public enlightenment. He told newsmen on April 25:

I think this is not the occasion, when the last American has barely left Saigon, to make an assessment of a decade and a half of American foreign policy, because it could equally well be argued that if five Administrations that were staffed, after all, by serious people, dedicated to the welfare of the country, came to certain conclusions, that maybe there was something in their assessment, even if for a variety of reasons the effort did not succeed. . . . [S]pecial factors have operated in recent years. But I would think that what we need now in this country . . . is to heal the wounds and to put Viet-Nam behind us and to concentrate on the problems of the future.[82]

During subsequent days both Ford and Kissinger responded to similar questioning with the plea that the time had come to look forward, not backward. Kissinger could explain with no greater precision what, with Saigon's fall, had become of the long-predicted falling dominoes. If the American people would demand no explanation of a failed policy at the moment of its collapse, they would not do so thereafter. For them, no less than for official Washington, Vietnam no longer mattered.

Kissinger, in defending an always questionable and ultimately disastrous policy to the end, became, in a sense, its final victim. For many, his claims to statesmanship would never survive that performance. Even as Saigon's fall threatened to sweep him from power, White House Press Secretary Ronald Nessen announced that the secretary would remain in office, at least until the end of the president's current term in January 1977. Whatever the decline in his national popularity, Kissinger, with President Ford's full backing, continued to wield scarcely diminished authority in Washington.[83] The secretary, moreover, had no desire to resign. As he confided to NBC's Barbara Walters in May, "to leave in a period of turmoil, when people are looking for a sense of direction, and when foreign nations are watching us—I think it would not be of service to the country."[84] To quiet his critics, Kissinger repeated his determination to establish closer rapport with Congress and, on occasion, acknowledged mistakes in U.S. policy toward Vietnam.[85]

What characterized some of the subsequent reconsideration of the Vietnam War was the renewed insistence that there had been nothing wrong with the war's design or the assumptions that motivated it. The tide of human misery that swept across Southeast Asia after the fall of Saigon seemed to demonstrate the justice of the American cause. If the war was neither ignoble nor immoral and successive presidents had acted solely to protect the interests of the United States, the accusations that one or more had behaved unwisely were without foundation. The United States had failed, not because of the ends that it pursued, but because of the insufficient and ineffective use of its power. The lessons of the war were strategic; another war, fought with a different strategy, would end in success and honor. Guenter Lewy's massive study, *America in Vietnam* (1978), arrived at the same conclusion: "The commitment to aid South Vietnam was made by intelligent and reasonable men who tackled an intractable problem in the face of great uncertainties, including the future performance of an ally and the actions and reactions of an enemy. The fact that some of their judgments in retrospect can be shown to have been flawed and that the outcome has been a fiasco does not make them villains or fools."[86]

For some critics of the war's official reporting, the United States lost the war, not on the battlefield, but on the home front. Writing in *Encounter*, journalist Robert Elegant argued that misreporting by a hostile press undermined a successful military effort. Elegant's judgment was severe:

For the first time in modern history, the outcome of a war was determined not on the battlefield, but on the printed page and, above all, on the television screen. Looking back coolly, I believe it can be said (surprising as it may still sound) that South Vietnamese and American forces actually won the limited military struggle. They virtually crushed the Viet Cong in the South ...; and thereafter they threw back the invasion by regular North Vietnamese divisions. None the less, the War was finally lost to the invaders *after* the United States disengagement because the political pressures built up by the media had made it quite impossible for Washington to maintain even the minimal material and moral support that would have enabled the Saigon regime to continue effective resistance.[87]

Lewy's judgment of the war critics was equally harsh, but typical of those who defended the war: "The opponents of the war had a consti-tutional right to express their views, but it was folly to ignore the con-sequences of this protest. American public opinion indeed turned out to be a crucial 'domino'; it influenced military morale in the field, the long-drawn-out negotiations in Paris, the settlement of 1973, and the cuts in aid to South Vietnam in 1974, a prelude to the final abandon-ment in 1975."[88] Thus, for the new critics, victory seemed possible, but denied.

That the loss of Vietnam had damaged the nation's security seemed unclear from the apparent evidence of few falling dominoes in Asia, Africa, and elsewhere. Yet State Department officer Lawrence S. Eagleburger declared in a *New York Times* interview: "I don't care what anybody says about the domino theory having been discredited in Southeast Asia. ... If you were a Cambodian or a Laotian you might argue that there was something in the theory."[89] Actually, the Communist-led turmoil in Laos and Cambodia erupted during the war itself; the American failure to control Vietnam permitted no occa-sion for resolving the other conflicts within the borders of the former Indochina. Beyond Indochina, the countries of Southeast Asia, the real dominoes of the Vietnam War because of the contiguity to Indochina and to each other, thrived in the war's aftermath as never before. Prosperous and confident of their future, they enjoyed an economic growth twice the global average. Certainly the sources of the scattered upheavals in Angola, Ethiopia, Nicaragua, and elsewhere did not lay in Vietnam. Finally, the concept of falling dominoes assumed the existence of a Communist monolith, an expansive force of unprecedented magnitude coordinated and directed by the Kremlin. The Sino-Soviet split, which antedated the Vietnam War, demonstrated that there was no monolith after all.

Studies of the inner history of all administrations from John F. Kennedy to Richard Nixon revealed that none of them was confident of success in Vietnam or developed any plan for victory. Each administration sought little more than the time required to pass the war on to the next administration. Nixon's Vietnamization program was not designed for victory, but rather to de-Americanize the war under conditions satisfactory to most Americans. As to the enemy, historical evidence suggested that the Viet Cong guerrillas were not popular with the peasants; their successes, it appears, were greatly exaggerated.[90]

The main body of the war's opponents never believed the Viet Cong autonomous, virtuous, or popular. For them the strategic restraints of the successive administrations were clear from the war's record itself. What troubled the war critics was not the quality of the strategy or leadership, but doubts that the United States could ever win the war in Southeast Asia at a cost acceptable to the American public and compatible with other, more important, national interests.[91]

* * *

Kissinger's Middle Eastern diplomacy of 1974, despite its outward brilliance, did not resolve any basic issue. By November the Arabs had compelled him to accept their decision to recognize the Palestine Liberation Organization (PLO) as the legitimate agency for "liberating" the Israeli-occupied West Bank. Undoubtedly the failure of the secretary's 16-day effort of March 1975 to secure an Egyptian-Israeli agreement in the Sinai weakened U.S. influence in the Middle East. Upon his return to Washington, he acknowledged that American influence in the region had seriously diminished.[92] Still Kissinger, in August, succeeded in obtaining an Egyptian-Israeli agreement on the strategic Mitla and Gidi passes, but at a potentially heavy price for the United States. The new agreement, heralded as another major diplomatic triumph, served to separate the armies and extend the period of peace, but, by assigning two hundred U.S. civilian technicians to surveillance stations along the vital passes, the agreement made the United States the keeper of peace in the Sinai. The agreement, along with the secret protocols that Kissinger termed binding, provided for military aid to Egypt and Israel which could amount to $15 billion over the first five years.[93]

This agreement satisfied Egypt's concern for peace and security, but other Arab states regarded it a sellout of their interests as it ignored such substantial issues as the Golan Heights, the Palestinians in the West Bank, and Jerusalem.[94] Mike Mansfield, the Senate majority leader, opposed congressional approval and reminded the Senate that "the sending of American technicians to the Sinai changes the nature of our involvement in the Middle East. By placing the American flag in the middle of the conflict the chances of our involvement in the next round of fighting, should it occur, will be greatly increased, as will the danger of confrontation with the Soviet Union."[95] Early in October, the Senate and House overwhelmingly approved the arrangement, largely because they had no alternative to offer.

Following the failed "Year of Europe," U.S. relations with Western Europe—and Japan—remained unsatisfactory. With such countries the ties of interest were strong, the existing relations intricate. Still, for Kissinger, U.S. relations with the Soviet Union remained far more challenging and essential than satisfactory communications with Britain, France, Germany, and Japan. Washington's unresolved differences with Europe were too complex and unpromising to permit any startling diplomatic triumphs. Kissinger's personal style, enhanced by a marked arrogance in his relations with those who could not injure him or his policies, permitted him alternately to ignore and imperil traditional American ties with the Western powers or Japan. The secretary criticized Europe's leaders publicly when they acted without consulting Washington in advance. At the same time, European leaders complained that he did not consult them on issues that affected their region. Peter Jenkins of the *Manchester Guardian* wrote that Kissinger "regards Europe as he regards the State Department—as an adjunct to his personal diplomacy, to be seen and not heard."[96] Europe demonstrated its divergent interests and independence when it refused to cooperate with the American effort to supply the Israelis during the Yom Kippur War. Kissinger attributed the need for speed and secrecy to the seriousness of the international crisis, yet it seemed illogical for Washington to operate secretly and unilaterally in a situation, proclaimed dangerous, without consulting its most important allies. Observers condemned the unilateralism in U.S. behavior toward the major powers of Europe.[97] Kissinger's shocks to Japan were equally notorious. He failed to inform Tokyo of either the new approaches to

China or basic American commercial and monetary decisions that affected Japan.

* * *

Simultaneously with the collapse of U.S. policy in Vietnam and the resurrection of unresolved challenges in the Middle East and Europe, the great expectations for détente with the Soviet Union began to fade. Throughout the spring of 1974, the forthcoming third summit, again in Moscow and scheduled for June 27, loomed as the critical test. Past agreements had not brought any measurable gains for human rights in the U.S.S.R. or any relaxation of the curbs on Jewish emigration. In 1972, Senator Henry M. Jackson of Washington took up the cause of the Soviet Jews. By 1974, he had tied his amendment for the abolition of Soviet emigration restrictions to the administration's trade bill with its pledge of most-favored-nation (MFN) status for the Soviet Union. So overwhelming was Jackson's support among both human rights activists and opponents of détente that Kissinger could not negotiate modifications in the Jackson amendment sufficient to save MFN.[98] Even as Nixon left for the Moscow summit, Jackson announced that he would submit new conditions on trade. This eliminated the issue from the summit agenda. At the same time, Jackson, armed with information from the Pentagon, accused the Soviets of violating Nixon-Kissinger's 1972 SALT I agreement. The charges, even if unproven, were sufficient to curtail any new arms negotiations in Moscow. Most available agreements had already been signed at the two previous summits. The domestic constraints on Nixon's diplomatic maneuverability merely assured a stalemate at Moscow.

After Nixon's resignation, President Ford and Soviet Premier Leonid Brezhnev met at Vladivostok in November 1974 in an attempt to keep the SALT process in motion. They signed a non–legally binding "agreement in principle," which listed agreed-to objectives—each side should be limited to 2,400 ICBMs, SLBMs, and long-range bombers, of which 1,320 could have MIRVed warheads. Soviets agreed to "equal aggregates" or parity; but it allowed them to continue their MIRVing and to keep their heavier ICBMs. Individuals on both sides were unhappy with the terms. Some Americans complained about the lack of reductions because the ceilings were set so high that both nations would have to build additional weapons to meet them. Others, such as Senator Jackson, were critical because the Soviet could protect their heavy ICBMs that could carry far more MIRVs than American missiles. Meanwhile, the United States continued increasing the accuracy of their missiles, pursuing a larger ICBM known as the "MX," and developing a sophisticated warhead, MARV (maneuverable reentry vehicle), which greatly increased the problems of a missile defense system—none of which pleased officials in Moscow. In 1976, Kissinger approached a SALT II treaty, building on the Vladivostok accords of November 1974, but became sidetracked by the presidential primary contest between Ford and California Governor Ronald Reagan. Despite Ford's boast in March 1976 that "in my presidency, I have proposed the two largest peacetime defense budgets in American history," Reagan and other conservative critics charged that the United States was becoming a second-rate power. "Under Kissinger and Ford," Reagan charged during a primary campaign visit to Florida, "this nation has become Number Two in a world where it is dangerous—if not fatal—to be second best. All I can see is what other nations the world over see: collapse of the American will and the retreat of American power." His experiences during the 1976 Republican presidential primaries did not leave Ford with a high opinion of Reagan whom he considered "superficial, disengaged, intellectually lazy showman who didn't do his homework and clung to a naïve, unrealistic and essentially dangerous world view."[99]

Stung by Reagan's criticisms and out of deference to Pentagon hardliners and their congressional allies, President Ford had backed away from a SALT II agreement. Negotiating the treaty, consequently, fell to the Carter administration. After reviewing the Vladivostok agreement, Carter officials found that the accord established numerical ceilings, even on MIRVed missiles, but that the ceilings were so high that both countries would have required additional weapons to reach them. Moreover, the Vladivostok formula avoided consensus on the weapons to be included in the count. Vice President Walter Mondale summed up the deal, "Kissinger says he put a cap on the arms race at Vladivostok. Well he did, but the cap was fifteen feet over the head. The Vladivostok agreement was basically a matter of taking the force levels of the two sides, adding fifteen percent, and stapling them together. It was certainly not real arms control."[100]

During a European trip in late summer 1975, President Ford visited Finland to sign the initial product of the Conference on Security and Cooperation in Europe (CSCE)—the Helsinki Final Act. This document was the result of two years of negotiations involving 33 European nations that formed three basic groups: NATO, the Warsaw Pact Organization, and the loosely organized neutral and unaligned states. Despite his claims in his *Years of Renewal*, in the beginning Kissinger showed little interest in the proceedings. He apparently saw it as a "loser

Figure 12.4
President Ford, Soviet Premier Brezhnev, and Secretary of State Kissinger,
behind Ford, at the Vladivostok Meeting (Courtesy: Gerald R. Ford Library)

for the West" and summed up his opinion in a quip at a December 1974 national security staff meeting: "They can write it in Swahili for all I care."

The initial product emerging from the CSCE was a political, not legally binding, document. Rather it consisted of three basic parts (or "baskets") dealing with: (1) Security in Europe; (2) Cooperation in the Fields of Economics, Science and Technology, and the Environment; and (3) Cooperation in Humanitarian and Other Fields. Basket One's formal acknowledgment of the Warsaw Pact by the West constituted a virtual recognition of the Soviet's Eastern European empire, Basket Two permitted commercial relations between East and West, and Basket Three provided for a free flow of information and visitations. If Moscow officials were delighted to finally obtain the West's recognition of the Soviet Union's dominate position in Eastern Europe, they were much concerned, as they should have been, with the relaxation of restrictions on the free flow of information and movement.

In his memoirs, the CIA's Robert Gates found mostly controversy, and little that was positive, in the Helsinki Final Act: "In the United States, especially, East European émigrés and conservatives more generally saw this as a one-sided concession by the West to keep détente alive. It was seen as a sellout of Eastern Europe by Ford. Nearly everyone saw Basket III, on human rights, as hortatory window dressing, a paper exercise of no consequence." Predictably, there was little enthusiasm for the Helsinki pact among certain politicians. Senator Jackson accused the president of "taking us backward, not forward, in the search for genuine peace" and Governor Reagan, gearing up for the new presidential primaries, declared: "I am against it [the Helsinki pact], and I think all Americans should be against it." Meanwhile, the *Wall Street Journal* pleaded, "Jerry, don't go" to Helsinki. The *New York Times* concluded the trip was "misguided and empty."

Despite these dismissive attitudes, the Helsinki Final Act would play a major role in opening the closed Soviet satellites and, in turn, spurring their sense of nationalism and their desire to free themselves from Moscow's domination. The United States lost little in legitimizing the Soviet hegemony in Eastern Europe in the 1975 Helsinki accords, but it eventually received much in exchange. "If it can be said there was one point when the Soviet empire began to crack," William Hyland later wrote, "it was at Helsinki."[101]

* * *

Some analysts and observers always denied the possibility of any meaningful détente with the Soviet Union. They argued that the U.S.S.R. had never ceased to be a revolutionary power. Anti-Soviet Harvard historian Richard Pipes spoke for many when he observed that the "Soviet aim is world hegemony." In February 1976, Paul Nitze and Charles Burton Marshall warned the nation, in the *New York Times*, that the profound disagreements on the meaning of peace demanded, not further efforts at détente, but a strategic approach to Soviet-American relations. "Détente has brought changes," they acknowledged, "but their sum amounts to modification and not mutation of relationships. The main change involves tone of discourse. In the U.S. version, détente dwells on concord, however slight, and soft-pedals differences, however basic."[102] Some critics wondered why the administration would even pursue reduced tensions with a dangerous antagonist. "Tension is, after all," wrote Warren Nutter, "the natural reaction to a perceived threat, and it alerts and stimulates the will to resist." What the country required, he concluded, was the restoration of "a healthy state of alert on appreciation of the external dangers threatening the Western way of life, and a sense of confidence that they can be overcome." The pact to eliminate nuclear war, many feared, merely encouraged Soviet expansionist ventures throughout the Third World. Equally troubling was Soviet naval expansion, which transformed the U.S.S.R. into a genuine global power.[103] Those who shared this skeptical view of détente could discover no genuine gains from the effort.

Kissinger defended the Nixon administration's search for détente, however limited its demonstrable successes. He countered, with considerable success, the charges that the administration gave too much away. He reminded the nation, in March 1976, that the capacity of both superpowers to devastate the world in a few hours compelled the U.S. government to guard its relations with the Kremlin. None of the critics, he complained, was very specific in enumerating Soviet gains and American losses emanating from the administration's diplomacy with the Kremlin. Nor did any of them suggest a precise alternative to administration policy. At the end, détente became another name for competitive coexistence, with all the limited expectations that the term implied. During the 1976 presidential campaign the Republic Party eliminated détente as a proper national objective.

Actually, détente's failure lay in the program's over-expectation of what Western power and ingenuity might achieve through diplomacy alone. Ultimately, it asked the Kremlin to cooperate in the creation of an international environment that conformed to U.S. interests and ideals. In its program of rewards and punishments, neither very effective, the administration always anticipated arrangements with the Soviet Union that embraced the acceptance of American rules. Kissinger made clear at the outset that détente rested on the imperative that the U.S.S.R. alter no situation to its advantage; every agreement would preserve U.S. primacy. That détente scored any successes at all measured the willingness of the Kremlin to accept some conditions favorable to the West as the price of transforming U.S.-Soviet relations, especially in Europe, toward increased relaxation, cooperation, and trade. Outside Europe, Washington never possessed the power to influence Soviet policies to its advantage. Here U.S. defense of the *status quo*, often binding the United States to unpromising regimes and objectives, had become expensive and divisive. Détente held out the promise that peaceful incentives would encourage the Kremlin to terminate its assistance to revolutionary movements and thereby resolve Washington's uniquely troublesome challenge of dealing with Third World upheavals. Kissinger would eliminate all regional tensions attributable to Communist expansionism through Soviet self-containment. Such hopes for détente imposed far greater restraints on Soviet than on American behavior, compelling the Kremlin to consider whether gains in the form of American attitudes and cooperation were sufficient to render the arrangement worthwhile.[104]

Ultimately, the United States discovered that it could not prevent unwanted Soviet activities in Africa, the Middle East, or Southeast Asia. Still, for those who took linkage seriously, détente ruled out U.S. acceptance of any apparent expansion of Soviet influence in the Afro-Asian world. That rejection was apparent, not in confrontations with the Kremlin over the flow of military supplies or the presence of Soviet advisers and Cuban mercenaries, especially in Africa, but in the administration's condemnation of the recipients of Soviet and Cuban aid. Kissinger left no doubt that he favored the prompt and effective use of force to counter Soviet gains, but he could never explain how Soviet-Cuban aid endangered U.S. security interests in Africa. Congress, conditioned by Vietnam against further Third World interventions, terminated the Ford administration's burgeoning effort of 1975 to intervene in Angola where the Soviets, using Cuban mercenaries, backed the victorious faction struggling for control of that country. Despite the widespread domestic opposition to U.S. involvement in African affairs, Kissinger warned the Kremlin that the United States would not accept any further Angolan-style Soviet interventions.[105] However severe détente's limitations, the Nixon-Kissinger experience with the U.S.S.R. faced the condemnation of both those who believed that it attempted too little and those who feared that it sought too much.

Anatoly Dobrynin, the longtime Soviet ambassador to Washington, was also concerned that Moscow's consistent attempt to put a policy of détente in place was in jeopardy. "Our foreign policy was unreasonably dominated by ideology," Dobrynin lamented in his memoirs, "and this produced continued confrontation especially through our involvement in regional conflicts 'to perform our international duty to other peoples'. . . . This was complicated by Soviet leadership's great-power aspirations and fraught with inevitably, but unnecessary, conflicts with the United States, though our diplomacy for years was trying to establish at least a minimum of trust between our two countries." He faulted Soviet policies and actions in Cuba and then, during the Ford years, in Africa that were "undermining the foundations of détente even as we tried to build them."[106]

The simultaneous search of the Nixon-Ford years for agreement with the Kremlin and support of all regimes reputedly anti-Communist led to ever-increasing charges of amorality in U.S. behavior. More than their predecessors, Nixon and Kissinger were willing to accept the changes wrought by the Soviet victories of 1944 and 1945, as well as the subsequent Communist triumph in China. They refused to criticize the Kremlin for its repression of Eastern Europe and its refusal to liberalize the Soviet political system. Much of the administration's approval, therefore, hinged on its lack of public concern for human rights inside the Soviet bloc, although it was Kissinger's conviction, often expressed, that he could serve those rights more effectively with policies aimed at relaxation rather than tension. Countless Americans, tired of Washington's former Cold War posture, which seemed to achieve so little, agreed. For them Kissinger's diplomacy was credible and praiseworthy. His critics, however, rejected his claims that the relaxation of international tension was more important than the pursuit of human rights, whether the pursuit brought results or not.

Much of the criticism of Kissinger's pragmatism centered less on his dealings with major powers and regions, where U.S. interests in peace and security loomed large, than on those with minor and more remote states where the acceptance of undemocratic and inhumane conditions, without any show of displeasure, seemed both cynical and unnecessary. Even as Washington boasted of gains for détente in achieving a higher degree of international stability, it continued, with extensive programs of economic and military aid, to underwrite its allegiance to a wide variety of repressive governments, some of which used torture to eliminate their opponents. Under the assumption that U.S. security interests demanded the support of all avowedly anti-Communist regimes, the United States continued to furnish military aid to countries whose armies had no useful purpose except to keep the recipients in power.[107]

In its deep concern for global defense against Communism in all its forms, the Nixon-Ford administration, with few exceptions, exerted no pressure toward freedom and humaneness in the regimes that it supported. Kissinger remained silent on the abuses perpetrated by such governments. He had explained in July 1974 that the United States continued to authorize economic and military assistance for the South Korean government, despite its declining reputation for humaneness and justice, because "where we believe the national interest is at stake, we proceed even when we do not approve." Having authorized the

Central Intelligence Agency $8 million to "destabilize" the Allende government of Chile, the United States supported the new military regime of Augusto Pinochet Ugarte, regarded one of the most repressive in the world, with by far the largest American aid program in South America.[108] The vast bulk of food aid went not to desperately needy countries but to a few military-political clients such as South Vietnam, Thailand, Iran, Israel, and Egypt.[109] Despite the Nixon Doctrine's promise of retrenchment everywhere, the United States, because of its lingering globalism, remained hostage to weak governments that could not sustain themselves without American aid.

* * *

For many analysts and Kissinger watchers, the secretary's elusive successes and declining prestige after 1974 resulted less from his personal style and idiosyncrasies than from conditions over which he had no control. Throughout Kissinger's troubling encounters after 1974, the American people generally remained content with him and his diplomacy.[110] Kissinger's contribution had been unique. He was the first secretary of state in three generations to think and act in political rather than judicial terms. Unlike his predecessors reaching back to William Jennings Bryan, Woodrow Wilson's first secretary of state, he did not search for rightness and wrongness in the policies of other countries. Even after his disappointing failure in the Middle East during March 1975, he implored the American people not to pass judgment on the contestants. He judged countries and dealt with them on the basis of interests and power.

What colored his judgment of both U.S. and Soviet interests and power was the continuing Cold War environment in which he operated. But his political approach to diplomacy and the arrangements that it permitted brought the widespread approval that he received. What was astonishing in this acceptance of Kissinger's basically pragmatic, amoral approach was the fact that it won the plaudits of the same population that had lauded the largely moralistic and legalistic policies of his predecessors. Perhaps the American people had developed some appreciation of the cost of policies that produced moral judgments and little else. They were ready for some measurable diplomatic achievements, and were prepared to praise them whether they were based on pragmatism or not.

Kissinger's chief critics were those of the center and left who believed that his policies lacked humaneness, and those of the right who believed that they failed to maintain the necessary tensions in

U.S.-Soviet relations. By late autumn of 1975 the domestic pressures on Kissinger began to mount. One congressional committee cited him for contempt because of his refusal to deliver subpoenaed State Department documents; another embarrassed him with questions about his role in covert U.S. operations in Chile. Clearly, Kissinger's influence in the White House had declined and with it his image as Washington's dominant personality. No longer did U.S. achievements abroad, both real and imagined, sustain his standing as a diplomat. President Ford's trip to China in late November 1975 achieved little, the peace campaign in the Middle East was stalled, and negotiations with the U.S.S.R. over strategic arms limitation made little progress and clouded the future of U.S.-Soviet summitry. Conscious of his growing vulnerability, Kissinger confided to a friend: "I received perhaps excessive praise at one stage—I may receive excessive criticism now."[111] Whatever his shortcomings, however, Kissinger still stood above the Washington crowd. Even as the criticism became more strident, only a minority of Americans cared to ponder the choice of a successor.

CHAPTER 13

The Carter Years

Journalists who had followed James Earl (Jimmy) Carter's rise from Georgia politics to the White House in 1977 assumed that he would concentrate on the immediate issues of inflation and unemployment. They discovered soon enough, however, that the new president had assembled a full spectrum of foreign policy objectives designed to achieve success where presumably his predecessors had failed. To Carter, the Nixon-Kissinger-Ford policies had divided the country and diminished the presidency by employing tactics abroad divorced from the nation's values. That approach had failed, demonstrated most graphically by the intellectual and moral poverty of the long U.S. engagement in Vietnam.[1] The nation's perennial anti-Communism had caused it to lose sight of the American mission. Convinced that previous administrations had exaggerated the Communist threat, he promised more relaxed, flexible, and rewarding relations with the U.S.S.R., anchored to the pursuit of U.S.-Soviet cooperation on a wide range of issues, including a SALT II treaty on arms control. Asian peace and security, believed Carter, required a more constructive Sino-American relationship.

To further his separation from past concerns with Cold War issues, Carter, as a member of the Trilateral Commission, accepted the need for greater unity in the Trilateral world of North America, Western Europe, and Japan. David Rockefeller had established the Trilateral Commission in 1973 in response to the growing fear among leaders of the advanced countries that economic nationalism endangered the vital unity and strength of the Western World. For Trilateralists, interdependence would more assuredly promote the economic and security interests of the Trilateral bloc than would the pursuit of national interests as defined by the Cold Warriors.[2] In their preference for the cultivation of the Trilateral world, they rejected totally Kissinger's emphasis on U.S.-Soviet relations. For example, the Commission's Executive Committee issued this warning in December 1974:

The international system is undergoing a drastic transformation through a series of crises. Worldwide inflation reflects, transmits and magnifies the tensions of many societies, while the difficulties produced by the abrupt change in oil prices are accompanied by the entry of major new participants onto the world scene.[3]

With 10 million American jobs dependent on exports, the promotion of the international economy appeared vital for the country's welfare and security. Trilateralism promised both economic growth and the recovery of America's former hegemony in the non-Communist world.

Beyond his concern for improved relations with the world's major states, the new president, unlike Nixon and Kissinger, hoped to address the problems and possibilities of the Third World states. Finally, Carter repeatedly announced his determination to base his policies on Americans values, especially human rights.[4] Such policies, Carter declared, required new faces and new ideas. "We are not going to get changes," he acknowledged, "by simply shifting around the

Figure 13.1
(L to R) National Security Advisor Zbigniew Brzezinski, Carter, and Secretary of State Cyrus Vance (Courtesy: Jimmy Carter Library)

same group of insiders, the same tired old rhetoric, the same unkept promises. . . . The insiders have had their chances, and they have not delivered."[5] Yet, Carter's actual appointees comprised a phalanx of familiar personalities tied to the Eastern Establishment, including Yale Law School graduate and former Pentagon official, Cyrus Vance, as secretary of state, and Columbia University's Zbigniew Brzezinski as national security advisor. Carter's broad goals envisioned striving for peace, prosperity, and human welfare, albeit at the price of incoherence.[6] In its promise of a better world, it unfortunately paid scant attention to the question of means.

For the new president, human rights was ideally suited to rebuild both the country's global leadership and the primacy of the White House in the areas of external affairs.[7] The issue of human rights would reestablish the nation's global status as the world's leading proponent of human welfare and, in the words of Vice President Walter Mondale, leave the American people "feeling good." Domestically, the president hoped to construct the necessary national consensus around those who objected to Nixon and Kissinger's disregard for the repressive behavior of certain countries aligned with the United States, and those who believed that they had failed to defend the interests of the United States in their search for détente with the U.S.S.R. Not only would the pursuit of human rights permit the president to provide a moral tone for U.S. relations abroad, but also provide the issue for admonishing the Soviet Union for its iniquities without a heavy expenditure of money nor an intricate, risk-laden foreign policy.

Congress had already taken up the cause of human rights. Under Nixon the vast bulk of U.S. economic aid went, not to desperately needy countries, but to military-political clients. During 1973 congressional condemnation of such practices began to mount. On March 24, 1974, Minnesota Congressman Donald Fraser's Subcommittee on International Organizations submitted a report to the House Committee on Foreign Affairs. It accused governments—right, left, and center—of gross human rights violations, condemned Washington's program of selective criticism of such violations, and recommended that the State Department treat the status of human rights as an essential element in foreign policy decision-making.[8] Deputy Secretary of State Robert Ingersoll warned Kissinger that if the Department "did not place itself ahead of the curve on this issue, Congress would take the matter out of the Department's hands."[9] That Congress did. The Foreign Assistance Act of 1974 denied economic and military assistance to any government that engaged "in a consistent pattern of

gross violations of internationally recognized human rights."[10] The
State Department responded by asking 68 U.S. embassies, in countries
receiving U.S. economic assistance, to report on human rights violations. The Foreign Assistance Act of 1976 declared: "A principal goal
of the foreign policy of the United States is to promote the universal
observance of internationally recognized human rights by all countries."[11] That year Kissinger acknowledged that the country could
not "be true to itself without moral purpose." At the same time he
warned that a policy excessively moralistic "may turn quixotic or
dangerous."[12]

* * *

Carter caught this emerging interest in human rights on the
upswing. "Because we are free," he declared in his inaugural address,
"we can never be indifferent to the fate of freedom elsewhere."
He reminded the permanent representatives of the United Nations
on March 17, 1977, "[N]o member of the United Nations can claim
that mistreatment of its citizens is solely its own business. Equally, no
member can avoid its responsibilities to review and to speak when torture or unwarranted deprivation occurs in any part of the world."[13]
At the University of Notre Dame, on May 22, Carter sought to define a
conceptual approach to America's new global role. The United States,
he said, could have a foreign policy that was democratic, based on fundamental values, and employed power and influence for humane purposes.
Democracy's example alone would be compelling, but beyond that, he
declared, the nation "would seek to inspire, to persuade, and to lead."
To ignore the worldwide trend toward human progress, he warned,
would lose America "influence and moral authority in the world. To lead
it will be to regain the moral stature we once had."[14]

At the core of the administration's human rights endeavor was the
State Department's Bureau of Human Rights and Humanitarian
Affairs, headed by Patricia Derian, a former civil rights activist.
In addition, deputy secretary of state Warren Christopher chaired
the Interagency Group on Human Rights and Foreign Assistance.
Derian was determined to make the United States the conscience of
the non-Communist world. Under her prodding—and that of others
—the president issued a secret directive in February 1978 that ordered
all agencies to consider the impact of their decisions on the status of
human rights abroad.[15] The administration, meanwhile, undertook
diplomatic initiatives to encourage countries to release political prisoners; it reduced or halted economic assistance programs to countries

engaged in serious violations or altered such programs to benefit the mistreated rather than ruling elites. It instructed its representatives in international lending agencies, such as the Asian Development Bank, to vote against loans to repressive regimes and worked to strengthen the Inter-American Commission on Human Rights as well as the human rights activities of the United Nations. Finally, it supported governments that demonstrated genuine concern for the status of human rights in their countries.

What troubled some critics was the administration's failure to distinguish between repression and the absence of self-government in other countries. Samuel Pisar, writing in the *New York Times*, condemned the tendency to identify U.S. purpose abroad with the universalization of democratic values and practices:

The posture that our new policy makers have struck toward the world conjures up the image of Don Quixote charging at windmills. It is one thing to speak out, in the name of America, against the systematic use of torture and brutality by repressive regimes, some of them in our own backyard. But to go further and urge our own political values and traditions on other nations, from China to Brazil and from Pakistan to Cuba, while the bulk of humanity is still groping for the right to work, housing, education and decent medical care, calls for extraordinary faith in the power of persuasion.[16]

There was little relationship, unfortunately, between most human rights that the administration advocated and the possibility of their achievement anywhere in the Third World. In few Third World countries could human rights be measured by Western standards of democracy and political freedom.[17]

Critics found that the president's appeals to human rights lacked a systematic analysis of either American intentions or the means available for pursuing them. As one state department official complained, "No one knows what the policy is, yet it pervades everything we do."[18] Whatever its goals, Carter's human rights crusade, like all crusades, would remain divorced from policy wherever repression existed outside the areas of direct U.S. influence. Obviously, no member of the Carter administration advocated military invasion or the overthrow of misbehaving governments. Economic pressures could be effective; they could also increase rather than diminish the extent of human misery. Even when totally ineffective, they could unleash charges that Washington was interfering in another country's internal affairs.[19] No government would acknowledge any immorality; nor would it agree that its behavior exceeded the bounds of necessity.

No ruling elite would adopt reforms that endangered its authority merely to obtain aid or to quiet the condemnation of others. There existed, finally, the risk of humiliation in declaring objectives that had no relationship to contemplated actions. Henry Kissinger reminded the president in April 1978: "If a nation constantly affirms human rights and then does not try to carry through with the ideals in policy, it can be regarded not as strength but as impotence."[20]

Few questioned the president's sincerity, but some wondered about his humility and sense of proportion. British scholar Robert McGeehan declared that Carter's "officious response to human rights violations abroad . . . led some to wonder just how many countries he wanted to govern."[21] How did the president, others asked, intend to reconcile his idealistic goals with the more traditional requirements of foreign policy? "I am not cynical enough," admitted French critic Raymond Aron, "to say that to have a good policy you cannot have *des bons sentiments*, but I would say that it is not enough to be a statesman to wish the best for everybody." The Carter administration, no less than others, carried a far greater obligation to political, economic, and strategic considerations than to human rights in the formulation of policy.[22] Secretary Vance reminded the Senate Foreign Operations Subcommittee as early as February 1977: "In each case we must balance a political concern for human rights against economic and security goals. No formula can resolve the larger conflict of commitments."[23]

The ultimate criticism of Carter's human rights program lay in the absence of consistency. Even as the proclamations on human rights proliferated in Washington, the administration refused to indict governments whose cooperation appeared essential for reasons of trade and security. However embarrassing the human rights record of South Korea and the Philippines, American security interests and military requirements rendered both countries too important to permit altering military arrangements with them. That the Shah of Iran ran a repressive regime was well known, but the U.S. need of Iranian oil rendered human rights violations there irrelevant.[24]

Secretary Vance himself acknowledged the limitations of any human rights policy. U.S. objectives, he said in April 1977, would of necessity be circumscribed by the willingness of other governments to tolerate outside investigation, by the prospects of effective action, and by the realization that violence could result in a loss rather than a gain for human rights. "[I]n pursuing a human rights policy," he declared, "we must always keep in mind the limits of our power and of our wisdom. A sure formula for defeat of our goals would be a rigid, hubristic attempt to impose our values on others."[25] Similarly, in May, Carter admonished his Notre Dame audience that the United States could not conduct its foreign policy "by rigid moral maxims. We live in a world," he added, "that is imperfect, and which will always be imperfect. ... I understand fully the limits of moral suasion."[26] Such admissions of limited influence almost explained away the entire human rights program.

Some Americans warned the administration that even the appearance of any intention to link the future of U.S. relations with the U.S.S.R. to changes in Soviet human rights policy would impede further progress toward an arms agreement. Still, during his first weeks in office Vance advised the Kremlin that the United States would "vigorously pursue human rights matters" that came under the East-West Helsinki Accord of 1975. Soon Washington issued statements criticizing the U.S.S.R. and Czechoslovakia for harassing and intimidating citizens who attempted to exercise their right of protest.[27]

Soviet leaders expressed anger at the Carter administration's decision to include the Soviet bloc in its human rights crusade. What troubled them especially was Washington's references to the human rights pronouncements in the Helsinki Accords. To the Soviets what mattered at Helsinki was the West's recognition of the Kremlin's predominant interests in Eastern Europe, not the issue of human rights. Georgi Arbatov, head of Moscow's famed Soviet Institute of U.S.A. and Canadian Studies, reminded Washington that there were many unsettled issues in Soviet-American relations of greater importance *than human rights.*[28] Soviet leader Leonid Brezhnev responded on March 21: "Washington's claim to teach others how to live cannot be accepted by any sovereign state." Foreign Minister Andrei Gromyko charged Carter with "poisoning the atmosphere [of détente]" and embracing the nation's Cold War tradition.[29] American critics complained that Carter threatened to undo the major achievement of the Nixon-Kissinger era: the elimination of ideology from the Soviet-American relationship which had enabled the two countries to address common and conflicting interests on their merits alone. Vance insisted that the administration would divorce the issue of human rights from its efforts to reach substantive agreements with the Kremlin; each question, he assured newsmen, would receive the attention it deserved.[30] It was not clear that the Kremlin would accept such distinctions.

Why Washington's pronouncements in behalf of Soviet dissidents would provoke determined Soviet resistance was obvious from the outset.[31] Columbia University's Marshall Shulman, Carter's key advisor on Soviet affairs, warned a Senate committee as early as 1974 that any U.S. effort to improve human rights in the U.S.S.R. would pose "conditions which the present Soviet regime cannot but regard as terms of surrender and of self-liquidation."[32] Similarly national security advisor Brzezinski, whose writings had never revealed much sympathy for the Soviet Union, admitted that even "a limited democratization of Soviet society . . . would threaten the present political leadership." Any major increase of either intellectual dissent or the region's historic nationalisms, he correctly observed, would endanger the Soviet Union's very existence.[33] Time would verify his assessment.

Late in 1977, the president sent Arthur Goldberg to represent the administration at the Belgrade Conference, called to review the compliance with the Helsinki Accord and its human rights provisions for Eastern Europe. In his opening address on October 6, Goldberg restated the U.S. position that a deepening of détente "cannot be divorced from progress in humanitarian matters and human rights. Rather, it can strengthen détente and provide a firmer basis for both security and cooperation."[34] Western Europeans, concerned with the improvement of East-West relations, displayed no interest in human rights at all. At Belgrade the limited criticism of human rights violations focused on three countries—the Soviet Union, Czechoslovakia, and East Germany. Not even the United States had any interest in damaging its relations with Poland, Hungary, and Rumania by dwelling on human rights violations in those states. The final Belgrade report contained no statement on human rights.[35] Late in December 1977, the *New York Times* observed that the Soviet human rights movement was at its lowest ebb in many years.[36]

Nothing demonstrated the Soviet determination to resist all external pressures for human rights as the trial of Soviet dissidents Anatoli B. Shcharansky and Aleksandr Ginzburg in July 1978. Shcharansky's crime lay in his sometimes obstreperous efforts to leave the country. Despite the worldwide clamor for the dissidents' acquittal, the Soviet court, in mid-July, sentenced Shcharansky to thirteen and Ginzburg to eight years at hard labor. The storm of protest, in some measure, was a gain for human rights. "The publicity given the trials is very encouraging," observed Valentin Turchin, a Soviet activist residing in the United States. "The awful thing about the Stalin era was that people just disappeared. . . . Now there is public reaction, and people understand what is happening. The struggle is worth the effort."[37] Still, the apparent ineffectiveness of American appeals to the Kremlin created a bitter mood in Washington. Senator Jacob Javits of New York took the lead in denouncing the Soviet action, calling the trial "an international disgrace." Noting the limits of American authority, House Speaker Thomas O'Neill of Massachusetts retorted, "I don't know what we can do other than express our deep concern, regret, and displeasure."[38]

President Carter's observations on the Shcharansky trial revealed the dilemma to which the human rights issue consigned his administration. "We have a deep commitment to human rights," he declared, "not only here but around the world." But he added quickly, "I have not embarked on a vendetta against the Soviet Union. We cannot interfere in their internal affairs."[39] While in Berlin during July 1978, the president fell into the trap between hope and reality. He assured a cheering audience: "No matter what happens, Berlin will remain free." Later at a town meeting he faced an elderly woman who asked, "Can you tell us how long we will have to live with the wall?" The president's response was candid: "I don't know. I can't give you a better answer, but that's the truth."[40]

What Washington achieved for human rights abroad defied accurate measurement. Mark L. Schneider, deputy assistant secretary for human rights, acknowledged, in October 1977, that "in very few instances can we assume that our policy or our expressions of concern are the crucial factors that have or can produce change. A variety of forces are at work. Our policy is one of them."[41] Beyond creating a global interest in human rights, the program had compelled some repressive governments to weigh the costs of their behavior and grant permission to international agencies to conduct investigations within their borders. Finally, the human rights program had changed the nation's self-image. Columnist Anthony Lewis of the *New York Times* expressed the reaction of many when he wrote: "After the dark years in which many of us became ashamed of the things done in America's name, it simply feels good to hear a president denounce torture and inhumanity in the most direct way." Because of Carter, Brzezinski averred, America was again seen as standing for its traditional values.[42]

* * *

When Carter entered the White House in 1977, U.S. forces on the Asian mainland were limited to South Korea. Vietnam, Laos, and Cambodia were under Communist control, SEATO was approaching its final demise, and Washington had unilaterally reduced its commitments to other regional allies, including Taiwan. In the absence of any measurable decline in the country's security, Americans could only conclude that successive administrations had exaggerated the dangers that led the country into Southeast Asia. After Saigon's fall, the United States remained the world's leading power, but now the troublesome issues that captured the headlines scarcely challenged traditional U.S. interests and thus defied the exertion of will or the creation of effective countering policies. Meg Greenfield, writing in *Newsweek* in February 1978, saw the dilemma that faced the country:

So what *are* we going to do about it if the rulers of Cambodia embark on a policy of national genocide, if the Cubans take up [Soviet] arms in Africa, if the Saudis lower production or increase the price of oil, if Southern Africa moves toward all-out racial war, if the Indians continue to build nuclear explosives, if the Western Europeans vote Communists into office? Is there anything we can do in an era in which we have even been admonished for expressing the hope that Italy remain a democracy? If that is regarded as an act of aggression, it tells you something about our role as a "superpower" in the post-Vietnam world.

The United States had approached the stage where it could neither admit that what happened abroad was not its concern nor act effectively when it did.

Carter met the challenge by acknowledging America's declining world role and, with that recognition, a diminution of the strategic importance of Asia, Africa, and Latin America. For the president, the Third World possessed the power and will to confound any serious Soviet threat. Carter rejected the traditional Cold War assumption that American interests were global. "Being confident of our own future," he said, "we are now free of that inordinate fear of communism which once led us to embrace any dictator who joined us in that fear."[43] In a world of triumphant nationalism, American power had no legitimate or necessary use. For arms negotiator Paul C. Warnke the country's security and international standing were not "so precarious that we are threatened when an alien people opts for a form of government organization that we find distasteful. ... The injection of American firepower into a local conflict is rarely compatible with our foreign policy interests. For the most part, investment in such forces will buy us nothing but trouble."[44] In deserting the old commitment to global containment, the Carter administration accepted Soviet activity in the Afro-Asian world with deep indifference. Most Americans initially welcomed Carter's relaxed, confident approach to the external world. Brzezinski attributed the public's widespread acceptance of the Carter policies to the fact that "the country, as a whole, [was] fatigued by the Vietnam War."[45]

Carter's non-ideological approach to the country's external relations enabled him to discard the Nixon-Kissinger notion of linkage and deal with the nations of Asia and Latin America as individual states. For Carter, Latin America comprised less a problem of security than one of reprehensible governments. As late as 1963 military dictatorships controlled only four small Latin American countries—El Salvador, Honduras, Nicaragua, and Paraguay. But Brazil fell to a military junta in 1964, Panama and Peru in 1968, Bolivia in 1969, Ecuador in 1972, Chile and Uruguay in 1973, and Argentina in 1976. Behind most of these dictatorships were officers who had trained either in U.S. military schools or academies, or in the Pentagon's School of the Americas, located in the Panama Canal Zone. Under the previous administration, these dictatorships, despite their known reliance on terrorism and torture, flourished with American aid. What mattered for Washington was simply their commitment to anti-Communism.

When the Carter administration accompanied its 1977 offer of $50 million in military aid to Brazil with the state department's report on the status of human rights in that country, the Brazilian government rejected the offer. Matters such a human rights, it reminded Washington, remained within the exclusive competence of Brazilian authorities.[46] Argentina, Uruguay, El Salvador, Chile, and Guatemala followed Brazil's lead. Together these countries spurned military credits totaling $74 million, but it was not clear against what external dangers these countries would defend the Western Hemisphere.[47] Pentagon officials, freed of their former anti-Communist restraints, informed Latin American governments that their behavior on human rights would determine future military relations.

President Carter's decision to separate the White House from Latin America's repressive regimes quickly established a new relationship. Elio Gaspari, the Brazilian journalist, recorded the change: "From the moment Latin Americans, Africans and Asians started looking at President Carter as a politician interested in human rights, the United States Embassy ceased being seen by thousands of third-world liberals as a headquarters for conservative maneuvers; it became identified with the nation it represents." Under Carter the United States was no longer the unconditional supporter of dictators and dictatorships as it had been under previous administrations. "For the last several years," Gaspari observed, "citizens of the third world couldn't quite understand why so many poisonous mushrooms grew in the shadow of the American foreign policy. Today, it is the mushrooms that do not realize that the shadow is gone."[48]

The Carter human rights program for Latin America affected some change. In July 1978, Grenada's vote established the Inter-American Court of Human Rights.[49] In its assessment of the status of human rights in the Americas the same month, the Council on Hemispheric Affairs questioned Washington's performance, but added: "The Carter Administration, through its human rights policy, has made a significant contribution to the cause of humanity in the hemisphere. ...We have now entered a period where no totalitarian regime can victimize its own people with impunity or in silence."[50] In Nicaragua, Washington targeted the repressive Anastasio Somoza Debayle regime by reducing military assistance and thereby emboldened Somoza's enemies.[51]

Carter also announced his desire for an early rapprochement with Castro's Cuba, thereby bringing U.S. policy into alignment with that of the hemisphere.[52] For reasons of trade and politics, in 1975, the OAS lifted its economic embargo, permitting each member state to determine its own economic and diplomatic relations with Cuba. That year Castro sent a delegation to Washington to discuss the expropriation of U.S. property in Cuba, as well as matters of diplomacy and trade. Cuba's involvement in Angola quickly terminated the exchanges. Within the United States, Castro faced a host of enemies, none more so than the thousands of Cuban exiles who favored his overthrow. Responding to pressures against any relaxation of official U.S. opposition to the Castro regime, the president made clear his refusal to normalize U.S. relations until Castro demonstrated his intention both to terminate Cuba's interference in hemispheric and African affairs and to improve its human rights record by releasing known political prisoners from Cuban jails.[53]

Nowhere in East Asia did regional rivalries respond to ideological imagery. China and the U.S.S.R. had long been at odds. The ongoing war in Southeast Asia between Vietnam and Cambodia added to the Sino-Soviet antagonism and destroyed whatever illusions of Communist unity still remained. Vietnamese occupied portions of Cambodia, not to expand Communism, but to challenge the Chinese presence. The Vietnamese government assigned Camrah Bay to the Soviet Union, but its ties to Moscow left little room for Kremlin influence in the renamed Ho Chi Minh City. Edwin O. Reischauer, Harvard's noted authority on Asian affairs, explained why East Asia had emerged as one of the world's most stable regions. "In my judgment," he wrote, "East Asia ... is stable because four of the five great power centers of the world—that is, all except Western Europe—are involved in this area, and these four produce a very stable balance between them because they all turn out to be *status quo* in their desires."[54] The Carter administration linked its regional objectives to Communist and non-Communist nations alike.

Confident in Vietnam's emergence as a permanent, stabilizing element in Southeast Asian, Carter set out to normalize relations with Hanoi. In March 1977 Carter sent Leonard Woodcock, president of the United Auto Workers, to Hanoi to discuss the issue of Americans missing in action (MIAs). Vietnamese officials countered with the demand that the United States, because of its responsibility for the war, compensate their country for the damage wrought by bombing.[55] During 1977 Vietnam entered the United Nations, but the movement toward normalization succumbed to the conflict between the U.S. demand for Vietnamese accountability regarding MIAs and Hanoi's insistence for greater U.S. accountability for Vietnam's wartime destruction.

Persuaded that South Korea could defend itself, the Carter administration, in May 1977, announced its intention to withdraw all 32,000 U.S. ground forces from South Korea, leaving only Air Force, support, and logistics personnel. Military experts quickly besieged the White House, predicting that the removal of U.S. forces would invite another invasion from the north and, with it, another American war in Asia. Both Beijing and Moscow made clear their preference for a strong U.S. presence in South Korea to discourage any unwanted North Korean expansionism.[56] So pervasive was the protest that the president reaffirmed the U.S. commitment to South Korea's defense and then slowed and finally terminated the American withdrawal.

Carter also moved logically toward the normalization of relations with China, a process inaugurated by Nixon's Shanghai Communiqué of 1972. The president addressed the question of China directly in his speech of May 1977: "We see the American-Chinese relationship as a central element in our global policy. . . . We wish to cooperate closely with the creative Chinese people on the problems that confront all mankind, and we hope to find a formula which can bridge some of the difficulties that still separate us."[57] To demonstrate his intentions, Carter sent Leonard Woodcock to head the U.S. mission in Beijing. At the same time he downgraded the U.S.-Taiwan relationship, severing contacts between the Chinese embassy and the State Department. He no longer recognized the Taiwanese ambassador as the official spokesman of China and, instead, turned to Huang Zhen, Beijing's liaison officer in Washington.

China's Mao Zedong and Chou En-lai shared Washington's desire to strengthen U.S.-Chinese relations, as a deterrent to Soviet armed expansion into Asia. The schism between Beijing and Moscow, as well as the profound mutual insecurities that it generated, began in the late 1950s; thereafter, the gap between the two countries on almost every foreign policy issue continued to widen. Although Europe was Moscow's major concern, Chinese leaders were troubled by the presence of 450,000 Soviet soldiers along the Sino-Soviet frontier. Moscow, moreover, had acquired naval bases along the Indian and Southeast Asian littoral.[58] Not without reason, China applauded Washington's efforts to strength NATO with deployment of theater nuclear weapons in Europe. Beijing sustained its strong presence in North Korea to dissuade that country from again invading the South, an act that would have unleashed another damaging confrontation with the United States.[59]

Carter approached the quest for normalization with caution. He understood that any profitable arrangement with China would force him to run the gauntlet of the pro-Taipei lobby in Congress and the press. For Carter and Vance, moreover, it was essential that the approach to China avoid any irritation of Moscow that might inhibit future negotiations. As Vance advised the president on April 5, 1977, "The Chinese must . . . be made to understand that we do not perceive our relations with them as one-dimensional, but that we also look at our relationship in the context of key bilateral and international issues."[60] In August, Vance flew to Beijing to advance the effort at normalization; however, he found Beijing's conditions remained in place: Washington's abrogation of its Mutual Defense Treaty with Taiwan, the severance of official U.S. relations with the Republic of China, and the withdrawal of all American military personnel from the island.[61] Still the political changes within China were hopeful. The moderate Deng Xiaoping, China's new vice premier, emerged that summer as the pivotal figure in opening the path to normalization.

In May 1978, President Carter sent Brzezinski to Beijing, instructing him to assure Chinese leaders that the Soviet Union remained in a competitive relationship with the United States. That relationship, he added, was "enduring, deep seated, and rooted in different traditions, history, outlook, interests, and geographical priorities. Hence the competition would not be terminated quickly." Brzezinski, unlike Vance, had long speculated that closer U.S.-China ties might deter Soviet aggressiveness in Asia. In Beijing, Brzezinski reminded the Chinese that the Shanghai Communiqué presumed shared concerns based on long-term strategic views of Asia. "The United States," he assured his listeners, "does not view its relationship with China as a tactical expedient. We recognize and share China's resolve to resist the efforts of any nation which seeks to establish global or regional hegemony." Amid provocative remarks concerning the Kremlin's international behavior, Brzezinski assured Chinese officials that the United States was fully committed to the normalization of relations.[62]

Deng Xiaoping and his associates accepted Brzezinski's assurances and agreed to terminate their public criticism of the United States. In turn, Carter dropped the sale of F-4 fighters to Taiwan and, in November, instructed Woodcock to present his final proposals to Beijing. The United States, the president concluded, would maintain its defense agreement with Taiwan for another year, continue some arms sales thereafter, and require Chinese guarantees for a peaceful settlement of the Taiwan issue. Deng accepted Carter's first proposal, balked at the second, and rejected the third. For Carter, Deng's response was satisfactory enough. On December 15, 1978, the president announced to the nation that the United States, in recognizing the Peoples Republic of China as that country's only government, was acknowledging a simple reality. Washington terminated the Mutual Defense Treaty with Taiwan and removed the remaining U.S. military advisors from the island. The new Sino-American relationship received additional impetus from agreements for scientific exchanges and limited sales of U.S. military equipment.[63]

Carter's concessions to China unleashed a storm of protest. On December 22, Senator Barry Goldwater and other Republicans filed an unsuccessful suit in Federal Court, challenging the president's authority to terminate the 1954 treaty with Taiwan without the approval of Congress. Senator Robert J. Dole of Kansas declared that the United States, in conceding its strategic interest in Taiwan, had gained little in its normalization of relations with the mainland. Nothing could reverse Carter's decision. Official relations between the United States and the Republic of China ended on January 1, 1979. That day Beijing announced unilaterally that it accepted the principle of a peaceful settlement of the Taiwan issue. Congress, still dissatisfied, responded with the Taiwan Relations Act of March 28, 1979, signed by the president on April 10. The act charged the United States government with responsibility to promote the peaceful settlement of the Taiwan issue and Taiwan's future security with adequate arms. Predictably, Beijing condemned the Taiwan Relations Act as an infringement on its agreement with the United States. Convinced that his formal recognition of Beijing comprised a major and necessary achievement, Carter ignored the congressional action.

Meanwhile, Washington moved to solidify its strategic position in the western Pacific. Vance had long argued that American policy toward China should threaten no one. Brzezinski preferred to play the "China card," however, exploiting Sino-Soviet tensions to enhance American security. With Brzezinski in command of China policy, Washington assured Beijing of its concern for Chinese security, offering the Chinese dual-use technology, air defense radars, transport planes, communication, and nonlethal military equipment. Brezhnev caught the message, complaining to *Time* in January 1979 that "attempts are being made to encourage ... with deliveries of modern weapons, material and military technology those who, while heading one of the biggest countries in the world, have openly declared their hostility to the cause of détente, disarmament and stability in the world."[64] By aligning openly with China, the administration lost much of its leverage in both Moscow and Beijing. The United States could not prevent China's inglorious, ill-fated invasion of Soviet-allied Vietnam shortly after Deng's visit to Washington in January 1979.[65]

* * *

Nowhere did the prospects for effective American leadership seem more propitious than in the Middle East. By 1977 both Arabs and Israelis, it seemed, had grown weary of their perennial quarrel. Secretary Vance informed the press on February 9 that much had changed in the previous year; the administration, he said, would "take advantage of these facts and press forward for a prompt and early resolution of the differences which obviously remain."[66] Carter, hoping to arrange another Geneva conference for the Middle East, would, as honest broker, negotiate the necessary Arab-Israeli agreements. The peace formula prepared by the Brookings Institution in 1975 offered a promising guide to a Middle Eastern settlement. It advised an Israeli withdrawal from occupied Arab lands (except those exempted by mutual agreement), the Arab recognition of Israeli sovereignty, the establishment of trade relations between Israel and the Arab states, and the resolution of the Palestinian question with either an independent Palestinian state or an autonomous Palestinian entity federated with Jordan.[67] The Palestinian cause was strengthened by the emergence in 1964 of the Palestinian Liberation Organization (PLO), with Yasser Arafat as its leader, committed to the destruction of the Jewish state and its replacement with an Arab nation of Palestine.[68] Still, any

West Bank settlement would require no less than a Palestinian recognition of Israel's existence. Whatever the attractiveness of the Brookings formula, past experience might have encouraged caution.

Secretary Vance discovered quickly on his trip to the Middle East in February 1977 that both Egyptian and Israeli positions remained as uncompromising as ever. Israel, its spokesmen assured him, would never return to the boundaries that existed before the 1967 war. Because of their strong bargaining position, the Israelis favored private negotiations with the Arab states where power, not principle, reigned.[69] Egypt supported Palestinian demands for an independent Palestinian state; Israel offered no more than Palestinian home rule under Israeli jurisdiction, with the added proviso that it would never negotiate with the PLO.[70]

Early in March, Israeli Prime Minister Yitzhak Rabin arrived in Washington. So vehement was his refusal to make concessions that Carter concluded that Israel was the real impediment to a Middle Eastern peace. He informed Rabin that the United States favored UN Resolution 242, with its demand that the Israelis withdraw from its occupied territories in exchange for defensible borders. Rabin agreed privately to give up some occupied territories, but publicly he showed no constraint: "Without any qualification, Israel will not return to the lines that existed before the 1967 war."[71] In Cairo, Egyptian President Anwar el-Sadat retorted that his country would not surrender "a single inch of Arab land."[72]

On April 4, Carter had his first meeting with Egypt's Sadat. His conversations with Sadat, whom he would come to admire, were so cordial that observers proclaimed his preference for the Arab cause. Immediately the pro-Israeli bloc in Congress closed in, compelling the president to retreat from his restrictions on arms sales to Israel. Carter observed that all Arab leaders encouraged him in his search for peace, but none, except Sadat, would defy the Arab world's hatred for Israel by supporting compromise publicly. On one occasion the President confessed to White House visitors: "I doubt that any foreign negotiating effort has ever been attempted that is more complicated, more thankless and more frustrating."[73]

In June 1977, Menachem Begin became Israel's new prime minister. His election, as a victory for Israel's most anti-Arab element, placed the entire peace process under a cloud. Begin asserted that he would not accept a Palestinian homeland, withdraw from any occupied territories, or tolerate a PLO presence at any forthcoming Geneva conference.[74] He quickly strengthened Israeli claims to the disputed region by authorizing new Jewish settlements. In response to Carter's suggestion that the PLO might attend as part of a pan-Arab delegation, American Jews again deluged the White House with protesting telegrams and letters. One accused the administration of "pointing a dagger at the heart of every Jew in the world." Aroused Jewish leaders warned the president that their community would revolt if the United States pressed Israel to accept PLO participation at Geneva. One Chicago lawyer accused the president of sacrificing Israel's interests in his quest for a needed foreign policy success. In early November, Carter assured the World Jewish Congress, while respecting the legitimate rights of the Palestinians, he did not favor an independent Palestinian state in the West Bank.[75]

Seeking to break a seemingly hopeless impasse, Sadat announced to the Egyptian parliament that he was prepared to take the issues directly to the Israeli Knesset. Sadat's unprecedented trip to Jerusalem in November 1977 comprised the first face-to-face exchange between principal Arab and Israeli leaders. The meeting occurred without Washington's prior knowledge. One White House officials observed, "We were expecting him to do something big, but not that big."[76] Sadat's reception in Jerusalem was tumultuous. In his speech before the Knesset, Sadat recognized the state of Israel, the first Arab leader to do so. But his demands for the return of all Arab lands were adamant: "There will be no lasting peace with the occupation of our land." In his response Begin referred to Israel's eternal rights. He admonished Sadat: "We know how to defend ourselves, our wives, our children, and our honor." Yet Begin assured his listeners that there would be no more war, bloodshed, or threats between Israel and Egypt.[77] Returning with that promise of peace, Sadat received a hysterical welcome from Cairo's masses. For Carter, Sadat's visit to Jerusalem broke the Arab shell that had sought the isolation of Israel; but also, it demonstrated again that Sadat and Begin could not resolve the Palestinian issue.[78] Arab leaders condemned Sadat's decision to undertake a diplomatic venture without the approval of other Arab states. In Beirut one Palestinian declared, "Nobody can forgive the biggest Arab leader for meeting the biggest Zionist terrorist, unless the leader brings back a Palestinian state."[79] Sadat had thrown the Arab world into confusion.[80]

Confronted with immovable Israeli opposition to the PLO and its demands, Carter moved to accommodate Begin. He informed the media, on December 28, that he favored, not an independent Palestinian state, but a Palestinian entity tied either to Israel or to Jordan. Begin appeared ready to give the Palestinians that choice; the arrangement would eliminate the PLO.[81] Arafat accused the president of trying to destroy the Palestinian movement, while Sadat reminded the president that Egypt would accept no less than full Israeli withdrawal from the West Bank and recognition of the inalienable rights of the Palestinian people.[82] Begin and Sadat remained separated by a chasm, but, for Washington, the PLO comprised the chief barrier to an agreement. Eliminating the PLO would not be easy; it constituted the only organized Palestinian voice. No West Bank settlement could ignore the presence and preferences of its million inhabitants; merely to proclaim them radical and over-demanding would resolve nothing.[83]

Diplomatically, Sadat and Begin—and the forces behind them—were too committed to antagonistic positions to permit any accommodation. For a year the two Middle Eastern leaders had come to Washington to argue their cases before the president.[84] Without any progress, Carter arranged direct negotiations between Begin and Sadat at Camp David. Beginning on September 5, 1978, Egyptian, Israeli, and American officials worked continuously for thirteen days in search of some agreement.[85] Sadat was prepared to settle for a declaration of principles that would recognize Arab sovereignty over the disputed lands. For the Israelis, such precepts spelled disaster. Israeli Foreign Minister Moshe Dayan had expressed his country's opposition: "Self-determination for the Palestinians means for us the destruction of the State of Israel in stages." The president acted as messenger and negotiator, keeping Begin and Sadat apart for a week of heavy negotiations. On September 17, the three leaders returned to the White House where they signed two agreements, one entitled "A Framework for Peace in the Middle East." Based on UN Resolution 242, the framework proposed essentially a five-year transition of the West Bank and Gaza to full autonomy. The Palestinians would have the right to participate in the determination of their future, while the Israelis would receive secure and recognized borders. Camp David's second document, "Framework for the Conclusion of a Peace Treaty between Egypt and Israel," provided for Egyptian sovereignty in the Sinai, the full withdrawal of Israeli military forces from that region, and the establishment of normal, peaceful Egyptian-Israeli relations, including mutual diplomatic recognition.[86]

In their failure to bridge the gap between principle and power, the Camp David accords settled very little. Sadat claimed a victory for principle, clearly stated: "Peace requires respect for the sovereignty, territorial integrity and political independence of every state in the area and their right to live in peace within secure and recognized boundaries free from threats or acts of force."[87] The fulfillment of those principles

Figure 13.2
Egypt's President Anwar Sadat shakes hands with Israel's Prime Minister Menachem Begin at Camp David (Courtesy: Jimmy Carter Library)

rested on the creation of self-governing authorities in the West Bank and Gaza. On the removal of Israeli settlements from Arab territory, a prerequisite to any peace treaty, the framework was silent. The Camp David accords provided no guarantee that Israel would carry out the provisions of the transitional process, leaving to that country the power to determine the outcome.[88] Still, the official and public euphoria over the Camp David accords was almost universal. Begin and Sadat received the Nobel Peace Prize. The *Wall Street Journal* observed: "President Carter has won a genuine achievement at the Camp David summit. ... Mr. Carter did revive hopes for peace in an atmosphere from which those hopes had all but disappeared, and that is no small cause for gratitude." The *New York Times* chided those who had underestimated the president. "What Jimmy Carter brought off in twelve long days at Camp David," ran its judgment, "demonstrates how skillful he has become at the substance of diplomacy—and how adept at political imagery to boot."[89] The *Washington Post* concluded that the President "did a beautiful piece of work. He saw possibilities that few others saw. . . . There will be a richly earned boost to his presidency and to the stature of the United States in the world."[90] Understandably, the Camp David accords produced little enthusiasm in the Arab world where writers and observers detected little gain for Palestinians.

Negotiations for a proposed Egyptian-Israeli Peace Treaty began in Washington on October 12 and continued intermittently into the following year. Vance and other U.S. officials traveled to the Middle East, but achieved little. Washington called a ministerial conference at Camp David, but it failed to advance the treaty-making process. On November 9, the president vented his frustration in his diary: "It is obvious that the negotiations are going backwards. . . . I told Cy to withdraw from the negotiations at the end of this week, to let the technicians take over. . . . It's obvious that the Israelis want . . . to keep the West Bank and Gaza permanently."[91] With Brzezinski leading the way, Carter set out to save the Camp David accords by traveling to the Middle East in March 1979. He conferred with Sadat in Cairo and Begin in Jerusalem. At breakfast with Begin on his final morning in Jerusalem, he broke the deadlock by meeting Israeli demands, largely by promising deliveries of Arab oil to Israel and arms to both countries. Sadat and Begin signed the peace treaty in Washington on March 26, 1979. The treaty declared a state of peace between the two countries. Israel agreed to withdraw all armed forces and civilians from the Sinai and behind the international boundary separating Egypt from mandated Palestine. The treaty established normal economic relations, including the sale of Arab oil to Israel.

There was no agreement on the Camp David processes relating to the West Bank and Gaza; but the two countries agreed, in an exchange of letters, to open negotiations on the creation of a self-governing authority in the West Bank and Gaza, preliminary to full autonomy. Again Sadat's efforts at bilateral negotiations with Israel alienated the Arab world. In their renewed imposition of heavy economic and political sanctions against Egypt, the Arabs understood that the treaty provided no infringements on Israel's power to command the future of the 1.1 million Palestinians residing in Israeli-controlled territory. Carter acknowledged that he spent more time dealing with the challenges of the Middle East than any other region, yet achieved little.[92]

* * *

President Carter confronted Europe with a program derived largely from his membership in the Trilateral Commission. Brzezinski had summarized the commission's two major premises: that the United States, under Nixon, had overemphasized the importance of U.S.-Soviet relations to the detriment of those with Western Europe and Japan. By exploiting its available power sources, the industrial world need not pay Nixon's price for Soviet cooperation.[93] The administration's Trilateral Commission's membership included not only the president, Vance, and Brzezinski, but also Vice President Walter Mondale, Defense Secretary Harold Brown, Treasury Secretary Michael Blumenthal, and arms negotiator Paul C. Warnke, as well as other high-ranking officials in the foreign and military services. Brzezinski explained that the external problems facing the country were so complex "that no single person can structure a response. A team effort is necessary."[94]

Carter's top officials had worked together on European issues over a period of years. Among these men were differences, even contrasts, in personality and disposition. Vance, not a seminal thinker, was moderate, gentlemanly, and generally optimistic in his world outlook, as was Warnke and other key members of Carter's younger foreign policy team. Brzezinski, who had spent an academic career studying the Soviet bloc, was less optimistic on matters of Soviet motives and dependability. As national security adviser, Brzezinski would not reinvent Kissinger's dominant role, but his nearness to the White House, added to his penchant for originality and readiness to formulate policy positions, rendered him first among equals.[95] Conscious of Brzezinski's bureaucratic advantages, Vance observed, "As long as I can debate my views, I have no problem at all."[96] Only a crisis, some predicted, would reveal who had the power.

Carter, during his first week in office, dispatched Vice President Mondale to the Trilateral world to outline the administration's foreign policy intentions. In Brussels on January 23, Mondale assured the NATO allies that the president was deeply concerned about the alliance and was "prepared to consider increased United States investment in NATO's defense." The vice president continued on to Bonn, Berlin, Rome, Paris, and Tokyo.[97] During a subsequent trip to London, the president urged NATO leaders to widen their economic cooperation, promote freer trade, strengthen the world's monetary system, and seek ways to avoid nuclear proliferation. Behind Carter's European policy was always the dual purpose of encouraging greater allied defense efforts and reassuring the Europeans of America's continuing commitment to their defense.[98] At the same time Carter rejected Kissinger's opposition to Eurocommunism. Vance assured French Socialists that the United States regarded the status of the Communist Party in any European country as a matter for the government and people of that country. The Communist parties of Yugoslavia, Italy, France, and Spain, he declared, pursued policies of their own and did not merit the term "Eurocommunism." What mattered for the United States was its ability to work cooperatively with the countries of Western Europe on matters of mutual concern.[99] Consequently, Carter could point to Europe where the Soviet-American competition ceased to have much meaning.

Amid his extended pursuit of an arms agreement with Moscow, Carter faced the critical NATO decision on the development and deployment of enhanced radiation (ER) weapons, or neutron bombs. The ER's destructive force would come, not from its explosion, but from its emission of intense radiation—killing troops without demolishing surrounding structures. Carter questioned the morality of such a weapon (popularly known as the "capitalist" bomb because it left property intact), but asked Congress for standby funding while he consulted the allies on the weapon's acceptability. German officials were prepared to deploy such weapons, convinced that they might render a nuclear war more bearable. Other countries were more equivocal. Carter's top officials subsequently advised him to proceed with the bomb's development, but by then he, like most European allies, had lost interest.[100] Eventually the German Bundestag approved the bomb's deployment by a narrow margin; Carter, unimpressed, proceeded to scuttle the whole neutron bomb program. Chancellor Helmut Schmidt objected, attributing the bomb's demise to habitual American unilateralism and the president's, not Europe's, vacillation.[101]

* * *

Initially for Carter, the competition between the United States and the U.S.S.R. remained intense, yet the danger of conflict had receded through the years. He accepted détente as a goal if not as a reality; like Nixon, he reminded the Kremlin that the two powers could not enjoy accommodation in one part of the world and promote conflict elsewhere. He recognized the importance of curtailing the arms race, a phenomenon he regarded wasteful, dangerous, and morally deplorable. Indeed, during his campaign for the presidency he unrealistically promised the total elimination of nuclear weapons from the world's arsenals. He pledged a reduction in national defense expenditures as well as arms sales to underdeveloped countries. Yet, on the critical issues of defense and Soviet relations, Carter faced a divided administration.

Much earlier members of Carter's foreign policy team had revealed a full spectrum of convictions regarding the Communist danger. The profound disagreements among his top advisers on the Vietnam War revealed totally antagonist concepts of Soviet power and influence in world affairs. Brzezinski had been a strong pro-war advocate, especially during the Vietnam teach-ins. Vance, Brown, and Warnke supported the war as Pentagon officials, but with rapidly declining enthusiasm. The president's total opposition to the war was expressed by his disbelief in falling dominoes. Some younger men in the administration had been active war protestors.[102] For Vance, the Cold War experience had long discredited the notion that the U.S.S.R. comprised a mortal threat to the non-Soviet world. His chief adviser on Soviet matters, Columbia University's Marshall Shulman, viewed the Cold War as a receding phenomenon. For him the Kremlin had developed a vested interest in participating constructively in the international community. Except for Brzezinski, who remained suspicious of the Kremlin, Carter's top advisers had become skeptical of traditional Cold War assumptions.[103] Vance and Brzezinski generally agreed on the largely unavoidable, risk-free responses available to them, none of which had much relevance to perceptions of danger. "I would say," Carter recalled, "that 95 percent of the time, or even more, they were completely harmonious in their policy recommendations."[104]

Nothing could deter the president's determination to pursue arms negotiations with the Soviet Union. The U.S. nuclear arsenal possessed over a million times the destructive power of the Hiroshima bomb. Vance believed that arms negotiations could vastly reduce defense expenditures and guide the two powers toward greater cooperation. Brzezinski favored arms limitations, not to spur cooperation, but to enhance U.S.-Soviet stability and limit the Soviet capacity to achieve a competitive advantage.[105] Kissinger and Ford had been unable to translate the Vladivostok accords of November 1974 into a SALT II treaty, largely due to Pentagon hawks and congressional opposition. Carter looked unfavorably on Vladivostok's established numerical ceilings that required building additional weapons, although he might have achieved an early arms agreement by adhering to the Vladivostok formula. The president preferred deep cuts in the number of strategic weapons, a freeze in the number of missiles with multiple independently targeted warheads, and a moratorium on the development of new missiles.[106]

In March 1977, Secretary Vance flew to Moscow with two proposals. One option built on the Vladivostok agreement, with a possible reduction of some 10 percent on weapons levels. The second, and preferred, proposal offered a major decrease in strategic weapons, protection against first strikes, constraints on testing, a balanced control of conventional weapons, and an agreement on the sale of arms to other countries.[107] In promptly rejecting the proposal, Soviet leaders questioned both the substance of Carter's elaborate formula and the manner in which the administration presented it. They had first learned of Vance's trip, moreover, through a Carter-Vance news conference and wondered how a public statement could advance such a difficult negotiation as that on nuclear arms limitation. Whether the administration's verbal support of Soviet dissidents, increased expenditures for Radio Free Europe and Radio Liberty, or Carter's accusations of human rights violations influenced the Soviet decision was not clear; however, they undoubtedly clouded the atmosphere in Moscow.[108]

Through 1977 the two countries continued their negotiations on arms issues that centered on Warnke's version of an acceptable SALT II agreement. Warnke, then also director of the U.S. Arms Control and Disarmament Agency, recommended a maximum of 2200–2250 strategic bombers and intercontinental missiles for each side, compelling the U.S.S.R. to reduce its forces. The treaty would impose a level of 1320 on each country's combined force of independently target reentry vehicles (MIRVs) and aircraft carrying strategic weapons. Soviet officials were reluctant, however, to negotiate away their strong bargaining posture based on the massive post-1965 Soviet arms buildup.[109] U.S. negotiators could not ignore the power of Congress and the press to defeat any arms agreement that failed to uphold their precepts of national security.

Vance assured the country, in late October 1977, that both the United States and the Soviet Union desired an agreement based on strategic parity; but, he added, they could not define parity.[110] The fundamental asymmetry in the military structures and requirements of the two countries rendered exceedingly formidable the task of measuring precisely what comprised strategic equality. Each side was stronger in some aspects of weaponry and recognized the advantages of other systems, but could not determine which of the different classes of weapons was the more effective. What rendered calculations even more difficult was the flow of technological innovation in weaponry and the relative importance of weapons modernization to two different strategic systems. The United States emphasized light but accurate nuclear weapons, including those designed to be launched from submarines; the Soviet Union relied on heavy land-based ballistic missiles. The geographic situations of the two powers offered a special mixture of strategic advantages and disadvantages. Moreover, the United States had only one enemy, the U.S.S.R., whereas the Soviet Union had China, Europe both East and West, and the United States.

Two competing weapons systems created special problems of measurement. For the Soviets the major complicating factor was the American air-launched cruise missile, a small, subsonic, low-flying weapon with a range of 1500 miles, of relatively low cost but high accuracy. For American negotiators the controversial Soviet bomber, code-named Backfire, was a long-range aircraft; to the Soviets the Backfire was of medium range and therefore properly excluded from all calculations.[111] The *New York Times*, in its editorial of September 18, 1977, posed the fundamental question: "Have the rival strategic forces developed along such divergent paths that real limitation agreements have become both intellectually and politically impossible?" The interim accord on offensive strategic weapons expired on October 3. In the absence of another agreement, both Washington and Moscow continued to respect the 1972 limitations.

Warnke, who took arms limitation seriously, explained on November 10 why the objective of arms reduction, based on parity, was worth pursuing. The country, he warned, had the simple choice of continuing the arms race, with the risk of Soviet military supremacy or of controlling the competition with arms limitation agreements. The United States, he acknowledged, led the Soviet Union in nuclear warheads, but both countries had far more weapons than targets. Both nations had long ago achieved overkill capacity. The principle of mutual deterrence presumed the continuing nonuse of nuclear weapons. Those, however, who believed that the Cold War continued to flourish, distrusted mutual deterrence despite the immensity of the nuclear arsenals. To them the proper objective of arms negotiations was not that of reassuring the enemy of good intentions by striking a balance but of maintaining an arsenal of weapons capable of deterring and, if necessary, winning a nuclear war.[112]

Despite Soviet unease over the Sino-American rapprochement, the SALT II discussions eventually produced an agreement in April 1979 as considerable time was spent correcting the mistakes of the 1972 Interim Agreement. Carter prepared carefully for his June meeting with Brezhnev in Vienna to sign the treaty. The Vienna summit, attended by two thousand reporters, commentators, anchormen, photographers, scriptwriters, and producers, outdid its predecessors as a media event, dwarfing Carter and Brezhnev in the process. On June 18, Carter and Brezhnev signed the Strategic Arms Limitation Treaty that sought to limit each superpower to 2250 strategic weapons. The Soviet's development and deployment of its ICBMs was significantly slowed; while both parties' number of MIRVs were limited for the first time. In addition to capping the arms race, the agreement included mutual rules, including a ban on telemetry encryption, that greatly aided verification.

Although the Senate Foreign Relations Committee voted 9–6 on November 9 to recommend ratification of the SALT II treaty, much opposition to the treaty had developed, especially among Republican Party members. On December 16, a group of 16 senators asked the president to delay the Senate vote on SALT II until after the presidential elections. Carter did not comply with this request, but following the Soviet action in Kabul on December 27, he asked the Senate to delay voting on SALT II. On June 6, 1980, the State Department announced that SALT II and Afghanistan were "inseparable." Thus, the Senate never voted on the ratification of SALT II. Nevertheless, America and the Soviet Union "remained within the limits prescribed by SALT II" until well into the Reagan administration.[113]

The treaty reflected mutual interests in arms limitation that far transcended the state of U.S.-Soviet relations or the Carter-Brezhnev display of cordiality. The five-day meeting received mixed reviews in the press. The *Wall Street Journal* condemned the SALT process, arguing "preoccupation with a dubious arms agreement erodes broader American security interests." Georgia's Sam Nunn, the Senate's leading military expert, declared that the answer to the Soviet military threat lay not in arms limitation but in larger military budgets.[114] What troubled the critics was Carter's pledge to abide by SALT II even if the Senate rejected it.

For Europeans, the arms control negotiations raised the issue of European security. For such Germans as Egon Bahr, the answer lay in acknowledging the absence of any Soviet military threat to Western Europe—an optimistic proposition not acceptable to most European leaders.[115] Those Europeans who relied on the deterrent power of American nuclear superiority could see little gain for European security in a SALT II agreement, with its emphasis on parity. European leaders doubted that a simple U.S. threat of massive retaliation would deter a European war. For them, NATO required credible deterrents positioned in Europe itself.[116] Europeans were especially troubled, therefore, by the Soviet deployment of new, highly accurate, SS-20 intermediate-range missiles, with three warheads each and a range of 3,000 miles. To counter the new Soviet weapons, NATO's Nuclear Planning Group, meeting during April 1979, agreed tentatively to deploy the two new American intermediate-range systems capable of reaching the U.S.S.R. from Western European bases. Both the Pershing II and the ground-launched cruise missiles had ranges of 1100 miles. In December 1979, the NATO partners agreed to deploy 108 Pershing II and 464 ground-launched cruise missiles unless the Soviets curtailed their medium-range deployments.[117]

* * *

What Soviet-American competition remained in Asia and Africa had proved to be costly and unsatisfactory for both countries. The Soviets had gained little from past efforts to affect Third World developments; while in opposing East Asian Communism, the United States had inflicted grievous injury on itself without commensurate rewards. The nations of the world, for better or worse, had long been moving in directions that had little relationship to world Communism, liberation, or containment. Only the Eastern European countries, under direct Soviet control, had not stepped fully out of the role to which the great powers had consigned them at the dawn of the Cold War. The United States had given the Kremlin incentives to accept the existing world when Nixon, in the SALT negotiations, acknowledged nuclear parity and Ford signed the Helsinki Declaration recognizing Soviet hegemony in Eastern Europe. Even so, throughout the 1970s the U.S.S.R. continued to spend some fifteen percent of total national output on defense, compared to only five percent in the United States. What the effort revealed of Soviet intentions or what it contributed to Soviet security, influence or prestige, remained highly elusive. The Kremlin's costly military effort rendered the U.S.S.R. strong enough to menace the West and reinforce American insecurities, but it did not eliminate the Soviet requirement for coexistence with its major antagonists.[118]

Western Sovietology presented the U.S.S.R. from Khrushchev to Brezhnev as a success story. It presumed that the Communist advances, under Brezhnev, in global acceptance, economic productivity, and increased consumerism flowed from a relaxed Soviet power structure— more democratic, innovative, and promising. Unfortunately, after Khrushchev, the Soviet system chose not to foster liberalization.[119] Yet whatever its advances under Brezhnev, the Soviet economy was not as efficient, powerful, or successful as it appeared. It could not overcome the inadequacies of a command economy, with its inefficiencies in production and organization and its lack of innovation required for the creation and marketing of better and more varied products. Western calculations of Soviet GNP exaggerated Soviet economic performance, often to demonstrate the growing danger of Soviet power. Unable to escape such measurements, the CIA, for many years, overestimated Soviet economic activity by as much as 60 percent.

For those Americans—many in high places—who had never detected any waning of the Kremlin's global ambitions, the confluence of the known surge of Soviet military capabilities and Carter's apparent readiness to accommodate Communist advances in the Third World presaged global disaster. This troubling trend toward moderation, beginning in the mid-1960s with the rise of multi-polarity, seemed to find its ultimate political expression in George McGovern's "New Politics." McGovern's nomination at the 1972 Democratic convention, followed by his overwhelming rejection by the American electorate, opened an inviting chasm in national politics for liberals. For them, Democratic leaders, as well as much of the nation's intellectual community, had gone too far in their abnegation of force in protecting the country's interests and willingness to assert the superiority of Western democratic values. By the mid-1970s, former liberals, designated neoconservatives, had launched an anti-Communist crusade to reassert America's role as defender of the free world.

In the neoconservative vanguard were Norman Podhoretz, editor of *Commentary*, Irving Kristol, coeditor of *Public Interest*, Senator Daniel Patrick Moynihan, writers and scholars Midge Decter, Jeane Kirkpatrick, Nathan Glazer, and Walter Laqueur. Podhoretz wrote off McGovern's followers as ideologues "hostile to the feelings and beliefs of the majority of the American people." For millions, added Jeane Kirkpatrick, McGovern "was a man who had gone over to the enemy."[120] Podhoretz, Decter, and other neoconservatives founded the Coalition for a Democratic Majority to recapture the Democratic Party. After the 1974 Democratic midterm convention in Kansas City institutionalized McGovern's antiestablishment program, Moynihan led the effort to embody neoconservatism in national political discourse.[121] By unfurling the banners of democracy, he declared, the United States could reestablish a vigorous, anti-Communist role in world affairs. As ambassador to the United Nations after April 1975, Moynihan won the plaudits of countless Americans for his undiplomatic ridicule of the frailties of Third World countries and leaders, such as Uganda's notorious dictator, Idi Amin, for their rejection of

Western policies and standards. The West, in its failure to defend its principles, Moynihan charged, was enabling the Soviets to establish their political dominance and military superiority.[122]

Led by Podhoretz and Kristol, the neoconservatives warned the country against the dangers of Soviet power and expansionism. Laqueur denounced the view that the U.S.S.R. had a major stake in the *status quo*. Rather, he asserted, the Soviets were out to win the global struggle.[123] Similarly, Kristol saw a growing Soviet menace and a dangerously weak U.S. response, leading to "an alarming upsurge of national delinquency and international disorder everywhere."[124] *Commentary* had emerged as the chief vehicle for the crusade against the country's alleged isolationism. Americans traumatized by Vietnam, Podhoretz declared in April 1976, no longer seemed willing to defend the free world from Soviet aggression. Glazer warned in July that the major threat to the independence of nations came "from Soviet Russia and communist China and the world movement over whose leadership they compete." Robert W. Tucker concluded, in March 1977, "our relationship with the Soviet Union constitutes today, as it has since the close of World War II, the central problem for American foreign policy." That month, military analyst Edward Luttwak informed the readers of *Commentary* that the Soviet buildup under Brezhnev "signified an expansionist intent."[125]

By 1976, the neoconservatives, after years of mutual distrust, found themselves aligned with the traditional right, characterized by such columnists as William Buckley, editor of *National Review*, George Will, William Safire, and Patrick Buchanan. This new coalition, bound together by their demand for an active, determined anti-Communist foreign policy, assumed that the security and prestige of the United States, as the lone defender of the international order against Soviet expansionism, required a constant readiness to employ force. They sought a public that would cheer the national assertiveness they advocated; how they intended to render that assertiveness effective in international affairs remained elusive. Largely unilateral in their approach, they condemned any official attention to allies or international law that might counsel caution or restraint.

This counterattack on the emerging common wisdom of a receding Cold War received added impetus when, in 1976, George H. W. Bush, then CIA Director, appointed an outside-government panel, headed by Richard E. Pipes of Harvard University, to prepare an estimate of Soviet military programs and intentions. The ten team members included Paul Nitze, the author of NSC 68, William Van Cleve, and

Foy Kohler. All members of Team B were selected deliberately because they reflected "a more somber view of the Soviet strategic threat than that accepted as the intelligence community's consensus." The Team B report, completed in December 1976, concluded that previous intelligence estimates had tended to misperceive Soviet motivations, underestimating their intensity, scope, and implicit danger. It accused the CIA of relying too heavily on data provided by cameras and listening devices, and not enough on the threatening private and public statements of Soviet officials. Team B concluded that the Soviet Union was bent on gaining military superiority over the United States as part of its preparation for a limited nuclear war that would destroy American society while losing no more than 20 million Soviet citizens.[126] The incoming Carter administration, finding little merit in the report, ignored it.

Another group in the vanguard of those who shared these burgeoning fears of Soviet power and expansionism was the Committee on the Present Danger (CPD). The committee's program was based largely on the Team B report. Led by Eugene Rostow and Paul Nitze, the CPD comprised largely former generals, admirals, state department officials, and academicians who were troubled by the persistent buildup of Soviet military power and the concomitant failure of the United States to oppose Soviet Third World activities, especially in Africa and the Middle East. On its executive committee were Richard V. Allen, Charles Burton Marshall, and Dean Rusk. Going public in October 1976, the CPD argued that the Soviet drive for dominance, based on unprecedented military preparations, required a much higher level of American defense expenditures. Its policy statement began, "Our country is in a period of danger and the danger is increasing."[127] CPD spokesmen, three days before Carter's victory in November, explained the danger of continued strategic inferiority: "If Soviet dominance of the strategic nuclear level is allowed to persist, Soviet policymakers may—and almost certainly will—feel freer to use force at lower levels, confident that the U.S. will shy away from a threat of escalation." Nitze summarized the argument for American nuclear superiority: "To have the advantage at the utmost level of violence helps at every lesser level.[128]

Carter disregarded the Committee on the Present Danger in making his advisory appointments. Forced outside government, the committee set out to mobilize the public against the new administration's predictable passivity toward the twin forces of Soviet preparedness and Third World nationalism. During subsequent weeks, the committee criticized Carter's

appointments and savagely attacked Warnke's nomination as arms negotiator. The committee challenged Carter's central assumption—that in a
world of triumphant nationalism U.S. power had no legitimate or necessary use—by arguing that the Kremlin stood behind every assault on
international stability.[129] For the CPD, American inaction in the Third
World was synonymous with weakness and retreat.

Much of the country's foreign policy elite challenged these burgeoning fears and predictions of doom. At issue in the debate over
national security and military adequacy were Soviet capabilities and
intentions. On both counts, the suppositions of the New Right,
Team B, and the CPD faced vigorous criticism. G. B. Kistiakowsky,
President Eisenhower's assistant for science and technology, denied
that the United States suffered from strategic inferiority or faced a
Soviet nuclear attack. Those who advocated an ever-larger nuclear
arsenal, Kistiakowsky observed, had no choice but to dwell on the fea-
sibility of nuclear war. He attacked the persistent worst-case view of
the Soviet danger, employed repeatedly after 1949, he charged, to
rationalize the continuing American military buildup. Never, he
noted, did the predicted disasters materialize. He discounted the dismal scenarios of Nitze and Pipes that the Soviet first-strike strategy
could produce victory in such a war. As he concluded: "It is difficult
to regard these dooms day scenarios as anything more than baseless
nightmares."[130] He wondered how the U.S.S.R. could better survive
a nuclear war than the United States; both sides, he declared, would
face absolute chaos. For Henry Kissinger the issue of nuclear strategy
was too complex and important to be subjected to doctrinaire and par-
tisan debate. "Those who talk about supremacy," he charged, "are not
doing this country a service."[131] Where it mattered, such writers
agreed, U.S. policies of containment had been effective. Nowhere
had the Kremlin risked a superpower military confrontation.

Soviet expert Raymond Garthoff pointedly denied Nitze's conten-
tion that the Soviets were seeking nuclear supremacy to fight a nuclear
war. Actually, he noted, Soviet military and political leaders had
repeatedly called for strategies of mutual destruction, based on parity,
and designed to avoid nuclear war.[132] Columbia scholar Robert
Legvold, writing in *Foreign Affairs*, October 1977, observed that the
Soviet military effort was designed largely to sanctify the Soviet
Union's status as a global power so that no international issue would
terminate to that country's disadvantage. George F. Kennan saw little
danger of war. He advised Americans to stop believing that the Soviets
contemplated an attack on Western Europe or that they would have

struck earlier except for the American nuclear deterrent. Kennan reminded Americans that when the Soviet Union "looks abroad it sees more dangers than inviting opportunities. . . . It has no desire for any major war, least of all for a nuclear one. It fears and respects American military power . . . and hopes to avoid a conflict with it."[133]

* * *

Such varied attempts to dispel the country's fears of Soviet power and expansionism quickly foundered before the pressure of events in Latin America, Africa, and the Middle East. Despite the accumulating constraints that time and change had imposed on Soviet policy, countless Americans believed the country's security and global standing to be under constant threat. Predictably, Carter's effort in 1977 to change the status of the Panama Canal raised a vigorous protest. The issue was not new; three previous administrations had wrestled with it. Nixon's negotiators had arranged a treaty as early as 1974. Carter, like his predecessors, was conscious of the growing antagonism throughout Latin America over the existing 1903 Panama Canal Treaty, which granted the United States full control of the canal. The new treaty, for which he campaigned, would eliminate the issue of American colonialism by turning over control of the canal to Panama in the year 2000.[134] What embittered the debate was less the control of the canal than the perceived decline in the country's international standing. A *New Yorker* cartoon illustrated the central issue. Two men are standing at a bar, one saying to the other: "What's wrong with me? For thirty years I never gave a thought to the Panama Canal. Now I can't live without it." Many critics feared that the Panamanians, once in control of the canal, would not operate it efficiently or fairly. Others doubted that the treaty guaranteed American access to the waterway in time of crisis. The treaty's defenders argued that it effectively balanced the country's security interests with rights granted the Panamanians.

No assurances, however, could overcome the strong conviction that the Panama Canal, as a remarkable American engineering triumph and controlled by the United States for over sixty years, was symbolic of American power.[135] The willingness to negotiate the canal away by treaty under the threat of violence and sabotage appeared, for many, ignominious in the extreme and further evidence of the nation's decline. Carter managed to secure Senate approval of the new Panama Canal Treaty in the spring of 1978, but the intense condemnation marked the administration as incapable of maintaining the country's role as a world power.

The accumulating convictions that Carter's Washington could not protect the country's security interests in the Caribbean surfaced again with the declining fortunes of Nicaragua's Anastasio Somoza. Through the decades since Franklin D. Roosevelt's administration, the Somoza family had served U.S. interests in Nicaragua faithfully, but had also grown rich by looting the country.[136] Carter was trapped after 1977 between the long U.S. record of support for the Somoza regime, reinforced by the knowledge that Somoza's chief enemies, the Sandinistas, received aid from Cuba, and his disgust with the regime's corruption and human rights violations. The murder of Pedro Joaquin Chamorro, Somoza's leading critic, in early 1978, created a negative reaction in Washington.[137] As Somoza's support disintegrated, Carter could identify no promising course of action to moderate the Sandinista-led opposition. At the NSC meeting on June 22, 1979, Brzezinski, advocating intervention, warned the president of the possible consequences of leftist victory over Somoza. The United States, he said, would be considered "incapable of dealing with problems in our own backyard and impotent in the face of Cuban intervention. This will have devastating domestic implications."[138] In his refusal to interfere boldly in Nicaraguan affairs, the president concluded that the Sandinistas held greater promise than others for a just and democratic society. Indeed, Mexico, Venezuela, Costa Rica, and Panama helped bring Somoza down and send him into exile in Paraguay where unknown enemies quickly assassinated him. Carter's critics charged that a more rapid and positive U.S. response to the Nicaraguan crisis could have deprived the Sandinistas of victory and thereby avoided the conversion of Nicaragua into a potential Cuba.[139]

Latin America's third challenge to American credibility came in July 1979 when Democratic Senator Richard Stone of Florida informed the president of the possible presence of Soviet combat forces in Cuba. Brzezinski requested CIA Director Stansfield Turner to verify the report. The troops were there—in apparent violation of the Cuban missile settlement of late 1962. Carter, who wanted no quarrel with the Soviets over the issue, kept it under wraps until Frank Church of Idaho, chairman of the Senate Foreign Relations Committee, learned of the Soviet brigade. Church, then in a tough reelection campaign because of his known moderation on external issues, demanded publicly that the Soviet forces be removed. Brzezinski now proclaimed the brigade evidence of Soviet adventurism. The president exacerbated the issue by declaring, "[W]e consider the presence of a Soviet combat brigade in Cuba to be a very serious matter and that this *status quo* is not acceptable.[140] For the press, the issue quickly became a major test of the President's crisis leadership.[141]

When confronted, Soviet leaders revealed that the brigade had been in Cuba since 1962. President Kennedy, they acknowledged, had asked the Soviets to remove the troops; when they failed to do so, he dropped the subject. Gromyko responded bluntly to Washington's prodding: "Our advice on this score is simple. It is high time you admit this whole matter is artificial and proclaim it to be closed." That ended the controversy.[142] The president assured troubled members of Congress that the United States could not order the Soviet troops out of Cuba, that their presence violated no treaty and comprised no danger. He criticized members of Congress and the press for habitually panicking when confronted by a Soviet issue. Critics, condemning the president's irresolution, attributed his inaction to the decline of American will.[143]

More than previous issues, Soviet behavior in Africa widened the ideological cleavage not only within the Carter administration but also within the country's ruling elites. In dispatching forces into the Horn of Africa in 1977, the U.S.S.R. and Cuba supported the Communist-led government of Ethiopia in its effort to save Ogaden province from Somali-supported insurgents. In Angola, Cuban-Soviet aid brought victory to the radical Popular Movement for the Liberation of Angola (MPLA). Then Cuban forces, joined by members of the MPLA, supported Katangese exiles in an invasion of Zaire's mineral-rich Shaba province.[144] While the threat to Zaire brought a concerted response from both Washington and Paris, enough to save the province for Zaire, writers nevertheless condemned Washington for its inaction. "Whenever American counter-measures of any kind are suggested," complained Robert Moss, "siren voices are raised to defend a policy of *passivism* in the face of Soviet encroachments in Africa." Moss acknowledged that the Soviets were unpopular in Africa, but they would not leave until the United States inflated the price of remaining.[145]

In Washington, Vance and much of the administration opposed any confrontation in Africa where the United States lacked leverage. Vance observed on July 1, 1977, "A negative, reactive American policy that seeks only to oppose Soviet or Cuban involvement in Africa would be both dangerous and futile." It would be more promising, he said, for the United States to seek solutions to the problems that invited Soviet-Cuban intervention. But as Soviet-Cuban activity in Africa continued to expand, amid charges of American weakness, Brzezinski advised the president, in early 1978, that Soviet action could be part of a broad strategic design. During the spring of 1978, U.S. officials charged the Kremlin with maintaining 37,000 Cuban military personnel in 20 African countries.[146] Finally, Carter, in his Annapolis address of June 7, 1978, crafted by both Brzezinski and Vance, accused Soviet leaders of waging an "aggressive struggle for political advantage" in Africa. He appealed to the Soviets to exercise restraint in troubled areas, but his final challenge was blunt: "The Soviet Union can choose either confrontation or cooperation. The United States is adequately prepared to meet either choice."[147] Many in Washington reveled in the president's show of toughness. In Moscow, *Pravda* wondered why Soviet maneuvering in Africa, far outside the American and Soviet spheres of strategic interest, should provoke Washington to such levels of hysteria.[148]

Some analysts challenged the fears that underwrote the administration's changing mood toward events in Africa. It seemed incredible that independent African countries that had long struggled for independence would willingly become puppets of Cuba or the Soviet Union. Most Africans could detect nothing objectionable in Soviet behavior, for the Soviet and Cuban personnel had gone only where they were invited. When New York Senator Moynihan and former Secretary Kissinger charged that the United States should not have permitted the Cubans to enter Ethiopia, the *New York Times* editorialized: "One man says threaten anything, no matter what the chances of making good on the threat. The other says never mind the particular stakes or possibilities, in geopolitics everything is tied to everything else ... There, we submit, walks the ghost of Vietnam.... Whatever the stakes on the ground, or the possibilities, for geopolitical reasons Hanoi had to be stopped.... To resurrect that logic against a President who seeks new techniques for applying American influence around the world is a dangerous game indeed."[149] Far better, said the *Times*, to portray the risks and costs to Moscow. If any of Carter's critics really wanted an American war in Africa, they never revealed it.

* * *

Strategically, the Middle East was another matter, made so by its gigantic stores of oil and its proximity to the Soviet Union. After the Suez crisis of 1956, the United States displaced Britain and France as the protector of Western interests in the critical area of southwest Asia. With direct access only to the region's periphery—Israel, Egypt, and the Gulf—Washington entrusted Middle Eastern stability to the transformation of Iran into a bastion of pro-Western power. Even as the Shah Mohammed Reza Pahlavi supported OPEC's manipulation of oil prices in 1973 to fill his treasury, to U.S. officials he could do no wrong. Nixon and Kissinger offered him whatever sophisticated arms and equipment his ample treasury could afford. Against what external dangers the Shah's insatiable pursuit of military hardware protected was never clear.

What rendered Washington's Middle Eastern strategy precarious was the pervading public dissatisfaction with the Shah's rule. His land reforms antagonized the landed gentry and drove multitudes of small farmers suffering from imposed ruin into the bulging Iranian cities. The income from oil did little for the masses but much for the Shah's military and personal establishments. The lavish Iranian court, added to the Shah's Westernization programs, deeply offended the fundamentalist Shi'ite Islamic clergy, led by the Ayatollah Ruhollah Khomeini. His unrelenting attacks on the Shah's rule led to his exile in France in 1964, from where he sustained his assault. Following the Shah's $300 million celebration of the 2500th anniversary of the Persian Empire in October 1971, Khomeini denounced the party and termed the Shah's title, King of Kings, as "the most hated of all titles, in the sight of God." Shielded by sycophants, the Shah remained largely ignorant of the growing disillusionment among his Moslem subjects.

Despite the Shah's vulnerability, Carter sustained the country's uncritical support of his regime. He toasted the Shah in Teheran on December 31, 1977: "Iran, under the great leadership of the Shah, is an island of stability in one of the most troubled areas of the world." Carrying the burden of U.S. objectives in the Middle East, the pampered Shah now obtained from Washington more military equipment than any other nation in the world.[150] Concerned with the Shah's survival, the president failed to challenge the horrendous reprisals of the Shah's notorious secret police, SAVAK, which kept the Shah in power. As late as August 1978, the CIA, in a long intelligence assessment, declared that Iran was "not in a revolutionary, or even in a pre-revolutionary situation."[151]

Unfortunately, Washington had failed to grasp the power of the Iranian revolution. In December, the Shah faced a general strike, with several hundred thousand demonstrators in the streets demanding his removal. Powerless to respond, the Shah's regime was doomed. The administration turned to Prime Minister Shapour Bahktiar to ease the Shah's retirement. While Sullivan pushed the Shah to abdicate, General Robert Huyser, U.S. military adviser in Teheran, moved to strengthen Iran's military ties to Bahktiar and thus stem the revolution.

The effort failed. On January 16, the Shah fled the country, never to return.[152] With the Shah's abdication, Khomeini's Islamic adherents recalled him to Teheran. He returned on February 1, 1979, not to take command of the government, but to establish himself as the driving force behind the changes that would quickly transform the country. Before Khomeini's arrival, Washington viewed the Iranian revolution as a local affair. Still, the upheaval had demonstrated that events beyond the control of U.S. power could seriously undermine strategies regarded vital.[153]

Yet, the administration reasserted the country's global interests. "The United States," declared Defense Secretary Harold Brown in late February, "is prepared to defend its vital interests with whatever means are appropriate, including military force where necessary, whether that's in the Middle East or elsewhere." Energy Secretary James Schlesinger added, "The United States has vital interests in the Persian Gulf. The United States must move in such a way that it protects those interests, even if that increases the use of military strength."[154] Brown assured Riyadh of America's continued support. That year, the administration sent Saudi Arabia $5 billion in military equipment including the latest early warning aircraft. It planned a stronger U.S. naval presence in the Persian Gulf and the creation of stronger ties in the Gulf region with both Iraq and the Gulf shiekdoms.[155]

Elsewhere in the Middle East, Washington faced challenges for which it could frame no easy response. By 1979, the People's Democratic Republic of Yemen, strategically located at the southern terminus of the Red Sea, had established strong ties with the Soviet Union. The desert country had become a huge arsenal for Soviet weapons, missiles, tanks, advanced aircraft, and naval stores. East German, Cuban, and Soviet personnel directed much of the country's civilian and military activity. With the fall of the Iranian Shah, Washington provided military aid to North Yemen to strengthen its defenses against assaults from South Yemen.[156]

On May 25, 1979, the West Bank-Gaza negotiations, required by the Israeli-Egyptian peace treaty, opened in Beersheba, Israel. Nothing in that treaty strengthened the claims of either the Syrians or the Palestinians against Israel's refusal to compromise. Again the Arab world held the United States responsible for the failed negotiations.[157] At the same time, much of the American Jewish community, led by its neoconservative writers, had long questioned Carter's pursuit of a Palestinian settlement. They suspected that the president's peace effort, if successful, would force Israel into a disadvantageous settlement. What troubled Jewish leaders was the widespread assumption that Israel, in antagonizing the Arabs and much of the Third World, was its own worst enemy.[158] Taking up the Israeli cause, Eugene Rostow argued in *Commentary* that Israel, the bulwark against Soviet-Arab aggression in the Middle East, required the occupied territories to guarantee its survival.[159] Carter anticipated Israeli territorial concessions, but he assured Jewish leaders that he regarded Israel's survival a "moral imperative." What terminated his uneasy truce with Jewish neoconservatives on the Palestinian issue was UN Ambassador Andrew Young's failure, in August 1979, to inform the State Department fully of his meeting with representatives of the PLO in July. Vance demanded Young's resignation. That decision ignited a massive anti-Israeli crusade among black leaders, who accused the president of removing the popular black official under Israeli pressure. Spokesmen of the major black organizations now condemned Israel for its support of the white racial regimes of South Africa and Southern Rhodesia.[160] On March 1, 1980, perhaps because of confused signals, the United States voted in favor of a UN Security Council resolution that condemned Israeli settlements in occupied Arab lands. Thereafter many neoconservatives, already at odds with the Carter administration on a full spectrum of Cold War issues, were prepared to break with the Democratic Party on the Palestinian issue alone.[161]

For the president the worst was yet to come. After his return to Iran, Khomeini directed his Islamic crusading zeal toward the United States. On May 13, 1979, Teheran radio announced that the Iranian government had rescinded the capitulations law that exempted all U.S. diplomatic personnel from Moslem jurisdiction. Over Teheran radio, on October 28, he recited his special grievances against Washington. "All of our problems," Khomeini said, "come from America. . . . All of the problems of the Moslems stem from America."[162] Under the urging of Kissinger and Chase Manhattan's David Rockefeller, Carter permitted the Shah to enter a New York hospital for cancer treatment. The U.S. embassy in Teheran had warned that the Shah's entry into the United States would ignite the anti-American sentiment in Iran. On November 4, Khomeini's militant followers occupied the U.S. embassy, taking hostage some fifty American diplomatic personnel and demanding the return of the Shah for trial and execution.[163]

This defiance of international law challenged the country's sensibilities, but not its security. Carter, with good reason, eliminated the option of force, but he warned Iran of grave consequences if harm came to any of the hostages. Washington's minimum response brought plaudits from those who believed that the president had no retaliatory policies available.[164] For others, the hostage crisis was another measure of the world's growing disrespect for the United States. The country had brought on the crisis, wrote columnist George Will, with policies of "right-mindedness, supplications and the scrupulous avoidance of conflict."[165] In late November, Marvin Stone passed judgment on Carter's abhorrence of force:

The U.S. has projected an image of weakness, indecision and vacillation. For the past three years, there has been a pattern in every international test of strength—tough talk followed by a shrinking from action. . . . Throughout, Carter has demonstrated a penchant for responding to challenges and rebuffs by turning the other cheek. . . . The cumulative effect of the Carter administration's behavior has been to debase the prestige of the United States and to invite insults—and worse—even from the pygmies of the international community.[166]

Iran's continuing refusal to release the American hostages merely aggravated the nation's belligerent mood. Norman C. Miller observed in the *Wall Street Journal* on January 31 that the Iranian fanatics had held the hostages for 89 days because they knew that the president would not retaliate. In March, Kraft advised Carter to "break negotiations with Iran, threaten ominous action, and make *them* worry about *our* next move." Polls revealed a sharp increase in support for stronger action against Iran. Under pressure to act, the president agreed to a hostage rescue mission in late April, an ill-fated venture that ended in the death of eight American servicemen on the Iranian desert.[167] One Shi'ite cleric close to Khomeini responded to the rescue attempt: "We wish and we welcome military aggression against us because it strengthens the revolution and rallies the masses around it."[168] On April 28, Vance, who had opposed the mission, resigned his position, much to the dismay of the nation's moderates. Vance was a major casualty of the end of détente. Early in the administration he had felt no rivalry, but his long effort to cushion the effect of the Soviet thrusts into Africa and Afghanistan could not withstand the increasing anti-Soviet sentiment within the administration, led by Brzezinski and buttressed by powerful voices on the outside.

Employing Algerian officials as intermediaries, U.S. negotiator Warren Christopher succeed in gaining the release of the 52 hostages on January 20, 1981 ending 444 days of captivity—minutes after Ronald Reagan was sworn in as president. Because the Shah was dead, the final arrangements largely involved dividing up his assets and releasing other frozen Iranian funds.[169]

* * *

Far more troubling for the Carter administration was Afghanistan where, by 1978, the Soviet Union was deeply, if reluctantly, involved in that neighboring country's political affairs. In April, pro-Soviet Afghan Communists overthrew the neutralist government of Mohammed Daoud. The victorious Communists immediately requested Soviet military assistance. Although the coup took the Kremlin by surprise, its proclaimed loyalty to the U.S.S.R. gave the Soviets little choice but to offer financial and technical assistance. By February 1979, the pro-Soviet regime was in deep trouble. The Communist Party had split along tribal lines. Herat fell to a Shi'ite Moslem rebellion, aided by a mutiny of Afghan troops who proceeded to kill some one hundred Soviet military personnel and their families. Afghan leader Mohammed Taraki, on March 18, asked for Soviet ground forces to rescue his government. Soviet Defense Minister Dmitri Ustinov and Foreign Minister Gromyko agreed to helicopter gunships, technicians, and grain on credit, with paratroops to guard the airport, but no ground forces. As Brezhnev explained, "We have examined this question from all sides . . . and I will tell you frankly: We must not do this. It would only play into the hands of enemies— both yours and ours." The aid strengthened Taraki's regime and permitted it to recapture Herat.[170] In Washington, President Carter could find neither the interests nor the occasion that would permit more than a rhetorical response to the Soviet presence in Afghanistan.

But this changed when, in late December 1979, Soviet forces seized Kabul and killed Taraki's successor Hafizullah Amin—only to find the intervention gave the resistance a patriotic appeal that soon placed the Soviets on the defensive. Already facing open challenges to its alleged loss of will, the administration reacted to the Soviet invasion of Afghanistan with bewilderment and rage. Afghanistan was not a Western interest; nor did the Soviet occupation alter the world's strategic balance. But for the first time since 1945 the Kremlin had used force outside Eastern Europe.[171] Carter acknowledged bitterly that Afghanistan taught him more about the Soviet Union than he had learned during three previous years in office.[172] Unable to ignore the Soviet action, the president faced an unfortunate decision. He could either inform the American people that the Soviet intervention to stabilize its borders, while irresponsible, did not touch any vital American or Western interest or declare Soviet behavior dangerous to all southwest Asia, thus demanding some form of retaliation.

Brzezinski warned the country that the Soviet Union now threatened American interests from the Mediterranean to the Sea of Japan, especially Pakistan and the states bordering the Persian Gulf.[173] On January 4, Carter revealed his concerns to the nation. "A Soviet-occupied Afghanistan" he said, "threatens both Iran and Pakistan, and is a stepping stone to possible control over much of the world's oil supplies.... If the Soviets ... maintain their dominance over Afghanistan and then extend their control to adjacent countries, the stable, strategic and peaceful balance of the entire world will be changed. This would threaten the security of all nations, including, of course, the United States."[174] Such apocalyptic rhetoric, in bringing back the dominos, isolated national policy from official perceptions of danger.

Soviet presence in Kabul, without visible evidence of dangers elsewhere, would not permit sanctions commensurate with the presumed dangers. The punishments available to Carter might enrage the Kremlin; however, they would not expel the Soviets from Kabul. Carter's sanctions, announced early in January, comprised reductions in the number of Aeroflot flights to the United States, reduced Soviet access to U.S. fishing waters, limited access to U.S. high technology equipment, a partial grain embargo, and $500 million in military aid to Pakistan to strengthen the Khyber Pass—an amount that the Pakistanis decided was not worth accepting. The president warned the Soviets that unless they evacuated Afghanistan, the United States would boycott the 1980 Moscow Olympics. Secretary Vance explained the threatened boycott: "To hold the Olympics in any nation that is warring on another is to lend the Olympic mantle to that nation's actions."[175] Washington could discover no effective response between acquiescence and military intervention.

Afghanistan vindicated those who had long charged U.S. policy with weakness. For them, the Kremlin's imperialistic behavior revealed a decline in the essential cautiousness of Soviet leaders and a diminishing respect for American power. Marvin Stone predicted that the president would be long on rhetoric but short on action.[176] Still, columnist Hugh Sidey saw special significance in the president's warning to the Kremlin: "History teaches perhaps few clear lessons. But surely one such lesson learned by the world at great cost is that aggression unopposed becomes a contagious disease." Within the administration's policy machinery, the crisis had apparently a bracing effect: "Afghanistan was a godsend.... It gave point and opportunity for action." Still, action meant no more than a confrontational attitude; no one suggested that the United States place an army in Afghanistan.[177]

On January 23, in his State of the Union message, the president set forth the Carter Doctrine: "Any attempt by any outside force to gain control of the Persian Gulf region will be regarded as an assault on the vital interests of the United States of America, and such an assault will be repelled by any means necessary, including military force."[178] The widespread assumption, proclaimed by the president, that the Soviet invasion exposed all southwest Asia to further Soviet encroachment, pushed American hawkishness to a new high. What mattered was not the reasons the Soviets had entered Afghanistan, but the presumption that they had gained a strategic position from which they could more easily threaten Pakistan, Iran, and the Persian Gulf states. When asked in a *New York Times* interview on February 10 what evidence he had that the Soviets would go further, Harvard's Richard Pipes, invoking an ideologically based analysis, replied: "No evidence except that it would make no sense to occupy Afghanistan for any other purpose. Afghanistan has no natural resources of importance, and the risk of antagonizing the West is very high for a bit of mountainous territory with a primitive economy, with a population that has never been sub-dued by any colonial power. To run all these risks for the sake of occu-pying this territory seems to make little sense—unless you have some ultimate, higher strategic objectives."[179]

Yet, the Carter Doctrine did not create a strategic policy for the Middle East. As the *New York Times* editorialized on January 27, 1980:

There is no firm terrain on which to build Mr. Carter's new wall of contain-ment. Military pacts and bases will not stand up well in the region's political, ethnic and religious storms. Importing American power will arouse as many radicals as it will reassure conservatives, without resolving their conflicts. . . . Stability in the region from Turkey to Pakistan is a long-term project that cannot be designed or paid for by Americans alone. The regimes that profit most from the area's oil, and the allies who crave it, need to be partners in defending that treasure. Less Western dependence on oil remains essential to any defense. And so, paradoxically, do relations with Moscow that could be used to induce future Soviet restraint.[180]

Vance observed that even for the United States the response to Afghanistan never came to grips with the perceived dangers it presented. He recalled in his memoirs that Afghanistan broke the tenuous balance between visceral anti-Sovietism and efforts at détente. "The scales," he wrote, "tipped toward those favoring confrontation, although in my opinion, the confrontation was more rhetorical than actual."[181]

Europe's hesitancy in sharing Washington's sense of alarm over Afghanistan sealed the fate of any effective strategy for southwest Asia. The European allies, no less than many U.S. observers, concluded that the president and his supporters had miscalculated the Soviet threat; they presumed from the outset that the Soviets acted to protect their borders, not to send forces to the Persian Gulf. They questioned the customary U.S. retreat to worst-case scenarios. To Carter, Germany was especially difficult. When, in March, Chancellor Schmidt visited Washington, he promised the president nothing. *Die Zeit* clarified Germany's detachment: "Europe must not become a zone of tension if tension prevails in other regions. . . . The West cannot win in Berlin the battle it lost in Afghanistan."[182] West European leaders had no interest in imposing sanctions on the U.S.S.R. over Afghanistan; détente with the Soviet Union was flourishing and they were determined to sustain it. Nicolas Krul, president of Gulf and Occidental, a German-based investment firm, observed that "Europe has too big a stake economically, financially, and politically to allow détente to collapse."[183]

For many American writers and public officials, however, the Soviet invasion of Afghanistan sounded the death knell of détente and the inauguration of a new Cold War. Polls as well as reports of newspaper correspondents around the country revealed the return of an assertive, Cold War mentality. The Soviet aggression and the president's response, the editors of *Business Week* noted, "have pushed relations between the two superpowers across a watershed from which there is no easy return." After mopping up in Afghanistan, the editors asked, would the Soviets turn on Pakistan or try, through coercion or subversion, to gain control of Iran and the entire region of the Persian Gulf?[184] To those who shared such reactions, the Soviet invasion recalled not the tragic misadventure in Vietnam but rather the early aggressions of Nazi Germany.

When Congress reconvened in late January, it quickly responded to the president's post-Afghan image of strength and leadership by displaying its own adherence to the new Cold War mood. In his State of the Union message, Carter called for additional military outlays of five percent above inflation (an increase of $15.3 billion), a stronger U.S. presence in the Arabian Ocean, naval and air facilities in northeast Africa and the Persian Gulf, medium-range nuclear forces for Western Europe, and revitalization of the draft.[185] With few dissenting voices, Congress backed the president's proposals for tightening American military facilities around the rim of the Indian Ocean, a region that Carter had once sought to demilitarize. "Even the most rational and most cautious members," declared Senator Edmund S. Muskie of Maine, "are going to ride this bandwagon no matter what their doubts about particular spending proposals. We've been aware all along that the Russians were close to the jugular of our oil supplies but practically no one thought they'd reach for the jugular. Now, there's the fear they might."[186]

* * *

Amid charges of weakness, Carter's apparent failure to prevent unwanted developments stretching from Nicaragua and Cuba, through most of Africa, to Iran, Yemen, and Afghanistan—all perceived as dangerous to U.S. and Western security—revolutionized much of the nation's outlook on world affairs. Gone was the growing conviction that the Cold War was receding into history. As early as June 1978 a CBS–*New York Times* poll revealed that over half of the American people favored a firmer approach to the Soviet Union. Critics complained that the Soviets would not have ventured into Africa with such little restraint had they anticipated a stronger reaction in the White House. Evans and Novak observed that whereas the Soviets could never be sure "whether Kennedy, Johnson, Nixon and Ford would suddenly choose force, they can be certain . . . that Carter will not." Such criticism reduced U.S. policy in the Third World to a dangerous game of bluff. What was uniquely troubling about the fall of the Shah was the fear that Washington, seemingly, no longer could care for the nation's business in a dangerous world.[187] To his critics, Carter's problem lay not in the absence of forceful responses to events in Africa and the Middle East, but primarily in the appearance of weakness, irresolution, and innocence that invited the abhorrent and threatening behavior.

Nowhere could the critics recommend policy alternatives beyond the resort to tougher words, but they clearly held the rhetorical advantage in their dramatic charges of weakness, supported by evidences of failure that were often superficial. Columnist David Broder's response was typical. He accused the president of giving "the nasties in the world . . . the dangerous notion that the United States is easy picking." It was time, he added, "for the United States to show the flag and Carter to show some backbone." Similarly *Washington Post* writer Joseph Kraft noted that the president's troubles were not accidental. "He comes on weak," wrote Kraft, "and whatever the merits of this or that policy, it seems beyond dispute that under his stewardship the country is very poorly prepared to meet a challenge as difficult as any we have faced since World War II." The *Wall Street Journal* reminded the administration that in "the world of geopolitics, if you lose in one place you will be tested in another. If you lose successively you will be tested in more and more ways. If you start not even to put up a fight, everyone will start to bully you."[188] Robert Elegant placed the blame squarely on the Vietnam-era media. Assuming that the West, but especially the United States, had been demoralized by the fall of Saigon, he wondered whether "Angola, Afghanistan, and Iran would have occurred *if* Saigon had not fallen amid nearly universal odium—that is to say, *if* the 'Viet Nam Syndrome,' for which the press ... was largely responsible, had not afflicted the Carter Administration and paralyzed American will."[189]

That polls revealed a surge in American opinion for larger defense budgets was not surprising. Amid the charges of national weakness, countless Americans embraced the warnings of previous years that the Soviets sought both conventional and nuclear superiority in quest of war-winning capability. Strategists complained that the Carter administration, relying on the good faith of the nation's adversaries, had decoupled Soviet ambitions, as demonstrated in Africa and the Middle East, from expanding Soviet power.[190] General George J. Keegan, retired head of Air Force intelligence, warned that the Soviet threat was real and that global conflict was in the making. At stake, added General Matthew B. Ridgway, was the nation's survival. Admiral Elmo R. Zumwalt concluded that, because of U.S. weakness, Soviet naval and air forces were clearly capable of gaining control of the western Pacific and the eastern Mediterranean. In Europe as well, he added, the balance had shifted against the West. No longer could NATO place its trust in either its conventional forces or the American nuclear umbrella.[191] Defense Secretary Brown acknowledged that the United States, for a decade, had pursued a policy of strategic restraint in building its missile and bomber forces, as well as its defense capabilities. Now, as Brzezinski's ally, he advocated a reversal of policy with the observation that Soviet military spending "has shown no response to U.S. restraint—when we build, they build; when we cut, they build." Kissinger, once a proponent of détente, advocated a renewal of strategic competition with Moscow.[192]

But in a succinct assessment, correspondent Peter Marin questioned the wisdom of the country's current outlook:

Whether it be the Nicaraguan revolution, the hostage crisis, the rise in OPEC prices, the Russian invasion of Afghanistan, or the fighting in Iraq and Iran, our inability to control events and our inept response to them have demanded from us a rethinking of our political and moral relation to the world. But we neglect this crucial task. Instead, we have lapsed happily into the familiar attitudes that marked the Cold War in the Fifties and the Asian debacle of the Sixties: we clench our fists and mutter comforting platitudes to ourselves, cheerfully lost among the same illusions that proved so disastrous a decade ago. It is fashionable now, in some circles, to see this renewed military hubris as both inevitable and necessary. We are told that we are merely leaving behind, as we must, guilt that paralyzed us for a decade after the war in Vietnam. But that, I think, misstates the case. What paralyzed us was not simply the guilt felt about Vietnam, but our inability to confront and comprehend that guilt: our refusal to face squarely what happened and why.[193]

Carter's undoctrinaire approach to external affairs still appealed to a broad segment of the country, but it exposed the administration to charges that it had discarded the Cold War strategy of containment. For Carter, the multipolar world demanded a multiplicity of policies that defied the formulation of any global strategy. Brzezinski explained to a New York audience in May 1979 that Carter had "sought to widen the scope of our primary relationships to encompass countries in Latin America, Africa, and Asia. Our purpose is to create a framework that is genuinely global, within which the individual needs of nations and of peoples can be more fully satisfied."[194] In contrast to such ambitions, the strategy of containment was exceedingly limited in scope and action. That strategy comprised a perennial effort to maximize the strength and will of countries opposed to the U.S.S.R., but it provided no strategic responses to events not perceived as Soviet threats or even to many that were. No previous administration, for example, had ever confronted the U.S.S.R. directly over any alleged Soviet Third World expansionism. No one who condemned the Carter administration for its lack of strategy could define one that integrated balance of power considerations with those of world order, or weigh the importance of sound bilateral relationships with major governments against the demands of security, economic welfare, nonproliferation, arms sales, and human rights. Even some who advocated more coherent and integrated foreign policies acknowledged that Carter faced external challenges so complex and ambiguous that any overriding strategy would have been unsuitable and confining.[195]

Still, critics could, with justice, accuse the president of undertaking too much without a clear set of priorities. What seemed to reinforce the lack of direction was the administration's chaotic system of policy formulation. Without a dominant foreign policy adviser, Carter looked to two power centers, the State Department and the NSC. Their often conflicting opinions impeded the process of decision-making, leading at times to confusion.[196] The administration possessed no balancing historical perspective; it revealed no interest in continuity or precedent, often ignoring previous efforts to deal with issues under consideration. Unable to recognize basic trends, it too often shifted from one policy option to another until it discovered that events had moved beyond its control and in directions that the nation regarded disastrous. Carter's failures lay as well in his general unconcern for public, congressional, and bureaucratic opinion. Initially, Carter's moderation captured the mind of Washington's bureaucracy, but he reached out neither to the bureaucracy nor to Congress; ultimately he lost the support of both. Except to his close friends, he conveyed no feeling of personal warmth.[197] His repeated efforts to democratize the presidency stripped the office of much of its symbolic authority and exposed him to public disrespect. Beleaguered, battered, and bewildered, the former governor of Georgia appeared a lost soul.

CHAPTER 14

Rise and Fall of the Second Cold War: Reagan and Gorbachev

Exploiting the nation's sense of futility caused by Iran's seizure of American hostages and the Soviet intervention in Afghanistan, Ronald Reagan embellished them and rode them to victory in November 1980. During his presidential campaign, he and other Republican leaders condemned the Carter administration for its "weakness, inconsistency, vacillation, and bluff" in the face of Islamist radicals and Moscow's alleged aggressive actions. Not only that, Reagan charged that the Democratic administration had permitted the Soviet Union to seize military supremacy from the United States. "We're already *in* an arms race," Reagan complained, "but only the Soviets are racing."[1] Even though America's economic and military strength continued to stabilize a divided Europe, to Cold War hawks the Carter administration had failed to restrain threatening Soviet expansionism in the Middle East, Africa, and Latin America. Pledging to rebuild the country's military forces, Reagan and his supporters during the campaign repeatedly declared their determination to reverse the country's decline.

Reversing that decline demanded far more than augmenting the armed forces. National security required, as well, rebuilding the American consensus broken by the Vietnam War. "[W]e must rid ourselves of the 'Vietnam Syndrome'," Reagan advised the nation—and only briefly—in April 1980. "It has dominated our thinking for too long."[2] During the campaign, he defended the Southeast Asian conflict as a "noble war," an unselfish American effort to help a new Asian country defend itself against a "totalitarian neighbor bent on conquest." The United States was not defeated in Vietnam, he assured his audience, the failure to achieve victory rested on the country's antiwar elements. His secretary of state designate, Alexander M. Haig, Jr., echoed this view, arguing that the United States would have triumphed had it employed all of its available military power. In seeking to transform the Vietnam conflict into a necessary, laudable, and winnable encounter, Reagan stressed the proposition that the United States dared not again abjure the use of adequate force in Third World crises. Neither dared it lose. By reinstituting its military supremacy and commitment to global containment, the United States would regain both the capability and the will to check Soviet expansionism. It would again be the defender of free world, challenging Communist advances in Central America, Africa, and the Middle East.

Long before he settled in at 1600 Pennsylvania Avenue, Reagan had a perfected, well-honed anti-Communist litany. Speaking to the Phoenix, Arizona, Chamber of Commerce in 1961, he declared, "Wars end in victory or defeat. One of the foremost authorities on communism in the world today has said we have ten years. Not ten years to make up our minds, but ten years to win or lose—by 1970 the world will be all slave or free." Reagan's rhetoric, especially of the early 1960s, combined the views of the populists and fundamental evangelicals, presenting in simple, uncomplicated language, what Frances Fitzgerald suggests as "the virtues still generally thought to be most quintessentially American: anti-elitism, distrust of experts, a belief in democratic values, in plain speaking and common sense." It also contained many of the characteristics of a "paranoid style," which historian Richard Hofstadter described in his masterful essay "The Paranoid Style in America Politics." The paranoid spokesman—focusing on a gigantic, sinister conspiracy driven by an almost demonic force—holds that he comprehends what others do not, that he is the protagonist in an apocalyptic drama.

In his trademark "standard speech," Reagan approached the Cold War much as many other strident anti-Communists. His view on international Communism was found at the end of the speech. "We are faced with the most evil enemy mankind has known in his long climb from the swamp to the stars." With this as a launching pad, he would go on to castigate American liberals for seeking accommodation with these evil forces. "We are being asked to buy our safety from the threat of the Bomb by selling into permanent slavery our fellow human beings enslaved behind the Iron Curtain." Reagan charged his opponents of "encouraging them to give up their hope of freedom because we are ready to make a deal with their slave masters." Reagan also denounced the various early superpower arms control negotiations.[3] While he never directly urged the United States to challenge the Soviet Union militarily, he never proposed any solutions to the dilemmas he presented.

Although it was not the first occasion he employed that term to describe the Soviet Union, Reagan's "evil empire" speech on March 8, 1983, to the National Association of Evangelicals, was the climax of his hostile rhetoric. During his campaign for a second term and after he met the new Soviet leader Mikhail Gorbachev, he greatly muted his criticisms of the Kremlin. Indeed, much to the dismay of his hard-line anti-Communist supporters, before he left the White House Reagan would declare the evil empire no longer existed.

By drawing on his colleagues from the Committee on the Present Danger, Reagan established a sympathetic advisory team during his first term committed to reasserting the country's global leadership. Prominently among the 51 Committee members that obtained positions in the new administration were former Team B members William R. Van Cleave, a defense analyst from the University of Southern California, Harvard historian Richard Pipes, and General Daniel O. Graham, former director of the Defense Intelligence Agency. Other principal advisers were Richard V. Allen, Soviet specialist, former member of Kissinger's national security council and Reagan's principal campaign coordinator for foreign policy; Fred C. Ikle, former director of the arms control agency; and Robert W. Tucker, political scientist at Johns Hopkins. Pipes, Tucker, and Van Cleave established the high-decibel anti-Communist tone of the group. The Kremlin, Pipes argued, "is driven by ideology, internal politics, and economic exigencies steadily to expand." Moreover, repeating the dismal findings of Team B, he warned in *Commentary* that the Soviets did not accept the idea of nuclear deterrence and were building forces designed to wage and win a nuclear war. Tucker suggested that America's lost of will to use its power had allowed Moscow to misbehave in various parts of the world. Van Cleave focused on what he saw as the United State's inexcusable decline in readiness, modernization, maintenance, and force levels. "Today," he declared in a *New York Times* interview of October 1980, "the United States is almost irrelevant."[4]

Downplaying President Carter's concern with human rights, the new administration placed its emphasis on U.S. security interests. Whether Third World governments had poor human rights records mattered less than their opposition to Communism. Jeane Kirkpatrick of Georgetown University entered the Reagan stable with a 1979 article in *Commentary* entitled, "Dictatorships and Double Standards." Appointed ambassador to the United Nations, Kirkpatrick joined with Ernest W. Lefever, also of Georgetown University, in arguing that there was a fundamental distinction between Communist totalitarianism and right-wing authoritarianism. The former, they pointed out, pursued ideological purity at the expense of human rights; authoritarian regimes ignored human rights to combat subversion or external pressure. Totalitarian regimes, they argued, never became democratized, whereas many autocracies did. What this distinction seemed to overlook was not the absence of reformist potential in Communist societies, as Hungary, Czechoslovakia, and Poland demonstrated, but the power of Soviet armies. Yet such distinctions greatly aided in rationalizing assistance to pro-Western dictatorships as well as the consistent opposition to Communist nations. Lefever insisted that the United States should support friendly governments, whatever their character. Nominated as an assistant secretary of state dealing with human rights matters, Lefever eventually withdraw his name from consideration in the face of Senate opposition.[5]

Fears of Soviet military power and global expansionism dominated the outlook of the Reagan team and fellow neoconservatives. The president defined these dangers at a White House news conference in late January 1981:

From the time of the Russian revolution until the present, Soviet leaders have reiterated their determination that their goal must be the promotion of world revolution and a one world socialist or communist state. . . . They have openly and publicly declared that the only morality they recognize is what will further their cause; meaning they reserve unto themselves the right to commit any crime; to lie [and] to cheat in order to obtain that.[6]

Secretary of State designate Alexander Haig endorsed this alarming view of the Kremlin's activities. At his January 1981 confirmation hearings, he warned members of the Senate Foreign Relations Committee that the years ahead would "be unusually dangerous. Evidence of that danger . . . [was] everywhere." The nation needed be vigilant and be prepared to expend the resources necessary to control future events. "Unchecked," he said, "the growth of Soviet military power must eventually paralyze Western policy altogether." Addressing the American Society of Newspaper Editors three months later, Haig declared that Washington needed to concentrate its policies on the Soviet Union because the Kremlin was "the greatest source of international insecurity today. . . . Let us be plain about it: Soviet promotion of violence as the instrument of change constitutes the greatest danger to world peace."[7] As with the president's claims, the secretary of state never supplied evidence to support their charges.

The Reagan administration presumed from the outset that unwanted developments everywhere resulted from Soviet expansionism. The Republican platform had detected "clear danger signals indicating that the Soviet Union was using Cuban, East German, and now Nicaraguan, as well as its own, military forces to extend its power to Africa, Asia and the Western Hemisphere."

* * *

Caught in the momentum of expanding fears and strategic concerns, the administration eventually set in motion the costliest defense program in the nation's peacetime history. Led by Van Cleave, a long-time critic of the nuclear arms limitation treaties, Reagan's military advisers pushed for higher levels of defense expenditures ignoring traditional review procedures and unwilling to reconsider the military utility of a project once authorized. Even Defense Secretary Caspar W. Weinberger, who had arrived with a well-earned reputation for cutting costs, endorsed the Pentagon's "wish list," with its projection that to meet the Soviet threat required nothing less than an annual seven percent increase in defense spending above inflation.[8] Most Americans seemed to accept the increase in arms expenditures as the best way for the United States to restore the nation's military predominance and, thus, to regain its capacity to shape events and support reliable friends.

Reagan agreed and included the inflated figure in his new budget. With new technologically advanced weapons Washington would deal from a position of greater strength, reassure allies, and, perhaps, enhance U.S. negotiations on nuclear weapons reduction. The proposed expenditures—$1.6 trillion in five years—would be spent to acquire new missile systems, especially the mobile MX, underwrite the nation's most ambitious naval program in history, update air force planes and facilities, and create a stronger, more mobile conventional force prepared for any global challenges.[9] Reiterating a long-held Pentagon truism, Secretary Weinberger insisted that Afghanistan demonstrated the United States always must be ready to fight several conventional wars simultaneously. "We have to be prepared," he argued, "to launch counteroffensives in other regions and to exploit the aggressor's weaknesses wherever we might find them. ... We must be prepared for waging a conventional war that may extend to many parts of the world." How the administration would obtain the necessary personnel to man its ships, tactical air wings, and divisions without some form of public service was not evident. But more immediate was the dilemma of distinguishing

Figure 14.1
(L to R) CIA director William Casey, Secretary of Defense Caspar Weinberger,
Reagan, Vice President George Bush, Secretary of State Alexander Haig,
and Ed Meese, in the Oval Office (Courtesy: Ronald Reagan Library)

weapons that were necessary, effective, and manageable from those that were merely expensive.[10]

The massive new military buildup was not without its critics. Among them were informed observers who charged that the Reagan administration's claim of Soviet overwhelming military power was nothing more than a myth. According to James Fallows, symbols unquestionably play a part in international politics. "The Russians have derived incalculable mileage from the impression that they have built a world-conquering military force, an impression they have been fostering, overtly and covertly, since 1945. But why should we help them create that impression," he questioned, "when it is at such variance with the facts, and when the real purpose of such warnings, I am convinced, is only to apply a scourge to the flaccid American soul? If the problem is the perception of American strengthen, why not assess that strength coolly rather that create exaggerated fears?" The administration's avoidance of readily available facts was evident. One of the many examples noted by Fallows was the Pentagon's alarm in the late 1960s regarding the Soviet Foxbat (MIG-25) that it reported could fly at 3.2 mach or better, with a combat range of 2,000 miles. Since officials asserted it would change the balance of air power, the U.S. Air Force ordered the F-15; indeed, only the MIG-25 could justify the expense of the F-15. A Soviet pilot seeking asylum in 1976 brought with him a MIG-25 where American technicians discovered the wings were not made of titanium and had rust spots and protruding rivets; the radio still had vacuum tubes; it could not fly faster than 2.5 mach; and it had a far shorter range than estimated. Christopher Paine pointed out in a fall 1982 edition of *Bulletin of the Atomic Scientists*, "85 percent of the Soviet submarine-launched ballistic missile force [is] usually in port on any given day" while only one-third of U.S. submarines were similarly in port. The *New York Daily News* reported in February 1982 that "morale among Soviet troops stationed in East Germany is so bad that some units are close to mutiny."[11] Not surprisingly, overly generous annual assessments of the Soviet armed forces published by the Pentagon, to justify its budgets during the early Reagan years, ignored such data.

There were also many businessmen and even Pentagon officials who questioned whether military projections transcended the requirements of national security. Could Defense Secretary Caspar Weinberger reduce the military's wasteful habits, could he ever persuade Pentagon to be accountable—to balance its books? Congressmen, equally troubled by the perennial rise in the cost of national defense, had difficultly arguing that specific expenditures were excessive when the experts, with their control of essential information, insisted that they were not. (Moreover, most congressmen benefited from the monies spent in their districts and realized substantial reductions of defense expenditures would result in the loss of jobs at home.) There existed in Washington a strange lack of concern for an effective distribution of allocated defense funds. Nonetheless, the expenditures themselves were seemingly expected to send a message to the Kremlin.

As with previous administrations, Reagan and his advisers anticipated far more than the perpetuation of the *status quo* from the country's costly defense efforts. The higher levels of U.S. preparedness, supplemented by a program to deny the U.S.S.R. the benefits of Western trade, credits, and technology, some thought, would bring about long-desired changes in Soviet behavior. Determined to assert the administration's revisionist goals in its dealings with the Kremlin, Reagan insisted that a discussion of the "imperialism of the Soviet Union" must be featured prominently at any future summit meeting. "We have a right, indeed a duty," Secretary Haig echoed, "to insist that the Soviets support a peaceful international order, that they abide by treaties, and that they respect reciprocity."[12]

With revisionist expectations, a senior administration official announced that a Soviet withdrawal from Afghanistan and Angola was not sufficient as a precondition for moderating the U.S. posture; he would demand nothing less than an extensive reduction in Soviet military spending. Others in Washington anticipated that when the United States achieved overwhelming nuclear supremacy, the Soviet Union would be coerced into accepting conditions everywhere that conformed to American design. In strong language, Reagan offered his administration's revisionist goals when he spoke before the British Parliament on June 8, 1982: "Let us now begin a major effort to secure the best—a crusade for freedom that will engage the faith and fortitude of the next generation. For the sake of peace and justice, let us move toward a world in which all people are at last free to determine their own destiny."[13] In some measure, Reagan's approach to the U.S.S.R. was a reaffirmation of the Eisenhower administration's concept of massive retaliation, with its underlying assumption that the Soviets could not, in the long run, survive American competition.

Critics' prediction that his administration would never link its fears of the Soviet Union with its actions was borne out by the record. Never did the Reagan team develop policies that focused on fulfilling its self-proclaimed global goals. Foreign policy rhetoric spewed about during the administrations early months were never the determinants of policy, for the occasions when American force might be used was never defined with any precision. Shooting down, in late 1981, two Libyan aircraft that challenged an American naval presence inside the Gulf of Sidra was scarcely a defining moment for the administration. Raising questions about his policy of toughness, Reagan, in early April 1981, terminated Carter's embargo on grain shipments to the Soviet Union. Much as Carter, Reagan coexisted—often quietly employing the CIA—with the Soviet activities in Afghanistan, Africa, and the Arabian Peninsula. The Reagan rhetoric was meant, critics logically concluded, not to form the basis of the tougher policy toward Moscow, but rather to assuage the American public.[14]

Soon it became apparent that the chasm between official words and official actions aggravated differences between the administration's pragmatists and the ideologues. Because of the lack of clearly defined objectives, Reagan received conflicting policy proposals from Haig's State Department, Weinberger's Defense Department, Richard Allen's National Security Council, Jeane Kirkpatrick's UN office, and Republicans everywhere. As a consequence, bitter bureaucratic struggles sprang up leading Haig to complain that the decision-making process was as "mysterious as a ghost ship; you heard the creak of the rigging and the groan of the timbers and even glimpsed the crew on deck. But which one of the crew was at the helm? It was impossible to know for sure."[15]

Still, contrary to critics' perception of his anti-Soviet rhetoric, Reagan ultimately expected much improved relations with the Kremlin. His inaugural address emphasized the American people's desire for peace: "We will negotiate for it, sacrifice for it, [but] we will not surrender for it, now or ever." The new president, however, was determined to negotiate from strength. His expanded military program, Reagan later explained, was aimed at gaining concessions from the Soviets. "I think that we can sit down and maybe have some more realistic negotiations because of what we can threaten them with," the president told reporters in October 1981. "But they know our potential capacity industrially, and they can't match it." It was questionable, however, whether Reagan ever lacked the military strength to negotiate. Negotiation always consists of more than assessing existing power, whatever its magnitude, when it carries no serious sign of impending hostile action. Successful negotiation entails compromises needed to establish a satisfactory agreement grounded on mutual interests, whether dealing with territory or arms reductions.[16]

* * *

Central America, specifically Nicaragua's radical Sandinista regime and El Salvadoran guerrillas, loomed as the Reagan administration's immediate challenge. Congress had decided in September 1979 to provide economic assistance to the Sandinistas, but the Nicaraguan government subsequently arrived at a better arrangement with Moscow. During 1980, the Sandinistas solidified their hold over the country and received military aid from Communist countries to strengthen their army against local counterrevolutionary forces. The Republican platform of 1980 had warned of the growing power of Communism in Central America as demonstrated by the Marxist takeover of Nicaragua and Marxist attempts to destabilize El Salvador, Guatemala, and Honduras. "As a result," noted the platform, "a clear and present danger threatens the energy and raw material lifelines of the Western world." Kirkpatrick condemned Carter's failure to assist Nicaragua's Anastasio Somoza, even if he was a dictator, because his pro-American government was a more acceptable ally. Since Somoza had created an efficient, urban political regime, she insisted Washington should have provided whatever support he needed to stay in power. In April 1981, the State Department ordered a halt to all American assistance to the Sandinistas, including shipments under the PL-480 food program.[17]

Even before assuming office, Reagan had designated El Salvador as a focal point of Soviet-American confrontation. Since it was well known that Cuba and other Soviet-bloc countries were supplying Salvadoran rebels with arms via Nicaragua, an administration counteroffensive would not only reassert American role in hemispheric defense, it could also do so without risking the introduction of U.S. combat forces. By supporting moderate Salvadoran reform activities in late 1979, the Carter administration had hoped to blunt the Communist-led insurgency. Unfortunately, the large landowners and the military, employing "death squads," ended the reform efforts with a bloody repression that resulted in the murder of thousands. Even suspect Americans did not escape the violence, as Salvadoran soldiers abducted, raped, tortured, and murdered four American churchwomen and buried them in a shallow grave. Yet, the Reagan administration refused to view the underlying causes of the struggle within El Salvador, ignoring the horrid indigenous conditions of widespread poverty, gross inequality, little peasant land ownership, political and judicial corruption, and vigorous repression of dissent.

Even though the insurgency had begun to wane by the end of 1980, the hard-liners in Washington feared the Moscow-sponsored Salvadoran threat had become hemispheric. Reagan resurrected the domino theory to emphasize the nature of the Soviet challenge. "What we're doing," he told newsmen, "is try to halt the infiltration into the Americas, by terrorists and by outside interference, and those who aren't just aiming at El Salvador but, I think, are aiming at the whole of Central America and possibly later South America and, I'm sure, eventually North America."[18] A February 1981 State Department report, endorsing Napoleon Duarte's ineffectual government, claimed the existence of an external conspiracy that threatened all of Central America. One government had already become a victim, the report stated, of "a well-coordinated, covert effort to bring about the overthrow of [its] established government and to impose in its place a . . . regime with no popular support." Now another nation had become a base for indirect armed aggression" against its neighbors. "In short," the report concluded, Central America had become "a textbook case of indirect aggression" that could endanger the entire hemisphere. Once again the domino theory surfaced. "[I]f the Sandinistas and the Salvadoran guerrillas are successful in overthrowing the Government in El Salvador," Lawrence Eagleburger, Reagan's Under Secretary of State for Political

Affairs worried, "that's the beginning, not the end, of the problem. The Costa Ricans, the Hondurans and the Guatemalans are certainly going to face the same sort of threat. I can't even say that the Mexicans wouldn't have a problem."[19]

Symbolizing the Central American situation as nothing less than a global crisis, Secretary Haig insisted that the Kremlin must control its clients in Cuba, Nicaragua, and El Salvador or assume responsibility for their activities. El Salvador was merely a single item on "a priority target list—a hit list, if you will, for the ultimate takeover of Central America," he informed the House Foreign Affairs Committee in mid-March. If the spread of this Soviet-sponsored terrorism was not halted, the secretary warned, "[We] will find it within our own borders tomorrow." With Nicaragua already under Moscow's domination, El Salvador, Guatemala, and Honduras would surely follow.[20] To many observers, however, the administration had overplayed its hand.

Administration officials were subsequently forced to recognize that the political realities of Central America were far more complex than Haig's hit list suggested. Despite their dramatic portrayal of hemispheric dangers, their rhetoric scarcely contained the elements of a national policy necessary to liberate Central America from the alleged Soviet influence. Critics questioned the notion that poverty-stricken and revolution-prone El Salvador somehow could be the keystone of hemispheric security. Haig took the position that defending U.S. interests in Central America required the elimination of the Castro regime. Despite all the talks of impending dangers, Reagan's advisers had no intention of deploying U.S. armed forces to Central America to secure the nation's safety. If Washington's policy objectives remained elusive, the means for effective U.S. action were equally so. In the absence of direct U.S. military involvement, Reagan, on March 9, 1981, issued a "finding" (written statement required by law) that authorized U.S. covert action in Central America through allies and surrogates.

CIA director William Casey and Reagan launched such an offensive in late 1981 to eliminate the pro-Soviet forces in Central America. The administration would provide covert support to the contras, the insurgent groups seeking to overthrow the Sandinista government in Nicaragua. While Washington's objective ostensibly was to halt the flow of arms into El Salvador from Nicaragua, CIA officials and others became skeptical as assistance was extended to anti-Sandinista insurgents operating out of Costa Rica and Honduras. It soon became evident that the administration desired to overthrow the Sandinista regime, when Reagan created Project Democracy and, in August 1982, gave the National Security Council (NSC) responsibility for achieving its objectives in Central America. In December 1982, Congress impeded the NSC's operation when it passed the Boland Amendment that specifically denied funds for overthrowing the Nicaraguan government. The State Department rescued the languishing contra war when it agreed with the CIA and decided that the contras could, with U.S. supplies and training, defeat the Sandinista forces.[21]

During 1982, the administration's counterrevolutionary program began to focus on Honduras, bordering both Nicaragua and El Salvador, as a desirable base of operations for the contras. In camps along the Nicaraguan-Honduran frontier, the United States set out to turn the contras, mostly exiled supporters of the former Nicaraguan dictator Somoza, into combat units capable of conducting raids across the border to undermine the Sandinista regime. By late in the year, these attacks into Nicaragua were almost daily occurrences. U.S. Ambassador John D. Negroponte played a major role in directing U.S. activities in Honduras. Following a major military exercise (Big Pine 2) in August 1983, the Pentagon left behind nearly a thousand U.S. troops in Honduras to guard the assets remaining there—radar stations, field hospitals, aircraft, and heavy equipment. Many inside and outside Central America feared the American military buildup was a prelude to wider hostilities in the region.

As efforts to overturn the Nicaraguan government continued into 1983, the president warned the America people of the serious events in Central America. Despite emphasizing that "the United States' national security" was at stake, Reagan insisted the nation's role in defending the hemisphere would remain strictly limited. "We will not Americanize this conflict," he said. "American combat troops are not going to El Salvador." Even so, the president continued to stress the vital importance of an anti-Communist Nicaragua in an April 17 address to the joint session of Congress. "The national security of all the Americas is at stake in Central America. If we cannot defend ourselves there, we cannot expect to prevail elsewhere. Our credibility would collapse, our alliances would crumble and the safety of our homeland would be put in jeopardy."

If the United States did not halt the insurgency in Central America, Secretary Weinberger feared, Washington might need to pull its forces out of Europe, Japan, and Korea, leaving these regions open to potential Soviet domination.[22]

* * *

Without warning, on October 25, 1983, Reagan informed the world that U.S. military forces had invaded the small island of Grenada in the eastern Caribbean with a population of 120,000. Ever since Maurice Bishop in a bloodless coup had seized control of the government in 1979 and established close ties with Cuba's Fidel Castro, Washington kept the island under close scrutiny. On a visit to the Caribbean in 1982, the president declared that the Soviet Union had brought Grenada, as well as Cuba and Nicaragua, under its influence in order to "spread the virus" of Marxism throughout the Caribbean.[23]

Washington opposed Grenada in the World Bank and staged massive naval maneuvers, even a mock invasion, near the island. Without U.S. economic assistance, Bishop turned to Venezuela, East Germany, North Korea, and Canada and created by 1983 a booming tourist trade. Hundreds of Cubans were brought in to construct a long airstrip, improve medical facilities, and build other public projects. In addition, Bishop imported large quantities of Cuban arms. These activities aroused suspicions within the Reagan administration. It condemned the 12,000-foot runway as one designed only for military use, although Barbados, the Bahamas, and Martinique all had longer airstrips to handle tourists. Bishop's ongoing verbal confrontation with Washington ended on October 19 with his assassination during a coup led by the deputy prime minister. In their success, the island's political extremists destroyed whatever legitimacy Bishop's revolution possessed.

Growing pressure to invade Grenada, Washington explained, came from frantic leaders of small island nations in the vicinity. Had the United States not sent in its military forces, a ranking administration official claimed, "no one would have taken . . . [the United States] seriously any more down there. What good are maneuvers and shows of force, if you never use it?" Fearing the possibility of chaos following Bishop's death, most of the island's population welcomed the arrival of U.S. forces and the promises of order and democracy that they offered. American students at the local medical college enthusiastically greeted what the president termed a rescue mission. Grenada's new leadership announced an election in November 1984.[24] If the American public overwhelming approved of the surprise invasion, as a military venture Operation Urgent Fury left much to be desired. The attacking U.S. force of 7,000 took three days to overwhelm fifty Cuban soldiers and a few hundred construction hands. The lack of a unified command found Army and Navy personnel failing to attend the other's planning sessions, equipping their attacking units with incompatible radios and, at least on one occasion, assaulting the other's positions. The commander of the

USS Guam refused to refuel Army helicopters unloading wounded soldiers. Nevertheless, the administration reveled in successfully preventing Grenada's incorporation into the Soviet-Cuban bloc and at limited cost. Much of the country seemed to agree. According to an ABC *Nightline* phone-in poll, Americans favored the invasion nine to one. Democratic leaders joined Republicans in lauding the Grenada operation.[25]

Later the president justified the U.S. invasion because it nipped Cuban occupation in the bud and kept Grenada from becoming a Soviet-Cuban colony that would export "terror and subversion" throughout Central America. Picking up the theme of Soviet expansionism aimed at Grenada, Ambassador Kirkpatrick argued that the Grenada and Nicaragua regimes were "committed not just to Marxism and socialism but integrated into the Soviet bloc." Joining in the praise, neoconservative critic Norman Podhoretz asserted that the administration had approached the challenge with the clarity of political and moral purpose. But he cautioned: "Grenada by itself cannot be taken to signify a resurgence of American power, especially given the demoralization evident in our response to the attack on our Marines in Beirut, . . . but if Lebanon shows us a United States still suffering from the shell-shocked condition that has muddled our minds and paralyzed our national will since Vietnam, Grenada points the way back to recovery and health." "The events in Lebanon and Grenada, though oceans apart," Reagan chimed in on October 27, "are closely related. Not only has Moscow assisted and encouraged violence in both countries, but it provides direct support through a network of surrogates and terrorists."[26]

There were, however, many Americans and Europeans who questioned the legality of the invasion and the interference in the domestic affairs of a small Caribbean country. Responding to the Grenada invasion, thousands of people gathered in Washington, during November, to protest the president's policies in Central America and the Caribbean. Western Europeans were also disturbed by the realization that Reagan again linked the U.S.S.R. to the whole of the instability of Africa, the Middle East, and Central America. European officials were more determined than ever to gain some influence in Washington and a more powerful voice in East-West relations. Sir Geoffrey Howe, British foreign secretary, responded to the Grenada invasion with the assertion that "there are times when Europe needs a voice independent even of its closest allies." Every Reagan decision delighted some and troubled others; the desired consensus remained as elusive as ever.[27]

* * *

Reagan's new globalism obligated Washington to challenge Moscow's putative expansionist activities not only in Central America but also in Africa and the Middle East. The Chinese mainland was exempt from any administration pressure to join in its anti-Soviet strategy because of the Taiwan Relations Act of 1979, which promised continued support for the island. Although conservative Republicans continued to endorse the Chinese nationalist cause, the administration sought to avoid the issue of military sales to Formosa in the face of Beijing's threat to break diplomatic relations. Such arms sales, Beijing warned, would provoke a crisis in the western Pacific. Finally, in mid-August 1982, Washington agreed to curtail arms sales, especially advanced equipment, to Taiwan. The necessity for better relations with Beijing was the danger, articulated forcefully by Admiral Robert L. Long, commander of U.S. forces in the Pacific and Indian Oceans, that the United States could no longer defend the periphery of South and Southeast Asia alone.

Much in the same vein, Robert Tucker warned in *Foreign Affairs* that the previous administration's failure to confront the Soviet intervention in Afghanistan "has laid bare as never before the vulnerability of the American position in a region of vital interests. . . . [T]he invasion of Afghanistan must signal, even for the most obtuse, that we have entered a very dangerous period." With such warnings, the Reagan administration uncritically endorsed the Carter Doctrine for the region, despite its dubious premises. When Secretary Haig visited the Middle East during April 1981, seeking bilateral agreements with Arab states to fend off Soviet adventurism, he found that Arab leaders considered the unresolved Palestinian question to be the basic threat to regional stability. Egypt flatly rejected any anti-Soviet strategy for the Middle East. The United States had more success in persuading Pakistan to accept a $3 billion military aid package; immediately, however, India sought to counter Washington's program, for they perceived it as a threat to the stability of South Asia. The administration's attempt substantially to improve Saudi Arabia military forces ran into fierce Israeli opposition. Recognition of Israel's strategic importance to U.S. objectives in the Middle East prompted the president's refusal to condemn that country for its air strikes against Soviet-equipped missile bases in Syria or its preemptive destruction in June 1981 of the nuclear facility at Osirak, in Iraq.[28]

To some critics, Washington's policy obviously overlooked larger questions. Against what common foe could Pakistan, Saudi Arabia, and Israel, cooperatively, be mobilized? What level of American expenditure or alliance making would garner the resources required to meet Soviet power in the region? If the Arab countries could not mount a military assault against Israel, how could they protect the Middle East from Soviet conventional military power? Fortunately, Moscow's caution and limited interests in the Middle East rescued a questionable American policy initiative.[29]

In a southern corner of Africa, Reagan attempted to transform what was clearly a local revolutionary conflict into a Soviet-American confrontation. The administration supported the Republic of South Africa's effort to confront the Soviet-backed, but United Nations–recognized, Southwest Africa People's Organization (SWAPO) in Angola. American multinational corporations, long welcomed by the Angolan government, had assisted in developing the country's resources, especially off shore oil fields. Washington protested the presence of Cuban troops in Angola, requested by the government, despite the fact that they also secured Western operations. In late August 1981, Pretoria, assured of U.S. cooperation, sent an armed force into Angola in pursuit of SWAPO forces. Following a brief campaign, South African forces claimed to have neutralized hundreds of SWAPO rebels, captured a Soviet officer and large quantities of Soviet-made equipment. When black African leaders insisted the United Nations invoke sanctions against South Africa, the State Department refused to condemn Pretoria's actions. Washington's decision reversed the United Nation's current anti-Moscow alignment resulting from its intervention in Afghanistan, costing the administration the support of many black African officials. The price was substantial, for South Africa controlled relatively little of the continent's population and resources.[30]

The Senate later eased the hostility when, without Reagan's support, it finally endorsed the United Nations' 1977 arms embargo of South Africa. Then a U.S. VELA nuclear detection satellite detected a double flash of light, somewhere in the South Atlantic, on September 22, 1979, suggesting a nuclear test. Because the CIA knew little about South Africa's nuclear program, it could not rule out a possible nuclear explosion. (A majority of the respondents to a later NSC study offered three, never confirmed, possibilities: a secret test by South Africa, a secret test by Israel, and a secret test by South Africa and Israel.) Washington did not publicly accuse Pretoria of violating the Non-Proliferation Treaty because American officials feared a revelation that South Africa might possess nuclear weapons could only exacerbate tensions throughout the continent. If black African states, sided by Moscow, demanded much stricter UN sanctions against Pretoria, Washington would be confronted with the prospect of taking an anti-Pretoria position which, in turn, might threaten important mineral exports to the United States. In the end, downplaying the incident served the administration best, although Washington did press Pretoria to honor its nonproliferation obligations.[31]

Meanwhile, events in the Middle East during 1982 undermined Washington's declared anti-Soviet strategy for the region and sent the administration in pursuit of peace arrangements. Not only did Europeans fail to support Reagan's strategic Middle East program, they questioned the U.S. shipment of arms to such would-be allies as Saudi Arabia, Egypt, and Pakistan. Repeatedly European officials reminded Washington that a comprehensive peace between Israel and the Arab world, including a settlement of the Palestinian question, was more essential for regional stability than attempting to build a military system to keep the Soviets out. Israel's annexation of the Golan Heights in late December 1981, seized from Syria in the 1967 war, prompted Washington to suspend its newly signed strategic cooperation agreement with Tel Aviv. Prime Minister Menachem Begin immediately castigated the United States for treating Israel like a "banana republic."[32]

Israel returned control of the Sinai to Egypt on April 25, 1982, as previously agreed; other events in the spring and summer of 1982, however, exacerbated the already tense relationship between Washington and Tel Aviv. Authorizing the construction of new Jewish settlements in the West Bank, Israel continued to assume the United States' often expressed commitment to Israel's survival gave it a free hand in dealing with its neighbors. Irritating Israel, the Palestinian Liberation Organization (PLO), headquartered in Beirut, kept up its harassment from bases in the south of Lebanon. Seizing upon the June 3 attempted assassination of its ambassador to London, Tel Aviv two days later sent its troops and tanks sweeping into southern Lebanon for the announced purpose of pushing back the PLO and, possibly with UN assistance, creating a neutral zone. Advancing beyond their initial objectives in the south, however, on June 13 Israeli forces encircled the PLO-occupied areas of Beirut and began subjecting the city to heavy aerial bombing and artillery barrages. The resulting civilian casualties and devastation—and not for the last time—dismayed a global audience.

Finding himself at odds with "quarreling, back-biting" senior members of administration, especially their rejection of his suggestions for resolving the crisis in Lebanon, Secretary Haig resigned in late June. Reagan immediately chose George P. Shultz for his new secretary of state[33] If the administration questioned Tel Aviv's strategy and urged a cease-fire, its divided council was seemingly powerless to control Israeli policy. Frustrated, Washington charged that Arab states were to blame, in part, for Beirut's destruction. Reagan expressed outrage, but he refused to antagonize Begin's supporters in the United States or compromise his demand that the PLO leave Lebanon—an objective that required an Israeli victory. Despite mixed signals from U.S. officials, the prolonged diplomatic efforts by America's negotiator Philip C. Habib managed, in August, to secure the evacuation of Palestinian forces from Beirut.[34] If PLO leader Yasser Arafat had been evasive and difficult, the Israeli commander Ariel Sharon was even more uncooperative. President Reagan announced the administration's first comprehensive Middle Eastern policy on September 1, 1982—a policy essentially resurrected from the Carter administration's various principles. Long-term peace, he stated, required halting new Israeli settlements in the West Bank and offering Palestinians self-government, not as an independent state but in association with Jordan. Tel Aviv's prompt rejection of Reagan's proposal, and the continued unwanted presence of Israeli forces in Lebanon, revealed Washington's lack of influence on its ally.

The administration's new focus on the Palestinian issue, in place of the earlier anti-Soviet strategy, was largely the result of Secretary Shultz's growing influence in Washington. A former successful businessman and secretary of treasury, Shultz was decidedly a conservative. Unlike many senior members of the administration, however, he was not an ideologue. Although he desired to be a team player, he would often find himself at odds with Defense Secretary Weinberger, NSC Adviser William Clark, and CIA Director William Casey. Gradually, however, he developed a working relationship with the president, enabling him to project the appearance of consensus among the nation's leaders. "Trading on close ties to Mr. Reagan and previous experience in Washington, Mr. Shultz set the right priorities." The *New York Times* offered in November 1982 that Shultz had "lowered the secretary's voice and raised his influence."[35]

In mid-September, Lebanese forces, with Israeli encouragement, entered the Sabra and Shatila Palestinian refugee camps and slaughtered scores of men, women, and children. On September 21, the president announced his decision to send U.S. Marines to join a multinational force in Beirut. A week later, he explained their mission: "They're there along with our allies, the French and the Italians, to give a kind of support and stability while the Lebanese Government seeks to reunite its people which have been divided for several years now into several [armed] factions, and bring about a unified Lebanon with a Lebanese army that will then be able to preserve order."[36] These goals appeared realistic and the administration expected to accomplish them by supporting Amin Gemayel's new Lebanese government, removing Syrian influence, and persuading Israel to withdraw its forces. Unfortunately for Washington's hopes, Gemayel, buoyed by the support of the peacekeeping forces, pressed his own agenda in defiance of the other political groups. In the subsequent bitter struggle for power, the Marines found themselves caught between the violent contending factions. While Congress worried that the position of U.S. forces in Lebanon was no longer simple or reassuring, it permitted the president to extend the Marines' stay 18 months.

In late October, Reagan's Lebanon commitment faced a serious challenge. On the 23rd, the French unit of the multinational force suffered the loss of 58 men to a suicide-squad. The same day, a suicide bomber drove a truck onto the U.S. Marine base, killing 241 servicemen and wounding another 130. The Marines had accomplished little, for they did not have the capacity to create needed political agreements that would bring stability to Lebanon. That was the responsibility of the Lebanese.[37] Nevertheless, the president tied U.S. credibility in the Middle East to the Marines' continued presence in Beirut until the situation had been stabilized. "We have vital interests in Lebanon," Reagan declared. "And our actions in Lebanon are in the cause of world peace. With our allies, England, France, and Italy, we're part of a multinational peacekeeping force seeking a withdrawal of all foreign forces from Lebanon and from the Beirut area." Lebanon was the key to America's security, the president insisted, employing the overworked domino threat. "If Lebanon ends up under the tyranny of forces hostile to the West [Syria and its allies]," he warned, "not only will our strategic position in the eastern Mediterranean be threatened but also the stability of the entire Middle East. Lebanon is central to our credibility on a global scale." Ignoring the feuding Lebanese factions, Reagan transformed the necessity of reestablishing order in Beirut into a confrontation with Soviet expansionism. "Can the United States and the free world stand by and see the Middle East incorporated into the Soviet bloc?" The United States had an obligation, the president reminded his audience, to guarantee Israel's security and to ensure that Western Europe and Japan received Middle Eastern petroleum.[38]

Affairs did not bode well for the Gemayel government despite the administration's continued verbal support. Syria had moved some

50,000 troops into Lebanon to protect Moslem dissidents. The Soviets had increased their presence in Syria. By early February 1984, Vice President George H. W. Bush, Secretary Weinberger, and the Joint Chiefs of Staff were in a rush to remove the Marines. The American forces left Lebanon with the Syrians dominating affairs in Beirut. Perhaps the administration's most serious miscalculation was supporting the Lebanese government, with deep anti-Moslem biases, that could not bring the country's quarreling factions together. However, Israeli Defense Minister Sharon's overbearing approach to affairs in Lebanon contributed greatly to preventing a possible favorable settlement in September and October 1982. In the end, Tel Aviv gained little from its massive, costly invasion of Lebanon. The Israelis could not remove the Syrians; meanwhile, their troops were bogged down in southern Lebanon. The PLO had been removed, but the Palestinian issue remained. Any hope of an Israeli-Arab peace conference lay shattered. "Lebanon is a quagmire," Yitzhak Rabin told Secretary Shultz in May 1983. "Anyone there will get drawn deeper and deeper into the engulfing morass."[39]

* * *

If Washington's relations with Europe were exacerbated by the Lebanese crisis, the relationship was even more strained by the Reagan administration's opposition to the Soviets' proposed Yamal natural gas pipeline. This episode vividly illuminated the growing U.S.-European differences in their perceptions of the possibilities for improved relations with Moscow. A $15 billion project, the pipeline was designed to convey three billion cubic meters of natural gas from the Yamal Peninsula, above the Arctic Circle, to West Germany, France, and Italy by 1984. The Europeans hailed the pipeline as a means of providing much-needed energy; consequently, led by West Germany's approval in 1980, they quickly endorsed the project. Predictably, Reagan opposed the pipeline and offered U.S. assistance in the form of coal and nuclear power. The president, having rejected détente, had no desire to encourage closer ties between Europe and the Kremlin. This project, he told a Western summit conference at Ottawa in July 1981, would enhance Soviet power and influence in Europe by providing Moscow a potential stranglehold over Western Europe's energy supplies. This the Soviets could exploit economically and politically. The Defense Department feared the $8 billion the Soviets earned annually would enhance the Soviet economy and provide for greater military spending.[40] White House adviser Richard Pipes argued that Washington should not assist the Soviet Union to sustain its "inefficient system ... and [instead] build up an aggressive military force and expand globally. Any attempt to help the Soviet Union out of its economic predicament both eases the pressures for internal reform and reduces the need for global retrenchment."[41]

None of these arguments and expectations played well in Western European capitals. Although the Soviet Union might not be an ideal source of energy, European leaders believed Moscow was preferable to the OPEC countries of the Middle East. With some 25 million unemployed in the West, the projected pipeline offered opportunities for much needed jobs and commerce. West European leaders believed that because the Soviets had a mutual interest with them in seeing the project succeed, the pipeline would lessen Kremlin aggressiveness. The Soviet need for hard currency, combined with the fact that natural gas sales would account for only two percent of Western Europe's combined energy requirements, increased the incentive to keep the pipeline open. Finally, Western Europeans doubted that any U.S. economic sanctions against the U.S.S.R., aimed at halting the pipeline, would alter Soviet behavior. The Kremlin already possessed sufficient nuclear weapons to destroy both Western Europe and the United States.[42]

Undeterred by these arguments, Reagan's decision to bar American corporations from supplying materials for the construction of the pipeline initially faced little opposition. Soon, however, internal concerns surfaced. Disagreement arose among U.S. officials over whether to extend the ban to European subsidiaries of American firms. The State Department worried that with Western European commitments to the pipeline, economic sanctions could seriously endanger the NATO alliance. Defense Secretary Weinberger and Pentagon officials, urging unilateral enforcement of a broad ban, were willing to risk alienating America's allies to prevent the Soviet Union from receiving any economic gain from the pipeline. Reagan finally dispatched a special mission to Europe in March 1982 to discuss his proposed sanctions. Everywhere the Reagan program faced rejection. Ultimately, on June 18, the president, in defiance of international law, authorized sanctions on U.S. firms, their European subsidiaries, and foreign companies producing equipment under U.S. licenses. Worried about their economies, officials in Bonn, Rome, Paris, and London announced separately that they would honor their pipeline contracts. The president's action prompted some Europeans to question why, if so concerned about bringing economic pressure on the U.S.S.R., Washington had not cancelled the sale of American grain to the Soviet Union. "We no longer speak the same language," France's Foreign Minister Claude Cheysson complained. "The United States seems wholly indifferent to our problems."[43]

As the controversy heated up, European governments instructed firms operating within their borders to fulfill their contracts with the Soviet Union. To West German Chancellor Helmut Schmidt, national sovereignty and the sanctity of contracts were at stake. Officials from the four countries directly involved met at London in September to organize a common policy of resistance to the Reagan sanctions. The dispute, said the *Times* (London), had "torn a nasty hole in the Western Alliance." The *Daily Mail* added, "The Atlantic Alliance is a genuine partnership of free and independent nations, not a superpower plus a gaggle of satellites."[44] In the United States, the National Association of Manufacturers insisted that Washington should acknowledge that a firm must obey the laws of the country in which it operated. Administration critics warned that strict application of the pipeline sanctions could bring about reprisals that would endanger U.S. investments in Europe and, indeed, the future of the alliance. Washington, some predicted, had created a crisis it could not contain. Reagan had stressed that unity of the Western alliance was vital to improve relations with Moscow. Now wasn't it also true, West Germany's Hans-Dietrich Genscher observed, that agreement within the alliance on policy toward Moscow was equally vital for coherent Western actions?[45] Opposed almost universally from the beginning to the unilateral bans, the State Department during the fall of 1982 planned a negotiated face-saving retreat. Before diplomatic action could begin, Reagan abruptly terminated the sanctions.

Other disagreements continued to plague Washington and its Western European allies: Reagan policies toward the Third World, especially Central America, and his administration's approach to the emerging Polish crisis. Many European leaders condemned every aspect of the White House's policies aimed at Third World challenges. They ridiculed the administration's claims that Soviet expansionism was the universal source of turmoil. "Americans see danger, revolution and terrorism everywhere," declared Germany's *Der Spiegel*, "and behind it all are the Russians." Why would the administration make Central America a focal point of U.S.-Soviet confrontation? Why support a notoriously repressive government in El Salvador, send assistance to suppress the civil war there, and seek to overturn the government of Nicaragua? Some European writers, such as Robert Held of the *Frankfurter Allgemeine Zeitung*, did endorse Reagan's cause.

"The Americans," he wrote, "simply cannot afford to let the land bridge to the South American continent become a hegemonical [*sic*] zone of the Soviet Union." A far larger number of critics questioned the U.S. commitment to the San Salvadoran government. If Rome's *Il Messaggero* feared this policy could lead to another American error in judgment, such as Vietnam, Amsterdam's conservative *De Telegraaf* warned that by introducing troops into El Salvador "[Reagan] would lose the right to criticize Moscow's involvement in Afghanistan and Poland."[46]

Ignoring Reagan's Central America policies, French President Mitterand announced the sale to Nicaragua's Sandinista regime of arms, equipment, helicopters, patrol boats, trucks, and rocket launchers. Rejecting the White House's plea to reconsider, Mitterand urged Reagan to follow the Mexican government's lead and seek a diplomatic solution to El Salvador's internal strife. Much like their American counterparts, European critics considered the political and social upheavals in Central America to be regional rather than global, indigenous rather than external. "President Reagan still sees in any Third World crisis the hand of the Soviet Union," complained Andre Fontaine, editor of Paris's *Le Monde*, in April 1982. "From here that appears ridiculous. You don't need Russians to create situations like Nicaragua and El Salvador." London's *Sunday Times* added, "The tendency to measure everything that happens in the world by the scale of East-West relationships ... has done much to increase the sense of disunity and mistrust within the alliance."[47] Since they could not find any serious threat to their security in Third World conflicts, Europeans found them of little concern.

Europeans also disagreed with Reagan's anti-Soviet crusade in Europe. Not surprisingly, the December 1981 unrest in Poland became a divisive issue. When Warsaw's Communist government announced a state of national emergency, established martial law, and called upon its military to crack down on the popular union-led Solidarity movement, European leaders expressed relief that Soviet armed forces were not involved. Whether or not Solidarity head Lech Walesa had attempted too much, Western Europeans expressed their sympathy and sent shipments of food. Washington officials, in contrast, held Moscow responsible for crushing Solidarity's efforts to gain power. German Foreign Minister Hans-Dietrich Genscher, however, refused to consider the administration's proposed sanctions to be levied against the Kremlin. Undaunted by Europe's refusal to cooperate, President Reagan, in late December, placed an embargo on all shipments of

American technology to the Soviet Union, suspended Aeroflot flights to the United States, and restricted Soviet access to U.S. ports. He also refused to renew exchange agreements in energy, science, and technology. Once again, the administration was reminded that in its imposition of economic sanctions against the U.S.S.R., it had failed to consult its allies.[48]

Most European leaders rejected the president's presumption that Moscow bore responsibility for the Polish government's harsh actions. With 450,000 German jobs and over 700 companies relying on trade with the Soviet bloc, Bonn declared it would ignore the sanctions unless the Soviets actually invaded Poland. Paris announced that while it did not approve of the sanctions, it would not undermine them. In Britain, the conservative London *Daily Telegraph* warned that the dispute over sanctions revealed "snarling and back-biting of a type not seen since NATO began [and that threatened] to bring the alliance to ruin." Why the White House failed to gain allied support for its initiative was obvious. Western Europeans, in keeping with the long-established principle, insisted that their interests required respect for the integrity of the European spheres of influence.[49]

* * *

The Reagan administration's ideological crusade, virtually rejecting "the Soviet Union's right to exist," had inexcusably heightened tensions between Washington and Moscow. Former ambassador to Moscow, Malcolm Toon, found relations with the Soviets worse than at any time since World War II.[50] Writing in the October 3, 1983, issue of the *New Yorker*, Soviet expert George F. Kennan noted that public discussion of Soviet-American relations seemed to indicate that only a military showdown could resolve the outstanding differences. "Can anyone mistake, or doubt," he asked, "the ominous meaning of such a state of affairs? The phenomena just described . . . are the familiar characteristics, the unfailing characteristics, of a march toward war—that, and nothing else." This grim assessment suggested that America was bent on creating a second, more dangerous Cold War.

Oddly, the administration's publicly stated insecurities arose at the same time Washington officials recognized the Soviet Union's internal weaknesses. Some Americans had long held the Soviet Union's status as a superpower to be a myth. Could a country be a superpower, if it could not provide the basic needs of its own people? Even many Cold Warriors believed the U.S.S.R. could not survive the West's combined political, economic, and military pressures. They would accelerate the Soviet Union's collapse by denying it Western trade, credits, and technology. One American naval officer argued, "We must pursue policies which aggravate its condition until it bleeds to death from within." Reagan confidently assured the British Parliament, on June 8, 1982, that the march of freedom and democracy would "leave Marxism-Leninism on the ash heap of history." Given time and strong leadership, he declared, the forces of good would triumph over evil. Climaxing his castigation of the Soviet Union, the president defined it as "the focus of evil in the Modern World." In a March 8, 1983, address to the National Association of Evangelicals, he warned that no nation could safely ignore "the aggressive impulses of an evil empire."[51]

Such harsh rhetoric was ill received in Moscow. Various Soviet spokesmen complained that the United States had neither accepted the Soviet Union as a great power with legitimate global interests of its own, nor accorded the Kremlin's view of the world any genuine or consistent attention, nor acted as though it realized the two powers would live together or die together on this planet. Even more frequently, Soviet diplomats pointed to the endless ring of military bases surrounding their nation from Japan to Norway. How could there be long-term coexistence without genuine U.S. acceptance of Soviet legitimacy? "How can we deal with a man," a Kremlin leader wondered, "who calls us outlaws, criminals, and the source of evil in the world?"[52]

Nowhere, critics pointed out, did the administration's alleged toughness result in diplomatic achievements that improved America's security. Reagan's ideological approach, Stanley Hoffmann argued in *Dead Ends* (1983), "has turned out to be utterly deficient as a strategy because it fails to address many real problems, it aggravates others, it provides no priority other than the anti-Soviet imperative, and precious little guidance even in connection with the new Cold War."[53] Because rhetoric would not cause the Soviets to either back down or go away, he wondered, how did it further the U.S. national interests for this animosity to close communications. The character of the Soviet power structure was irrelevant to the requirement of dealing openly and frankly with the Kremlin. "Like Mount Everest," wrote *Newsweek*'s Meg Greenfield, in September 1983, "the Russians are there. And, like Mount Everest, their features are not exactly a mystery. We need to stop gasping and sighing and exclaiming and nearly dying of shock every time something truly disagreeable happens. We have to grow up and confront them—as they are."

Meanwhile, on September 1, 1983, the Soviets shot down a Korean commercial airliner (KAL 007) that had strayed over Russian territory.

To Washington officials, the incident was additional evidence of Soviet paranoia and unconcern for human life. While the State Department called the disaster "brutal and unprovoked," the president drafted a statement for the media. "What can we think of a regime that so broadly trumpets its vision of peace and global disarmament and yet so callously and quickly commits *a terrorist act*? What can be said about *Soviet credibility* when they so *flagrantly lie about such a heinous act* [italics in original]?" The Soviet airline Aeroflot was ordered to close its American offices. New York and New Jersey denied Foreign Minister Andrei Gromyko landing rights to attend the opening session of the UN General Assembly, the first he missed in twenty years.[54]

In perhaps the most comprehensive and categorical top-level Soviet denunciation of any U.S. administration since the early Cold War, Soviet premier Andropov condemned Reagan's attitude toward the superpower relationship. The president's ideological challenges risked the prospect of actual war, the Soviet leader declared on September 28. "To turn the battle of ideas into military confrontation would be too costly for the whole of mankind. But those who are blinded by anticommunism are evidently incapable of grasping this," Andropov continued. "Starting with the bogey of a Soviet military threat, they have now proclaimed a crusade against socialism as a social system."[55]

The reality of Andropov's warning came two months later. Without notifying the Warsaw Pact countries, NATO had scheduled a command post exercise, code-named Able Archer, for November 2–11, 1983, to test nuclear release procedures. Uninformed of the exercise's purpose, the Soviet Union went on a strategic intelligence alert. Days passed, and the attack did not come; the Soviets had apparently exaggerated the danger. Throughout the crisis—although they were aware of the turmoil in Moscow—Washington offered the Soviets no explanation. On November 16, Alexander Bovin, *Izvestia*'s political commentator, accused American leaders, blinded by their hatred of Communism, of ignoring the security interests of the Soviet Union and compelling the two countries to walk "the edge of the missile precipice." From mid-1983 into 1984, according to CIA reports, senior officials in Moscow took "very seriously" the threat of a U.S. preemptive nuclear attack.[56]

Former diplomat W. Averell Harriman accurately summarized the situation. He warned Reagan on January 1, 1984, that his program of emphasizing military strength while denigrating diplomacy could lead to disaster. Blaming the Kremlin for the world's current instabilities was, he wrote, "not a strategy or a policy.... It will not reshape the

Russian nation; it will not bring down the Iron Curtain; and, above all, it will not reduce the nuclear threat that hangs over every American."[57]

The "war scare" and subsequent criticism of the administration's handling of the Able Archer episode may have moderated Reagan's later comments about the Soviet Union. He was quite surprised to learn that "many people at the top of the Soviet hierarchy were genuinely afraid of America and Americans." Why would the Soviets have such fears, Reagan wondered: "I'd always felt that from our deeds it must be clear to anyone that Americans were a moral people who starting at the birth of our nation had always used our power only as a force of good in the world."[58]

* * *

With its early emphasis on increasing America' nuclear armaments, its lack of interest in arms control and its harsh anti-Soviet rhetoric, the administration and its supporters fed the anxieties of antinuclear movements from the United States across Western Europe. Untroubled by the collapse of détente, ardent anti-Communists openly acknowledged the possibility of hostilities. Reagan's arms control chief, Eugene Rostow, noted, "We are living in a prewar and not a postwar world." Even the president appeared ambivalent. Reagan had many times voiced his desire to see nuclear weapons eliminated; yet, in 1981, he told reporters that "the exchange of tactical [nuclear] weapons against troops in the field" need not bring "either of the major powers to pushing the button." If Caspar Weinberger believed nuclear wars were not winnable, the defense secretary nevertheless insisted, "We are planning to prevail if we are attacked." Echoing this opinion, White House advisor Thomas C. Reed, added, "Prevailing with pride is the principal new ingredient of American foreign policy."[59] West Germans, at the potential center of any European firestorm, were understandably upset with the apparent nonchalance in Washington about the prospects of fighting and winning a nuclear war.[60]

The rapidly expanding antinuclear movements failed to see how additional nuclear weapons could serve Western security or world peace. With U.S. strategic forces capable of striking Soviet targets with some 10,000 hydrogen warheads, many observers rejected the claim that the United States lacked a credible deterrence against a Soviet first strike. Stimulating the crusade against continuing the nuclear arms race was the obvious consequences the use of these weapons posed to the future of civilization. Jonathan Schell's *The Fate of the Earth* (1982), followed by George Kennan's *The Nuclear Delusion* (1982), aggravated the growing anxieties—as well as hopes. Although a cataclysmic nuclear conflict could result in the extinction of human life on the planet, Schell wrote, the danger lay not in intentional governmental action but in the chance of miscalculation. Four distinguished American students of strategy—McGeorge Bundy, George Kennan, Robert McNamara, and Gerard Smith—argued in *Foreign Affairs* (Spring 1982) that the United States, to limit the possibilities of nuclear war, should reverse its policy of three decades and promise never to use nuclear weapons first. It did not happen.

To offset Moscow's deployment of SS-20s, a significantly upgraded intermediate missile carrying three nuclear-tipped warheads, the United States began preparing in 1979 to counter with 108 Pershing II and 464 ground-launched cruise missiles (GLCMs) to West Germany, Belgium, Britain, the Netherlands, and Italy. Fear of a renewed nuclear arms race by the superpowers, who seemed to have no desire to control it, set off the powerful European peace movement of 1981. Washington's exaggeration of the Soviet menace had clearly backfired as over two million Europeans joined antinuclear, and largely anti-American, demonstrations. In Bonn on October 10, 1981, nearly 250,000 demonstrators denounced NATO plans to modernize its nuclear defenses. One poster read, "Only Schmidt and the Cowboy Need Nuclear Protection." Another German peace activist complained, "Talking to the superpowers about disarmament is like talking to drug dealers about stopping drug deliveries." Similar protest sprang up in London and Paris. Some European neutralists opposed Soviet weapons no less than American. The marchers—churchmen, youth groups, and citizens of all classes and persuasions—were too numerous to be dismissed as a fringe movement. Chancellor Schmidt favored the emplacement of theater weapons and thought the protests to be "rubbish." He argued, however, that mutual limitation of the Euromissiles were a very important priority.[61]

Unfortunately, he was addressing an administration that showed little enthusiasm for controlling arms. The president was on record opposing the 1963 Test Ban pact, the 1968 Non-Proliferation Treaty, the 1972 SALT I and ABM agreements, and the Helsinki Accords. During the 1980 presidential campaign, Reagan denounced SALT II as "fatally flawed," and claimed that it allowed the Soviet Union a "window of vulnerability" against U.S. land-based nuclear forces. Consequently, his administration spent its early months concerned with expanding and modernizing U.S. forces to offset the supposed Soviet military superiority. However, pressure from antinuclear protesters in NATO countries and the nuclear freeze movement at home prompted the administration, in late 1981, to review the ongoing intermediate nuclear forces (INF) negotiations. These discussions stemmed from an earlier NATO decision for the United States to deploy the designated Pershing IIs and ground-launched cruise missiles if the Soviets could not be persuaded to remove their SS-20s. Attempting to pacify European demonstrators, the Reagan administration casually offered its "zero option" concept—the United States would cancel the deployment of its intermediate-range missiles, scheduled for two years in the future, in exchange for the Soviet's withdrawal of its deployed SS-20s carrying some 1,100 warheads.[62]

In May 1982, Reagan unveiled his two-phased proposal for the promised Strategic Arms Reduction Talks (START) that emphasized a "practical phased reduction" of strategic nuclear systems. Phase I would reduce warheads by a third and significantly cut back the number of ballistic missiles. It required the Soviets substantially to reduce their land-based ICBMs—their most effective strategic weapons—while the United States would retain most of its land-based Minutemen and deploy a hundred new large MX missiles in similar silos. In addition, the United States could deploy its cruise missiles and modernize its submarine and bomber fleets. Subsequently, Phase II would require Soviets to reduce by almost two-thirds the aggregate throw weight of their missiles, while the United States suffered no cuts at all. If general public response was favorable, knowledgeable observers found the START formula, as with the earlier "zero option," to be so one-sided it was nonnegotiable. "This proposal is so stacked against the Soviets," the sponsor of the House's nuclear freeze resolution Congressman Edward J. Markey complained, "there is little chance they will accept it." Not surprisingly, Moscow ignored both of Washington's proposals, while negotiations on nuclear weaponry limped along.[63]

To what extent Reagan actually understood the administration's two proposals was open to question. On several occasions, his "allergy to detail" apparently resulted in his failure to grasp arms control issues. The president shocked congressional leaders in the fall of 1983 when it was evident he did not realize that most of the Soviet's intercontinental nuclear missiles were land-based. Then, later, Reagan acknowledged that he "forgot" the America's long-range bombers and cruise missiles carried nuclear warheads. When George Shultz became secretary of state in 1982, his basic disagreements with CIA Director Casey, Secretary Weinberger and National Security Adviser Clark prevented getting arms control issues on track. "Beginning in 1983 an internecine war began," an insider wrote, "over how to deal with the Soviets that would rage for two years and smolder the rest of the Reagan administration."[64]

Neither Washington nor Moscow was prepared for Reagan's March 23, 1983, plea for a defense against nuclear-tipped missiles targeting American cities. After noting the nation's security currently depended on nuclear deterrence, Reagan told his television audience:

Let me share with you a vision of the future which offers hope. It is that we embark on a program to counter the awesome Soviet military threat with measures that are defensive. . . . What if free people could live secure in the knowledge that their security did not rest on the threat of instant U.S. retaliation to deter a Soviet attack, that we could intercept and destroy strategic ballistic missiles before they reached our own soil or that of our allies?" Without actually understanding the technological challenges ahead, Reagan called "upon the scientific community in this country, who gave us nuclear weapons . . . to give us the means of rendering these weapons impotent and obsolete.[65]

The program was officially named the Strategic Defense Initiative (SDI) in January 1984, while critics quickly dubbed it "Star Wars."

Later the president suggested that SDI "could be the greatest inducement to arms reduction." Through the SDI, he added, "We seek the total elimination one day of nuclear weapons from the face of the earth." Reaction to Reagan's proposal was understandably mixed. Favoring needed funding of SDI research, undersecretary of defense Richard Delauer nonetheless worried it was becoming a "half-baked political travesty." Facing the media, Minority Whip Robert Michel of Illinois thought the speech's promises might be "a bit of overkill." Yet, while many U.S. military leaders and most scientists believed a successful Star Wars program lay far in the future, its existence initially posed problems to Moscow. Yuri Andropov, Soviet leader since November 1982, viewed SDI as a program to bury the 1972 Anti-Ballistic Missile (ABM) treaty and unleash an arms race in offensive and defensive weapons. "Engaging in this is not just irresponsible, it is insane," Andropov charged in a March 27 *Pravda* interview, "Washington's actions are putting the entire world in jeopardy." The SDI project would raise questions about the status of the ABM Treaty, haunt future arms control negotiations, and compete with other Pentagon agencies for funding.[66]

* * *

With mounting congressional and public criticism of his Central American policies, Reagan, in July 1983, enlisted former Secretary of State Henry Kissinger to head a bipartisan commission examining the region's political environment. In its January 1984 report, the commission urged the administration to adopt a program of economic and military assistance designed to build a consensus for U.S. policy in the area. The commission found that past revolutions and pressures for change were indigenous and therefore no real danger to hemispheric security. The global balance of power, however, was essentially dependent upon the inherent security of the North American continent. Moscow's efforts to exploit those vulnerable hemisphere areas now endangered this balance. "From the standpoint of the Soviet Union," the report warned, "it would be a strategic coup of major proportions to impose on the United States the burden of landward defenses. If they succeeded in doing so they would have out-maneuvered us on a global scale." Nicaragua posed a particular threat. It was, the commission added, "the indispensable stepping stone for the Cuban and Soviet effort to promote armed insurgency in Central America. With both an Atlantic and Pacific coast, Nicaragua.... [was] uniquely well-placed" to provide bases for Soviet activity designed to subvert the entire region, including Panama.

Sounding much like the justification for Vietnam, the report concluded, "The triumph of hostile forces in what the Soviets call the 'strategic rear' of the United States would be read as a sign of U.S. impotence. It would signify our inability to manage our policy or exercise our power." Communist forces were testing "not so much the ability of the United States to provide large resources but rather the realism of ... [its] political attitudes."[67] Agreeing with established policy, the commission never questioned the right of the United States to intervene in the civil wars of Nicaragua and El Salvador. The report called for increased military aid to El Salvador to counter what it depicted as a "direct threat to U.S. security interests" and sufficient military assistance should be dispatched to Honduras "to build a credible deterrent." The commission's language of fear raised the stakes in Central America so high that the United States dared accept nothing less than a military victory over the Communist enemy.[68]

Critics in Congress balked at the request for a substantial increase in military aid. More weaponry would achieve nothing, noted Congressman Michael Barnes of Maryland, chairman of the House Subcommittee on Latin American Affairs, except "more death, destruction, and suffering." Senator Christopher Dodd of Connecticut concurred, insisting that the commission failed "to address the fundamental economic, social and political reform necessary to make any aid program effective within the region. . . . There is rhetoric to satisfy every imaginable constituency, but there is no policy." Chiming in, the occasionally hawkish Senator Daniel P. Moynihan of New York claimed that the report provided little evidence for its charge that U.S. security interests in the hemisphere were seriously endangered by the Soviet-Cuban connection. Media critics responded similarly. "The same fears about impotence and credibility," the *New York Times* editorialized, "were the stuff of a thousand speeches justifying American involvement for a generation in the lost war in Indochina."[69]

Perhaps the most severe critic of the commission was former Idaho Senator Frank Church. Not long before his death in early 1984, he recalled that the United States had intervened in Vietnam to contain China and the Soviet Union, only to discover that these two Communist countries were not the problem in Southeast Asia. Such mistaken judgments, he argued, cost the nation a high price:

It is this idea that the communist threat is everywhere that has made our government its captive and its victim . . . This country has become so conservative—so fearful—that we have come to see revolution anywhere in the world as a threat to the United States. It's nonsense. And yet that policy we have followed has cost us so many lives, so much treasure, such setbacks to our vital interests, as a great power ought not to endure. Until we learn to live with revolution, we will continue to blunder, and it will work to the Soviets' advantage. It will put them on the winning side, while we put ourselves on the side of rotten, corrupt regimes that end up losing. And each time one of those regimes is overthrown, it feeds the paranoia in this country about the spread of communism.[70]

Except for the hard-liners, in and out of Congress, who still clung to the validity of the Vietnam conflict, opinion throughout the country was no more favorable toward Reagan's Central American policies than it was toward U.S. policy in Vietnam during its moment of ultimate failure. An April 1984 Gallup survey found that only 29 percent of the people interviewed endorsed the president's policies. That same month a *New York Times*–CBS News poll indicated that only one-third of respondents supported the administration. A month later, a *Washington Post* poll confirmed these results. That poll revealed, additionally, that almost half of those interviewed did not know which side the U.S. government supported in El Salvador.[71] Vietnam had destroyed the guideposts to which all administrations from Truman to Ford had attached their containment policies; despite his efforts, Reagan failed to reconstitute them.

Nevertheless, the Pentagon continued to build a substantial military infrastructure, based largely in Honduras, without public announcements and congressional authorizations that normally accompanied such foreign commitments. For Washington, this support was necessary, in lieu of sending U.S. combat units, to support the forces fighting leftists in Nicaragua and El Salvador. If initially American aid to the contras had been limited to small groups raiding Sandinista outposts, by 1984, some 18,000 U.S.-supported contras were conducting full-scale field operations. One officer explained, "If Salvador falls, that's the time the United States would have to decide whether to send troops or withdraw completely and fortify the Rio Grande."[72]

In early April, the administration became directly implicated in the mining of Nicaraguan harbors. This activity, part of a CIA plan to cripple the Nicaraguan economy, for the first time openly involved the United States in the war against the Sandinistas. The Senate rebuked the administration for mining the harbors by a vote of 84 to 12. Republican Senator Barry Goldwater of Arizona complained to CIA Director Casey that the mining violated international law. "It is an act of war," he declared. "For the life of me, I don't see how we are going to explain it." House Speaker "Tip" O'Neill (D-MA) added, "I have contended that the Reagan Administration's secret war against Nicaragua was morally indefensible. Today it is clear that it is legally indefensible as well."

The Sandinista government appeared before the International Court of Justice at The Hague, charging that the United States was "directing military and paramilitary actions" in an attempt to destabilize and overthrow its government. Washington, however, had informed The Hague it refused to recognize the Court's jurisdiction over Central American disputes. For the British and French governments, no less than for members of Congress, this was an admission of guilt. "[Critics] ignore the most relevant fact," Reagan responded, "Central America has become the stage for a bold attempt . . . to install communism by force."[73]

By February 1985 Reagan's crusading efforts on behalf of anti-Communist guerrillas blossomed into the Reagan Doctrine. In his State of the Union address, the president declared: "We must not break faith with those who are risking their lives on every continent from Afghanistan to Nicaragua to defy Soviet-supported aggression and secure rights which have been ours from birth." Echoing this policy, Secretary Shultz claimed the United States, as leader of the free world, had a moral responsibility to assist popular insurgencies against any and all Communist regimes. Reversing the Truman Doctrine, which ultimately justified intervening to protect governments threatened by Communists, the Reagan Doctrine proclaimed the right, indeed an obligation, to subvert existing Communist regimes.[74] Emphasizing the global focus of his new doctrine, Reagan told Polish-Americans at the White House on August 17, 1984, that he rejected "any interpretation of the Yalta agreement" indicating "American consent for the division of Europe into spheres of influence." CIA director Casey spelled out the dimensions of this proposed global rollback in May 1985 speech: "In the occupied countries— Afghanistan, Cambodia, Ethiopia, Angola, and Nicaragua—in which Marxist regimes have been either imposed or maintained by external force ... [there] has occurred a holocaust comparable to that which Nazi Germany inflicted on Europe some forty years ago."[75]

Those on the right who had long strived for an offense against the Soviet Union and its alleged clients everywhere were delighted with Reagan's new doctrine, which they saw as the antithesis of the Brezhnev Doctrine's assertion that Soviet gains were irreversible. To Charles Krauthammer, the Reagan Doctrine rested on America's support of justice, necessity, and tradition: justice because anti-Communist revolutionaries were fighting tyranny; necessity because any defeat for freedom fighters assigned a country irrevocably to Soviet dominance; and tradition because the United States, throughout its history, had supported the cause of freedom abroad. All three assumptions, however, revealed a dubious understanding of U.S. history. Yet, for Krauthammer and his ilk, it was no longer prudent or moral for the country to ignore the cause of freedom in deference to national sovereignty.[76]

Critics of Reagan's doctrine pointed to Washington's habit of exaggerating the dangers posed by Communist regimes, as well as available capacity to eliminate them. Robert Tucker questioned the doctrine's core tenet that all Marxist-Leninist governments lacked legitimacy and that the United States had a moral responsibility to support rebels who opposed them. The Nicaraguan government, he noted, served its people far better than several of those in Central America supported by the United States. "What the Reagan Doctrine requires, in theory," political scientist Kenneth Thompson warned, "is indiscriminate intervention to overturn Communist regimes regardless of calculations of interest and power." In the absence of such calculations, policies would either be abandoned, as in Lebanon, or pursued in the face of public disillusionment, as in Vietnam.[77]

In practice, the Reagan Doctrine unleashed limited war by proxy, for there were no commitments of U.S. forces. It provided the rationale for Washington's economic and military assistance to the mujahedeen resistance in Afghanistan, to rebel factions in Cambodia, and, following the repeal of the Clark Amendment in 1985, to Jonas Savimbi's guerrilla forces in Angola. Here the U.S. contribution was the risk-free funding of low-cost mercenaries, whose devotion to democratic principles and prospects of success remained dubious.[78]

The new doctrine's main thrust, of course, sought to justify the president's special obsession for the Nicaraguan contras as a means of halting the Kremlin's global advances. "They are our brothers, these freedom fighters, and we owe them our help," he observed on March 1, 1985, "They are the moral equivalent of the Founding Fathers and the brave men and women of the French Resistance. We cannot turn away from them. For the struggle is not right versus left, but right versus wrong." Unfortunately, few contras leaders possessed democratic credentials; some ultimately faced trial and execution for murder and other crimes. These insurgents killed thousands of peasants and rendered other thousands homeless, but all the death and destruction failed to overthrow the Sandinista regime. Still, their constant threat forced the Sandinistas to become dependent upon Soviet equipment, including tanks, trucks, artillery, and heavy weapons. Addressing the nation on March 16, 1986, Reagan stressed that the Soviets and Cubans, using Nicaragua as a base, threatened to become the dominant force in the crucial corridor between North and South America. "Established there," he warned, "they will be in a position to threaten the Panama Canal, interdict our vital Caribbean sea lanes, and, ultimately, move against Mexico." When support in Congress stalled, Wyoming's Dick Cheney criticized those who held back: "You can't have foreign policy carried out by 435 House members and 100 Senators. There are times when the president needs strong support, and debate has to stop at the water's edge."[79]

Reagan found little support in Europe for his crusade against the Sandinistas. At the Bonn economic summit of May 1985, the Europeans rejected Reagan's plea for support of his trade embargo against Nicaragua. When he visited Madrid after the summit, the president faced massive anti-American demonstrations. In deliberate defiance of the U.S. embargo, the European Economic Community several days later doubled its aid to Nicaragua. When the World Court, in June 1986, criticized Washington for supporting the Nicaraguan contras and violating the UN Charter, Europe's rejection of American policy became complete. "That the U.S. did not even consider it necessary to make an appearance before the World Court in the [sic] Hague is more than arrogant flouting of the international court," the *Frankfurter Rundschau* complained, "it sets a negative precedent for other states to follow." It seemed unconscionable to international lawyer John Norton Moore, who joined Reagan in believing Nicaragua had become another Cuba, that the United States' European allies and the United Nations chose not to support the United States. Outraged that democratic allies refused to support the United States in the Security Council, wrote Moore in October 1986, reflected "an advanced deterioration of the global deterrent system."[80]

Meanwhile, the administration's policy toward the Third World, based on Jeane Kirkpatrick's questionable distinction between authoritarian and totalitarian regimes, had started to unravel. Authoritarian governments, often labeled by Washington as democratic, had readily escaped chastisement for their repressive actions. In practice, the administration endorsed notoriously oppressive authoritarian governments in Argentina, Chile, Guatemala, El Salvador, Haiti, and the Philippines. For example, at the UN Human Rights Commission only the United States voted to exonerate Argentina's military dictatorship for the abduction, torture or murder of thousands of its citizens by government death squads. As repressive Washington-supported governments dissolved, the president decided that the United States would no longer attempt to distinguish between authoritarian and totalitarian governments. The administration would, he informed Congress in March 1986, oppose all dictatorships, right and left.[81] His decision in effect, indicated a belated recognition that Third World struggles were indigenous and that the perpetuation of friendly governments was not vital for American security.

Ironically, the so-called Iran-Contra affair not only embarrassed the administration and slightly tarnished the president, it wrote the concluding chapter to Reagan's Central American crusade. Iraq's invasion of Iran on September 22, 1980 went well until the Iranians regrouped. Fearing Iraq was in danger of losing the war, Reagan dispatched Donald Rumsfeld to Baghdad in December 1983. After meeting Saddam Hussein, Rumsfeld cabled the White House that "the development of U.S.-Iraqi relations" could benefit America's "posture in the region." Subsequently, the United States, U.S.S.R., France, and England provided sophisticated military equipment and financial aid. Yet while the administration was openly assisting Iraq, it was also secretly selling arms, especially antiaircraft weapons, to Iran in the hope of gaining funds to help the Nicaraguan contras and, at the same time, achieving the release of Americans held hostage by radical Islamist groups.[82]

After the Iran-Contra affair became public, congressional investigations began in May 1987 to learn whether U.S. laws had been violated. National Security adviser John Poindexter and a staff member Lt. Colonel Oliver North became the focal point. Over initial objections by Shultz and Weinberger, North directed Project Democracy that evolved into a parallel, largely secret, foreign policy apparatus, with its own sources of funds, communications systems, secret envoys, leased ships and airplanes, and Swiss bank accounts. Testifying in July, decorated and defiant, an unrepentant Colonel North blamed Congress for the loss of Vietnam and the failure to confront enemy aggression in Central America. Similarly Poindexter declared that the security of the United States was not safe in the hands of the State Department, the Defense Department, or Congress. Both men were convicted and pardoned.[83]

But the fallout did not end there. The administration's long crusade to eliminate the Sandinistas and subdue the Salvadoran guerrillas was about to come to an end. An independent Costa Rican peace process emerging in 1987 found more in common among the Marxist-oriented Sandinistas and the other Central American governments than any they could discover in Washington's anti-Soviet crusade. That the Central Americans had minds, wills, and interests of their own was something that the Reagan administration had not recognized. Nicaragua ceased to be an issue when, in 1990, a free election drove the Sandinistas from power.[84]

* * *

As early as February 12, 1983, Reagan lamented that he had not visited Moscow or Beijing. Secretary Shultz explained such trips needed significant improvement in Washington's relations with leaders of the Communist powers. Three days later Shultz invited longtime Soviet ambassador Anatoly Dobrynin to the White House for discussion with the president on ways to improve U.S.-Soviet relations, arms control, and human rights. The two-hour meeting was Reagan's first serious encounter with a Soviet official. In the Kremlin officials ignored the conversation, which they found a serious contradiction between Reagan's military buildup, verbal abuse of the U.S.S.R., and his desire for better relations. In March, the president began exchanging messages with Soviet Premier Yuri Andropov. In his July 11 letter, Reagan emphasized his long-held antipathy toward nuclear weapons and noted that both leaders shared "an enormous responsibility for the preservation of stability in the world." In October, Robert McFarlane, who had succeeded Clark as head of National Security Council, advised the president that it was time for the United States to exploit its military buildup by negotiating arms limitations with the Soviet Union.[85]

Continuing his conciliatory efforts on January 25, 1984, Reagan pointed out that Soviets and Americans had never been at war. "And if we Americans have our way," he declared, "they never will." At Georgetown University on April 6, the president commented that increased U.S. military power paved the way for successful negotiations. "If the new Soviet leadership is devoted to building a safer and more humane world, rather than expanding armed conquests," he stated, "it will find a sympathetic partner in the West." Both countries needed to accept the huge challenge of reducing the risk of nuclear war because, he warned, "a nuclear war cannot be won and must never be fought." Again in June the president expressed his willingness to meet Soviet leaders at a summit or anywhere else.[86] Reagan ended his campaign for a second term determined to pursue closer ties with Moscow. In a speech before the United Nations, on October 24, he promised, if reelected, to seek an arms agreement with Moscow.

Fortunately for Reagan and Shultz, during early 1985 a new, more promising, leadership was emerging in Moscow. A rising star, Mikhail Gorbachev seemed destined to become head of the Soviet state because Konstantin Chernenko, who had succeeded Andropov in February, was old and ill. When Gorbachev, with his wife Raisa, visited London in mid-December 1984, Prime Minister Margaret Thatcher detected in Gorbachev's predictable elevation new diplomatic opportunities. "I can do business with this man," she informed the press.[87] Following Chernenko's death in March 1985, Gorbachev emerged as secretary general of the party, with a better grasp of the realities of international life than did his predecessors. His basic challenges lay in maintaining the U.S.S.R.'s international status while rescuing it from its present, overextended, debilitating global role—especially in Afghanistan—and stimulating a stagnate economy. Even as Gorbachev, an ardent admirer of Lenin and dedicated socialist, struggled with the Kremlin's internal troubles, the full spectrum of his "new thinking" on foreign affairs began to emerge. In his campaign to cut Soviet losses abroad and military spending at home, while maintaining his international standing,

Afghanistan with its massive physical and emotional drain on the Soviet people headed Moscow's list of expendable commitments.[88]

The Kremlin's unpopular war in Afghanistan, producing some 10,000 Soviet casualties a year without demonstrable success, sought only political stabilization. If officials in Moscow anticipated accurately the tenacity of the popular resistance, they overestimated the acceptability of the Kabul government. During 1985–1986, Gorbachev intensified the military operations, installed a stronger Afghan leader, and sought to save "Soviet credibility" before withdrawing. While the failed Afghanistan venture did not reach the stage of a "Russian Vietnam," it comprised an endless draining of resources and public tolerance, and stood as a barrier to improved U.S.-Soviet relations. If Gorbachev focused less on Third World issues, he nevertheless was annoyed by what he saw as Reagan hypocrisy. In an April 23, 1985, speech, he pointed to Washington's protesting of Moscow's intervention in Afghanistan while claiming its "right to interfere" in Grenada and Nicaragua.[89] When the issue of Central America was raised in later talks with Reagan or his staff, the Soviet leader retorted, talk with Castro—which Washington refused to do.

By the summer of 1985, Reagan finally found someone in the Kremlin willing to discuss the possibility of reducing the threat of nuclear war, for Gorbachev had decided to move quickly to find ways of curbing the nuclear arms race. To the beleaguered Soviet leader, the only real solution for his country's internal and external dilemmas lay in shifting resources away from the military-industrial complex to address shortages of food and other necessities. Moreover, he believed that "the policy of total, military confrontation has no future," and that the "arms race, as well as nuclear war, cannot be won." Equally significant, Gorbachev saw "the task of building security appears to be a political task, and it can be resolved only by political means." This approach evoked criticism from veteran Soviet policy-makers, one of whom grumbled, "Are you against force, which is the only language that imperialism understands?" But Gorbachev's "new thinking" overturned Stalin's doctrine of "two camps" that had ruled Moscow since 1947.[90]

Following eight months of discussions, Reagan and Gorbachev prepared to meet at a Geneva Summit in November 1985. Gorbachev had made it clear he wanted to concentrate on curtailing the arms race. Perhaps inspired by his wife's astrologer, historian Raymond Garthoff noted, "a limited but interesting transformation occurred in [Reagan's] statements on the source and nature of the difficulties in American-Soviet relations." Departing Washington for Geneva, the president said he hoped both nations would "seek to reduce the suspicions and mistrust that had led us to acquire mountains of strategic weapons." He even conceded that nuclear weapons, not an evil opponent, posed "the greatest threat in human history to survival of the human race" and declared "a nuclear war cannot be won and must never be fought." Seeking to sabotage the meeting, Secretary Weinberger deliberately leaked a letter to the president on the eve of the summit that emphasized alleged Soviet violations of earlier arms control treaties, while carefully ignoring U.S. evasions, and urged Reagan not to agree to any limits on the anti-missile program.[91]

The Geneva summit, the first in six years, was essentially a media event. Gorbachev pressed arms control issues, especially limits on the Strategic Defense Initiative and maintaining SALT II and new arms reductions but found Reagan refusing to offer concessions on any of contested points. However, Reagan found that he could hold his own with the Soviet leader; even more, he saw Gorbachev as one with whom he shared "a kind of chemistry." The most significant outcome of the summit undoubtedly was the rapport that developed between the two heads of state. They agreed to meet in Washington in 1987 and in Moscow during 1988. Not since the Nixon-Brezhnev summits of 1972 and 1973 did Soviet-American relations appear more hopeful.[92]

In the months following the Geneva meeting, Gorbachev continued to stress the absurdity of the costly and potentially dangerous arms race. In an address to the United Nations in January 1986, he offered a grand plan for arms reductions, along with extensive Soviet concessions on nuclear weaponry. He would eliminate medium-range missiles, set aside the issue of French and British forces, and cut strategic weapons by 50 percent, including the SS-18 heavy missiles. According to a close adviser, Gorbachev had "already decided, come what may, to end the arms race. . . . because [he believes that] nobody is going to attack us even if we disarm completely." Gorbachev's ambitious economic modernization program, endorsed by the 27th Party Congress, in February–March, required the reduced military spending that would follow arms cuts. For him the Soviet objective was the attainment of mutual security at the lowest possible strategic balance.[93]

The president, in late May 1986, announced that the United States would no longer be bound by the SALT II formula at the end of the year unless the Kremlin undertook undefined "constructive steps." Critical Europe reaction followed. *Le Figaro* complained that Washington did not bother to ask Europe's opinion. "It's a disaster," fumed Helmut Kohl. The *Times* (London) declared that the president had "come close to making one of the most controversial decisions in his six years in the White House. . . . Its impact on the Western alliance could be serious." The *Economist* noted that half the Britons polled distrusted Reagan's judgment and considered Americans equal to the Soviets as a threat to peace. In Washington, officials insisted that the president was justified in his action because of apparent Soviet cheating, but also acknowledged they had not anticipated Europe's reaction. Gorbachev recognized Europe's anxiety and offered a series of new arms proposals, which Pentagon officials routinely rejected. *New York Times* columnist James Reston noted the preference for "ideological confrontation and warrior diplomacy . . . at the Pentagon and the White House." To columnist Andrew J. Glass, "[T]he national security apparatus in the White House remains thoroughly fractionated. With so many hawks and pseudo-hawks flapping about in the Reagan aviary, it will muster all the administration's ability in diplomatic falconry merely to fashion a cogent response to the latest Soviet initiative."[94] Meanwhile, Gorbachev topped European polls as the man of peace. In late August 1986, Reagan announced the United States would not exceed the limits imposed by the 1979 SALT II treaty before the October summit.[95]

In October, the two leaders met at Reykjavik, Iceland, initially focusing on the issue of intermediate-range missiles in Europe. Gorbachev opened negotiations by proposing to scrap all SS-20s in Europe, while retaining one hundred in Asia and allowing the United States one hundred similar missiles in Alaska. The final session took the Soviets by surprise. Reagan presented the "sweeping" U.S. proposals to eliminate all nuclear warheads by 2000, which his advisors were confident Gorbachev would reject. Startling everyone, the Soviet leader responded, "Yes." He would accept Reagan's proposal if the president agreed to limit SDI research to "laboratories" for at least five years. Reagan rejected Gorbachev's counter offer, declaring he would not compromise his missile defense project.[96]

One is left with the impression that Reagan had confused his priorities, for, when his long-held desire to eliminate nuclear weapons loomed, he clung to the Strategic Defense Initiative. This system was still essentially in the planning stage, there was no evidence if it would work and, if it eventually should, when it might be available. Faced with such uncertainty, he might have compromised and satisfied his wish to eliminate the nuclear threat. Reagan and Gorbachev departed Reykjavik, both disappointed and exhausted. However, Western military strategists and political leaders—and most certainly Soviet marshals—were shaken by news of a near-agreement to abolish nuclear weapons. Prime Minister Margaret Thatcher hurried to Washington, warning Reagan that the nuclear deterrence strategy had been the bedrock of almost forty years of U.S. and European security.[97]

* * *

While not everyone agreed, Gorbachev's strategy of ending the Cold War by reducing the nuclear threat did find widespread popular approval. He surprised Pentagon hard-liners, on February 28, 1987, by accepting their proposal to eliminate all intermediate-range nuclear missiles in Europe. Secretary of State Shultz immediately accepted Gorbachev's offer. Negotiators subsequently agreed to destroy 2,611 intermediate-range missiles with flight ranges from 300 to 3,440 miles or 500 to 5,000 kilometers, including U.S. Pershing IIs and cruise missiles and Soviet SS-4s, SS-12s, SS-20s, and SS-23s.[98]

When Defense Secretary Weinberger and other hard-liners demanded on-site inspections, Gorbachev agreed to an "intrusive verification" plan where each power would inspect the other's facilities to fulfill Intermediate Nuclear Force (INF) Treaty terms. Soviet enthusiasm for intrusive inspections gave pause to the Pentagon, the National Security Agency, and the CIA. They realized they did not want the Soviets prowling U.S. defense plants, nuclear-armed submarines, and missile sites. As Weinberger's replacement, Frank Carlucci, admitted, "[V]erification has proven to be more complex than we thought it would be. The flip side of the coin is its application to us. The more we think about it, the more difficult it becomes." Now the United States desired less intrusive procedures.[99]

The Washington summit of December 1987, to sign the INF Treaty, turned out to be a Reagan-Gorbachev triumph as the media coverage was hugely favorable. The Soviet leader and his wife were so enthusiastically greeted in the normally blasé capital, that it prompted *Washington Post* columnist Tom Shales to observe the city was seized by "Gorby fever." When Gorbachev expressed concern about the criticism that Reagan was receiving from hard-liners, Shultz reassured him, "[T]he vast majority of American support what President Reagan is doing."

"For the first time in history," Reagan declared when signing the INF treaty on December 8, "the language of 'arms control' was replaced by 'arms reduction' in this case, the complete elimination of an entire class of U.S. and Soviet nuclear missiles." The treaty offered "a big chance at last to get onto the road leading away from the threat of catastrophe,"

Figure 14.2
Soviet Chairman Mikhail Gorbachev and President Reagan sign the INF Treaty,
December 8, 1987 (Courtesy: Ronald Reagan Library)

Gorbachev added. "It is our duty . . . to move forward toward a nuclear-free world . . . [that is] without fear and without a senseless waste of resources on weapons of destruction." Although the INF pact eliminated only four percent of the superpowers' nuclear arsenal, it would eventually launch serious arms negotiations.[100]

Critics of the treaty wasted no time weighing in. Richard Nixon and Henry Kissinger, writing jointly, insisted the pact damaged relations with European allies, increased the threat from Soviet conventional forces, and failed to reduce the Kremlin's long-range nuclear arsenal. For William F. Buckley, the INF treaty constituted unilateral disarmament, threatening to leave the West naked before the Soviet enemy. The most hysterical outburst came from two of the right's leading activists, Richard Viguerie and Howard Phillips. "It is with deep regret that we who have supported President Reagan in so many battles during the past 20 years now must begin to publicly separate ourselves from our former leader," Viguerie observed bitterly. "We feel alienated, abandoned and rejected." Phillips simply denounced Reagan as "a useful idiot for Soviet propaganda."[101]

The signing of the INF treaty failed to spur the talks toward a strategic arms reduction treaty. Although the Soviets offered several concessions, interminable bureaucratic delays hampered Washington's attempts to substantially modify its initial START proposal—indeed an agreement would not be reached until 1991. Meanwhile, the intractability of various American bureaucracies over the specific terms was frequently more intense than the negotiations with Moscow. This bickering led an unhappy member of the National Security Council to suggest, "Even if the Soviets did not exist, we might not get a START treaty because of disagreements on our side." If the Soviets "came to us," another high-ranking U.S. official complained, "and said, 'You write it, we'll sign it,' we still couldn't do it."[102]

The Kremlin's concern about Reagan's strategic missile defense program gradually dissipated. Andrei Sakharov persuaded Gorbachev there was no defense that could stop a barrage of intercontinental ballistic missiles carrying decoys and multiple warheads. He argued that SDI was a kind of "Maginot line in space," a line that could not defeat concentrated missile attacks anymore than the French Maginot defense line stopped the German blitzkrieg in 1940. Soviet scientists recognized that the SDI program was a "fuss about nothing." As Roald Z. Sagdeyev, the head of the Soviet Institute for Space Research, told Strobe Talbott, "We came to realize that we had not helped ourselves by screaming so much about SDI. . . . we had over-estimated how much damage SDI could do to strategic stability in the short run and even in the medium term."[103]

With the vast majority of the Senate favoring the INF treaty and Reagan's assurance that he was negotiating from strength, ratification came on May 29, 1988, as the president left for the Moscow summit. The significance of this triumphant meeting was the reintroduction of détente. On Sunday, May 29, 1988, as Reagan received a warm wel-come at the Kremlin, Gorbachev declared, "[H]istory has objectively bound our two countries by a common responsibility for the destinies of mankind." On Tuesday, as Reagan walked through Red Square, he commented publicly that the two leaders had "decided to talk to each other instead of about each other. It's working just fine." In the Kremlin, when asked by a reporter what became of the 1983 "evil empire," the president replied, "I was talking about another time, another era." Since the U.S. Senate approved the INF treaty, Gorbachev and Reagan signed the ratification documents at the final ceremony.[104] If short on achievement, the summit had been long on goodwill.

Predictably, the right once again criticized Reagan's actions. Buckley continued to assert that the Soviet Union, with its human rights violations, remained the evil empire. George Will's judgment of the

Moscow summit served for most hawks. To fellow conservatives, he wrote, "Ronald Reagan's foreign policy has produced much surprise but little delight. His fourth and, one prays, final summit is a suitable occasion for conservatives to look back with bewilderment and ahead with trepidation." In his final White House years, as Will saw it, the president had ruined his earlier, superb foreign and military policy.[105] Among anti-Soviet hard-liners, inside and outside Washington, the ultimate Reagan triumphs had emerged with the Reagan Doctrine, followed in 1986 by the vote for contra aid, the warm White House welcome for Angola's Jonas Savimbi, and the destructive bombing of Libyan targets in response to Qaddafi's alleged terrorist activities in Europe.

Despite criticism from the right, it seemed apparent that moderates were gaining the ascendancy in the administration's turf wars over foreign policy. Secretary of State Shultz had organized the State Department into an effective group for conducting negotiations with the Soviets. Together with Frank Carlucci as the new secretary of defense and Colin L. Powell as national security adviser, the Reagan administration finally had three top advisers who were in general agreement. As one administration spokesman phrased it in March 1988, "Over the past three years we have established a broad, active, and quietly developing relationship, almost from a cold start in '85." For the president, the move toward moderation appeared to be less a broad philosophical change than the slow, pragmatic evolution of policy.[106] The pragmatists understood that there was no choice but to coexist on the planet with the U.S.S.R. and regarded Gorbachev a durable Soviet leader. They agreed with his December 7, 1988, address before the United Nations, where he criticized the reliance on nuclear arms. Gorbachev, at this time, reached the high point of his global leadership by pledging the unilateral reduction of Soviet military forces by 500,000 men and withdrawing forces from Afghanistan.

Meanwhile, Reagan departed the White House convinced that the Cold War was over, and Gorbachev awaited initiatives from the new president that would continue easing American-Soviet tensions and reducing nuclear arsenals.

CHAPTER 15

The Final Days of the Cold War

The transition from Reagan to George H. W. Bush was not as smooth as might have been expected. Both men were staunch Republicans, but their personalities and foreign policy experiences contrasted sharply. As vice president, Bush remained quiet about his personal dislike of Reagan's harsh anti-Soviet rhetoric and his concern that Reagan went too far in restoring a détente with Moscow based on a personal friendship with Gorbachev. The new president understandably desired to step out of Reagan's shadow and, consequently, was determined to establish policies and programs that bore his own imprint. He removed most of the "Reaganites" from the cabinet and other senior positions in his administration, a decision that might indicate a new toughness toward the Kremlin to please the domestic right-wing. Neoconservatives and Cold War hawks alike had become skeptical of Reagan and George Shultz's coziness with Gorbachev and Soviet foreign minister Eduard Shevardnadze.

Upon assuming the presidency in January 1989, Bush installed a new national security and foreign policy team. Less than a week after the election, Bush told George Shultz to look for another job, indicating that a longtime friend, James A. Baker III, would be his secretary of state. Baker had a low opinion of Shultz's ability to negotiate with the Soviets, suggesting that he had given away what the Kremlin would have offered for free. This attitude filtered through the Bush administration, according to Michael Beschloss and Strobe Talbott, to such an extent that it became commonplace to denounce Shultz as the "worst secretary of state since [Edward] Stettinius" in the 1940s. Bush also appointed another close friend, Brent Scowcroft, as national security advisor and, after the Senate rejected John Tower, named Richard Cheney as secretary of defense. Scowcroft brought in Robert M. Gates, a former deputy director of the CIA, as his assistant. Bush and all of his senior staff initially had their suspicions of Gorbachev and were skeptical of Reagan's insistence that the Cold War was over.[1]

For a half decade the signs of emerging tensions within the Soviet bloc were apparent everywhere, yet George Bush entered the presidency in January 1989 not persuaded that the Cold War was receding. Even as its twin pillars—the presumption of a powerful and aggressive Soviet Union and an American economy sufficiently vibrant to carry the concomitant burden of global containment—were crumbling, the new president and his senior staff were hesitant. They insisted that time was needed to develop a well-thought-out strategy before formally addressing Mikhail Gorbachev's desire to continue improved relations between Washington and Moscow.

Bush had met the Soviet leader earlier. At the funeral of Konstantin Chernenko, Vice President Bush listened to Gorbachev make it clear that the Soviet Union did not seek a confrontation with the United States. The new Soviet leader also voiced his hope that Washington would join in the serious nuclear arms limitation talks going on in Geneva. Bush came away from this initial meeting impressed that Gorbachev was a young, tough man who "wants to change the Soviet Union." As Gorbachev was ending his first visit to the United States

Figure 15.1
(L to R) President George H. W. Bush, National Security Advisor Brent Scowcroft, John Sununu (Courtesy: George Bush Library)

in December 1987, Vice President Bush explained to the Soviet leader that he was in a heated race for the Republican nomination to run for president in 1988. Bush was optimistic that he had an excellent chance of gaining the presidency, and informed Gorbachev that if he were elected he wanted to improve the relations between the two countries. However, he asked the Soviet leader to ignore his harsh rhetoric that would emerge in the forthcoming election, as he would have to confirm his conservative anti-Communist credentials. Gorbachev indicated he understood. Years later, when his staff believed that Bush showed too much concern about the feeling of Republican conservatives, Gorbachev recalled his 1987 talk with the then–vice president. "Don't worry. His heart is in the right place."[2]

Gorbachev and Reagan had seemingly become partners in the informal winding down of the Cold War. Bush, however, had been privately dismayed at the president's "sentimentality" about Gorbachev, especially when Reagan, visiting Moscow in June 1988, retracted his description of the U.S.S.R. as an "evil empire." Bush's contradictory response to reporters was: "The Cold War isn't over." In December 1988, Reagan and president-elect Bush met with Gorbachev at Governors Island in New York Harbor for lunch shortly after the latter had addressed the United Nations. The Soviet leader hoped to continue his close and productive relationship with the incoming president. Political advisers, however, urged Bush to show a slight distance and skepticism in order not to prejudice his administration's future negotiations with the Kremlin. For his part, the Soviet leader largely ignored Reagan, as he focused his attention on Bush. After dodging Gorbachev's questions, the vice president finally asked: "What assurance can you give me that I can pass on to American businessmen who want to invest in the Soviet Union that *perestroika* and *glasnost* will succeed?" Gorbachev responded indignantly: "Not even Jesus Christ knows the answer to that question." He then indicated to Bush that he knew advisers were warning the president-elect "to go slow, you've got to be careful, you've got to review, that you can't trust us, that we're doing all this for show." However, he continued, "You'll see soon enough that I'm *not* doing this for show . . . or to take advantage of you."[3]

Still, the path to a post–Cold War world appeared uncertain. Some Americans failed to see in the Reagan-Gorbachev meetings any significant shift in Soviet-American relations. In Washington especially there was a reluctance to recognize or encourage change. The anti-Communist elite had grown accustomed to a vast body of Cold War policy that few cared to question. Bush's national security adviser, Brent Scowcroft, advised the country that the Cold War was not over. Such suspicions of the Kremlin also characterized the outlook of his deputy, Gates, as well as Defense Secretary Cheney and Soviet experts in the CIA.

The new administration expressed concerned with the "lulling" effect of Gorbachev's repeated proposals that seemingly put an end to the Cold War. In February, Soviet forces left Afghanistan, a point the president noted, yet he warned, "It is important not to let these encouraging changes, political and military, lull us into a sense of complacency. Nor can we let down our guard against a worldwide threat. . . . Military challenges to democracy persist in every hemisphere." Scowcroft agreed. The administration must be wary of the "clever bear syndrome" that could lull the public into a false sense of security. In keeping with a long-held Washington theme, he insisted that "only when we've been scared to death" have the American people sustained their vigilance. Former Secretary of State Henry A. Kissinger added to the chorus warning the American people that it would be naïve to assume that an American president, dealing personally with a receptive Soviet leader, could quickly resolve decades of formidable differences. Mikhail Gorbachev's moderate policies, for Kissinger, was not an indication that the Kremlin had retreated from its global ambitions.[4]

In his inaugural address of January 1989, Bush emphasized the continued need for vigilance and strength in dealing with the Soviets. Three weeks later, addressing a joint session of Congress, the president stressed caution in dealing with Gorbachev:

[I]t's a time of great change in the world, and especially in the Soviet Union. Prudence and common sense dictate that we try to understand the full meaning of the change going on there, review our policies, and then proceed with caution. But I've personally assured General Secretary Gorbachev that at the conclusion of such a review we will be ready to move forward. We will not miss any opportunity to work for peace. The fundamental facts remain that the Soviets retain a very powerful military machine in the service of objectives which are still too often in conflict with ours. So, let us take the new openness seriously, but let's also be realistic. And let's always be strong.

The president again dwelled on the dangers confronting the country at the swearing-in ceremonies of Secretary James A. Baker.[5] The new administration's insistence on reexamining U.S.-Soviet relations was a not-too-subtle indication that Bush questioned Reagan's soft approach toward Gorbachev during the last months of his presidency.

The new president and his advisers not only approached the new Soviet-American relationship with considerable caution; they also slowed the momentum of exchanges between Washington and Moscow. A cautious man by nature, Bush rarely questioned conventional wisdom or was given to innovative actions. In concert with his old friend and now Secretary of State James Baker, the president was determined not to be rushed into a summit with Gorbachev, much to the latter's increasing concern. Bush and Baker recalled ill-considered examples of moving too fast: John Kennedy's early unpleasant summit with Nikita Khrushchev, in Vienna, and Jimmy Carter's ill-fated arms control initiative proposed to Moscow shortly after his inauguration. The skeptical Scowcroft continued to endorse a cautious approach. In a January 22nd appearance on ABC television, he warned that Gorbachev appeared "interested in making trouble within the Western alliance. And I think he believes that the best way to do it is a peace offensive, rather than to bluster, the way some of his predecessors have." Moscow apparently was trying to buy time to revive its economy and enhance its military prowess before undertaking a new offensive against the West. "Until we have better evidence to the contrary," he argued, "we ought to operate on that expectation." Relations with the Kremlin might be improving, but Scowcroft made it clear he believed "the Cold War is not over."

Five days later in his initial press conference, President Bush responded to a question regarding Scowcroft's pessimism by seeking to elaborate on the administration's position. "Let's take our time now," he declared. Yet Bush did not think the phrase "Cold War" was wholly appropriate since it did not "properly give credit to the advances that have taken place in this relationship. . . . Do we still have problems, are there still uncertainties, are we still unsure in our predictions on Soviet intentions? I'd have to say 'Yeah, we should be cautious'." However, Bush continued: "I don't think the Soviets see that as foot-dragging. I'm confident they don't. Indeed, I made that clear to General Secretary Gorbachev just this week in a rather long talk with him."[6]

Thus the president stressed to an impatient American audience and an anxious Gorbachev that he and his staff needed to undertake a broad assessment of American-Soviet relations before moving ahead. The president told business leaders at a White House luncheon on February 3, 1989, that in dealing with Moscow, "I don't want to miss an opportunity, but I don't want to do something that's imprudent either." While it would require a certain amount of time for Baker and Scowcroft to monitor the policy review, "when we do go forward," he added, "whether it's on conventional arms control, or strategic weapons, or whatever else it is—the economic front, regional problems, human rights—we're going to be marching together in this administration."[7]

On February 13, the president examined a directive prepared by Scowcroft and his staff, calling on the State Department to undertake a "national security review" suggesting new U.S. policies toward the Kremlin for the next four to eight years. Bush felt that the draft did not go far enough. "Let's see if we can't come up with something more forward-looking. Let's push it out at least into the next century." In approving the revised instructions two days later the president acknowledged that while Gorbachev was a "historically formidable person," his staff needed to understand that the Soviet leader was "still a Russian and a Communist, which counts for more in the final analysis."[8]

On March 14, the State Department's 31-page policy review (NSR-3) reached the president. It was, in Scowcroft's words, a "big disappointment." It essentially presented a broad survey of affairs, but failed to provide any detailed, creative initiatives that the administration might employ to produce significant improvements in Soviet-American relations. NSC staff members, led by Condoleezza Rice, promptly drafted a memorandum that evolved into a four-point blueprint that Scowcroft believed should guide U.S. policy in dealing with Moscow. First, the American people must be shown that U.S. foreign policy was "driven by clear objectives." Second, the administration needed to shore up its relations with its allies, especially to emphasize the need to modernize NATO's nuclear deterrent and develop a joint formula for the upcoming negotiations on conventional arms reductions. Because it was important for the United States to demonstrate competence in arms control activities, Washington must "prepare carefully" for the renewed bilateral START talks. Third, after revisiting a review of policy for Eastern Europe, the administration might offer some new initiatives as Soviet influence there waned. Fourth, Washington should seek Moscow's cooperation to achieve regional stability, especially in Central America.

These four themes formed the general basis upon which the administration initially sought to construct its policies. Because of the ever-changing political environment in Eastern Europe, specific initiatives related to the four themes took months more to surface. These delays prompted considerable domestic and overseas criticism. In her normal direct manner, British prime minister and a solid friend of the United States, Margaret Thatcher, indicated to Secretary Baker her dissatisfaction with the slow-moving relaxed manner that Washington officials were approaching their policy review. "I'm sure," she added, "Mr. Gorbachev is, too." The U.S. ambassador to Moscow, Jack Matlock, who witnessed the historical changes taking place in the Soviet Union, would later title his chapter on this initial period of the

Bush administration, "Washington Fumbles." Gorbachev's advisor Anatoly Chernyaev was not so kind in calling the last chapter in his memoirs "The Lost Year."[9]

* * *

Stirrings of democratic forces, grounded in traditional nationalism, began rippling through Eastern Europe even as the Bush family was settling in the White House. On January 16, 1989, crowds gathered in Prague to witness the twentieth anniversary of the death of a young Czech, Jan Palach, who had set himself on fire to protest the 1968 Soviet intervention. Lech Walesa's earlier attempt with the Solidarity movement to challenge Poland's Communist structure fell to martial law in 1981; however, eight years later it had gathered strength and was challenging a weakened Communist leadership. When the June election placed the Communist regime on the ropes, the Kremlin made no effort to prevent its fall. In May, after Hungary dismantled its border with Austria, thousands of migrating East Germans crossed the open border and continued on their way to West Germany. When the East German government attempted to halt the exodus, it succeeded only in unleashing an uncontrollable protest, centering in Leipzig. Meeting leaders of the Warsaw Pact in Bucharest on July 7, Gorbachev reiterated his promise of December 1988—that the Soviets would not employ force in the pursuit of external goals. Thus, he essentially informed them that Moscow would not use its armed forces to halt the political changes taking place in Poland and Hungary. In repealing the Brezhnev Doctrine—that a Communist state could not renounce Communism—Gorbachev was, in effect, encouraging the collapse of Soviet hegemony in Eastern Europe. The mere withdrawal of Soviet power exposed all Communist Eastern European governments to immediate destruction.

"The United States—and let's be clear on this—has never accepted the legitimacy of Europe's division," President Bush noted in a speech at Hamtramck, Michigan, on April 17. Ignoring the U.S. concessions in the Helsinki Declaration, he continued, "the Cold War began in Eastern Europe and if it is to end," it must end there. However, "the winds of change" were reshaping Europe's destiny as "Eastern Europe is awakening to yearnings of democracy, independence, and prosperity," he declared on the same day that the legal status of the Solidarity political movement was recognized in Poland. And with new leaders emerging in Hungary, reforms were taking place "that may permit a political pluralism that only a few years ago would have been absolutely unthinkable."

In laying out the administration's policy, the president announced that Washington would "with prudence, realism, and patience ... promote the evolution of freedom." More specifically, he said, "I've carefully considered ways that the United States can help Poland. And we will not act unconditionally. We're not going to offer unsound credits. We're not going to offer aid without requiring sound economic practices in return. ... I will ask Congress to join me in providing Poland access to our Generalized System of Preferences, which offers selective tariff relief to beneficiary countries. We will work with our allies and friends in the Paris Club to develop sustainable new schedules for Poland to repay its debt, easing a heavy burden so that a free market can grow." While the aid being offered was largely technical, Washington's basic criteria were evident. Assistance would be linked, Scowcroft's assistant Robert Gates emphasized, "to the forward progress of the reform process."[10] In July, Bush visited Poland and Hungary for five days to encourage the reform process, but carefully avoided gloating at the Kremlin's problems in the region.

By autumn, Eastern European Communist governments—artificial creations of Joseph Stalin's Soviet Russia following World War II and possessing few popular bases of support—were falling with amazing speed. Nowhere had Soviet ideology successfully challenged the force of nationalism. Global television revealed the stark contrasts between the failures of Communism and the triumphs of Western democracy. When asked to explain the fall of Communism across Eastern Europe, Solidarity's chief simply pointed to a TV set. The communications revolution had broken the information barrier, providing Eastern Europeans the knowledge on which to act.

Foreign observers understood that the Soviet's Eastern Europe satellite empire had been lagging economically, but only the lifting of the Iron Curtain revealed how inadequate its economic performance had been and how dismal its standard of living. The price of Communist rule had been horrendous, creating economic challenges that lay beyond the ability of the new national governments to resolve. Before 1939, Czech prosperity was approximately equal to that of Italy and Austria; after four decades of Communism its standard of living, though still the best in Eastern Europe, was scarcely a third of Austria's.[11] During these years obsolete, coal-burning plants in Poland, East Germany, and Czechoslovakia had turned out shoddy, noncompetitive, subsidized goods, and sustained workers without marketable skills. An industrial belt stretching eastward from southern East Germany through Poland and northern Czechoslovakia held towering smokestacks that released plumes of bright yellow, jet black, and hazy brown smoke, scattering sulfur dioxide over the countryside. An unfortunate by-product of these factories were poisonous gases and toxic dust in abundance, producing widespread cancer, lung and heart diseases, eye and skin ailments, asthma, emphysema, pneumonia, and shortened lives. One-third of Poland's population lived in areas of ecological disaster.[12]

Protecting their populace from the normal consequences of low productivity, the Communist governments had provided countless subsidies and, often, cheap housing. Any shift to a free market would eliminate not only countless nonproductive jobs but also the full spectrum of public subsidies that had sustained life. Rising prices outstripped the desired productivity and assured only further destitution. Countless Eastern Europeans found themselves incapable of functioning successfully in a competitive economy. The price of freedom, they complained, was too high. "The freedom we wanted," wrote Czech scholar Erazim Kohak, "was freedom from care, freedom from responsibility. We wanted to be free of reality's persistent demands." A popular joke circulated that the Czechs wanted "to consume like the Germans, be provided for like the Swedes, and work like the Russians." Not surprisingly, large numbers of Eastern Europeans faltered under the new system of free market pricing of food, clothing, housing, and energy. By early 1990, low productivity and scarcity sent prices soaring, placing many basic necessities beyond reach. Finding gasoline no longer affordable, thousands of Polish car owners quit driving. Large homeless populations became squatters in major cities of Eastern Europe. With central planning discontinued, Hungarian officials predicted that by the end of 1990, 100,000 Hungarians would be unemployed.[13]

Unfortunately, a populace cast adrift by Communism's collapse, and struggling for survival in a starkly competitive environment, was scarcely prepared to create a democratic, free market paradise. As the countries of Eastern Europe, with the exception of Czechoslovakia, rarely possessed publicly involved, democratic governments, the post-Communist regimes faced profound barriers. The implications of democracy, with its accent on skills, effort, and individual responsibility, were scarcely appealing to people who had long relied on governmental dispensations for survival. They were simply not prepared for the disagreement and tension that characterized the democratic process. If elites and foreign observers proclaimed the coming triumph of democracy, the reality was confusion, detachment, demagoguery, and often the return to power of former Communists. One Polish leader complained, "Achieving democracy seemed so simple. But, in fact, it's like building a house from the roof down."[14]

Nor were Eastern Europeans prepared for the heavy costs of free market reform. Price liberalization and privatization were the only apparent alternatives to continued economic stagnation, but the cost could be exorbitant. The International Monetary Fund dictated the move toward privatization by making it the criterion for Western credits. Poland ventured slowly into a program of privatization; Czechoslovakia, Hungary, and Bulgaria followed. Suffering continued as everywhere the people experienced the resulting pain of unemployment and rising prices. In February 1990 a leading Polish publisher recorded the impact of economic change on his country:

You'd think we could bask in our glorious triumph these days. But the fact is that we're facing an absolute catastrophe—especially those of us involved in Polish culture. It's a terrible paradox: we are quickly becoming the victims of the free market we fought to establish. Prices have shot up enormously for everything—food, housing, energy. But salaries are strictly controlled. So during the month of January people's standard of living dropped fifteen percent, and this month it still appears to be falling sharply.[15]

Gorbachev's repeal of the Brezhnev Doctrine in December 1988— to abjure the use of force to crush rebellious elements in Communist states—set the standard for Soviet behavior in the political upheavals of 1989. If the U.S.S.R. commanded the military power to halt the "reform" processes at their inception, a half-decade of rising demands for political and economic self-determination had taken their toll on Soviet energy and political will. For Gorbachev, who essentially had invited the Eastern Europeans to revolt, the price of Soviet impositions on the peoples of Eastern Europe had become both physically and morally exorbitant. At the end, the Soviet leader encouraged the disintegration of the Soviet empire.

As the events in Eastern Europe saturated the Soviet press, the collapse of Soviet hegemony created no public outcry. For most Soviet citizens the domination of Eastern Europe never served any fundamental, even recognizable, Soviet interests. Meanwhile, Eastern European leaders, especially those of Poland, Hungary, and Czechoslovakia, demanded the withdrawal of Soviet forces and termination of the Warsaw Pact as the essential conditions for establishing normal relations with Moscow. By March 1990, Soviet forces began to depart.[16]

* * *

As the East German Communist regime crumbled in November 1989, huge demonstrations demanded a reunified Germany. Public opinion in the United States and Britain favored German unification overwhelmingly, in France less so. Many other Europeans were concerned that a Germany of 80 million people might again dominate Europe because its economy alone could be sufficient to elevate the country to superpower status. Gunter Grass, the noted German novelist, warned against reunification. "[N]o one of sound mind and memory," he wrote, "can ever again permit such a concentration of power in the heart of Europe."[17]

President Bush favored unification as a right but insisted that a unified Germany be tied to the West economically, politically, and militarily. With East Germany now independent, Gorbachev asked only that the Soviet Union gain necessary security guarantees before unification became a reality. Secretary of State Baker insisted on Germany's membership in NATO. In Moscow, on February 8, he warned Gorbachev that a neutral Germany would be free to develop nuclear weapons. While Gorbachev initially objected to any extension of NATO's jurisdiction, the White House pursued a different plan: all German territory would be in NATO, but only German forces would be stationed in East Germany. Gorbachev accepted that arrangement and thereby gave some sanction to NATO expansion. The two sides never discussed the possibility that Poland, Hungary, or other Central European states might one day enter NATO.[18]

At the Ottawa Foreign Ministers Conference of February 1990, the administration endorsed the so-called two-plus-four formula for German unification. The two Germanies would negotiate all internal reunification issues; while the four powers resolved all external aspects of German unity. Helmut Kohl moved quickly to exploit the favorable international environment with a trip to Moscow. There, in West German foreign minister Hans-Dietrich Genscher's words, the chancellor made an offer that Gorbachev could not refuse. It included German financial support for the 380,000 Soviet forces remaining in East Germany, forces supported by the East German government at the cost of $400 million a year. Finally, Kohl promised to honor all East German contracts with Moscow. Subsequently, at the March two-plus-four talks in Bonn, the delegations acknowledged Poland's demands that Germany offer guarantees on the future of the Polish-German border. At the Potsdam Conference of 1945, Poland had been given a slice of Germany as compensation for the loss of eastern Poland to the Soviet Union. Reluctantly, Kohl agreed that a united Germany would not levy territorial demands on Poland. In return, he insisted that Warsaw make no demands on Germany for reparations covering Polish forced labor during World War II.[19]

On May 18, 1990, the two Germanies agreed on a currency, economic, and social union, to become effective in July. For Washington, only the Kremlin's objections to a united Germany within NATO stood in the way of unification. Previously, President Bush had rejected a Soviet proposal that Germany join both NATO and the Warsaw Pact. Meanwhile, when the foreign ministers of the two Germanies as well as Britain, France, the United States, and the U.S.S.R. had gathered earlier in Bonn on May 5, there was unanimous agreement that the issue of German unification must be dealt with quickly. Soviet minister Eduard A. Shevardnadze, however, worried about the impact of how German membership in NATO would affect Soviet security interests—would it upset the European balance of power, and create, for the U.S.S.R., a dangerous military-strategic situation? Although the Kremlin accepted German unity, Shevardnadze reminded the other ministers that the Soviet Union still possessed its victor's rights in Germany.[20] Seeking to eliminate the final roadblock to a unified Germany, the initial Bush-Gorbachev summit at Washington opened on May 31, 1990, to endless hours of often fruitless discussions. Unable to convince the Soviet delegation that the U.S. presence in Europe, with a unified Germany in NATO, comprised no threat to the Soviet Union, President Bush finally reminded Gorbachev that under principles of the ongoing Conference Security and Cooperation in Europe, especially its Stockholm Agreement of 1986, all countries possessed the right to choose their own alliance. Gorbachev agreed. "The United States and the U.S.S.R.," he conceded, "are in favor of Germany deciding herself in which alliance she would like to participate." The United States desired Germany's membership in NATO, Bush reiterated, but he was prepared to accept any German decision. When Gorbachev concurred, the agitated Soviet delegation vocally questioned the decision. To his amazement, Bush later recalled, Marshal Sergei Akhromeyev and senior policy adviser Valentin Falin appeared in virtual "rebellion" against the Soviet leader.[21] However, Gorbachev's decision carried.

Negotiations during July, between Kohl and Gorbachev, confirmed the latter's consent to German membership in NATO. Kohl meanwhile agreed to limit German weaponry and military manpower and to permit Soviet troops to remain in East Germany for several years. Additionally, two-plus-four discussions resulted in a guarantee of Poland's existing western border along the Oder-Neisse line. On August 21, the two

Germanies signed a Treaty of Unification and the next month, on September 12, the United States, Britain, France, and the Soviet Union terminated the responsibility they had exercised over Berlin since 1945. The newly united nation had achieved full sovereignty. The Final Settlement treaty provided for German membership in NATO, set limits on future German troop levels, and prohibited Germany's acquisition of nuclear, biological, and chemical weapons. With the treaty's ratification on October 3, 1990, on paper at least, a sovereign and reunited Germany came into existence.[22] For the Bush administration, the resolution of the German unification was a major triumph. The new, enlarged Germany that emerged was a country firmly limited in its ambitions and behavior by its membership in NATO.

The reality of German unification came on that fateful evening of November 8–9, 1990, when East Germany citizens were officially told they could leave the country without formal permission. That night sections of the Berlin Wall were breached and thousands of people surged through gaps in the ugly twenty-eight-year-old concrete barrier. They danced and sang to the melodies of jazz bands playing under the searchlights mounted on the wall that had previously sought out fleeing fugitives. Germans from the former eastern and western states toasted with beer and champagne as they hauled off pieces of the despised wall as souvenirs. Television relayed accounts of the participants and the joyous celebration throughout the world. In Washington, President Bush watched the events from a small room off the Oval Office, fully understanding the significance of the occasion. "If the Soviets are going to let the Communists fall in East Germany," he informed his aides, "they've got to be really serious—more serious than I realized."[23]

* * *

The Bush administration had reacted to the challenge of a disintegrating Soviet empire with remarkable restraint. Indeed, the president's response to the long-awaited triumph of self-determination in Eastern Europe and the looming collapse of the Soviet economy was generally passive, with no soaring rhetoric, exultation, or bold initiatives. The Eastern European upheaval never became a matter of controversy between Washington and Moscow. Congress and the press loudly protested the president's failure to suggest programs to deal with the new government's substantial political and economic problems. In the Senate, Republican Robert Dole of Kansas proposed to divert some of the current foreign aid funds allotted to Israel and Egypt to the struggling Eastern European nations. From the other side of the aisle, Bill Bradley of New Jersey suggested that the administration could significantly improve its ties to Eastern Europe with a modified Marshall Plan. In the House, Democratic majority leader Richard Gephardt of Missouri pointed out that the United States had offered less money to the newly freed nations than the cost of one major savings and loan bailout. The United States, he pointed out, had spent $125 billion in 1989 to defend the NATO bloc. Many private groups, such as the U.S. Chamber of Commerce, the American Bar Association, and the International Executive Service Corps, had already begun assisting these countries. While these efforts were commendable, columnist David Broder noted on March 21, 1990, they could neither meet the needs of the Eastern European state nor take advantage of the opportunities available to the United States. Surely the Bush administration could do more than encourage these voluntary efforts, he complained, to aid the countries of Eastern Europe.[24]

Even as his public approval rating soared to 80 percent, the president maintained a cautious approach to the challenges of Eastern Europe and the Soviet Union. The popular mood recognized no foreign threats and it was no longer concerned with events abroad. The administration's disinterest in advancing any sizeable funds to either party was due largely to the national indebtedness and opposition to new taxes. Meanwhile, most Western nations scrambled to develop multibillion-dollar aid programs for their newly formed, neighboring democracies. Even after being pressured by the Democratic Congress, the Bush administration would only offer a paltry grant of $500 million for Eastern Europe, less than one-twelfth of what newly united Germany provided.

The State Department no longer showed much concern for the region. In rejecting any shift of military funds to an aid package, Secretary Baker argued that American taxpayers were willing to provide any needed monies for defense, but not for foreign economic assistance. In July, economist Henry Kaufman concluded that the country's substantial deficits and rejection of new taxes simply ruled out any extensive U.S. investments in Eastern Europe. "The European Development Bank," he wrote, "will extend credits but not give grants. Thus it is not clear that the Eastern European countries are going to obtain the aid they need."[25]

Even more bleak perhaps was the outlook for any economic assistance to the U.S.S.R. Although Bush repeatedly stated that improvement of America's relations with the Soviet Union rested on Gorbachev's actions, he rejected any aid to Moscow. The president also threatened to boycott the new East European Bank if it extended major loans to that country. "For U.S. taxpayers to finance lending to the Soviet Union," one Treasury official explained, "is not politically acceptable." Looking more realistically at the bigger picture, Czech president Vaclav Havel urged the extending of economic aid to the ailing Soviet Union. "You can help us most of all," he argued, "if you help the Soviet Union on its irreversible but immensely complicated road to democracy." Although many of Gorbachev's reforms were failing, there were many observers who believed that is was even more important for Washington to assist him in order to achieve a less threatening world. Yet when Congressman Gephardt pressed his program of substantial aid for the Soviet Union to ease the transition from Communism to democracy, even if it appeared to the Kremlin's advantage, Senator Alan K. Simpson of Wyoming dismissed the idea. Two-thirds of the American people, he claimed, rejected providing any large amount of aid to Moscow. The administration refused to believe that shortages were the U.S.S.R.'s basic problem; instead, it insisted that they were the result of poor distribution and excessive military and foreign expenditures. Others argued that the primitive Soviet and Eastern European markets were unlikely to successfully absorb foreign aid and investments. For members of the American right, such as Patrick J. Buchanan, any aid to Communist-controlled governments would simply be wasted.[26]

Not all Americans believed that the radical changes taking place within the Soviet bloc advanced Western security. Many senior Washington officials were still skeptical of Gorbachev's motives and his ability to hold on to power long enough to merit the full support of the United States. It was evident to Paul H. Nitze, who had held various positions in several administrations, that the collapse of Soviet influence in Eastern Europe during 1989 had undercut the presumption that Marxist-Leninist ideology was destined for worldwide acceptance. Writing in January 1990, he nevertheless advised readers of the *Washington Post* that the Soviet Communist structure, with its heavy concentration of power, would continue to grant Soviet leaders a sense of identity and purpose. He also believed it would convince them that they possessed a superior organization for managing and conducting international conflict. Gorbachev's determination to preserve the Communist organization, Nitze believed, indicated that the Soviet leader had deferred Communism's long-term ideological struggle with the West, while awaiting the return of conditions that would give Communist parties "a decisive edge in dealing with a potentially fragmented world." He argued that any effort to reinstall Communist discipline would demand America's unambiguous opposition even at the price of chaos and disruption within the Soviet Union. Bush himself warned in February, "It is important not to let these encouraging changes, political and military, lull us into a sense of complacency. Nor can we let down our guard against a worldwide threat. . . . Military challenges to democracy persist in every hemisphere."[27]

* * *

Yet by 1990 Moscow's economic and political systems were on the verge of bankruptcy. The collapse of Communism in Eastern European gradually revealed the long known, but often discounted, deficiencies in the Soviet economy and the institutional resistance to change needed for Gorbachev's reforms to take hold. As early as 1979, Haverford College economist Holland Hunter pointed out the Soviet Union's centrally dominated command economy, seeking to maintain a full work force, had resulted in padded rosters, declining efficiency, unsatisfactory products, and chronic shortages. As Hunter explained: "[Market competition] forces old technology off the stage, penalizing with bankruptcy those who fail to adapt . . . , long standing Soviet tradition preserves old capital plant and equipment to an extraordinary extent." The institutional structure of the Soviet system, with its powerful vested interests, failed to allow for necessary changes to more efficient processes and enhanced products. "A systems approach to technological innovation," he noted, "would concede major initiative to plant management. . . . [E]nterprise-level initiative would permit 'localist tendencies' to divert resources from the Party's priorities."[28] Innovation, in short, would threaten the structure of centralized power.

Yet official American analysts viewed the Soviet economy quite differently. From the 1950s, CIA reports consistently placed the Soviet economic base at a much superior level than that of the United States. These estimates claimed that Moscow was investing in its economy at a rate similar to that of West Germany and Japan, twice that of the United States. This extraordinary bias, grounded on the notion of Soviet superiority and deluded by highly questionable Soviet statistics, prevailed into the 1970s, leading to the prediction that the Soviet economy would grow faster than that of America. But Hunter had not been alone in his cautionary observations. Returning from a visit to Moscow, Jack P. Ruina, a leading scientist in the Kennedy administration, wondered how, behind its fifteenth-century façade, the Soviets could develop a dynamic twenty-first-century economy. Swedish economist Anders Aslund viewed the U.S.S.R. as "a reasonably well-developed Third World country," while other observers placed it in the same category with India. Analyst Robert B. Hawkins, Jr., concluded, "Soviet national income, generally thought to be about half that of the United States, is, in fact, less than a third. That puts the Soviet military burden at as much as 25 percent of GNP." Clearly the Soviet defense bill far exceeded what the country could afford. Without the benefit of sophisticated intelligence-gathering equipment, Senator Daniel Moynihan predicted, in 1979, that the Soviet Union was headed for extinction.[29]

Soviet analysts belonging to the "new thinking" reformist school, from which Gorbachev drew, were equally critical. In their view, the Soviet economy began faltering soon after 1975, falling far behind the advanced nations in productivity, scientific development, and the employment of high technology. Even the Soviet's once enormously productive agricultural economy, which fell behind as a result of collectivization, could not produce sufficient food to feed its citizens. Czarist Russia exported grain, but during the 1970s Moscow had to import millions of tons of grain to prevent starvation.[30] By the 1990s, the Soviet economy was nearing the tipping point. The economic havoc cascading across Eastern Europe had made the situation in the Soviet Union even more grim. For the first time in 45 years the Soviet economy, in 1990, experienced a fall in both industrial and agricultural production. The drop in industrial output was especially disastrous in the metallurgical and energy sectors, as both oil and coal production fell sharply. It gradually became apparent that Gorbachev's efforts at reform, limited to what the Communist establishment would accept, could not stem the downward spiral of the Soviet economy.[31]

Equally bankrupt was the Soviet political system. By 1990 the Communist Party was a moribund organization, with its concern focused on its prerogatives. Moreover, the Soviet authoritarian political system was less and less compatible with the desire of its better-educated population for policy innovations, civil rights, and individual freedoms. The growing irrelevance of the political structure led Gorbachev in January 1990 to terminate the Communist Party's monopoly on political power, paving the way for a multiparty system. Yet the opening of a multiparty system was no panacea. To maintain order and reduce the prospect of anarchy, the Soviet leadership designed a new constitution that fashioned a Western-looking presidential form of government, with a legalized multiparty political system.[32] In March, Gorbachev chose to have himself elected president by a discredited parliament;

he could not claim a popular mandate for his authority. Pledges to use his new powers to improve the economy faltered before the self-imposed limits on his economic initiatives. A cartoon of Gorbachev and a sailor standing on the deck of a sinking ship was captioned: "Captain Gorbachev, the gala to celebrate your vastly increased authority has been moved to the lifeboat."[33]

The nationalist spirit continued to exert itself in May 1990, when the speaker of the Supreme Soviet of the Russian Soviet Federative Socialist Republic, and Gorbachev opponent, Boris Yeltsin, declared that the republic of Russia no longer would be subordinated to the Kremlin's central authority. "Our state, our country," he said, "will only be strong if the republics are strong."[34] If Gorbachev sought to block Russia's attempt to gain its sovereignty, Yeltsin warned it might employ its constitutional right to secede from the union. During subsequent months, nationalist pressures intensified and exposed dangers that defied solution. By late 1990 the very semblance of the U.S.S.R., which had existed for 70 years, was fading into history. The U.S.S.R. was an empire that comprised over one hundred ethnic and language groups, all held together by the raw power of the Communist Party. The looming retreat of Kremlin authority unleashed long pent-up nationalist demands for self-determination across much of the Soviet Union. Gorbachev's reforms, aimed at stimulating the staggering economy and reviving the moribund Communist Party, actually contributed to the Soviet Union's slide to oblivion by the end of 1991.

* * *

The secessionist urge that swept through Eastern Europe also encompassed Ukraine, Georgia, Estonia, Latvia, and Lithuania. Lithuania, however, became a special case as nationalists launched efforts in January 1990 to escape from the Kremlin's direct authority. Because Lithuania was added to the Russian Empire in the late 1800s, claimed its independence at the end of World War I, and was reacquired by the U.S.S.R. under the Nazi-Soviet Pact of 1939, Moscow had a stronger claim there than to the states of Eastern Europe. The West, which had endorsed Lithuania's 1918 independence movement, had consistently opposed the Soviet's acquisitions under the 1939 pact and had strongly supported Lithuania's claim for independence throughout the Cold War. Consequently, Gorbachev was faced with a most difficult decision: permitting Lithuania to leave the union or risking his carefully constructed foreign relations with the West. Lithuania's unchallenged departure was fraught with devastating consequences, among which included serious damage to the fragile Soviet economy and the initiating of secessionist activity that could threaten the existence of the Soviet Union of Socialist Republics. Gorbachev sought to halt the process of Soviet disintegration by pleading with the Lithuanians to remain within the union and by reminding them that their countries were fused to the Soviet economy and political structure, its factories managed by Soviet ministries, burning Soviet oil, producing goods for Soviet customers.[35] Because large segments of the Lithuanian work force were ethnic Russians, their abandonment would likely be more politically perilous for the Gorbachev government than the desertions of Eastern Europe states. "My personal fate," Gorbachev recognized, "is linked to this choice." Reminded of his endorsement of any people's right of self-determination, he assured the Lithuanians he would not resort to force.[36]

On March 11, 1990, the Lithuanian parliament unilaterally declared its independence. As Gorbachev demanded that the parliament retract its declaration, Soviet armored units began rolling into Vilnius, the Lithuanian capital, despite the Soviet leader's earlier assurances he would not employ force. Seeking to avoid a bloody confrontation, Lithuanian leaders informed Moscow that the parliament desired no more than a gradual transfer of power and suggested a negotiated settlement. The crisis mounted when Estonia threatened to take similar action and Gorbachev warned its leaders not to challenge Soviet authority. Turning to Lithuania, he charged that the parliament had acted illegally and in violation of the constitution, and imposed an economic blockade seeking to compel the Lithuanians to accept Moscow's terms.[37]

The Bush administration viewed Lithuania's demand for independence cautiously, recognizing that the American people had neither the interest nor the will to rescue the Baltic state from Soviet military force. The president hoped to achieve a reluctant Soviet recognition of Lithuanian independence. "That," declared one senior U.S. official, "requires a negotiating process that's likely to take months before anyone can tell where it's going, and for the United States to rush in with heavy-handed statements will only make it harder for both sides to work their way through this."[38]

Approaching the crisis even more cautiously, European leaders feared that a major confrontation over Lithuania could unhinge the whole process of removing Soviet control over the Eastern European states.[39] Meanwhile, Senator Edward M. Kennedy of Massachusetts, after visiting Moscow, relayed to the White House Gorbachev's complaint that Western devotion to Lithuania was undermining his reform efforts. Gorbachev, Kennedy added, faced intense domestic pressure to retain Lithuania. The Bush administration understood from Kennedy's and other accounts that its encouragement of the Lithuanians could only exacerbate U.S.-Soviet relations. The president had come to recognize that the Soviet threat to regional peace receded with Gorbachev's successes, not his failures.[40]

When Baltic-American spokesmen, on April 11, finally met with the president, Bush flatly rejected their plea for formal U.S. recognition of Lithuanian independence. Following the meeting, White House spokesman Marlin Fitzwater informed the press: "Our policy, we believe, is the correct one, and it does not involve recognition." Bush repeated his support for self-determination, but added, "The U.S. must avoid taking actions that would inadvertently make Lithuania's task more difficult by inflaming the situation." The president obviously had no desire to repeat the fiasco of 1956 when the United States encouraged the Hungarian uprising and then stood by helplessly as Soviet forces crushed the rebellion.[41] The Bush administration, meanwhile, continued to acknowledge Gorbachev as a vital figure on the international scene, although his authority was being contested. The White House looked forward to promising negotiations at the impending May 30–June 2 summit at Washington.

For the champions of American anti-Communist orthodoxy, however, Gorbachev and his reform efforts remained an aberration, compelled by adverse circumstances.[42] They insisted that with a revitalized Soviet economy, Moscow's aggressive actions would increase global insecurity and reestablish a Cold War climate. To the steadfast Cold Warriors, therefore, it was essential that the administration take advantage of Soviet vulnerabilities, that it aggressively challenge the Kremlin and avoid compromises that merely perpetuated Moscow's former illusions of power. These critics rejected the White House's argument that the only choice was between Gorbachev and the return of Communist hard-liners and, consequently, the wisdom of placing all hopes for finally burying the Cold War on the Soviet leader. "Conservatives," observed Representative Dana Rohrabacher of California, "do not see keeping Gorbachev in power [as] a laudable goal. Most see him as communism's last gasp."[43] The administration's insistence that Gorbachev was indispensable, some charged, actually impeded Russian reform efforts and prevented Washington from fully exploiting Soviet weakness. Bush rejected suggestions that Gorbachev would come to a summit weakened by his unanswered political and economic troubles.

"It is not a question of who is stronger, who is weaker," he said, "[It is a question of trying] to convince him where we differ that our position is correct, just as he will be trying to convince me." The administration needed to deal forthrightly with Gorbachev, the *Washington Post* advised, because the Soviet leader was dealing with the immense but significant challenge of guiding Europe's transition to the post–Cold War era.[44]

* * *

When Bush assumed the presidency, it was expected by virtually everyone that he would expedite the arms control process begun by Reagan and Gorbachev. Earlier negotiators had toiled long over such basic issues as totally eliminating nuclear testing, outlawing chemical weapons, reducing conventional weapons in Europe, and, especially, the nuclear weapons systems. However, because Bush thought Reagan had casually granted too many concessions to Gorbachev, he and Scowcroft did not contact the Soviet leader regarding arms control matters until nearly five months after his inauguration.

After weeks of temporizing, Bush, in early December 1989, approached the Malta summit with Gorbachev understanding that success in achieving Western goals depended on Gorbachev. With winds howling and waves crashing in a wild Mediterranean storm, the two leaders met for the first time aboard the Soviet cruise ship *Maxim Gorky*, recently refurbished to provide quarters for the Soviet delegation. At Gorbachev's invitation, the president opened the discussion with a 50-minute gambit in which he spelled out a 20-point program. Pausing to respond, Gorbachev replied optimistically: "This is interesting. It shows the Bush Administration has already decided what to do." During subsequent sessions, Bush and Gorbachev defined an ambitious program for cooperation and speedy progress on arms control, enhanced trade relations, and a Washington summit in late spring 1990. The discussions had been congenial and frank. Bush felt that the meeting's most "positive effect" was "upon my personal relationship with Gorbachev." Yet the president and his advisers resisted reporters' invitations to declare the Cold War over. At a final press conference, Gorbachev declared, "[T]he world is leaving an era of cold war and entering another. This is just the beginning . . . of a long peaceful period." Bush responded, "Now, with reform under way in the Soviet Union, we stand at the threshold of a brand new era in U.S.-Soviet relations."[45]

Gorbachev arrived in Washington on May 30, 1990, beleaguered and profoundly unpopular at home but determined to sustain his image of confidence, enthusiasm, and authority. He and Bush formally acknowledged verification protocols to nuclear testing pacts that had been signed nearly two decades earlier—the Threshold Test Ban Treaty (1974) and Peaceful Nuclear Explosions Treaty (1976)—and now, finally, permitted their ratification. But Bush balked at considering a comprehensive nuclear test ban; indeed, he had issued a policy statement earlier in January that his administration had "not identified any further limitations on nuclear testing . . . that would be in the United States' national security interest." The two leaders, nevertheless, pressed ahead with other issues, establishing a framework that would lead to future arms reductions—the Treaty on Conventional Forces in Europe (CFE) in November 1990 and the Strategic Arms Reductions Treaty (START I) in August 1991.

Bush felt passionately about one arms control measure—the long-talked-about abolition of chemical weapons. "I want to get rid of chemical weapons," the president told Gorbachev at the November Malta summit, "I mean it." Bush urged the Soviet leader to support the chemical warfare initiative spelled out in his September speech at the United Nations. The Chemical Weapons Convention (CWC) finally reached fruition—reducing the chemical weapons arsenals of both countries by 80 percent—in January 1993. Eventually some 180 enthusiastic nations signed on giving the CWC global coverage.[46]

Negotiations seeking to limit European conventional military forces began in the early 1970s and limped on for nearly twenty years. The imbalance between the vastly larger Soviet and Warsaw Pact forces and U.S. and NATO forces meant that Moscow held the upper hand in the discussions and, not surprisingly, Soviet leaders resisted offering substantial concessions. Accelerated discussions between 1989 and 1990 finally resolved most major areas of disagreement and pointed toward a CFE agreement. Several factors contributed to this progress: France joined the talks; Gorbachev unilaterally withdrew troops and equipment from forward areas; the Warsaw Pact disintegrated; and the reunited Germany agreed to troop limitations. Unwilling to attend the Paris summit unless a CFE treaty was awaiting signatures, President Bush pressed delegates to resolve the lingering issues. In the end, Soviet and American negotiators in Moscow held marathon sessions to finalize the verification regime and to narrow differences on definitions and agreed limits—despite the continued opposition of the Soviet military. President Bush signed the CFE pact at Paris on November 19, 1990, placing limits on tanks, artillery, armored combat vehicles, aircraft, helicopters, and military personnel stationed in Europe from the Atlantic Ocean to the Ural Mountains.

Figure 15.2
Presidents Bush and Gorbachev at Malta meeting, December 1, 1989 (Courtesy: George Bush Library)

In the long, tortuous history of arms control, historian Michael Beschloss and foreign policy expert Strobe Talbott have written, the CFE treaty was a "most impressive accomplishment" in that a few years earlier such an agreement would have been unthinkable. Yet the treaty also vividly demonstrated events had overtaken the efforts of diplomats. At the president's urging, Brent Scowcroft, in early 1989, suggested that if the West should inject a bold proposal into the CFE discussions, Moscow might be persuaded to remove all of its ground units from Eastern Europe. But before the signatures were dry on the CFE treaty, Beschloss and Talbott noted, "Soviet units were already committed to a complete pullout from Hungary and Czechoslovakia in 1991 and from the eastern parts of Germany in 1994. . . . [O]f the original twenty three states involved in the [CFE] negotiations, one—the German Democratic Republic—had ceased to exist, and five others had changed their names," an indication of their independence from Moscow. With the Warsaw Pact in tatters, a U.S. delegate to the CFE negotiations later claimed the treaty had "ended the Cold War" because Europe was now truly at peace.[47]

In January 1989, Bush's White House found the basic framework of a START pact already laid out by the Reagan administration, but several unresolved details had become dormant because of incessant bickering over technicalities between government agencies. One major hurdle, for example, was how to verify whether sea-launched cruise missiles (SLCMs) were actually aboard warships, but U.S. naval officers rebelled at the idea of Soviet inspectors snooping about their newest nuclear submarines. Tossing aside Reagan's often repeated Russian proverb "Trust but verify," the United States proposed that each side declare the number of SLCMs it planned to deploy. Dissatisfied with this solution, Moscow continued to press for intrusive verification procedures. This attitude again unsettled Pentagon officials and U.S. intelligence agencies who resisted the thought of Soviets inspectors prowling U.S. defense factories and other installations. Washington's decades-long insistence on an intrusive inspection system became less rigid.[48]

To stir up the moribund START talks, the president urged his arms control team to look for new ideas for the looming Malta summit. Secretary Baker and national security adviser Scowcroft suggested that Bush could put his stamp on the process, and at the same time win bipartisan congressional approval, by proposing a ban on mobile missiles equipped with nuclear-tipped Multiple Independently Targeted Reentry Vehicles (MIRVs). Surprising his advisers, the normally cautious president suggested going for broke—let's offer the Soviets a ban on all the threatening, vulnerable land-based MIRVed intercontinental missiles. When Secretary of Defense Cheney and Pentagon officials learned of the proposed ban, an intramural struggle began and soon Baker and Scowcroft retreated. The idea of a total MIRV ban was dropped. With modest progress at the Malta summit toward moving START I forward, perhaps the most significant accomplishment was the fact Bush considered the meeting a great success.[49]

Finally, on July 31, 1991, after eight and a half frustrating years, President Bush and Soviet President Gorbachev signed a detailed 750-page START I treaty. Basically, it limited each side to the deployment of 1,600 ballistic missiles and long-range bombers, carrying 6,000 "accountable" warheads, and established further sub-limits. This was the first agreement that called upon each side to make significant cuts in their strategic arsenals. Almost 50 percent of the nuclear warheads carried on ballistic missiles would be eliminated. Additionally, the agreement established a complex verification system that would satisfactorily serve future accords on strategic weaponry.[50]

* * *

It was clear that the Soviet decline had offered unprecedented possibilities for imaginative policy, but the administration seemed torn between its desire to support Gorbachev and the possibility that the Cold War was not really ending, requiring the United States to continue enhancing its military forces. The president had presumed, moreover, that any improvement in American-Soviet relations mattered far more to the Soviet Union than to the United States. Not until the Berlin Wall came down in November 1989 did the president fully understand that Gorbachev was no traditional Soviet leader. At the earlier Malta and Washington summits, consequently, U.S. leaders had hesitated to acknowledge the ending of the Cold War.

Accepting the challenge, the NATO summit's London Declaration of July 6, 1990, proclaimed the Cold War's demise. The Atlantic community, seeking to build a new partnership with all the countries of Europe, offered its former adversaries "the hand of friendship." NATO delegates told members of the Warsaw Pact: "[W]e are no longer adversaries and reaffirm our intention to refrain . . . from acting in any other manner inconsistent with the purpose and principles of the United Nations Charter." The declaration invited the Warsaw Pact nations to come to NATO, establish diplomatic liaisons with its members, and enter reciprocal pledges of nonaggression and against use of force. As the Soviet forces withdrew from Eastern Europe, NATO would field smaller, restructured active forces, reduce its nuclear deterrents, eliminate all nuclear artillery shells, and diminish its reliance on nuclear weapons. Gorbachev praised the London Declaration for its promise of a peaceful, unified Europe.[51]

Uncertainty had prevailed regarding the actual end of the Cold War. Some have pointed to the Paris summit of November 19, 1990, where Gorbachev, Bush, and other European leaders signed a treaty for the reduction of conventional forces in Europe that removed the fear of a conventional war on the continent—the last major obstacle to the ending of the Cold War. Others might choose the dismantling of the Berlin Wall or the formal reunification of Germany in October 1990 or the dissolution of the U.S.S.R in December 1991 as the end of the 40-year contest.

Perhaps closer to historical reality was Bush's recollection of his 1990 trip to Eastern Europe where he saw "the many uplifted bright faces" in Warsaw, Gdansk, Prague, and Budapest where Communist power was ended in 1989 with the support of Gorbachev. The president noted at the time: "This was their victory. We all were winners, East and West." Bush believed that his relations with Gorbachev smoothed developments at a critical time. These changes were "the culmination of many years of efforts by many people, both in the United States and elsewhere. . . . From those who served in our military to those who played and implemented policy across succeeding administrations, all had a hand in bringing the Cold War to a peaceful conclusion."[52] Whatever the actual date, the end of the Cold War—or, more precisely, the end of Moscow-dominated Communism—caused the world to rejoice that it had ended with treaties and understandings, not a violent series of mushroom clouds.

CHAPTER 16

Reflections

Throughout its long, tumultuous history, America's Cold War comprised essentially a rhetorical exercise. It emerged and thrived on images of a global Communist expansion and an impending nuclear holocaust. The fundamental portrayal of the Soviet menace and America's eagerness to challenge that menace became the overwhelming focus of the United States' ill-defined Cold War policies. Lost in the rhetoric was a realistic sorting out of the nation's vital interests from secondary or illusionary ones, and a connection between attainable policy objectives and means necessary to achieve them.

The country's emerging anti-Communist elite was grounded in an antiradical legacy that blossomed in the first "Red Scare" of 1919–1920 that briefly threatened the nation's cherished civil liberties. At that time many Americans feared that socialists, radicals, and labor organizers were inspired, if not led, by Communists who aimed to subvert American society. To strident American anti-Communists, the post–World War II Soviet danger lay not only in military aggression but even more in the limitless prospect of Moscow's ideological expansion aimed at world domination. To them the U.S.S.R.'s self-assigned leadership of world Communism possessed the power and will to incite and support Communist-led revolutions everywhere, imposing on them its influence, if not its direct control. This presumption assigned to the Soviet Union the unprecedented power to extend its presence over vast distances *without* military force. To counter Moscow's ideological threat, Washington actively stimulated its own ideological foundation—a blind, knee-jerk anti-Communism that frequently bordered on what political scientist Howard Ball called "control hysteria." From Truman to Reagan, America's political establishment conducted a "war on communism" that refused to consider any resolution short of the Soviet Union's surrender.

"Before we can hope to stabilize international relations with the Communists or have a peaceful environment in which to seek a resolution of differences between countries," Senator Strom Thurman of South Carolina insisted, "the Communists have got to abandon their goal of world domination." In similar fashion, Robert Strausz-Hupé declared the "desirability of such . . . dealing with an opponent who seeks world domination and frequently speaks of burying us is questionable." Constant reminders of the threat posed by a godless Communism and a disastrous nuclear war to Western Civilization sprang from the media, the pulpit, and politicos of almost every stripe. "For more than four decades," Strobe Talbott concluded in the January 1, 1990, issue of *Time*, "Western policy has been based on a grotesque exaggeration of what the U.S.S.R. could do if it wanted, therefore what it might do, and therefore what the West must be prepared to do in response. . . . Worst-case assumptions about Soviet intentions were fed . . . [by] worst-case assumptions about Soviet capabilities."[1]

If the nuclear arsenals best symbolized the long Soviet-American rivalry, they never realistically reflected any clash of interests whose resolution demanded a resort to such levels of violence. No issue that divided the two superpowers was worth an hour of nuclear war, even of conventional war. Yet never did the nation's role as special defender of the free world monopolize its interests or activities as the Cold War, for most Americans, remained an abstraction, acknowledged but not understood. It levied few impositions on the vast majority who lived through it— confident, untouched, secure—conscious only of the unprecedented opportunities that the long experience provided.

Despite America's constant dramatic portrayal of the alleged expansive power of Soviet Communism, the actual danger posed by the U.S.S.R. remained so imprecise that no Washington official cared to define it. Fear of Moscow's seemingly limitless ability to project its ideology around the world transformed this power into an international phenomenon of unprecedented expansive power. But ideology was no expansive force. Nationalism and the demands of self-determination, sweeping much of the former colonial world, comprised a universal defense against Soviet ideological expansion. Rhetorically, Washington's view of the Soviet threat was global but, except in bordering Afghanistan, nowhere—not in Europe, the Middle East, Asia, Africa, or Latin America—did Moscow reveal any ambition or interest of sufficient importance to merit a resort to military force or a showdown with the United States. Nowhere did the Kremlin threaten direct military aggression against any region regarded vital to the security of the United States or its Western allies. Even the occasional encounters remained provisional, usually conducted by alleged proxies whose interests were always indigenous.

If the world avoided a major conflict since 1945, the unresolved questions between East and West had been considerably less than vital for one side or the other. The stability of Europe, especially, reflected the realization among Western and Soviet leaders alike that the issues of the Cold War were better left unresolved than disposed of through war. The balance of power in Europe had after all succeeded in establishing and perpetuating a stable division of the continent. There had been innumerable incidents and provocation, even some minor wars, but no nation possessing nuclear-striking power had passed, or perhaps approached, the point of no return. Most lines of demarcation had been well established through tradition and prudence, if not by diplomatic agreement; few, if any, could have been tampered with without setting off a war.

What characterized world politics in the post–World War II era, therefore, was a remarkable stability, produced partially by the dangers of thermonuclear war but especially by the relative absence of vital conflicting interests. There were no apparent problems that lay outside the power of astute diplomacy to compromise, provided that governments were permitted the freedom to maneuver. The forces that lead to war are varied and illusive, and the ultimate decision to fight—and fight totally—is more often the product of fears and emotions than of clear and measured judgments of national interest. In the long run, therefore, peace rests on the ability of nations to distinguish with considerable accuracy their essential rights, upon which hinge their security and welfare, from demands of secondary importance that are always proper questions for negotiation and compromise.

Yet Washington and Moscow were arming for a war that nobody wanted and over issues that few considered critical. "We are trapped," Thomas Powers summed the continuing rivalry in the January 1984 issue of the *Atlantic Monthly*, "in a tightening spiral of fear and hostility. We don't know why we have got into this situation, we don't know how to get out of it, and we have not found the humility to admit we don't know. In desperation, we simply try to manage our enmity from day to day."[2]

* * *

If the day-to-day policies of the superpowers recognized the limits of their capacity to perform, Washington's ultimate goals were attached to abstractions that had little relationship to America's national interests. If the Soviets introduced uncertainty and abused the normal privileges and methods of diplomacy by maintaining a varied political, economic, and psychological assault on the non-Communist world, the United States warred on the Soviet bloc through appeals to the doctrine of self-determination. It was against such tendencies that William Graham Summer, the noted Yale sociologist, warned over half a century ago. He wrote:

Doctrines are the most frightful tyrants to which men are ever subject, because doctrines get inside of a man's own reason and betray him against himself. . . . Doctrines are always vague; it would ruin a doctrine to define it, because then it could be analyzed, tested, criticized, and verified; but nothing ought to be tolerated which cannot be tested. . . . What can be more contrary to sound statesmanship and common sense than to put forth an abstract assertion which has no definite relation to any interest of ours now at stake, but which has in it any number of possibilities of producing complications which we cannot foresee, but which are sure to be embarrassing when they arise![3]

Arguing from the principle of self-determination, the West refused to recognize the Soviet sphere of influence in East-Central Europe, established with the destruction of Nazi Germany in 1944 and 1945. Throughout World War II, Western leadership did nothing to prevent this transferal of power to the Soviet Union, yet it refused to accept it as the basis of negotiation at the conclusion of the war. In large measure, the Kremlin, in establishing Soviet political and economic control over Slavic Europe, was mistaken in its wartime and postwar estimate of Western purpose.

Since 1947 Western policies had been defensive in nature. Yet the persistent attachment of containment policies to the rhetoric of rollback and liberation sustained the impression of an offensive purpose that appeared to deny to the Russians the tangible fruits of victory and to aim at the actual destruction of Soviet influence in European affairs. What this posture of not recognizing the massive changes that had occurred in Eastern Europe had achieved, beyond its contribution to postwar tensions, is not clear. It liberated no one. And it is conceivable that many of the unfortunate aspects of the Cold War, including the nuclear arms race itself, might have been avoided by more realistic policies based on interests rather than doctrines that have never really been applicable. The United States demonstrated its capacity to maintain the *status quo* where it appeared essential; it had not demonstrated any power—moral, economic, or military—to alter it appreciably.

The West, under the mantle of American preparedness, could have what it needed; it could not have had much more.

Nor was more demanded. The United States and the West coexisted with the Kremlin and its satellite empire for more than four decades with remarkable success. It would have been well for the Cold War antagonists to dwell less on the failure of their ideals and doctrines in the unfolding history of the postwar era and more on the decades' unprecedented achievements. By almost every standard of accomplishment, the world passed through one of the greatest periods of history. This was true not only for the developments in science and technology and in material progress but also for the genuine gains in the realm of politics and even of self-determination. This era had been marked less by the antagonism between the Western and Communist worlds than by the creation of dozens of new nations, comprising more than a billion people, as well as by the sheer economic expansion on both sides of the Iron and Bamboo curtains.

Even the more mundane diplomacy of the Cold War had been characterized by an essential and hopeful conservatism. Eighteen years after the 1919 Versailles Treaty, the world was inescapably on the way to a second world war. Without the benefit of any general postwar settlement, the great powers since 1945 maintained a reasonable peace. With all its confusion of interests with abstractions, postwar diplomacy performed far more successfully than did the diplomacy of the interwar period. There remained many arrangements in the world that defied the principle of self-determination; and no American could have taken any pleasure in their existence. But the United States simply lacked the power—and therefore the obligation—to serve humankind in general. Any attempt to eliminate from the world those factors that to many Americans appeared immoral would have terminated in the destruction of a civilization that has reached unprecedented achievements in most areas of human endeavor.

China remained a special problem. It was here, perhaps, that the genuine statesmanship of the future would be tested. Since mid-century, the United States had attempted to limit, if not eliminate, the Chinese challenge to Far Eastern stability through policies of diplomatic isolation and military alliance. Neither course proved effective. Nonrecognition of the Beijing regime, the core of American policy, had not returned Chiang Kai-shek and his Nationalists to power; nor had it undermined the strength of the mainland. Indeed, China evolved into a greater rather than a lesser danger to the postwar status of Asia. Whatever the internal problems and the agricultural and industrial failures of China, that nation grew to represent a far more formidable power than that which drove Chiang from the mainland in 1949 and opposed the United States in Korea. U.S. attitudes, moreover, had achieved no mitigation of Chinese animosity towards the West. And if there was little affection for China among the nations of the world, there existed an ever-increasing conviction that diplomatic isolation in itself had achieved nothing.

If Communist China did not unleash a more determined and wide-ranging assault on Southeast Asia, it must be explained by either the threat of American nuclear retaliation or the perennial overestimation of Chinese intention. To defend the periphery of China with conventional forces against a full-scale Chinese attack would have been impossible in some areas and difficult everywhere. On the Asian mainland, it was China, not the United States, that held the strategic advantage. What happened when China became a first-rate military power was always going to be a problem. The perennial devotion of Cold War America to the Republic of China on Formosa had presented no real alternative to the ultimate necessity of coming to terms, diplomatically and militarily, with the power of the mainland. The nation could not escape the stark choice of fitting China into a world pattern of coexistence or sitting on the Chinese pressure pot until it exploded in the face of humanity.

* * *

Neither side in the Cold War can escape responsibility for its part in prolonging a rivalry that dominated the second half of the twentieth century. Before there could be a genuine relaxation of tension, both sides first had to free their policies of ideological, universal objectives. As long as Khrushchev proclaimed the right of the Soviet Union, under conditions of coexistence, to wage war on the values of the Western world until they were destroyed, Western leaders could hardly regard coexistence as a hopeful arrangement. Unfortunately, the choices confronting the West were limited. Whatever the disagreement on the meaning of peaceful coexistence, the West had no alternative to coexistence, even on Soviet terms, but war. There was, moreover, a vast discrepancy between Soviet rhetoric and the Soviet capacity to achieve an international Communist society. It remained well within the power of the West to preserve a world that was, in the words of Secretary of State Dean Rusk, "safe for freedom."

The Cold War reflected the stark fact that the world could, indeed, exist half slave and half free. It has always been so. The abstract ideals of universal freedom and justice could never establish the foundations of national policy. To eliminate the control of one people over another does not guarantee political progress or even the survival of freedom. The world is unfortunately replete with examples of political and economic retrogression that followed the achievement of self-determination. To free a people from its external masters, moreover, required nothing less than war, and to establish a country's vital interest in the freedom of a nation or group of nations, long held in subjugation, was never simple. The price required to achieve such an objective, under conditions of nuclear stalemate, would undoubtedly come very high indeed.

The United States had no genuine stake in the destruction of the Soviet hegemony in East-Central Europe or in the elimination of the Beijing regime for which it was willing to risk a war. This was amply demonstrated through years of carefully sustained inaction during moments of crisis behind the Iron and Bamboo curtains. That experience, spanning as it did a period of unprecedented material progress and almost untrammeled freedom, demonstrated that any war fought over the future of either East-Central Europe or the Beijing regime would have scarcely reflected the vital interests of the United States. Any war that involved the major powers, moreover, could easily have escalated into a grand nuclear confrontation.

* * *

What measured the true magnitude of the Soviet-American rivalry over the decades most visibly was the nuclear arms race. The United States, in Secretary of State Dean Acheson's often repeated words, must only "negotiate from strength," but, in spite of constructing the world's most deadly arsenal, Washington never concluded that it had sufficient strength to undertake negotiation of basic political issues with Moscow. Nonetheless, each successive presidential administration after 1945—despite frequent misgivings—engaged in protracted negotiations seeking to limit, outlaw, or reduce specific weaponry.

Novelists, scientists, and scholars who described the horrors of nuclear war seldom bothered to explain weapons may be troublesome, even dangerous, but they were not central to the status of war and peace. Weapons do not cause war; they determine only its nature. Historically nations rarely, if ever, engaged in war over competition for military supremacy but over conflicting fundamental purposes that engaged their perceived interests and transcended the possibilities of negotiated settlements. Overwhelmingly the wars of modern Europe involved contests over territory or strategic entrances to major bodies of water.

National ambitions were sufficiently specific to render most war predictable.

Despite their extensive consideration of various nuclear war fighting strategies, the United States and U.S.S.R., through more than four decades of high tension and mutual recrimination, did not confront one another with force. Indeed, leadership of the two superpowers did not even approach such a decision, and the Cuban missile crisis of October 1962 was no clear exception. Thus nuclear weapons rather quickly lost their military utility as senior civilian officials in Washington and Moscow grasped that the catastrophic consequences of a nuclear exchange would be so appalling that no political or ideological objectives could justify it. "Nuclear weapons," Robert McNamara wrote in the September 1983 issue of *Foreign Affairs*, "serve no military purpose whatsoever. They are totally useless—except to deter one's opponents from using them." The stark reality of "mutual assured destruction," grounded on recognition of nuclear parity, led to an informal nuclear weapon taboo. As professor Nina Tannenwald has concluded in *The Nuclear Taboo: The United States and the Non-Use of Nuclear Weapons Since 1945* (2008), the "moral opprobrium" that gradually arose in Washington created a "*de facto* prohibition against the first use of nuclear weapons."[4] Clearly Moscow also found no utility in the use of this weaponry.

Yet as both nations spent several trillion dollars on their strategic arsenals and nuclear weapons, these instruments took on a political nature. In Washington, officials assumed that the buildup of its military forces would contain Russian expansionism and compel the Soviets ultimately to accept some resolution of the Soviet-American conflict largely on Western terms. As this did not occur, the continued acquisition of nuclear-tipped weapons acquired a momentum of its own. The growing nuclear arsenals assumed an increasingly significant *political* role in the discussions between Moscow and Washington. Consequently, by the 1960s the superpowers began exploring various arms control measures to rein in expanding nuclear weaponry, a diplomatic activity that would dominate negotiations between the superpowers from John Kennedy to George H. W. Bush. In point of fact, arms control had become for years the primary if not the only area of political dialogue between the two powers.

Secretary of State Dean Rusk noted that even if arms control deliberations went badly, "they provided a forum in which Soviet and American officials sat across from each other at long tables, sipped mineral water and discussed military matters that used to be the stuff spies were paid and shot for. So in that sense, even ... [the] disagree-ments were often salutary. The process was the product." An official in several presidential administrations and strident Cold Warrior, Paul H. Nitze acknowledged that arms control endeavors had played a major role in negotiations between Moscow and Washington. "Of course," he wrote, "Soviet-American arms control was not the sole cause of the relaxation of superpower tensions and the end of the Cold War. However, given the lack of diplomatic negotiations dealing with other basic political differences, arms control became the princi-pal conduit for Soviet-American relations." Emphasizing the signifi-cant role that arms control negotiations played as a political conduit during the Cold War, Nitze wrote: "Even in times of [political] tension, arms control trudged ever on in some form."[5]

* * *

What ultimately defined the limited role of the American-Soviet con-flict in world politics was its perennial failure to dominate the behavior and outlook of international society. Common interests in trade, invest-ment, and other forms of global activity governed international life far more than did the fears of Soviet aggression and war. The flourishing of world commerce after mid-century was totally without precedent. By most standards of human progress, the Cold War years comprised the most pervading, most prosperous golden age in history. The prodi-gious investment of human and physical resources assumed a fundamental international security that, despite the recurrence of limited aggression and war, permitted the evolution of the complex, dynamic, technology-driven civilization that emerged during the age of the Cold War. Peoples and governments assumed that the varied forces underwriting international stability were dominant enough, whatever the official state of U.S.-Soviet relations, to sustain the material gains of the age, symbolized graphically by the changing skyline of every major city in the Western World. Even as the perennial Cold War rhetoric warned insistently that the country and the world were in danger of global Communist conquest, every modern nation built with the confidence that its civilization was secure, and none more so than the United States itself.

By the mid-1960s, the continuing Cold War with the U.S.S.R. faced rejection amid the changing realities of international life. Europe had long recovered from the damages of war and had achieved levels of pros-perity and wealth unprecedented in its history. Its very stability erased fears of Soviet aggression. The U.S.S.R. and China, the Communist giants, had become the world's most bitter rivals, demonstrating that the Communist bloc no longer existed. Rhetorically, the Soviet threat was global, but, except in bordering Afghanistan, nowhere—not in Europe, the Middle East, Asia, Africa, or Latin America—did the Soviets reveal any ambition or interest of sufficient importance to merit a resort to military force of a showdown with the United States. Even the occasional encounters remained provisional, usually conducted by alleged proxies whose interests always remained indigenous. In 1983, George Kennan reminded a Washington audience of the absence of any perceptible dangers in the continuing, costly, and divisive Soviet-American conflict. "There are no considerations of policy—no aspirations, no ambitions, no anxieties, no defensive impulses," he declared, "that could justify the continuation of this dreadful situation."[6]

Western economic and military predominance, with the creation of NATO, established containment of the U.S.S.R. as a reality. At the same time, there appeared no way in which the anti-Communist world could eliminate the undesirable attributes of the Communist system until it failed from its own incongruities. That left no room but coexistence, the fundamental condition in U.S.-Soviet relations throughout the Cold War, one that neither side dared to challenge. The emergence of a totally acceptable East-West stability lay not in a quest for military predominance, with its corresponding rhetoric of fear and defiance, but in accommodation. In time, these possibilities for a formal coexistence became obvious amid the continuing internal collapse of the Soviet Union.

While the Kremlin never presented Washington a crisis that demanded military action, neither did the United States ever make any serious attempt to "free" Eastern Europe, China, or the Soviet Union. Behind the reality of an acceptable superpower coexistence was the fundamental American decision to ignore the dictates of ideology and pursue the limited goal of containment, with its acceptance of the *status quo*, where it mattered, as well as a careful avoidance of direct and unnecessary conflict with China and the Soviet Union. On none of the key objectives driving the long Cold War—the liberation of Eastern Europe, China, Vietnam, and Korea—could Washington command the means to succeed. And on every issue the realist projections, not necessarily Washington's policies, proved to be accurate. The Western contribution to the Soviet demise remained one of maintaining the lines of containment, permitting its weaknesses and inconsistencies within the Soviet system, their precise fulfillment unpredictable, to produce the collapse.

Ronald Reagan caught the revival of Cold War fears, unleashed largely by Jimmy Carter's unanswered Afghan crisis of 1979, at high tide, and rode them to victory. He entered office, in January 1981, committed to the enhancement of the country's security through tougher anti-Communist rhetoric and massive military expansion. In practice, he maintained the same defense posture of previous administrations. He made no direct effort to recover Carter's alleged losses in Afghanistan, Africa, Cuba, and Central America. Even before Reagan's inauguration, the Soviet Union had entered its long, predictable disintegration that, in 1985, produced Mikhail Gorbachev and the possibility of a genuine U.S.-Soviet détente, one that Reagan and Gorbachev achieved in their four summits from 1986 to 1988.

Professional Cold Warriors, blinded by their ideological bent, refused to admit that the joint policies of Bush and Gorbachev, after the two began cooperating, had brought the Cold War to an end. After 1991, Gates and Weinberger as well as such pundits as George Will and Irving Kristol argued that Ronald Reagan's military buildup and SDI program had played the dominate role in the collapse of the Soviet Union. But while this myth received extensive publicity during the 1990s, respected scholars investigating U.S.-Soviet relations have since dismissed these claims as much oversimplified. As we have argued in our previous study, *Reagan, Bush, Gorbachev: Revisiting the End of the Cold War*, even with all the contributions of Reagan and Bush it is most unlikely the Cold War would not have ended when it did and how it did without the determination of Mikhail Gorbachev.[7] After nearly a half century, the Cold War had exited quietly, without ceremony.

* * *

Unfortunately for the United States, the heavy price of success threatened its global leadership. The economic primacy of the post–World War II decade had given way by the 1980s to massive deficits at home, huge adverse trade balances abroad, and the rise of powerful, competing economies, especially in Japan and Germany. Not even in its industrial innovation and efficiency had the United States sustained its long-unchallenged primacy. Foreign investments underwrote much of the U.S. deficit, prompting C. Fred Bergsten, director of the Institute for International Economics, to observe that the United States was caught between increasing dependence on "external economic forces and a shrinking capacity to influence those forces." In the changing world of 1989 and 1990, economic power defined the role of nations.[8]

At the Houston economic summit of July 1990, budgetary constraints compelled President Bush to avoid any joint economic policy toward Eastern Europe and the Soviet Union.[9] Recognizing the diminution of American economic leadership, Michael Mandelbaum, spokesman for the Council on Foreign Relations, defined 1990 as "a time when the American nuclear surplus will be less and less important and the American fiscal deficit will be more important." Similarly, Bergsten observed that the United States was "perilously close to being unable to play a serious role—let alone a leading one—on a growing number of global issues.[10]

Still, as long as the U.S.S.R. had appeared to Americans and Europeans alike as an aggressive antagonist, military power assured the United States a pervading role in world affairs. America's global leadership would be challenged, however, by the disintegration of the Soviet bloc in 1989 and 1990. Mikhail Gorbachev's termination of the old East-West rivalry eliminated the confrontations that had, as the *New Yorker* observed:

automatically yielded us a more sharply defined sense of ourselves in relation to a belligerent, untrustworthy Soviet Union. They gave us a gratifying self-image, and an important, dramatic place in the world. In contrast, Gorbachev's actions threatened to deprive us of an identity. ... [W]e become less the defender of the free world and more a nation among nations. We lose a role, we lose a script, we lose a language by which we have come to be known to others and to ourselves.[11]

The mirror by which the United States had defined itself was gone. The unraveling of the Soviet system in Eastern Europe deepened the identity crisis because it threatened to unravel Washington's role in Western Europe as well. Throughout the Cold War, America's European role demanded the presence of a threatening East; the Iron Curtain, now gone, had symbolized the presence of that danger. In the post–Cold War days the United States faced the task of discovering a new identity.

Amid such profound challenges to its economic and military leadership, Washington faced the critical decision whether to perpetuate its Cold War role, based on power and the readiness to use it, or to reexamine its interests in a changing world and accept the traditional workings of the international system and the historic limitations that it imposed. President Bush reminded a Texas audience on May 12, 1989, that containment had succeeded. "Now it is time," he added, "to move beyond containment, to a new policy for the 1990s, one that recognizes the full scope of change around the world, and in the Soviet Union itself."[12] William Colby, former CIA director, observed in February 1990, "This is the end of an era of threat and danger and the time for building a new world." For Robert McNamara the country faced "the greatest opportunity in forty years to shift from Cold War thinking to a new vision of the world, a post–Cold War vision."[13] Economist Peter Drucker noted that the disintegration of the Cold War required total change in American foreign policy and desertion of the assumptions on which it had rested.

Senator Daniel Patrick Moynihan of New York, in the June 28, 1990, issue of *The New York Review of Books*, reflected on the ending of the Cold War. "How do we demobilize?" he asked. "How do we move from the national security state to a government that merely asks what are our interests abroad and our needs at home, and calmly and openly pursues them?" For many American analysts, the United States had no choice but to judge its interests carefully, avoid involvements in external affairs that did not touch its interests directly, seek accommodation with nations large and small as it found them, and address forthrightly its debilitating and inescapable challenges at home.

Much in the country's Cold War experience lent credence to a reduced role in international affairs. Despite its extensive power and international commitments, the United States, throughout the Cold War, had faced unassailable barriers to its will in the sovereignty of nations. During the Reagan years, when American power was almost beyond challenge, there was little in the international realm that it could control. Even as the United States expended trillions in defending Europe, the European states played an ever-diminishing and increasingly independent role in international affairs, seldom supporting the United States on issues that mattered to it. Emerging from years of the greatest prosperity in history, Europe again seemed to possess the strength and capability to create a self-contained equilibrium that would permit the United States to escape its long commitment to Europe's peace and stability. Both the United States and the Soviet Union had found their competitive interventions in the Third World inhibited, frustrating, and unprofitable. The so-called Reagan Doctrine, in its program of supporting Third World democracies and anti-Communist regimes, proved to be ephemeral and politically unsustainable. Without perceptible threats to national security or external challenges that the United States alone could resolve, the events of 1990 seemed to offer the occasion for a thorough reevaluation of the U.S. role in world affairs.

Still, the end of the Cold War raised critical and pervading issues regarding the disposal of the huge Cold War establishment (suddenly without a mission), the nature and purposes of U.S. policy in the new post–Cold War world, the size and shape of the defense structure, and the role of the intelligence agencies—all created to defend the world against Soviet aggression. Clearly, the country's powerful Cold War legacies were hard to relinquish, especially its newfound and often exhilarating role as a superpower, now the only remaining super-power, and the ingrained sense of obligation, one amplified by the long Cold War experience, that reflected its wealth, its power, and its self-assigned mission to serve the cause of peace, freedom, and humanity. What underwrote the widespread conviction that the United States must continue to play a leading role in world affairs was the supposition, held by many, that U.S. power, not the flaws in the Communist system, had brought the Soviet Union to its knees. That same power, still largely unused, added to the toughness required to employ it, could now domi-nate a unipolar world, assuring its future peace and security against what-ever dangers and challenges might arise. Harvard's Joseph S. Nye, Jr., observed that the United States was far too rich and powerful to enjoy a free ride in the international system. It was essential that it exercise an influence in world politics commensurate with its size and stake in the spread of open societies. But he warned against any American hegemonic mission to lead the world. "Leadership is not hegemony," he wrote. "It means taking responsibility for one's long-term political and economic interests."[14]

For much of the country's foreign policy elite, nothing in the passing of the Cold War seemed to dictate a careful, precise reexamination of the nation's role as world leader and guarantor of international security. Even as the Berlin Wall was being dismantled in the late autumn of 1989, observers noted that Washington officials approached the post–Cold War challenges in accordance with principles that had guided U.S. policy throughout the Cold War. The country's recommitment to international leadership demanded the perpetuation of large military appropriations, renewed commitments to Cold War alliances, poten-tially heavy involvements abroad, and renewal of the CIA—now rendered more important than ever by the presence of international terrorism and the intense competition among the world's economic powers. As early as October 1989, in the *Atlantic Monthly*, Harvard's Stanley Hoffmann criticized members of the American foreign policy establishment for their refusal to desert the precepts of containment, clinging, he complained, to obsolete strategies and notions of global responsibility. "And yet," he wrote, "this is the moment coolly to reevaluate American interests in the world. For many years our percep-tions (often mistaken) of the Soviets drove our policy and defined, or distorted, our interests." Clearly, the time had come for America to rethink anew its position on the world stage.

Notes

PREFACE

1. Norman A. Graebner, *A Twentieth Century Odyssey: Memoir of a Life in Academe* (Claremont, CA: Regina Books, 2002), 151.

2. See Joseph M. Siracusa, "The 'New' Cold War History and the Origins of the Cold War," *Australian Journal of Politics and History* 47 (2000), 149.

3. The authors of this study have briefly touched on the significance of the end of the Cold War in Norman A. Graebner, Richard Dean Burns, and Joseph M. Siracusa, *Reagan, Bush, Gorbachev: Revisiting the End of the Cold War* (Westport, CT: Praeger Security International, 2008).

4. Scott Lucas and Kaseten Mistry, "Illusions of Coherence: George F. Kennan, U.S. Strategy and Political Warfare in the Early Cold War, 1946–1950," *Diplomatic History* 33, 1 (2009): 63.

INTRODUCTION

1. For examples of early predictions of Soviet expansionism, with the concomitant danger of war, see Joseph C. Grew, *Turbulent Era: A Diplomatic Record of Forty Years, 1904–1945*, ed. Walter Johnson (Boston: Houghton Mifflin, 1952), II: 1446; Mark Ethridge's memorandum on Bulgaria and Rumania, Dec. 7, 1945, *Foreign Relations of the United States, Diplomatic Papers* (hereafter *FRUS*), 1945; V (Washington, DC: U.S. G.P.O., 1967), 637; John D. Hickerson to James Byrnes, Dec. 10, 1945; ibid., IV (Washington, 1968), 407; Joint Chiefs of Staff quoted in Melvyn P. Leffler, *A Preponderance of Power* (Stanford, CA: Stanford University Press, 1992), 50.

2. Joseph and Stewart Alsop, "Tragedy of Liberalism," *Life* 20 (May 20, 1946): 69.

3. Edwin G. Wilson to Byrnes, Mar. 18, 1946, *FRUS, 1946: VII* (Washington, DC: G.P.O., 1969), 818–819; George Lewis Jones to Loy Henderson, Aug. 9, 1946, ibid., 830; Acheson to Byrnes, Aug. 15, 1946, ibid., 840–841.

4. As quoted in Michael S. Sherry, *In the Shadow of War: The United States since the 1930s* (New Haven: Yale University Press, 1995), 117; Lippmann quote in Stanley Meisler, "Soviet Union's End Deprives Americans of a Top Attraction," *Los Angeles Times*, Jan. 4, 1992.

5. For Kennan's Long Telegram of Feb. 22, 1946, see George F. Kennan, *Memoirs: 1925–1950* (Boston: Little, Brown, 1967), 547–559.

6. On the fears of Matthews and other U.S. officials see John Lewis Gaddis, *The United States and the Origins of the Cold War, 1941–1947* (New York: Columbia University Press, 1972), 319; John Foster Dulles, "Thoughts on Soviet Foreign Policy and What to Do About It,"*Life* 20 (June 3, 1946): 113–126; (June 10, 1946): 119–120 (quotation, 119); William C. Bullitt, *The Great Globe Itself: A Preface to World Affairs* (New York: Scribner's Sons, 1946), 100–102, 175.

7. The Clifford-Elsey Report, "American Relations with the Soviet Union," in Arthur Krock, *Memoirs: Sixty Years on the Firing Line* (New York: Funk & Wagnalls, 1968), 427, 431.

8. Harry S. Truman's message to Congress, Mar. 12, 1947, *Department of State Bulletin* 16 (Mar. 23, 1947): 536.

9. Howard Jones, *"A New Kind of War": America's Global Strategy and the Truman Doctrine in Greece* (New York: Oxford University Press, 1989), 191–226.

10. For the negotiations leading to the establishment of the Federal Republic of Germany, Mar.–Apr. 1949, see *FRUS, 1949: III* (Washington, DC: G.P.O., 1974), 156–177; Acheson to George W. Perkins, Oct. 13, 1949, ibid., IV (Washington, DC: G.P.O., 1975), 469–470.

11. Norman A. Graebner, "The United States and NATO: Ends Without Means," in Graebner, *America as a World Power: A Realist Appraisal from Wilson to Reagan* (Wilmington, DE: Scholarly Resources, 1984): 1949–1950.

12. For America's economic predominance see Harold J. Laski, "America–1947," *The Nation* 165 (Dec. 13, 1947): 641; Robert Payne quoted in *Newsweek* (Jan. 11, 1993): 36; Haynes Johnson, "The War that Remade America," the *Washington Post National Weekly Edition*, Aug. 14–20, 1995, 9.

13. For a critical evaluation of the Soviet system and the postwar attitudes of Soviet citizens toward it, see Nina Tumarkin, "The Great Patriotic War as Myth and Memory," *The Atlantic Monthly* 267, June 1991: 26–44. Edward Crankshaw discusses the failure of the Soviet system in "Russia's Power: Not Ideas but Force," the *New York Times Magazine*, June 3, 1951, 29–30.

14. Report by the National Security Council on the Position of the United States with Respect to Soviet-Directed World Communism (NSC 7), Mar. 30, 1948, *FRUS, 1948: I*, Pt. 2 (Washington, DC: G.P.O., 1976), 546.

15. U.S. Objectives with Respect to the USSR to Counter Soviet Threats to U.S. Security (NSC 20/4, in Thomas H. Etzold and John Lewis Gaddis, eds., *Containment: Documents on American Policy and Strategy, 1945–1950* (New York: Columbia University Press, 1978), 204.

16. NSC 68: United States Objectives and Programs for National Security, Apr. 14, 1950, in Joseph M. Siracusa, *Into the Dark House: American Diplomacy and the Ideological Origins of the Cold War* (Claremont, CA: Regina Books, 1998), 213.

17. NSC 20/4, Etzold and Gaddis, *Containment*, 209–210.

18. NSC 68, Siracusa, *Into the Dark House*, 217, 227.

19. Cabot to W. Walton Butterworth, Feb. 6, 1948, *FRUS*, 1948: VIII (Washington, DC: G.P.O., 1973), 468.

20. Memorandum prepared by the research division of the Department of State, enclosed with Acting Secretary of State to Certain Diplomatic and Consular Offices, Oct. 13, 1948, ibid., I, Pt. 2, p. 643.

21. Letter of Transmittal, July 30, 1949, *United States Relations with China, With Special Reference to the Period 1944–1949* (Washington, DC: G.P.O. 1949), xvi, xvii.

22. Stanton to Secretary of State, June 14, 1949, *FRUS*, 1949: VII (Washington, DC: G.P.O., 1975), 50–51, italics added.

23. The State Department's Policy Planning Staff concluded as early as September 1948 that China's future rested with the Chinese. See U.S. Policy Toward China (PPS 39), Sept. 7, 1948, *FRUS* , 1948: VIII 146–155.

24. Truman's Statement on the Situation in Korea, June 27, 1950, *Public Papers of the Presidents of the United States (hereafter PPP); Harry S. Truman, 1950* (Washington, DC: G.P.O., 1965), 492.

25. Louis W. Koenig, ed. *The Truman Administration, Its Principles and Practice* (New York: New York University Press, 1956), 286; Goran Rystad, *Prisoners of the Past? The Munich Syndrome and Makers of American Foreign Policy in the Cold War Era* (Lund, Sweden: CWK Gleerup, 1982), 35.

26. Aaron Singer, ed., *Campaign Speeches of American Presidential Candidates, 1928–1972* (New York: Ungar, 1976), 245.

27. Acheson's speech in Cleveland, Nov. 29, 1950, *Department of State Bulletin* 23 (Dec. 18, 1950): 964; Truman's statement to the press, Nov. 30, 1950, ibid., 23 (Dec. 11, 1950): 925–926.

28. For further assumptions of Soviet dominance of China see Minutes, Truman-Attlee meeting, Dec. 7, 1950, *FRUS*, 1950: VII, 1456; Norman A. Graebner, *Cold War Diplomacy: American Foreign Policy, 1945–1975* (New York: D. Van Nostrand, 1977), 52.

29. Annual Message on the State of the Union, Jan. 8, 1951, *PPP: Harry S. Truman, 1951* (Washington, DC: G.P.O., 1965), 7.

30. Dulles's address before the China Institute of New York, May 18, 1951, *Department of State Bulletin* 24 (May 28, 1951), 844.

31. Eisenhower's News Conference, Apr. 7, 1954, *PPP: Dwight D. Eisenhower, 1954* (Washington, DC: G.P.O., 1960), 383.

32. See McArthur's speech to Congress, Apr. 4, 1954, *Reminiscences* (Greenwich, CN: Fawcett Publications, 1965), 400.

33. Kennedy quoted in Rystsad, *Prisoners of the Past?* 40.

34. Eisenhower's speech at Gettysburg College, Apr. 4, 1959, *Department of State Bulletin* 40 (Apr. 27, 1959), 580–581.

35. Rusk's address to the American Society of International Law, Apr. 13, 1964, ibid., 52, May 10, 1965, 699.

36. Thomas J. Dodd's speech in the Senate, Feb. 23, 1965, *Congressional Record*, 89th Cong., 1st Sess. (Vol. III, Part 3), 3350.

37. *Department of Defense, United States-Vietnam Relations, 1945–1967* (Washington, DC: G.P.O., 1971), II, 664.

38. Siracusa, *Into the Dark House*, x–xi.

CHAPTER 1

1. For the view that the democracies could not win an unsullied victory see George F. Kennan, *American Diplomacy* (Chicago, 1951), 74–85.

2. Atlantic Charter, Aug. 12, 1941, *Foreign Relations of the United States (hereafter FRUS)*, Diplomatic Papers, 1941, I (Washington, 1958), 368. The full document is found in Joseph M. Siracusa, ed., *The American Diplomatic Revolution: A Documentary History of the Cold War* (New York, 1976). See also Theodore A. Wilson, *The First Summit: Roosevelt and Churchill at Placentia Bay 1941* (1969); Robert Dallek, *Franklin D. Roosevelt and American Foreign Policy, 1932–1945* (New York, 1979), 281–285; Winston S. Churchill, *The Second World War, II: The Grand Alliance* (Boston, 1950), 433–444; James MacGregor Burns, *The Soldier of Freedom* (New York, 1970), 126–131.

3. Hull to John Winant, Dec. 5, 1941, *FRUS*, 1941: I, 194–195. For Sumner Welles's telling criticism of postponement, see Sumner Welles, *Seven Decisions that Shaped History* (New York, 1950), 123–145.

4. Hull's radio address, July 23, 1942, *The Department of State Bulletin*, 7 (July 25, 1942), 639; Roosevelt's news conference at Casablanca, Jan. 24, 1943, Norman A. Graebner, ed., *Ideas and Diplomacy: Readings in the Intellectual Tradition of American Foreign Policy* (New York, 1964), 656–657; Gaddis Smith, *American Diplomacy During the Second World War, 1941–1945* (New York, 1965), 53–56. For Roosevelt's address to Congress, Jan. 7, 1943, see Louis J. Halle, "Our War Aims Were Wrong," the *New York Times Magazine*, Aug. 22, 1965, 13. For Churchill's reaction see John L. Chase, "Unconditional Surrender Reconsidered," *Political Science Quarterly*, 70 (June 1955), 258–279; Herbert Feis, *Churchill, Roosevelt, Stalin: The War They Waged and the Peace They Sought* (Princeton, 1957), 108–111.

5. *Foreign Relations of the United States: The Conferences at Washington, 1941–1942, and Casablanca, 1943* (Washington, 1968), 834–835. Unconditional surrender became a subject of controversy. Churchill accepted it in the interest of Allied unity, convinced that the Allies had no choice but to destroy German power. See Winston S. Churchill, *The Second World War, IV: The Hinge of Fate* (Boston, 1950), 684–688. Raymond G. O'Connor upheld unconditional surrender as the only approach to victory over Germany that would have held the alliance together. See O'Connor, *Diplomacy for Victory: FDR and Unconditional Surrender* (New York, 1971), 100–104. For assaults on the doctrine as responsible, if not for the prolongation of the war, at least for the destruction of the balance of power, see Hanson W. Baldwin, *Great Mistakes of the War* (New York, 1950); Chester Wilmot, *The Struggle for Europe* (New York, 1952); Hans Rothfels, *The German Opposition to Hitler*

An Appraisal, trans. Lawrence Wilson (Chicago, 1962); and especially Anne Armstrong, *Unconditional Surrender: The Impact of the Casablanca Policy Upon World War II* (New Brunswick, NJ, 1961).

6. On the formation of the alliance see Churchill, *The Grand Alliance*, 377–614; Edward M. Bennett, *Franklin D. Roosevelt & the Search for Victory: American-Soviet Relations, 1939–1945* (Wilmington, 1990), 39–50; Feis, *Churchill, Roosevelt, Stalin*; Robin Edmonds, *The Big Three: Churchill, Roosevelt, and Stalin in Peace & War* (New York, 1991), 253–266; David Reynolds, ed., *The Origins of the Cold War in Europe: International Perspectives* (New Haven, 1994); John Charmley, *Churchill's Grand Alliance* (London, 1995); and Robert Beitzell, *The Uneasy Alliance: America, Britain, and Russia, 1941–1943* (New York, 1972), 3–27.

7. For Churchill's conversations with John R. Colville on his motivations in offering aid to Moscow see Winston S. Churchill, *The Second World War: The Grand Alliance* (Boston, 1950), 370, 380–381; Hopkins's observations appear in Robert E. Sherwood, *Roosevelt and Hopkins: An Intimate History* (New York, 1948), 309–311.

8. Maisky's address of September 24, 1941, in Leland M. Goodrich, ed., *Documents in American Foreign Relations*, Vol. IV, 1941–1942 (Boston, 1942), 214–216; *FRUS*, 1941: I, 378; Vojtech Mastny, *Russia's Road to the Cold War* (New York, 1979), 40–42. For the Declaration's failure to recognize the position of the U.S.S.R. in the Grand Alliance as well as its known territorial objectives see Burns, *Soldier of Freedom*, 183–187.

9. Harley A. Notter, *Postwar Foreign Policy Preparation, 1939–1945* (Washington, 1950); Lynn Etheridge Davis, *The Cold War Begins: Soviet-American Conflict over Eastern Europe* (Princeton, NJ, 1974), 70–88. Johns Hopkins President Isaiah Bowman, a member of the planning group, warned his colleagues from time to time that the United States would have no influence in the postwar Eastern Europe settlement and had no choice but to accept the reality of Soviet postwar dominance in the region. See ibid., 80–81, 98, 134–135.

10. Anthony Eden, *The Reckoning* (Boston, 1965), 335–343.

11. Churchill to Lord Privy Seal, Dec. 20, 1941, Winston S. Churchill, *The Grand Alliance* (Boston, 1950), 630.

12. Churchill to Eden, Jan. 8, 1942, ibid., 695.

13. Churchill to Roosevelt, Mar. 7, 1942, *The Hinge of Fate* (Boston, 1950), 327.

14. Cordell Hull, *Memoirs* (New York, 1948), II, 1168.

15. Ibid., 1172.

16. Churchill to Roosevelt, May 27, 1942, Churchill, *The Hinge of Fate*, 339; Hull, *Memoirs* 1173–1174; Eden, *The Reckoning*, 381–382.

17. Hull, *Memoirs*, II, 1179–1180.

18. See Michael D. Pearlman, *War-making and American Democracy: The Struggle over Military Strategy, 1700 to the Present* (Lawrence, Kansas, 1999), 229.

19. See, for example, Roosevelt to Stalin, Dec. 28, 1942, Ministry of Foreign Affairs of the U.S.S.R., *Stalin's Correspondence with Roosevelt and Truman, 1941–1945* (New York, 1965), 45–46; Roosevelt to Stalin, Feb. 5, 1943; ibid., 53; Stalin to Roosevelt, Feb. 6, 1943; ibid., 54; Roosevelt to Stalin, Feb. 23, 1943,

ibid., 57–58; press clipping for Feb. 1944, President's Secretary's File (PSF): Russia, Box 68, Franklin D. Roosevelt Library, Hyde Park. These exchanges expressed both cordiality and mutual confidence that the combined U.S.-Soviet military successes assured the final and total defeat of the common enemy.

20. On the mistreatment of the Poles see George F. Kennan, *Memoirs: 1925–1950* (Boston, 1967), 199–200; Louis J. Halle, *The Cold War as History* (New York, 1967), 59–60. For Poland's policy toward the U.S.S.R. see Edward J. Rozek, *Allied Wartime Diplomacy: A Pattern in Poland* (New York, 1958), 56; R. Umiastowski, *Poland, Russia, and Great Britain, 1941–1945: A Study of the Evidence* (London, 1946), 92–93; Stanislaw Mikolajczyk, *The Pattern of Soviet Domination* (London, 1948); M. K. Dziewanowski, *The Communist Party of Poland: An Outline of History* (Cambridge, Mass., 1959); W. W. Kulski, "The Lost Opportunity for Russian-Polish Friendship," *Foreign Affairs*, 25 (1946–1947), 676.

21. Churchill, *The Grand Alliance*, 391–392; Kennan, *Memoirs: 1925–1950*, 201.

22. Anthony Eden, *The Memoirs of Anthony Eden: The Reckoning* (Boston, 1965), 335; Ambassador Bogomolov to Count Raczynski, Feb. 7, 1943, communicated in Jan Ciechanowski to Sumner Welles, Feb. 19, 1943, PSF: Poland, FDRL.

23. Standley to Hull, Mar. 9, 1943, 760C.61/1007 T1244, National Archives; Memorandum on the Urgency of British and American Reaction to USSR Territorial Demands, Mar. 25, 1943, PSF: Poland, FDRL. Sikorski was equally adamant when he visited Moscow in December 1941, refusing to discuss the question of Poland's postwar boundaries with Stalin. See Jan Ciechanowski, *Defeat in Victory* (New York, 1947), 78; Rozek, *Allied Wartime Diplomacy: A Pattern in Poland*, 82–94.

24. Churchill, *The Grand Alliance*, 392–393.

25. For example, U.S. Ambassador to Poland, A. J. Drexel Biddle, Jr., reported that a London audience's response to Polish Prime Minister Wladyslaw Sikorski's appeal for support on Jan. 28, 1943, "bore signs of a steadied attempt to reveal no sense of emotion or interest; their eyes were rigidly fixed either on the tips of their shoes or on the floor directly in front of them." See Biddle's report to Hull, Feb. 15, 1943, PSF: Poland, FDRL.

26. Standley to Hull, Mar. 9, 1943, U.S. Department of State Files, Record Group 59, Decimal File 760C.61/1007, National Archives, Washington, DC (Hereafter cited as DSF); Memorandum of conversation between Durbrow and Davies, Feb. 3, 1943, DSF 711.61/2-343, National Archives; Memorandum on Polish-Soviet Relations, Mar. 22, 1943, PSF: Poland, FDRL.

27. Memorandum of conversation, Mar. 15, 1943, Records of Harley A. Notter 1939–1945, Box 19, National Archives; Anthony Eden, *The Memoirs of Anthony Eden: The Reckoning* (Boston, 1965), 432.

28. Harry Hopkins memorandum of Roosevelt-Eden conversation, Mar. 15, 1943, *FRUS*, 1943: III (Washington, 19), 13–18; Warren F. Kimball, *The Juggler: Franklin Roosevelt as Wartime Statesman* (Princeton, NJ, 1991); Robert E. Sherwood, *Roosevelt and Hopkins: An Intimate History* (New York, 1948), 709–710; Eden, *The Reckoning*, 432; Feis, *Churchill, Roosevelt, Stalin: The War They Waged and the Peace They Sought* 192. On the Polish temperament see Halle, *The Cold War as History*, 55–59. Shortly after Eden's departure Sikorski pleaded with Roosevelt not to

abandon Poland. Roosevelt assured him that he was seeking a course of action that would be most helpful. Roosevelt to Sikorski, Apr. 6, 1943, PSF: Poland, FDRL.

29. Churchill to Stalin, Apr. 24, 1943, DSF 760.61/2032, National Archives; Halle, *The Cold War as History*, 61–62.

30. Stalin to Roosevelt, Apr. 21, 1943, *Stalin's Correspondence with Roosevelt and Truman*, 60–61; Stalin to Churchill, Apr. 25, 1943, DSF 760C.61/2033; William H. Standley to Hull, Apr. 26, 1943, DSF 760C.61/1035; Sikorski to Roosevelt, May 4, 1943, PSF: Poland, FDRL; Biddle to Hull, June 3, 1943, DSF 760C.61/ 2038, National Archives. Although Soviet scholars agreed that the Polish officers died in 1940 before the Germans arrived, it was not until October 1992 that the Russian government revealed documents from the secret archives of the Communist Party showing that Stalin's Politburo, meeting on Mar. 5, 1940, directly ordered the execution ("the supreme punishment") of more than 25,000 Poles, including clergymen, factory owners, policemen and the thousands of Polish Army officers. *International Herald Tribune*, Oct. 1992, 8.

31. Roosevelt to Churchill, June 9, 1943, DSF 760C.61/2056.

32. OSS Report, No. 132, on the Polish press in the United States, DSF 760C.61/2058, National Archives.

33. Stalin to Roosevelt, Apr. 29, 1943, *Stalin's Correspondence with Roosevelt and Truman*, 62; Stalin to Churchill, enclosed in Eden to British Embassy in Washington, May 7, 1943, DSF 760C.61/2035; Special Report IDS, No. 260, May 17, 1943, DSF 760C.61/2057, National Archives.

34. Joseph Goebbels, *The Goebbels Diaries, 1942–1943*, ed. and trans. Louis P. Lochner (Garden City, N.Y., 1948), 259, 272, 318, 461.

35. See Edmund Stillman, "'Containment' Has Won, But . . . ," the *New York Times Magazine* May 28, 1967, 23.

36. For the Quadrant Conference see *FRUS: The Conferences at Washington and Quebec, 1943* (Washington, 1970), 849–967; Beitzell, *The Uneasy Alliance*, 111–117; Arthur Bryant, *A History of the War Years Based on the Diaries of Field Marshal Lord Alanbrooke, Chief of the Imperial General Staff, I: The Turn of the Tide* (Garden City, N.Y., 1957), 577–581.

37. Stalin to Roosevelt, Aug. 22, 1943, U.S.S.R. Ministry of Foreign Affairs, *Correspondence Between the Chairman of the Council of Ministers of the U.S.S.R. and the Presidents of the U.S.A. and the Prime Ministers of Great Britain During the Great Patriotic War of 1941–1945* (2 vols., Moscow, 1957), II, 84; Roberto G. Rabel, *Between East and West: Trieste, the United States, and the Cold War, 1941–1954* (Durham, N.C., 1988), 26.

38. Gerhard L. Weinberg, *A World at Arms: A Global History of World War II* (New York, 1994), 462–463, 602–607; Sherwood, *Roosevelt and Hopkins*, 748. Churchill expressed a similar judgment of the U.S.S.R. in a letter to Field Marshal Jan Smuts, Sept. 5, 1943, Churchill, *The Second World War, V: Closing the Ring* (Boston, 1951), 129.

39. Robert I. Gannon, *The Cardinal Spellman Story* (Garden City, N.Y., 1962), 223–224.

40. On the formation of the Anglo-American alliance see Jean Laloy, *Yalta: Yesterday, Today, and Tomorrow* (New York, 1988), 15. For Churchill's efforts to

diminish the Soviet role in the alliance see Henry Butterfield Ryan, *The Vision of Anglo-America: The US-UK Alliance and the Emerging Cold War, 1943–1946* (Cambridge, 1987), 39–53; Robert M. Hathaway, *Ambiguous Partnership: Britain and America, 1944–1947* (New York, 1981), 36–44; D. Cameron Watt, *Succeeding John Bull: America in Britain's Place, 1900–1975* (Cambridge, 1984), 103. William Hardy McNeill labeled the U.S.S.R. as "half an ally." See McNeill, *America, Britain, and Russia, 1941–1946* (London, 1953). Churchill's distrust of the U.S.S.R. began with the Soviet demands for the ethnic border of Poland without the sanction of a general peace agreement. See Laloy, *Yalta*, 17.

41. Bernard Brodie, *War and Politics* (New York, 1973), 369.

42. John Lewis Gaddis, *The United States and the Origins of the Cold War, 1941–1947* (New York, 1972), 82–83; John R. Deane, *The Strange Alliance: The Story of Our Efforts at Wartime Cooperation with Russia* (New York, 1947), 89–91, 98–99; George C. Herring, "Lend-Lease to Russia and the Origins of the Cold War, 1944–1945," *The Journal of American History* 66 (June 1969), 94–97; Herring, *Aid to Russia, 1941–1946: Strategy, Diplomacy, the Origins of the Cold War* (New York, 1973); Robert Huhn Jones, *The Roads to Russia: United States Lend-Lease to the Soviet Union* (Norman, Okla., 1969).

43. Standley to Roosevelt, May 3, 1943, *FRUS*, 1943, British Commonwealth, 521; Randall Bennett Woods, *A Changing of the Guard: Anglo-American Relations, 1941–1946* (Chapel Hill, 1990), 5–7, 107; Bruce Kuklick, *American Policy and the Division of Germany: The Clash with Russia over Reparations* (Ithaca, N.Y., 1972), 96–98; William H. Standley and Arthur A. Ageton, *Admiral Ambassador to Russia* (Chicago, 1955), 341; Deane, *Strange Alliance*, 98–99.

44. Warren F. Kimball, "Lend-Lease and the Open Door: The Temptation of British Opulence, 1937–1942," *Political Science Quarterly*, 86 (1971), 232–259; David Reynolds, *The Creation of the Anglo-American Alliance, 1937–1941: A Study in Competitive Co-operation* (London, 1981), 274.

45. Cordell Hull, *The Memoirs of Cordell Hull* (New York, 1948), II, 1307; Averell Harriman to Hull, Nov. 5, 1943, *FRUS*, 1943: I (Washington, 1963), 699; W. Averell Harriman and Elie Abel, *Special Envoy to Churchill and Stalin, 1941–1946* (New York, 1975), 236; Thomas T. Hammond, ed., *Witnesses to the Origins of the Cold War*, 284–285; Beitzell, *The Uneasy Alliance*, 141, 170–245. Hull's address to Congress, Nov. 18, 1943, Department of State *Bulletin*, 9 (Nov. 20, 1943), 343.

46. See Eduard Benes, *Memoirs of Dr. Eduard Benes* (Boston, 1954), 1954; Special Report IDS, No. 254, May 15, 1943, DSF 760C.61/2057.

47. Cordell Hull, *The Memoirs of Cordell Hull* (New York, 1948), II, 1271, 1315; Hull to Roosevelt, Nov. 23, 1943, PSF: Poland, FDRL. Unfortunately the Soviets already had plans to incorporate the Union of Polish Patriots, supported by the Communist Polish Workers Party, into the London Polish government. See Rozek, 144; Dziewanowski, 163.

48. John Charmley criticizes Churchill for relying too heavily on Roosevelt and permitting the president to undermine Britain's historic position. Unfortunately, Churchill, dealing from weakness, made concessions to both the United States and the U.S.S.R., out of necessity, to assure at least a British victory over Germany and some role for Britain in the postwar world. See Charmley, *Churchill,*

the End of Glory: A Political Biography (New York, 1993). For varied judgments of Churchill's wartime defense of British interests see Geoffrey Wheatcroft, "The Savior of His Country," the *Atlantic Monthly*, (Feb. 1994), 116–123.

49. John Ehrman, *Grand Strategy, Vol. V: Aug. 1943–September 1944* (London, 1956), 166–181; Winston S. Churchill, *The Second World War, V: Closing the Ring* (Boston, 1951), 344–358, 366–373, 382–384; Beitzell, *The Uneasy Alliance*, 332–336; Burns, *Soldier of Freedom*, 407–411; Edmonds, *The Big Three*, 350–356; Richard M. Leighton, "OVERLORD versus the Mediterranean at the Cairo-Teheran Conferences," Kent Roberts Greenfield, ed., *Command Decisions* (Washington, 1990), 271–278

50. Isaac Deutscher, *Stalin: A Political Biography* (New York, 1949), 508; John A. Lukacs, *The Great Powers and Eastern Europe* (New York, 1953), 523–524, 556; J. F. C. Fuller, *The Second World War, 1939–1945* (New York, 1949), 305–313, 324–325. Chester Wilmot develops the same theme in *The Struggle for Europe*.

51. *FRUS: Conferences at Cairo and Teheran*, 513; Churchill, *The Hinge of Fate*, 689–691; Bennett, *Franklin D. Roosevelt and the Search for Victory*, 125; John P. Glennon, " 'This Time Germany Is a Defeated Nation': The Doctrine of Unconditional Surrender and Some Unsuccessful Attempts to Alter It, 1943–1944," Gerald N. Grob, ed., *Statesmen and Statecraft in the Modern World: Essays in Honor of Dwight E. Lee and H. Donaldson Jordon* (Barre, Mass., 1967).

52. Bohlen's notes of Roosevelt-Stalin conversation, Dec. 1, 1943, *Foreign Relations of the United States: Conferences at Cairo and Teheran, 1943* (Washington, 1961), 594–595; Churchill, *Closing the Ring*, 407.

53. Keith Sainsbury, *The Turning Point: Roosevelt, Stalin, Churchill, and Chiang Kai-Shek, 1943: The Moscow, Cairo, and Teheran Conferences* (New York, 1985), 322; American Embassy, Moscow, to Hull, Dec. 14, 1943, PSF Russia, Box 68, FDRL; Samuel I. Rosenman, ed., *The Public Papers and Addresses of Franklin D. Roosevelt, 1943* (Washington, 1950), XIII, 32, 135–136.

54. William C. Bullitt, "How We Won the War and Lost the Peace," *Life 25* (Aug. 30, 1948), 941.

CHAPTER 2

1. On the postponement of Mikolajczyk's visit to Washington see Churchill to Roosevelt, Dec. 27, 1943, Map Room, Box 12, FDRL; Roosevelt to Mikolajczyk, Dec. 28, 1943, ibid.; Roosevelt to Churchill, Dec. 28, 1943, ibid.

2. Biddle to Roosevelt, Oct. 18, 1943, PSF: Biddle, Box 34; Durbrow to Matthews, Dunn, and Hull, Dec. 27, 1943, 860C.00/12-2743, National Archives; Churchill to Roosevelt, Dec. 27, 1943, Map Room, Box l2, FDRL; Churchill to Stalin, Jan. 28, 1944, Francis L. Loewenheim, Harold D. Langley, and Manfred Jonas, eds., *Roosevelt and Churchill: Their Secret Wartime Correspondence* (New York, 1975), 420–421; Mikolajczyk's broadcast in Rudolf E. Schoenfeld to Hull, Jan. 21, 1944, 780C.61/2201, National Archives.

3. On the State Department's response to Roosevelt's decision to avoid Ciechanowski, Bohlen to Stettinius, Feb. 17, 1944, 760C.61/2232, T1244-2, National Archives; Memorandum of conversation between James Dunn and

Jan Ciechanowski, Jan. 13, 1944; Edward R. Stettinius Papers, Series ll, Box 725, Alderman Library, University of Virginia. For the acceptability of a Polish regime without its anti-Soviet elements see Harriman to Hull, Jan. 22, 1944, 760C.61/2188, National Archives; Roosevelt's exchange with Stalin in Roosevelt to Stalin, Feb. 11, 1944, *Stalin's Correspondence* 119–120; Stalin to Roosevelt, Feb. 16, 1944, ibid., 120–121; Woodward, *British Foreign Policy*, III, 178.

4. Roosevelt to Ciechanowski, Feb. 18, 1944, Stettinius Papers, Series 11, Box 725; Hull to Stettinius, Feb. 18, 1944, Stettinius Papers, Series 4, Box 218; Hull's report on Ciechanowski's desire to see the president, Feb. 19, 1944, Stettinius Papers, Series 4, Box 216, Alderman Library.

5. Mikolajczyk to Roosevelt, Mar. 18, 1944, PSF: Poland, Box 66, FDRL; Churchill to Roosevelt, Feb. 20, 1944, Loewenheim, Langley, and Jonas, *Roosevelt and Churchill*, 441–443.

6. On the invitation of Mikolajczyk to visit Washington see Churchill to Roosevelt, Mar. 4, 1944, Warren F. Kimball, ed., *Churchill and Roosevelt* (Princeton, 1974), III, 21; Churchill to Roosevelt, Apr. 1, 1944, ibid., 69; Memorandum for the president, May 16, 1944, PSF: Poland, Box 66, FDRL; Memorandum of conversation between Stettinius and Gromyko, June 6, 1944, Stettinius Papers, Series ll, Box 725, Alderman Library; Harriman to Roosevelt, June 7, 1944, PSF: Russia, Box 68, FDRL.

7. For this exchange see Stanislaw Mikolajczyk, *The Pattern of Soviet Domination* (London, 1948), 65–66; Hull, *Memoirs*, II, 1444–1445. Roosevelt promised Mikolajczyk a free Poland in Roosevelt to Mikolajczyk, Apr. 26, 1944, PPF 78, FDRL.

8. Memorandum of conversation on the Polish situation, June 13, 1944, Stettinius Papers, Series ll, Box 725. Mikolajczyk raised the issue of moral support with Under Secretary Sumner Welles as well. See Memorandum for the president, June 14, 1944, DSF 860C.002/6-1444, National Archives. At the airport Stettinius delivered a letter from Roosevelt that lauded Polish valor and predicted that the forces of liberation would "march to certain victory and the establishment of a peace based upon the principles of freedom, democracy, mutual understanding, and security for all liberty-loving people." Hull to Roosevelt, June 13, 1944, President's Personal File (PPF) 78, FDRL. Roosevelt reported Mikolajczyk's visit to Stalin in Roosevelt to Stalin, June 19, 1944, *Stalin's Correspondence.* 146–147.

9. Eden, *The Reckoning*, 539–540.

10. Churchill to Roosevelt, July 25, 1944, Loewenheim, Langley, and Jonas, *Roosevelt and Churchill*, 554; Churchill to Roosevelt, Feb. 5, 1944, ibid., 428; Roosevelt to Churchill, Feb. 7, 1944, ibid., 430; Churchill to Roosevelt, Feb. 20, 1944, ibid., 442–443; Churchill to Roosevelt, Mar. 4, 1944, ibid., 461; Churchill to Roosevelt, Mar. 21, 1944, Kimball, *Churchill and Roosevelt*, III, 61; for Washington's lack of concern for any specific Polish boundary or Polish government see Policy for Liberated Poland, June 20, 1944, PWC-216 (CAC 220), T1222-3, Harley Notter Papers, National Archives.

11. Eden, *The Reckoning*, 541; Stalin to Churchill, July 23, 1944, *Stalin's Correspondence*, 152; Churchill to Roosevelt, July 25, 1944, Loewenheim, Langley, and Jonas, *Roosevelt and Churchill*, 555–556; Churchill to Roosevelt, July 29, 1944, ibid., 556–557; Churchill to Stalin, July 25, 1944, Kimball, *Churchill and Roosevelt*, III,

255; Churchill to Stalin, July 27, 1944, ibid., 261; Harriman to Hull, July 26, 1944, 760C.61/7-2644, T1244, National Archives; Adam Ulam, *Expansion and Coexistence* (New York, 1968), 376.

12. Harriman to Roosevelt, Aug. 12, 1944, PSF: Poland, Box 66, FDRL. For Stalin's rejection of Mikolajczyk's views see Stalin to Roosevelt, June 24, 1944, *Stalin's Correspondence*, 148.

13. Harriman to Roosevelt, Aug. 4, 1944, ibid.; Churchill to Roosevelt, Aug. 10, 1944, Loewenheim, Langley, and Jonas, *Roosevelt and Churchill*, 558–559; Churchill to Roosevelt, Aug. 11, 1944, ibid., 561; Harriman to Roosevelt, Aug. 10, 11, 1944, PSF: Poland, Box 66, FDRL; Memorandum of conversation between Stettinius and Ciechanowski, Aug. 9, 1944, Stettinius Papers, Series ll, Box 725. Kennan recorded the hopelessness of Mikolajczyk's position in Moscow in his *Memoirs: 1925–1950*, 206–210. For Kennan the repeated assurances of ultimate success given to the Polish premier by British and American diplomats were so hollow as to be frivolous. I wished, he recalled, "that instead of mumbling words of official optimism we had had the judgment and the good taste to bow our heads in silence before the tragedy of a people who have been our allies, whom we have helped to save from our enemies, and whom we cannot save from our friends." Ibid., 210.

14. Stalin to Roosevelt, June 24, 1944, *Stalin's Correspondence*, 148; Harriman to Hull, Aug. 17, 1944, DSF 740.0011 EW/8-1744, National Archives; Churchill to Roosevelt, Aug. 18, 1944, Loewenheim, Langley, and Jonas, *Roosevelt and Churchill*, 563; Winant to Hull, Aug. 18, 1944, 760.61/8-1844, National Archives; Jan Ciechanowski, *The Warsaw Rising of 1944* (Cambridge, 1974); Churchill, *Triumph and Tragedy*, 128–131. Stalin later told Churchill, at their subsequent October meeting, that Red Army's inaction at the time had been influenced by a major reverse in the Vistula sector during August and the extent of that reverse had to be kept secret at the time for operational reasons. Norman Davies, *Rising '44: 'The Battle of Warsaw'* (London: Macmillan, 2003), 444.

15. Harriman to Roosevelt, Aug. 15, 1944, PSF: Poland, Box 66, FDRL; Harriman to Roosevelt, Aug. 17, 1944, ibid.; Harriman to Hull, Aug. 17, 1944, DSF 740.0011 EW/8-1744, National Archives; Roosevelt to Mikolajczyk, Aug. 18, 1944, PSF: Poland, Box 66, FDRL; Winant to Roosevelt, Aug. 24, 1944, ibid.; Winant to Hull, Sept. 2, 1944, ibid.

16. Roosevelt and Churchill to Stalin, Aug. 20, 1944, *Stalin's Correspondence*, 156; Roosevelt to Mikolajczyk, Aug. 23, 1944, DSF 740.0011 EW/8-1844, National Archives; Roosevelt to Churchill, Aug. 24, 1944, Kimball, *Churchill and Roosevelt*, III, 294; for Roosevelt's view that the United States and Britain can still save Poland see Roosevelt to Churchill, Sept. 5, 1944, ibid., 313. For Churchill's plan to aid Warsaw with flights from Britain and Roosevelt's refusal to support him in the interest of sustaining Soviet support, see Churchill, *Triumph and Tragedy*, 132–141; *Newsweek*, Aug. 1, 1995, 39.

17. Harriman to Roosevelt, Aug. 15, 17, 1944, PSF: Poland, Box 66, FDRL.

18. Harriman to Hopkins, Sept. 10, 1944, Hopkins Papers, Box 157, FDRL; Harriman to Hopkins, Sept. 11, 1944, Map Room, Box 13, FDRL; Hopkins to Harriman, Sept. 11, 1944, ibid.; W. Averell Harriman and Elie Abel, *Special Envoy to Churchill and Stalin, 1941–1946* (New York, 1975), 535–536; Rudy Abramson,

Spanning the Century: The Life of W. Averell Harriman, 1891–1986 (New York, 1992). In retrospect Harriman concluded that the Soviet decision not to enter Warsaw was not a political plot, but a military necessity. See Isaacson and Thomas, *The Wise Men*, 231–232.

19. For the long, if futile, efforts of U.S. officials to return Bulgaria to freedom from both German and Soviet control see Michael M. Boll, "U.S. Plans for a Postwar Pro-Western Bulgaria: A Little-Known Wartime Initiative in Eastern Europe," *Diplomatic History*, 7 (Spring 1983), 118–134. On Bulgarian efforts to leave the war see Churchill to Roosevelt, Feb. 9, 1944, Map Room, Box 35, FDRL; Harriman to Roosevelt, Feb. 16, 1944, ibid.

20. For the Rumanian, Hungarian, and Italian roles in the Nazi invasion of the U.S.S.R. see Mario Fenyo, "The Allied Axis Armies and Stalingrad," *Military Affairs*, 29 (Summer 1965), 57–72. Washington objected to even these limited Soviet demands on Rumania. See Chronological Survey of Events Regarding Rumanian Peace Efforts, Aug. 26, 1944, Map Room, Box 164, FDRL; Hull, *Memoirs*, II, 1451–1452.

21. U.S. Charge in the Soviet Union to Hull, May 9, 1944, *FRUS*, 1944: IV, 870. See also ibid., III, 515–520.

22. Churchill, *Triumph and Tragedy*, 72–73.

23. Hull, *Memoirs*, II, 1452.

24. Churchill, *Triumph and Tragedy*, 74–77; Hull, *Memoirs*, II, 1452–1453; Churchill to Roosevelt, June 11, 1944, Map Room, Box 164, FDRL.

25. Memorandum from the Department of State to the British Embassy, June 12, 1944, DSF 870.00/48, National Archives; Roosevelt to Churchill, June 12, 1944, Map Room, Box 164, FDRL; Roosevelt to Churchill, June 13, 1944, Churchill, *Triumph and Tragedy*, 76–81. Hull did not discover Roosevelt's acceptance of the three-month trial until U.S. diplomats in Europe began to inquire about the apparent change in American policy. When Hull confronted Roosevelt with this evidence, Roosevelt, to Hull's dismay, revealed his private correspondence with Churchill. See Hull to Roosevelt, June 29, 1944, Map Room, Box 164, FDRL; Roosevelt to Hull, June 30, 1944, ibid.

26. For a graphic account of the invasion see Joseph Balkoski, *Utah Beach: The Amphibious Landing and Airborne Operations on D-Day, June 6, 1944* (Stackpole, 2005). The standard work on OVERLORD is Stephen E. Ambrose, *D-Day June 6, 1944: The Climactic Battle of World War II* (New York, 1994).

27. David Eisenhower, "D-Day Remembered," Foreign Policy Research Institute, publication 5, No. 3 (June 2004), 2.

28. Vojtech Mastny, *Russia's Road to the Cold War: Diplomacy, Warfare, and the Politics of Communism, 1941–1945* (New York, 1979), 161–167; Churchill to Roosevelt, June 9, 1944, Kimball, *Churchill and Roosevelt*, III, 172–173; Stalin to Roosevelt, June 21, 1944, *Stalin's Correspondence*, 145, 147.

29. Churchill to Hopkins, Aug. 6, 1944, Map Room, Box 13, FDRL; Lord Moran, *Churchill Taken from the Diaries of Lord Moran: The Struggle for Survival, 1940–1965* (Boston, 1966), 73.

30. Mark W. Clark, *Calculated Risk* (New York, 1950), 348–349; Harry C. Butcher, *My Three Years with Eisenhower: The Personal Diary of Captain Harry C. Butcher, USNR, Naval Aid to General Eisenhower, 1942 to 1945* (New York, 1946), 644.

31. Hanson W. Baldwin, "Churchill Was Right," *The Atlantic Monthly*, 194 (July 1954), 30.

32. Churchill to Roosevelt, Aug. 1, 1944, Warren F. Kimball, ed., *Churchill and Roosevelt: The Complete Correspondence, III: Alliance Declining, February 1944–April 1945* (Princeton, NJ, 1984), 279; Moran, *Diaries of Lord Moran*, 185.

33. Albert Resis, "The Churchill-Stalin Secret 'Percentages' Agreement on the Balkans, Moscow, October 1944," *The American Historical Review*, 83 (Apr. 1978), 378–381.

34. For the background of Churchill's decision to go to Moscow see Joseph M. Siracusa, "The Night Stalin and Churchill Divided Europe: The View from Washington," *The Review of Politics*, 43 (July 1981), 381–409; Churchill, *Triumph and Tragedy*, 206–218; Churchill to Roosevelt, Sept. 29, 1944, Kimball, *Churchill and Roosevelt*, III, 341; Churchill to Roosevelt, Oct. 3, 1944, ibid., 342. On Roosevelt's response see Roosevelt to Churchill, Oct. 4, 1944, ibid., 344; Churchill to Roosevelt, Oct. 5, 1944, ibid., 345; Churchill, *Triumph and Tragedy*, 219–220.

35. For Washington's decision not to fight in the Balkans see Report of the Office of European Affairs, July 15, 1944, Stettinius Papers, Series 4, Box 216; Report on American Policy in Eastern Europe, Sept. 26, 1944, Records of Policy and Planning Committee, Harley A. Notter Papers, Box 137, National Archives. On the Roosevelt-Stalin exchange see Hugh de Santis, *The Diplomacy of Silence: The American Foreign Service, the Soviet Union, and the Cold War, 1933–1947* (Chicago, 1980), 125; Resis, "The Churchill-Stalin Secret 'Percentages' Agreement," 386. To Resis, Roosevelt's letter of October 4, with its claim to equal authority in the Balkans, was the beginning of the Cold War.

36. Warren F. Kimball, "Naked Reverse Right: Roosevelt, Churchill, and Eastern Europe from TOLSTOY to Yalta—and a Little Beyond," *Diplomatic History*, 9 (Winter 1985), 5.

37. Churchill, *Triumph and Tragedy*, 227; Joseph M. Siracusa, "The Meaning of TOLSTOY: Churchill, Stalin, and the Balkans Moscow, October 1944," *Diplomatic History*, 3 (Fall 1979), 443–463; Sir Llewellyn Woodward, *British Foreign Policy in the Second World War* (5 vols., London, 1971), III, 146–153. For a full analysis of the background and decisions of the Churchill-Stalin meeting of October 9 see John A. Lukacs, "The Night Stalin and Churchill Divided Europe," the *New York Times Magazine*, Oct. 5, 1969, 37–50. On Molotov's changes see Resis, "The Churchill-Stalin Secret 'Percentages' Agreement," 375–376.

38. Harriman to Hull, Oct. 17, 1944, *FRUS*, 1944: III, 459; Resis, "The Churchill-Stalin Secret 'Percentages' Agreement," 376–378, 382–383.

39. Churchill to the Cabinet, Oct. 12, 1944, Churchill, *Triumph and Tragedy*, 234; Discussion of European Events, Oct. 18, 1944, Records of Policy and Planning Committees, Records of Harley A. Notter, 1939–1945, Box 137, National Archives; Churchill to Hopkins, Oct. 12, 1944, Map Room, Box 13, FDRL; Kimball, "Naked Reverse Right," 5–6.

40. Churchill to Roosevelt, Oct. 11, 1944, Churchill, *Triumph and Tragedy*, 228–229; Churchill to Roosevelt, Oct. 11, 1944, Kimball, *Churchill and Roosevelt*, III, 353; Churchill to Roosevelt, Oct. 18, 1944, ibid., C-799; Roosevelt to Stalin, Oct. 24, ibid., R-635. Clearly, as Elisabeth Barker notes, the percentages agreement of

October 9 vastly understated actual Soviet predominance in the Balkans. See Barker, *British Policy in South-East Europe in the Second World War* (London, 1976), 146–147. State Department officials agreed that the United States, acting alone, could achieve nothing in the Balkans. See U.S. Policy toward Eastern Europe and the Near East, Office of European Affairs, Oct. 14, 1944, Stettinius Papers, Series 4, Box 216.

41. Churchill, *Triumph and Tragedy*, 226–227, 237–238; Mikolajczyk, *The Pattern of Soviet Domination*, 97–99?; Eden, *The Reckoning*, 563–564. Roosevelt accepted TOLSTOY'S limited agreements on Poland. See Churchill to Roosevelt, Oct. 22, 1944, Kimball, *Churchill and Roosevelt*, III, C-801; Roosevelt to Churchill, Oct. 22, 1944, ibid., R-632. For Churchill's bitter exchanges with Mikolajczyk, on October 14–15, over the Polish premier's refusal to compromise, see Alfred M. de Zayas, *Nemesis at Potsdam* (London, 1979), 46–49; Rozek, 277, 283, 285; Mikolajczyk, 97–99; Churchill, *Triumph and Tragedy*, 235.

42. For Soviet military advances in the summer of 1944 see Weinberg, *A World at Arms*, 704–705, 710–711; Leahy quoted in Norman A. Graebner, *Cold War Diplomacy: American Foreign Policy, 1945–1975* (New York, 1977), 9; Kennan, *Memoirs, 1925–1950*, 226, 506.

43. Mastny, *Russia's Road to the Cold War*, 308; British scholar Edward H. Carr echoed McCormick's view of Soviet military expansion. See Norman A. Graebner, "Cold War Origins and the Continuing Debate; A Review of Recent Literature," *The Journal of Conflict Resolution*, 13 (Mar. 1969), 127. Kennan stressed the importance of opportunity and historic Russian interests in determining Soviet policy in 1944. Kennan, *Memoirs, 1925–1950*, 226–228, 520–522. Walter Lippmann argued later against those who attributed Soviet expansionism to Leninist ideology, seeing it rather the result of the destruction of the powers that historically had held Russia in check. Lippmann to Arthur M. Schlesinger, Jr., Sept. 25, 1967, John Morton Blum, ed., *Lippmann*, 615–616.

44. Harriman to Roosevelt, Jan. 9, 1944, DSF 711.61/968; Roosevelt to Stalin, Feb. 7, 1944, enclosed in Hull to Harriman, Feb. 9, 1944, DSF 711.61/977A, National Archives.

45. Harriman to Hopkins, Sept. 9, 1944, Map Room, Box 13, FDRL; Harriman to Hopkins, Sept. 11, 1944, ibid.

46. Bennett, *Franklin D. Roosevelt and the Search for Victory*, 125–126.

47. Hull, *Memoirs*, II, 1459–1460; Hull to Harriman, Sept. 1944, *FRUS*, 1944: IV, 991.

48. Writers generally hold the view that Soviet policy in Eastern Europe and the Balkans responded to the perceived interests to be served in filling the vacuum of power across the heart of Europe. See, for example, Philip E. Mosely, "American Policy Toward East Central Europe," Roger Pethybridge, ed., *The Development of the Communist Bloc* (Boston, 1965), 4–5; Hammond, *Witnesses to the Origins of the Cold War*, 288–289; Woods, *A Changing of the Guard*, 252–253; Halle, *The Cold War as History*, 48–49.

49. Halle, *The Cold War as History*, 62; for Stalin's speech see Milovan Djilas, *Conversations with Stalin*, trans. Michael B. Petrovich (New York, 1962), 114. William C. Bullitt outlined what the Soviets had taken and intended to keep in Bullitt to Roosevelt, Aug. 10, 1943, Bullitt, 596–597.

50. *FRUS*, 1944, 1025–1026; Eduard Mark, "Charles E. Bohlen and the Acceptable Limits of Soviet Hegemony in Eastern Europe: A Memorandum of 18 October 1945," *Diplomatic History*, 3 (Spring 1979), 204.

51. Eduard Mark, "American Policy toward Eastern Europe and the Origins of the Cold War, 1941–1946," *The Journal of American History*, 68 (Sept. 1981), 315; Mark, "Charles E. Bohlen and the Acceptable Limits of Soviet Hegemony in Eastern Europe," 203.

52. *FRUS*, 1944: IV, 815–817, 824–825, 951, 1035, 1037.

53. Ibid., 994–997, 1053; Kuklick, *American Policy and the Division of Germany*, 102–107.

54. On Harriman see Deborah Welch Larson, *Origins of Containment: A Psychological Explanation* (Princeton, NJ, 1985), 111; Harriman to Hull, Sept. 20, 1944, *FRUS*, 1944: IV, 933. For Kennan's views see Kennan, *Memoirs: 1925–1950*, 61; Kennan, "The View from Russia," Thomas T. Hammond, ed., *Witnesses to the Origins of the Cold War* (Seattle, 1982), 29.

55. Berry to Hull, Nov. 30, 1944, PSF: Russia, Box 68, FDRL.

56. *FRUS*, 1944: IV, 992–999; Anders Stephanson, *Kennan and the Art of Foreign Policy* (Cambridge, Mass., 1989), 38.

57. Arthur Bliss Lane, *I Saw Poland Betrayed* (Indianapolis, 1948), 65–67; Thomas M. Campbell and George C. Herring, eds., *The Diaries of Edward R. Stettinius, Jr., 1943–1946* (New York, 1975), 214; Daniel Yergin, *Shattered Peace: The Origins of the Cold War and the National Security State* (Boston, 1977), 57–58.

58. Sherwood, *Roosevelt and Hopkins*, 818.

59. For the tasks facing the Allies see Gordon A. Craig and Alexander L. George, *Force and Statecraft: Diplomatic Problems of Our Time* (New York, 1983), 104–111.

60. Kuklick, *American Policy and the Division of Germany*, 26–32.

61. Kennan, *Memoirs: 1925–1950*, 164–167; Churchill to Roosevelt, Sept. 23, 1944, 334; Ryan, *The Vision of Anglo-America*, 14.

62. Kimball, *Churchill and Roosevelt*, III, 316–317; *FRUS: The Conference at Quebec* (Washington, 1972), 98–100; Henry L. Stimson, 571–573; John Morton Blum, ed., *From the Morgenthau Diaries* (3 vols., Boston, 1961), I, 540; Warren F. Kimball, *Swords or Ploughshares? The Morgenthau Plan for Defeated Nazi Germany, 1943–1946* (Philadelphia, 1976); Hathaway, *Ambiguous Partnership*, 55–64; Kuklick, *American Policy and the Division of Germany*, 47–59; John L. Chase, "The Development of the Morgenthau Plan Through the Quebec Conference," *Journal of Politics*, 16 (May 1954), 329–333; Walter Dorn, "The Debate over American Occupation Policy in Germany in 1944–1945," *Political Science Quarterly*, 72 (Dec. 1957), 481–501. For Roosevelt's bitter rejection of Stimson's moderate views toward German reconstruction see Gaddis, *The United States and the Origins of the Cold War*, 119.

63. Roosevelt to Robert Murphy, Sept. 1944, Robert Murphy, *Diplomat among Warriors* (New York, 1964), 227.

64. Kennan, *Memoirs: 1925–1950*, 177–179.

65. These guidelines for employment later created serious problems of hiring and retention. See Robert Murphy, *Diplomat Among Warriors* (New York, 1964), 284.

66. Walter Isaacson and Evan Thomas, *The Wise Men: Six Friends and the World They Made* (New York, 1986), 235–236. On the elusiveness of American

strategic thinking in wartime see Colin S. Gray, "National Style in Strategy: The American Example," *International Security*, 6 (Fall 1981), 30–31.

67. B.K. Madan, "Echoes of Bretton Woods," *Finance and Development*, 6 (June 1969), 30–38; *The Economist*, 332 (July 9, 1994), 69–70; Hull, *Memoirs*, II, 1681; Alfred E. Eckes, Jr., *A Search for Solvency: Bretton Woods and the International Monetary System, 1941–1971* (Austin, 1975); Armand van Dormael, *Bretton Woods: Birth of a Monetary System* (London, 1978); Lloyd C. Gardner, *Economic Aspects of New Deal Diplomacy* (Madison, 1964); Richard N. Gardner, *Sterling-Dollar Diplomacy: The Origins and Prospects of Our International Order* (London, 1969); Woods, *A Changing of the Guard*, 130–145, 168–173; E. F. Penrose, *Economic Planning for the Peace* (Princeton, 1953); Robert Kuttner, *The End of Laissez-Faire: National Purpose and the Global Economy After the Cold War* (New York, 1991), 24–38.

68. For Law's statement see Campbell and Herring, *The Diaries of Edward R. Stettinius*, 92–94. On Morgenthau and Roosevelt, John Morton Blum, ed., *From the Morgenthau Diaries* (3 vols., Boston, 1961–1967), I, 308, 310; D. Cameron Watt, *Succeeding John Bull: America in Britain's Place, 1900–1975* (Cambridge, 1984), 82–83, 95. Britain's Lord Beaverbrook observed in October: "For the first time, the English are not sure of themselves. They are anxious about their future." Quoted in Hathaway, *Ambiguous Partnership*, 36.

69. Blum, *From the Morgenthau Diaries*, I, 313–314; Hathaway, *Ambiguous Partnership*, 64–67; Hull, *Memoirs*, II, 1614. In the final Lend-Lease negotiations of November 1944, State Department and congressional opposition to the Quebec agreement compelled Roosevelt to compromise on nonmilitary assistance. See Hathaway, *Ambiguous Partnership*, 74–85.

70. "Mr. Hull," *Life*, 17 (Dec. 11, 1944), 26; Julius W. Pratt, *Cordell Hull* (New York, 1964), II, 765–766.

71. On the intricate maneuvering in Congress and the administration in behalf of an international peace organization see Robert A. Divine, *Second Chance: The Triumph of Internationalism in America During World War II* (New York, 1971), 89–219. Sumner Welles lauds Roosevelt's role in the creation of the United Nations in Welles, *Seven Decisions That Shaped History*, 172–198.

72. *FRUS: Conferences at Cairo and Teheran*, 530–531.

73. Bennett, *Franklin D. Roosevelt and the Search for Victory*, 127–131; Divine, *Second Chance*, 220–228. Maxim Litvinov explained the Soviet demand for the veto by noting that the U.S.S.R. had never been accepted in European councils on the basis of equality. See Edgar Snow to Grace Tully, Dec. 28, 1944, PSF: Russia, FDRL. For Stalin's apprehension of anti-Soviet prejudices see Stalin to Roosevelt, Sept. 14, 1944, *Stalin's Correspondence with Roosevelt and Truman*, 160.

74. Churchill to Roosevelt, Sept. 25, 1944, Kimball, *Churchill and Roosevelt*, III, 335; Roosevelt to Churchill, Sept. 28, 1944, ibid., 339; Robert C. Hilderbrand, *Dumbarton Oaks: The Origins of the United Nations and the Search for Postwar Security* (Chapel Hill, 1990). For the impasse on the veto and the Soviet emphasis on unanimity see Campbell and Herring, *The Diaries of Edward R. Stettinius*, 137–139; Kennan, *Memoirs: 1925–1950*, 220–221.

75. Churchill speech of Dec. 15; Roosevelt to Stalin, Dec. 16, 1944, Kimball, *Churchill and Roosevelt*, R–675.

76. Kennan, *Memoirs: 1925–1950*, 214; Roosevelt to Stalin, Dec. 20, 1944, *Stalin's Correspondence*, 175–176; Stalin to Roosevelt, Dec. 27, 1944, ibid., 180–181; Roosevelt to Stalin, Dec. 30, 1944, ibid., 182–183.

77. State Department press conference, Jan. 5, 1945, Stettinius Papers, Series 11, Box 721, Alderman Library; *Manchester Guardian*, Jan. 12, 1945, 17–18; Churchill, *Triumph and Tragedy*, 336–337.

78. Executive Committee of the Polish American Democratic Organization to Stettinius, Dec. 20, 1944, PSF: Poland, FDRL; Stettinius memorandum for the president, Jan. 4, 1945, ibid.; Arciszewski to Roosevelt, Feb. 3, 1945, Map Room, Box 21, FDRL.

79. Vandenberg's speech before the Senate, Jan. 10, 1945; Arthur H. Vandenberg, Jr. and Joe Alex Morris, eds., *The Private Papers of Senator Vandenberg* (Boston, 1952), 134; Bennett, *Franklin D. Roosevelt and the Search for Victory*, 146; Memorandum for the Secretary of State, Jan. 2, 1945, Stettinius Papers, Series 4, Box 222.

80. Churchill to Stalin, Jan. 6, 9, 1945, U.S.S.R., Ministry of Foreign Affairs, *Correspondence between the Chairman of the Council of Ministers of the USSR and the Presidents of the U.S.A. and the Prime Ministers of Great Britain during the Great Patriotic War of 1941–1945* (2 vols., Moscow, 1957), I, 294–295.

81. For this German offensive see Max Hastings, *Armageddon: The Battle for Germany, 1944–1945* (New York, 2004).

82. Statement on military progress, Jan. 15, 1945, Map Room, Box 23; Stalin to Roosevelt, n.d., PSF: Russia, Box 68, FDRL; Larry H. Addington, *The Pattern of War Since the Eighteenth Century* (Bloomington, 1984), 221; for the Soviet surge see Joseph C. Harsch in *The Christian Science Monitor*, Jan. 30, 1995, 9; Stalin to Roosevelt, Jan. 15, 1945, *Stalin's Correspondence*, 184; *The Nation*, 160 (Jan. 13, 1945), 291.

83. *Time*, Feb. 5, 1945, 4, 34; Reston in the *New York Times*, Feb. 11, 1945, E5.

84. *FRUS: The Conferences of Malta and Yalta*, 1945 (Washington, 1955), 94–96.

85. Walter Lippmann, "Today and Tomorrow," *New York Herald-Tribune*, Jan. 9, 1945, 17, as quoted in Robert Max Berdahl, "The Emergence of American Cold War Policy," 1945–1947, M.A. Thesis, University of Illinois, 1959, 8; Bohlen, *Witness to History*, 176–177.

86. Russell D. Buhite, in a superb account of the Yalta Conference, argues that the Western powers had so little to gain at the Yalta summit that they should have held no conference at all. The agreements, easily oversold, could create little but disillusionment. See Russell D. Buhite, *Decisions at Yalta: An Appraisal of Summit Diplomacy* (Wilmington, Del., 1986), 129–136.

87. Eden, *The Reckoning*, 597; views on the Polish-German borders, Jan. 3, 1945, CAC- 341, PWC-216, The Papers of Harley A. Notter, National Archives; *FRUS: Conferences of Malta and Yalta*, 680, 716–717, 792, 869, 905, 938, 973–974, 980; Churchill, *Triumph and Tragedy*, 374, 377.

88. *FRUS: Conferences at Malta and Yalta*, 667–670; Roosevelt to Stalin, Feb. 6, 1945, Soviet documents, 187–188.

89. On the Polish settlement see Martin F. Herz, *Beginnings of the Cold War* (Bloomington, 1966), 80–85; Edward R. Stettinius, Jr., *Roosevelt and the Russians:*

The Yalta Conference, ed. Walter Johnson (Garden City, N.Y., 1949), 251–252; *FRUS: Conferences at Malta and Yalta*, 788, 846, 848, 872, 973, 980.

90. Kimball, "Naked Reverse Right," 7–8; Churchill to Hopkins, Dec. 11, 1944, Kimball, *Churchill and Roosevelt*, III, C-850-1; Roosevelt to Churchill, Dec. 13, 1944, ibid., R-673; Churchill to Roosevelt, Dec. 26, 1944, ibid., C-858; Roosevelt to Stalin, Dec. 30, 1944, ibid., R-684. For U.S. condemnation of Britain for its unilateral action in both Greece and Italy, see Hathaway, *Ambiguous Partnership*, 90–95.

91. Harriman to Hull, Jan. 10, 1945, PSF: Russia, Box 68, FDRL.

92. On the Declaration on Liberated Europe and related issues see *FRUS: Conferences at Malta and Yalta*; Diane Shaver Clemens, *Yalta* (New York, 1970); Charles F. Delzell, "Russian Power in Central-Eastern Europe," in John L. Snell, ed., *The Meaning of Yalta* (Baton Rouge, La., 1956), 115–122; Stettinius, *Roosevelt and the Russians*, 253; Buhite, *Decisions at Yalta*, 114–118.

93. Eden, *The Reckoning*, 572–574.

94. Yalta Conference protocols, Feb. 11, 1945, *FRUS: Conferences of Malta and Yalta*, 978–980.

95. Moran, *Diaries of Lord Moran*, 246; *FRUS: The Conferences at Malta and Yalta*, 632; For the Yalta debates on reparations see Kuklick, *American Policy and the Division of Europe*. 80–81; Robert Maddox, "Reparations and the Origins of the Cold War," *Mid-America: An Historical Review*, 67 (Oct. 1985), 125–131; Thomas G. Paterson, *Soviet-American Confrontation* (Baltimore, 1973), 251–252; Laloy, *Yalta*, 73.

96. George A. Lensen, "Yalta and the Far East," Snell, *The Meaning of Yalta*, 147–166. Lensen agrees with Stettinius that Roosevelt gave nothing away in the Far East and had good reasons to make his agreements with Stalin.

97. Kimball, *Churchill and Roosevelt*, III, 527.

98. Among the many books that place responsibility for the division of Europe, not on Yalta, but on subsequent Soviet decisions that the West could not control are Laloy, *Yalta*, 81; Vladislav Zubok and Constantine Pleshakov, "The Soviet Union," Reynolds, *The Origins of the Cold War in Europe*, 60; Graebner, *Cold War Diplomacy*, 13; John L. Snell, *Illusion and Necessity: The Diplomacy of Global War, 1939–1945* (Boston, 1963); Stettinius, *Roosevelt and the Russians*, 272–283.

99. On Jebb and Roosevelt's behavior toward Stalin at Yalta see Anthony Lewis in the *New York Times*, Feb. 8, 1970, 28; Hathaway, *Ambiguous Partnership*, 113, 115; Adam B. Ulam, *The Rivals: America and Russia Since World War II* (New York, 1971), 57; Moran, *Churchill Taken from the Diaries of Lord Moran*. For indictments of Yalta as the cause of Europe's subsequent division see Ferenc Nagy, *The Struggle Behind the Iron Curtain* (New York, 1948); Stanislaw Mikolajczyk, *The Rape of Poland: Pattern of Soviet Aggression* (New York, 1948); Lane, *I Saw Poland Betrayed*; Athan Theoharis, *Yalta*; Chamberlin; Zbigniew Brezezinski, "The Future of Yalta," *Foreign Affairs*, 63 (Winter 1984/85), 287–288; George Konrad, "A Path Toward Peace," *The Atlantic Monthly*, 253 (Mar. 1984), 71.

100. Cadogan quoted in Hathaway, *Ambiguous Partnership*, 121; Adam B. Ulam, *Stalin: The Man and His Era* (New York, 1973), 608–609.

101. Arciszewski to Roosevelt, Feb. 18, 19445, Map Room, Box 22, FDRL; Norman A. Graebner, *Cold War Diplomacy: American Foreign Policy, 1945–1975*

(New York, 1977), 14; Zbigniew Brzezinski, "The Future of Yalta," *Foreign Affairs*, 63 (Winter 1984/85), 287.

102. *Manchester Guardian*, Feb. 16, 1945, 89; *Newsweek*, Feb. 19, 1945, 37; *Time*, Feb. 19, 1945, 15; Daniels to Early, Feb. 13, 1945, Map Room, Box 21, FDRL; Brzezinski, "The Future of Yalta," 287.

103. Churchill's address to the House of Commons, Feb. 27, 1945, Churchill, *Triumph and Tragedy*, 400–401; Roosevelt's report to Congress, Mar. 1, 1945, in *The Department of State Bulletin*, 12 (Mar. 4, 1945), 361; Sherwood, *Roosevelt and Hopkins*, 870 (emphasis added); James F. Byrnes, *Speaking Frankly* (New York, 1947), 45.

CHAPTER 3

1. For a graphic German view of the destructiveness of Allied bombing of German cities throughout the spring of 1945 see Hugh Trevor-Roper, ed., *The Diaries of Joseph Goebbels: The Final Entries, 1945* (New York, 1978), passim. Also see, Jorg Friedich: *Fire: The Bombing of Germany, 1940–1945* (New York: Columbia University Press, 2007).

2. Robert L. Messer, *The End of an Alliance: James F. Byrnes, Roosevelt, Truman, and the Origins of the Cold War* (Chapel Hill, 1982), 50–51; Martin F. Herz, *Beginnings of the Cold War* (Bloomington, 1966), 80–85; Edward R. Stettinius, Jr., *Roosevelt and the Russians: The Yalta Conference*, ed. Walter Johnson (Garden City, N.Y., 1949), 251–252; Vladislav Zubok and Constantine Pleshakov, "The Soviet Union," David Reynolds, ed., *The Origins of the Cold War in Europe: International Perspectives* (New Haven, 1994), 60.

3. Joseph Grew to W. Averell Harriman, Feb. 27, 1945, *Foreign Relations of the United States, Diplomatic Papers* (hereafter *FRUS*), 1945: V (Washington, 1967), 483; Burton Y. Berry to Vyshinsky, Feb. 28, 1945, ibid., 486–488; Berry to Edward R. Stettinius, Feb. 28, Mar. 2, 7, 1945, ibid., 492–493, 502–503.

4. On Hungary see Louis Mark, Jr., "The View from Hungary," Thomas T. Hammond, ed., *Witnesses to the Origins of the Cold War* (Seattle, 1982), 186–208. Mark, who arrived in Hungary during April 1945, insists that American officials in Hungary were not anti-Soviet and attempted unsuccessfully to convince the Soviets that Western goals in Hungary did not threaten Soviet interests. Hammond's volume offers a full evaluation of all Soviet takeovers across East-Central Europe and the Balkans. Note especially Hammond's long conclusion.

5. Harriman to Roosevelt, Mar. 15, 1945, President's Secretary's File (PSF): Russia, Box 68, Franklin D. Roosevelt Library, Hyde Park (FDRL).

6. Messer, *The End of an Alliance*, 54–58.

7. See David Carlton, *Anthony Eden: A Biography* (London, 1981), 254–255.

8. J. M. Mackintosh, *Strategy and Tactics of Soviet Foreign Policy* (London, 1962), 6–7.

9. Warren F. Kimball, "Naked Reverse Right: Roosevelt, Churchill, and Eastern Europe from TOLSTOY to Yalta—and a Little Beyond," *Diplomatic History*. 9 (Winter 1985), 18; Henry Butterfield Ryan, *The Vision of Anglo-America: The US-UK Alliance and the Emerging Cold War, 1943–1946* (Cambridge, 1987), 91.

10. Martin Gilbert, *Winston S. Churchill, VII: Road to Victory, 1941–1945* (Boston, 1986), 1230–1231; Geir Lundestad, *The American "Empire" and Other Studies of US Foreign Policy in a Comparative Perspective* (Oxford, 1990), 152; Ryan, *The Vision of Anglo-America*, 89.

11. Churchill to Roosevelt, Mar. 8, 1945, Warren F. Kimball, ed., *Churchill & Roosevelt: The Complete Correspondence* (3 vols., Princeton, NJ, 1984), III, 547–551; Winston S. Churchill, *The Second World War, VI: Triumph and Tragedy* (Boston, 1953), 421–423; Ryan, *The Vision of Anglo-America*, 92.

12. Messer, *The End of an Alliance*, 60.

13. Harriman to Stettinius, Feb. 24, 1945, *FRUS*, 1945: V, 124; Harriman to Stettinius, Feb. 27, 1945, ibid., 129–130; Harriman to Stettinius, Mar. 1, 1945, ibid., 134; Churchill, *Triumph and Tragedy*, 362–363.

14. Charles E. Bohlen, *Witness to History, 1929–1969* (New York, 1973), 207–208; Harriman to Stettinius, Mar. 7, 1945, *FRUS*, 1945: V, 145.

15. Robert Murphy, *Diplomat Among Warriors* (Garden City, N.Y., 1964), 227.

16. Roosevelt to Churchill, Mar. 11, 1945, Kimball, *Churchill & Roosevelt*, III, 562; Roosevelt to Churchill, Mar. 12, 1945, ibid., 563; Roosevelt to Churchill, Mar. 15, 1945, ibid., 568–569.

17. Anthony Eden, *The Reckoning* (Boston, 1965), 603, 606–607; Churchill to Roosevelt, Mar. 27, 1945, *FRUS*, 1945: V, 189; Ryan, *The Vision of Anglo-America*, 94–95.

18. Roosevelt to Stalin, Mar. 31, 1945, PSF: Russia, Box 68, FDRL; Roosevelt to Stalin, Apr. 1, 1945, *FRUS*, 1945: V, 194–196.

19. Churchill to Roosevelt, Apr. 5, 1945, Kimball, *Churchill & Roosevelt*, III, 613; Roosevelt to Churchill, Apr. 6, 1945, ibid., 617.

20. Stalin to Roosevelt, Apr. 7, 1945, Ministry of Foreign Affairs of the U.S.S.R., *Correspondence Between the Chairman of the Council of Ministers of the U.S.S.R. and the Presidents of the U.S.A. and the Prime Ministers of Great Britain During the Great Patriotic War of 1941–1945* (hereafter *Stalin's Correspondence*) (New York, 1965), 211–213.

21. Memorandum of William Leahy to Roosevelt, Mar. 31, 1945, Map Room, Box 23, FDRL.

22. Roosevelt to Stalin, Apr. 5, 1945, Map Room, Box 9, FDRL; Stalin to Roosevelt, Apr. 3, 7, 1945, Map Room, Box 23, FDRL; Roosevelt to Churchill, Apr. 11, 1945, Map Room, Box 9, FDRL.

23. Churchill to Roosevelt, Apr. 1, 1945, Winston S. Churchill, *Memoirs of the Second World War* (Boston, 1959), 936; Churchill to Roosevelt, Apr. 5, 1945, Map Room, Box 7, FDRL.

24. Stephen E. Ambrose, *Eisenhower and Berlin, 1945: The Decision to Halt at the Elbe* (New York, 1967), 88–89; Forrest C. Pogue, "The Decision to Halt at the Elbe," Kent Roberts Greenfield, ed., *Command Decisions* (New York, 1959), 479–492.

25. On Harriman's growing concern regarding Soviet intentions during March and April see Walter Isaacson and Evan Thomas, *The Wise Men: Six Friends and the World They Made* (New York, 1986), 247–250; Stettinius to Harriman, Apr. 3, 1945, Department of State File (DSF) 711.61/4-345, National Archives,

Washington, DC; Harriman to Stettinius, Apr. 4, 1945, PSF: Russia, Box 68, Franklin D. Roosevelt Library (FDRL); Harriman to Stettinius, Apr. 6, 1945, DSF 711.61/4-645, National Archives.

26. Minutes of the Secretary of State's Staff Committee, Apr. 20, 1945, *FRUS*, 1945: V, 841.

27. Stettinius's calendar notes, Apr. 13, 1945, Thomas M. Campbell and George C. Herring, eds., *The Diaries of Edward R. Stettinius, Jr., 1943–1946* (New York, 1975), 318; Harry S. Truman, *Memoirs, I: Year of Decisions* (Garden City, N.Y., 1955), 26, 64; Harriman to Stettinius, Apr. 17, 1945, *FRUS*, 1945: V, 225–226; Kennan to Stettinius, Apr. 21, 1945, ibid., 229–234; William D. Leahy, *I Was There* (New York, 1950), 349.

28. Truman, *Year of Decisions*, 71–72; Walter Millis, ed., *The Forrestal Diaries* (New York, 1951), 47; Bohlen memorandum of Truman-Harriman conversation, Apr. 20, 1945, *FRUS*, 1945: V, 231–234.

29. Stettinius and Truman quoted in Truman, *Year of Decisions*, 76–77; for the White House meeting of April 23 see Millis, *Forrestal Diaries*, 50–51. That day the State Department urged the President to avoid any agreement with the U.S.S.R. that did not guarantee a Polish government representative of all the Democratic elements among the Polish people. See Dunn and Bohlen to Truman, Apr. 23, 1945, Series 11, Box 721, Stettinius Papers, University of Virginia Library, Charlottesville. For the views of Stimson and Marshall see Millis, *Forrestal Diaries*, 50–51; Truman, *Year of Decisions*, 77–79; Bohlen's memorandum of conversation, Apr. 23, 1945, *FRUS*, 1945: V, 253–255; Henry L. Stimson and McGeorge Bundy, *On Active Service in Peace and War* (New York, 1948), 609.

30. Conversations with Molotov, Apr. 23, 1945, Truman, *Year of Decisions*, 81–82.

31. Stalin to Truman, Apr. 24, 1945, *Stalin's Correspondence*, 219–220. Stalin reminded Truman that Poland bordered on the Soviet Union, not on Britain or the United States.

32. W. Averell Harriman and Elie Abel, *Special Envoy to Churchill and Stalin, 1941–1946* (New York, 1975), 448; Vandenberg diary, Apr. 24, 1945, Arthur H. Vandenberg, Jr., and Joe Alex Morris, eds., *The Private Papers of Senator Vandenberg* (Boston, 1952), 176; Leahy, *I Was There*, 352.

33. Millis, *Forrestal Diaries*, 49; Forrestal to Homer Ferguson, May 14, 1945, ibid., 57.

34. Quoted in Joseph C. Grew, *Turbulent Era: A Diplomatic Record of Forty Years, 1904–1945*, ed. Walter Johnson (Boston, 1952), II, 1446.

35. Sumner Welles, *The Time for Decision* (New York, 19445), 374; Vandenberg and Morris, *Private Papers of Senator Vandenberg*, 150–158; Walter Lippmann, "Today and Tomorrow," *New York Herald-Tribune*, Mar. 31, 1945, 13.

36. Vandenberg and Morris, *Private Papers of Senator Vandenberg*, 178–182, 206–208; C. L. Sulzberger in the *New York Times Magazine*, July 8, 1945, 43; Anthony Eden, "Birth of the U.N.," ibid., June 20, 1965, 12–13, 53–57. For analyses of the U.N.'s limitations see Drew Middleton, "The U.N. Tries Hard, But—," ibid., Jan. 9, 1966, 28–29, 78–80; Hans J. Morgenthau, "The U.N. of Dag Hammarskjold Is Dead," ibid., Mar. 14, 1965, 32, 37–40.

37. Winston S. Churchill, *Memoirs of the Second World War* (Boston, 1959), 948; Martin Gilbert, *Winston S. Churchill, VII: Road to Victory* (Boston, 1969), 1350.

38. Richard A. Best, Jr., *"Co-Operation With Like-Minded Peoples": British Influences on American Security Policy, 1945–1949* (New York, 1986), 22; Richard Law quoted in Ryan, *The Vision of Anglo-America*, 27.

39. Michael S. Sherry discusses the postwar views of American military leaders toward the Soviet Union in *Preparing for the Next War: American Plans for Postwar Defense, 1941–1945* (New Haven, 1977), 168, 185; Hanson W. Baldwin in the *New York Times*, May 28, 1945, 4; Walter Lippmann, "Today and Tomorrow," *New York Herald-Tribune*, May 8, 1945, 13, quoted in Robert Max Berdahl. "The Emergence of American Cold War Policy, 1945–1947," M.A. Thesis, University of Illinois, 1961, 37–38.

40. George F. Kennan, *Memoirs: 1925–1950* (Boston, 1967), 256; John Fischer, "Odds Against Another War," *Harper's Magazine*, 191 (Aug. 1945), 97–106.

41. *The New Republic*, 112 (June 4, 1945), 771–772; 113 (July 9, 1945), 39; Henry A. Wallace, *The Price of Vision*, ed., John Morton Blum (New York, 1973), 450; Archibald MacLeish, "United States-Soviet Relations," *Department of State Bulletin* (May 27, 1945), 951; W.J. Gallman to H. Freeman Matthews, May 2, 1945, DSF 711.61/5-245; H. Schuyler Foster to MacLeish, May 24, 1945, DSF 711.61/5-2445; MacLeisah to Grew, May 26, 1945, DSF 711.61/5-2645, National Archives.

42. Lippmann to George Fielding Elliot, June 14, 1945, John Morton Blum, ed., *Public Philosopher: Selected Letters of Walter Lippmann* (New York, 1985), 467–468.

43. Churchill to Truman, May 11, 1945, *Foreign Relations of the United States, Diplomatic Papers: The Conference of Berlin, 1945*, I (Washington, 1960), 6; Churchill to Truman, May 12, 1945, ibid., 9.

44. Charles E. Bohlen, *Witness to History* (New York, 1973), 215; Messer, *The End of an Alliance*, 82.

45. Bohlen's report on the Hopkins-Stalin conversations, May 26–27, 1945, *FRUS: Berlin*, 1945: I, 26–28, 37–40. Quotation on page 39.

46. Harriman to Truman, June 8, 1945, ibid., 61.

47. Hopkins was delighted with the list. See Hopkins to Truman, May 31, 1945, *FRUS*, 1945: V, 308. Mikolajczyk and the British were equally convinced that an agreement based on the Declaration of Poland was now possible. Schoenfeld to Stettinius, June 2, 1945, ibid., 316.

48. Harriman to Stettinius, June 28, 1945, ibid., 728. On the movement toward a Polish settlement see the *New York Times*, June 14, 1945, 1; Bohlen, *Witness to History*, 219; "Solution in Poland," *The New Republic*, 113 (July 2, 1945), 6.

49. White House Press Release, July 5, 1945, *FRUS: Berlin*, 1945: I, 735.

50. Messer stresses this point in *The End of an Alliance*, 6–7, 96.

51. Stalin to Truman, May 27, 1945, *Stalin's Correspondence*, 239; Harriman to Stettinius, May 30, 1945, *FRUS*, 1945: V, 548; Memorandum of Elbridge Durbrow, May 30, 1945, quoted in Lynn Ethridge Davis, *The Cold War Begins: Soviet-American Conflict over Eastern Europe* (Princeton, NJ, 1974), 283–284;

Truman to Stalin, June 2, 1945, *FRUS*, 1945: V, 550; see also *Stalin's Correspondence*, 241–242.

52. Churchill, *Triumph and Tragedy*, 636; Meeting of Foreign Ministers, July 20, 1945, *FRUS: Berlin*, 1945: II, 152–155; James F. Byrnes, *Speaking Frankly* (New York, 1947), 73.

53. Bohlen, *Witness to History*, 234–235; Leahy, *I Was There*, 428–429; Department of State *Bulletin*, 13 (Aug. 5, 1945), 159.

54. For the evolution of U.S. policy toward Germany after Yalta see Richard J. Barnet, "Annals of Diplomacy: Alliance, I," *The New Yorker*, Oct. 10, 1983, 53–61; Truman to Churchill, June 24, 1945, *FRUS: Berlin*, 1945: I, 612; Byrnes to Pauley, July 3, 1945, ibid., 633.

55. Department of State *Bulletin*, 13 (Aug. 5, 1945), 153–160; *FRUS: Berlin*, 1945: II, 210–215; "Potsdam," *London Observer*, Aug. 5, 1945, 4; Lippmann to Forrestal, Sept. 24, 1945, Blum, *Public Philosopher*, 475. Lippmann saw clearly that after Potsdam the U.S.S.R. carried the major burden for curtailing German power. Germany's subsequent division, if unfortunate, was, like the Soviet hegemony elsewhere across East-Central Europe, not the result of any Big Three decisions, but simply a consequence of the war.

56. Truman, "The Berlin Conference," *Department of State Bulletin*, 13 (Aug. 12, 1945), 213.

57. Quoted in Joseph M. Siracusa and David G. Coleman, *Depression to Cold War: A History of America from Herbert Hoover to Ronald Reagan* (Westport, CT: Praeger, 2002), 113.

58. See Maurice Matloff, *Strategic Planning for Coalition Warfare, 1943–1944* (Washington, DC, 1959), 5.

59. On LeMay's fire-bombing campaign see Richard Rhodes, "Annals of the Cold War: The General and World War III," the *New Yorker*, June 19, 1995, 47–48; Richard L. Harwood, "War Was Hell," the *Washington Post National Weekly Edition*, Aug. 7–13, 1995, 6–9; Murray Sale, "Letter from Hiroshima: Did the Bomb End the War?" the *New Yorker*, July 31, 1995, 47.

60. Ronald H. Spector, *Eagle Against the Sun* (New York, 1985), 502–505.

61. Hanson W. Baldwin, *Battles Lost and Won: Great Campaigns of World War II* (New York, 1966), 380. For a full account of Okinawa see Roy E. Appleman *et al*, *Okinawa: The Last Battle* (Washington, DC, 1948); Robert Leckie, *Okinawa: The Last Battle of World War II* (New York, 1995).

62. See Edward J. Drea, *MacArthur's ULTRA: Codebreaking and the War Against Japan, 1942–1945* (Lawrence, Kansas, 1992), 207–209; James MacGregor Burns, "Kyushu, the War-Ending Invasion That Wasn't," the *New York Times*, Aug. 13, 1995, E6; John Ray Skates, *The Invasion of Japan: Alternative to the Bomb* (Columbia, S.C., 1994).

63. For statements of top Japanese officials, as obtained by the United States Strategic Bombing Survey, see Robert P. Newman, "Ending the War with Japan: Paul Nitze's 'Early Surrender' Counterfactual," *Pacific Historical Review*, 64 (Dec. 1995), 178–189.

64. Leahy, *I Was There*, 384–385; Ernest J. King and Walter Whitehill, *Fleet Admiral King: A Naval Record* (New York, 1952), 598.

65. H. H. Arnold, *Global Mission* (New York, 1949), 595–596. For the larger debate over strategy for victory see Charles F. Brower IV, "Sophisticated Strategist: General George A. Lincoln and the Defeat of Japan, 1944–45," *Diplomatic History*, 15 (Summer 1991), 322–326.

66. Louis Morton, "The Decision to Use the Atomic Bomb," Kent Roberts Greenfield, ed., *Command Decisions* (Washington, DC, 1990), 501–502; Brower, "Sophisticated Strategist," 322–326.

67. Morton, "The Decision to Use the Atomic Bomb," 504–506; Murray Sale, "Letter From Hiroshima: Did the Bomb End the War?" the *New Yorker*, July 31, 1995, 52; Robert J. C. Butow, *Japan's Decision to Surrender* (Stanford, Calif., 1954), 75, chap. 6; *FRUS: Berlin*, 1945: I, 873–883; Robert P. Newman, *Truman and the Hiroshima Cult* (East Lansing, Mich., 1995), 12–13; for the many unofficial Japanese efforts at peace in April and May 1945 see Hanson W. Baldwin, "How the Decision to Drop the Bomb Was Made: 'Little Boy's' Long, Long Journey," the *New York Times Magazine*, Aug. 1, 1965, 6–7, 44.

68. For Grew's appeal see Martin J. Sherwin, "Hiroshima and Modern Memory," *The New Republic* (Oct. 10, 1981), 352; Morton, "The Decision to Use the Atomic Bomb," 506–507; Truman, *Year of Decisions*, 416–417; Joseph C. Grew, *Turbulent Era*, II, chap. 36.

69. For Sato's failures in Moscow see John A. Harrison, "The USSR, Japan, and the End of the Great Pacific War," *Parameters*, 14 (Summer 1984), 76–85.

70. Richard Rhodes, *The Making of the Atomic Bomb*; Robert Gilpin, *American Scientists and Nuclear Policy* (Princeton, NJ, 1962); Robert Jungk, *Brighter Than a Thousand Suns: A Personal History of the Atomic Scientists* (New York, 1958); Ruth Moore, *Niels Bohr: The Man, His Science, and the World They Changed* (New York, 1966), 342–343; S. Rozenthal, ed., *Niels Bohr: His Life and Work as Seen by His Friends and Colleagues* (New York, 1967). Ian Christopher Graig traces the effort of Bohr, other scientists, and U.S. leaders to advance the international control of atomic weapons in "A Missed Opportunity: The Pursuit of the International Control of Atomic Weapons, 1943–1946," Ph.D. Dissertation, University of Virginia, 1987.

71. Barton J. Bernstein, "Hiroshima Reconsidered—Thirty Years Later," *Foreign Service Journal*, (Aug. 1975), 8–9; Martin J. Sherwin, "Scientists, Arms Control, and National Security," Norman A. Graebner, ed., *The National Security: Its Theory and Practice, 1945–1960* (New York, 1986), 111–113.

72. Morton, "The Decision to Use the Atomic Bomb," 496–497; Bernstein, "Hiroshima Reconsidered," 9–10.

73. Morton, "The Decision to Use the Atomic Bomb," 498; Bernstein, "Hiroshima Reconsidered," 10; Interim Committee discussion of May 31, Barton J. Bernstein, *The Atomic Bomb: The Critical Issues* (Boston, 1976), 24; McGeorge Bundy, *Danger and Survival: Choices About the Bomb in the First Fifty Years* (New York, 1983), 67; Baldwin, "How the Decision to Drop the Bomb Was Made," 45–46.

74. For the Franck Report see Bernstein, *The Atomic Bomb: The Critical Issues*, 25–29; Morton, "The Decision to Use the Atomic Bomb," 498; Berstein, "Hiroshima Reconsidered," 10. For commentary on the Franck Report see Sherwin, "Scientists, Arms Control, and National Security," 115–116.

75. Stimson, "The Decision to Use the Atomic Bomb," 101.

76. Morton, "The Decision to Use the Atomic Bomb," 499–500; Bernstein, "Hiroshima Reconsidered," 10; Sherwin, "Scientists, Arms Control, and National Security," 116.

77. For the July 2 memorandum see Stimson, "The Decision to Use the Atomic Bomb," 103–105.

78. Joseph M. Siracusa, *Nuclear Weapons: A Very Short Introduction* (Oxford: Oxford University Press, 2008), 20. Also see, Richard G. Hewlett and Oscar E. Anderson, *The New World, 1939–1946: A History of the United States Atomic Energy Commission*, I (University Park, Pa., 1962), 389; Martin J. Sherwin, *A World Destroyed: The Atomic Bomb and the Grand Alliance* (New York, 1975); and Editorial, the *New York Times*, Aug. 6, 1945, E 14.

79. Henry L. Stimson and McGeorge Bundy, *On Active Service in Peace and War* (New York, 1948), 637; Churchill, *Triumph and Tragedy*, 638–639; Truman, *Year of Decisions*, 458; Eden, *The Reckoning*, 635.

80. Japan's peace feelers remained vague and uncompromising, although at Potsdam it mattered little. See Barton J. Bernstein, "Roosevelt, Truman, and the Atomic Bomb, 1941–1945: A Reinterpretation," *Political Science Quarterly*, 90 (Spring 1975), 57–58; for Soviet decisions, see David Holloway, *Stalin and the Bomb: The Soviet Union and Atomic Energy, 1939–1956* (New Haven: Yale University Press, 1994), chap 6 & 7.

81. For Byrnes's desire to keep the Soviet Union out of the Pacific war see Byrnes, *Speaking Frankly*. 207–208; James F. Byrnes, *All in One Lifetime* (New York: Harper and Bros., 1958), 305–307; Herbert Feis, *Between War and Peace: The Potsdam Conference* (Princeton, NJ, 1960), 113; Truman, *Year of Decisions*, 401.

82. Harriman and Abel, *Special Envoy to Churchill and Stalin*, 483; Byrnes, *Speaking Frankly*, 205; N. S. Khrushchev, *Khrushchev Remembers: The Glasnost' Tapes* (Boston, 1990), 81.

83. Newman, *Truman and the Hiroshima Cult*, 69–72; Kase Toshikazu, *Journey to the Missouri*, ed. David N. Rowe (New Haven, 1950), 209–210; Kato Masuo, *The Lost War* (New York, 1946), 233; Weinberg, *A World at Arms*, 888.

84. Sherwin, *A World Destroyed*, 235 (check); Sherwin, "Hiroshima and Modern Memory," 352; Leon V. Sigal, *Fighting to a Finish: The Politics of War Termination in the United States and Japan, 1945* (Ithaca, N.Y., 1988), 144–145; Gar Alperovitz, *The Decision to Use the Atomic Bomb and the Architecture of an American Myth* (New York, 1995); Skates, *The Invasion of Japan*, 249–252. Skates declared that unconditional surrender "drove the war to extremes of violence in 1945 and made the atomic bomb seem almost a benign alternative to an invasion." For observations on the Potsdam Declaration's failure to strengthen Japan's peace party see Baldwin, *Great Mistakes of the War*, 88–102, 107; Nicholas D. Kristof's interview with Akihiro Takahashi in the *New York Times*, Aug. 6, 1995, 10.

85. Weinberg, *A World at Arms*.

86. Kazuo Kawai, "Mokusatu, Japan's Response to the Potsdam Declaration," *Pacific Historical Review*, 19 (Nov. 1950), 409–414; William Craig, *The Fall of Japan* (New York, 1967); Kase, *Journey to the Missouri*; Stanley Weintraub, *The*

Last Great Victory: The End of World War II, July/August 1945 (New York, 1995); Butow, *Japan's Decision to Surrender*; Suzuki's reply of July 28, 1945, *FRUS: Berlin, 1945*: II, 1293.

87. Siracusa, *Nuclear Weapons*, 23. For the argument that the Nagasaki bomb had no real effect on Japanese policy and therefore served no purpose, see Barton J. Bernstein, "Doomsday II," the *New York Times Magazine*, July 27, 1975, 7, 21–29. To historian John W. Dower the Nagasaki bomb was unnecessary and thus comprised a war crime. See Dower, "Hiroshima, Nagasaki, and the Politics of Memory," *Technology Review* (MIT), 98 (Aug./Sept. 1995), 49. For Sato's ultimate failure in Moscow see Sale, "Letter from Hiroshima," 56.

88. For the long debate within the Japanese Supreme Council on August 9–10 see Sale, "Letter from Hiroshima," 57–58; Walter Pincus, "Defiance Between the Bombs," *The Washington Post National Weekly Edition*, Aug. 7–13, 1995, 10–11; Butow, *Japan's Decision to Surrender*, 244; Swiss charge to Secretary of State, Aug. 10, 1945, *FRUS*, 1945: VI: The British Commonwealth (Washington, 1969), 627.

89. Byrnes to Swiss Charge, Aug. 11, 1945, *FRUS*, 1945: VI, 631–632; Barton Bernstein, "The Perils and Politics of Surrender: Ending the War with Japan and Avoiding the Third Atomic Bomb," *Pacific Historical Review*, 46 (Nov. 1977), 23–27. Bernstein believed Byrnes's note of August 11 unnecessarily dangerous because its limitations on the Emperor's role played into the hands of Tokyo's extremists. See also Sale, "Letter from Hiroshima," 59.

90. Bernstein, "The Perils and Politics of Surrender," 23–27; Pincus, "Defiance Between the Bombs," 11. On the attempted coup see Pacific War Research Society, *Japan's Longest Day* (Tokyo, 1968).

91. Fred Charles Ikle, *Every War Must End* (Rev. ed., New York, 1991), 93–94; Paul Kecskemeti, *Strategic Surrender* (New York, 1964), 199–200; Sale, "Letter from Hiroshima," 59; Japanese surrender, Swiss charge to Byrnes, Aug. 14, 1945, *FRUS*, 1945: VI, 662–663. On the Emperor's address see Dan van der Vat, *The Pacific Campaign: The U.S.-Japanese Naval War 1941–1945* (New York, 1991), 398.

92. Morton, "The Decision to Use the Atomic Bomb," 494; and Robert H. Ferrell, *Harry S. Truman and the Modern American Presidency* (Boston: Little, Brown, 1983), 56–57. Also see Truman's conversation with Admiral Walter C. Mott in *The Daily Progress* (Charlottesville), Aug. 6, 1995, D1, D6; and Godfrey Sperling's interview with Truman in 1953, *Christian Science Monitor*, Sept. 12, 1995, 19.

93. For the military's response to the Hiroshima bombing see I. B. Holley, Jr., "Second-Guessing History," *Technology Review* (MIT), 98 (Aug./Sept. 1995), 52–53; Alexander Burnham, "Okinawa, Harry Truman, and the Atomic Bomb," *The Virginia Quarterly Review*, 71 (Summer 1995), 389–392.

94. USSBS, *Summary Report (Pacific War)* (Washington, DC, 1946), 26, also quoted in Newman, *Truman and the Hiroshima Cult*, 36; USSBS, *Japan's Struggle to End the War* (Washington, 1946), 6–13. Both this volume and Paul Nitze's memoirs, *From Hiroshima to Glasnost: At the Center of Decision* (New York, 1989), 36–37, argue that the Japanese would have surrendered by November 1 without the bomb. For the views of Nimitz, Arnold, and Chenault see Morton, "The Decision to Use the Atomic Bomb," 517.

95. Macdonald in *Politics*, II (Aug.–Sept. 1945), 225, 257–260; *U.S. News & World Report*, July 31, 1995, 54–55; Pincus, "Defiance Between the Bombs," 10; Baldwin, *Great Mistakes of the War*, 105–7.

96. For the horrors of Hiroshima see John Hersey, "Hiroshima," the *New Yorker*, Aug. 31, 1946; John W. Dower, "Hiroshima, Nagasaki, and the Politics of Memory," *Technology Review* (MIT), 98 (Aug./Sept. 1995), 49; Dower, *Japan in War and Peace* (New York, 1995); Nicholas D. Kristof's interview with Akihiro Takahashi in the *New York Times*, Aug. 6, 1995, 10; *The Economist*, 336 (July 29, 1995), 63. On official U.S. efforts to protect the American public from the realities of the bombs see Robert Jay Lifton, *Death in Life* (New York, 1968); Robert Jay Lifton and Greg Mitchell, *Hiroshima in America: Fifty Years of Denial* (New York, 1995).

97. Sale, "Letter from Hiroshima," 64; Skates, *The Invasion of Japan*, 249–252; Kecskemeti, *Strategic Surrender*, 199–200; Sigal, *Fighting to a Finish*. In general these writers agree with the USSBS's rejection of the role of the Hiroshima bomb in ending the war.

98. For criticism of the immediate dropping of the Hiroshima bomb see Norman Cousins and Thomas K. Finletter, "A Beginning for Sanity," *Saturday Review of Literature*, 29 (June 15, 1946), 7; P. M. S. Blackett, *Fear, War, and the Bomb: Military and Political Consequences of Atomic Energy* (New York, 1949), 130–143; Baldwin, *Great Mistakes of the War*, 88–107.

99. For criticism that the administration never gave sufficient consideration to an alternative see Gabriel Kolko, *The Politics of War: The World and United States Foreign Policy, 1943–1945* (New York, 1968), 595–600. Such scientists as Robert Oppenheimer and Edward Teller never opposed the making and use of the atomic bomb, but they agreed that the administration failed to issue sufficient warnings and assurances. See William L. Laurence, "Would You Make the Bomb Again?" The *New York Times Magazine*, Aug. 1, 1965, 8–9, 52–53. Teller, in a letter to Szilard of July 2, 1945, absolved the scientists of any responsibility for the use of the bomb, but believed that the American public should know the results of what the scientists had achieved as a warning against another war, a revelation that might come most instructively through its combat-use.

100. Karl T. Compton, "If the Atomic Bomb Had Not Been Used," the *Atlantic Monthly*, 178 (Dec. 1946), 54–56; Henry L. Stimson, "The Decision to Use the Atomic Bomb," *Harper's*, 194 (Feb. 1947), 97–107; Samuel Eliot Morison, "Why Japan Surrendered," the *Atlantic Monthly*, 206 (Oct. 1960), 41–47. General Leslie R. Groves defended the use of the bomb in *Now It Can Be Told: The Story of the Manhattan Project* (New York, 1962); see also Herbert Feis, *The Atomic Bomb and the End of World War II* (Rev. ed., Princeton, NJ, 1966), 190–201. The defense of the Hiroshima decision may be found in Norman Polmar and Thomas B. Allen, *Code-Name Downfall: The Secret Plan to Invade Japan and Why Truman Dropped the Bomb* (New York, 1995); Stanley Weintraub, *The Last Great Victory: The End of World War II, July/August 1945* (New York, 1995); and Robert P. Newman, *Truman and the Hiroshima Cult* (East Lansing, 1995). In 1965 Baldwin refused to pass judgment on the Hiroshima decision. See Baldwin, "How the Decision to Drop the Bomb Was Made," 51.

101. Bundy, *Danger and Survival*, 94–97; Thomas Powers, "Was It Right?" the *Atlantic Monthly*, 276 (July 1995), 20–23; *The Economist*, 336 (Aug. 1995), 16.

102. Bernstein, "Hiroshima Reconsidered," 10–11; on Truman see Jonathan Daniels, *The Man From Independence* (Philadelphia, 1950), 266; Byrnes quoted in Leo Szilard, "A Personal History of the Atomic Bomb," *The University of Chicago Round Table*, 601 (Sept. 25, 1949), 14–15; Leo Szilard, "Reminiscences," Donald Fleming and Bernard Bailyn, eds., *The Intellectual Migration* (Cambridge, Mass., 1969), 124–26; Alice K. Smith, *A Peril and a Hope: The Scientists' Movement in America* (Chicago, 1965), 29; Truman, *Year of Decisions*, 87; Morton, "The Decision to Use the Atomic Bomb," 510.

103. Hewlett and Anderson, *The New World*, 419–421; Truman, *Year of Decisions*, 525–529; The *New York Times*, Sept. 22, 1945, 1.

104. For views that the bomb decision and the rivalry that it unleashed contributed to the Cold War, see Martin J. Sherwin, "The Atomic Bomb and the Origins of the Cold War: U.S. Atomic-Energy Policy and Diplomacy, 1941–1945," *The American Historical Review*, 78 (Oct. 1973), 966–968; Bernstein, *Hiroshima and Nagasaki Reconsidered*, 24–26.

105. See, for example, Adam Ulam, *Expansion and Coexistence: The History of Soviet Foreign Policy* (London, 1968).

106. *The Department of State Bulletin*, 13 (Sept. 30, 1945), 478.

107. Byrnes, *Speaking Frankly*, 97–101.

108. Ethridge to Byrnes, Dec. 7, 1945, *FRUS*, 1945: V, 633–637; Byrnes, *Speaking Frankly*, 107; Millis, *Forrestal Diaries*, 124.

109. Eduard Mark, "Charles E. Bohlen and the Acceptable Limits of Soviet Hegemony in Eastern Europe: A Memorandum of October 18, 1945," *Diplomatic History*, 3 (Spring 1979), 206–209; Robert L. Messer, "Paths Not Taken: The United States Department of State and Alternatives to Containment, 1945–1946," ibid., 1 (Fall 1977), 301–304.

110. Truman's speech of November 27, 1945, *Public Papers of the Presidents of the United States: Harry S. Truman, 1945* (Washington, 1961), 434; Byrnes's address of Oct. 31, 1945, *The Department of State Bulletin*, 13 (Nov. 4, 1945), 709–711.

111. Walter Lippmann, "Today and Tomorrow," *New York Herald-Tribune*, Oct. 30, 1945, 25, quoted in Berdahl, "The Emergence of American Cold War Policy, 1945–1947," 65–66.

112. Bohlen quoted in Fraser J. Harbutt, *The Iron Curtain: Churchill, America, and the Origins of the Cold War* (New York, 1986), 132; Harriman and Abel, *Special Envoy*, 461–462; Melvyn P. Leffler, *A Preponderance of Power: National Security, the Truman Administration, and the Cold War* (Stanford, 1992), 33, 46–47; Lyon, 387.

113. Ethridge memorandum, Dec. 7, 1945, *FRUS*, 1945: V, 637; Hickerson to Byrnes, Dec. 10, 1945, ibid., IV, 407; Joint Chiefs of Staff quoted in Leffler, *A Preponderance of Power*, 50.

CHAPTER 4

1. For a brief survey of the Iranian question see Joseph Marion Jones, *The Fifteen Weeks: An Inside Account of the Genesis of the Marshall Plan* (New York, 1955), 48–52. The warnings of the Iranian ambassador were reported in Acheson to Harriman, Dec. 21, 1945, *FRUS*, 1945: VIII (Washington, 1969), 508.

2. Henderson quoted in Daniel Yergin, *Shattered Peace: The Origins of the Cold War and the National Security State* (Boston, 1977), 152.

3. Truman, *Year of Decisions*, 522–553; "What Is Happening in Iran," *The New Republic*, 113 (Dec. 3, 1945), 731–732.

4. Byrnes, *Speaking Frankly*, 109. In Moscow, Kennan opposed the conference, convinced that Byrnes would achieve nothing substantial. See George F. Kennan, *Memoirs: 1925–1950* (Boston, 1967), 284–286.

5. The United States recognized Rumania's Groza regime in Jan. 1946, when it admitted two members from opposition parties and promised free elections. Meeting resistance to its demands in Bulgaria, the United States did not recognize that country's government until October 1947.

6. Kennan, *Memoirs: 1925–1950*, 284; Davis, *The Cold War Begins*, 332; Philip R. Mosely, *The Kremlin and World Politics: Studies in Soviet Policy and Action* (New York, 1960), 217.

7. Byrnes, *Speaking Frankly*, 111–112. Some members of the press, like Harriman and Bohlen, believed Byrnes's concessions at Moscow essential, permitting the Big Three to move forward toward a general postwar settlement. See, for example, "Concessions and Confidence," *Manchester Guardian*, Jan. 4, 1946, 2–3; "Good News from Moscow," *The New Republic*, 114 (Jan. 7, 1946), 3–4.

8. On American-British relations at Moscow see Harbutt, *The Iron Curtain*, 120–123; James L. Gormly, *The Collapse of the Grand Alliance, 1945–1948* (Baton Rouge, La., 1987), 133; Best, *"Cooperation With Like-Minded Peoples"*, 26; Kennan, *Memoirs: 1925–1950*, 286.

9. Ryan, *The Vision of Anglo-America*, 55–56; Robin Edmonds, *Setting the Mould: The United States and Britain, 1945–1950* (New York, 1986), 99; Richard N. Gardner, *Sterling-Dollar Diplomacy in Current Perspective* (New York, 1980), passim; Vandenberg and Morris, *Private Papers of Senator Vandenberg*, 230–231.

10. Ryan, *The Vision of Anglo-America*, 58; Edmonds, *Setting the Mould*, 100–103.

11. John Lewis Gaddis, *The United States and the Origins of the Cold War, 1941–1947* (New York, 1972), 282–290; Truman, *Year of Decisions*, 549; Gormly, *The Collapse of the Grand Alliance*, 135.

12. Truman to Byrnes, Jan. 5, 1946 (unsent), Robert H. Ferrell, ed., *Off the Record: The Private Papers of Harry S. Truman* (New York, 1980), 79–80; Truman, *Year of Decisions*, 552.

13. Gormly, *The Collapse of the Grand Alliance*, 135–136; Harbutt, *The Iron Curtain*, 144.

14. Stalin, "New Five-Year Plan for Russia," *Vital Speeches of the Day*, 12 (Mar. 1, 1946), 300–301.

15. Harriman and Abel, *Special Envoy*, 547; *Newsweek*, Feb. 18, 1946, 47; *Time*, Feb. 18, 1946, 29–30; Douglas quoted in Millis, *Forrestal Diaries*, 134.

16. "The Capabilities and Intentions of the Soviet Union as Affected by American Policy," SDF 711.61/12-1045; Durbrow and Matthews memorandum, Feb. 14, 1946, SDF 711.61/2-1446, National Archives, in Messer, "Paths Not Taken," 304–313.

17. For Kennan's Long Telegram see Kennan, *Memoirs: 1925–1950*, 547–559.

18. Messer, "Paths Not Taken," 314n; Matthews to Caffery, Feb. 26, 1946, quoted in Gimbel, *Origins*, 131; Isaacson and Thomas, *The Wise Men*, 354–355; Louis J. Halle, *The Cold War As History* (New York, 1967), 105; Millis, *Forrestal Diaries*, 136.

19. Kennan's *Memoirs: 1925–1950*, 550. For a critique of Kennan's Long Telegram see Anders Stephanson, *Kennan and the Art of Foreign Policy* (Cambridge, Mass., 1989), 46–53; and Joseph M. Siracusa, *Into the Dark House: American Diplomacy and the Ideological Origins of the Cold War* (Claremont, CA: Regina Books, 1998), 31–56.

20. For Republican attacks on the Truman administration for its failure to control Soviet actions, especially in Eastern Europe, see Bradford Westerfield, *Foreign Policy and Party Politics: Pearl Harbor to Korea* (New Haven, 1955), 204–209; *New York Times*, Dec. 6, 1945, 18; Clare Booth Luce in ibid., Feb. 13, 1946, 18. For examples of Catholic opinion see Norman A. Graebner, *America as a World Power: A Realist Appraisal from Wilson to Reagan* (Wilmington, Del., 1984), 134–135.

21. Vandenberg's address in Vandenberg and Morris, *Private Papers of Senator Vandenberg*, 247–248; Byrnes's speech in the Department of State *Bulletin*, 14 (Mar. 10, 1946), 358. On American opinion in the spring of 1946 see Martin Kriesberg, "Dark Ages of Ignorance," Lester Markel, ed., *Public Opinion and Foreign Policy* (New York, 1949), 54; Thomas G. Paterson, *On Every Front: The Making of the Cold War* (New York, 1979), 119–121. Paterson notes that much of the American elite endorsed the tough approach.

22. For the evidence of the country's unconcern for means see the *London Observer*, Mar. 14, 1946, 4; Anne O'Hare McCormick, "Foreign Affairs," the *New York Times*, July 3, 1946, 24; *The New Republic*, 114 (Mar. 11, 1946), 348; Larson, 262–263. In addressing the Senate, Vandenberg found the means for controlling Soviet policy in Poland in the "organized conscience of the world." See Vandenberg and Morris, *Public Papers of Senator Vandenberg*, 244–245.

23. Churchill's Fulton speech of Mar. 5, 1946, *Vital Speeches of the Day*, 12 (Mar. 15, 1946), 329–332. For the background and context of the speech see Henry B. Ryan, "A New Look at Churchill's 'Iron Curtain' Speech," *The Historical Journal*, 22, No. 4 (1979), 894–910; Donovan, *Conflict and Crisis*, 190; Harry S. Truman, *Memoirs, II: Years of Trial and Hope* (New York, 1965), 117.

24. Gaddis, *The United States and the Origins of the Cold War*, 307–309; Halle, *The Cold War As History*, 102–103; Gormly, *The Collapse of the Grand Alliance*, 152; Harbutt, *The Iron Curtain*, 212.

25. Best, *"Co-operation With Like-Minded Peoples"*, 121–122; *FRUS*, 1946: I (Washington, 1972), 1165–1166.

26. David S. McLellan, *Dean Acheson: The State Department Years* (New York, 1976), 92–95. For the loan debate in Congress see Robert M. Hathaway, *Ambiguous Partnership: Britain and America, 1944–1947* (New York, 19891), 244–247; Herter quoted in Gardner, *Sterling-Dollar Diplomacy*, 250; Reston quoted in the *New York Times*, May 31, 1946, 8.

27. John H. Crider in the *New York Times*, Apr. 21, 1946; Thomas G. Paterson, "The Abortive American Loan to Russia and the Origins of the Cold War, 1943–1946," *The Journal of American History*, 56 (June 1969), 86–88.

28. For the opening debates see "Paris," *Manchester Guardian*. Apr. 26, 1946, 110; "The Atlantic Report—Europe," *The Atlantic Monthly*, 177 (June 1946), 13; Saville Davis, "Soviet Policy at Paris," *The New Republic*, 114 (May 20, 1946), 722; "One Year After," ibid., 715; Vandenberg and Morris, *Private Papers of Senator Vandenberg*, 271–272.

29. Bohlen, *Witness to History*, 253–255; Byrnes, *Speaking Frankly*, 280–281; Norman A. Graebner, *Cold War Diplomacy: American Foreign Policy, 1945–1975* (2nd. ed., New York, 1977), 31.

30. For observations on the absence of agreement in Paris see "A Warning," *Manchester Guardian*, May 31, 1946, 279; Vandenberg and Morris, *Private Papers of Senator Vandenberg*, 279; Thomas T. Connally, *My Name Is Tom Connally* (New York, 1954), 297; "Paris Post-Mortem," *The New Republic*, 114 (June 3, 1946), 788; Saville Davis, "Power Politics at Paris," ibid., 114 (May 13, 1946), 685; C. L. Sulzberger in the *New York Times*, May 16, 1946, 1; *Newsweek*, May 20, 1946, 34, 40. For a detailed account of the first session art Paris see Patricia Dawson Ward, *The Threat of Peace: James F. Byrnes at the Council of Foreign Ministers, 1945–1956* (New York, 1979), 78–102. Her portrayal delineates the frustrations of the successive sessions as recorded by the participants.

31. On the French problem see Gimbel, *Origins*, 44–47, 86–89.

32. "East and West," *Manchester Guardian*, May 24, 1946, 262; Gimbel, *Origins*, 1223–1225. Vandenberg discussed the German problem at length in his report to the Senate, July 16, 1946, *Vital Speeches of the Day*, 12 (Aug. 1, 1946), 613 620. For Byrnes's Stuttgart speech see Department of State *Bulletin*, 14 (Sept. 15, 1946), 496–501.

33. On Byrnes's determination see *Time*, May 27, 1946, 26; "Problems of Paris," *The New Republic*, 114 (June 17, 1946), 853; Vandenberg and Morris, *Private Papers of Senator Vandenberg*, 292. For the problems and gains of the second session at Paris see Saville Davis, "Costly Harmony at Paris," *The New Republic*, 115 (July 15, 1946), 38; "The Atlantic Report—Europe," *The Atlantic Monthly*, 178 (Aug. 1946), 3; Ward, *The Threat of Peace*, 103–126.

34. "Paris in Review," *Manchester Guardian*, Oct. 18, 1946, 202; "The Atlantic Report—Paris," *The Atlantic Monthly*, 178 (Oct. 1946), 3–7; "Washington," ibid., 15; "Byrnes, Hull and Peace," *The New Republic*, 115 (Oct. 14, 1946), 467; "What Blocks World Peace," ibid., 115 (Oct. 21, 1946), 501; J. Alvarez del Vayo, "Will Russia Break with the West?" *The Nation*, 163 (Aug. 24, 1946), 204; Ward, *The Threat of Peace*, 127–151.

35. Department of State *Bulletin*. 16 (Feb. 2, 1947), 183–186; "Too Much Blue," *The New Republic*, 115 (Nov. 15, 1946), 676–677; "Trieste Compromise," *Manchester Guardian*, Dec. 6, 1946, 310; "Change of Mind," ibid., Dec. 13, 1946, 326; Ward, *The Threat of Peace*, 152–169.

36. Clyde Eagleton, "The Beam In Our Own Eye," *Harper's Magazine*, 192 (June 1946), 483; Wallace to Truman, July 23, 1946, President's Secretary's File, Papers of Harry S. Truman, Harry S. Truman Library, Independence. Henry Wallace's Madison Garden speech, Sept. 12, 1946, *Vital Speeches of the Day*, 12 (Oct. 1, 1946), 738–741; Henry A. Wallace, "The Path to Peace with Russia," *The New Republic*, 115 (Sept. 30, 1946), 401–403. On Wallace's dismissal see

Vandenberg and Morris, *Private Papers of Senator Vandenberg*, 300–302; "After the Wallace Dismissal: Crisis in Foreign Policy," *The New Republic*, 115 (Sept. 30. 1946), 395–396; Claude Pepper in the *New York Times*, Sept. 13, 1946, 1; Joseph C. Harsch in *The Christian Science Monitor*, Oct. 4, 1946, 18.

37. Reinhold Niebuhr, "Europe, Russia, and America," *The Nation*, 163 (Sept. 14, 1946), 288–289; Walter Lippmann, "A Year of Peacemaking," *The Atlantic Monthly*, 178 (Dec. 1946), 35–40.

38. Truman's address to Congress, Jan. 6, 1947, Department of State *Bulletin*, 16 (Jan. 19, 1947), 123; Byrnes's statements in ibid., 87, 123; ibid., 16 (Mar. 23, 1947), 541.

39. Best, *"Co-operation With Like-Minded Peoples"*, 38–41; J. Alvarez del Vayo, "Will Russia Break With the West?" *The Nation*, 163 (Aug. 24, 1946), 205–206.

40. Hugh De Santis, *The Diplomacy of Silence: The American Foreign Service, the Soviet Union, and the Cold War, 1933–1947* (Chicago, 1980); Thomas Hammond, ed., *Communist Take-Overs*, 302ff.

41. Joseph and Stewart Alsop, "Tragedy of Liberalism," *Life*, 20 (May 20, 1946), 69. See also Ernest R. May, *The "Lessons" of History: The Use and Misuse of the Past in American Foreign Policy* (New York, 1973), 34–35.

42. *FRUS*, 1946: VII, 507–509; ibid., 529–536.

43. For a detailed account of the growth of the U.S. commitment to Iran after March 1946 see Richard Pfau, "Containment in Iran, 1946: The Shift to an Active Policy," *Diplomatic History*, 1 (Fall 1977), 361–372.

44. *FRUS*, 1946: VII, 818–819, 830, 840–841; Leffler, *A Preponderance of Power*, 124–125; Melvyn P. Leffler, "Strategy, Diplomacy, and the Cold War: The United States, Turkey, and NATO, 1945–1952," *The Journal of American History*, 71 (Mar. 1985), 810–811.

45. Some U.S. officials and analysts, including Durbrow, doubted that the Soviets intended to use force against Turkey. See Leffler, *A Preponderance of Power*, 124. Leffler notes that Moscow no less than Washington viewed Turkey as strategically important in "Strategy, Diplomacy, and the Cold War," 813.

46. For a discussion of the Turkish episode see Jonathan Knight, "American Statecraft and the 1946 Black Sea Straits Controversy," *Political Science Quarterly*, 90 (Fall 1975), 460ff; Kuniholm, *The Origins of the Cold War in the Near East*, 316–317, 356; Ulam, *Expansion and Coexistence*, 430–431; Truman, *Years of Trial and Hope*, 97; Millis, *Forrestal Diaries*, 192, 196–197, 211; Acheson, *Present at the Creation*, 195–196.

47. James McCormack to Henderson, Sept. 6, 1946, Leffler, *A Preponderance of Power*, 125–126; Henderson's memorandum, Oct. 21, 1946, *FRUS*, 1946: VII, 520–521.

48. Acheson to MacVeagh, *FRUS*, 1946: VII, 286; McLellan, *Dean Acheson: The State Department Years*, 112–124.

49. Millis, *Forrestal Diaries*, 127–128; Gaddis, *The United States and the Origins of the Cold War*, 319. For similar expressions of danger see Smith to Byrnes, May 31, 1946, *FRUS*, 1946: VI, 758; Durbrow to Byrnes, Oct. 31, 1946, ibid., 797; Davies to Smith, Nov. 18, 1946, ibid., 806.

50. John Foster Dulles, "Thoughts on Soviet Foreign Policy and What To Do About It," *Life*, 20 (June 3, 1946), 113–126; (June 10, 1946), 119–120. Quotation

in ibid., 119. See also Dulles's speech at the College of the City of New York, June 19, 1946, *Vital Speeches of the Day*. 12 (July 15, 1946), 593–595. William C. Bullitt, *The Great Globe Itself: A Preface to World Affairs* (New York), 100, 102, 175.

51. The Clifford-Elsey report, "American Relations with the Soviet Union," in Arthur Krock, *Memoirs: Sixty Years on the Firing Line* (New York, 1968), 427, 431, 468, 478, 482; Leffler, *A Preponderance of Power*, 131–133; Best *"Cooperation With Like-Minded Peoples"*, 122–124; Margaret Truman, *Harry S. Truman* (New York, 1973), 347. Clifford recalled that Truman ordered all copies of the report destroyed except his own. In his book, *Counsel to the President: A Memoir* (New York, 1991), Clifford quotes Truman as saying, "If it (the report) leaked it would blow the roof off the Kremlin."

CHAPTER 5

1. Howard Jones, *"A New Kind of War"*: *America's Global Strategy and the Truman Doctrine in Greece* (New York, 1989), 38–39; Joseph M. Jones, *The Fifteen Weeks (February 21–June 5, 1947)* (New York, 1955); Stephen G. Xydis, *Greece and the Great Powers, 1944–1947* (Thessaloniki, 1963); Dean Acheson, *Present at the Creation: My Years in the State Department* (New York, 1969); Edgar O'Ballance, *The Greek Civil War, 1944–1949* (New York, 1966).

2. Melvyn P. Leffler, *A Preponderance of Power* (Stanford, Calif., 1992), 143–144; Eisenhower Papers, VIII, 1581; Meeting of the Secretaries of State, War, and Navy, Mar. 12, 1947, *FRUS*, 1947: V, 109–110; Jones, *The Fifteen Weeks*, 162. For Kennan's countering view of Turkey's importance see George F. Kennan, *Memoirs: 1925–1950* (Boston, 1967), 316–317.

3. Jones, *The Fifteen Weeks*, 153–154; *Foreign Relations of the United States: Diplomatic Papers, 1947*, V (Washington, 1955), 76–77, 121–221.

4. Larson, 330–331.

5. For Marshall's statement see *FRUS*, 1947: V, 60–62. By nature and conviction Marshall was too moderate to elaborate on the evils and ambitions of the U.S.S.R. with much enthusiasm. See Mark A. Stoler, *George C. Marshall: Soldier-Statesman of the American Century* (Boston, 1989), 159; Forrest C. Pogue, *George C. Marshall: Statesman, 1945–1959* (New York, 1973), 151–152.

6. Acheson, *Present at the Creation*, 219.

7. Frederick J. Dobney, ed., *Selected Papers of Will Clayton* (Baltimore, 1971), 138–142; Department of State *Bulletin*, 16 (Mar. 16, 1947), 493.

8. Truman's message to Congress, Mar. 12, 1947, Department of State *Bulletin*, 16 (Mar. 23, 1947), 536. Full text found in Joseph M. Siracusa, *American Diplomatic Revolution: A Documentary History of the Cold War* (New York: Holt, Rinehart and Winston, 1976), 225–229.

9. In defending the Truman Doctrine, Howard Jones observes that the administration used the best analysis of the Greek situation available. It had no choice but to act on the circumstantial evidence and suspicions of Soviet involvement in Greek affairs. U.S. officials, he notes, assumed that aid reached the Greek guerrillas through Albania, Yugoslavia, and Bulgaria, not from the Soviet Union, but they feared that the U.S.S.R. would exploit any gains won by the guerrillas.

Thus in Greece the United States faced a "new kind of war" in which it did not confront the Soviet Union directly, but presumed indirect Soviet involvement which it could not ignore. At the same time, the administration behaved as if the struggle for Greece was a civil conflict and thus limited to Greece itself. "[E]ven if the Soviets were not guilty of the motives and actions attributed to them by American policymakers," Jones concludes, "the perception was more important than whatever the reality might have been." See Jones, *"A New Kind of War"*, 3–6, 46. Other books that defend the Truman Doctrine are Robert H. Ferrell, *George Marshall* (New York, 1966), vol. XV of Samuel F. Bemis and Robert H. Ferrell, eds., *The American Secretaries of State and Their Diplomacy*; Ferrell, *Harry S. Truman and the Modern American Presidency* (Boston, 1983); Herbert Feis, *From Trust to Terror: The Onset of the Cold War, 1945–1950* (New York, 1970); David S. McLellan, *Dean Acheson: The State Department Years* (New York, 1976); John Lewis Gaddis, *The Long Peace: Inquiries into the History of the Cold War* (New York, 1987); Bruce R. Kuniholm, *The Origins of the Cold War in the Near East: Great Power Conflict and Diplomacy in Iran, Turkey, and Greece* (Princeton, NJ, 1980); Walter Isaacson and Evan Thomas, *The Wise Men: Six Friends and the World They Made* (New York, 1986).

10. Larson, 309; Charles E. Bohlen, *Witness to History, 1929–1969* (New York, 1973), 261.

11. Vandenberg to John B. Bennett, Mar. 5, 1947, Arthur H. Vandenberg, Jr. and Joe Alex Morris, eds., *The Private Papers of Senator Vandenberg* (Boston, 1952), 340; Vandenberg to R. F. Moffett, Mar. 12, 1947, ibid., 342. Also see Joseph M. Siracusa, "Munich Analogy," in *Encyclopedia of American Foreign Policy*, 2d ed., eds., Alexander DeConde *et al* (3 vols., New York: Charles Scribner's Sons, 2001), II, 443–454.

12. George quoted in Richard J. Barnet, *Intervention and Revolution: The United States in the Third World* (New York, 1968), 123.

13. Larson, 317–318; C. L. Sulzberger, Nov. 4, 1947, Sulzberger, *Long Row of Candles* (New York, 1969), 364–365.

14. George F. Kennan, *Memoirs: 1925–1950* (Boston, 1967), 316; Alexander Werth, "Two Worlds in Moscow," *The Nation*, 164 (Mar. 22, 1947), 322.

15. Lippmann to Robert Waldo Ruhl, June 17, 1947, John Morton Blum, ed., *Public Phiosopher: Selected Letters of Walter Lippman* (New York, 1985), 496; Ronald Steel, *Walter Lippmann and the American Century* (Boston, 1980), 438–439; Lippmann, "Today and Tomorrow," *New York Herald Tribune*, Mar. 23, 1947, 25.

16. Senate Foreign Relations Committee, *Senate Hearings on Assistance to Greece and Turkey*, 80th Cong., 1st Sess. (Washington, 1947), 30; Hearings before the Senate Foreign Relations Committee on the Greek-Turkish Aid Bill, Department of State *Bulletin*, 16 (Apr. 3, 1947), 878; Jones, *"A New Kind of War"*, 55.

17. Clifford quoted in John Lewis Gaddis, *The United States and the Origins of the Cold War, 1941–1947* (New York, 1972), 350; Jones, *The Fifteen Weeks*, 190.

18. *Congressional Record*, 80th Cong., lst Sess., XCIII, 3195, 3276, 3325.

19. Ibid., 3768, 3771, 3484, 3683, 3753.

20. Ibid., 3281.

21. Leffler, *A Preponderance of Power*, 70, 101–102; Truman, *Off the Record*, 56; Irwin Wall, *French Communism*, 26–51; Caffery to Byrnes, Feb. 9, 1946, *FRUS*, 1946: V, 413; ibid., 432–433, 441–446. Alfred J. Rieber argues that Moscow's concern for French independence from the United States encouraged French Communists to work within the system and support policies that would strengthen French patriotism, reconstruction, and unity. This permitted them to play a leading and constructive role in French politics. See Rieber, *Stalin and the French Communist Party* (New York, 1962), 212–237.

22. Leffler, *A Preponderance of Power*, 120–121; Irwin Wall, *The United States and the Reshaping of Postwar France*, chaps. 2–3.

23. Melvyn P. Leffler, "The United States and the Strategic Dimensions of the Marshall Plan," *Diplomatic History*, 12 (Summer 1988), 279–280; High Strategy of the French Communist Party, May 10, 1946, Department of State File 851.00B/5-1046, Record Group 59, National Archives; Hickerson to Matthews, Feb. 17, 1947, DS/F 761.00/2-1747, ibid.; Cohen memorandum for the Secretary, June 28, 1947, DS/F 851.00/6-2847, ibid.; Caffery to Marshall, May 12, 1947, *FRUS*, 1947: III, 712.

24. Acheson, *Present at the Creation*, 226; Jones, *The Fifteen Weeks*, 199–201; *FRUS*, 1947: III, 197–199.

25. Report of the Special "Ad-Hoc" Committee of the State-War-Navy Coordinating Committee, Apr. 21, 1947, *FRUS*, 1947: III, 204–219.

26. Walt W. Rostow, *The Division of Europe After World War II: 1946* (Austin, 1981), 51, 55, 60; John Gimbel, *The Origins of the Marshall Plan* (Stanford, 1976), 112.

27. Forrest C. Pogue, *George C. Marshall: Statesman, 1945–1959* (New York, 1973), 157, 171, 178; Gimbel, *Origins of the Marshall Plan*, 194, 197–198. For the French problem at Moscow see *FRUS*, 1947: II, 189–195.

28. Charles E. Bohlen, *Witness to History, 1929–1969* (New York, 1973), 262–264. On April 15 Stalin responded to Marshall's regret over the lack of progress by suggesting that after the contestants had exhausted themselves in the opening skirmishes they would recognize the need for compromise. See Jones, *The Fifteen Weeks*, 222–223.

29. Walter Bedell Smith, *My Three Years in Moscow* (Philadelphia, 1950), 211; Hadley Arkes, *Bureaucracy, the Marshall Plan, and the National Interest* (Princeton, NJ, 1972), 41; Gimbel, *Origins of the Marshall Plan*, 194; Pogue, *George C. Marshall: Statesman*, 197–199; Alexander DeConde, "George Marshall," in Norman A. Graebner, ed., *American Secretaries of State in the Twentieth Century* (New York, 1961), 253–255; Speech of the Secretary, Apr. 28, 1947, *Department of State Bulletin*, 16 (May 11, 1947), 919–924. For an amusing view of the absence of accomplishment at Moscow see Interview with John Wills Tuthill, Dec. 18, 1987, Association for Diplomatic Studies/Foreign Service History Center, Georgetown University Library, Washington, DC.

30. Jones, *The Fifteen Weeks*, 240–241; Kennan, *Memoirs: 1925–1950*, 325–336; Acheson, *Present at the Creation*, 228.

31. Acheson, *Present at the Creation*, 227–228; Jones, *The Fifteen Weeks*, 274–281; Walter Isaacson and Evan Thomas, *The Wise Men: Six Friends and the World They Made* (New York, 1986), 409–410.

32. Kennan, *Memoirs: 1925–1950*, 343; Anna Kasten Nelson, ed., *The State Department Policy Planning Staff Papers* [1947–1949] (3 vols., New York, 1983).

33. Clayton quoted in Herbert Feis, *From Trust to Terror* (New York, 1970), 229; Dobney, *Select Papers of Will Clayton*, 206; *FRUS*, 1947: III, 701–702.

34. Dobney, *Select Papers of Will Clayton*, 493–503. Joseph Jones noted the impact of Clayton's report: "Not only Acheson, but others in the Department testify to the vividness and impressiveness of Clayton's recitals during those days; to the sense of urgency he imparted for taking immediate action." Jones, *The Fifteen Weeks*, 249.

35. Acheson, *Present at the Creation*, 232; Jones, *The Fifteen Weeks*, 249–254; Thomas G. Paterson, *Soviet-American Confrontation: Postwar Reconstruction and the Origins of the Cold War* (Baltimore, 1973), 211–212.

36. Marshall's speech of June 5, 1947, *FRUS*, 1947: III, 239; Jones, *The Fifteen Weeks*, 281–284; Pogue, *George C. Marshall, Statesman*, 212–214; Robin Edmonds, *Setting the Mould: The United States and Britain, 1945–1950* (New York, 1986), 161–162. Full text available in Siracusa, *American Diplomatic Revolution*, 255–257.

37. Bohlen believed the invitation to the Soviets a gamble that could drown the whole enterprise. Kennan favored the invitation but doubted that the Soviets could afford to accept it. See Kennan, *Memoirs: 1925–1950*, 339–341; Isaacson and Thomas, *The Wise Men*, 413–414.

38. Edmonds, *Setting the Mould*, 165–169.

39. Gimbel, *Origins of the Marshall Plan*, 175, 196, 225–226; Edmonds, *Setting the Mould*, 167; Michael J. Hogan, *The Marshall Plan: America, Britain, and the Reconstruction of Western Europe, 1947–1952* (Cambridge, 1987), 62.

40. Gimbel, *Origins of the Marshall Plan*, 226–227, 231–233, 243–246, 250–251.

41. Arkes, *Bureaucracy, etc.*, 55–56; Department of State *Bulletin*, 17 (Oct. 5, 1947), 681–683; Gimbel, *Origins of the Marshall Plan*, 258.

42. Djilas, 128–129, 175; M.S. Handler, "The Cominform, Instrument of the Kremlin," the *New York Times Magazine*, Oct. 9, 1949, 62–63.

43. Douglas Kinnard, "Civil-Military Relationships: The President and the General," in Norman A. Graebner, ed., *The National Security: Its Theory and Practice, 1945–1960* (New York, 1986), 199–200; Leffler, *A Preponderance of Power*, 175–178.

44. "The Sources of Soviet Conduct," *Foreign Affairs*, 25 (July 1947), 566–582.

45. The "X" article created the underpinning for the Truman administration's burgeoning hard line as proclaimed in the Truman Doctrine. See Charles Gati, "What Containment Meant," *Foreign Policy*, 7 (Summer 1972), 36.

46. Lippmann published these columns in a small book, *The Cold War* (New York, 1947).

47. Lippmann to Quincy A. Wright, Jan. 23, 1948, Blum, *Public Philosopher: Selected Letters of Walter Lippmann*, 505.

48. Lippmann to Luce, Nov. 14, 1947, Blum, 499; Ronald Steel, *Walter Lippmann and the American Century* (Boston, 1980), 447.

49. Lippmann, *The Cold War*, 168.

50. Steel, *Lippmann*, 444–449.

51. *Department of State Bulletin*, 17 (Nov. 30, 1947), 1025; ibid., (Dec. 28, 1947), 1247.

52. Report of the Policy Planning Staff, Nov. 6, 1947, *FRUS*, 1947: I, 770–771; Kennan, *Memoirs: 1925–1950*, 378.

53. Leffler, *A Preponderance of Power*, 198–199; Edmonds, 169; Arkes, 41.

54. Papers of the Presidents: Truman, 1947, 516–517.

55. Leffler, *A Preponderance of Power*, 200; Gimbel, 268, 272–273.

56. Hogan, 92–93. For the debate on the Marshall Plan and the economic configuration of the elements in American society who favored and opposed the plan see Hogan, 89–99; Arkes, 166–171.

57. Kennan memorandum, Jan. 20, 1948. *FRUS*, 1948: III, 7; Marshall to Inverchapel, Jan. 20, 1948, ibid., 9; Pogue, *George C. Marshall: Statesman*, 289, 318; Bullock, 516–522.

58. *Parliamentary Debates* (Commons), 5th Series, 446 (1947–1948), 383–410; Bullock, Bevin, 483–97.

59. Edmonds, 172–73; Lovett to Inverchapel, Feb. 2, 1948, *FRUS*, 1948: III, 18.

60. Edmonds, 173.

61. Paul Tigrid, "The Prague Coup of 1948: The Elegant Takeover," Thomas T. Hammond, ed., *The Anatomy of Communist Takeovers* (New Haven, 1975), 398–432.

62. There were no real surprises for Harriman. See Siracusa, *The American Diplomatic Revolution*, 56–57.

63. Edmonds, 174–175.

64. Edmonds, 174–175; Douglas to Marshall, Feb. 26, 1948, *FRUS*, 1948: III, 18, 23.

65. John Baylis, *Anglo-American Defense Relations, 1939–1984: The Special Relationship* (London, 1984).

66. Vandenberg; Edmonds, 175–176; Kaplan, 73ff.; Armin Rappaport, "The United States and European Integration," *Diplomatic History*. 5 (1981), 129.

67. Kennan, *Memoirs: 1925–1950*, 404–411.

68. PPS, II, 491; Gaddis, 65, Kaplan 86.

69. Timothy Irland, *Creating the Entangling Alliance: The Origins of the North Atlantic Treaty Organization* (London, 1981), 7, 71, 87; Achilles memorandum of conversation, Feb. 13, 1948, *FRUS*, 1948: II, 64.

70. Citation for NATO.

71. Norman A. Graebner, "The United States and NATO: Ends Without Means," Graebner, *American as a World Power: A Realist Appraisal from Wilson to Reagan* (Wilmington, 1984), 149–150.

72. Gregg Herken, *The Winning Weapon* (New York, 1980); Eisenhower in Graebner, *The National Security* (New York, 1986), 43–44.

73. See Gregg F. Herken, "Atomic Diplomacy Reversed and Revised," Barton Bernstein, ed., *The Atomic Bomb: The Critical Issues* (Boston, 1976), 136–142.

74. Graebner, National Security, No. 49.

75. Graebner, National Security, No. 50.

76. JCS 1844/13, July 21, 1948, Thomas H. Etzold and John Lewis Gaddis, eds., *Containment: Documents on American Policy and Strategy, 1945–1950*

(New York, 1978), 315–323; NSC 30, Sept. 10, 1948, ibid., 339–343; JCS 1952/1, Dec. 21, 1948, ibid., 357; Report of the Army-Navy-Air Force committee headed by General H.R. Harmon, May 11, 1949, ibid., 361–363.

77. Graebner, "The United States and NATO: Means Without Ends," 151–152.

78. Adam B. Ulam, *Expansion and Coexistence* (London, 1968), 440–447.

79. Kennan, *Memoirs, 1925–1950*, 429–442; *FRUS*, 1949: III, 694–751.

80. Kennan, *Memoirs: 1925–1950*, 428–429, 433.

81. Kennan, *Memoirs: 1925–1950*, 423–424, 443–445.

82. *FRUS*, 1949: III, 187–361; Acheson to George Perkins, Oct. 19, 1949, IV, 469–470.

83. Leffler, *A Preponderance of Power*, 158; Dur, *Caffery*, 42; Caffery to Marshall, May 12, 1947, *FRUS*, 1947: III, 710–712; Royal and Forrestal to Marshall, Sept. 5, 1947, ibid., V, 328–329; Memorandum of the Policy Planning Staff, Sept. 24, 1947, ibid., III, 977–981; Matthews to Lovett, July 11, 1947, ibid., 717–721.

84. Leffler, *A Preponderance of Power*, 503–505; Rieber.

85. *FRUS*, 1947: III, 889–892.

86. Jones, 191–226.

87. Leffler, *A Preponderance of Power*. 238–239.

88. Haynes Johnson, "The War That Remade America," *The Washington Post National Weekly Edition*, Aug. 14–20, 1995, 9; Harold J. Laski, "America—1947," *The Nation*, 165 (Dec. 13, 1947), 641. Article dated at London, Nov. 30, 1947.

89. Robert Payne quoted in *Newsweek*, Jan. 11, 1993, 36.

90. Quite naturally those directly involved in the evolution of U.S. policy between 1946 and 1949 took great pride in the decisions. See, for example, Jones, *The Fifteen Weeks*, 259. Reserve their special praise for Harriman, McCloy, Acheson, Lovett, Kennan, and Bohlen for their creativity in helping to design the U.S. policies toward Europe. See *The Wise Men*, 18–35.

91. Gerhard Weinberg, 894–895.

92. Browder quoted in Arthur Schlesinger, Jr., "Some Lessons from the Cold War," *Diplomatic History*, 16 (Winter 1992), 49.

93. For an evaluation of the Soviet system and the attitudes of Soviet citizens toward it at the close of the war and after, see Nina Tumarkin, "The Great Patriotic War as Myth and Memory," *The Atlantic Monthly*, 267 (June 1991), 26–44. Edward Crankshaw discusses the failure of Soviet indoctrination in "Russia's Power: Not Ideas but Force," the *New York Times Magazine*, June 3, 1951, 9, 31–36.

94. Journalist Walter Graebner analyzed well the wartime motivations of the Soviet troops in *Round Trip to Russia* (Philadelphia, 1943), 177–187.

95. Crankshaw, "Russia's Power: Not Ideas but Force," 29–30.

96. Report by the National Security Council on the Position of the United States with Respect to Soviet-Directed World Communism (NSC 7), Mar. 30, 1948, *FRUS*, 1948: I, 546.

97. Ibid.

98. For NSC 20/1 see Etzold and Gaddis, *Containment*, 184–185.

99. Ibid. 212.

100. For the assurances of NSC 20/1 see ibid., 183.

101. NSC 20/4 in *FRUS*, 1948: I, part 2, 663–669.

102. Killan, 56–61.

103. Miscamble, *George F. Kennan*, 347–355.

104. Kennan, *Memoirs: 1925–1950*, 379–380.

105. Churchill quoted in Norman A. Graebner, *Cold War Diplomacy: American Foreign Policy, 1945–1975* (New York, 1977), 57.

106. Acheson quoted in McLellam, *Dean Acheson: The State Department Years*, 163.

CHAPTER 6

1. Isaacs quoted in *Newsweek* (May 28, 1945): 50; *The New Republic* (May 28, 1945): 736.

2. Thomas M. Campbell, *Masquerade Peace: America's UN Policy, 1944–1945* (Tallahassee: Florida State University Press, 1973), 139, 170; Thomas M. Campbell and George C. Herring, eds., *The Diaries of Edward R. Stettinius, Jr., 1943–1946* (New York: New Viewpoints, 1975), 210–211; Michael S. Sherry, *Preparing for the Next War: American Plans for Postwar Defense, 1941–1945* (New Haven: Yale University Press, 1977), passim.

3. Department of State *Bulletin* XIII (Sept. 23, 1945): 423–430.

4. Russell Buhite, ed., *The Dynamics of World Power: A Documentary History of United States Foreign Policy, 1945–1973*, Vol. IV:*The Far East* (New York: Chelsea House Publishers, 1973), 21; on the Russian position in postwar Japan see Harold J. Noble, "The Russians Are Very Busy in Japan," *The Saturday Evening Post* 219 (Nov. 23, 1946): 14–15, 115–120.

5. Louis B. Halle notes the traditional strategic importance of Korea to China, Russia, and Japan and the predictable trouble for U.S. policy there in "The Conduct Versus the Teaching of International Relations," *The Virginia Quarterly Review* 53 (Spring 1977): 213–214.

6. Norman A. Graebner, ed., *Nationalism and Communism in Asia: The American Response* (Lexington, MA: Heath, 1977), xii; see also G.W. Seabridge's address, delivered in Cape Town on Sept. 6, 1944, "Some Problems of the White Man's Return to South-East Asia," *International Affairs* 21 (Apr. 1945): 196–205.

7. On the bases on Asian nationalism see Graebner, *Nationalism and Communism in Asia*, viii–xi.

8. Statement of Feb. 23, 1945, Samuel I. Rosenman, ed., *The Public Papers and Addresses of Franklin D. Roosevelt*, 13 vols. (New York: Random House, 1938–1950).

9. Jefferson Caffrey to Edward R. Stettinius, Mar. 13, 1945, in *Foreign Relations of the United States*, 1945 (Washington, DC: GPO, 1969), VI: 300. Hereafter cites as *FRUS*.

10. Draft Memo by G. H. Blakeslee, Department of State, Apr. 1945; Draft Memo for the President, Division of European Affairs, Apr. 20, 1945; Joseph Grew to Jefferson Caffrey, May 6, 1945; all in Gareth Porter, ed., Gareth Porter, ed., *Vietnam: The Definitive Documentation of Human Decisions*, 2 vols. (Stanfordville, NY: E.M. Coleman, 1979 (Stanfordville, NY: E.M. Coleman, 1979), I: 23–27, 40–41, 46–47, respectively. Also see Joseph M. Siracusa, "The United States, Vietnam,

and the Cold War: A Reappraisal," *Journal of Southeast Asian Studies* 5 (1974): 82–101.

11. Truman to Chiang Kai-shek, Aug. 12, 1945; Caffrey to Byrnes, Sept. 12, 1945; Proclamation by General D.D. Gracey, Saigon, Sept. 21, 1945; all in Porter, *Vietnam*, I:56, 73–74, 78–79.

12. Clyde Edwin Pettit, *The Experts* (Secaucus, NJ: L. Stuart, 1975), 19, 21.

13. U.S. Department of Defense, *The Pentagon Papers: The Defense Department History of United States Decision Making on Vietnam: The Senator Gravel Edition*, 5 vols. (Boston: Beacon, 1971–1972), I: 42–43.

14. On Ho Chi Minh's nationalism see Graebner, *Nationalism and Communism in Asia*, xiii-xiv; *The Pentagon Papers ... The Senator Gravel Edition*, I: 48–49.

15. See Harold Isaacs, *No Peace for Asia* (New York: Macmillan, 1947).

16. For Ho's letters see Porter, *Vietnam*, I, 94ff.

17. Stanley Karnow, *Vietnam: A History* (New York: Viking, 1983), 147.

18. Gravel, I:3; Conversation between George M. Abbott, first secretary in the U.S. embassy in Paris, and Ho Chi Minh, Sept. 12, 1946, Pettit, *The Experts*, 26.

19. Caffrey to Acheson, Nov. 29, 1946, *FRUS*, 1946: III, 63; Acheson to Consul in Saigon, Dec. 5, 1946, ibid., 67.

20. Marshall to Caffrey, Feb. 3, 1947, *FRUS*, 1947 (Washington, DC: GPO, 1972), VI: 67–68.

21. For Moffat's views see Graebner, *Nationalism and Communism in Asia*, 24–33

22. *FRUS*, 1947: VI, 111–112; O'Sullivan to Marshall, July 21, 1947, ibid., 121–123; Department of State Policy Statement on Indochina, Sept. 27, 1945, Porter, *Vietnam*, I:80.

23. *The Pentagon Papers ... The Senator Gravel Edition*, I, 4–5.

24. Bollaert quoted in *Le Monde*, May 17, 1947, Pettit, *The Experts*, 29.

25. Department of State Policy Statement on Indochina, Sept. 27, 1948, Porter, *Vietnam*, I, 180.

26. The Elysee Agreements: President Vincent Auriol to Bao Dai, Mar. 9, 1949, ibid., I: 184–185.

27. Robert Lovett to Caffrey, Jan. 17, 1949, *FRUS*, 1949 (Washington, DC: GPO, 1975), VI, pt. 1: 4–5; Acheson to the Embassy in France, Feb. 25, 1949, ibid., 8–9; Caffrey to Acheson, Mar. 16, 1949, ibid., 12–14; Achilles to John D. Hickerson, Mar. 25, 1949, Porter, *Vietnam*, I:195.

28. Acheson to the consulate in Hanoi, May 20, 1949, *FRUS*, 1949: VII, 29–30.

29. Ambassador to Thailand to Acheson, June 14, 1949, *FRUS*, 1949: VII, 50–51; Butterworth to Acheson, Oct. 20, 1949, ibid., 93; Ronald L. McGlothlen, *Controlling the Waves: Dean Acheson and U.S. Foreign Policy in Asia* (New York: Norton, 1993), 179.

30. Memorandum of conversation between Acheson and Schuman, Sept. 15, 1949, and among Acheson, Schuman, and Ernest Bevin, Sept. 17, 1949, *FRUS*, 1949: VII, 86–89.

31. Porter, *Vietnam*, I:195; Abbott to Acheson, May 6, 1949, *FRUS*, 1949: VII, pt. 1: 22–23; Caffery to Acheson, May 7, 1949, ibid., 23; Ogburn to Reed and O'Sullivan, June 28, 1949, quoted in Andrew J. Rotter, *The Path to Vietnam:*

Origins of the American Commitment to Southeast Asia (Ithaca, NY: Cornell University Press, 1987), 98.

32. Memorandum by Raymond B. Fosdick for Ambassador at Large Philip Jessup, Nov. 4, 1949, Porter, I: 214–215.

33. Buhite, *The Far East*, 103–104.

34. U.S. Department of State, *United States Relations with China* (Washington, DC: GPO, 1949), 86–92. Hereafter cited as *Relations with China*.

35. Chester J. Pach, *Arming the Free World: the Origins of the United States Military Assistance Program, 1945–1950* (Chapel Hill: University of North Carolina Press, 1991): 76–77.

36. Ibid., 78, 84.

37. For a superb, detailed analysis of Marshall's dilemma in confronting the military division of China see ibid., 163–197; Russell D. Buhite, *Soviet-American Relations in Asia, 1945–1954* (Norman: University of Oklahoma Press, 1981), 37–55. Marshall's refusal of any Communist bid for power. See Draft Memorandum, U.S. Embassy in China, Sept. 6, 1946, *FRUS*, 1946: X: 148.

38. Pettit, *The Experts*, 28.

39. See Walter S. Poole, "From Conciliation to Containment: The Joint Chiefs of Staff and the Coming of the Cold War, 1945–1946," *Military Affairs* 42 (Feb. 1978): 15.

40. Colonel Marshall S. Carter to General Marshall, Aug. 14, 1946, *FRUS*, 1946 (Washington, DC: GPO, 1972), X. 27–28. Emphasizing the Asian side of the early Cold War is Akira Iriye, *The Cold War in Asia: A Historical Introduction* (Englewood Cliffs, NJ: McGraw-Hill, 1974).

41. *Relations with China*, 187; Tang Tsou, *America's Failure in China*, 1941–1950 (Chicago: University of Chicago Press, 1963), 356–357, 369–371.

42. Memorandum of the Joint Chiefs of Staff, June 9, 1947, *FRUS*, 1947: VII, 707, 741–759, 845; *Relations with China*, 773; Norman A. Graebner, *The New Isolationism: A Study in Politics and Foreign Policy Since 1950* (New York: Ronald, 1956), 51. Marshall found Wedemeyer's report so confused that he buried it.

43. NSC report of Mar. 1948 quoted in Akira Iriye, "Was There a Cold War in Asia?" in John Chay, ed., *The Problems and Prospects of American-East Asian Relations* (Boulder, CO: Westview, 1977), 7–8; Memorandum of the Policy Planning Staff (NSC 34), Sept. 7, 1948, *FRUS*, 1948: VIII, 147.

44. Stuart to Marshall, May 1948, *Relations with China*, 865.

45. PPS 39, U.S. Interests in China, Sept. 7, 1948, *FRUS*, 1948: VIII, 146–155; NSC, Draft Report on U.S. Policy Toward China, Nov. 2, 1948, Butterworth to Lovett, Nov. 3, 1948, ibid., 185–189; George F. Kennan, *Memoirs, 1925–1950* (Boston: Little, Brown, 1967), 373–374.

46. Document published in *Relations with China*, 280–285.

47. See memorandum of Marshall's meeting with Madame Chiang Kai-shek, Dec. 27, 1948, *FRUS*, 1948: VIII, 302–304.

48. Rotter, *The Path to Vietnam*, 16, 26.

49. Truman quoted in Thomas G. Paterson, "If Europe, Why Not China? The Containment Doctrine, 1947–1949," *Prologue: Journal of the National Archives* 13 (Spring 1981): 32.

50. Arthur H. Vandenberg, Jr., and Joe Alex Morris, eds., *The Private Papers of Senator Vandenberg* (Boston: Houghton Mifflin, 1952), 531.

51. Acheson to Connally, Mar. 15, 1949, *Relations with China*, 1053–1054.

52. Ross Y. Koen, *The China Lobby in American Politics* (New York: Macmillan, 1960), 31–32.

53. Alfred Kohlberg, "Stupidity and/or Treason," *The China Monthly* 9 (June 1948): 151. The repeated theme of *The China Monthly* was the betrayal of China by those who would hinder the return of Chiang Kai-shek to the mainland. See, for example, Colonel W. Bruce Pirnie, "Who Hamstrings U.S. Military Aid to China," ibid., 9 (Oct. 1948): 288–291. Another writer branded all Americans as traitors who were unsympathetic to the Nationalist cause. Mark Tsai, "Now It Can Be Told," ibid., 9 (Sept. 1948), 255.

54. William C. Bullitt, "A Report to the American People on China," *Life* (Oct. 13, 1947): 35–37, 139–154; *Life* (Dec. 20, 1948) quoted in Robert J. Donovan, *Tumultuous Years: the Presidency of Harry S. Truman, 1949–1953* (New York: Norton, 1982), 31.

55. *United States Relations with China*, xiv-xv.

56. Ibid., xvi. This uncompromising conclusion was submitted by consultant Nathanial Peffer of Columbia University. See Robert P. Newman, "The Self-Inflicted Wound: The China White Paper of 1949," *Prologue: Journal of the National Archives* 14 (Fall 1982): 144.

57. *Manila Evening News*, Jan. 9, 11, 1950.

58. *The New Statesman and Nation*, 38 (Oct. 8, 1949): 374. Senator Knowland declared that British recognition of the mainland regime would be the greatest blow to peace since the Munich agreement of 1938. See Australia's *Sydney Morning Herald*, Dec. 2, 1949.

59. On Indian recognition see Loy Henderson to Secretary of State, Dec. 19, 1949, *FRUS*, 1949: IX, 227.

60. The Chinese government announced that it had no interest in recognition except on the bases of the withdrawal of foreign troops, national equality, mutual benefit, mutual respect for independence and territorial integrity, and withdrawal of recognition from the Nationalist government. *The Manchester Guardian Weekly* 60 (June 16, 1949).

61. Cabot to W. Walton Butterworth, Feb. 6, 1948, *FRUS*, 1948: VIII, 467–469; Memorandum prepared by the research division of the Department of State, enclosed with Acting Secretary of State to Certain Diplomatic and Consular Offices, Oct. 13, 1948, ibid., I: 643.

62. *United States Relations with China*, xvi.

63. *The Manchester Guardian Weekly* 61 (Aug. 11, 1949): 8; *The New Statesman and Nation* 38 (Dec. 23, 1949): 751.

64. Ibid.

65. Newman, "The Self-Inflicted Wound," 154–155.

66. Kennan's address of Aug. 22, 1949, Department of State *Bulletin* XXI (Sept. 5, 1949): 324.

67. Newman, "The Self-Inflicted Wound," 150, 152.

68. Quoted in Graebner, *Nationalism and Communism in Asia*, xix.

69. Quoted in Gordon H. Chang, *Friends and Enemies: the United States, China, and the Soviet Union, 1948–1972* (Stanford, CA: Stanford University Press, 1990), 37.

70. Alistair Cooke, "United States and China," *The Manchester Guardian Weekly* 61 (Aug. 11, 1949): 3.

71. Newman, "The Self-Inflicted Wound," 148–149.

72. Vandenberg, *Private Papers*, 538.

73. Buhite, *The Far East*, 70–71.

74. *FRUS*, 1949: VI, 50–51.

75. Rankin to Department of State, Nov. 16, 1949, in Karl Lott Rankin, *China Assignment* (Seattle: University of Washington Press, 1964), 35.

76. Report of the National Security Council on the Position of the United States with Respect to Asia, Dec. 23, 1949 (NSC 48/1), *United States-Vietnam Relations, 1945–1967: Study Prepared by Department of Defense*, 12 Bks (Washington, DC: GPO, 1971), 8:227–228.

77. For an account of U.S. intentions and efforts to produce rifts in Sino-Soviet relations see John Lewis Gaddis, "Dividing Adversaries: The United States and International Communism, 1945–1958," in his *The Long Peace: Inquiries Into the History of the Cold War* (New York: Oxford University Press, 1987), 147–194.

78. *FRUS*, 1945: VI, 1176.

79. *FRUS*, 1945: VI, 1190; *FRUS*, 1946: VIII, 844; *FRUS*, 1947: VI, 1006.

80. *FRUS*, 1947: VI, 1072, 1088.

81. Robert A. Lovett to Frank Graham, *FRUS*, 1947: VI, 1100.

82. *FRUS*, 1948: VI, 207, 227–228; ibid., 394.

83. *FRUS*, 1948: VI, 345.

84. Wilson D. Miscamble, *George F. Kennan and the Making of American Foreign Policy, 1947–1950* (Princeton, NJ: Princeton University Press, 1992), 274.

85. For a superb account of U.S. policy and Indonesian independence, highly critical of Washington's long refusal to accept the reality of Indonesian nationalism, see Robert J. McMahon, *Colonialism and the Cold War: The United States and the Struggle for Indonesian Independence, 19445–1949* (Ithaca, NY: Cornell University Press, 1981). See also Alastair M. Taylor, *Indonesian Independence and the United Nations* (Ithaca, NY: Cornell University Press, 1960); and George McTurnan Kahin, *Nationalism and Revolution in Indonesia* (Ithaca, NY: Cornell University Press, 1952). On why the Indonesian experience varied from that of Indochina, see Evelyn Colbert, "The Road Not Taken: Decolonization and Independence in Indonesia and Indochina," *Foreign Affairs* 51 (Apr. 1973): 608–628.

86. On Nehru's Washington visit see Dean G. Acheson, *Present At the Creation: My Years in the State Department* (New York: Norton, 1969), 334–336. Ambassador to India Loy W. Henderson shared Acheson's view Nehru as difficult and snobbish. To Henderson, as to others, Nehru appeared evasive and utopian in his refusal to see danger in Asian Communism. See H. W. Brands, *Inside the Cold War: Loy Henderson and the Rise of the American Empire, 1918–1961* (New York: Oxford University Press, 1991), 204–205.

87. Kennan's review of current trends, Feb. 24, 1948, *FRUS*, 1948 (Washington, DC: GPO, 1976), I, Pt 2:525.

88. The Director of the PPS to the Secretary of State, Mar. 14, 1948, ibid., 531–538.

89. Memorandum by the Director of the PPS, Oct. 14, 1947, *FRUS*, 1947, 233.

90. Kennan, *Memoirs: 1925–1950*, 375–375, 381, 388–389.

91. Kennan, *Memoirs: 1925–1950*, 375–375, 381, 388–389.

92. Edwin Martin, *The Allied Occupation of Japan* (Westport, CT: Greenwood, 1972), v-vii.

93. Miscamble, *George F. Kennan*, 266–267; *FRUS*, 1948: VI, 857–862; McGlothlin, *Controlling the Waves*, 36–37; Michael Schaller, *The American Occupation of Japan: the Origins of the Cold War in Asia* (New York: Oxford University Press, 1985),155.

94. Kennan, *Memoirs: 1925–1950*, 393; William Sebald, *With MacArthur in Japan* (New York: Norton, 1965) and Charles A. Willoughby, *MacArthur, 1941–1951* (New York: McGraw-Hill, 1954). Both Sebald and Willoughby, close MacArthur associates, make no mention of the changing policies.

95. Miscamble, *George F. Kennan*, 270–271; Roger Dingman, "Strategic Planning and the Policy Process: American Plans for War in East Asia, 1945–1950," *Naval War College Review* 32 (Nov./Dec. 1979): 4–21; Kennan, *Memoirs: 1925–1950*, 392–394; Acting Political Adviser in Japan to Secretary of State, Aug. 20, 1949, *FRUS*, 1949: VII, 831; Memorandum of Conversation by Acting Political Adviser in Japan, Sept. 21, 1949, ibid., 862; Enclosure, NSC 49, Report by Joint Chiefs of Staff, June 9, 1949, ibid., 771–777.

96. For a superb evaluation of the defense perimeter concept see John Lewis Gaddis, "The Strategic Perspective: The Rise and Fall of the 'Defensive Perimeter' Concept, 1947–1951," in Dorothy Borg and Waldo Heinrichs, eds., *Uncertain Years: Chinese-American Relations, 1947–1950*(New York: Columbia University Press, 1980), 64; Acheson, *Present at the Creation*, 357; Strategic Evaluation of United States Security Needs in Japan," June 9, 1949, *FRUS*, 1949: VII, 774–775; Memorandum for the Chief of Staff, U.S. Army, June 23, 1949, ibid., 1056–1057.

97. *FRUS*, 1949: IX, 369–377, 460–461, 464, 468.

98. For Merchant's views see *FRUS*, 1949: IX, 324–326, 337–341, 463–467. On Knowland see *FRUS*, 1950 (Washington, DC: GPO, 1976), VI: 258–263. Truman's statement of Jan. 5, 1950, ibid., 264.

99. For a detailed account of the Formosa issue see McGlothlen, *Controlling the Waves*, 92–125; Buhite, *The Far East*, 91–99.

100. David S. McLellan, *Dean Acheson: The State Department Years* (New York: Dodd, Mead, 1976), 261–262; Norman A. Graebner, *Nationalism and Communism in Asia*, xviii.

101. The position of the United States with Respect to Asia, NSC 48/1, Dec. 23, 1949, U.S. Department of Defense, *United States-Vietnam Relations, 1945–1967*, 12 vols. (Washington, DC: GPO, 1971), VIII: 226–227; NSC 48/2, Dec. 31, 1949, ibid., 265–272.

102. NSC 48/2, Thomas H. Etzold and John Lewis Gaddis, eds. *Containment: Documents on American Policy and Strategy, 1945–1950*(New York: Columbia University Press, 1978), 270–276.

103. Acheson's speech before the National Press Club, Jan. 12, 1950, Department of State *Bulletin*, 22 (Jan. 23, 1950), 116.

104. For Acheson's Europe-first views see Etzold and Gaddis, *Containment*. 114.

CHAPTER 7

1. For a contemporary reaction to these events see Walter Taplin, "The Next Stage in Foreign Policy," *The Listener* 43 (Mar. 9, 1950): 411–412.

2. *Public Papers of the Presidents of the United States: Harry S. Truman, 1949* (Washington, DC: GPO, 1955), 489.

3. *Report Prepared for the Commission on Organization of the Executive Branch by the Committee on the National Security Organization* (Washington, DC: GPO, 1949), 3, 49.

4. *New York Times*, Jan. 16, 1949, 13.

5. John Lewis Gaddis, *Strategies of Containment: A Critical Appraisal of American National Security Policy during the Cold War* (New York: Oxford University Press, 1982), 92–93.

6. Carl Vinson, speech in the House of Representatives, Apr. 4, 1950, in *Cong. Record, 1950*, Vol. 96, Pt 4, 4681–4683.

7. Thomas H. Etzold and John Lewis Gaddis, *Containment: Documents on American Policy and Strategy, 1945–1950* (New York: Columbia University Press, 1978), 366–368.

8. For a detailed account of the nuclear bomb decision see Joseph M. Siracusa, *Into the Dark House: American Diplomacy and the Ideological Origins of the Cold War* (Claremont, CA: Regina Books, 1998), 57–89.

9. Ibid., 373; Harry S. Truman, *Memoirs*, 2 vols. (Garden City, NY: Doubleday, 1955) II: 309–311; David Alan Rosenberg, "American Atomic Strategy and the Hydrogen Bomb Decision," *Journal of American History* 66 (June 1979): 62, 85–87.

10. Kennan's long memorandum against the hydrogen bomb, Jan. 20, 1950, Etzold and Gaddis, *Containment*, 374–381. Kennan regarded this document perhaps the most important of his public career, Kennan, *Memoirs, 1925–1950* (Boston: Little, Brown, 1967), 472. For Acheson's outspoken rejection, see David S. McLellan, *Dean Acheson: The State Department Years* (New York: Dodd, Mead, 1976),176–177.

11. For Truman's announcement on the nuclear bomb program, see *Public Papers of the Presidents: Harry S. Truman, 1950* (Washington, DC: GPO, 1965), 138.

12. The President to the Secretary of State, Jan. 31, 1950, S. Nelson Drew, ed., *NSC-68: Forging the Strategy of Containment* (Washington, DC: National Defense University, 1994), 33; and Joseph M. Siracusa, "NSC 68: A Reappraisal," *Naval War College Review* 33:6 (1980), 4–14.

13. For Nitze's views see ibid., 7–16; Nitze, "Recent Soviet Moves," (Secret study dated Feb. 8, 1950), *FRUS*, 1950: I, 145–146; Nitze in the "Report of State-Defense Review Group Meeting, February 27, 1950," ibid., 171; and Joseph M. Siracusa, "Paul H. Nitze, NSC 68, and the Soviet Union," in *Essays in Twentieth-Century*

American Diplomatic History Dedicated to Professor Daniel M. Smith, C. O. Egan, ed. (Washington, DC: University Press of America, 1982), 192–210.

14. NSC 68 in Etzold and Gaddis, *Containment*, 385–387.

15. Ibid., 413.

16. Ibid., 391, 402.

17. Dean Acheson, *Present at the Creation: My Years in the State Department* (New York: Norton, 1969), 451, 488.

18. Charles E. Bohlen, "Memorandum to the Director of the Policy Planning Staff (Nitze), Apr. 5, 1950, *FRUS*, 1950: I, 224.

19. Drew, *NSC 68*, 56–57.

20. Ibid.

21. NSC 68, Etzold and Gaddis, *Containment*, 422–423, 429.

22. Acheson's press conference on Feb. 8, 1950, Department of State *Bulletin* 22 (Feb. 20, 1950). Coral Bell analyzed the concept of negotiating from strength in her book, *Negotiation from Strength: A Study in the Politics of Power* (New York: Knopf, 1963).

23. Moscow statement in Anders Stephanson, *Kennan and the Art of Foreign Policy* (Cambridge, MA: Harvard University Press, 1989), 107–108; Acheson's Washington address in Department of State, *Strengthening the Forces of Freedom* (Washington, DC: GPO, 1950), 1.

24. Department of State *Bulletin* 22 (Jan. 23, 1950): 115.

25. For the full treaty of Feb. 14, 1950, see Buhite, 162–164. Mao observed Stalin's hesitancy to sign the treaty in Fox Butterfield's article on Mao's secret documents in the *New York Times*, Mar. 1, 1970. Acheson's reaction appears in Department of State *Bulletin* XXII (Mar. 27, 1950): 468.

26. Harrison E. Salisbury in Yonosuke Nagai and Akira Iriye, eds. *The Origins of the Cold War in Asia*(New York: Columbia University Press, 1977), 64–65. Salisbury was in Moscow at the time.

27. Department of State *Bulletin*, XXII (Mar. 27, 1950): 469–472.

28. Loy Henderson's speech before the Indian Council of World Affairs, New Delhi, Mar. 27, 1950, ibid. 22 (Apr. 10, 1950): 563. For a critique of the speech and Henderson's views see H.W. Brands, *Inside the Cold War: Loy Henderson and the Rise of the American Empire, 1918–1961*(New York: Oxford University Press, 1991), 208–209. For Jessup's statement see Department of State *Bulletin* 22 (Apr. 10, 1950): 562; ibid. 22 (Apr. 24, 1950): 627.

29. Alan G. Kirk to Walter Lippmann, Apr. 26, 1950, in John Blum, ed., *Public Philosopher: Selected Letters of Walter Lippmann* (New York: Ticknor & Fields, 1985), 551. For this theme of American omnipotence, with its accompanying theme of conspiracy, see also Charles Burton Marshall, "Foreign Policy Illusions," *The Commonweal* (Oct. 1, 1954): 623–626; Dennis W. Brogan, "The Illusion of American Omnipotence," *American Aspects* (London: H. Hamilton, 1964); and Richard Hofstadter, "The Paranoid Style in American Politics," *Harper's Magazine* (Nov. 1964): 77–86.

30. Hans J. Morgenthau quoted in Norman A. Graebner, *The New Isolationism: A Study in Politics and Foreign Policy Since 1950* (New York: Ronald, 1956), 127.

31. See O. Edmund Clubb, "Security Risks: National Security and the State Department," *Worldview* 16 (Aug. 1973): 43.

32. "Britain and China," *The Economist* 159 (June 24, 1950): 1375; *The New Statesman and Nation* 41 (June 16, 1951): 670.

33. Nancy B. Tucker, Patterns *in the Dust: Chinese-American Relations and the Recognition Controversy, 1949–1950* (New York: Columbia University Press, 1983), 167.

34. Statement by Acheson, Feb. 1, 1950, Department of State *Bulletin* 22 (Feb. 13, 1950): 244.

35. Rusk's testimony of June 8, 1950, in Gareth Porter, ed., *Vietnam: The Definitive Documentation of Human Decisions*, 2 vols. (Stanfordville, NY: E.M. Coleman, 1979), I:266.

36. Russell Buhite, ed., *The Dynamics of World Power: A Documentary History of United States Foreign Policy, 1945–1973*, Vol. IV:*The Far East* (New York: Chelsea House Publishers, 1973), 204; Griffin, encouraged by what he learned in Indochina, observed in Singapore on March 16: "I do not think conditions in Indo-China are hopeless at all. They could become very good." Pettit, *The Experts*, 31.

37. McLellan, *Dean Acheson*, 264.

38. Ibid.

39. Memorandum by Assistant Secretary of State for Far Eastern Affairs to Secretary of State, Apr. 26, 1950, *FRUS*, 1950: VI, 333–335; Memorandum by Rusk to Acheson, May 30, 1950, ibid., 350–351.

40. MacArthur's memorandum on Taiwan's strategic significance, June 14, 1950, *FRUS*, 1950, *Korea* (Washington, DC: GPO, 1976), VII: 161–165.

41. Owen Lattimore, "Our Failure in China," *The Nation* 169 (Sept. 3, 1949): 226; Lippmann quoted in Gilbert C. Fite and Norman A. Graebner, *Recent United States History* (New York: McGraw-Hill, 1972), 577.

42. *Manila Evening News*, June 23, 1950.

43. *The Manchester Guardian Weekly* 61 (Oct. 20, 1949): 3.

44. "America Put to the Test," ibid. 64 (Feb. 8, 1951): 15; "Life and Learning," *The Listener* 41 (Apr. 28, 1949): 1.

45. China Under the Communists," *The Economist* 156 (June 25, 1949): 1189.

46. Patrick O'Donovan, "Asia in Revolt," *The Listener* 42 (Sept. 15, 1949): 430.

47. John King Fairbank, "Toward a New China Policy," *The Nation* 168 (Jan. 1, 1949): 5–8.

48. Nathaniel Peffer, "China in the Long Haul," *Harper's Magazine* 200 (Apr. 1950): 81–82. For Peffer, China was not tied to the Soviet Union, and the United States had no choice but to come to terms with the new regime.

49. J.R. Clementin, "The Nationalist Dilemma in Vietnam," *Pacific Affairs* 23 (Sept. 1950): 295–308.

50. *The New Statesman and Nation* 38 (July 9, 1949): 31; Thomas Cadett, "France's Problem in Indo-China," *The Listener* 43 (May 18, 1950): 859.

51. See Charles DeBenedetti, "The American Peace Movement and Asia, 1941–1961," *Pacific Historical Review* 50 (May 1981): 202.

52. *The Atlantic Monthly*, 263 (Apr. 1989), 40; Wilson D. Miscamble, *George F. Kennan and the Making of American Foreign Policy, 1947–1950* (Princeton, NJ: Princeton University Press, 1992), 277.

53. *FRUS*, 1950: VI, 839.

54. Truman to the Executive Secretary of the National Security Council, Apr. 12, 1950, ibid., I: 234–235.

55. *FRUS*, 1950: VII, 158.

56. Truman's address of June 27, 1950, ibid., 202–203; Acheson to the Embassy in the United Kingdom, June 27, 1950, ibid., 187. Britain and India objected strenuously to Washington's unilateral defense of Formosa. "Plain Words on Formosa," *The New Statesman and Nation* 40 (July 22, 1950): 1.

57. See Norman A. Graebner, "The President as Commander in Chief: A Study in Power," in Joseph G. Dawson, III, ed., *Commanders in Chief: Presidential Leadership in Modern Wars* (Lawrence: University Press of Kansas, 1993), 37–39.

58. John Merrill, *Korea: The Peninsular Origins of the War* (Newark, DE: University of Delaware Press, 1989), chap. 1; James I. Matray, "Civil War of a Sort: The International Origins of the Korean Conflict," in Daniel J. Meador, ed., *The Korean War in Retrospect: Lessons for the Future* (Lanham, MD: University Press of America, 1998), 3–30.

59. Chong-Sik Lee and Ki-wan Oh, "The Russian Faction in North Korea," *Asian Survey* 8 (Apr. 1968): 270–288.

60. Nikita Khrushchev, *Khrushchev Remembers* (Boston: Little, Brown, 1970), 367–373.

61. Ibid., 202–203.

62. Draft Policy Statement Prepared by the Secretary of State, *FRUS*, 1950: I, 217; JCS to MacArthur, June 29, 1950, ibid., 241.

63. Kennan to Acheson, Aug. 8, 1950, *FRUS*, 1950: I, 361; Kennan to Acheson, Aug. 21, 1950, *FRUS*, 1950: VII, 625.

64. Douglas MacArthur, *Reminiscences* (New York: McGraw-Hill, 1964), 341; Buhite, *The Far East*, 385–386.

65. Minutes of Bohlen's meeting with British and French representatives, Paris, Aug. 4, 1950, *FRUS*, 1950 VI, 420.

66. Department of State *Bulletin* 23 (Sept. 18, 1950): 463; Judd quoted in John Lewis Gaddis, *The Long Peace: Inquiries Into the History of the Cold War* (New York: Oxford University Press, 1987), 169.

67. For Dulles's defense of the military advance see his address, "The Search for a Bond of Fellowship Between the Free East and the Free West," Department of State *Bulletin* 25 (Dec. 17, 1951): 973.

68. "The Price of Partnership," *The Economist* 159 (Dec. 2, 1950): 925.

69. Acheson in the *New York Times*, Nov. 30, 1950; Truman's statement in Public *Papers of the Presidents: Harry S. Truman, 1950* (Washington, 1965), 725.

70. Minutes, Truman-Attlee meeting, Dec. 7, 1950, *FRUS*, 1950: VII, 1456.

71. Quoted in Norman A. Graebner, *Cold War Diplomacy: American Foreign Policy, 1945–1975* (New York: Van Nostrand, 1977), 52.

72. *FRUS*, 1950: VII, 1300, 1243, 1776.

73. The *New York Times*, Dec. 15, 1950, 10.

74. *FRUS*, 1950: VII, 477–478.

75. Associated Press in the *New York Times*, Dec. 19, 1950, 20.

76. Ibid., Dec. 25, 1950, 5.

77. *FRUS*, 1950: VII, 1631.

78. Rusk's address before a regional conference on American foreign policy, sponsored by the World Affairs Council of Philadelphia, on Febr. 9, 1951, Department of State *Bulletin* 24 (Feb. 19, 1951): 295.

79. "Ourselves and America," *The New Statesman and Nation* 40 (Dec. 16, 1950): 616.

80. "America and the Resurgence of Asia," *The Manchester Guardian Weekly* 64 (Feb. 1, 1951), 1. For an Asian view of recognition see Tillman Durdin, "Southeast Asia Divided," the *New York Times*, Nov. 26, 1950.

81. "The Crazy Path to War," *The New Statesman and Nation* 41 (Jan. 1, 1951), 1; *The Economist* 159 (Dec. 2 1950): 925; "Bull in China," ibid. 160 (Feb. 3, 1951): 261–262.

82. For NSC 68/2, Sept. 30, 1950, see Drew, *NSC-68*, 111–112.

83. NSC-68/4, Dec. 14, 1950, ibid., 120–127.

84. Herbert Hoover, Radio and Television Address to the American People, the *New York Times*, Dec. 21, 1950. For Taft see Gaddis, *Strategies of Containment*, 119–120.

85. John T. Woolley and Gerhard Peters, *The American Presidency Project* [online]. Santa Barbara, CA: University of California (hosted), Gerhard Peters (database). World Wide Web: http://www.presidency.ucsb.edu/ws/?pid=13683.

86. *New York Times*, Dec. 13, 1950.

87. *New York Times*, Jan. 9, 1951.

88. For a brief survey of U.S. efforts to bring West Germany into NATO, see Lawrence S. Kaplan, "The United States and the Atlantic Alliance: The First Generation," in John Braeman, Robert H. Bremner, and David Brody, eds., *Twentieth-Century American Foreign Policy* (Columbus: Ohio State University Press, 1971), 317–321.

89. Department of State *Bulletin* 24 (Jan. 22, 1951): 123.

90. Dulles's address before the China Institute of New York, May 18, 1951, Department of State *Bulletin* 24 (May 28, 1951): 844; Rusk's speech in Philadelphia, etc.

91. NSC 48/5, United States Objectives, Policies and Courses of Action in Asia, May 17, 1951, *FRUS*, 1951: VI, 35–37.

92. For these optimistic statements see Pettit, *The Experts*, 40–41.

93. Melvyn P. Leffler, *A Preponderance of Power: National Security, the Truman Administration and the Cold War* (Stanford, CA: Stanford University Press, 1992), 471, 474–475.

94. U.S. Department of Defense. *The Pentagon Papers: The Defense Department History of United States Decision Making on Vietnam: The Senator Gravel Edition.* 5 vols. (Boston: Beacon, 1971–1972), I: 375–380.

95. William Pfaff, *Barbarian Sentiments: How the American Century Ends* (New York: Hill & Wang, 1989), 12; "Basic Issues Raised by Draft NSC 'Reappraisal of U.S. Objectives and Strategy for National Security," n.d., *FRUS*, 1952–1954: II, 64–65. See also Acheson to McCloy, Apr. 12, 1951, ibid., 7, 206.

96. Leffler, *A Preponderance of Power*, 488–492.

97. For a major contemporary analysis of the nature of the Soviet threat see Hans J. Morgenthau, "The Real Issue Between Russia and the United States," *The University of Chicago Magazine* (Apr. 1951): 5–8, 25.

98. Louis J. Halle, *The Cold War as History* (New York: Harper & Row, 1971), 416–417.

99. Quoted in Edward Crankshaw, "China and Russia," *The Atlantic Monthly* (June 1956): 27.

100. Edward Crankshaw, "The Kremlin Retools Its Foreign Policy," the *New York Times Magazine* (July 15, 1951): 5, 29.

101. For a critique of anti-Communism as a guide to policy see the *New York Times Magazine* (Dec. 6, 1970: 161.

102. Geir Lundestad, *The American "Empire" and Other Studies of U.S. Foreign Policy in a Comparative Perspective* (New York: Oxford University Press, 1990), 37.

103. See Frank Costigliola, *France and the United States: The Cold War Alliance since World War II* (New York: Twayne, 1992); also see Joseph M. Siracusa and David Coleman, *Australia Looks to America: Australian-American Relations since Pearl Harbor* (Claremont, CA: Regina Books, 2006), 32–50.

104. Schlesinger in *Diplomatic History* 16 (Spring 1992): 49; Ernest R. May in ibid., 270.

105. Richard J. Barnet, *Roots of War* (New York: Atheneum, 1972), 18–19, 57; Bernard Brodie, *War and Politics* (New York: Macmillan, 1973), 359–360.

106. *Public Papers of the Presidents, Truman, 1952–1953*, 1201.

CHAPTER 8

1. For an evaluation of the public opinion that underwrote the Cold War consensus see Ralph B. Levering, *The Public and American Foreign Policy, 1918–1978* (New York: Morrow, 1978), 94–98. James R. Burnham of Georgetown University argued that the U.S. could not survive unless it destroyed Communist power. See Burnham, *The Coming Defeat of Communism* (New York: Day, 1950), 138.

2. Much has been written on Dulles's background before becoming secretary of state in 1953. See, for example, Louis L. Gerson, *John Foster Dulles* (New York: Cooper Square, 1967), 9–97; John Robinson Beal, *John Foster Dulles: A Biography* (New York: Harper, 1957), 16–128; and Townsend Hoopes, *The Devil and John Foster Dulles* (Boston: Little, Brown, 1973), 17–133.

3. John Foster Dulles, "A Policy of Boldness," *Life* (May 19, 1952): 146–157. For Dulles's views on America's moral powers and obligations in external affairs see Henry Van Dusen, ed., *The Spiritual Legacy of John Foster Dulles: Selections From His Articles and Addresses* (Freeport, NY: Books for Libraries, 1960, 1972), passim. In many respects Dulles's precepts coincided with those of Woodrow Wilson. In *War and Peace* (New York: Macmillan, 1950) Dulles expressed repeatedly his faith in moral force in a morally divided world.

4. *U.S. News & World Report* (July 18, 1952): 83–84.

5. *New York Times*, Aug. 26, 1952, 12. For Eisenhower's adoption of liberation see also Norman A. Graebner, *The New Isolationism: A Study in Politics and Foreign Policy Since 1950* (New York: Ronald, 1956), 99–100.

6. Dulles quoted in the *New York Times*, Aug. 27, 1952, 15.

7. The European press quoted in the *New York Times*, Aug. 26, 1952, 12. See also ibid., Aug. 27, 1952, 15.

8. *The Economist* (London) 164 (Aug. 30, 1952): 503.

9. *The Economist* 164 (Sept. 13, 1952): 623; Truman's Parkersburg speech in the *New York Times*, Sept. 23, 1952, 20.

10. *New York Times*, Sept. 4, 1952, l, 20. One critic noted that Soviet armies did not occupy Yugoslavia and therefore Tito's successful defiance of Stalin and the Cominform was no valid example of what peaceful liberation might achieve, ibid., Sept. 5, 1952, 26. David Lawrence reminded his readers that liberation did not require force but rather the encouragement of the oppressed to free themselves. See *U.S. News & World Report* (Sept. 12, 1952): 92.

11. Hearings before the Committee on Foreign Relations, United States Senate, Eighty-third Congress, First Session, on the Nomination of John Foster Dulles, Secretary of State - Designate, Jan. 15, 1953 (Washington, DC: GPO, 1953), 5–6.

12. State of the Union message, Feb. 2, 1953, Department of State *Bulletin* 28 (Feb. 9, 1953), 207–211.

13. David Lawrence in *U.S. News & World Report* (Feb. 13, 1953): 100; Freda Kirchwey, "Where Are We Going?" *The Nation* 176 (Feb. 21, 1953): 159–160.

14. See Department of State, *American Foreign Policy: Basic Documents, 1950–1955*, 2 vols. (Washington, DC: GPO, 1957), II, 1958–1959; Dulles's statement, Feb. 26, 1953, ibid., 1959.

15. For the Senate's reaction see Graebner, *The New Isolationism*, 147–148.

16. Dulles speech of Apr. 18, 1953, Department of State *Bulletin* 0 28 (Apr. 27, 1953): 606.

17. Robert H. Ferrell, ed., *The Eisenhower Diaries* (New York: Norton, 1981), 222–223 (Jan. 6, 1953); John Colville, *Footprints in Time* (London: Collins, 1976), 235–236. For Churchill's continuing effort to establish a special Anglo-American relationship and Eisenhower's continued rejection see Robin Edmonds, *Setting the Mould: The United States and Britain, 1945–1950* (New York: Norton, 1986), 228–229.

18. Peter G. Boyle, ed., *The Churchill-Eisenhower Correspondence, 1953–1955* (Chapel Hill: University of North Carolina Press, 1990), 31–32.

19. Boyle, *The Churchill-Eisenhower Correspondence*, 36, 46–47.

20. 515 House of Commons Debates, col. 897, 11 May 1953.

21. David Lawrence in *U.S. News & World Report* (Mar. 13, 1953): 108; Memorandum of Discussion at a Special Meeting of the National Security Council, Mar. 31, 1953, *Foreign Relations of the United States, 1952–1954 (FRUS)* (Washington, 1984), II, Pt. l: 267–268.

22. Emmet John Hughes, The Ordeal of Power: A Political Memoir of the Eisenhower Years (New York: Athenaeum, 1963), 95–96, 120; Department of State, American Foreign Policy, 1950–1955, II:1746.

23. For a good survey of Project Solarium see William B. Pickett, "The Eisenhower Solarium Notes," The Society for Historians of American Foreign Relations *Newsletter* 16 (June 1985): 1–8.

24. Summaries Prepared by the NSC Staff of Project Solarium Presentations and Written Reports, *FRUS*, 1952–1954: II, Pt. 1: 400, 401, 414, 416–419; for the conclusions of the July 30 report see Pickett, "The Eisenhower Solarium Notes," 4–7; Memorandum by the Special Assistant to the President for National Security Affairs (Cutler), July 31, 1953, ibid., 441.

25. Draft Statement of Policy Proposed by the National Security Council, Sept. 30, 1953, ibid., 493. During 1954 the Eisenhower administration appeared to adopt goals and attitudes as conservative as those of the Truman years. During a discussion of NSC 5440, dated Dec. 13, 1954, Dulles acknowledged that during the 1952 campaign he had advocated a more dynamic foreign policy, but concluded "it was not easy to go very much beyond the point that this Administration had reached in translating a dynamic policy into courses of action . . . ." There had been and would be no liberation. Ibid., 833.

26. John Colville, The Fringes of Power: 10 Downing Street Diaries, 1939–1955 (New York: Norton, 1985), 673.

27. Quoted by Richard Wilson in the *Des Moines Register*, Dec. 1, 1953.

28. Colville, *The Fringes of Power*, 683.

29. The Bermuda Declaration of Dec. 7, 1953, in Department of State *Bulletin* 29 (Dec. 21, 1953): 852.

30. Department of State, *American Foreign Policy, 1950–1955*, II, 1747–1748, 1843–1844.

31. Ibid., 1850–1852, 1854–1855.

32. Graebner, *The New Isolationism*, 131; Memorandum of Discussion at the 138th Meeting of the National Security Council, Mar. 25, 1953, *FRUS*, 1952–1954: II, 260.

33. Graebner, *The New Isolationism*, 130–131; Eisenhower's Defense Reorganization message, Apr. 30, 1953, *Public Papers of the Presidents of the United States: Dwight D. Eisenhower, 1953* (Washington, DC: GPO, 1960), 225–238; President's meeting with congressional leaders, Apr. 30, 1953, *FRUS*, 1952–1954: II, 317; Memorandum of Discussion at the 140th Meeting of the National Security Council, Apr. 22, 1953, ibid., 297.

34. Ferrell, *The Eisenhower Diaries*, 235; *Newsweek* (May 11, 1953): 28. For Republicans generally the president's emphasis on budgetary restraints was highly attractive. Some such as Ohio's Robert A. Taft did not believe the cuts sufficient.

35. Report to the National Security Council by the Executive Secretary (Lay), Apr. 29, 1953, *FRUS*, 1952–1954: II 307; Memorandum of Discussion at the 160th Meeting of the National Security Council, Aug. 27, 1953, ibid., 447–450.

36. Memorandum of Discussion at the 168th Meeting of the National Security Council, Oct. 29, 1953, ibid., 572; Memorandum by the President to the Secretary of State, Sept. 8, 1953, ibid., 460–462.

37. Review of Basic National Security Policy (NSC 162), Oct. 7, 1953, ibid., 532; Memorandum of Discussion of the 166th Meeting of the National Security Council, Oct. 13, 1953, ibid., 545–546; Report to the National Security Council by the Executive Secretary (NSC 162/2), Oct. 30, 1953, ibid., 583, 591.

38. Dulles's New York address, Jan. 12, 1954, Department of State *Bulletin* 30 (Jan. 25, 1954): 107–110.

39. Hanson W. Baldwin in the *New York Times*, Nov. 1, 1953, Jan. 24, 1954; Hans J. Morgenthau, "Instant Retaliation: Will It Deter Aggression," *The New Republic* 130 (Mar. 29, 1954): 11–14; Dean Acheson, " 'Instant Retaliation': The Debate Continued," the *New York Times Magazine*, Mar. 28, 1954, 78; Thomas R. Phillips, "Our Point of No Return," *The Reporter* 12 (Feb. 24, 1954): 118–124. For Matthew Ridgway's rejection of massive retaliation, see Norman A. Graebner, "Matthew B. Ridgway: Cold War Statesman," in Henry S. Bausum, ed., *Military Leadership and Command: The John Biggs Cincinnati Lectures, 1987* (Lexington, VA: VMI Foundation, 1987), 173–177.

40. John Foster Dulles, "Policy for Security and Peace," *Foreign Affairs* 32 (Apr. 1954): 353–364.

41. Elmer Davis, *Two Minutes Till Midnight* (Indianapolis, 1955), 36–37; Humphrey quoted in Graebner, *The New Isolationism*, 132; William F. Knowland, "The 'Instant Retaliation" Policy Defended," the *New York Times Magazine* (Mar. 21, 1954): 74ff.

42. C.L. Sulzberger in the *New York Times*, Dec. 20, 1953; Woodrow Wyatt. "Geography Closes in on the British," the *New York Times Magazine* (Oct. 17, 1954): 68–71.

43. Drew Middleton noted Dulles's efforts to find the necessary compromises in the *New York Times*, Oct. 3, 1954.

44. For the United States-West German mutual defense agreement of June 30, 1955 see Department of State *Bulletin* 33 (July 25, 1955): 142–144; James B. Conant, ambassador to the Federal Republic, discussed the evolution of United States-West German relations, Mar. 23, 1956, in ibid. 34 (Apr. 9, 1956): 585–587.

45. Colville, *The Fringes of Power*, 691–703; Colville, *Footprints in Time*, 241–243.

46. Eisenhower, in his last letter to Churchill of Mar. 29, 1955, demonstrated his continuing ideological view of the world: "The Communist sweep over the world since World War II has been much faster and much more relentless than the 1930's sweep of the dictators." Boyle, *The Churchill-Eisenhower Correspondence*, 206.

47. For an analysis of the coming of the Geneva Conference, Eisenhower's reluctance to attend, and Senator Joseph McCarthy's unsuccessful efforts to scuttle the conference with a congressional resolution demanding the freedom of Eastern Europe, see Graebner, *The New Isolationism*, 209–230.

48. For the important innovations in Khrushchev's perceptions of successful Communist rule see Harry Schwartz, "Marx to Khrushchev: A Four-Act Drama," the *New York Times Magazine* (Nov. 12, 1961): 117–118. Dulles viewed Khrushchev's address as a threat to Western security because of the greater flexibility it seemed to provide for Soviet action. See Department of State *Bulletin* 34 (Mar. 5, 1956): 364–365; ibid., 35 (July 2, 1956): 3–5; ibid., 35 (July 23, 1956): 145.

49. Harrison E. Salisbury noted the critical choice that faced Khrushchev, whether to feed the yearning for freedom or re-Stalinize and risk an explosion. See Salisbury, "The Dilemma That Haunts the Kremlin," the *New York Times Magazine* (Jan. 27, 1957): II: 52–56.

50. *Daedalus*(1992): 46.

51. For contemporary analyses of possible dangers in the new Soviet policies, based on economic power, see Harry Schwartz, "Khrushchev's Purge and Our

Grandchildren," the *New York Times Magazine*, July 14, 1957, 5, 41–44; Edward Crankshaw, "Russia's Imperial Design," *The Atlantic Monthly* (Nov. 1957): 39–45; Louis J. Halle, "The Basic Aim of the Kremlin," the *New York Times Magazine* (June 28, 1959): 5, 41–43. For Halle, the Soviet threat was limited; he argued that Soviet power could not reach beyond the reach of Soviet armies.

52. Robert Legvold, "War, Weapons, and Foreign Policy," Seweryn Bialer and Michael Mandelbaum, eds., *Gorbachev's Russia and American Foreign Policy* (Boulder, CO: Westview, 1988), 101;for Dulles's views of the new Soviet approach see Department of State *Bulletin* 34 (Apr. 2, 1956): 550. On Murphy's statement that the Soviet new look policy was an effort to skirt the Western alliance system see ibid. 34 (Jan. 20, 1956): 170. See also Murphy's statement of Mar. 24 in ibid. (Apr. 2, 1956): 557–558, and of Apr. 2 in ibid. (Apr. 16, 1956): 648. On Harriman see "The Soviet Danger and American Policy," *The Atlantic Monthly* 197 (Apr. 1956): 42.

53. Waldemar A. Nielsen saw the "Russian drive for world domination" as a genuine economic threat. Because the threat was economic, not ideological, in nature, the proper response lay in a concerted effort to build the American economy to its full capacity. See Waldemar A. Nielsen, "Why We Are Losing the Ruble War," *Harper's Magazine* (Sept. 1958): 25–31. Similarly Barbara Ward took seriously Khrushchev's boast that the U.S.S.R. could maintain a growth rate double that of the West and warned the free world to reexamine its needs and methods. See Barbara Ward, "Now the Challenge of an Economic Sputnik," the *New York Times Magazine* (Feb. 8, 1959): 7, 62–64.

54. Khrushchev's statements appear in Norman A. Graebner, *Cold War Diplomacy: American Foreign Policy, 1945–1975*, 2d ed. (New York: Van Nostrand, 1977), 102–103.

55. Ibid., 58. For Khrushchev's final interpretation and argument for coexistence see Nikita S. Khrushchev, "On Peaceful Coexistence," *Foreign Affairs* 38 (Oct. 1959): 1-18.

56. Graebner, *Cold War Diplomacy*, 112–115.

57. Dulles's Executive Session testimony, June 26, 1956, *Historical Series: Eighty-Fourth Congress, Second Session, 1956* (Washington ,DC: GPO, 1956), 501, 503; on the causes of the Polish uprising see Cold War International History Project *Bulletin* (Spring 1995): 10–21.

58. Dulles, speech at Dallas Council on World Affairs, Oct. 27, 1956, Department of State *Bulletin* 35 (Nov. 5, 1956): 697.

59. Statements by President Eisenhower and Secretary Dulles, "U.S. Concern for Hungarian People, ibid., 700–701; for information from the Soviet side, see also Cold War International History Project *Bulletin* (Spring 1995): 22–57 and William Taubman, *Khrushchev: The Man and His Era* (New York: Norton, 2003), 298–294. Eisenhower had authorized a covert program using East European émigrés for paramilitary missions, see Stephen E. Ambrose, *Ike's Spies: Eisenhower and the Espionage Establishment* (Garden City, NY: Doubleday, 1981), 237–239.

60. Department of State *Bulletin* 35 (Nov. 12, 1956): 743–747; State Department statement, Sept. 14, 1957, ibid., 36 (Sept. 30, 1957): 515; Statement by Henry Cabot Lodge, Jr., "U.N. to Seek Improvement of Situation in Hungary," Dec. 12, 1958, in ibid., 38 (Jan. 12, 1959): 517.

61. See Elmer Plische, "Eisenhower's 'Correspondence Diplomacy' with the Kremlin - Case Study in Summit Diplomatics," *The Journal of Politics* 30:1 (Feb. 1968): 146–158.

62. Khrushchev's note of Nov. 27, 1958, in Department of State *Bulletin* 40 (1959): 81–89; Marc Trachtenberg, *History and Strategy* (Princeton, NJ: Princeton University Press, 1993), 169–197; Vladislav M. Zubok, "Khrushchev and the Berlin Crisis (1958–1962)," *Cold War International History Project Working Papers* 6 (May 1993).

63. U.S. rejected Soviet proposal for free city of Berlin on Dec. 31, 1958, Trachtenberg, *History and Strategy*, 169–197.

64. For two views of Khrushchev's trip to the U.S., see Taubman, *Khrushchev*, 416–441 and Eisenhower, *Waging Peace*, 432–449.

65. Chester J. Pach, Jr. and Elmo Richardson, rev. ed., *The Presidency of Dwight D. Eisenhower* (Lawrence: University Press of Kansas, 1991), 209–210; Eisenhower, *Waging Peace*, 485–513.

66. For U-2 incident and May 16, 1960 summit, see Robert A. Divine, Eisenhower and the Cold War (New York: Oxford University Press, 1981), 146–152; Eisenhower, *Waging Peace*, 543–559. The U.S. had long been invading Soviet air space, see William E. Burrows, *By Any Means Necessary: America's Secret Air War in the Cold War* (New York: Farrar, Straus & Giroux, 2001), esp. 20.

67. George F. Kennon, *Russia, the Atom and the West* (London: Oxford University Press, 1958); Polish foreign minister Adam Rapacki issued his initial proposal on Oct. 2, 1957 and repeated it on Mar. 28, 1962, for text see U.S. Arms Control and Disarmament Agency, *Documents on Disarmament, 1962* (Washington, DC: GPO, 1963), 201–204.

68. Dean Acheson, "The Illusion of Disengagement," *Foreign Affairs* 36 (Apr. 1958), 371–382.

69. Graebner, *Cold War Diplomacy*, 72–77.

70. Walter Millis was among those who advocated a genuine search for accommodation rather than pursue the arms race. See Millis, "How to Compete with the Russians," the *New York Times Magazine* (Feb. 2, 1958): 12, 53–54.

71. Ferrell, ed., *The Eisenhower Diaries*, 223; Dulles used this explanation of Soviet expansionism repeatedly, see for example Department of State *Bulletin* 30 (Apr. 12, 1954): 539.

72. Rankin to George V. Allen, July 29, 1953, Karl L. Rankin, *China Assignment* (Seattle: University of Washington Press, 1964), 173.

73. Quoted in Graebner, *The New Isolationism*, 124–125.

74. Ibid., 157–158.

75. Julius W. Pratt, Vincent De Santis, and Joseph M. Siracusa, *A History of United States Foreign Policy*, 4th ed. (Englewood cliffs, NJ: Prentice-Hall, 1980), 449.

76. Robert J. Donovan, *Eisenhower: The Inside Story* (New York: Harper, 1956), 132.

77. Papers of John Foster Dulles, Telephone Calls Series, Dwight D. Eisenhower Library, Abilene, Kansas. Note especially Dulles's conversations with Judd or Knowland for Apr. 9, 1953, Aug. 1, 1953, Nov. 14, 1953, Feb. 20, 27,

1954, Aug. 20, 1954, Nov. 20. 1954, Jan. 27, 1955, Apr. 27, 1955, Aug. 1, 1955, and Apr. 2, 1956.

78. Dwight D. Eisenhower, *Mandate for Change, 1953–1956: The White House Years* (Garden City, NY: Doubleday, 1963), 463–464.

79. Quoted in Graebner, *The New Isolationism*, 178.

80. President Eisenhower to Congress on Defense of Formosa, Jan. 24, 1955, Russell Buhite, ed., *The Dynamics of World Power: A Documentary History of United States Foreign Policy, 1945–1973*, Vol. IV:*The Far East* (New York, 1973), 211.

81. A. M. Rosenthal in the *New York Times*, Feb. 13, 1955; Eisenhower, *Mandate for Change*, 483.

82. Dwight D. Eisenhower, *Waging Peace, 1956–1961: The White House Years* (Garden City, NY: Doubleday, 1965), 299–300. For the Sept. 4 memorandum in full see ibid., 691–693.

83. For Khrushchev's warning against nuclear war see Bernard Brodie, *Strategy in the Missile Age*(Princeton, NJ: Princeton University Press, 1959), 256n–57n.

84. Eisenhower to Senator Green, Oct. 2, 1958, Buhite, *The Far East*, 253.

85. Robert Divine, *Eisenhower and the Cold War*(New York: Oxford University Press, 1981), 65ff.

86. Memorandum of meeting, Dec. 7, 1953, *FRUS*, 1952–1954: V, 1808–1818.

87. Minutes, NSC meeting, Aug. 18, 1954, *FRUS*, 1952–1954: XIV, 534; Notes on Dulles-Yeh conversation, Feb. 10, 1955, *FRUS*, 1955–1957: II, 254; Memorandum, Dulles-Lloyd conversation, Jan. 31, 1956, ibid., III, 292; Dulles's speech at San Francisco, June 28, 1957, ibid., 564.

88. Walter McConaughy, "China in the Shadow of Communism," ibid. 30 (Jan. 11, 1954): 41; Dulles' statement on U.S. China policy, Canberra, Mar. 12, 1957, ibid. 36 (Apr. 1, 1957): 531; Robertson's speech, Mar. 13, 1959, ibid. 40 (Apr. 6, 1959): 474.

89. Karl Lott Rankin, *China Assignment* (Seattle: University of Washington Press, 1964), 311, 315, 323.

90. For U.S. views of the Sino-Soviet conflict see Donald S. Zagoria, *The Sino-Soviet Conflict, 1956–1961* (Princeton: Princeton University Press, 1962), 152–221. A. Doak Barnett treats the Sino-Soviet relationship as a normal alliance under severe strain by 1960. See A. Doak Barnett, *Communist China and Asia: A Challenge to American Policy* (New York: Harper, 1960), 337–377.

91. See Richard H. Immerman for Mao's reasons for settling the conflict, *Dulles: Piety, Pragmatism and Power in U.S. Foreign Policy*(Wilmington, DC: Scholarly Resources, 1999), 72.

92. Dulles' survey of foreign policy problems, Jan. 27, 1953, Department of State *Bulletin* 28 (Feb. 9, 1953): 213; Nixon's radio and television address, Dec. 23, 1953, ibid. 30 (Jan. 4, 1954): 12.

93. See Robert Griffith, "Dwight D. Eisenhower and the Corporate Commonwealth," *American Historical Review* 87 (Feb. 1982): 119.

94. Address before the American Friends of Vietnam, Washington, June 1, 1956, Department of State *Bulletin* 34 (June 11, 1956): 972.

95. Meeting at the airport, May 8, 1957, ibid. 36 (May 27, 1957): 854; Joint statement, May 11, 1957, ibid., 851.

96. Speech at Gettysburg College, Apr. 4, 1959, ibid. 40 (Apr. 27, 1959): 580–581.

97. Such Eisenhower advisers as Andrew Goodpaster and Arthur Larson, in conversation with the author, insisted that Eisenhower would never have led the United States into an Indochinese war.

98. For a brief discussion the Iranian episode see Richard J. Barnet, *Intervention and Revolution: The United States and the Third World* (New York: World, 1968), 265–267; for a positive view of Mossadegh by a Cold War hawk, see Paul Nitze, *From Hiroshima to Glasnost: At the Center of Decision–A Memoir* (New York: Grove Weidenfeld, 1989), 129–137.

99. Speech before the General Federation of Women's Clubs, Washington, Oct. 14, 1953, Department of State *Bulletin* 29 (Oct. 26, 1953): 556.

100. Quoted in Richard H. Immerman, *The CIA in Guatemala: The Foreign Policy of Intervention* (Austin: University of Texas Press, 1982), 5.

101. Daniel Graham, "Castillo's Guatemala," *The Nation* 180 (May 21, 1955): 440.

102. For the Democratic and Republican reactions to the Eisenhower Doctrine see William S. White in the *New York Times*, Feb. 3, 1957.

103. *Foreign Policy Briefs*, May 30, 1958, 1.

104. Thomas Karis, "United States Policy toward South Africa," in Gwendolen M. Carter and Patrick O'Meara, eds., *Southern Africa: The Continuing Crisis* (Bloomington: Indiana University Press, 1982), 323.

105. See Gary W. Reichard, "The Domestic Politics of National Security," in Norman A. Graebner, ed., *The National Security: Its Theory and Practice, 1945–1960* (New York: Oxford University Press, 1986), 267–268.

106. Strobe Talbott, *The Master of the Game: Paul Nitze and the Nuclear Peace* (New York: Knopf, 1988), 68–70; Richard Aliano, *American Defense Policy from Eisenhower to Kennedy, 1957–1961*(Athens, OH: Ohio University Press, 1975), passim for politics of missile gap myth; also see Levering, *The Public and American Foreign Policy*, 114.

107. For the evolution of American nuclear strategy under Eisenhower see David G. Coleman and Joseph M. Siracusa, *Real-World Nuclear Deterrence: The Making of International Strategy* (Westport, CT: Praeger Security International, 2006), 19–43.

108. Eisenhower's Farewell Address, Jan. 17, 1961, see *Public Papers of the Presidents: Eisenhower, 1960–1961* (Washington, DC: GPO, 1961), 1038.

CHAPTER 9

1. "The Inaugural Address of President Kennedy," in John T. Woolley and Gerhard Peters, *The American Presidency Project* [online] Santa Barbara, CA: University of California (hosted), Gerhard Peters (database). Available from World Wide Web: http://www.presidency.ucsb.edu/ws/?pid=8032

2. Senator Goldwater's remarks in the Senate, July 14, 1961, *Congressional Record*, 87th Cong. 1st Sess., Vol. 107, No. 118, 11690.

3. "Editorial," *Life Magazine* (Jan. 27, 1961):16.

4. Michael R. Beschloss, *The Crisis Years: Kennedy and Khrushchev, 1960–1963* (New York: Harper Collins, 1991), 25.

5. *New York Times*, Aug. 25 and Sept. 24, 1960; "Annual Message to the Congress on the State of the Union, Jan. 30, 1961," in Woolley and Peters, *The American Presidency Project*: http://www.presidency.ucsb.edu/ws/?pid=8045

6. For a discussion of Kennedy's advisors, see John C. Donovan, *The Cold Warriors: A Policy-Making Elite* (Lexington, MA: Heath, 1974): chap. 7 & 8.

7. David Halberstam, *The Best and Brightest* (New York: Random House, 1992), 60.

8. Speech of June 14, 1960, U.S. Senate, Allan Nevins, ed., *John F. Kennedy: The Strategy for Peace*, 2nd ed. (New York: Harper & Row, 1960).

9. "Special Message to the Congress on the Defense Budget, March 28th, 1961," in Woolley and Peters, *The American Presidency Project*: http://www.presidency.ucsb.edu/ws/?pid=8554

10. Fred Kaplan, *The Wizards of Armageddon* (New York: Simon & Schuster, 1983), 268–272, 325.

11. See George Ball, *Diplomacy for a Crowded World: An American Foreign Policy* (Boston: Little, Brown, 1976), 60–61.

12. "Special Message to Congress on the Peace Corps, March 1, 1961," in Woolley and Peters, *The American Presidency Project*: http://www.presidency.ucsb.edu/ws/?pid=8515; see also Elizabeth Cobbs Hoffman, *All You Need Is Love: The Peace Corps and the Spirit of the 1960s* (Cambridge, MA: Harvard University Press, 1998).

13. Gerard C. Smith, *Disarming Diplomat: The Memoirs of Ambassador Gerard C. Smith* (Lanham, NJ: Madison, 1996), 28–29; Richard H. Immerman, *John Foster Dulles: Piety, Pragmatism and Power in U.S. Foreign Policy* (Wilmington, DE: Scholarly Resources, 1999), 52–55, 135.

14. Smith, *Disarming Diplomat*, 54–55; Matthew Evangelista, "Disarmament Negotiations in the 1950s," *World Politics* 42 (July 1990): 502–518; H. W. Brands, Jr. "Harold Stassen and the Perils of Disarmament," in *Cold Warriors: Eisenhower's Generation and American Foreign Policy*(New York: Columbia University Press, 1988), 138–162; "Dwight D. Eisenhower, Statement on Disarmament Presented at the Geneva Conference, July 21, 1955," in Woolley and Peters, *The American Presidency Project*: http://www.presidency.ucsb.edu/ws/?pid=10306.

15. State of the Union Message, Jan. 30, 1961, in Woolley and Peters, *The American Presidency Project*: http://www.presidency.ucsb.edu/ws/?pid=8045

16. Text is contained in U.S. Congress, Committee on Foreign Relations, Senate, Committee on Foreign Affairs, *Legislation on Foreign Relations Through 1989*, vol. 2 (Washington, DC. GPO, 1990).

17. Arthur M. Schlesinger, *A Thousand Days: John F. Kennedy in the White House* (Boston: Houghton Mifflin, 1965), 478–479, 484–486; see Glenn T. Seaborg, *Kennedy, Khrushchev and the Test Ban* (Berkeley: University of California Press, 1981), chap. 3 & 4.

18. "Address at a White House Reception for Members of Congress and for the Diplomatic Corps of the Latin American Republics," Mar. 13, 1961 in Woolley and Peters, *The American Presidency Project*: http://www.presidency.ucsb.edu/ws/?pid=8531; see also Teodoro Moscoso, "Progress Report on the

Alliance for Progress," the *New York Times Magazine* (Aug. 12, 1962): 11, 59–63; Jerome Levinson and Juan de Onís, *The Alliance That Lost Its Way* (Chicago: Quadrangle Books, 1970), 77–87, 166.

19. See Peter Wyden, *Bay of Pigs: The Untold Story* (New York: Simon & Schuster, 1979).

20. Quoted in ibid., 121.

21. Paul H. Nitze, *From Hiroshima to Glasnost: At the Center of Decision - A Memoir* (New York: Grove Weidenfeld, 1989), 183–184.

22. Lawrence Freedman, *Kennedy's Wars: Berlin, Cuba, Laos, and Vietnam* (New York: Oxford University Press, 2000), 134–135.

23. Wyden, *Bay of Pigs*, chap. 5–7 describes Kennedy's concerns, the landing and surrender.

24. Quoted in ibid, 8.

25. *New York Times*, Sept. 9, 1962; "Address Before the American Society of Newspaper Editors," Apr. 20, 1961, in Woolley and Peters, *The American Presidency Project*: http://www.presidency.ucsb.edu/ws/?pid=8076

26. "Lessons of Cuba," *New York Times*, Sept. 9, 1962.

27. Taylor Branch and George Crile III, "The Kennedy Vendetta: How the CIA Waged a Silent War Against Cuba," *Harpers Magazine* 251 (Aug. 1975): 49–63; see Chapter 17, "Mongoose," in Freedman, *Kennedy's Wars*, 153–160.

28. "Text of Rusk's Speech Urging Inter-American Action to Punish Cuban Regime," *New York Times*, Jan. 26, 1962, 4; for text of resolutions, see 87th Cong. 2d Sess., Committee Report, *Punta Del Este Conference, January 1962, Report of Senators Wayne Morse and Bourke B. Hickenlooper to the Committee on Foreign Relations, United States Senate* (Washington, DC: GPO, 1962).

29. Quoted in Nitze, *From Hiroshima to Glasnost*, 184.

30. Schlesinger, *A Thousand Days*, 348; Freedman, *Kennedy's Wars*, 57.

31. "Radio and Television Report to the American People on Returning from Europe," June 6, 1961 in Woolley and Peters, *The American Presidency Project*: http://www.presidency.ucsb.edu/ws/?pid=8180

32. Schlesinger, *A Thousand Days*, 380–382.

33. Ibid., 297; "Radio and Television Report to the American People on the Berlin Crisis," July 25, 1961, Woolley and Peters, *The American Presidency Project*: http://www.presidency.ucsb.edu/ws/?pid=8259

34. See Robert M. Slusser, "The Berlin Crises of 1958–59 and 1961," in Barry M. Blechman and Stephen S. Kaplan, eds., *Force Without War: U.S. Armed Forces as a Political Instrument* (Washington, DC: Brookings Institution, 1973), 343–439.

35. Kaplan, *The Wizards of Armageddon*, 294.

36. Richard Ned Lebow and Janice Gross Stein, *We All Lost the Cold War* (Princeton, NJ: Princeton University Press, 1994), 68, 73; John Lewis Gaddis, *We Now Know: Rethinking Cold War History* (New York: Oxford University Press, 1997), 260–264; Mary McAuliffe, ed., *CIA Documents on the Cuban Missiles Crisis, 1962*(Washington, DC: CIA History Staff, 1992), 45–97; Arthur Krock, *Memoirs* (New York: Funk & Wagnalls, 1968), 378–380.

37. For statement of Sept. 4, 1962, see Department of State *Bulletin* (Sept. 24, 1962): 450; "The President's News Conference of September 13th, 1962," in

Woolley and Peters, *The American Presidency Project*: http://www.presidency .ucsb.edu/ws/?pid=8867

38. Graham T. Allison, *Essences of Decision: Explaining the Cuban Missile Crisis* (Boston: Little, Brown, 1971), 235–237.

39. Senator Keating, *Congressional Record*, 88th Cong. 2nd. Sess., vol. 108, 18359–18361

40. Kennedy response in Allison, *Essences of Decision*, 193; Beschloss, *The Crisis Years*, 451.

41. Lester H. Brune, *The Cuba-Caribbean Missile Crisis of October 1962* (Claremont, CA: Regina Books, 1996), 55–56.

42. Beschloss, *The Crisis Years*, 385.

43. McNamara quoted in Lebow and Stein, *We All Lost the Cold War*, 98.

44. Freedman, *Kennedy's Wars*, 171.

45. See Henry Pachter, *Collision Course: The Cuban Missile Crisis and Coexistence* (New York: Praeger, 1963).

46. Freedman, *Kennedy's Wars*, 178–180, 190; Gilpatric quote in Sorensen, *Kennedy*, 694.

47. "Radio and Television Report to the American People on the Soviet Arms Buildup in Cuba, October 22, 1962," Woolley and Peters, *The American Presidency Project*: http://www.presidency.ucsb.edu/ws/?pid=8986

48. Freedman, *Kennedy's Wars*, 203.

49. Laurence Chang and Peter Kornbulh, *The Cuban Missile Crisis: A National Security Archive Documents' Reader* (New York: New Press, 1992), 185–188.

50. Allison, *Essence of Decision*, 223–230.

51. Arthur M. Schlesinger, Jr., *Robert Kennedy and His Times*, 2 vols. (Boston: Houghton Mifflin, 1978), 545–546; Freedman, *Kennedy's Wars*, 217.

52. Freedman, *Kennedy's Wars*, 204–205.

53. Walt Rostow, "The Test: Are We the Tougher," *New York Times Magazine* (June 7, 1964): 21ff.

54. *New York Times*, Oct. 29, 1962.

55. Brune, *The Cuba-Caribbean Missile Crisis*, 88–90; Raymond Garthoff, *Reflections on the Cuban Missile Crisis*, rev. ed. (Washington, DC: Brookings Institution, 1989), 140–149.

56. Quoted in Beschloss, *The Crisis Years*, 563.

57. "Address at Independence Hall, Philadelphia, July 4, 1963," cited in Woolley and Peters, *The American Presidency Project*: http://www.presidency .ucsb.edu/ws/?pid=8756

58. See Secretary of State Rusk, "The State of the North Atlantic Alliance," Department of State *Bulletin* 49:1258 (Aug. 5, 1963): 192–193.

59. "Excerpts from McNamara's Address, *New York Times*, June 17, 1962, 26; McGeorge Bundy, "Friends and Allies," *Foreign Affairs* (Oct. 1962): 21.

60. McGeorge Bundy, *Danger and Survival: Choices About the Bomb in the First Fifty Years* (New York: Random House, 1988), 476–481.

61. Schlesinger, *A Thousand Days*, 842–846.

62. Ibid., 867–888.

63. For the administration's view of Skybolt, see Schlesinger, *A Thousand Days*, 856–862.

64. U.S. Senate, Committee on Foreign Relations, Staff Study: *Problems and Trends in Atlantic Partnership II, June 17, 1963*, Washington, DC: GPO, 1963, 15, 54–56; for an brief, but pointed discussion see Frank Costingliola, "Lyndon B. Johnson, Germany, and the End of the Cold War," in Warren I. Cohen and Nancy Bernkopf Tucker, eds. *Lyndon Johnson Confronts the World: American Foreign Policy, 1963–1968* (New York: Cambridge University Press, 1994), 179–192.

65. Staff Study: *Problems and Trends in Atlantic Partnership II*, 60–62.

66. Ibid., 2–4; for text of treaty, see ibid., 50–53.

67. "The President's News Conference of February 7th, 1963," in Woolley and Peters, *The American Presidency Project*: http://www.presidency.ucsb.edu/ws/?pid=9550

68. Schlesinger, *A Thousand Days*, 953–956.

69. *New York Times*, June 30, 1963, 2E; see also Department of State, *Foreign Policy Briefs* 12:26 (July 8, 1963).

70. Schlesinger, *A Thousand Days*, 479–481; Department of State *Bulletin* 45 (July 31, 1961): 179.

71. Department of State *Bulletin*, 46 (Jan. 15, 1962): 109, 112.

72. John Bartlow Martin, *Adlai Stevenson and the World* (Garden City, NY: Doubleday, 1978), 662–663, 671, 682–684; Schlesinger, *A Thousand Days*, 486.

73. Department of State *Bulletin* 48 (Feb. 4, 1963), 162; For Rusk's statement see ibid., (Apr. 29, 1963): 644.

74. Ibid., (Feb. 25, 1963): 274.

75. Ibid., 49 (July 8, 1963), 44; ibid., 50 (Jan. 6, 1964), 11–17.

76. "Toward a Strategy of Peace," Address at the American University, June 10, 1963, Department of State *Bulletin* 49:1253 (July 1, 1963): 3–4.

77. The negotiations are detailed by Glenn T. Seaborg, who was chairman of the Atomic Energy Commission and directly involved, in his *Kennedy, Khrushchev and the Test Ban*.

78. U.S. Senate Committee on Foreign Relations, *Hearings on the Nuclear Test Ban Treaty*, 88th Cong., 1st Sess. (Washington, DC: GPO, 1963): 564; also see Jacqueline M. Bird, *Scientists in Conflict: Hans Beth, Edward Teller and the Shaping of United States Nuclear Weapons Policy, 1945–1972* (Regina Books, Claremont, CA, 2008), 160–164.

79. See Richard D. Burns, ed., *Encyclopedia of Arms Control and Disarmament*, 3 vols. (New York: Scribners, 1992): II: Hot Line pacts, 847–854; Outer Space, 877–886: Nonproliferation Treaty, 855–876.

80. For Fulbright's observations on Kennedy's efforts at detente, see Norman A. Graebner, *Ideas and Diplomacy: Readings in the Intellectual Tradition of American Foreign Policy* (New York, 1964), 863.

81. "Address at the University of Maine," Oct. 19, 1963 in Woolley and Peters, *The American Presidency Project*: http://www.presidency.ucsb.edu/ws/?Pid=9483; "Remarks at the Breakfast of the Fort Worth Chamber of Commerce," Nov. 22, 1963, ibid., =9538

CHAPTER 10

1. Kennedy quoted in Norman A. Graebner, *Ideas and Diplomacy: Readings in the Intellectual Tradition of American Foreign Policy*(New York: Oxford University Press, 1964), 794; for Rusk's statement see Norman A. Graebner, ed., *The Cold War: A Conflict of Ideology and Power*, 2nd ed. (New York: Van Nostrand, 1976), xxiv.

2. Acheson's press conference, Feb. 8, 1950, Department of State *Bulletin* 22 (Feb. 20, 1950): 273.

3. *New York Times*, Sept. 25, 1962.

4. See Fulbright's noted address, "Old Myths and New Realities," in the *New York Times*, Mar. 26, 1964, reprinted in Graebner, *Ideas and Diplomacy*, 862–864.

5. Quotes in Norman A. Graebner, "Can a Nuclear War Be Avoided?" *The Annals of the American Academy of Political and Social Science* 351 (Jan. 1964): 133–135.

6. George F. Kennan, "'X' Plus 25," *Foreign Policy* 7 (Summer 1972).

7. For Shulman's statement, see *Detente: Hearings Before the Committee on Foreign Relations, United States Senate, 93rd Cong., 2nd Sess., on United States Relations with Communist Countries, August 15, 20, and 21, September 10, 12, 18, 19, 24, and 25, and October 1 and 8, 1974* (Washington, DC: GPO, 1975), 102–110. See also Shulman's *Beyond the Cold War* (New Haven, 1966). For Morgenthau's analysis of a changing world see "Changes and Chances in American-Soviet Relations," *Foreign Affairs* 49 (Apr. 1971): 429–441; also see Edmund Stillman and William Pfaff, *The New Politics: America and the End of the Postwar World*(New York: Coward McCann, 1961).

8. Graebner, *The Cold War*, 183.

9. Kennan in Graebner, *The Cold War*, 183.

10. Louis J. Halle, "The Basic Aim of the Kremlin," the *New York Times Magazine* (June 28, 1959): 5, 41–43.

11. Kennan in Graebner, *The Cold War*, 183.

12. Thomas Alan Schwartz, *Lyndon Johnson and Europe: In the Shadow of Vietnam* (Cambridge, MA: Harvard University Press, 2003), 18–19, 21–28; Thomas W. Zeiler, *Dean Rusk: Defending the American Mission Abroad* (Wilmington, DE: Scholarly Resources, 2000), 56.

13. Speech, Sept. 7, 1964, *Public Papers of the President: Lyndon B. Johnson 1963–1964* (Washington, DC: GPO, 1965), 1049–1052.

14. See H.W. Brands, ed., *The Foreign Policies of Lyndon Johnson: Beyond Vietnam* (College Station: Texas A&M University Press, 1999), 4–5, 8.

15. Joseph S. Tulchin, "The Promise of Progress: U.S. Relations with Latin America During the Administration of Lyndon B. Johnson," in Warren I. Cohen and Nancy Bernkopf Tucker, eds., *Lyndon Johnson Confronts the World: American Foreign Policy, 1963–1968* (New York: Cambridge University Press, 1994), 211, 229; Tad Szulc, *Twilight of the Tyrants* (New York: Holt, 1959).

16. Jerome Levinson and Juan de Onís, *The Alliance That Lost Its Way: A Critical Report on the Alliance for Progress* (Chicago: Quadrangle Books, 1970): 87–88.

17. Tulchin, "The Promise of Progress," 218, 227.

18. Ibid., 228–231.

19. Ibid., 235–236.

20. Quoted in Peter Felten, "Yankee, Go Home and Take Me with You: Lyndon Johnson and the Dominican Republic," in Brands, ed., *The Foreign Policies of Lyndon Johnson*, 103.

21. Philip Geyelin, *Lyndon B. Johnson and the World*(New York: Praeger, 1966), 238, 257–258.

22. Tulchin, "The Promise of Progress," 240–242.

23. Nancy Bernkopf Tucker, "Threats, Opportunities and Frustrations in East Asia," in Warren I. Cohen and Nancy Bernkopf Tucker, eds., *Lyndon Johnson Confronts the World: American Foreign Policy, 1963–1968* (New York: Cambridge University Press, 1994), 108; Department of State *Bulletin* 53 (Dec. 13, 1965): 941–943.

24. Lin Piao, "Long Live the People's War," *Peking Review* 8 (Sept. 3, 1965).

25. Tucker, "Threats, Opportunities and Frustrations in East Asia," 103; Rusk quoted in the *New York Times*, Apr. 17, 1966.

26. Tucker, "Threats, Opportunities and Frustrations in East Asia," 106–108; see also Stanley Bachrack, *The Committee of One Million* (New York, 1976).

27. Frank Costigliola, "Lyndon B. Johnson, Germany, and "the End of the Cold War," in Warren I. Cohen and Nancy Bernkopf Tucker, eds., *Lyndon Johnson Confronts the World: American Foreign Policy, 1963–1968* (New York: Cambridge University Press, 1994), 180–187.

28. Tucker, "Threats, Opportunities and Frustrations in East Asia," 102.

29. Schwartz, *Lyndon Johnson and Europe*, 93–107.

30. Douglas Brinkley, *Dean Acheson: The Cold War Years, 1953–1971* (New Haven: Yale University Press, 1992), 228–235.

31. "Factors Affecting U.S. Policy Toward the Near East," 19 Aug. 1958, Papers of Dwight D. Eisenhower, White House Office Files, Special Asst. National Security Affairs, 1952–1961, National Security Council Series, Policy Papers Subseries, box 23, Dwight D. Eisenhower Library, Abilene, Kansas; reiterated by William B. Quandt, *Decade of Decisions: American Policy Toward the Arab-Israeli Conflict, 1967–1976* (Berkeley: University of California Press, 1977), 14ff.

32. Memorandum of Conversation, 27 Dec. 1962, *FRUS* (1961–1963), 18:280.

33. Memorandum for McGeorge Bundy, Dec. 21, 1962, Papers of Lyndon Baines Johnson (hereafter PLBJ), National Security File (hereafter NSF), National Security Council History—The Middle East Crisis (hereafter NSCH), box 21, Lyndon Baines Johnson Library (hereafter LBJL), Austin, Texas.

34. Memorandum of Conversation, 2 Aug. 1966, PLBJ, NSF, NSCH, box 21, LBJL.

35. Quoted in Candace Karp, *Missed Opportunities: U.S. Diplomatic Failures and the Arab-Israeli Conflict, 1947–1967* (Claremont, CA: Regina Books, 2004), 184.

36. Quoted in Warren I. Cohen, "Balancing American Interests in the Middle East: Lyndon Baines Johnson vs. Gamal Abdul Nasser," in Warren I. Cohen and Nancy Bernkopf Tucker, eds. *Lyndon Johnson Confronts the World: American Foreign Policy, 1963–1968* (New York: Cambridge University Press, 1994), 294.

37. Ibid., 279–80.

38. Memorandum for the White House, 4 June1967, PLBJ, NSF, NSCH, box 18, LBJL.

39. Cohen, "Balancing American Interests in the Middle East," 283–284; Nadav Safran, *Israel, the Embattled Ally* (Cambridge, MA: Belknap, 1978), 383.

40. Cohen, "Balancing American Interests in the Middle East," 284–285; see also George Lenczowski, *American Presidents and the Middle East* (Durham, NC: Duke University Press, 1990), 92–105

41. Lyndon B. Johnson, *The Vantage Point* (New York: Holt, Rhinehart & Winston, 1971), 288.

42. Karp, *Missed Opportunities*, 186–187; Cohen, "Balancing American Interests in the Middle East," 294–295.

43. For Secretary-General U Thant's explanation of his decision to accede to Nasser's request and remove the force, see U Thant, *View From the UN* (London: David & Charles, 1977), 220–252;

44. Quotes in Karp, *Missed Opportunities*, 187.

45. Quandt, *Decade of Decisions*, 60–68; Cohen, "Balancing American Interests in the Middle East," 301; Tom Wicker, *JFK and LBJ: the Influence of Personality Upon Politics* (New York: Morrow, 1968), 196–199.

46. Quandt, *Decade of Decisions*, 48–54; Cohen, "Balancing American Interests in the Middle East," 302–309; Lenczowski, *American Presidents and the Middle East*, 108–115.

47. Frank Constigliola, "LBJ, Germany, and the End of the Cold War," in Warren I. Cohen and Nancy Bernkopf Tucker, *Lyndon Johnson Confronts the World: American Foreign Policy, 1963–1968*(New York: Cambridge University Press, 1994), 193–195.

48. Cohen, "Introduction," ibid., 1; *New York Times*, Aug. 12, 1964; "Guidelines for Cold War Victory," *American Security Council Forum* (Aug. 1964); see also Richard Dean Burns and Lester H. Brune, *The Quest for Missile Defenses, 1944–2003* (Claremont, CA: Regina Books, 2003).

49. Hal Brands, "Progress Unseen: U.S. Arms Control Policy and the Origins of Détente, 1963–1968," *Diplomatic History* 30 (Apr. 2006): 253–57.

50. Ibid., 258–61; see also Raymond L. Garthoff, "The Outer Space Treaty: 1967 to the Present," in Richard Dean Burns, ed., *Encyclopedia of Arms Control and Disarmament*, 3 vols. (New York: Scribners, 1993), II: 877–886.

51. Brands, "Progress Unseen," 270–273; Thomas Graham, Jr., *Disarmament Sketches: Three Decades of Arms Control and International Law* (Seattle: University of Washington Press, 2002), xvii-xviii; see also Joseph S. Nye, Jr., "The Superpowers and the Non-Proliferation Treaty," in Albert Carnesale and Richard N. Haass, eds., *Superpower Arms Control: Setting the Record Straight* (Cambridge, MA: Ballinger, 1987), 165–190.

52. *Foreign Relations, 1952–1954*, II: 837.

53. Burns and Brune, *The Quest for Missile Defenses*, 19–30, 55–57.

54. Brands, "Progress Unseen," 277–285.

55. John Prados, "Prague Spring and SALT: Arms Limitation Setbacks in 1968," in Brands, ed., *The Foreign Policies of Lyndon Johnson*, 19–36; Edward H. Judge and John W. Langdon, A Hard and Bitter Peace: A Global History of the Cold War (Upper Saddle River, NJ: Prentice Hall, 1996), 208–210.

CHAPTER 11

1. John F. Kennedy, "The War in Indochina," *Vital Speeches* (May 1, 1954): 419–420; Kennedy, "America's Stake in Vietnam," ibid. (Aug. 1, 1956): 618.

2. David Halberstam, *The Best and The Brightest* (New York: Random House, 1969), 185.

3. Memorandum from the Deputy Assistant Secretary of State for Far Eastern Affairs to Secretary of State-Designate Rusk's Liaison (McGhee), Jan. 18, 1961, *Foreign Relations of the United States, 1961–1963: Southeast Asia* (Washington, DC: GPO, 1994), XXIII: 1–2. See also Memorandum From Secretary of State Rusk to President Kennedy, Feb. 24, 1961, ibid., 841.

4. Brief Prepared in the Joint Staff, Joint Chiefs of Staff, Mar. 28, 1961, ibid., 3.

5. Memorandum From Secretary of State Rusk to President Kennedy, Feb. 24, 1961, ibid., 841; American Aide-Memoire to Thailand's Foreign Minister, Apr. 3, 1961, ibid., 845–846.

6. Memorandum From the Joint Chiefs to Secretary of Defense McNamara, May 9, 1961, ibid., 852–853. For a review of U.S. policy toward Thailand, see Ambassador Kenneth T. Young's report in ibid., 870–873.

7. Telegram From Secretary of State Rusk to the Department of State, Mar. 28, 1961, ibid., 5.

8. See editorial notes, ibid., 8, 12.

9. Memorandum of Conversation, Oct. 3, 1961, ibid., 890.

10. Memorandum From the President's Special Assistant for National Security Affairs (Bundy) to President Kennedy, Mar. 5, 1962, ibid., 922–923; ibid., 891–892.

11. Memorandum for the Record, Feb. 13, 1962, ibid., 46.

12. Telegram From the Department of State to the Embassy in Thailand, Feb. 4, 1962, ibid., 906–907; Telegram From the Department of State to the Embassy in Indonesia, Feb. 15, 1962, ibid., 908–909.

13. Memorandum From the Deputy Under Secretary of State for Political Affairs (Johnson) to Secretary of State Rusk, Feb. 10, 1962, ibid., 38. Memorandum of Conversation, Mar. 2, 1962, ibid., 920

14. Memorandum for the Record, Feb. 13, 1962, ibid., 45–46.

15. For the Rusk-Thanat communiqué see Paper Prepared in the Bureau of Far Eastern Affairs, Nov. 7, 1962, Ibid., 981; Department of State, *American Foreign Policy: Current Documents, 1962* (Washington, DC: GPO, 1963), 1093.

16. Memorandum of Conversation, May 14, 1962, *FRUS*, 1961–1963: XXIII, 936; Memorandum From President Kennedy to Secretary of State Rusk, May 14, 1962, ibid., 937; Memorandum From the Director of Intelligence and Research (Hillsman) to the President's Special Assistant for National Security Affairs (Bundy), May 15, 1962, ibid., 65–66; Memorandum of Conversation (Kennedy and Sarasin), Sept. 28, 1962, ibid., 968.

17. Circular Telegram from Department of State to Certain Embassies, Mar. 28, 1963, ibid., 80.

18. Memorandum of Conversation, Bangkok, Feb. 26, 1962, ibid., 916; Memorandum of Conversation, Washington, Mar. 2, 1962, ibid., 921.

19. Paper Prepared in the Bureau of Far Eastern Affairs, Nov. 7, 1962, ibid., 981; Telegram from the Embassy in Thailand to Department of State, Jan. 10, 1963, ibid., 987.

20. Memorandum from Michael V. Forrestal of the National Security Council Staff to President Kennedy, Sept. 24, 1962, ibid., 965.

21. Telegram from Embassy in Thailand to Department of State, Mar. 29, 1963, ibid., 990–992.

22. James C. Thomson, Jr., "How Could Vietnam Happen? An Autopsy," *The Atlantic Monthly* 221 (Apr. 1968): 47–53.

23. Arthur M. Schlesinger, Jr., *The Bitter Heritage: Vietnam and American Democracy, 1941–1966*(Boston: Houghton Mifflin, 1967), 13.

24. On this theme see Halberstam, *The Best and the Brightest*, 97; Larry Berman, *Planning a Tragedy: The Americanization of the War in Vietnam* (New York: Norton, 1982), 19; Loren Baritz, *Backfire: A History of How American Culture Led Us Into Vietnam and Made Us Fight the Way We Did* (New York: Morrow, 1985), 112–113; Thomson, "How Could Vietnam Happen?" 48; Norman Podhoretz, *Why We Were in Vietnam* (New York: Simon & Schuster, 1982), 51.

25. Halberstam, *The Best and the Brightest*, 185.

26. Ibid., 128.

27. Brief Prepared in the Joint Staff, Joint Chiefs of Staff, Mar. 28, 1961, *FRUS*, 1961–1963: XXIII, 3.

28. For the Johnson report see *FRUS*, 1961–1963: XXIII, 7–9; U.S. Department of Defense, *United States-Vietnam Relations, 1945–1967*, 12 vols. (Washington, DC: GPO, 1971), Bk 11, 159–166.

29. Halberstam, *The Best and the Brightest*, 155–156.

30. Memorandum From the Ambassador to Thailand (Young) to the President's Military Representative (Taylor), Oct. 27, 1961, *FRUS*, 1961–1963: XXIII, 28.

31. Halberstam, *The Best and the Brightest*, 169–172.

32. Theodore C. Sorensen, *Kennedy* (New York: Harper & Row, 1965), 654.

33. Kennedy quoted in Schlesinger, *The Bitter Heritage*, 22.

34. Ibid., 31.

35. Daniel Ellsberg, *Papers on the War* (New York: Simon & Schuster, 1972), 59–60.

36. Editorial note, *FRUS*, 1961–1963: XXIII, 37.

37. On the escalation without any strategy to win, see Donald Zagoria, *Vietnam Triangle: Moscow, Peking, and Hanoi* (New York: Pegasus, 1968), 29; Podhoretz, *Why We Were in Vietnam*, 57–63; Ellsberg, *Papers on the War*, 67–71; Leslie H. Gelb and Richard K. Betts, *The Irony of Vietnam: The System Worked* (Washington, DC: Brookings Institution, 1979), 77; Chester Cooper, *The Lost Crusade: America in Vietnam* (New York: Dodd, Mead, 1970), 409.

38. "Special Message to the Congress on the Defense Budget, Mar. 28, 1961, *Public Papers: Kennedy, 1961* (Washington, DC: GPO, 1962), 236; Halberstam, *The Best and the Brightest*, 124.

39. Bernard B. Fall, *The Two Vietnams: A Political and Military Analysis* (New York: Praeger, 1967), 340–343, 374–380. For Nolting's claims for success

in the strategic hamlet program see Frederick Nolting, *From Trust to Tragedy* (New York: Praeger, 1988), 54–56.

40. Memorandum From the Under Secretary of State (Bowles) to President Kennedy, June 13, 1962, *FRUS*, 1961–1963: XXIII, 69.

41. John Kenneth. Galbraith, *Ambassador's Journal: A Personal Account of the Kennedy Years*(Boston: Houghton Mifflin, 1969), 132–133; 231–234.

42. Anatole Shub, *Washington Post*, Dec. 8, 1970; Russell Buhite, ed., *The Dynamics of World Power: A Documentary History of United States Foreign Policy, 1945–1973*, Vol. IV: *The Far East* (New York: 1973), 507.

43. Robert Shaplen, *The Lost Revolution: The U.S. in Vietnam, 1946–1966* (New York: Harper & Row, 1966), 154; John Mecklin, *Mission in Torment* (Garden City, NY: Doubleday, 1965), 38–43. See "Bargaining Between Saigon and Washington: Dilemma of Linkage Politics During War," *Orbis* 18 (Fall 1974): 837–843.

44. For Washington's official optimism see Norman A. Graebner , *America as a World Power: A Realist Appraisal from Wilson to Reagan* (Wilmington, DE: Scholarly Resources, 1984), 233; Mecklin, *Mission in Torment*, 18–19; Clyde Edwin Pettit, *The Experts* (Secaucus, NJ: L. Stuart, 1975), 125–180.

45. Halberstam, *The Best and the Brightest*, 304–306; Neil Sheehan, *A Bright Shining Lie: John Paul Vann and America in Vietnam* (New York: Random House, 1988), 289.

46. *Public Papers of the Presidents: Kennedy, 1963* (Washington, DC: GPO, 1964), 11.

47. Chalmers M. Roberts, "Our 25 Years in Vietnam," *Washington Post*, June 2, 1968, B5.

48. Stanley Karnow, *Vietnam: A History* (New York: Viking, 1984), 259–263; Sheehan, *A Bright Shining Lie*, 203–262; Nolting, *From Trust to Tragedy*, 97.

49. On the negative reporting, see George C. Herring, *America's Longest War: The United States in Vietnam, 1950–1975* (New York: Wiley, 1979), 91–92; Malcolm W. Browne, *The New Face of War* (Indianapolis, IN: Bobbs, Merrill, 1965); Mecklin, *Mission in Torment*, 99–151.

50. Sheehan, *A Bright Shining Lie*, 298–301, 316–317, 328–331.

51. Chester Cooper, quoted in George McT. Kahin, *Intervention: How America Became Involved in Vietnam* (New York: Knopf, 1986), 142–143.

52. Interview with Walter Cronkite, Sept. 2, 1963; Department of State *Bulletin* 49 (Sept. 30, 1963): 499.

53. On the coup see Kahin, *Intervention*, 146–181; Sheehan, *A Bright Shining Lie*, 358–371; Herring, *America's Longest War*, 103–106; Joseph Buttinger, *Vietnam: A Dragon Embattled*, 2 vols. (New York: Praeger, 1967), II, 1001–1002; Shaplen, *The Lost Revolution*, 188–212.

54. Nolting, *From Trust to Tragedy*, 124–138.

55. Kenneth O'Donnell, "LBJ and the Kennedys," *Life* 69 (Aug. 7, 1970): 51–52.

56. Ellsberg, *Papers on the War*, 97, 102.

57. Gelb and Betts, *The System Worked*, 186; Sheehan, *A Bright Shining Lie*, 375.

58. Sheehan, *A Bright Shining Lie*, 372–373.

59. Ibid., 374–375.

60. Ibid., 376–379; Baritz, *Backfire*, 135–137.

61. Theodore Draper, *The Abuse of Power* (New York: Viking, 1967), 61; Gelb and Betts, *The System Worked*, 98–100; Karnow, *Vietnam: A History*, 336–338.

62. Karnow, *Vietnam: A History*, 344–345; Baritz, *Backfire*, 138; Kahin, *Intervention*, 210–211.

63. On the Gulf of Tonkin Resolution, see Draper, *Abuse of Power*, 64–66; Kahin, *Intervention*, 219–223; Baritz, *Backfire*, 140–141; George W. Ball, *The Past Has Another Pattern* (New York: Norton, 1982), 379–380; Karnow, *Vietnam: A History*, 366–376. Also see Joseph C. Goulden, *Truth Is the First Casualty: The Gulf of Tonkin Affair—Illusion and Reality* (Chicago: Rand McNally, 1965); Eugene G. Windchy, *Tonkin Gulf* (Garden City, NY: Doubleday, 1971); John Galloway, *The Gulf of Tonkin Resolution* (Rutherford, NJ: Fairleigh Dickinson University Press, 1970), a documentary history, including the congressional debates.

64. Draper, *Abuse of Power*, 66–67.

65. Khanh's pressure for a bombing campaign, see Kahin, *Intervention*, 215; Karnow, *Vietnam: A History*, 378–379; Draper, *Abuse of Power*, 68–70.

66. Baritz, *Backfire*, 145; Sheehan, *A Bright Shining Lie*, 380; Draper, *Abuse of Power*, 70–71.

67. Baritz, *Backfire*, 145; Lyndon Baines Johnson, *The Vantage Point: Perspectives of the Presidency, 1963–1969* (New York: Holt, Rhinehard & Winston, 1971), 151–152.

68. Kahin, *Intervention*, 271–275; Berman, *Planning a Tragedy*, 45; Richard Goodwin, *Triumph and Tragedy: Reflections on Vietnam* (New York: Random House, 1966), 31; Berman, *Planning a Tragedy*, 36–37. On George Ball's doubts, see Karnow, *Vietnam: A History*, 404–405; Berman, *Planning a Tragedy*, 45–46.

69. Kahin, *Intervention*, 281–283; Draper, *Abuse of Power*, 73; Bundy's statement and Thomson's rebuttal in Berman, *Planning a Tragedy*, 43–45.

70. *Time* (Feb. 26, 1965): 20; John W. Finney, "Vietnam: A Debate over U.S. Role," the *New York Times*, Feb. 28, 1965, E3; Thomson, "How Could Vietnam Happen?" 50–51. See especially Reston, the *New York Times*, Feb. 14, 1965.

71. Karnow, *Vietnam: A History*, 382–386; Baritz, *Backfire*, 173; Berman, *Planning a Tragedy*, 70; Kahin, *Intervention*, 293–305; Draper, *Abuse of Power*, 85. For doubts regarding Rolling Thunder, see Berman, *Planning a Tragedy*, 47; Baritz, *Backfire*, 163–164; Kahin, *Intervention*, 314. McCone cited in Harrison E. Salisbury, ed., *Vietnam Reconsidered: Lessons From a War* (New York: Harper & Row, 1984), 55; also see Kathleen J. Turner, *Lyndon Johnson's Dual War: Vietnam and the Press* (Chicago: University of Chicago Press, 1985), 119–132.

72. Joseph Buttinger, *Vietnam: The Unforgettable Tragedy* (New York: Horizon, 1977), 77.

73. See Adam B. Ulam, *The Rivals: America and Russia Since World War II* (New York: Viking, 1976), 385; Rusk restated his defense of the war in Richard Rusk, *As I Saw It*, ed. Daniel S. Papp (New York: Norton, 1990).

74. William J. Duiker, *The Communist Road to Power in Vietnam* (Boulder, CO: Westview, 1981), 221–233; Guenter Lewy, *America in Vietnam* (New York: Oxford University Press, 1979), 40; Podhoretz, *Why We Were in Vietnam*, 74–76.

75. For defense of the White Paper by Norman Podhoretz, William V. O'Brien, Whittle Johnston, and Guenter Lewy, see John Norton Moore, ed., *The Vietnam Debate: A Fresh Look at the Arguments* (Lanham, MD: University Press of America, 1990), 24, 64–67, 89–96, 99–134.

76. Kahin, *Intervention*, 290–291; Hans J. Morgenthau, the *New York Times Magazine* (Apr. 18, 1965) charged the assertions supporting the White Paper bordered on the grotesque; also see Cooper, *The Lost Crusade*, 264–265.

77. Ball, *The Past Has Another Pattern*, 392–393. For the continuing pressure of Westmoreland and the JSC for troops, see Berman, *Planning a Tragedy*, 68–71.

78. Kahin, *Intervention*, 356.

79. Ibid., 311–313, 356–357, 361.

80. Ball, *The Past Has Another Pattern*, 383, 387, 398. Halberstam analyzed McNamara's advantages in confronting Ball with evidence that Ball's staff could never find for study and review, *The Best and the Brightest*, 705–706.

81. Berman, *Planning a Tragedy*, 100–103; Kahin, *Intervention*, 360–365.

82. Ibid., 375, 387. Berman, *Planning a Tragedy*, 109, 121; Thomas L. Hughes, "The Power to Speak and the Power to Listen: Reflections on Bureaucratic Politics and a Recommendation on Information Flows," in Thomas M. Franck and Edward Weisband, eds., *Secrecy in Foreign Policy* (New York: Oxford University Press, 1974), 34–38.

83. Karnow, *Vietnam: A History*, 420–426; Kahin, *Intervention*, 389; Draper, *Abuse of Power*, 85.

84. Kahin, *Intervention*, 397–398; White House press conference, July 28, 1965, *Department of State Bulletin* 53 (Aug. 16, 1965): 263–264.

85. Baritz, *Backfire*, 166; Berman, *Planning a Tragedy*, 128.

86. See Alexander George, David Hall, and William Simons, *The Limits of Coercive Diplomacy: Laos, Cuba, Vietnam.* (Boston: Little, Brown, 1971), 22, 26.

87. Johnson's speech in *Current* No. 59 (May 1965): 6. On Mar. 15, 1965, seventeen nonaligned countries asked both Washington and Hanoi to seek peace through negotiations, *Vietnam Perspective* 1 (Nov. 1965): 42–43, 46–47.

88. General Maxwell Taylor in "The Cause in Vietnam Is Being Won," the *New York Times Magazine* (Oct. 15, 1967): 36.

89. Thomson's views in Kahin, *Intervention*, 288–289, 327; Ball's warnings in Ball, *The Past Has Another Pattern*, 391, and Berman, *Planning a Tragedy*, 47; Lippmann's critique in Ronald Steel, *Walter Lippmann and the American Century* (Boston: Little, Brown, 1980), 562–564.

90. Wallace J. Thies, When Governments Collide: Coercion and Diplomacy in the Vietnam Conflict, 1964–1968 (Berkeley: University of California Press, 1980), 262.

91. Kahin, *Intervention*, 326. Hanoi, on Apr. 7, proclaimed its goal of self-determination to restore Vietnam's territorial integrity and independence, see *Vietnam Perspectives*, I (Nov. 1965), 44–45. Hanoi's purposes were as inflexible as those of the United States, see John M. Gates, "Vietnam: The Debate Goes On," *Parameters* 14 (Spring 1984); Stanley Karnow, "Giap Remembers," the *New York Times Magazine* (June 24, 1990): 36.

92. See Thies, *When Governments Collide*, 270, 278–281.

93. Gelb and Betts, *The System Worked*, 267, 283, 291–293; Karnow, *Vietnam: A History*, 479. By 1967 the Vietnam War was costing only three percent of the GNP compared to twelve percent during the Korean War, Ibid., 487. On the Johnson strategy—F. Charles Parker IV, *Vietnam: Strategy of Stalemate* (New York: Paragon House, 1989); Vaughn Davis Bornet attributes Johnson's no-win war in Vietnam to domestic constraints in *The Presidency of Lyndon B. Johnson* (Lawrence: University Press of Kansas, 1983), 253–282.

94. Gelb and Betts, *The System Worked*, 353–354. The system achieved a continuing war that avoided defeat. See also, Graebner, "Presidential Power and Foreign Affairs," 183–187.

95. Washington repeated its inflexible demands, see Ball, *The Past Has Another Pattern*, 405–406. The administration did not take the peace efforts seriously, see David Kraslow and Stuart H. Loory, *The Search for Peace in Vietnam* (New York: Random House, 1968), 5–88; Karnow, *Vietnam: A History*, 492–498; Gelb and Betts, *The System Worked*, 151–153.

96. On pacification, see U.S. Department of Defense. *The Pentagon Papers: The Defense Department History of United States Decision Making on Vietnam: The Senator Gravel Edition.* 5 vols. (Boston: Beacon, 1971–1972), II: 515–623; report of meeting at Honolulu, Feb. 6–8, 1966, *Department of State Bulletin* 54 (Feb. 28, 1966): 302–307; Denis Warner, "Vietnam: The Ordeal of Pacification," *Reporter* 35 (Dec. 1966): 25–28.

97. See Bui Diem, "Vietnam: Your War, Our Tragedy," *The Washington Post*, Aug. 30, 1987. Bui Diem was South Vietnam's ambassador to the United States from 1967 to 1972.

98. McNaughton's memorandum, Neil Sheehan, et al., *The Pentagon Papers as published by the New York Times* (New York: Quadrangle, 1971), 502.

99. Ibid., 503. Kennan's testimony before the Senate Foreign Relations Committee in Feb. 1966, raised the question of the country's reputation, see "Opinion at Home and Abroad," the *New York Times*, Feb. 13, 1966. Writer Jonathan Schell termed McNaughton's rationale a "psychological domino theory." Also see, Hans J. Morgenthau, "U.S. Misadventure in Vietnam," *Current History* 54 (Jan. 1968): 34.

100. Rusk's address to the American Society of International Law, Apr. 13, 1965, *Department of State Bulletin* 452 (May 10, 1965): 697.

101. Johnson's address before the Navy League of Manchester, New Hampshire, Aug. 20, 1966, *Department of State Bulletin* 55 (Sept. 12, 1966): 368.

102. For press opposition, see Turner, *Lyndon Johnson's Dual War*, 134–211; for Galbraith's and Kennan's criticisms, see Berman, *Planning a Tragedy*, 152–153; *The Atlantic Monthly* 263 (Apr. 1989): 40.

103. Pettit, The Experts, 305–341; F. M. Kail, What Washington Said: Administration Rhetoric and the Vietnam War, 1949–1969 (New York: Harper & Row, 1973), 238–241.

104. Ball, *The Past Has Another Pattern*, 407. Westmoreland appeared before Congress on Apr. 28, 1967, see "The Week in Review," the *New York Times*, Apr. 30, 1967, E1, also "Vietnam: How Much to Hold the Initiative?" the *New York Times*, Sept. 9, 1967; address to the National Press Club, Nov. 21, 1967, Department of State *Bulletin* 57 (Dec. 11, 1967): 788.

105. Gelb and Betts, *The System Worked*, 169–170; Townsend Hoopes, *The Limits of Intervention* (New York, 1969), 125; Karnow, *Vietnam: A History*, 498–507.

106. Halberstam, *The Best and the Brightest*, 701, 773–774; Harry Brandon, *Anatomy of Error: The Inside Story of the Asian War on the Potomac, 1954–1969* (Boston: Gambit, 1969), 100–117.

107. Don Oberdorfer, *Tet!* (Garden City, NY: Doubleday, 1971), 329–330; Podhoretz, *Why We Were in Vietnam*, 116–117; Hoopes, *The Limits of Intervention*, 149. Peter Braestrup, *Big Story: How the American Press and Television Reported and Interpreted the Crisis of Tet 1968 in Vietnam and Washington*, 2 vols. (Boulder, CO: Westview, 1977), agrees that Tet was a disaster for the Viet Cong and the North Vietnamese. Also see Salisbury, *Vietnam Reconsidered*, 168.

108. Gelb and Betts, *The System Worked*, 171; Baritz, *Backfire*, 180–181; Karnow, *Vietnam: A History*, 547–549; Cronkite quoted in Podhoretz, *Why We Were in Vietnam*, 125.

109. Hoopes, *The Limits of Intervention*, 146.

110. On the opening of the peace negotiations see Rowland Evans and Robert Novak in *The Washington Post*, Apr. 17, 1968; Joseph Kraft in ibid., May 19, 1968; *Newsweek* (Apr. 22, 1968): 40–45; Hendrick Smith and Henry Tanner in the *New York Times*, May 5, 1968. On Xuan Thuy's demands see Anthony Lewis in ibid., May 19, 1968. See also, Hans J. Morgenthau, "Bundy's Doctrine of War Without End," *The New Republic* 159 (Nov. 2, 1968): 18–20.

111. Bernard Weintraub, "Saigon's Reaction," the *New York Times*, May 5, 1968; A. J. Langguth, "Thieu and Ky Think About the Unthinkable," the *New York Times Magazine* (Apr. 14, 1968): 21.

112. For Paris talks see *Vietnam and the Paris Negotiations: Report of Senator Mike Mansfield to the Committee on Foreign Relations, September 1968*, 90th Cong., 2nd Sess. (Washington, DC: GPO, 1968). Mansfield suggested the U.S. modify Saigon's objectives to facilitate some agreement with the North Vietnamese. See also *Newsweek* (June 3, 1968): 40–41; Joseph Kraft in *The Washington Post*, July 14, 1968; and Ross Terrill, "A Report on the Paris Talks," *The New Republic* 159 (July 13, 1968): 15–18.

113. For continuing disagreements in Paris, see "Confusion over the Bombing Issue," the *New York Times*, Aug. 4, 1968, E4; Tom Wicker, ibid., Aug. 18, 1968, E15; Gene Roberts ibid., Oct. 20, 1968, 1; "The Week in Review," ibid., E1; "Hanoi Nibbles, But Has Not Yet Taken the Bait," ibid., Oct. 27, 1968, E3; and Murrey Marder, "Our Paris Foe Is Courtly," *The Washington Post*, Sept. 8, 1968, B1.

114. For reaction to the President's announcement, see Zalin B. Grant, "The Bombing Halt," *The New Republic* 159 (Nov. 9, 1968), 13–15. One reason for Johnson's failure to secure Saigon's approval. Thieu's bitter reaction appears in *The Washington Post*, Nov. 5, 1968, A19.

115. On the impasse in Paris, see "What Hanoi Wants at Paris," the *New York Times*, Nov. 10, 1968, E3; Chalmers M. Roberts, "Vietnam's Bitter Kernel Is Exposed," *The Washington Post*, Nov. 17, 1968, B1-B2; "Saigon Balks," *Newsweek* (Nov. 11, 1968): 46; "Paris: A Long Way to Go," ibid., 52–53; for Nixon's actions, see Stanley I. Kutler, ed. *Encyclopedia of the Vietnam War* (New York: Scribners, 1996), 369.

116. "Statements by Xuan Thuy," the *New York Times*, Nov. 3, 1968, 1; on Mrs. Binh's arrival in Paris, see *The Washington Post*, Nov. 4, 1968.

117. For the debate on the shape of the table, see the *Washington Post*, Dec. 8, 1968, A6; "The Peace Talks in Saigon," *The Washington Post*, Nov. 10, 1968, B6. On Ky, see Murrey Marder ibid., Dec. 18, 1968. See George C. Wilson, "Clifford Controversy," ibid., Dec. 29, 1968; The *New York Times*, Dec. 25, 1968, E3. Ky rebuked Clifford for accusing Saigon of intransigence, *The Washington Post*, Dec. 18, 1968, A20; "The Week in Review," the *New York Times*, Dec. 1, 1968, D1; *Newsweek* (Dec. 9, 1968): 27–28.

118. Paul Hofmann, the *New York Times*, Jan. 5, 1969; "The Sudden Breakthrough," *Newsweek* (Jan. 27, 1969): 36–37.

119. Ulam, *The Rivals*, 386; also see Walter Lippmann, *Newsweek* (Jan. 13, 1969): 11; Robert L. Heilbroner, "Making a Rational Foreign Policy Now," *Harper's Magazine* 237 (Sept. 1968), 64–71.

CHAPTER 12

1. Interview with Pierre Salinger of *L'Express* (France), Apr. 12, 1975, U.S. Department of State, Bureau of Public Affairs, Office of Media Services.

2. Henry Kissinger, *White House Years* (Boston: Little, Brown, 1979), 114–125.

3. Richard Nixon, *U.S. Foreign Policy for the 1970s: A New Strategy for Peace*, Report to Congress, Feb. 18, 1970 (Washington, DC: GPO, 1970), 2–3; Seyom Brown, *The Crisis of Power: An Interpretation of United States Foreign Policy During the Kissinger Years* (New York, 1979), 4–5.

4. Kissinger interview with Pierre Salinger, Apr. 12, 1975, U.S. Department of State, Bureau of Public Affairs, Office of Media Service; Halperin in *Newsweek* (Dec. 14, 1970): 40–43; Richard M. Nixon, *RN: The Memoirs of Richard Nixon* (New York: Grosset & Dunlap, 1978), 343 (later as Nixon, *RN*); also see Kissinger, *White House Years*, 1143.

5. Kissinger, *White House Years*, p. 129; Nixon, *RN*, 346.

6. Department of State *Bulletin* 69 (Oct. 29, 1973): 528.

7. William Safire, "Puppet as Prince," *Harper's Magazine* 250 (Mar. 1975): 12–17; Marvin Kalb and Bernard Kalb, *Kissinger* (Boston: Little, Brown, 1974), 4–7; Henry Brandon, *The Retreat of American Power* (New York: Dell, 1974), 33–34; Kissinger, *A World Restored: Metternich, Castlereagh and the Problems of Peace, 1812–1822* (Boston: Houghton Mifflin, 1957), 1–2.

8. For the administration's view, see Kissinger, *White House Years*, 407–411.

9. Ibid., 635ff, esp. 647; Nixon, *RN*, 485–489.

10. Richard N. Nixon, *Third Annual Report to the Congress on United States Foreign Policy* (Feb. 9, 1972).

11. Charles C. Flowerree, "Chemical and Biological Weapons and Arms Control," Richard Dean Burns, *Encyclopedia of Arms Control and Disarmament*, 3 vols. (New York: Scribners, 1992), II: 1005, also see Thomas Graham, Jr. *Disarmament Sketches: Three Decades of Arms Control and International Law* (Seattle: University of Washington Press, 2002), Chap. 2.

12. See "The President's News Conference," Oct. 12, 1971, Woolley and Peters, *The American Presidency Project*: http://www.presidency.ucsb.edu/ws/?pid=3736. Strobe Talbott, *Endgame: The Inside Story of SALT II* (New York: Harper & Row, 1979), 19.

13. Quoted in Gerard C. Smith, *Doubletalk: The Story of SALT I* (Garden City, NY: Doubleday, 1980), 16.

14. Aleksandr' G. Savel'yev and Nikolay N. Detinov, *The Big Five: Arms Control Decision-Making in the Soviet Union* (Westport, CT: Praeger, 1995), 7–8; Raymond L. Garthoff, *A Journey Through the Cold War: a Memoir of Containment and Coexistence* (Washington, DC: Brookings Institution, 2001), 206; "President's News Conference," Jan. 27, 1969, Woolley and Peters, *The American Presidency Project*: http://www.presidency.ucsb.edu/ws/?pid=1942.

15. Savel'yev and Detinov, *The Big Five*, 9.

16. Thomas Graham, Jr. *Disarmament Sketches: Three Decades of Arms Control and International Law* (Seattle: University of Washington Press, 2002), 44.

17. Graham, *Disarmament Sketches*, 53–54.

18. Kissinger, *White House Years*, 1132, 1150–1151; Anatoly Dobrynin, *In Confidence: Moscow's Ambassador to America's Six Cold War Presidents* (New York; Random House, 1995), 251–252.

19. John Newhouse, *Cold Dawn: The Story of SALT* (New York: Holt, Rinehart, Winston, 1973), 262–263.

20. Kissinger, *White House Years*, 391–402.

21. Ibid., 425–429, 1273–1274.

22. Kissinger, *Years of Upheaval* (Boston: Little, Brown, 1982), 142.

23. Ibid., 146–147.

24. Richard N. Nixon, *Third Annual Report to the Congress on the United States' Foreign Policy*, Feb. 9, 1972.

25. Kissinger, "Energy: European Problems," *Vital Speeches of the Day* 40:6 (Jan. 1, 1974): 166.

26. Richard M. Nixon, "Asia After Viet Nam," *Foreign Affairs* (Oct. 1967): 121.

27. Nixon, *RN*, 344.

28. Ibid., 545, 548.

29. Marvin Kalb and Bernard Kalb, *Kissinger* (Boston: Little, Brown, 1974), 239–240, 251.

30. William Pfaff, "Reflections (American Vietnam Policy),"*The New Yorker* (June 3, 1972): 79.

31. Nixon, *Third Annual Report to Congress* . . . . (Washington, DC: Feb. 8, 1972).

32. Nixon quoted by Clark Clifford, "Political Compromise—the only Solution in Vietnam," *New York Times*, May 25, 1970, 7; Kissinger, *White House Years*, 228–229.

33. Henry Kissinger, "The Viet Nam Negotiations," *Foreign Affairs* (Jan. 1969): 211–234.

34. Kissinger, *White House Years*, 238–239.

35. Ibid, 243–254.

36. George Ball, *The Past Has Another Pattern* (New York: Norton, 1982), 410–11.

54. Joseph Kraft, *Washington Post*, Sept. 9, 1973.

37. Nixon, *RN*, I, 482, 493–495; David Landau, *Kissinger: The Uses of Power* (Boston: Houghton Mifflin, 1972), 228.

38. Kissinger, *White House Years*, 281–82; Nixon, *RN*, I, 489–90. For the background of Kissinger's meeting with Xuan Thuy and later Le Duc Tho, see Kalb and Kalb, *Kissinger*, 137–139, 149–151.

39. Kalb and Kalb, *Kissinger*, 143–146.

40. Richard Nixon, "Address to the Nation on the Situation in Southeast Asia," May 30, 1970, Woolley and Peters, *The American Presidency Project*. http://www.presidency.ucsb.edu/ws/?pid=2490.

41. *Department of State Bulletin* 64 (June 21, 1971): 799.

42. Kalb and Kalb, *Kissinger*, 172–173; Nixon, "Address to the Nation on the Situation in Southeast Asia," Apr. 7, 1971, Woolley and Peters, *The American Presidency Project*. http://www.presidency.ucsb.edu/ws/?pid=2972.

43. Ellsworth Bunker, "A Review of Progress and Problems in Viet-Nam," *Department of State Bulletin* 64 (Feb. 15, 1971): 206, 207; Nixon, "President Nixon Reiterates Policy on Withdrawal From Indochina," ibid. 65 (Dec. 6, 1971): 658.

44. William Safire, "Puppet as Prince," *Harper's Magazine* 250 (Mar. 1975): 12. In explaining his decision to bomb Haiphong, Nixon declared that the United States was "faced with the specter of defeat, and I had to make a choice, a choice of accepting that defeat and going to Moscow hat in hand, ort of acting to prevent it. I acted." See Kalb and Kalb, *Kissinger*, 306.

45. Kissinger, *The White House Years*, 1341–1342.

46. See Ibid., 1378–1392.

47. Nixon, *RN*, 718.

48. Ibid., 749–750.

49. Nixon, "Address to the Nation About Vietnam and Domestic Problems," Mar. 29, 1973, Woolley and Peters, *The American Presidency Project:* http://www.presidency.ucsb.edu/ws/?pid=4161.

50. Alton Frye, *A Responsible Congress: The Politics of National Security* (New York: McGraw-Hill, 1975), 210–212; also see Alton Frye and Jack Sullivan, "Congress and Vietnam: the Fruits of Anguish," in Anthony Lake, ed. *The Vietnam Legacy: American Society and the Future of American Foreign Policy* (New York: New York University Press, 1976), 194–215.

51. See Nixon, *RN*, 772, 887–889.

52. See George W. Ball, *Newsweek* (Nov. 20, 1972): 21.

53. Leslie H. Gelb in the *New York Times*, Sept. 23, 1974.

55. For Kissinger's special challenges as secretary of state see Joseph Kraft, "Secretary Henry," the *New York Times Magazine* (Oct. 28, 197): 21.

56. For Kissinger's successful maneuver to gain control of Middle Eastern policy, see Kalb and Kalb, *Kissinger*, 450–478.

57. Ibid., 529–542.

58. Kissinger, *Years of Upheaval* (Boston: Little, Bown, 1982), 1125.

59. Nixon, *RN*, 1010–1018.

60. See Cyrus L. Sulzberger in the *New York Times*, Mar. 24, 1974.

61. John M. Crewdson, the *New York Times*, Sept. 29, 1974; see *Newsweek* (June 24, 1974): 25–28; Nixon, *RN*, 1009.

62. Gerald R. Ford, *A Time to Heal: The Autobiography of Gerald R. Ford* (New York: Harper & Row, 1979), 29–30.

63. Quoted in Norman A. Graebner, "Henry Kissinger and American Foreign Policy: A Contemporary Appraisal," *Australian Journal of Politics and History* 22 (Apr. 1976): 12.

64. James Reston in the *New York Times*, Feb. 17, 1974.

65. See Kraft in *The Washington Post*, Nov. 5, 1974. For a critical examination of Kissinger's diplomacy see Simon Head, "The Hot Deals and Cold Wars of Henry Kissinger," the *New York Times Magazine* (Oct. 26, 1975): 13.

66. Press Conference at the Western White House, News Release, Aug. 23, 1974, Bureau of Public Affairs, Office of Media Services, Department of State.

67. Murrey Marder and Marilyn Berger in *The Washington Post*, Oct. 6, 1974.

68. See Leslie Gelb in the *New York Times*, June 16, 1974.

69. See James Reston in Ibid., Feb. 9, 1975; Stephen S. Rosenfeld in the Cleveland *Plain Dealer*, Oct. 15, 1974; Meg Greenfield in *Newsweek* (Nov. 11, 1974): 46.

70. News release, Jan. 24, 1975, Department of State, Bureau of Public Affairs, Office of Media Services; Gelb in the *New York Times*, Jan. 26, 1975.

71. Marder in the *Philadelphia Inquirer*, Oct. 12, 1975. Frances R. Hill complained that Kissinger, as secretary of state, seemed destined, like Bismarck, to leave what Kissinger called "a heritage of unassimilated greatness." See *Worldview* 17 (Oct. 1974), 33.

72. Göran Rystad, "Eurocommunism in American Foreign Policy during the 1970s," *Scandia*, band 50:2 (1984): 191–196; see Jean-François Revel, "The Myths of Eurocommunism," *Foreign Affairs* 2 (1978): 295ff.

73. Ford quote in Kissinger, *Years of Renewal*, 629; David Binder, "Kissinger Sees NATO End If Europeans Elect Reds," and "Summary of Kissinger Speech to U.S. Ambassadors," the *New York Times*, Apr. 7, 1976.

74. Raymond L. Garthoff, *Détente and Confrontation: American-Soviet Relations from Nixon to Reagan*, rev. ed. (Washington, DC: Brookings Institution, 1994), 538–541.

75. Ford's speech, "America's Strength and Progress toward Freedom and Peace," in Department of State *Bulletin* 73 (Sept. 15, 1975): 12; Kissinger, "American Unity and the National Interest," Ibid., 393.

76. Garthoff, *Détente and Confrontation*, 543–544.

77. George W. Ball, *Diplomacy for a Crowded World: An American Foreign Policy* (Boston: Little, Brown, 1976), 78.

78. Tom Wicker in the *New York Times*, Mar. 16, 1975.

79. See Gary Wills in *The Washington Post*, Mar. 31, 1975. For President Gerald Ford's warning of falling dominoes, issued at the University of Notre Dame in March, see Reston in the *New York Times*, Mar. 20, 1975.

80. News release, Apr. 15, 1975, U.S. Department of State, Bureau of Public Affairs, Office of Media Services.

81. Quoted in *Newsweek* (Mar. 24, 1975): 92.

82. Quoted in Fox Butterfield, "The New Vietnam Scholarship," *New York Times Magazine* (Feb. 13, 1983): 54; also see Joseph M. Siracusa, "Lessons of

Viet-Nam and the Future of American Foreign Policy," *Australian Outlook* 30 (Aug. 1976), 232.

83. *Washington Star*, Mar. 31, 1975; *Chicago Tribune*, May 3, 1975; *The Daily Progress* (Charlottesville), June 12, 1975; Rowland Evans and Robert Novak in Ibid., Jan. 16, 1975.

84. *Time* (May 19, 1975): 69.

85. Kraft in *The Washington Post*, June 22, 1975; Dana Adams Schmidt in *The Christian Science Monitor*, Oct. 17, 1975.

86. Guenter Lewy, *America in Vietnam* (New York: Oxford University Press, 1978), 440; Norman Podhoretz took this view in his book, *Why We Were in Vietnam* (New York: Simon & Schuster, 1982).

87. Robert Elegant, "How to Lose a War: Reflections of a Foreign Correspondent," *Encounter* 57 (Aug. 1981): 73.

88. Lewy, *America in Vietnam*, 436.

89. Interview with David Binder and Bernard Gwertzman in "The Week in Review," the *New York Times*, Apr. 22, 1984.

90. For a valuable, but generally uncritical, survey of the recent literature on the Vietnam War, see Fox Butterfield, "The New Vietnam Scholarship," the *New York Times Magazine*, Feb. 13, 1983, 26–35, 45–62.

91. See letters to the editor, especially that of Stanley Hoffmann, Ibid., Mar. 20, 1983, 110.

92. See Joseph Kraft in *The Washington Post*, Nov. 11, 1974. For a review of Kissinger's failure of March see Ibid., Mar. 23, 1975; Henry Kamm in the *New York Times*, Mar. 9, 1975.

93. The *New York Times*, Sept. 7, 1975.

94. See *Newsweek* (Sept. 15, 1975): 33.

95. *Philadelphia Inquirer*, Oct. 12, 1975.

96. See Kraft in *The Washington Post*, May 27, 1973; Chalmers M. Roberts in Ibid., Aug. 26, 1973; Reston in the *New York Times*, Feb. 28, 1974.

97. Kenneth Thompson in *Worldview* 17 (July 1974): 61.

98. *Robert G. Kaufman, Henry M. Jackson: A Life in Politics* (Seattle: University of Washington Press, 2000), 280–283.

99. Ford, *A Time to Heal*, 373; Thomas M. DeFrank, *Write It When I'm Gone: Remarkable Off-the-Record Conversation With Gerald R. Ford* (New York: Putnam's Sons, 2007.

100. Ford quoted in James E. Goodby, *At the Borderline of Armageddon: How American Presidents Managed the Atom Bomb* (Lanham, DE: Rowman & Littlefield, 2006), 104; Mondale in Strobe Talbott, *Endgame: The Inside Story of SALT II* (New York: Harper & Row, 1979), 32–37, 52.

101. John Fry, *The Helsinki Process: Negotiating Security and Cooperation in Europe* (Washington, DC: National Defense University Press, 1993): Jussi M Haminäki, " . . . 'Dr. Kissinger' or 'Mr. Kissinger'? Kissingerology, Thirty Years and Counting," *Diplomatic History* 27:5 (2003): 654; Ford, *A Time to Heal*, 300–301; William G. Hyland, *Mortal Rivals* (New York: Random House, 1982), 128; Robert M. Gates, *From the Shadows: The Untimate Insider's Story of Five Presidents and How They Won the Cold War* (New York: Simon & Schuster, 1996), 86.

102. Paul Nitze and Charles Burton Marshall in the *New York Times*. Feb. 8, 1976.

103. Nutter quoted by Marder in the *Philadelphia Inquirer*, Oct. 12, 1975

104. Kissinger, *Years of Renewal*, 93–103; Garthoff, *Détente and Confrontation*, 326–335.

105. Kissinger, *Years of Renewal*, 914–915, 921; for an American and Soviet perspective on Angola, see Garthoff, *Détente and Confrontation*, 574–588.

106. Dobrynin, *In Confidence*, 472.

107. See Lorrin Rosenbaum, "Government by Torture," *Worldview* 18 (Apr. 1975): 21–27. Assistant Secretary Philip C. Habib insisted in June 1975 that the U.S. government was concerned with human rights. See news release, June 24, 1975, U.S. Department of State, Bureau of Public Affairs, Office of Media Services.

108. *The Washington Post*, May 18, 1975.

109. See Kissinger's interview with Bill Moyers in *Worldview* 18 (Mar. 1975): 37–45.

110. For the widespread approval of Kissinger's role see *The Washington Post*, June 29, 1975; *U.S. News & World Report* (Oct. 6, 1975): 12.

111. For a review of Kissinger's declining prestige and popularity see *The Wall Street Journal*, Nov. 5, 1975; *Newsweek* (Dec. 8, 1975): 36–37.

CHAPTER 13

1. Address at the University of Notre Dame, May 22, 1977, Department of State *Bulletin* 76 (June 13, 1977): 622.

2. Laurence H. Shoup, *The Carter Presidency and Beyond: Power and Politics in the 1980s* (Palo Alto, CA: Ramparts Press, 1980), 141, 144–145; Paul Lewis in the *New York Times*, Feb. 13, 1977, E5.

3. Quoted in Shoup, *The Carter Presidency and Beyond*, 109.

4. For a survey of Carter's foreign policy goals see Anthony Lake, "Pragmatism and Principle in U.S. Foreign Policy," Department of State, Bureau of Public Affairs, Office of Media Services, June 13, 1977, 1–7; Jimmy Carter, *Keeping Faith: Memoirs of a President* (New York: Bantam Books, 1982), 143–144; Carter, *Why Not the Best?* (Nashville: Broadman Press, 1975), 1–6.

5. Donald C. Spencer, *The Carter Implosion: Jimmy Carter and the Amateur Style of Diplomacy* (New York: Praeger, 1988), 25–27.

6. Stanley Hoffmann, "A View from At Home: The Perils of Incoherence," *Foreign Affairs* 57 (1979): 485.

7. Richard J. Barnet, "Carter's Patchwork Doctrine," *Harper's* (Aug. 1977): 27.

8. U.S. House of Representatives, Committee on Foreign Affairs, *Human Rights in the World Community: A Call for U.S. Leadership, March 27, 1974* (Washington, DC: GPO), 1974, 1–3.

9. Arthur Schlesinger, Jr., "Human Rights and the American Tradition," *Foreign Affairs* 57:3 (1978): 512.

10. On the 1974 Foreign Assistance Act see Ernest W. Lefever, "The Trivialization of Human Rights," *Policy Review* 3 (Winter 1978): 13.

11. Sandy Vogelgesang, *American Dream Global Nightmare: The Dilemma of U.S. Human Rights* (New York: Norton, 1980), 128; Norman A. Graebner, "Human Rights and Foreign Policy: The Historic Connection," in Kenneth W. Thompson, ed., *The Moral Imperatives of Human Rights: A World Survey* (Lanham, MD: University Press of America, 1980), 50.

12. Henry Kissinger, *American Foreign Policy* (New York: Norton, 1977), 121.

13. Carter's Inaugural Address, *Department of State Bulletin* 76 (Feb. 14, 1977): 121; Carter's Address, Mar. 17, 1977, The Department of State, Bureau of Public Affairs, Office of Media Services, 1–4; also Carter's speech before the United Nations, Oct. 4, 1977, News Release, The Department of State, Bureau of Public Affairs, Office of Media Services, 6.

14. Address at Notre Dame University, May 22, 1977, Department of State *Bulletin* 76 (June 13, 1977): 621–623.

15. On Patricia Derian see Spencer, *The Carter Implosion*, 58–59; *Newsweek* (May 16, 1977): 70.

16. Samuel Pisar, "Let's Put Détente Back on the Rails," the *New York Times Magazine* (Sept. 25, 1977): 32.

17. On the limited validity and usefulness of Western political principles, see George F. Kennan, *The Cloud of Danger: Current Realities of American Foreign Policy* (Boston: Little, Brown, 1977), 43; Schlesinger, "Human Rights and the American Tradition," 517–518. For sources of international human rights, see Paul Battersby and Joseph M. Siracusa, *Globalization and Human Security* (Lanham. MD: Rowan & Littlefield, 2009), 145–173.

18. Elizabeth Drew, *The New Yorker*, 36; C.L. Sulzberger in the *New York Times*, Aug. 7, 1977.

19. Sandy Vogelgesang, "What Price Principle? U.S. Policy on Human Rights," *Foreign Affairs* 56 (July 1978): 819; Vogelgesang, "Principle's Price," the *New York Times*, June 28, 1978.

20. "Dr. Kissinger on World Affairs," *Encounter* (Nov. 1978): 11.

21. *The World Today* 33 (July 1977): 241–243.

22. Hans J. Morgenthau, *Human Rights and Foreign Policy* (New York: Council on Religion & International Affairs 1979), 7; Vogelgesang, "What Price Principle? U.S. Policy on Human Rights," 827–828.

23. Statement, Feb. 24, 1977, Secretary of State, Bureau of Public Affairs, Office of Media Services, 1–3; Vance Press Conference, Mar. 4, 1977, The Secretary of State, Bureau of Public Affairs, Office of Media Services, 1.

24. Stanley Hoffmann, "The Hell of Good Intentions," *Foreign Policy* 29 (Winter 1977–1978): 3–26; Spencer, *The Carter Implosion*, 52–53; Evans and Novak, "A Double Standard on Human Rights," *The Washington Post*, Apr. 12, 1978; Bernard Gwertzman in the *New York Times*, Mar. 6, 1977; C. L. Sulzberger in ibid., Aug. 7, 1977. Also see Richard H. Ullman, "Human Rights and Economic Power: The United States Versus Idi Amin," *Foreign Affairs* 56 (Apr. 1978), 531–543; Morgenthau, *Human Rights and Foreign Policy*, 6–7.

25. Schlesinger, "Human Rights and the American Tradition," 515; Bernard Gwertzman, "Vance Asks Realism in Human Rights Policy," the *New York Times*, May 1, 1977, 1, 12.

26. Carter's Address, May 22, 1977, *Department of State Bulletin* 76 (June 13, 1977): 623.

27. The Economist [London] (Jan. 30, 1977).

28. For early Soviet responses see David K. Shipler in the *New York Times*, Jan. 13, 1977; Christopher S. Wren in ibid., Jan. 30, 1977; Victor Zorza in *The Washington Post*, Jan. 5, 1977.

29. The *New York Times*, Mar. 21, 1977, 1, 14; ibid., Apr. 1, 1977, 9; John M. Howell, "The Carter Human Rights Policy as Applied to the Soviet Union," *Presidential Studies Quarterly* 13 (Spring 1983): 286–295; Karl Helicher, "The Response of the Soviet Government and Press to Carter's Human Rights Policies," ibid., 296–304.

30. Interview, Feb. 3, 1977, Secretary of State, Bureau of Public Affairs, Office of Media Services, 2. *Public Papers of the Presidents of the United States: Jimmy Carter, 1977, Part II* (Washington, DC: GPO, 1978), 1168.

31. See Bernard Gwertzman in the *New York Times*, Feb. 13, 1977; Spencer, *The Carter Implosion*, 44; Malcolm W. Browne, "Silent Fall," the *New York Times Magazine* (Oct. 23, 1977): 66–85; Lefever, "The Trivialization of Human Rights," 15–23; George Lister in *Current Policy* No. 973: U.S. Human Rights Policy: Origins and Implementation, United States Department of State, Bureau of Public Affairs, Washington, DC, 1–3.

32. Shulman quoted in Reston, the *New York Times*, Jan. 30, 1977.

33. Zbigniew Brzezinski, *The Permanent Purge: Politics in Soviet Totalitarianism* (Cambridge, MA: Harvard University Press, 1956), 174; *Time*, Dec. 17, 1976, 14; Spencer, *The Carter Implosion*, 43.

34. Speech, Oct. 6, 1977, The Department of State, Bureau of Public Affairs, Office of Media Services, 1; *Newsweek* (Oct. 10, 1977): 48–50.

35. David A. Andelman, "Accord in Belgrade: To Meet Again, Period," the *New York Times*, Mar. 12, 1978; Ambassador Goldberg's address, Mar. 8, 1978, Department of State, Bureau of Public Affairs, Office of Public Communication, 2–3.

36. The *New York Times* cited in Lefever, "The Trivialization of Human Rights," 14.

37. "After the Russian Trials," *U.S. News & World Report* (July 24, 1978): 12–16; *Newsweek* (July 24, 1978): 20–23; *Time* (July 24, 1978): 8–9, 24–31. For the administration's response see Carter, *Keeping Faith*, 220; Graham Hovey in the *New York Times*, July 9, 1978, 1, 6. Quoted in the *New York Times*, July 16, 1978, 3.

38. Quoted in *The Daily Progress*, July 15, 1978, A3.

39. Helen Thomas in *The Washington Post*, July 21, 1978; *Time* (July 24, 1978): 8, 13.

40. Terence Smith in the *New York Times*, July 16, 1978, 1, 10; *Time* (July 24, 1978): 13; *Newsweek* (July 24, 1978): 19.

41. Mark L. Schneider, "Human Rights Policy Review," Department of State, Bureau of Public Affairs, Office of Media Services, Oct. 25, 1977, 3.

42. Anthony Lewis quoted in Graebner, "Human Rights and Foreign Policy," 64; Zbigniew Brzezinski, *Power and Principle: Memoirs of the National Security Advisor, 1977–1981* (New York: Farrar, Straus, Giroux, 1983), 515. Also see Carter, *Keeping Faith*, 150–151.

43. *Department of State Bulletin* 76 (June 13, 1977): 621.

44. Paul Warnke, "Apes on a Treadmill," *Foreign Policy* (Spring 1975): 18–21; Andrew Young, "Why I Support Jimmy Carter," *The Nation* (Apr. 3, 1976): 397.

45. Brzezinski quoted in Graebner, "American Foreign Policy After Vietnam," John Schlight, ed., *The Second Indochina War* (Washington, DC: Center for Military History, 1986), 204.

46. Juan de Onis in the *New York Times*, Mar. 13, 1977.

47. Bernard Gwertzman in ibid., May 22, 1977.

48. Elio Gaspari, "Carter, Si!," the *New York Times*, Apr. 30, 1978; Graebner, "Human Rights and Foreign Policy," 56–58.

49. Tom Wicker in the *New York Times*, July 23, 1978, E19; Graham Hovey in ibid., July 2, 1978.

50. Wicker in the *New York Times*, July 23, 1978, E19.

51. Alan Riding in the *New York Times*, May 22, 1977; Willima M. LeoGrande, "The Revolution in Nicaragua: Another Cuba?" *Foreign Affairs* 58 (Fall 1979): 31.

52. David Binder in the *New York Times*, Feb. 13, 1977.

53. *International Herald Tribune*, Apr. 13, 1977.

54. Robert A. Scalapino, "Pacific Prospects," *The Washington Quarterly* 4 (Spring 1981): 5–8.

55. *International Herald Tribune*, May 18, 1977.

56. Donald S. Zagoria, "Why We Can't Leave Korea," the *New York Times Magazine* (Oct. 2, 1977): 17–18, 86–95.

57. *Department of State Bulletin* 76 (June 13, 1977): 625.

58. Scalapino, "Pacific Prospects," 10.

59. Robert L. Pfaltzgraff, Jr., "China, Soviet Strategy, and American Policy," *International Security* 5 (Fall 1980): 24–31.

60. Scalapino, "Pacific Prospects," 11.

61. Cyrus Vance, *Hard Choices*, 76–77.

62. Brzezinski, *Power and Principle*, 211.

63. Pfaltzgraff, "China, Soviet Strategy, and American Policy," 44.

64. L. I. Brezhnev, *Our Course: Peace and Socialism* (Moscow, 1980), 10.

65. Raymond L. Garthoff, *Detente and Confrontation: American-Soviet Relations from Nixon to Reagan* (Washington, DC: Brookings Institution, 1985), 1049–1050; Shoup, *The Carter Presidency*, 150–152; Aleksandr Solzhenitsyn, "Misconceptions About Russia Are a Threat to America," *Foreign Affairs* (Spring 1980): 819.

66. Interview, Feb. 9, 1977, The Department of State, Bureau of Public Affairs, Office of Media Services, 1.

67. For Carter's 1977 Middle Eastern efforts, see Stanley Karnow, "Carter's Long Mideast Ordeal," the *New York Times Magazine* (Jan. 15, 1978): 8, 35–46, 60.

68. See Barry Rubin, *Revolution Until Victory? The Politics and History of the PLO* (Cambridge, MA: Harvard University Press, 1994).

69. Kenneth Hunt in the *New York Times*, Feb. 13, 1977.

70. *Newsweek* (Feb. 21, 1977): 27.

71. H. D. S. Greenway in *The Washington Post*, Mar. 12, 1977.

72. Sadat quoted in Karnow, "Carter's Long Mideast Ordeal," 11.

73. Carter quoted in Karnow, "Carter's Long Mideast Ordeal," 10.

74. Carter, *Keeping Faith*, 288.

75. Bernard Gwertzman in the *New York Times*, Aug. 7, Oct. 9, 1977; *Newsweek* (Aug. 15, 1977): 27–28; Karnow, "Carter's Long Mideast Ordeal," 44; William E. Farrell in the *New York Times*, Sept. 18, 1977; Marvine Howe in ibid., Oct. 23, 1977; Hedrick Smith in ibid., Oct. 9, 1977; Terrence Smith in ibid., Oct. 30, 1977.

76. Karnow, "Carter's Long Mideast Ordeal," 46; for Sadat's trip to Jerusalem see Carter, *Keeping Faith*, 297–298.

77. For Sadat's Israeli venture see *Newsweek* (Nov. 28, 1977): 37–38, 41.

78. Carter, *Keeping Faith*, 298.

79. Marvine Howe in the *New York Times*, Nov. 20, 1977.

80. Bernard Gwertzman and David Binder in ibid., Dec. 11, 1977.

81. News Release, Dec. 28, 1977, Department of State, Bureau of Public Affairs, Office of Media Services, 3.

82. Marvine Howe in the *New York Times*, Jan. 1, 1978.

83. For the Palestinian issue see Stanley Hoffmann in the *New York Times*, Jan. 22, 1978.

84. *Newsweek* (Feb. 6, 1978): 41–42.

85. Carter, *Keeping Faith*, 337–401. Begin arrived at the summit with no proposals, see ibid., 337.

86. *Public Papers of the Presidents of the United States: Jimmy Carter, 1978, Part II*, 1519–1520.

87. "Framework for Peace in the Middle East, Agreed at Camp David, September 17, 1978," *Department of State Bulletin* (Oct. 2, 1978): 7–11.

88. William Quant, a member of the NSC staff, saw the problem of future negotiations clearly in *Camp David: Peacemaking and Politics* (Washington, DC: Brookings Institution, 1986), 256, 292–319; Vance, *Hard Choices*, 232–255.

89. "Mr. Carter's Achievement," *Wall Street Journal*, Sept. 19, 1978, 22; "Twelve Days in September," the *New York Times*, Sept. 19, 1978, 92.

90. "The Jimmy Carter Conference," *The Washington Post*, Sept. 19, 1978, A20; For these and other press opinions see Mark J. Rozell, *The Press and the Carter Presidency* (Boulder, CO: Westview, 1989), 96–101.

91. Carter, *Keeping Faith*, 409.

92. Ibid., 426–429.

93. Barnet, "Carter's Patchwork Doctrine," 30.

94. Marilyn Berger, "Vance and Brzezinski: Peaceful Coexistence or Guerrilla Warfare?" the *New York Times Magazine* (Feb. 13, 1977): 19–23.

95. For a judgment of Brzezinski's many written predictions and analyses, see Kenneth L. Adelman, "The Runner Stumbles: Carter's Foreign Policy in Year One," *Policy Review* 3 (Winter 1978): 95.

96. Berger, "Vance and Brzezinski," 23.

97. Charles Mohr in the *New York Times*, Jan. 9, 1977; Paul Lewis in ibid., Feb. 13, 1977.

98. For Carter's renewed commitment to NATO see *Department of State Bulletin* 76 (June 6, 1977): 597–600; Barnet, "Carter's Patchwork Doctrine," 52.

99. Oswald Johnson in the *International Herald Tribune*, Apr. 8, 1977; C. L. Sulzberger in the *New York Times*, Nov. 6, 1977.

100. Carter, *Keeping Faith*, 225–229.

101. Helmuth Schmidt, *Men and Power* (New York, 1989), 63–64, 186–187, 213; Sam Cohen, *The Truth About the Neutron Bomb* (New York: Morrow, 1983), 174–175.

102. Adelman, "The Runner Stumbles: Carter's Foreign Policy," 93.

103. Cyrus Vance, *Hard Choices*, 441; Marshall Shulman, "On Learning to Live with Authoritarian Regimes," *Foreign Affairs* (Jan. 1977): 334–338; John Ehrman, *The Rise of Neoconservatism: Intellectuals and Foreign Affairs 1945–1994* (New Haven, CT: Yale University Press, 1995), 100–101.

104. Kenneth W. Thompson, ed., *The Carter Presidency* (Lanham, MD: University Press of America, 1990), 6.

105. Strobe Talbott, *Endgame: The Inside Story of SALT II* (New York: Harper & Row, 1980), 48–49.

106. Ibid., 49–50.

107. Carter, *Keeping Faith*, 219; James Reston in the *New York Times*, Mar. 27, 1977.

108. The Soviet complaint appeared in the *New York Times*, Apr. 3, 1977; Spencer, *The Carter Implosion*, 114–115.

109. *Newsweek* (Oct. 24, 1977): 53; Richard Burt in the *New York Times*, Feb. 19, 1978.

110. Interview, Oct. 31, 1977, Secretary of State, Bureau of Public Affairs, Office of Media Services, 2.

111. David K. Shipler in the *New York Times*, Feb. 12, 1978.

112. Adelman, "The Runner Stumbles: Carter's Foreign Policy," 96–97.

113. Thomas Graham, Jr., *Disarmament Sketches: Three Decades of Arms Control and International Law* (Seattle: University of Washington Press, 2002), p. 56, 76–99; Hugh Sidey in *Time* (June 25, 1979): 11; Carter, *Keeping Faith*, 243–260.

114. *The Wall Street Journal*, May 31, 1979, 24; ibid., June 4, 1979, 18; Rozell, *The Press and the Carter Presidency* 127; Robert Kaiser in *The Guardian* [Manchester], May 4, 1979.

115. John Palmer in *The Guardian*, May 9, 1979, 13.

116. Richard R. Burt, "Washington and the Atlantic Alliance: The Hidden Crisis," in Thompson, *The Carter Presidency*, 114–115.

117. Gregory Treverrton in *The Observer* [London], Apr. 29, 1979; Hella Pick in *The Guardian*, May 1, 1979, 7; Burt, "Washington and the Atlantic Alliance," 117.

118. Anatole Shub, *The New Russian Tragedy* (New York: Norton, 1969), 87–88, 112–113, 120.

119. Martin Malia, "Leninist Endgame," *Daedalus* 121 (Spring 1992): 59–60.

120. Norman Podhoretz, "What the Voters Sensed," *Commentary* (Jan. 1973): 6; Jeane Kirkpatrick, "The Revolt of the Masses," ibid., (Feb. 1973), 59–60.

121. John Ehrman, *The Rise of Neoconservatism: Intellectuals and Foreign Affairs* (New Haven, CT: Yale University Press, 1995), 60–61.

122. Ehrman, *The Rise of Neoconservatism*, 79–92; Daniel Patrick Moynihan, "The United States in Opposition," *Commentary* (Mar. 1975), 31–40.

123. Mark J. Rozell and James F. Pontuso, eds., *American Conservative Opinion Leaders* (Boulder, CO: Westview, 1990); Norman Podhoretz, *Breaking Ranks: A Political Memoir* (New York: Harper & Row, 1979); Walter Laqueur, "The

Gathering Storm," *Commentary* (Aug. 1974), 24–33; Laqueur, "The West in Retreat," ibid. (Aug. 1975), 44, 50.

124. Irving Kristol, "American Intellectuals and Foreign Policy," *Foreign Affairs* (July 1967): 609; Kristol, "We Can't Resign as 'Policeman of the World,'" the *New York Times Magazine* (May 12, 1968): 26–27.

125. Norman Podhoretz, "Making the World Safe for Communism," *Commentary* (Apr. 1976): 32, 35; Nathan Glazer, "American Values & American Foreign Policy," *ibid.* (July 1976): 33–34; Robert W. Tucker, "Beyond Detente," ibid. (Mar. 1977): 45; Edward Luttwak, "Defense Reconsidered," ibid. 57–58.

126. Murray Marder in *The Washington Post*, Jan. 2, 1977; Don Oberdorfer in ibid., Oct. 12, 1992, A11; Anne Hessing Cahn, "Team B: The Trillion," *The Bulletin of the Atomic Scientists* (Apr. 1993): 22–27; Paul Nitze, *From Hiroshima to Glasnost: At the Center of Decision—A Memoir* (New York: Grove Weidenfeld, 1989), 350–353; Oberdorfer in *The Washington Post*, Oct. 12, 1992, A11.

127. Linda Charlton in the *International Herald Tribune*, Apr. 5, 1977.

128. These two quotations are taken from Jerry W. Sanders, "Para-Institutional Elites and Foreign Policy Consensus," a paper prepared for a conference at the White Burkett Miller Center for Public Affairs, University of Virginia, Sept. 28–29, 1984, 11.

129. David Callahan, *Dangerous Capabilities: Paul Nitze and the Cold War* (New York: Harper & Row, 1990), 19–21, 389–395.

130. G. B. Kistiakowsky, "The Arms Race: Is Paranoia Necessary for Security?" The *New York Times Magazine* (Nov. 27, 1977); Paul Nitze, "Assuring Strategic Stability in an Era of Detente," *Foreign Affairs* 54 (Jan. 1976); Richard Pipes, "Why the Soviet Union Thinks It Can Fight and Win a Nuclear War," *Commentary* (July 1977).

131. Kissinger in the *New York Times*, Jan. 11, 1977; Callahan, *Nitze*, 380.

132. Raymond Garthoff, "Mutual Deterrence and Strategic Arms Limitation in Soviet Policy," *International Security* 3 (Summer 1978): 139.

133. Kennan, *The Cloud of Danger*, 200.

134. Walter LaFeber, *The Panama Canal: The Crisis in Historical Perspective* (New York: Oxford University Press, 1978), 180–195.

135. See Michael L. Conniff, *Panama and the United States: The Forced Alliance* (Athens: University of Georgia Press, 1992).

136. See Anthony Lake, *Somoza Falling* (Boston: Houghton Mifflin, 1989).

137. Spencer, *The Carter Implosion*, 92; *Newsweek* (Mar. 13, 1989): 72.

138. Robert Pastor, *Condemned to Repetition: The United States and Nicaragua* (Princeton, NJ: Princeton University Press, 1987), 147–148.

139. Spencer, *The Carter Implosion*, 95–96; see Jeane J. Kirpatrick, *Dictatorships and Double Standards: Rationalism and Reason in Politics* (New York: Simon & Schuster, 1982).

140. Carter, *Keeping Faith*, 263–264; Spencer, *The Carter Implosion*, 106–107.

141. Rozell, *The Press and the Carter Presidency*, 144–145.

142. Reston in the *New York Times*, Sept. 16, 1979.

143. George F. Will in *Newsweek* (Oct. 1, 1979): 84; editorial, *The Washington Post*, Oct. 3, 1979; Richard E. Neustadt and Ernest R. May, *Thinking in Time: The Uses of History for Decision-Makers* (New York: Free Press, 1986), 92–96.

144. *Newsweek* (Mar. 13, 1978): 36–37; Robert Moss, "On Standing Up to the Russians in Africa," *Policy Review* 5 (Summer 1978): 97–99; Peter Vanneman and Martin James, "Soviet Intervention in the Horn of Africa: Intentions and Implications," ibid., 15–31.

145. Moss, "On Standing Up to the Russians," 102, 107.

146. *Newsweek* (Apr. 24, 1978): 47; Vance, *Hard Choices*, 74–75; Brzezinski, *Power and Principle*, 147, 150, 182; David Ottaway, "Africa: U.S. Policy Eclipse," *Foreign Affairs* 58:3 (1980): 637–638; Anthony Lake, "Carter's Foreign Policy: Success Abroad, Failure at Home," in Thompson, *The Carter Presidency*, 152.

147. Carter, *Keeping Faith*, 229–230; *U.S. News & World Report* (June 19, 1978): 37; Robert A. Strong, "Anecdote and Evidence: Jimmy Carter's Annapolis Address on U.S.-Soviet Relations," *Miller Center Journal* [University of Virginia], I (Spring 1994): 35–50; Vance, *Hard Choices*, 102; Brzezinski, *Power and Principle*, 520.

148. David K. Shipler in the *New York Times*, June 18, 1978, 1, 10.

149. "The Ghosts of Vietnam," the *New York Times*, June 4, 1978.

150. Roy Parviz Mottahedeh, "Iran's Foreign Devils," *Foreign Policy* (Spring 1980): 90–92; Spencer, *The Carter Implosion*, 68–71; Shoup, *The Carter Presidency*, 118.

151. For Iran's human rights violations see Flora Lewis, "U.S. Policy On Rights Gets a Crucial Test," the *New York Times*, Nov. 12, 1978; Carter, *Keeping Faith*, 439.

152. *Ibid.*, 445–447; *Newsweek* (Mar. 14, 1983): 34–35; see also William Shawcross, *The Shah's Last Ride: The Fate of an Ally* (New York: Simon & Schuster, 1988); Charles-Philippe David, Nancy Ann Carrol, and Zachary A. Selden, *Foreign Policy Failure in the White House: Reappraising the Fall of the Shah and the Iran-Contra Affair* (Lanham, MD: University Press of America, 1993).

153. "America's Role in a Turbulent World," Department of State *Bulletin* 79 (Mar. 1979), 21.

154. Brown and Schlesinger quoted by Donald E. Nuechterlein in the *New York Times*, Mar. 14, 1979, A22.

155. See *The Washington Post*, July 1, 1979.

156. Spencer, *The Carter Implosion*, 104: Shoup, *The Carter Presidency*, 123–124.

157. Department of State *Bulletin* (Aug. 1979): 48–49; *Time* (Sept. 3, 1979); 14.

158. For an exposition of this view see George W. Ball, "How to Save Israel in Spite of Herself," *Foreign Affairs* (Apr. 1977): 459–470.

159. Eugene V. Rostow, "The American Stake in Israel," *Commentary* (Apr. 1977): 37–40.

160. Thomas A. Johnson, "Black Leaders Air Grievancers on Jews," the *New York Times*, Aug. 23, 1979, 12; Samuel Allis, "U.S. Jewish Leaders Lash Back After Criticism by Blacks," *The Washington Post*, Aug. 24, 1979, A16.

161. Ehrman, *The Rise of Neoconservatism*, 123–135.

162. Mottahedeh, "Iran's Foreign Devils," 92–93; William F. Hickman, "Did It Really Matter?" *Naval War College Review* 36 (Mar.–Apr. 1983): 24.

163. *Newsweek* (Dec. 10, 1979): 24, 49–50.

164. *The Washington Post*, Dec. 4, 1979, A20.

165. "Nightmare in Iran," *U.S. News & World Report* (Nov. 19, 1979): 23; George Will in *Newsweek* (Dec. 24, 1979): 84; Spencer, *The Carter Implosion*, 80.

166. Marvin Stone, "Iran and After," *U.S. News & World Report* (Nov. 26, 1979): 108; Rozell, *The Press and the Carter Presidency*, 146–147.

167. Norman C. Miller, "A Real Debate," *The Wall Street Journal*, Jan. 31, 1980, 14; Joseph Kraft, "Who's Conning Whom?" *The Washington Post*, Mar. 13, 1980, A19; On the aborted rescue mission see Carter, *Keeping Faith*, 501–21; Allan J. Mayer, "A Mission Comes to Grief in Iran," *Newsweek* (May 5, 1980): 24–27.

168. Quoted in Hickman, "Did It Really Matter?" 24–25.

169. Tom Wicker, "Mr. Carter's Loss," the *New York Times*, Apr. 29, 1980, A23; Hedrick Smith, "A Political Jolt for Carter," ibid., A1, A15; Rozell, *The Press and the Carter Presidency*, 163–165; Lake, "Carter's Foreign Policy," 149; Leslie Gelb, "The Vance Legacy," *The New Republic* (May 10, 1980): 14–15; *Time* (May 12, 1980): 13–14; Carter, *Keeping Faith*, 594.

170. Michael Dobbs, "The Afghan Archive," *The Washington Post*, Nov. 15, 1992, A1, A32.

171. Michael Dobbs, "The Afghan Archive: Into the Quagmire," *The Washington Post*, Nov. 11, 1992, A1, A32.

172. Adam B. Ulam, "Soviet-American Relations: Where Do We Go From Here?" Prosser Gifford, ed., *The National Interests of the United States in Foreign Policy* (Lanham, MD: University Press of America, 1981), 7.

173. Reston in the *New York Times*, Dec. 30, 1979.

174. Carter, *Keeping Faith*, 472–473.

175. Carter, *Keeping Faith*, 474–475; Spencer, *The Carter Implosion*, 110–111; *Current Policy* No. 137: Secretary Vance, Statement on Olympic Games, Feb. 9, 1980, United States Department of State, Bureau of Public Affairs, Washington, DC, 1.

176. Joseph Kraft, "Unhappy New Year," *The Washington Post*, Jan. 1, 1980, A17; Marvin Stone, "Meaning of Afghanistan," *U.S. News & World Report* (Jan. 14, 1980): 84.

177. Hugh Sidey in Spencer, *The Carter Implosion*, 109–110; Robert Dudney, "Carter's U-Turn In Foreign Policy," *U.S. News & World Report* (Jan. 20, 1980): 23–26; W. Scott Thompson, "Toward a Strategic Peace," Thompson, *The Carter Presidency*, 483.

178. Leslie Gelb, "Beyond the Carter Doctrine," the *New York Times Magazine* (Feb. 10, 1980): 18–19.

179. *Current Policy*, No. 138: "The U.S. and the Nonaligned Movement," Feb. 4, 1980, United States Department of State, Bureau of Public Affairs, Washington, DC, 1; interview with Richard E. Pipes in "The Week in Review," the *New York Times*, Feb. 10, 1980.

180. Editorial, the *New York Times*, Jan. 27, 1980.

181. Vance, *Hard Choices*, 394.

182. Carter, *Keeping Faith*, 500; Peter Jay, "Europe and America," *Atlantic Community Quarterly* 18 (Summer 1980): 141; Leonard Downie, Jr., in *The Washington Post*, Jan. 15, 1980.

183. Krul quoted in *Business Week*, Jan. 21. 1980, 80. For Europe's reaction to Afghanistan see Hedrick Smith in "The Week in Review," the *New York Times*, Jan. 27, 1980.

184. *Business Week*, Jan. 21, 1980, 78.

185. *Business Week*, Jan. 21, 1980, 82; *Current Policy* No. 132: President Carter, State of the Union Address, Jan. 23, 1980, United States Department of State, Bureau of Public Affairs, Washington, DC, 2–3; "New Mood on Capitol Hill," *Time* (Feb. 4, 1980): 17.

186. See Hedrick Smith in "The Week in Review," the *New York Times*, Jan. 17, 1980.

187. Evans and Novak in *The Washington Post*, Feb. 21, 1979, A15; Lake, "Carter's Foreign Policy," 155.

188. Broder, Kraft, and *The Wall Street Journal* quoted in Marvin Stone, "Carter vs. a Dangerous World," *U.S. News & World Report* (Mar. 5, 1979): 88; Rozell, 127.

189. Robert Elegant, "How to Lose a War: Reflections of a Foreign Correspondent," *Encounter* 57 (Aug. 1981) 73.

190. Adelman, "The Runner Stumbles: Carter's Foreign Policy," 98; W. Scott Thompson, "Introduction," Thompson, *The Carter Presidency*, 13.

191. Keegan quoted in *The Washington Post*, Mar. 12, 1977; Ridgway in *The Daily Progress*, Jan. 30, 1977; Elmo R. Zumwalt, Jr., "Heritage of Weakness: An Assessment of the 1970s," Thompson, *The Carter Presidency*, 19–37.

192. Richard Burt, "Reassessing the Strategic Balance," *International Security* 5 (Summer 1980), 39; George F. Will in *Newsweek* (June 25, 1979): 104; Kissinger in Stephen S. Rosenfeld, *The Washington Post*, Aug. 3, 1979.

193. Peter Marin, "Coming to Terms with Vietnam," *Harper's* 261 (Dec. 1980): 41.

194. Harold Jackson in *The Guardian*, May 3, 1979.

195. William J. Barnds, "Carter and the World: The First Two Years," *Worldview* 22 (Jan.–Feb. 1979), 39.

196. David M. Alpern, "Feeling Helpless," *Newsweek* (Feb. 26, 1979): 22–25.

197. Lake, "Carter's Foreign Policy," 146.

CHAPTER 14

1. *Newsweek* (Sept. 1, 1980): 18; Anthony Lewis in *The Daily Progress* (Charlottesville), Oct. 31, 1980.

2. Reagan quoted in George C. Herring, "The 'Vietnam Syndrome' and American Foreign Policy," *Virginia Quarterly Review* 57 (Autumn 1981): 612.

3. Frances Fitzgerald, *Way Out in the Blue: Reagan, Star Wars and the End of the Cold War* (New York: Simon & Shuster, 2000), 27–31.

4. For a superb evaluation of the Reagan foreign policy team see Hedrick Smith in the *New York Times*, May 25, 1980; Van Cleave interview in The Week in Review, ibid, Oct. 12, 1980; see also Richard Pipes, "Why the Soviet Union Thinks It Could Fight & Win a Nuclear War." *Commentary* 64:1 (July 1977) 21–34. Richard Burt offers a long discussion of the Reagan view of Soviet power in the *New York Times*, Dec. 7, 1980.

5. John A. Marcum, "The United States at the U.N.: The Kirkpatrick Era," *Worldview* 24 (June 1981): 20; *Newsweek* (Mar. 30, 1981): 32.

6. Reagan quoted in *Newsweek*, Feb. 9, 1981, 45.

7. Opening Statement at Confirmation Hearings, Jan. 9, 1981, U.S. Department of State, Bureau of Public Affairs, *Current Policy No. 257*; *New York Times*, May 3, 1981.

8. Steven R. Weisman, "Reaganomics and the President's Men," *New York Times Magazine* (Oct. 24, 1982): 83–85.

9. Drew Middleton, *New York Times*, Jan. 3, 1982; Richard Halloran, *New York Times*, Apr. 11, 1982.

10. Middleton, *New York Times*, June 21, 1981 and Feb. 14, 1982.

11. James M. Fallows, *National Defense* (New York: Random House, 1981), 70–71, 163; Christopher Paine, "A False START," *Bulletin of the Atomic Scientists* 38 (Aug./Sept. 1982): 13; *New York Daily News*, "Report from Munich," Feb. 20, 1982, 6.

12. *U.S. News & World Report* (Nov. 3, 1980): 62; Lou Cannon and Lee Lescaze in *The Washington Post*, Mar. 29, 1981; "A New Direction in U.S. Foreign Policy," (Apr. 24, 1981), U.S. Department of State, Bureau of Public Affairs, *Current Policy No. 275*, 2; Haig quoted in *The Daily Progress*, May 10, 1981.

13. Seweryn Bialer and Joan Afferica, "Reagan and Russia," *Foreign Affairs* 61 (Winter 1982–1983): 71; "Promoting Democracy and Peace," U.S. Department of State, Bureau of Public Affairs, *Current Policy No. 399*, 3–5.

14. Anthony Lewis in *The Daily Progress*, May 6, 1981; Helen Thomas in ibid., May 16, 1981; James Reston in the *New York Times*, July 17, 1981.

15. Alexander M. Haig, Jr., *Caveat, Realism, Reagan and Foreign Policy* (New York: Macmillan, 1984).

16. Also see Joseph M. Siracusa and David G. Coleman, *Depression to Cold War: A History of America from Herbert Hoover to Ronald Reagan* (Westport, CT: Praeger, 2002), 249–250; *Public Papers of the Presidents: Ronald Reagan, 1981* (Washington, DC: GPO, 1981), I, 957, 958.

17. Walter LaFeber, *Inevitable Revolutions: The United States and Central America* (New York, 1983), 240; *New York Times*, Mar. 23, 1980, 8; ibid., July 13, 1980, 14; ibid., Apr. 2, 1981, 3.

18. Reagan quoted in Alexander Cockburn, *Wall Street Journal*, Mar. 12, 1981.

19. Quotes in Siracusa and Coleman, *Depression to Cold War*, 260, 261–264.

20. Ibid., 261–264; Karen de Young, *Washington Post*, Mar. 8, 1981; *Newsweek*, Mar. 16, 1981, 34–38; Mar. 30, 1981, 20–21.

21. Nestor D. Sanchez, "The Communist Threat," *Foreign Policy* 52 (Fall 1983): 41–43.

22. Remarks on Central America and El Salvador at the Annual Meeting of the National Association of Manufacturers, Mar. 10, 1983, John T. Woolley and Gerhard Peters, *The American Presidency Project* [online]. Santa Barbara, CA: University of California at http://www.presidency.ucsb.edu/ws/?pid=41034; Address Before a Joint Session of the Congress on Central America, Apr. 17, 1983, ibid., http://www.presidency.ucsb.edu/ws/?pid=41245.

23. Ronald Reagan, "Remarks . . . following a Luncheon Meeting with Leaders of Eastern Caribbean Countries," in *Public Papers of the Presidents, Ronald Reagan, 1982*, Book 1 (Washington: GPO, 1983), 448.

24. J. Thomas, *New York Times*, Oct. 30, 1983; Bernard Gwertzman, *New York Times*, Oct. 30, 1983, 1.

25. Nicholas von Hoffman, "Terrestrial Wars," *The Spectator* (Apr. 13, 1985): 8–9; Norman A. Graebner, "The Uses and Misuses of Power: The 1980s." *Dialogue: A Magazine of International Affairs* 1:1 (Mar. 1988): 29.

26. Hedrick Smith, "The Week in Review," *New York Times*, Oct. 30, 1983, F1; Stuart Taylor, Jr., ibid., Nov. 6, 1983, 20; Francis Clines, "The Week in Review," ibid., Feb. 5, 1984; Michael D. Barnes, "Grenada: The Invasion Was Right," *Washington Post National Weekly*, Nov. 21, 1983, 32; editorial, *New York Times*, Oct. 30, 1983; Podhoretz, *New York Times*, Oct. 30, 1983; Lou Cannon, *President Reagan: The Role of a Lifetime* (New York: Public Affairs, 1991), 391–393.

27. For Moyniham, the Grenada invasion was illegal, Daniel Patrick Moynihn, *On the Law of Nations* (Cambridge: Harvard University Press, 1990), 122, 127–131; John Wylee, "The West at a Crossroads," *World Press Review* 31 (Feb. 1984): 35.

28. Bernard Gwertzman, *New York Times*, June 21, 1981 and Mar. 14, 1982; Robert W. Tucker, "America in Decline: The Foreign Policy of 'Maturity,' " *Foreign Affairs* 58(3) (1980): 480, 484; *Newsweek*, June 15, 1981.

29. See Kiguel Schapira, "Wanted: A Foreign Policy," *World Press Review* (Jan. 1982); Roger Fisher, *New York Times*, Mar. 30, 1980.

30. See editorial, the *New York Times*, Mar. 22, 1981.

31. Walto Stumpt, "South Africa's Nuclear Weapons Program: From Deterrence to Dismantlement," *Arms Control Today* (Dec. 1995/Jan. 1996): 3–8. In 1993, President F. W. DeKlerk admitted that South Africa had built six atomic bombs, since dismantled, but did not shed any light on the 1979 incident.

32. Peter Jay, "Europe and America: Europe's Ostrich and America's Eagle," *Atlantic Community Quarterly* 18 (Summer 1980): 141–142; Robert Lacey, "How Stable Are the Saudis?" *New York Times Magazine* (Nov. 8, 1981): 35–38, 118–121.

33. David K. Shipler, *New York Times*, Mar. 28, July 25, 1982; for internal conflict, see Robert M. Gates, *From the Shadows: The Ultimate Insider's Story of Five Presidents and How They Won the Cold War* (New York: Simon & Shuster, 1996), 284–285.

34. Eric Pace, *New York Times*, July 4, 1982.

35. Gates, *From the Shadows*, 283; Bernard Gwertzman, *New York Times*, Oct. 10, 1982; see also George P. Shultz, *Turmoil and Triumph: My Years As Secretary of State* (New York: Scribners, 1993), 96–97.

36. "The Week in Review," *New York Times*, Jan. 1, 1984; Shultz, *Turmoil and Triumph*, 110–111, makes it clear it was Reagan's decision to send in the Marines.

37. Thomas J. Friedman, "America's Failure in Lebanon," *New York Times Magazine* (Apr. 8, 1984): 32–33; Shultz, *Turmoil and Triumph*, 227–228.

38. "The Week in Review," *New York Times*, Jan. 1, 1984; Bernard Gwertzman, *New York Times*, Oct. 9, 1983, E1, 6; Hedrick Smith, *New York Times*, Oct. 30, 1983, E1.

39. Marvin Howe, *New York Times*, Aug. 29, 1982; Shultz, *Turmoil and Triumph*, 233.

40. For the Ottawa Conference, see Leslie H. Gelb, *New York Times*, July 19, 26, 1981.

41. Pipes quoted by Stephen S. Rosenfeld, *Washington Post*, Oct. 8, 1982.

42. Reston, *New York Times*, Feb. 7, 1982.

43. For the debate within the administration, see Bernard Gwertzman, *New York Times*, Feb. 21, 1982; For the Reagan announcement and the bitter European reaction, see *World Press Review* 29 (Aug. 1982): 4; Flora Lewis, *New York Times*, June 27, 1982.

44. Steven Ratner, *New York Times*, Aug. 29, 1982.

45. Hans-Dietrich Genscher, "Toward an Overall Western Strategy for Peace, Freedom, and Progress," *Foreign Affairs* 61 (Fall 1982): 42.

46. Quoted in *World Press Review* 29 (Apr. 1982): 12.

47. *Newsweek*, Mar. 22, 1982, 42.

48. *Times Herald Record*, Dec. 24, 1981; see also, Norman A. Graebner, "Western Disunity: It's Challenge to America," *The Reynolds Distinguished Lecture Series*, Davidson College, Fall 1982, 34.

49. *Manchester Guardian* quoted in *World Press Review* 29 (Feb. 1982): 14; Ronald Steel, *New York Times*, Jan. 3, 1982.

50. Lawrence T. Caldwell and Robert Legvold, "Reagan through Soviet Eyes," *Foreign Policy* 52 (Fall 1983): 5

51. Remarks to Members of the British Parliament, June 8, 1982, *Public Papers of the Presidents: Reagan, 1982*, I (Washington, DC: GPO, 1983), 747–748; Remarks at the annual convention of the National Association of Evangelicals, Mar. 8, 1983, *Public Papers of the Presidents*, 363–364.

52. Graebner, "The Soviet-American Conflict," 583; *Christian News*, Apr. 18, 1983, 1.

53. Leslie H. Gelb, "The Week in Review," *New York Times*, May 1, 1983, E.1; Stanley Hoffmann, *Dead Ends: American Foreign Policy in the New Cold War* (Cambridge, MA: Ballinger, 1983), 154–155.

54. Reagan's Address to Congress, Sept. 5, 1983, *American Foreign Policy: Current Documents, 1983* (Washington, DC: GPO, 1985), 544–547.

55. Strobe Talbott, *The Russians and Reagan* (New York: Vintage, 1984), 122, appendix.

56. Alexander Bovin quoted in *World Press Review* 31 (Jan. 1984): 53; for the impact of "Able Archer," see Gates, From the Shadows, 270–273.

57. *New York Times*, Jan. l, 1984, E13.

58. Ronald Reagan, *Ronald Reagan: An American Life* (New York: Pocket Books, 1990), 588–589.

59. Richard J. Barnet, *New Yorker* (Oct. 17, 198): 153; Christopher Paine, "A False START," BAS 38 (Aug/Sept 82): 14; see also Douglas C. Waller, *Congress and the Nuclear Freeze* (Amherst: The University of Massachusetts Press, 1987).

60. Barnet, *New Yorker*, 156.

61. Ibid.; Judith Miller, *New York Times*, Aug. 23, 1981. Steve Breyman, *Why Movements Matter: The West German Peace Movement and U.S. Arms Control Policy* (Albany, NY: State University of New York Press, 2001), 47, 93–95.

62. Fitzgerald, *Way Out There in the Blue*, 88–96; Waller, *Congress and the Nuclear Freeze*, 14; Thomas Graham, Jr., *Disarmament Sketches: Three Decades of Arms Control and International Law* (Seattle: University of Washington Press, 2002), 103.

63. Fitzgerald, *Way Out There In The Blue*, 153–154; Waller, *Congress and the Nuclear Freeze*, 94–97, 99.

64. Leslie Gelb, "The Mind of the President," *New York Times Magazine* (Oct. 6, 1985): 21ff; Lou Cannon, "Dealings with the Soviets Raise Uncomfortable Questions," *Washington Post*, July 2, 1984, A13; Gates, *In the Shadows*, 287, 289.

65. Edward Reiss, *The Strategic Defense Initiative* (New York: Cambridge University Press, 1992); McGeorge Bundy, *Danger and Survival: Choices About the Bomb in the First Fifty Years* (New York: Random House, 1988), 571; Reagan, *An American Life*, 571–572.

66. John Tirman, "The Politics of Star Wars," in John Tirman, ed., *The Empty Promise: the Growing Case Against Star Wars* (Boston, MA: Beacon, 1986); Union of Concerned Scientists, *The Fallacy of Star Wars* (New York: Vintage, 1984); and Richard Dean Burns and Lester M. Brune, *The Quest for Missile Defenses, 1944–2003* (Claremont, CA: Regina Books, 2003), 77ff.

67. Mary McGrory, "Struggles over a Kissinger Report That Will Change Nothing," *Washington Post National Weekly*, Jan. 23, 1984, 23; Seymour M. Hersh, *New York Times*, Jan. 8, 1984, 1, 16.

68. *New York Times*, Feb. 4, 1984; Joanne Omang, "The Play of Light and Shadow Hides the Truth in El Salvador," *Washington Post National Weekly*, Apr. 16, 1984, 16.

69. *Newsweek*, Jan. 23, 1984, 28; Editorial, *New York Times*, Jan. 15, 1984, E22.

70. David S. Broder, "Frank Church's Challenge," *Washington Post National Weekly*, Feb. 6, 1984, 4.

71. David Schribman, *New York Times*, Apr. 29, 1984.

72. Fred Hiatt, "The U.S. Military Buildup Continues," *Washington Post National Weekly*, Apr. 30, 1984, 16.

73. Philip Taubman, *New York Times*, Apr. 18, 1984, 1, 12; For a legal defense of the Reagan policy, see John Norton Moore, *The Secret War in Central America: Sandinista Assault on World Order* (Frederick, MD: University Publications of America, 1987).

74. *New York Times*, Feb. 24, 1985; George P. Shultz, "Shaping American Foreign Policy: New Realities and New Ways of Thinking," *Foreign Affairs* (Spring 1985): 713.

75. Also see Siracusa and Coleman, *Depression to Cold War*, 263.

76. George Will, *Washington Post*, Dec. 12, 1985, A19.

77. Robert W. Tucker, "Intervention and the Reagan Doctrine," *Intervention and the Reagan Doctrine* (New York: The Council on Religion and International Affairs, 1985), 16–17.

78. *Newsweek*, Dec. 23, 1985, 32–34.

79. *Chronology of the Cold War, 1917–1992*, compiled by Lester Brune and edited by Richard Dean Burns (New York: Routledge, 2006), 483; Dickey, Christopher, *With the Contras: A Reporter in the Wilds of Nicaragua* (New York: Simon & Schuster, 1987), 10–11; *The Sandinista Military Build-Up*, Inter-American Series 119 (Washington, DC: Dept. of State, 1985); and *The Soviet-Cuban Connection in Central America and the Caribbean* (Washington, DC: Dept. of State and Dept. of Defense, 1985); Cheney quoted in Steven V. Roberts, *New York Times*, May 25, 1986, E1.

80. John Norton Moore, *The Struggle for Peace in Central America: And the Deterioration of the Global Deterrent System* (Washington, DC: Washington Institute for Values in Public Policy), 2, 42.

81. Elliott Abrams, director of the State Dept.'s Bureau of Human Rights and Humanitarian Affairs, in *Foreign Policy* 52 (Fall 1983): 122, 124; *Foreign Policy*, 53 (Winter 1983–1984): 175; Charles Maechling, Jr., "Human Rights Dehumanized," *Foreign Policy* 52 (Fall 1983): 118–135; Guillermo M. Ungo, "The People's Struggle," *Foreign Policy* 52 (Fall 1983): 51–63; Flora Lewis, *New York Times*, Mar. 16, 1986, E25.

82. John Keegan, *The Iraq War* (New York: Vintage Books, 2005), 58–63; James Mann, *Rise of the Vulcans: The History of Bush's War Cabinet* (New York: Penguin Books, 2004), 123–126; Michael T. Klare, "Fueling the Fire: How We Armed the Middle East, *Bulletin of the Atomic Scientists* 47 (Jan./Feb. 1991): 19–26.

83. Draper, *A Very Thin Line*, 333, 344–345; Also see Siracusa and Coleman, *Depression to Cold War*, 270.

84. George Black, *The Good Neighbor: How the United States wrote the History of Central America and the Caribbean* (New York: Pantheon Books, 1988), 179–180.

85. State of the Union Address, Jan. 25, 1984, *American Foreign Policy: Current Documents, 1984* (Washington, DC: GPO, 1986), 28; Address at Georgetown University, Apr. 6, 1984, *American Foreign Policy*, 8.

86. James Reston in *New York Times*, June 17, 1984, E21; Address on U.S.-Soviet Relations, Jan. 16, 1984, *Public Papers of the Presidents: Ronald Reagan, 1984*, I (Washington, DC: GPO, 1986), 42; John Newhouse, "Annals of Diplomacy: The Abolitionist—II," *New Yorker* (Jan. 9, 1989): 51.

87. For Gorbachev in London, *New York Times*, Dec. 16, 1984, 1, 5.

88. See Robert D. English, *Russia and the Idea of the West: Gorbachev, Intellectuals & the End of the Cold War* (New York: University of Columbia Press, 2000), esp. chap. 6 and Vladislav M. Zubok, *A Failed Empire: The Soviet Union in the Cold War from Stalin to Gorbachev*(Chapel Hill: University of North Carolina, 2007), 278ff.

89. Adam Ulam, *Dangerous Relations: The Soviet Union in World Politics* (New York: Oxford University Press, 1983), 266–267; Zubok, *A Failed Empire*, 283–284.

90. Quoted in Zubok, *A Failed Empire*, 286.

91. Shultz, *Turmoil and Triumph*, 598; Raymond L. Garthoff, *The Great Transition: American-Soviet Relations and the End of the Cold War* (Washington, DC: Brookings Institution, 1994), 235–238.

92. See Shultz, *Turmoil and Triumph*, 596–607; Matlock, *Reagan and Gorbachev*, chap. 6.

93. English, *Russia and the Idea of the West*, 206; Philip Taubman, *New York Times*, Apr. 6, 1986.

94. For compliance, see John Newhouse, *New Yorker* (Jan. 9, 1989): 59–61; James Reston, *New York Times*, Apr. 6, 1986, E23.

95. Michael R. Gordon, *New York Times*, June 7, 1987, 7; *New York Times*, Aug. 29, 1986.

96. Garthoff, *The Great Transition*, 252–267; Shultz, *Turmoil and Triumph*, 751–755; Mikhail Gorbachev, *Reykjavik: Results and Lessons*, (Madison, CT:

Sphinx Press, 1987); also see "The Reykjavik File: Previously Secret Documents from U.S. and Soviet Archives on the 1986 Reagan-Gorbachev Summit," posted Oct. 13, 2006 by the National Security Archive, George Washington University at http://www.nsarchive.org.

97. David K. Shipler, "The Week in Review," *New York Times*, Oct. 26, 1986, E1.

98. Garthoff, *Transition*, 327n.64; Shultz, *Turmoil*, 1009–1015; Fitzgerald, *Way Out There in the Blue*, 426.

99. Newhouse, *New Yorker* (Jan. 9, 1989): 65–66; Lou Cannon, *President Reagan: The Role of a Lifetime* (New York: Public Affairs, 1991), 694; Fitzgerald, *Way Out There in the Blue*, 444–445.

100. Lou Cannon and Gary Lee, *Washington Post*, May 30, 1988, A1, A21.

101. *Washington Post*, Oct. 12, 1987, A19; For a critique of Phillips and Viguerie, see James J. Kilpatrick, *Washington Post*, Dec. 15, 1987, A23.

102. Quoted in Fitzgerald, *Way Out There In The Blue*, 445.

103. Andrei Sakarov, *Moscow and Beyond* (New York: Alfred A. Knopf, 1991), 21–42; Strobe Talbott, *Master of the Game: Paul Nitze and the Nuclear Peace* (New York: Alfred A. Knopf, 1988), 306.

104. Lou Cannon and Gary Lee, *Washington Post*, May 30, 1988, A1, A21; Don Oberdorfer, *Washington Post*, June 1, 1988, A1.

105. *Washington Post*, June 7, 1988, A23; ibid., May 29, 1988, C7

106. *New York Times*, July 10, 1988, E30; see David K. Shipler, ibid., May 29, 1988, E1, E3

CHAPTER 15

1. Raymond L. Garthoff, *The Great Transition: American-Soviet Relations and the End of the Cold War* (Washington, DC: Brookings Institution Press, 1994): 380–388; George P. Shultz, *Turmoil and Triumph: My Years as Secretary of State* (New York: Scribners, 1993): 1137; James A. Baker, III, *The Politics of Politics of Diplomacy* (New York: G.P. Putnam, 1995): 17–18; Shultz quote in Michael R. Beschloss and Strobe Talbott, *At The Highest Levels: The Inside Story of the End of the Cold War* (Boston: Little, Brown, 1993), 28. Also see Norman A. Graebner, Richard Dean Burns, and Joseph M. Siracusa, *Reagan, Bush, Gorbachev: Revisiting the End of the Cold War* (Westport, CT: Praeger Security International, 2008), 113.

2. Beschloss and Talbott, *At The Highest Levels*, 3–4.

3. Ibid., 9–11.

4. *Newsweek* (May 15, 1989): 22; Department of State *Bulletin* 89 (Apr. 1989): 4–5; *Washington Post*, Feb. 13, 1990, A1, A9; Beschloss and Talbott, *At The Highest Levels*, 12–13,17–19; Robert M. Gates, *From the Shadows: The Ultimate Insider's Story of Five Presidents and How They Won the Cold War* (New York: Simon & Schuster, 1996).

5. For Bush's inaugural see John T. Woolley and Gerhard Peters, *The American Presidency Project* [online] at http://www.presidency.ucsb.edu/ws/?pid=16610; "Address on Administration Goals Before a Joint Session of Congress," Feb. 9, 1989, at http://www.presidency.ucsb.edu/ws/?pid=16660; Department of State *Bulletin* 89 (Apr. 1989): 2, 4.

6. Beschloss and Talbott, *At The Highest Levels*, 17–18; Woolley and Peters, *The American Presidency Project* [online] at http://www.presidency.ucsb.edu/ws/?pid=16629.

7. Remarks at Woolley and Peters, *The American Presidency Project* [online] at http://www.presidency.ucsb.edu/ws/?pid=166248; Beschloss and Talbott, *At The Highest Levels*, 24.

8. George Bush and Brent Scowcroft, *A World Transformed* (New York: Knopf1998), 40–41; Thatcher quoted in Beschloss and Talbott, *At The Highest Levels*, 29.

9. Jack F. Matlock, Jr., *Autopsy on an Empire* (New York: Random House, 1995), p. 177; Anatoly Chernyaev, *My Six Years With Gorbachev* (University Park, PA: Penn State University Press, 2000), p. 201.

10. Woolley and Peters, *The American Presidency Project* [online] at http://www.presidency.ucsb.edu/ws/?pid=16935; Robert M. Gates, *From the Shadows: The Ultimate Insider's Story of Five Presidents and How They Won the Cold War* (New York: Simon & Schuster, 1996), 465.

11. *Newsweek*, Dec. 25, 1989, 40; *The Economist* (London) 330 (Feb. 12, 1994), Survey, 4.

12. Craig R. Whitney, *New York Times*, Jan. 7, 1990, E3 and Apr. 8, 1990, 14; *Washington Post*, Apr. 16, 1990, A1, A20.

13. Erazim Kohak, "Ashes, Ashes … Central Europe after Forty Years," *Daedalus* 121 (Spring 1992): 207; Whitney, *New York Times*, Jan. 7, 1990, E3; also see Lonnie R. Johnson, *Central Europe: Enemies, Neighbors, Friends* (New York: Oxford University Press, 1996).

14. *Newsweek*, Sept. 10, 1990, 36.

15. Girard C. Steichen, "Bulgaria Slips Deeper into Economic Crisis," *The Christian Science Monitor*, Mar. 5, 1991, 5; *New Yorker*, Feb. 19, 1990, 33.

16. On Gorbachev's leadership, see Stanley Hoffmann, "A Case for Leadership," *Foreign Policy* 81 (Winter 1990–1991): 20–22; Alexander Dallin, *Washington Post*, Jan. 15, 1990, A19; Meg Greenfield, *Newsweek*, Feb. 5, 1990, 75 and Mar. 12, 1990, 63; *Washington Post*, Jan. 19, 1990, A14.

17. *New York Times*, Dec. 1, 1989, Y9; Judt, "New Germany, Old NATO," 40; Henry Ashby Turner, *New York Times*, Feb. 11, 1990, E25; Elizabeth Pond, *Washington Post*, Feb. 25, 1990, B2; *Newsweek*, Feb. 26, 1990, 17–18; Jim Hoagland, *Washington Post*, Mar. 22, 1990, A23 and Apr. 1, 1990, A1, A32; *New York Times*, Jan. 7, 1990, E25.

18. *Washington Post*, Jan. 20, 1990, A15; *Washington Post*, Feb. 3, 1990, A20; *Washington Post*, Feb. 7, 1990, A19; *New York Times*, Feb. 21, 1990, 1; on NATO expansion, see Philip Zelikow and Condoleezza Rice, *Germany Unified And Europe Transformed: A Study in Statecraft* (Cambridge, MA: Harvard University Press, 1996); Michael R. Gordon, "The Anatomy of a Misunderstanding," *New York Times*, May 25, 1997, E3.

19. *Newsweek*, May 28, 1990, 27; Stephen S. Rosenfeld in *Washington Post*, Nov. 1, 1996, A25; *Boston Globe*, Mar. 1, 1990, 18; *Washington Post*, Mar. 9, 1990, A25; Mar. 15, 1990, A29; and Mar. 22, 1990, A1, A35. For assurances to the Poles, see *New York Times*, Mar. 11, 1990, 14.

20. *Washington Post*, Apr. 12, 1990, A38; for the Bonn meeting, see Serge Schmemann in *New York Times*, May 6, 1990, 1, 20; *Newsweek*, May 28, 1990, 27.

21. James A. Baker, III, *The Politics of Diplomacy: Revolution, War and Peace* (New York: Putnam, 1995), 253; Michael Boll, "Superpower Diplomacy And German Unification: The Insiders' Views," *Parameters* 26 (Winter 1996–1997): 119–120; Bush and Scowcroft, *A World Transformed*, 282–283.

22. Judt, "New Germany, Old NATO," 40; Elizabeth Pond, *Beyond the Wall: Germany's Road to Unification* (Washington: Brookings Institution Press, 1993); Tadeusz Pieciukiewicz, "Security in Central and Eastern Europe: A View from Warsaw," *Parameters* 26 (Winter 1996–1997): 127.

23. Bush quoted in Beschloss and Talbott, *At The Highest Levels*, 132.

24. Michael Mandelbaum, "The Bush Foreign Policy," *Foreign Affairs* 70 (1990–1991): 5–8; Editorial, *Washington Post*, Jan. 18, 1990, A22 and, Mar. 28, 1990, A23; Broder, *Washington Post*, Mar. 21, 1990, A21.

25. *Washington Post*, Jan. 27, 1990, A13, A15; On the State Department, *Washington Post*, Mar. 16, 1990, A34; David Gergen, "America's Missed Opportunities," *Foreign Affairs* 71, no. 1 (1991–1992), 3; Henry Kaufman, *Washington Post*, July 10, 1990, A19.

26. *Washington Post*, Mar. 16, 1990, A34; On Havel, see *Boston Globe*, Feb. 23, 1990, 12; *New York Times*, Feb. 11, 1990, E25; *New York Times*, Mar. 18, 1990, E3; Editorial, *New York Times*, Jan. 21, 1990, E20; Editorial, *New York Times*, Jan. 21, 1990, E20.

27. Editorial, *New York Times*, Jan. 14, 1990, 22; Paul H. Nitze, "Gorbachev's Plan For a Communist Comeback," *Washington Post*, Jan. 10, 1990, A19; Feb. 7, 1990, A18; and Feb. 13, 1990, A1, A9.

28. Holland Hunter, "Soviet Economic Problems and Alternative Policy Responses," *Soviet Economy in a Time of Change*, A Compendium of Papers Submitted to the Joint Economic Committee, Congress of the United States, Vol. I, Oct. 10, 1979 (Washington, DC: GPO, 1979), 27.

29. Daniel Patrick Moynihan, "The Soviet Economy: Boy, Were We Wrong!" *Washington Post*, July 11, 1990, A19.

30. Marshall Goldman, *What Went Wrong With Perestroika* (New York: Norton, 1991), 48–49.

31. *Chicago Tribune*, Apr. 10, 1990, 8; *Atlantic Monthly* 265 (Feb. 1990): 20–24; *New Yorker*, Jan. 13, 1992, 21.

32. James H. Billington, "The Crisis of Communism and the Future of Freedom," *Ethics & International Affairs* 5 (1991): 87–97; *Washington Post*, Jan. 14, 1990, A1 and Feb. 8, 1990, A10; *New York Times*, Mar. 13, 1990, E1; *Washington Post*, Feb. 5, 1990, A1, A15; Stanislav Kondrashov, *Washington Post*, Feb. 15, 1990, A25.

33. *Newsweek*, Mar. 26, 1990, 13; *Washington Post*, Mar. 16, 1990, A1.

34. *Washington Post*, May 31, 1990, A1, A19.

35. Stephen S. Rosenfeld, *Washington Post*, Mar. 30, 1990, A25; *New York Times*, Jan. 14, 1990, E3; *Newsweek*, Jan. 22, 1990, 32–33 and Feb. 19, 1990, 29.

36. *New York Times*, Jan. 14, 1990, E3; editorial, *Washington Post*, Jan. 14, 1990, B6; *The Atlantic Monthly* 265 (Mar. 1990): 32–40.

37. *New York Times*, Jan. 14, 1990, E3; *Newsweek*, Apr. 2, 1990, 26; *Washington Post*, Apr. 3, 1990, A12; Apr. 4, 1990, A33; Apr. 5, 1990, A1; Apr. 10, 1990, A1; and Apr. 14, 1990, A1.

38. *Washington Post*, Mar. 13, 1990, A21.

39. Ibid., Mar. 23, 1990, A19 and, Mar. 29, 1990, A31.

40. Ibid., Mar. 30, 1990, A1, A20; Stephen S. Rosenfeld, *Washington Post*, Apr. 6, 1990, A15.

41. Tom Wicker, *Daily Progress*, Apr. 2, 1990, A4 and Apr. 12, 1990, A1; *Washington Post*, Apr. 12, 1990, A33 and Apr. 14, 1990.

42. Bill Keller, "Gorbachev's Need: To Still Matter," *New York Times*, May 27, 1990, 1, 10; William G. Hyland, *The Cold War Is Over* (New York: Random House, 1991); Walter Laqueur, ed., *Soviet Union 2000: Reform or Revolution?* (New York: St. Martin's Press, 1991); Caspar Weinberger, *AARP Bulletin* 31 (Feb. 1990): 16.

43. Stephen S. Rosenfeld, "Lighten Up, Fellows," *Washington Post*, May 25, 1990, A21; Dan Balz, "Conservatives: Victory or Vigilance?" *Washington Post*, May 26, 1990, A1, A14.

44. William Safire, "Gorbachev's Strength Is Weakness," *Daily Progress*, June 3, 1990, A5; Ann Devroy, *Daily Progress*, May 28, 1990, A19; Editorial, "With Mikhail Gorbachev," *Daily Progress*, May 29, 1990, A22; T. R. Reid, "Giving Gorbachev Credit," *Daily Progress*, May 27, 1990, A1, A25.

45. *Newsweek*, Dec. 11, 1989, 28–32, 39; editorial, *New York Times*, Dec. 1, 1989, Y30; *New York Times*, Dec. 4, 1989; Elizabeth Drew, "Letter From Washington," *New Yorker*, Jan. 1, 1990, 80–83; Bush and Scowcroft, *A World Transformed*, 164, 173.

46. Quote in Bush and Scowcroft, *A World Transformed*, 163; also see Charles C. Flowerree, "Chemical and Biological Weapons and Arms Control," in Richard Dean Burns, ed., *Encyclopedia of Arms Control and Disarmament*, 3 vols. (New York: Scribner's, 1993), II: 999–1020.

47. Thomas Graham Jr., *Disarmament Sketches: Three Decades of Arms Control and International Law* (Seattle: University of Washington Press, 2002), 190–205, 209; Beschloss and Talbott, *At the Highest Levels*, 288–289.

48. Quotes in Frances Fitzgerald, *Way Out There in the Blue: Reagan, Star Wars and the End of the Cold War* (New York: Simon & Schuster, 2000), 444–445; Raymond L. Garthoff, *The Great Transition: American-Soviet Relations and the End of the Cold War* (Washington, DC: The Brookings Institution, 1994), 252–337, 553–557; Graham, *Disarmament Sketches*, 102–142.

49. Beschloss and Talbott, *At the Highest Levels*, 166–167; Gates, *From the Shadows*, 482–483.

50. Jeffrey A. Larsen and James M. Smith, *Historical Dictionary of Arms Control and Disarmament* (Lanham, MD: Scarecrow Press, 2005), 204–205.

51. For the London Declaration, see *Current History* 89 (Oct. 1990): 334; Raymond L. Garthoff, "The Bush Administration's Policy toward the Soviet Union," *Current History* 90 (Oct. 1991), 314.

52. Bush and Scowcroft, *A World Transformed*, 564–565.

CHAPTER 16

1. Ball quote from Gordon R. Mitchell, *Strategic Deception* (East Lansing: Michigan State University Press, 2000), 81; see Fredrik Logevall, "A Critique of Containment," *Diplomatic History* 28 (Sept. 2004): 473, 482; U.S. Senate Preparedness Investigation Subcommittee of the Committee on Armed Services, *Hearings on the Military Aspects and Implications of Nuclear Test Ban Proposals and Related Matters*, 88th Cong., 1st Sess. (Washington, DC: GPO, May–Aug. 1963): 644; Strobe Talbott, "Rethinking the Red Menace," *Time* 135 (1 Jan. 1990): 36–38.

2. Quoted in Graebner, Burns, and Siracusa, *Reagan, Bush, Gorbachev*, 138.

3. William Graham Sumner, "War," *Essays of William Graham Sumner*, Albert Galloway Keller and Maurice R. Davie, eds. (New Haven, CT: Yale University Press, 1934), I: 169–175.

4. Robert McNamara, "The Military Role of Nuclear Weapons: Perceptions and Misperceptions," *Foreign Affairs* (Fall 1983): 68–72; Nina Tannenwald *The Nuclear Taboo: The United States and the Non-Use of Nuclear Weapons Since 1945* (New York: Cambridge University Press, 2007).

5. George Bush and Brent Scowcroft, *A World Transformed* (New York: Knopf, 1998), xi; Rusk quoted in Strobe Talbott, *Endgame: The Inside Story of SALT II* (New York: Harper & Row, 1979), 19–20; Paul H. Nitze, "Foreword," in Aleksandr' G. Savel'yev and Nikolay N. Detinov, *The Big Five: Arms Control Decision-Making in the Soviet Union* (Westport, CT: Praeger, 1995), xi–xii.

6. Kennan quoted in Norman A. Graebner, "The Soviet-American Conflict: A Strange Phenomenon," *The Virginia Quarterly Review* 60:4 (1984): 569.

7. See Graebner, Burns and Siracusa, *Reagan, Bush, Gorbachev: Revisiting the End of the Cold War* (Westport, CT: Praeger Security International, 2008).

8. Writers who noted the economic basis of America's apparent decline as a world power are Paul M. Kennedy, *The Rise and Fall of the Great Powers: Economic Change and Military Conflict from 1500 to 2000* (New York: Random House, 1987); David P. Calleo, *Beyond American Hegemony: The Future of the Western Alliance* (New York: Basic Books, 1987); James Fallows, *More Like Us: Making America Great Again* (Boston: Houghton Mifflin, 1989); Russell Mead, *Mortal Splendor: The American Empire in Transition* (Boston: Houghton Mifflin, 1987); and David Halberstam, *The Reckoning* (New York: Morrow, 1986); C. Fred Bergsten, "The World Economy After the Cold War," *Foreign Affairs* 69 (Summer 1990): 96–112; Samuel P. Huntington, "America's Changing Strategic Interests," *Survival* 33 (Jan./Feb. 1991), 16; C. Fred Bergsten, "The Primacy of Economics," *Foreign Policy* No. 87 (Summer 1992): 4. On Germany's economic leadership see Richard Cohn in *The Washington Post*, July 18, 1990, A23; R.W. Appel, Jr., in the *New York Times*, July 8, 1990, E1.

9. *Newsweek* (July 9, 1990): 29; David Hoffman and Dan Balz in *The Washington Post*, July 12, 1990, A8.

10. Bergsten, "The Primacy of Economics," 13; Joel Kotkin in *The Washington Post*, May 20, 1990, B1, B4. Some writers pointed to American culture and other forms of soft influence, and argued, with considerable prescience, that low productivity and budgetary problems were only temporary. See Kenneth Auchincloss in *Newsweek* (July 16, 1990): 31; Henry R. Nau, *The Myth of America's*

Decline: Leading the World Economy into the 1990s (New York: Oxford University Press, 1990); Joseph S. Nye, Jr., *Bound to Lead: The Changing Nature of American Power* (New York: Basic Books, 1990).

11. *The New Yorker*, Mar. 13, 1989, 25.

12. Bush quoted in *The Washington Post*, May 13, 1989, A15.

13. Elliot Carlson and Ray Stephens, "Cold War Thaw?" *AARP Bulletin*, 31 (Feb. 1990): 20; David Broder in *The Washington Post*, May 2, 1990, A23.

14. Joseph S. Nye, Jr., "The Misleading Metaphor of Decline," *The Atlantic Monthly* 265 (Mar. 1990): 93.

Selected Bibliography

GENERAL ACCOUNTS

Alexander, Charles. *Holding the Line: The Eisenhower Era, 1952–1961*. Bloomington: Indiana University Press, 1975.

Bacevich, Andrew, J. *The Long War: A New History of U.S. National Security Policy since World War II*. New York: Columbia University Press, 2007.

Beschloss, Michael. *The Crisis Years: Kennedy and Khrushchev, 1960–1963*. New York: Edward Burlingame Books, 1991.

Boyle, Peter G. *American-Soviet Relations: From the Russian Revolution to the Fall of Communism*. New York: Routledge, 1993.

Brands, H. W. *The Devil We Knew: Americans and the Cold War*. New York: Oxford University Press, 1993.

Buckingham, Peter H. *America Sees Red: Anticommunism in America, 1870s to 1980s: A Review of Issues and References*. Claremont, CA: Regina Books, 1988.

Cohen, Warren I. *America in the Age of Soviet Power, 1945–1991*. Vol. 4: *The Cambridge History of American Foreign Relations*, 4 vols. New York: Cambridge University Press, 1993.

Coleman, David G., and Joseph M. Siracusa. *Depression to Cold War: A History of America from Herbert Hoover to Ronald Reagan*. Westport, CT: Praeger, 2002.

Dumbrell, John. *The Carter Presidency: A Re-evaluation*. 2nd ed. New York: St. Martin's Press, 1995.

Flanagan, Jason C. *Imagining the Enemy: American Presidential War Rhetoric from Woodrow Wilson to George Walker Bush*. Claremont, CA: Regina Books, 2009.

Gaddis, John Lewis. *The Long Peace: Inquires into the History of the Cold War*. New York: Oxford University Press, 1987.

———. *We Now Know: Rethinking Cold War History*. New York: Oxford University Press, 1997.

Garthoff, Raymond L. *Détente and Confrontation: American Relations from Nixon to Reagan*. rev. ed. Washington, DC: Brookings Institution, 1994.

———. *A Journey Through the Cold War*. Washington, DC: Brookings, 2001.

Gorodetsky, Gabriel, ed. *Soviet Foreign Policy, 1917–1991: A Retrospective*. Portland, OR: Frank Cass, 1994.

Greene, John Robert. *The Limits of Power: The Nixon and Ford Administrations*. Bloomington: Indiana University Press, 1993.

Heale, M. J. *McCarthy's Americans: Red Scare Politics in State and Nation, 1935–1965*. Athens, GA: University of Georgia Press, 1998.

Hogan, Michael J. *A Cross of Iron: Harry S. Truman and the Origins of the National Security Sate, 1945–1954*. New York: Cambridge University Press, 1998.

Hyland, William G. *Mortal Rivals: Superpower Relations from Nixon to Reagan*. New York: Random House, 1987.

Kennedy-Pipe, Caroline. *Stalin's Cold War: Soviet Strategies in Europe, 1943 to 1956*. New York: St. Martin's Press, 1995.

LaFeber, Walter. *America, Russia, and the Cold War, 1945–1996*. 8th ed. New York: McGraw-Hill, 1997.

Larson, Deborah Welch. *Anatomy of Mistrust: U.S.-Soviet Relations during the Cold War*. Ithaca, NY: Cornell University Press, 1997.

Leffler, Melvyn P. *For the Soul of Mankind: The United States, the Soviet Union, and the Cold War*. New York: Hill & Wang, 2007.

Lundestad, Geir. *East, West, North, South: Major Developments in International Politics since 1945*. Trans. by Gail Adams Kvam. 4th ed. New York: Oxford University Press, 1999.

McCormick, Thomas J. *America's Half Century: United States Foreign Policy in the Cold War and After*. 2nd ed. Baltimore: Johns Hopkins University Press, 1995.

Mower, A. Glenn, Jr. *Human Rights and American Foreign Policy: The Carter and Reagan Experiences*. New York: Greenwood Press, 1987.

Nelson, Harvey W. *Power and Insecurity: Beijing, Moscow and Washington, 1949–1988*. Boulder, CO: Lynne Rienner Publishers, 1989.

Nelson, Keith, *The Making of Détente: Soviet-American Relations in the Shadow of Vietnam*. Baltimore, MD: Johns Hopkins University Press, 1995.

Painter, David S. *The Cold War: An International History*. New York: Routledge, 1999.

Patterson, Thomas G. *Meeting the Communist Threat: Truman to Reagan*. New York: Oxford University Press, 1988.

Perkins, John H. *Geopolitics and the Green Revolution: Wheat, Genes and the Cold War*. New York: Oxford University Press, 1997.

Powaski, Ronald E. *The Cold War: The United States and the Soviet Union, 1917–1991*. New York: Oxford University Press, 1998.

Radosh, Ronald. *Prophets on the Right: Profiles of Conservative Critics of American Globalism*. New York: Simon & Schuster, 1975.

Sakwa, Richard. *The Rise and Fall of the Soviet Union, 1917–1991*. New York: Routledge Press, 1999.

Schrecker, Ellen W. *Many Are the Crimes: McCarthyism in America*. Boston: Little, Brown, 1998.

Seppain, Hélène. *Contrasting US and German Attitudes to Soviet Trade, 1917–91: Politics by Economic Means*. New York: St. Martin's Press, 1992.

Shaw, Tony. *Hollywood's Cold War*. Amherst: University Massachusetts Press, 2007.

Smith, Tony. America's Mission: *The United States and the Worldwide Struggle for Democracy in the Twentieth Century*. Princeton, NJ: Princeton University Press, 1994.

Stevenson, Richard W. *The Rise and Fall of Détente: Relaxations of Tension in U.S.-Soviet Relations, 1954–84*. Urbana: University of Illinois Press, 1985.

Tyroler, Charles II, ed. Committee on the Present Danger. *Alerting America: The Papers of the Committee on the Present Danger*. Washington, DC: Pergamon-Brassey's, 1984. (Attacks Carter's arms control policies.)

Ulam, Adam B. *Expansion and Coexistence: Soviet Foreign Policy, 1917–73*. 2nd ed. New York: Praeger, 1974.

Waller, Douglas C. *Congress and the Nuclear Freeze: An Inside Look at the Politics of a Mass Movement*. Amherst: The University of Massachusetts Press, 1987.

Weihmiller, Gordon R. *U.S.-Soviet Summits: An Account of East-West Diplomacy at the Top, 1955–1985*. Lanham, MD: University Press of America, 1986.

Wittner, Lawrence S. *Cold War America: From Hiroshima to Watergate*. New York: Praeger, 1974.

Wohlforth, William Curti. *The Elusive Balance: Power and Perceptions during the Cold War*. Ithaca, NY: Cornell University Press, 1993.

Zubok, Vladislav M. *A Failed Empire: The Soviet Union in the Cold War From Stalin to Gorbachev*. Chapel Hill: The University of North Carolina Press, 2007.

Zubok, Vladislav M., and Constantine Pleshakov. *Inside the Kremlin's Cold War: From Stalin to Khrushchev*. Cambridge, MA: Harvard University Press, 1996.

ORIGINS OF THE COLD WAR

Alperovitz, Gar. *Atomic Diplomacy: Hiroshima and Potsdam. The Use of the Atomic Bomb and the American Confrontation*. New York: Vintage Books, 1967.

Bills, Scott L. *Empire and Cold War: The Roots of US-Third World Antagonism, 1945–47*. New York: St. Martin's Press, 1990.

Boll, Michael M. *Cold War in the Balkans: American Foreign Policy and the Emergence of Communist Bulgaria, 1943–1947*. Lexington: University of Press of Kentucky, 1984.

Davis, Lynn Etheridge. *The Cold War Begins: Soviet-American Conflict over Eastern Europe*. Princeton, NJ: Princeton University Press, 1974.

Edmonds, Robin. *The Big Three: Churchill, Roosevelt, and Stalin in Peace & War*. New York: Norton, 1991.

Frazier, Robert. *Anglo-American Relations with Greece: The Coming of the Cold War, 1942–47*. New York: St. Martin's Press, 1991.

Gaddis, John Lewis. *The United States and the Origins of the Cold War, 1941–1947*. New ed. New York: Columbia University Press, 2000.

Gori, Francesca, and Silvio Pons, eds. *The Soviet Union and Europe in the Cold War, 1943–53*. New York: St. Martin's Press, 1996.

Gormly, James L. *From Potsdam to the Cold War: Big Three Diplomacy, 1945–1947*. Wilmington, DE: SR Books, 1990.

Harbutt, Fraser J. *The Iron Curtain: Churchill, America, and the Origins of the Cold War*. New York: Oxford University Press, 1986.

Hinds, Lynn Boyd, and Theodore Otto Windt, Jr. *The Cold War as Rhetoric: The Beginnings, 1945–1950*. New York: Praeger, 1991.

Hogan, Michael J. *The Marshall Plan: America, Britain, and the Reconstruction of Western Europe, 1947–1952*. New York: Cambridge University Press, 1987.

Kaplan, Karel. *The Short March: The Communist Takeover in Czechoslovakia, 1945–1948*. New York: St. Martin's Press, 1987.

Kuniholm, Bruce R. *The Origins of the Cold War in the Near East: Great Power Conflict and Diplomacy in Iran, Turkey and Greece*. Princeton, NJ: Princeton University Press, 1980.

Leffler, Melvyn P. *The Specter of Communism: The United States and the Origins of the Cold War, 1917–1953*. New York: Hill & Wang, 1994.

Linz, Susan J., ed. *The Impact of World War II on the Soviet Union*. Totowa, NJ: Rowman & Allanheld, 1985.

Messer, Robert L. *The End of an Alliance: James F. Byrnes, Roosevelt, Truman, and the Origins of the Cold War*. Chapel Hill: University of North Carolina Press, 1982.

Miscamble, Wilson D. *From Roosevelt to Truman: Potsdam, Hiroshima, and the Cold War*. New York: Cambridge University Press, 2007.

Nadeau, Remi. *Stalin, Churchill and Roosevelt Divide Europe*. New York: Praeger, 1980.

Neumann, William L. *After Victory: Churchill, Roosevelt, Stalin and the Making of the Peace*. New York: Harper & Row, 1967.

Offner, Arnold A. *Another Such Victory: President Truman and the Cold War, 1945–1953*. Stanford, CA: Stanford University Press, 2002.

Paul, Allen. *Katyn: The Untold Story of Stalin's Polish Massacre*. New York: Charles Scribner's Sons, 1991.

Reid, Escott. *Time of Fear and Hope: The Making of the North Atlantic Treaty, 1947–1949*. Toronto: McClelland Publishers, 1977.

Reynolds, David, ed. *The Origins of the Cold War in Europe: International Perspectives*. New Haven, CT: Yale University Press, 1994.

Reynolds, David, Warren F. Kimball, and A. O. Chubarian, eds. *Allies at War: The Soviet, American and British Experience, 1939–1945*. New York: St. Martin's Press, 1994.

Risse-Kappen, Thomas. *Cooperation Among Democracies: The European Influence on U.S. Foreign Policy*. Princeton, NJ: Princeton University Press, 1997.

Roman, Eric. *Hungary and the Victor Powers, 1945–1950*. New York: St. Martin's Press, 1996.

Senarclens, Pierre de. *From Yalta to the Iron Curtain: The Great Powers and the Origins of the Cold War*. Trans. by Amanda Pingree. Washington, DC: Berg, 1995.

Siracusa, Joseph M. *Into the Dark House: American Diplomacy & the Ideological Origins of the Cold War*. Claremont, CA: Regina Books, 1998.

Siracusa, Joseph M. *The American Diplomatic Revolution: A Documentary History of the Cold War, 1941–1947*. New York: Holt, Rinehart and Winston, 1976.

Sirgiovanni, George. *An Undercurrent of Suspicion: Anti-Communism in America during World War II*. New Brunswick, NJ: Transaction Publishers, 1990.

Stavrakis, Peter J. *Moscow and Greek Communism, 1944–1949*. Ithaca, NY: Cornell University Press, 1989.

Ward, Patricia Dawson. *The Threat of Peace: James F. Byrnes and the Council of Foreign Ministers, 1945–1946*. Kent, OH: Kent State University Press, 1979.

Yergin, Daniel. *Shattered Peace: The Origins of the Cold War*. Rev. & update of 1977 edition. New York: Penguin Books, 1990.

END OF THE COLD WAR

Beschloss, Michael R., and Strobe Talbott. *At the Highest Level: The Inside Story of the End of the Cold War*. Boston: Little, Brown, 1993.

Carrere d'Encausse, Helene. *The End of the Soviet Empire: The Triumph of the Nations*. New York: Basic Books, 1993.

English, Robert D. *Russia and the Idea of the West: Gorbachev, Intellectuals and the End of the Cold War*. New York: Columbia University Press, 2000.

Fitzgerald, Frances. *Way Out There in the Blue: Reagan, Star Wars and the End of the Cold War*, New York: Simon & Schuster, 2000.

Garthoff, Raymond L. *The Great Transition: American-Soviet Relations and the End of the Cold War*, Washington, DC: Brookings Institution, 1994.

Hogan, Michael J., ed. *The End of the Cold War*. New York: Cambridge University Press, 1992, See especially Richard J. Barnet, "A Balance Sheet: Lippman, Kennan and the Cold War," and Denise Artaud, "The End of the Cold War: A Skeptical View."

Hough, Jerry F. *Russia and the West: Gorbachev and the Politics of Reform*. New York: Simon & Schuster, 1987.

Hutchings, Robert S. *American Diplomacy and the End of the Cold War, An Insider's Account of U.S. Policy in Europe, 1989–1992*. Baltimore, MD: Johns Hopkins University Press, 1997.

Kaiser, Robert G. *Why Gorbachev Happened: His Triumphs and His Failure*. New York: Simon & Schuster, 1991.

LeBow, Richard, and Janice Gross Stein. *We All Lost the Cold War*. Princeton, NJ: Princeton University Press, 1994.

Lebow, Richard Ned, and Thomas W. Risse-Kappen, eds. *International Relations Theory and the End of the Cold War*. New York: Columbia University Press, 1995.

Lundberg, Lirsten. *The CIA and the Fall of the Soviet Empire: The Politics of "Getting it Right."* Cambridge, MA: Kennedy School of Government, Harvard University, 1994.

Mann, James. *The Rebellion of Ronald Reagan: A History of the End of the Cold War*. New York: Viking, 2009.

Matlock, Jack F. *Autopsy of an Empire: The American Ambassador's Account of the Collapse of the Soviet Union*. New York: Random House, 1995.

Matlock, Jack F., Jr. *Reagan and Gorbachev*. New York: Random House, 2004.

Meneges, Constantine C. *Inside the National Security Council: The True Story of the Making and Unmaking of Reagan's Foreign Policy*. New York: Simon & Schuster, 1988.

Rowen, Henry S., and Charles Wolf, Jr., eds. *The Impoverished Superpower: Perestroika and the Soviet Military Burden*. San Francisco CA: Institute for Contemporary Studies, 1990.

Schweizer, Peter. *Victory: the Reagan Administration's Secret Strategy that Hastened the Collapse of the Soviet Union*. New York: The Atlantic Monthly Press, 1994.

Shelton, Judy. *The Coming Soviet Crash: Gorbachev's Desperate Pursuit of Credit in Western Financial Markets*. New York: Free Press, 1988.

Summy, Ralph, and Michael E. Salla, eds. *Why the Cold War Ended: A Range of Interpretations*. Westport, CT: Greenwood Press, 1995.

Talbott, Strobe. *The Russians and Reagan*. New York: Vintage, 1984.

Walt, Stephen M. "The Gorbachev Interlude and International Relations Theory." *Diplomatic History* 21:3 (Summer 1997). Review of Lebow and Risse-Kappen and defends "realist" interpretation.

Zubok, Vladislav M. "New Evidence of the End of the Cold War." *The Cold War International History Bulletin*, Issue 12/13 (Fall/Winter 2001): 5–23. (An excellent overall source on the Cold War's end.)

PERSONALITIES

American

Ambrose, Stephen E. *Eisenhower: Soldier and President*. New York: Simon & Schuster, 1990.

Abramson, Rudy. *Spanning the Century: The Life of W. Averell Harriman, 1891–1986*. New York: William Morrow, 1992.

Acheson, Dean. *Present At the Creation: My Years in the State Department*. New York: W.W. Norton, 1969.

Baker, James A., III. *The Politics of Diplomacy*. New York: G. P. Putnam's Sons, 1995.

Bornet, Vaughn Davis. *The Presidency of Lyndon B. Johnson*. Lawrence: The University Press of Kansas, 1983.

Bowie, Robert R., and Richard H. Immerman. *Waging Peace: How Eisenhower Shaped an Enduring Cold War Strategy*. New York: Oxford University Press, 1998.

Brands, H. W., ed. *The Foreign Policies of Lyndon Johnson: Beyond Vietnam*. College Station: Texas A & M University Press, 1999.

Brzezinski, Zbigniew. *Power and Principle: Memoirs of the National Security Adviser, 1977–1981*. New York: Farrar Straus Giroux, 1983.

Bundy, William. *A Tangled Web: The Making of Foreign Policy in the Nixon Presidency*. New York: Hill & Wang, 1998.

Bush, George, and Brent Scowcroft. *A World Transformed*. New York: Alfred A. Knopf, 1998.

Callahan, David. *Dangerous Capabilities: Paul Nitze and the Cold War*. New York: Harper & Row, 1990.

Canon, Lou. *President Reagan: The Role of a Lifetime*. New York: Simon & Schuster, 1991.

Carter, Jimmy. *Keeping the Faith: Memoirs of a President*. New York: Bantam, 1982.

Chace, James. *Acheson: The Secretary of State Who Created the American World*. New York: Simon & Schuster, 1998.

Clifford, Clark, with Richard C. Holbrook. *Counsel to the President: A Memoir*. New York: Random House, 1991.

Cohen, Warren I., and Nancy Bernkopf Tucker, eds. *Lyndon Johnson Confronts the World: American Foreign Policy, 1963–1968*. New York: Cambridge University Press, 1994.

Cohen, William S., and Mitchell, George J. *Men of Zeal: A Candid Inside Story of the Iran Contra Hearings*. New York: Viking, 1988.

Dallek, Robert. *Flawed Giant: Lyndon Johnson and His Times, 1961–1973*. New York: Oxford University Press, 1998.

———. *Nixon and Kissinger: Partners in Power*. New York: HarperCollins, 2007.

Deaver, Michael K. *A Different Drummer: My Thirty Years with Ronald Reagan*. New York: HarperCollins, 1987.

Diggins, John Patrick. *Ronald Reagan: Fate, Freedom, and the Making of History*. New York: W.W. Norton, 2006.

Dunn, Dennis J. *Caught Between Roosevelt & Stalin: America's Ambassadors to Moscow*. Lexington: University Press of Kentucky, 1998.

Eisenhower, Dwight D. *Mandate for Change, 1953–1956*. Garden City, NY: Doubleday, 1963.

———. *Waging Peace, 1956–1961*. Garden City, NY: Doubleday, 1965.

Ford, Gerald R. *A Time to Heal: The Autobiography of Gerald R. Ford*. New York: Harper & Row, 1979.

Gates, Robert M. *From the Shadows: The Ultimate Insider's Story of Five Presidents and How They Won the Cold War*. New York: Simon & Schuster, 1996.

Haig, Alexander M., Jr. *Caveat: Realism, Reagan and Foreign Policy*. New York: Macmillan, 1984.

Hartmann, Robert T. *Palace Politics: An Inside Account of the Ford Years*. New York: McGraw-Hill, 1980.

Helms, Richard, with William Hood. *A Look Over My Shoulder: A Life in the CIA*. New York: Random House, 2003.

Hixson, Walter L. *George F. Kennan: Cold War Iconoclast*. New York: Columbia University Press, 1989.

Immerman, Richard H., ed. *John Foster Dulles and the Diplomacy of the Cold War*. Princeton, NJ: Princeton University Press, 1990.

Isaacson, Walter, and Evan Thomas. *The Wise Men: Six Friends and the World They Made*. New York: Simon & Schuster, 1986.

Kaufman, Robert G. *Henry M. Jackson: A Life in Politics*. Seattle: University of Washington Press, 2000.

Kaufman, Scott. *Plans Unraveled: The Foreign Policy of the Carter Administration*. Dekalb, IL: Northern Illinois University Press, 2008.

Kearns, Doris. *Lyndon Johnson & the American Dream*. New York: Harper & Row, 1976.

Kennan, George F. *Memoirs*. 2 vols. Boston: Little, Brown, 1967, 1972.

Kissinger, Henry. *White House Years*. Boston: Simon & Schuster, 1979.

———. *Years of Renewal*. New York: Simon & Schuster, 1999.

———. *Years of Upheaval*. Boston: Simon & Schuster, 1982.

McLellan, David S. *Dean Acheson: The State Department Years*. New York: Dodd, Mead, 1976.

McFarlane, Robert C., with Zofia Smardz. *Special Trust*. New York: Cadell & Davies, 1994.

Meese, Edwin III. *With Reagan: The Inside Story*. Washington, DC: Regnery Gateway, 1992.

Miscamble. Wilson D. *George F. Kennan and the Making of American Foreign Policy, 1947–1950*. Princeton, NJ: Princeton University Press, 1992.

Nitze, Paul H., with Steven L. Rearden and Ann M. Smith. *From Hiroshima to Glasnost: At the Center of Decisions, A Memoir*. New York: Weidenfeld & Nicolson, 1898.

Nixon, Richard. *RN: The Memoirs of Richard Nixon*. New York: Grosset & Dunlap, 1978.

Offner, Arnold A. *Another Such Victory: President Truman and the Cold War, 1945–1953*. Stanford, CA: Stanford University Press, 2002.

Reagan, Ronald. *An American Life: The Autobiography*. New York: Simon & Schuster, 1990.

Rearden, Steven L. *The Evolution of American Strategic Doctrine: Paul H. Nitze and the Soviet Challenge*. Boulder, CO: Westview Press, 1984.

Ognibene, Peter J. *Scoop: The Life and Politics of Henry M. Jackson*. New York: Stein & Day, 1975.

Robertson, David. *Sly and Able: A Political Biography of James F. Byrnes*. New York: Norton, 1994.

Schlesinger, Arthur M. *A Thousand Days: John F. Kennedy in the White House*. Boston: Houghton Mifflin, 1965.

Schoenbaum, Thomas J. *Waging Peace and War: Dean Rusk in the Truman, Kennedy and Johnson Years*. New York: Simon & Schuster, 1988.

Schulzinger, Robert D. *Henry Kissinger: Doctor of Diplomacy*. New York: Columbia University Press, 1989.

Shultz, George Pratt. *Turmoil and Triumph: My Years as Secretary of State*. New York: Scribners, 1993.

Talbott, Strobe. *Master of the Game: Paul Nitze and Nuclear Peace*. New York: Knopf, 1988.

Truman, Harry S. *Memoirs*. 2 vols. Garden City, NY: Doubleday, 1955–1956.

Vance, Cyrus. *Hard Choices: Critical Years in America's Foreign Policy*. New York: Simon & Schuster, 1983.

Wallison, Peter J. *Ronald Reagan: The Power of His Conviction and the Success of His Presidency*. Boulder: Westview Press, 2003.

Weinberger, Caspar. *Fighting for Peace: Seven Critical Years in the Pentagon*. New York: Warner Books, 1990.

Soviet

Berezhkov, Valentin M. *At Stalin's Side: His Interpreter's Memoirs from the October Revolution to the Fall of the Dictator's Empire*. Trans. by Sergei M. Mikheyev. Seacaucus, NJ: Carol Publishing Group, 1994.

Blacker, Coit D. *Hostage to Revolution: Gorbachev and Soviet Security Policy, 1985–1991*. New York: Council on Foreign Relations Press, 1993.

Chernyaev, Anatoly S. *My Six Years with Gorbachev*. University Park: The Pennsylvania State University Press, 2000.

Dobrynin, Anatoly. *In Confidence: Moscow's Ambassador to America's Six Cold War Presidents*. New York: Times Books, 1995.

Djilas, Milovan. *Conversations with Stalin*. Trans. by Michael B. Petrovich. New York: Harcourt, Brace and World, 1962.

Fursenko, Aleksandr, and Timothy Naftali. *Khrushchev's Cold War: The Inside Story of an American Adversary*. New York: Norton, 2006.

Gorbachev, Mikhail. *Memoirs*. London: Doubleday, 1995.

———. *Reykjavik: Results and Lessons*. Madison, CT: Sphinx Press, 1987.

Gorlizki, Yoram, and Oleg Khlevniuk. *Cold Peace: Stalin and the Soviet Ruling Circle, 1945–1953*. New York: Oxford University Press, 2004.

Gromyko, Andrei. *Memories*. Trans. by Harold Shukman. New York: Doubleday, 1989.

Khrushchev, Sergei N. *Nikita Khrushchev and the Creation of a Superpower*. Trans. by Shirley Benson. University Park: University of Pennsylvania Press, 2000.

Palazchenko, Pavel. *My Years with Gorbachev and Shevardnadze: The Memoir of a Soviet Interpreter*. University Park: Pennsylvania State University Press, 1997.

Resis, Albert, ed. *Molotov Remembers: Inside Kremlin Politics: Conversations with Felix Chuey*. Chicago: Ivan R. Dee, 1993.

Sakarov, Andrei. *Moscow and Beyond*. New York: Knopf, 1991.

Schecter, Jerrold L., with Vyacheslav V. Luchkov, ed. and trans. *Khrushchev Remembers: The Glasnost Tapes*. Boston: Little, Brown, 1990.

Talbott, Strobe, ed. and trans. *Khrushchev Remembers*. Boston: Little, Brown, 1970.

———. *Khrushchev Remembers: The Last Testament*. Boston: Little, Brown, 1974.

Taubman, William. *Khrushchev: The Man and His Era*. New York: Norton, 2003.

———. *Stalin's American Policy: From Entente to Détente to Cold War*. New York: Norton, 1982.

Volkogonov, Dmitri A. *Stalin: Triumph and Tragedy*. Trans. by Harold Shukman. New York: Grove Weidenfeld, 1991.

ARMS CONTROL

Adelman, Kenneth L. *The Great Universal Embrace: Arms Summitry—a Skeptic's Account*. New York: Simon & Schuster, 1989.

Alibek, Ken, and Stephen Handelman. *Biohazard: The Chilling True Story of the Largest Covert Biological Weapons Program in History—Told from the Inside by the Man Who Ran It*. New York: Random House, 1999.

Bird, Jacqueline M. *Scientist in Conflict: Hans Bethe, Edward Teller and the Shaping of United States Nuclear Weapons Policy, 1945–1972*. Claremont, CA: Regina Books, 2008.

Carnesale, Albert, and Richard H. Haass, eds. *Superpower Arms Control: Setting the Record Straight*. Cambridge, MA: Ballinger, 1987.

Duffy, Gloria. *Compliance and the Future of Arms Control*. Cambridge, MA: Ballinger, 1988.

Foerster, Schuyler. "The Reagan Administration and Arms Control: Redefining the Agenda." In *Defense Policy in the Reagan Administration*. William P. Snyder and James Brown, eds. Washington, DC: National Defense University Press, 1988, pp. 5–44.

Graham, Thomas, Jr. *Disarmament Sketches: Three Decades of Arms Control and International Law*. Seattle: University of Washington, 2002.

Kartchner, Kerry M. *Negotiating START: Strategic Arms Reduction Talks and the Quest for Strategic Stability*. New Brunswick, NJ: Rutgers University, 1992.

Landais-Stamp, Paul, and Paul Rogers. *Rocking the Boat: New Zealand, the United States and the Nuclear-Free-Zone Controversy in the 1980s*. New York: Berg Publishers, 1989.

Miller, Judith, Stephen Engelberg, and William Broad. *Germs: Biological Weapons and America's Secret War*. New York: Simon & Schuster, 2001.

Miller, Richard L. *Under the Cloud: The Decades of Nuclear Testing*. New York: Free Press, 1986.

Mosher, David, and Michael O'Hanlon. *The START Treaty and Beyond*. Washington, DC: Congressional Budget Office, 1991.

Scheer, Robert. *With Enough Shovels: Reagan, Bush and Nuclear War*. New York: Random House, 1982.

Seagrave, Sterling. *Yellow Rain*. New York: M. Evans, 1981.

Shimko, Keith L. *Images and Arms Control: Perceptions of the Soviet Union in the Reagan Administration*. Ann Arbor: University of Michigan Press, 1991.

Sims, Nicholas Roger Alan. *The Evolution of Biological Disarmament.* Oxford and
    New York: Oxford University Press, 2001.
Smith, Gerard C. *Doubletalk: The Story of the First Strategic Arms Limitation Talks.*
    New York: Doubleday, 1980.
Talbott, Strobe. *Deadly Gambits: The Reagan Administration and the Stalemate in
    Nuclear Arms Control.* New York: Knopf, 1984.
———. *Endgame: The Inside Story of SALT II.* New York: Harper & Row, 1979.

INTELLIGENCE, MILITARY FORCES, AND STRATEGY

Burns, Richard Dean, and Lester M. Brune, *The Quest for Missile Defenses, 1944–
    2004.* Claremont, CA: Regina Books, 2004.
Burrows, William E. *By Any Means Necessary: America's Secret Air War in the Cold
    War.* New York: Farrar, Straus and Giroux, 2001.
Cahn, Anne Hessing. *Killing Détente: The Right Attacks the CIA.* University Park:
    Pennsylvania State University Press, 1998.
Carney, John T., and Benjamin F. Schemmer, *No Room for Error: The Covert Oper-
    ations of Special Tactics Units From Iran to Afghanistan.* New York: Ballantine
    Books, 2003.
Coleman, David G., and Joseph M. Siracusa. *Real-World Nuclear Deterrence: The
    Making of International Strategy.* Westport, CT: Praeger, 2006.
Coll, Steve. *Ghost Wars: The Secret History of the CIA, Afghanistan, and Bin Laden
    from the Soviet Invasion to September 10, 2001.* New York: Penguin Press,
    2004.
Crile, George. *Charlie Wilson's War: The Extraordinary Story of the Largest Covert
    Operation in History.* New York : Atlantic Monthly Press, 2003.
Firth, Noel E., and James H. Noren, *Soviet Defense Spending: A History of CIA
    Estimates, 1950–1990.* College Station, TX: Texas A & M Press, 1998.
Freedman, Lawrence. *Kennedy's Wars: Berlin, Cuba, Laos and Vietnam.* New York:
    Oxford University Press, 2000.
Gervasi, Tom. *The Myth of Soviet Military Supremacy.* New York: Harper & Row,
    1986.
Graebner, Norman A., ed. *The National Security: Its Theory and Practice, 1945–
    1960.* New York: Oxford University Press, 1986.
Grau, Lester W. *The Bear Went Over the Mountain: Soviet Combat Tactics in
    Afghanistan.* London: Frank Cass, 1998.
Herken, Gregg. *Cardinal Choices: Presidential Science Advising from the Atomic Bomb
    to SDI.* New York: Oxford University Press, 1992.
———. *Counsels of War.* New York: Knopf, 1985.
———. *The Winning Weapon: The Atomic Bomb in the Cold War, 1945–1950.* New
    York: Knopf, 1980.
Higgins, Trumbull. *The Perfect Failure: Kennedy, Eisenhower, and the CIA at the Bay
    of Pigs.* New York: Norton, 1987.
Holloway, David. *The Soviet Union and the Arms Race.* New Haven, CT: Yale Uni-
    versity Press, 1983.

Holloway, David. *Stalin and the Bomb: The Soviet Union and Atomic Energy, 1939–1956.* New Haven, CT: Yale University Press, 1996.

Kaplan, Lawrence S. *NATO and the United States: The Enduring Alliance.* Updated ed. New York: Twayne Publishers, 1994.

Lakoff, Sanford, and Herbert F. York. *A Shield in Space? Technology, Politics, and the Strategic Defense Initiative.* Berkeley, CA: University of California Press, 1989.

Mathers, Jennifer G. *The Russian Nuclear Shield from Stalin to Yeltin.* New York: St. Martin's, 2000.

McGwire, Michael. *Military Objectives in Soviet Foreign Policy.* Washington, DC: Brookings Institution, 1987.

Mendel, Richard A. *The Defense Game: An Insider Explores the Astonishing Realities of America's Defense Establishment.* New York: Harper & Row, 1986.

Nolan, Janne E. *Guardians of the Arsenal: The Politics of Nuclear Strategy.* New York: Basic Books, 1989.

Odom, William E. *The Collapse of the Soviet Military.* New Haven, CT: Yale University Press, 1998.

Podvig, Pavel, ed. *Russian Strategic Nuclear Forces.* Cambridge, MA: MIT Press, 2001.

Prados, John. *Presidents' Secret Wars: CIA and Pentagon Covert Operations from World War II through the Persian Gulf.* Rev. and expanded ed. Chicago, IL: I. R. Dee, 1996.

Pratt, Erik K. *Selling Strategic Defense: Interests, Ideologies, and the Arms Race.* Boulder, CO: Lynne Rienner, 1990.

Randlagh, John. *The Agency: The Rise and Decline of the CIA.* Rev. and updated ed. New York: Simon & Schuster, 1987.

Roman, Peter J. *Eisenhower and the Missile Gap.* Ithaca, NY: Cornell University Press, 1995.

Rowen, Henry S., and Charles Wolf, Jr., eds. *The Impoverished Superpower: Perestroika and the Soviet Military Burden.* San Francisco CA: Institute for Contemporary Studies, 1990.

Sokov, Nikolai, *Russian Strategic Modernization: Past and Present.* Lanham, MD: Rowman & Littlefield, 2000.

Stone, David. *Wars of the Cold War, Campaigns and Conflicts, 1945–1990.* London: Brassey's, 2004.

Winkler, David F. *Cold War at Sea: High-Seas Confrontation between the United States and the Soviet Union.* Annapolis, MD: Naval Institute Press, 2000.

York, Herbert F. *The Race To Oblivion: A Participant's View of the Arm Race.* New York: Simon & Schuster, 1970.

AFRICA

Clough, Michael. *Free at Last? U.S. Policy toward Africa and the End of the Cold War.* New York: Council on Foreign Relations Press, 1992.

———. ed. *Reassessing the Soviet Challenge in Africa.* Berkeley: Institute of International Studies, University of California, 1986.

Emerson, Rupert. *Africa and United States Policy*. Englewood Cliffs, NJ: Prentice-Hall, 1967.

Gleijeses, Piero. *Conflicting Missions: Havana, Washington and Africa, 1959–1976*. Chapel Hill: University of North Carolina Press, 2002.

Klinghoffer, Arthur J. *The Angolan War: A Study in Soviet Policy in the Third World*. Boulder, CO: Westview Press, 1980.

Korn, David A. *Ethiopia, the United States and the Soviet Union*. Carbondale: Southern Illinois University Press, 1986.

Laïdi, Zadi. *The Superpowers and Africa: The Constraints of a Rivalry, 1960–1990*. Trans. by Patricia Baudoin. Chicago, IL: University of Chicago Press, 1990.

Lefebvre, Jeffrey A. *Arms for the Horn: U.S. Policy in Ethiopia and Somalia, 1953–1991*. Pittsburgh, PA: University of Pittsburgh Press, 1993.

Marte, Fred. *Political Cycles in International Relations: The Cold War and Africa, 1945–1990*. Amsterdam: VU University Press, 1994.

Noer, Thomas J. *Cold War and Black Liberation: The United States and White Rule in Africa, 1948–1968*. Columbia: University of Missouri Press, 1985.

Smock, David R., ed. *Making War and Waging Peace: Foreign Intervention in Africa*. Washington, DC: United States Institute of Peace Press, 1993.

Windrich, Elaine. *The Cold War Guerrilla: Jonas Savimbi, the U.S. Media and the Angolan War*. New York: Greenwood Press, 1992.

ASIA

Carter, Carolle J. *Mission to Yenan: American Liaison with the Chinese Communists, 1944–1947*. Lexington: University Press of Kentucky, 1997.

Chang, Gordon H. *Friends and Enemies: The United States, China and the Soviet Union, 1948–1972*. Stanford, CA: Stanford University Press, 1990.

Chen Jian. *China's Road to the Korean War: The Making of the Sino-American Confrontation*. New York: Columbia University Press, 1994.

Cumings, Bruce. *The Origins of the Korean War, 1947 to 1950*. 2 vols. Princeton, NJ: Princeton University Press, 1990.

Foot, Rosemary. *The Practice of Power: US Relations with China since 1949*. New York: Oxford University Press, 1995.

———. *A Substitute for Victory: The Politics of Peacemaking at the Korean Armistice Talks*. Ithaca, NY: Cornell University Press, 1990.

———. *The Wrong War: American Policy and the Dimensions of the Korean Conflict, 1950–1953*. Ithaca, NY: Cornell University Press, 1985.

Gallicchio, Marc S. *The Cold War Begins in Asia: American East Asian Policy and the Fall of the Japanese Empire*. New York: Columbia University Press, 1988.

Goncharov, Sergei N., John W. Lewis, and Xue Litai. *Uncertain Partners: Stalin, Mao and the Korean War*. Stanford, CA: Stanford University Press, 1993.

Guangqiu Xu. *Congress and the U.S.-China Relationship, 1949–1979*. Akron, OH: University of Akron Press, 2007.

Iriye, Akira, *The Cold War in Asia: A Historical Introduction*. Englewood Cliffs, NJ: Prentice-Hall, 1974.

Kaufman, Victor S. *Confronting Communism: U.S. and British Policies toward China.* Columbia: University of Missouri Press, 2001.

Keith, Ronald C. *The Diplomacy of Zhou Enlai.* New York: St. Martin's Press, 1989.

Larkin, Bruce D. *China and Africa, 1949–1970: The Foreign Policy of the People's Republic of China.* Berkeley: University of California Press, 1971.

Lee, Steven Hugh. *Outposts of Empire: Korea, Vietnam, and the Origins of the Cold War in Asia, 1949–1954.* Montreal: McGill-Queen's University Press, 1995.

Lerner, Mitchell B. *The Pueblo Incident: A Spy Ship and the Failure of American Foreign Policy.* Lawrence: University Press of Kansas, 2002.

McIntyre, W. David. *Background to the Anzus Pact: Policy-making, Strategy and Diplomacy, 1945–55.* New York: St. Martin's Press, 1995.

McMahon, Robert J. *The Cold War on the Periphery: The United States, India and Pakistan.* New York: Columbia University Press, 1994.

Mayers, David. *Cracking the Monolith: U.S. Policy against the Sino-Soviet Alliance, 1949–1955.* Baton Rouge: Louisiana State University Press, 1986.

Peck, James. *Washington's China: The National Security World, the Cold War and the Origin of Globalism.* Amherst: University of Massachusetts Press, 2006.

Yafeng Xia. *Negotiating with the Enemy: U.S.-China Talks during the Cold War, 1949–1972.* Bloomington: Indiana University Press, 2006.

Yu, Maochun. *OSS in China: Prelude to Cold War.* New Haven: Yale University Press, 1996.

Zhang, Shu Guang. *Mao's Military Romanticism: China and the Korean War, 1950–1953.* Lawrence: University Press of Kansas, 1995.

Southeast Asia

Anderson, David L. *Trapped by Success: The Eisenhower Administration and Vietnam, 1953–1961.* New York: Columbia University Press, 1991.

Berman, Larry. *No Peace, No Honor: Nixon, Kissinger, and Betrayal in Vietnam.* New York: Free Press, 2001.

Halberstam, David. *The Best and the Brightest.* New York: Random House, 1972.

Herring, George C. *America's Longest War: The United States and Vietnam, 1950–1975.* 4th ed. New York: John Wiley, 1979.

Kaplan, Lawrence S., Denise Artaud, and Mark R. Rubin, eds. *Dien Bien Phu and the Crisis of Franco-American Relations, 1954–1955.* Wilmington, DE: SR Books, 1990.

Kiernan, Ben. *The Pol Pot Regime: Race, Power, and Genocide in Cambodia Under the Khmer Rouge, 1975–1979.* New Haven, CT: Yale University Press, 2008.

Levine, Alan J. *The United States and the Struggle for Southeast Asia, 1945–1975.* Westport, CT: Praeger, 1995.

Logevall, Fredrik. *Choosing War: The Lost Chance for Peace and the Escalation of the War in Vietnam.* Berkeley: University of California Press, 1999.

McNamara, Robert S., James G. Blight, and Robert K. Brigham. *Argument Without End: In Search of Answers to the Vietnam Tragedy*. New York: Public Affairs, 1999.

Moise, Edwin E. *Tonkin Gulf and the Escalation of the Vietnam War*. Chapel Hill: University of North Carolina Press, 1996.

O'Balance, Edgar. Malaya: The Communist Insurgent War, 1948–60. Hamden, CT: Archon Books, 1966.

Preston, Andrew. *The War Council: McGeorge Bundy, the NSC and Vietnam*. Cambridge, MA: Harvard University Press, 2006.

Ross, Robert S. *Negotiating Cooperation: The United States and China, 1969–1989*. Stanford, CA: Stanford University Press, 1995.

Schulzinger, Robert D. *A. Time for Peace: The Legacy of the Vietnam War*. New York: Oxford University Press, 2006.

———. *A Time for War: The United States and Vietnam, 1941–1975*. New York: Oxford University Press, 1997.

Shawcross, William. *Sideshow: Kissinger, Nixon and the Destruction of Cambodia*. New York: Simon & Schuster, 1979.

Statler, Kathryn C. *Replacing France: The Origins of American Intervention in Vietnam*. Lexington: University Press of Kentucky, 2007.

Stevenson, William, and Monika Jensen-Stevenson. *Kiss the Boys Goodbye: How the United States Betrayed Its Own POW's in Vietnam*. New York: Plume, 1991.

Tucker, Nancy Berkopf, ed. *China Confidential: American Diplomats and Sino-American Relations, 1943–1996*. New York: Columbia University Press, 2001.

U.S. Department of Defense. *The Pentagon Papers: The Defense Department History of United States Decision Making on Vietnam. The Senator Gravel Edition*. 5 vols. Boston: Beacon, 1971–1972.

CARIBBEAN, SOUTH AND CENTRAL AMERICA

Adams, Jan S. *A Foreign Policy in Transition: Moscow's Retreat from Central America and the Caribbean, 1985–1992*. Durham, NC: Duke University Press, 1992.

Adkin, Mark. *Urgent Fury: The Battle for Grenada*. Lexington, MA: D. C. Heath, 1989.

Arnson, Cynthia. *Crossroads: Congress, the Reagan Administration, and Central America*. New York: Pantheon, 1989.

Beck, Robert J. *The Grenada Invasion*. Boulder, CO: Westview Press, 1993.

Burrowes, Reynold A. *Revolution and Rescue in Grenada: An Account of the U.S.-Caribbean Invasion*. New York: Greenwood Press, 1988.

Byrne, Hugh. *El Salvador's Civil War*. Boulder, CO: Lynne Rienner, 1996.

Cockbury, Leslie. *Out of Control: The Story of the Reagan Administration's Secret War in Nicaragua*. New York: Atlantic Monthly Press, 1987.

Coleman, Kenneth M., and George C. Herring, Jr., eds. *Understanding the Central American Crisis: Sources of Conflict, U.S. Policy and Options for Peace*. Wilmington, DE: SR Books, 1991.

Cullather, Nick. *Secret History: The CIA's Classified History of Its Operations in Guatemala, 1952–1954*. Stanford, CA: Stanford University Press, 2000.

Immerman, Richard H. *The CIA in Guatemala: The Foreign Policy of Intervention*. Austin: University of Texas Press, 1982.

Kagan, Robert. *A Twilight Struggle: American Power and Nicaragua, 1977–1990*. New York: Free Press, 1996.

Konbluh, Peter. *Nicaragua: The Price of Intervention*. Washington, DC: Institute for Policy Studies, 1987.

Landau, Saul. *The Guerrilla Wars of Central America: Nicaragua, El Salvador and Guatemala*. New York: St. Martin's Press, 1993.

LeoGrande, William M. *Our Own Backyard: The United States and Central America, 1977–1992*. Chapel Hill: University of North Carolina Press, 1998.

Miller, Nicola. *Soviet Relations with Latin America, 1959–1987*. New York: Cambridge University Press, 1989.

Moreno, Dario. *U.S. Policy in Central America: The Endless Debate*. Miami: Florida International University Press, 1990.

O'Shaughnessy, Hugh. *Grenada: An Eyewitness Account of the U.S. Invasion and the Caribbean History That Provoked It*. New York: Dodd, Mead, 1984.

Pavlov, Yuri I. *The Soviet-Cuban Alliance, 1959–1991*. New Brunswick, NJ: Transaction Publishers, 1994.

Rabe, Stephen G. *Eisenhower and Latin America: The Foreign Policy of Anticommunism*. Chapel Hill: University of North Carolina Press, 1988.

Scheman, L. Ronald, ed. *The Alliance for Progress: A Retrospective*. New York: Praeger, 1988.

Sigmund, Paul E. *The Overthrow of Allende and the Politics of Chile, 1964–1976*. Pittsburgh, PA: University of Pittsburgh Press, 1977.

Walker, Thomas W., ed. *Reagan versus the Sandinistas: The Undeclared War on Nicaragua*. Boulder, CO: Westview, 1987.

Wiarda, Howard J., and Mark Falcoff, et al, eds. *The Communist Challenge in the Caribbean and Central America*. Washington, DC: American Enterprise Institute for Public Policy Research, 1987.

Cuban Missile Crisis

Allison, Graham T., and Philip D. Zelikow. *Essence of Decision: Explaining the Cuban Missile Crisis*. 2nd ed. New York: Longman, 1999.

Blight, James G., and David A. Welch. *On the Brink: Americans and Soviets Reexamine the Cuban Missile Crisis*. New York: Hill & Wang, 1989.

Dobbs, Michael. *One Minute to Midnight: Kennedy, Khrushchev, and Castro on the Brink of Nuclear War*. New York: Knopf, 2008.

Frankel, Max. *High Noon in the Cold War: Kennedy, Khrushchev, and the Cuban Missile Crisis*. New York: Ballantine Books, 2004.

Fursenko, Alexsandr, and Timothy Naftali. *"One Hell of a Gamble": Khrushchev, Castro, and Kennedy, 1958–1964, The Secret History of the Cuban Missile Crisis*. New York: Norton, 1997.

Gribkov, Anatoli I., and William Y. Smith. *Operation Anadyr: U.S. and Soviet Generals Recount the Cuban Missile Crisis*. Berlin: Verlags-GMBH, 1994.

Kennedy, Robert. *Thirteen Days: A Memoir of the Cuban Missile Crisis*. New York: Norton, 1969.

Nathan, James A., ed. *The Cuban Missile Crisis Revisited*. New York: St. Martin's, 1992.

EUROPE

Allin, Dana H. *Cold War Illusions: America, Europe and Soviet Power, 1969–1989*. New York: St. Martin's Press, 1995.

Blinken, Antony J. *Ally versus Ally: America, Europe and the Siberian Pipeline Crisis*. New York: Praeger, 1987.

Boll, Michael M. *Cold War in the Balkans: American Foreign Policy and the Emergence of Communist Bulgaria, 1943–1947*. Lexington: University of Press of Kentucky, 1984.

Breyman, Steve. *Why Movements Matter: The West German Peace Movement and U.S. Arms Control Policy*. Albany: State University of New York Press, 2001.

Costigliola, Frank C. *France and the United States: The Cold Alliance since World War II*. New York: Twayne Publishers, 1992

Creswell, Michael. *A Question of Balance: How France and the United States Created Cold War Europe*. Cambridge MA: Harvard University Press, 2006.

Goldstein, Walter, ed. *Reagan's Leadership and the Atlantic Alliance: Views from Europe and America*. Washington, DC: Pergamon-Brassey, 1986.

Heuser, Beatrice. *Western "Containment" Policies in the Cold War: The Yugoslavia Case, 1948–53*. New York: Routledge, 1989.

Hitchcock, William I. *France Restored: Cold War Diplomacy and the Quest for Leadership in Europe, 1944–1954*. Chapel Hill: University of North Carolina Press, 1998.

Hofmann, Arne. *The Emergence of Détente in Europe: Brandt, Kennedy and the Formation of Ostpolitik*. New York: Routledge, 2007.

Iatrides, John O. *Revolt in Athens: The Greek Communist "Second Round," 1944–1945*. Princeton, NJ: Princeton University Press, 1972.

Kirk, Roger, and Mircea Raceanu. *Romania versus the United States: Diplomacy of the Absurd, 1985–1989*. New York: St. Martin's Press, 1994.

Kovrig, Bennett. *Of Walls and Bridges: The United States and Eastern Europe*. New York: New York University Press, 1991.

Krebs, Ronald P. *Dueling Visions: U.S. Strategy toward Eastern Europe under Eisenhower*. College Station: Texas A & M University Press, 2001.

Large, David Clay. *Germans to the Front: West German Rearmament in the Adenauer Era*. Chapel Hill: University of North Carolina Press, 1996.

Mawby, Spencer. *Containing Germany: Britain and the Arming of the Federal Republic*. New York: St. Martin's Press, 1999.

Rabel, Roberto G. *Between East and West: Trieste, the United States and the Cold War, 1941–1954*. Durham, NC: Duke University Press, 1988.

Ruddy, T. Michael, ed. *Charting an Independent Course: Finland's Place in the Cold War and in U.S. Foreign Policy*. Claremont, CA: Regina Books, 1998.

Smith, Arthur L., Jr. *Churchill's German Army: Wartime Strategy and Cold War Politics, 1943–1947*. Beverly Hills, CA: Sage Publications, 1977.

Sodaro, Michael J. *Moscow, Germany and the West from Khrushchev to Gorbachev.* Ithaca, NY: Cornell University Press, 1990.

Zelikow, Philip D., and Condoleezza Rice. *Germany Unified and Europe Transformed: A Study in Statecraft.* Cambridge, MA: Harvard University Press, 1995.

Berlin Crises

Morris, Eric. *Blockade: Berlin and the Cold War.* New York: Stein and Day, 1973.

Schick, Jack M. *The Berlin Crisis, 1958–1962.* Philadelphia: University of Pennsylvania Press, 1971.

Tusa, Ann, and John Tusa. *The Berlin Airlift.* New York: Atheneum, 1988.

MIDDLE EAST AND SOUTH ASIA

Alteras, Isaac. *Eisenhower and Israel: U.S.-Israeli Relations, 1953–1960.* Gainesville: University Press of Florida, 1993.

Barrett, Roby C. *The Greater Middle East and the Cold War: US Foreign Policy under Eisenhower and Kennedy.* London: I.B. Tauris, 2007.

Bradsher, Henry. *Afghan Communism and Soviet Intervention.* New York: Oxford University Press, 1999.

Brands, H. W. *Into the Labyrinth: The United States and the Middle East, 1945–1993.* New York: McGraw-Hill, 1994.

Brune, Lester H. *America and the Iraqi Crisis, 1990–1992.* Claremont, CA: Regina Books, 1993.

Fain, W. Taylor. *American Ascendance and British Retreat in the Persian Gulf Region.* New York: Palgrave Macmillan, 2008.

Freedman, Lawrence, and Efraim Karsh. *The Gulf Conflict, 1990–1991: Diplomacy and War in the New World Order.* Princeton, NJ: Princeton University Press, 1993.

Freedman, Robert O. *Moscow and the Middle East: Soviet Policy since the Invasion of Afghanistan.* New York: Cambridge University Press, 1991.

Gasiorowski, Mark J. *U.S. Foreign Policy and the Shah: Building a Client State in Iran.* Ithaca, NY: Cornell University Press, 1991.

Gerges, Fawaz A. *Superpowers and the Middle East: Regional and International Politics, 1955–1967.* Boulder, CO: Westview Press, 1994.

Golan, Galia. *Soviet Policies in the Middle East: From World War Two to Gorbachev.* New York: Cambridge University Press, 1990.

Hiro, Dilip, *The Longest War: The Iran-Iraq Military Conflict.* New York: Routledge, 1991.

Jentleson, Bruce W. *With Friends Like These: Reagan, Bush and Saddam, 1982–1990.* New York: W.W.Norton, 1994.

Kakar, M. Hassan. *Afghanistan: The Soviet Invasion and the Afghan Response.* Berkeley: University of California Press, 1995.

Keddie, Nikki R., and Mark J. Gasiorowski, eds. *Neither East nor West: Iran, the Soviet Union and the United States.* New Haven, CT: Yale University Press, 1990.

Kyle, Keith. *Suez*. New York: St. Martin's Press, 1991.

Lesch, David W., ed. *The Middle East and the United States: A Historical and Political Reassessment*. 2nd ed. Boulder, CO: Westview Presss, 1999.

Persson, Magnus. *Great Britain, the United States and the Security of the Middle East: The Formation of the Baghdad Pact*. Lund, Sweden: Lund University Press, 1998.

Quandt, William B. *Peace Process: American Diplomacy and the Arab-Israeli Conflict since 1967*. Washington, DC: Brookings Institution Press, 2001.

Sick, Gary. *All Fall Down: America's Tragic Encounter with Iran*. New York: Random House, 1985.

Simpson, Bradley R. *Economists with Guns: Authoritarian Development and U.S.-Indonesian Relations, 1960–1968*. Stanford, CA: Stanford University Press, 2008.

Smolansky, Oles M., and Bettie M. Smolansky. *The USSR and Iraq: The Soviet Quest for Influence*. Durham, NC: Duke University Press, 1991.

REFERENCE WORKS

Beisner, Robert L., ed. *American Foreign Relations since 1600: A Guide to Literature*. 2 vols. 2nd ed. Santa Barbara, CA: ABC-Clio, 2003.

Brune, Lester, comp., and Richard Dean Burns, ed. *Chronology of the Cold War, 1917–1992*. New York: Routledge, 2006.

Bulletins of the International Cold War History Project from no. 1, Spring 1991, to 2004 and beyond. Washington, DC: Woodrow Wilson Center.

Burns, Richard Dean, ed. *Encyclopedia of Arms Control and Disarmament*. 3 vols. New York: Scribners, 1993.

Burns, Richard Dean, and Joseph M. Siracusa. *Historical Dictionary of the Kennedy-Johnson Era*. Lanham, MD: Scarecrow, 2007.

DeConde, Alexander, Richard Dean Burns, Fredrik Logevall, and Louise Ketz, eds. *Encyclopedia of American Foreign Policy*. 3 vols. 2nd. ed. New York: Scribners, 20002.

Geyer, David C., and Douglas E. Selvage, eds; Edward C. Keefer, supervisory ed. *Soviet-American Relations: The Détente Years, 1969–1972*. Washington, DC: GPO, 2007.

Higham, Robin, and Donald J. Mrozek, eds. *A Guide to the Sources of United States Military History* and Supplements I to IV. Hamden, CT: Archon Books, 1975 to 1998.

Siracusa, Joseph M. *Presidential Profiles: The Kennedy Years*. New York: Facts on File, 2004.

U.S. Department of State. *[Papers Relating to the] Foreign Relations of the United States*. Washington, DC: GPO, 1861–.

U.S. President. *Public Papers of the Presidents of the United States*. Washington, DC: GPO, 1961–.

Index

Abbott, George M., 160
Able Archer, 466–67
ABMs (antiballistic missiles), 309–10, 351, 468, 470. *See also* Nuclear weapons
Abrams, Creighton, 334
Acheson, Dean: Acheson-Lilienthal Report, 136–37; on Berlin, 264; China White Paper, 168, 169, 170, 189, 234; Chinese Civil War, 166, 169; on Chinese-Soviet relations, 187–88, 196–97, 198, 199; Cuban missile crisis, 268; Cyprus crisis, 302; on European economy, 106, 122, 123–24; on Formosa, 178, 190, 191; on French declarations of independence, 298; on Greece and Turkey, 1–2, 111, 112, 115, 116, 118, 119–20; on Indochina, 159–60, 192–93, 204; Kennan's thesis criticized by, 232; on Korea War, 194, 200; McCarthy's Communist conspiracy in Washington, 189; on NATO, 135–36, 137–38, 232; negotiation from strength concept, 186, 214–15, 283, 519; Nehru's advice to, 176; on nuclear weapons

program, 183; photograph, 338; on Soviet atomic weapons, 181; on stabilization of Europe, 150, 151–52; on Truman's national defense policy, 184–87; on U.S. policy in Asia, 9, 11, 179, 180, 204; on Vietnam, 157, 189, 190, 337
Achilles, Theodore, 134
Act of Bogota, 258–59
Adenauer, Konrad, 221, 264, 276–77
Aeroflot, 434, 464, 466
Afghanistan: Carter years, 419, 433–37; Reagan years, 441, 448, 455, 475; Soviet withdrawal from, 448, 478–79, 485, 490; UN intervention, 456
Africa: Carter years, 427; Eisenhower years, 246; Ford years, 389; Reagan years, 455, 456–57. *See also specific countries by name*
Agency for International Development, 294
Akhromeyev, Marshal Sergei, 498
Alamogordo, New Mexico, 86, 92
Alanbrooke, Lord, 34
Albania, 6, 112
Algeria, 274, 432

Allen, George V., 233
Allen, Richard V., 423–24, 443
Allende, Salvador, 373, 391
Alliance for Progress, 258–59, 291–92, 294
Allied Control Council, 81
Allied Reparations Commission, 80
Allies. *See* the Grand Alliance
Allison, Graham T., 270
Allison, John M., 197
Alperovitz, Gar, 88
Alsop, Joseph, 1, 110, 167, 247
Alsop, Stewart, 1, 110, 167, 364
America in Vietnam (Lewy), 380
American Security Council, 306–7
Amin, Hafizullah, 433
Amin, Idi, 421–22
Anami, Korechika, 84, 88, 89
Anders, Wladyslaw, 28
Anderson, Rudolph, Jr., 270
Andropov, Yuri, 466, 470, 478
Anglo-American Nassau agreement, 276
Anglo-Iranian Oil Company, 110–11, 242
Anglo-Soviet pact (1942), 31
Angola, 389–90, 404, 427, 448, 456, 475
Annam. *See* Bao Dai regime
Antiballistic missiles (ABMs), 309–10, 351, 468, 470. *See also* Nuclear weapons
Anti-Communist elite, 209, 210, 253, 513
Antiwar movement, 336, 339, 361–62
ANZUS pact, 205
Ap Bac, 323–24
Arab-Israeli conflict. *See* Middle East
Arafat, Yasser, 408–9, 458. *See also* PLO (Palestine Liberation Organization)
Arbatov, Georgi, 399
Arbenz Guzman, Jacobo, 243
Arciszewski, Franciszek, 56, 57, 63
Argentina, 259, 403, 476
Armas, Carlos Castillo, 243

Arms control and disarmament: ABM agreements, 468, 470; anxieties of antinuclear movements, 467–70; Atoms for Peace program, 256; Bush administration, 507–10; Carter administration, 385, 416–20, 491; Chemical Weapons Convention (CWC), 508; Eisenhower administration, 256–57; European peace movement of 1981, 468; Geneva Summit (1985), 479–81; Helsinki Accord (1975), 468; Intermediate Nuclear Force (INF) Treaty, 482–84, 483f; Johnson administration, 307–10, 350; Kennedy administration, 256–58, 307; Moscow test-ban negotiations, 281; Nuclear Non-Proliferation Treaty (1968), 468; Paris summit (1990), 511; Peaceful Nuclear Explosions Treaty, 508; post-Cuban missile crisis relations, 280–82; Rapacki Plan for a nuclear-free zone, 232–33; Reagan administration, 445–47, 507, 509–10; Reykjavik Summit, 481–82; SALT treaties, 350–53, 384–85, 386f, 416–20, 468, 480, 481; Star Wars (SDI/Strategic Defense Initiative), 470, 480, 481–82, 523; Strategic Arms Reduction Talks (START), 469, 484, 508–10; Test Ban pact, 468; Threshold Test Ban Treaty, 508; "throw-weight" issue, 350–51; Treaty on Conventional Forces in Europe (CFE), 508–9; U.S. Arms Control and Disarmament Agency, 258, 307; verification, 482, 508, 510; Washington summit (1987), 482–84. *See also* Nuclear weapons
Arnold, Henry H., 83, 90
Aron, Raymond, 29, 398
ARVN (South Vietnamese) forces, 323–24
Aslund, Anders, 503
Aswan Dam, 224, 245

Atcheson, George, 161
Atlantic Charter, 17–18, 18f, 20–22, 27, 31, 32–33, 49–50, 55
Atomic Energy Act, 274
Atomic Energy Commission, 136–37, 183, 256–57, 307
Atomic weapons: Acheson-Lilienthal Report, 136–37; Manhattan Project, 84–93; military prepared-ness vs. Soviet expansionism, 136; Moscow Conference, 136; Soviet atomic project expanded as a result of, 92–93; Soviet's first atomic explosion, 181; UN Atomic Energy Commission, 136–37, 183, 256–57, 307. See also Nuclear weapons
Atoms for Peace program, 256
Attlee, Clement, 79, 99, 199
Austin, Warren R., 165f, 204
Australia, 205, 241
Austria, 35, 222, 256–57
Axis powers. See World War II
Azerbaijan, 97–98, 104, 110–11

Backfire, 418
Badoglio, Pietro, 29
Baghdad Pact, 245
Bahktiar, Shapour, 429
Bahr, Egon, 419
Baker, James A., III, 487, 490–91, 497, 500, 510
Balaguer, Joaquin, 294
Balance of power in Europe, 515
Baldwin, Hanson W., 45, 75, 83, 90, 182, 204, 220, 553 n.100
Balkan states: Axis powers, 42; Churchill-Stalin agreements, 46–47, 49, 60, 66; Soviet postwar expansion plans, 42–46; Soviet suc-cesses on the Eastern Front, 57–58; TOLSTOY meeting, 46, 50–51, 66; U.S. on Soviet influence, 60, 65, 77–78, 98–99; Yalta Conference, 65. See also specific nations by name
Ball, George: on Bosch, 293; Cyprus crisis, 302; photograph, 338;

quarantine of Cuba, 268; on Vietnam War, 327–28, 330, 331, 332, 360, 378
Ball, Howard, 513
Baltic states, Soviet annexation of, 20, 21–22, 27, 36. See also specific states by name
Bangkok, 315–16, 317
Bao Dai regime, 156, 157, 159, 176, 189–90, 192–93
Bard, Ralph, 85
Barker, Elisabeth, 539–40 n.40
Barnes, Michael, 471
Barr, Egan, 354
Baruch, Bernard, 137, 257
Basic Principles of Relations agreement, 351–52
Batista, Fulgencio, 244
Bay of Pigs, 260–61, 272
Beaverbrook, Lord, 542 n.68
Begin, Menachem, 409–13, 411–13, 412f, 457
Belgium, 96. See also Benelux countries
Belgrade Conference, 400
Benelux countries, 131, 133
Benes, Eduard, 33, 132
Bennett, W. Tapley, 294
Benton, William, 102–3
Bergsten, C. Fred, 523, 524
Beria, Lavrenti, 216
Berlin, Germany. See Germany
Berlin Conference (1954), 218
Berlinguer, Enrico, 375–76
Bermuda Conference, 217, 236–37
Bern, Switzerland, 69
Bernstein, Barton, 552 n.89
Berry, Burton Y., 51
Beschloss, Michael, 487, 509
Bessarabia, 20, 42
Bevin, Ernest: Chinese government recognized by, 168; on consolidation of Western Europe, 131, 133; on economic aid to Germany, 123; on France's postwar vulnerability to Communism, 121;

Iranian crisis, 104; the Marshall Plan, 125, 126–27; Treaty of Dunkirk, 123; U.S.-British relations, 99
Bidault, Georges, 125, 126–27, 131
Biddle, A. J. Drexel, Jr., 532 n.25
Bierut, Boleslaw, 48, 78
Big Four Foreign Ministers conference, 222–23, 223f
Biological weapons, 349, 499
Bipolarism, 286–87
Bishop, Maurice, 453
Blackett, P. M. S., 91
The Black Sea Straits, 100
Blum, Leon, 121
Blumenthal, Michael, 414
Bohlen, Charles: on Chinese-Soviet relations, 196, 267; on Kennan's Long Telegram, 102; on Korean War, 194; the Marshall Plan, 124, 562 n.37; Moscow Conference, 123; on NSC 68, 185; Paris Foreign Ministers Conference, 107; on Poland, 39, 58, 71; on postwar Soviet threat, 58, 95, 101–2, 185; on Stalin-Byrnes meeting, 98, 555 n.7
Bohr, Niels, 84
Boland Amendment, 452
Bolivia, 403
Bollaert, Emile, 158
Bolshevik revolution, 2
Bonn economic summit, 475, 498
Bosch, Juan, 293–94
Boun Oum, 314
Bovin, Alexander, 466
Bowles, Chester, 253, 260, 322
Bowman, Isaiah, 531 n.9
Bradley, Bill, 500
Bradley, Omar, 194, 330, 338f
Brandenburg Gate, 264
Brandon, Henry, 347
Brands, H. W., 291
Brandt, Willy, 348, 354
Brazil, 259, 403
Bretton Woods Conference, 53–54
Brezhnev, Leonid: Afghanistan, 433;

Brezhnev Doctrine, 311–12, 377, 474, 493–94, 496; détente policy, 351–53; economy and trade, 420–21; on human rights, 399, 400; military expenditures, 420; Moscow Summit, 351–53; new directions of Soviet policy outlined by, 348; Nixon-Kissinger approach to the Soviet Union, described, 343–49; photograph, 352, 386; Prague Spring, 310, 344, 350, 377; SALT II treaty, 384–85, 386f, 418–19; on U.S-China relations, 408; Washington summit (1973), 353; Western Sovietology on, 420–21
Bridge building policy, 306–8
Bridges, Styles, 167
Broder, David, 437, 500
Brookings Institution, 408–9
Browder, Earl, 145
Brown, Harold, 414, 416, 430, 438
Bruce, David K. E., 362–63
Brussels Pact, 133, 134, 135
Bryan, William Jennings, 391
Brzezinski, Zbigniew: on Afghanistan, 433–34; China policy, 406–7, 408; on criticism of Carter policies, 438, 439; on human rights, 401; Middle East issues, 413; Nicaraguan crisis, 426; on nuclear weapons, 416; personality and disposition, 414, 432; photograph, 394; on Soviet-Cuban involvement in Africa, 427–28; the Trilateral Commission, 414; on Vietnam War, 416
Buchanan, Patrick, 422, 501
Buckley, William, 422, 483, 484
Buhite, Russell D., 543 n.86
Bulganin, Nikolay, 223, 223f, 224
Bulgaria: economy, 496; London Foreign Ministers Conference, 93; postwar reconstruction, 43–44, 46–47, 79, 93–94, 106–7, 109; Soviet occupation, 45, 57, 61, 65, 66; Stalin-Byrnes meeting, 98–99;

TOLSTOY meeting, 46; U.S. recognition policy, 79, 93–94, 95, 98–99, 100; World War II, 42
Bulletin (U.S. State Department), 204
Bullitt, William C., 4, 36, 113, 234
Bunche, Ralph, 302
Bundy, McGeorge: anti-Communist Establishment represented by, 253; Cuban missile crisis, 266, 268, 271; on nuclear weapons, 273, 298, 468; Panama Canal, 293; photograph, 338; on U.S.-Soviet cooperation, 307; Vietnam War, 326, 328
Bundy, William, 326, 327, 338f
Bunker, Ellsworth, 294, 334, 336, 363
Burdick, Usher, 201
Burma, 155, 227
Burnham, James R., 578 n.1
Bush, George H. W., 487–512; on 1990 trip to Eastern Europe, 511–12; arms control negotiations, 507–10; as CIA director, 422–23; on German reunification, 497, 497–99; on Gorbachev's intentions, 488–89; Houston economic summit, 523–24; on Lebanon, 460; on Lithuanian independence, 505–6; Malta summit (1989), 507, 509f, 510; national security and foreign policy team, 487–88, 490–92; Paris summit (1990), 511; personality and foreign policy experiences, 487; personal relationship with Gorbachev, 488–89; photographs of, 446, 488, 509; on Reagan-Gorbachev relationship, 489; on redefining U.S. policy following fall of Communism, 524; response to disintegrating Soviet empire, 499–502, 511; transition from Reagan administration to, 487–93; as vice president, 487, 488–89; Washington summit (1990), 506–8, 511
Bush, Vannevar, 85
Business Week, 436

Butcher, Harry C., 45
Butterworth, Walton, 159
Byelorussia, 62
Byrnes, James F.: on Chinese-Soviet relations, 86–87; on German economy, 107; Iranian crisis, 104; on Japan, 89; London Foreign Ministers Conference, 93–94; Manhattan Project, 85, 92; Moscow Conference, 136; Paris Foreign Ministers Conference, 106–7, 108; peace treaties negotiated by, 106–7, 108–9; photograph, 39; Potsdam, 79–80; on Soviet concern for friendly bordering states, 95; Stalin meeting, 98–99, 100–101; on Stalin's Moscow address of February 9, 101; Trieste agreement, 108; on Turkey, 104–6; Wallace's speech, 108; Yalta Conference, 64, 66, 67

Cabot, John Moors, 9, 168–69, 243
Cadogan, Alexander, 63
Caffery, Jefferson, 121, 141, 157
Cairo Conference, 161, 178
Cambodia, 159, 240, 360, 362, 366, 378–82, 401–2, 475
Camp David accords, 411–13, 412f
Canada, 134, 135
Captive Nations Week, 264
Caribbean, 292–94, 453–54, 479
Carlucci, Frank, 482, 485
Carpentier, Marcel, 193
Carter, Jimmy, 393–440; advisors, 395, 414, 416, 423–24; Afghanistan, 433–37; Africa, 426–28; American Jewish lobby, 430–31; on America's declining world role, 402–3; arms control negotiations, 385, 416–20, 491; on Berlin Wall, 401; burgeoning fears of Soviet power and expansionism, 421–24; Cambodia, 401–2; Camp David accords, 411–13, 412f; Carter Doctrine, 434–36, 455; China, 405–8; criticism of Carter policies, 437–

40; Cuba, 404, 426–28; on domino theory, 416, 434; East Asia, 404–8; embargo on grain shipments to the Soviet Union, 448; European issues, 414–15, 435–36; Helsinki Accord (1975), 399, 400; on human rights, 395–401, 403–4, 443–44; Iranian revolution, 428–32; Latin America, 403, 449, 450; Middle East, 408–13; military expenditures, 420; Moscow Olympics, 434; neoconservatives vs., 421–23, 431, 443; nuclear weapons, 416–20; oil issues, 436–37; Panama, 293, 425–26; photograph, 394; separation from past concerns with Cold War issues, 393–95, 403, 414, 415–16; South Korea, 405; Taiwan, 405, 406–8; Team B report, 423, 424, 443; Trilateral Commission, 393–95, 414; U.S.-Soviet relations, 399–401, 408, 415–20; on Vietnam, 404–5, 416
Casablanca Conference, 19
Casey, William, 451, 458, 469–70, 473, 474
Castro, Fidel, 244, 259–62, 292, 404. *See also* Cuba
Castro, Raul, 265
Catholic journals, 103
Catholic World, 103
Cavert, Samuel McCrea, 90
Central America during the Reagan years, 449–52, 461–64, 471–77, 479. *See also specific countries by name*
Central Intelligence Agency (CIA): Arbenz's overthrow, 242, 243; creation of, 128; Iran, 242; powerful bureaucratic interests developed vs. Soviet threat, 208
Ce Soir, 213
Ceylon, 155
CFE (Treaty on Conventional Forces in Europe), 508–9
Chamorro, Pedro Joaquin, 426
Charmley, John, 534 n.48

Chemical weapons, 349, 499, 508
Chemical Weapons Convention (CWC), 508
Chenault, Claire L., 90
Cheney, Dick, 475, 487, 490, 510
Chennault, Anna, 340
Chernenko, Konstantin, 478, 488
Chernyaev, Anatoly, 493
Cheysson, Claude, 462
Chiang Kai-shek, 161–71; China Lobby, 166–67, 170, 189, 233–36, 296, 297–98; China White Paper, 167–70; Chinese Civil War, 160–71, 178; Eisenhower's China policy, 233–38; McCarthy's support for, 188–89; overview of Chinese challenge, 517–19; Roosevelt on, 156
Chiang Kai-shek, Madame, 165
Chiari, Roberto, 293
Chicago Tribune, 63, 132
Chile, 373, 391, 403
China: Carter years, 405–8; China Lobby, 166–67, 170, 189, 233–36, 296, 297–98; China White Paper, 167–70, 189; Chinese-Soviet Pact, 161; Chinese Titoism, 172–73; civil war, 160–71, 178; Committee of One Million, 298; Democratic Republic of Vietnam recognized by, 189; diplomatic defeat of U.S. by, 188; Eisenhower's China policy, 233–38; Ford's trip to, 392; France on U.S. China policy, 298, 299; independence from Soviet influence, 344; India attacked by, 279; international recognition of Communist-led government, 168–71, 176; Johnson administration on, 295–98; Kennedy years, 278–80; Korean War, 195–98, 198f, 204, 239; lack of evidence of Soviet influence over, 191–92; Lin Piao's call for revolutionary action, 296–97; nationalism, 191–92; Nixon years, 298, 355–58, 371–72, 405; nuclear weapons, 295–96, 308; offshore

islands, 235–37, 238; overview of Chinese challenge, 517–19; perceptions of Soviet influence over, 9–10, 11, 163–69, 170–73, 179, 198–200, 203, 233–37; ping-pong diplomacy, 356–58; Roosevelt's plans for Four Policemen, 55; Shanghai Communiqué, 404, 406–7; Single Integrated Operational Plan (SIOP-62) directed towards, 254–55; Sino-Soviet alliance during Khrushchev years, 238; Sino-Soviet rift during Kennedy years, 278–79, 278–80; Sino-Soviet Treaty of Friendship and Alliance, 88, 187–88; Taiwan Relations Act, 407–8, 455; UN membership status, 279; UN Security Council membership, 200; U.S. nonrecognition policy, 198, 200, 204, 237–38, 278–79, 296, 357; U.S. perimeter defense policy in East Asia, 179–80; U.S. recognition of exiled Republic of China, 171; White Paper, 9, 189; WWII, 160–61; Yalta Conference, 86. *See also* Chiang Kai-shek; Formosa (Taiwan); Mao Zedong

The China Lobby in American Politics (Koen), 167

Chou En-lai, 162f, 356, 357f, 406

Christian Century, 90

Christopher, Warren, 396, 432

Church, Frank, 426, 472

Churchill, Winston S.: on Allied policy of unconditional surrender, 19, 35; Atlantic Charter, 17–18, 18f, 20–22, 31, 49–50; on the Balkans, 43–44, 45, 46–47, 66; Bermuda summit meeting, 217; on Bern meeting, 70; Bretton Woods Conference, 54; Churchill-Stalin agreements, 46–47, 49, 51; Declaration of Four Nations, 33, 50; dependence on U.S., 30–31, 67, 68–69, 74–75, 76–77; distrust of Soviet intentions, 31, 32, 44, 67, 74–75, 76–77, 104; on Dulles, 215; Eisenhower and, 215, 222; Fulton College speech, 104, 105f; on German reparations, 80; on Kremlin-instituted Polish regimes, 28; on Lend-Lease agreements, 99–100; Malenkov regime and, 215–16, 222; Manhattan Project, 84, 86; Molotov meeting, 222; on Montreux Convention revisions, 47; Munich syndrome, 67; on Nazi invasion of the U.S.S.R., 20; on OVERLORD's success, 44; photographs of, 18, 60, 79, 105; on Polish-Soviet relations, 33, 37, 38–40, 41, 47–48, 56, 66–67, 81; Potsdam, 78–79, 81–82, 86; Quadrant Conference, 29, 33; Roosevelt and, 31, 34; on second front, 24–25; on stabilization of Europe, 151; succession, 79; Teheran Conference, 34–35, 47–48; TOLSTOY meeting, 46, 50–51, 66; Yalta Conference, 59–69

CIA (Central Intelligence Agency): Arbenz's overthrow, 242, 243; creation of, 128; Iran, 242; powerful bureaucratic interests developed vs. Soviet threat, 208

Ciechanowski, Jan, 33–34, 37–38

Clark, Mark, 44–45, 306–7

Clark, William, 458, 469–70

Clark Amendment, 475

Clark Kerr, Archibald, 41, 60, 68, 69

Clay, Lucius D., 107, 123, 138, 139

Clayton, William, 85, 116, 119, 124, 125

Clementin, J. R., 192

Clifford, Clark, 4, 113, 119, 120, 283–84, 331, 337, 339

Clifford-Elsey report, 113, 119

Cline, Ray S., 266, 271

Coalition for a Democratic Majority, 421

Cohen, Benjamin V., 121, 124

Cohen, Warren, 302

Colby, William, 524

Cold War, overview: absence of vital conflicting interests, 515; abstract ideals of universal freedom and justice, 519; the Chinese challenge, 517–19; Cold War as rhetorical exercise, 6, 513–14; failure to dominate the behavior and outlook of international society, 521–23; fear of Soviet military aggression at root of anti-Communist sentiments, 3–5; lack of unity in world Communism, 285–86; nuclear arms race, 519–21; redefining U.S. policy following fall of Communism, 524–26; U.S. refusal to recognize Soviet sphere of influence, 516–17; vagueness of doctrines, 516

Cold War elite, 209, 210, 253, 513

Colombia, 243–44

Colonial powers, 155, 174–75

Colville, John Rupert, 217

Cominform (Communist Information Bureau), 127, 142

Commentary, 421, 422, 431, 443

Committee of One Million, 298

Committee on the Present Danger (CPD), 202, 423–24, 443

Common Market, 272, 275, 276, 277–78, 354

The Commonweal, 90, 103

Communications revolution, 494

Communism, overview: Cold War as rhetorical exercise, 513–14; fear of Soviet military aggression at root of anti-Communist sentiments, 3–5; lack of unity in world Communism, 285–86; post-WWII movements, 96; Red Scare (1919–1920), 2–3, 513; Red Scare (1950–1954), 3–5

Communist Information Bureau (Cominform), 127, 142

Communist Polish Workers Party, 534 n.47

Compton, Karl, 85, 91

Conant, James B., 85, 202

Conference of the Committee on Disarmament, 349

Conference Security and Cooperation in Europe, 498

Connally, Tom, 106, 120, 166

Containment policy: described, 5, 206–7; during Eisenhower years, 217, 314; evaluation of, 210, 344; international support for U.S. policy, 208; Kennan's "X" article, 128–30; Korean War, 194–98, 200, 202, 204; Truman administration, 215

CORONET invasion, 83

Corporatism, 133

Costa Rica, 451, 477

Council of Foreign Ministers, 79

Council on Hemispheric Affairs, 404

Counterinsurgency in Vietnam, 321–23

Cowles, John, 338f

CPD (Committee on the Present Danger), 202, 423–24, 443

Crimea Conference, 67

Cripps, Stafford, 22

Crisis hot line communication system, 281, 305

Cronkite, Walter, 337

Cuba: Alliance for Progress as counterweight to, 292; Bay of Pigs, 260–61, 272; Castro, 244, 259–62, 292, 404; Cuban missile crisis, 265–72, 271f, 281, 354; Cuban troops in Angola, 389, 404, 427–28, 456; Eisenhower years, 244, 259; Grenada invasion, 453–54, 479; human rights, 404; Johnson administration, 292–95; Kennedy years, 259–62, 265–72, 268–71, 294–95; Kissinger's bipartisan commission report on U.S. policy, 471; the Mann doctrine, 292; Operation Mongoose, 261, 272; Panamanian challenge, 293; Salvadoran rebels supplied arms by, 450, 451, 475; Soviet specialists in

Cuba, 265, 426–27; Soviet submarines within Cuban water, 348; Standing Group on Cuba, 292; U-2 pilot shot down by SAM missile, 270

Cunhal, Alvaro, 376–77

Curzon line, 21, 26, 33, 35, 37–38, 47–48, 59

CWC (Chemical Weapons Convention), 508

Cyprus, 302–3, 372–75

Czechoslovakia, 33; Communist government, 96, 132–34, 228; Czech arms procured by Soviets for Arab states, 224; economy, 494–95; human rights, 399, 400; nationalism, 306; Palach, Jan, 493; postwar reconstruction (WWII), 43; Prague Spring, 310, 344, 350, 377; withdrawal of Soviet power from, 496; World War II, 57, 70, 132

Daily Mail, 462

Daily Mirror, 213

Daily Telegraph, 462

Dallek, Robert, 291

Dalton, Hugh, 99

Daoud, Mohammed, 433

Davies, John Paton, 161, 173–74

Davies, Joseph E., 26–27, 32, 72, 77

Dayan, Moshe, 411

D-Day, 35, 44

Dead Ends (Hoffman), 465

Dean, Acheson, 338f

Dean, Gordon, 183, 349–50

Deane, John, 32

The Decision to Use the Bomb (Alperovitz), 88

Declaration of Four Nations, 32–34, 50

Declaration of San Jose, 244

Declaration on Liberated Europe, 61

Decter, Midge, 421

Defense Reorganization message, 219

De Gaspari, Alcide, 141

de Gaulle, Charles: anti–Anglo-Saxon crusade, 276–78; Berlin crisis 1961, 264; Franco-German treaty, 276–77; on Indochina, 156; on Kennedy's Grand Design for Europe, 274; Kennedy warned about Vietnam by, 322; on nuclear weapons, 275, 276; Paris Summit, 231; resignation (1946), 121; Soviet relations with, 306; U.S. China policy challenged by, 298, 299; withdrawal from NATO, 298, 299–300. *See also* France

DeKlerk, F. W., 614 n.31

Delauer, Richard, 470

Democratic Convention in Chicago, 339

Deng Xiaoping, 406–7, 408

Denmark, 135

Derian, Patricia, 396

Der Spiegel, 462

De Telegraaf, 463

Détente, 343–92; arms control negotiations, 350–53, 384–85, 386f; failure of, 387–90, 435–36; Ford administration, 375–78, 378–82, 385–87, 415; Johnson administration, 306, 310; Middle East diplomacy, 368–69, 382–83; Moscow Summit (1974), 384–85; Nixon administration, 343–49, 354–55, 371–72, 383; reintroduced by Reagan and Gorbachev, 484–85, 487, 523; Vietnam War, 358–67, 378, 382

Deutscher, Isaac, 34–35

Dewey, Thomas, 3, 199

Diem, Ngo Dinh, 240, 241–42, 313, 318, 323–24, 324. *See also* Vietnam/Vietnam War

Dillon, Douglas, 266, 268

Disarmament. *See* Arms control and disarmament

Dobrynin, Anatoly, 269, 270, 351, 389–90, 477–78

Doctrines, vagueness of, 516

Dodd, Christopher, 471–72
Dodd, Thomas J., 12–13, 335
Dole, Robert J., 407, 499–500
Dominican Republic, 293–94, 310–11
Domino theory: applied to Vietnam
    War, 11–13, 313, 318, 331–32, 335,
    341, 381–82, 416; Carter on, 416,
    434; as rhetorical extension to the
    doctrine of anti-Communism, 6;
    Truman Doctrine and, 118
Dong, Pham Van, 332
Donovan, Robert J., 234–35
Douglas, Lewis, 126, 133
Douglas, Paul, 298
Douglas, William O., 101
Dower, John W., 552 n.87
Draper Committee report, 177
Drucker, Peter, 525
Duarte, Napoleon, 450
Dubcek, Alexander, 310, 377
Du Bois, Coert, 174
Dulles, John Foster: Bermuda summit
    meeting, 217, 236–37; on China,
    11, 170, 234, 235, 236–37;
    Churchill on, 215; on Communism
    vs. nationalism, 233; domino
    theory, 241; faith in moral force
    in a morally divided world, 212–13;
    on German reunification, 218;
    Japanese peace treaty, 205; on
    Khrushchev, 226–27; on Korean
    War, 197, 239–40; on liberation
    policies, 213–14, 216; Middle
    Eastern policy, 245; on nuclear
    weapons, 219–20, 274; photograph,
    220; "A Policy of Boldness," 212;
    prior to becoming secretary of state,
    210–11; resignation due to illness,
    229; Rhee meeting, 194; Rusk vs.,
    253; San Francisco speech, 237; on
    Soviet emphasis on coexistence,
    225; on Soviet expansionism, 4,
    112–13, 203; Tenth Inter-American
    Conference, 243; vs. Truman's
    containment policies, 211; on Viet-
    nam War, 240

Dumbarton Oaks, 55, 62, 73
Dunn, James C., 50, 64, 73, 141
Durbrow, Elbridge, 26–27, 50, 101,
    102, 318
Duverger, Maurice, 248

Eagleburger, Lawrence S., 381,
    450–51
Eagleton, Clyde, 108
Eagleton, Thomas F., 373
East Asia, 153–80; Carter years, 401,
    404–8; Chinese Civil War, 160–71,
    178; decolonization, 155–60;
    Elysee Agreements, 159; Johnson
    administration, 295–98; Melby-
    Erskine mission, 193; nationalism,
    154–55, 157–58, 174–76, 191–92;
    Roosevelt on France's empire in
    Southeast Asia, 155–56; Soviet
    exploitation of local Communist-
    led revolutions, 9–10; Truman
    administration, 194; U.S. air and
    naval bases, 82–83, 84, 153, 176,
    178, 179–80, 191, 205. See also
    specific countries and regions by name
Easter offensive, 364
East European Bank, 501
East German Democratic Republic.
    See Germany
Eastland, James O., 120
Eban, Abba, 304
Eberstadt Committee, 182
Economic Cooperation
    Administration (ECA), 133
Economist (London), 100, 155, 197,
    213, 481
Economy and trade: Act of Bogota,
    259; aid to Italy to combat
    communism, 141–42; Alliance for
    Progress, 258–59, 291–92, 294;
    Berlin blockade, 6–7, 138–39,
    140f; Bretton Woods Conference,
    53–54; British postwar economic
    conditions, 106, 115; Byrnes's
    advocacy of a unified German
    economy, 107–8; Common Market,

272, 275, 276, 277–78, 354; embargo vs. Nicaragua, 475; European Economic Community (EEC), 275; financial and military assistance to Greece and Turkey, 115, 116, 118, 120, 142; Foreign Assistance Acts of 1974 and 1976, 395–96; Houston economic summit, 523–24; Hungary's postwar economic conditions, 66; Japan's postwar economic recovery, 176–77; Kennedy's Grand Design for Europe, 272–73; Lend-Lease agreements, 31–32, 54, 99–100; Marshall Plan, 6, 124–27, 130–31, 132, 133; massive deficits during the 1980s, 523; Nixon-Kissinger approach to the Soviet Union, described, 349; postwar economic conditions in France, 124, 126–27; post-WWII aid to Germany, 122–23; post-WWII aid to Soviets, 50; price of Communist rule, 494–95; Soviet post-Cold War economy, 495–96, 499–501, 502–3, 504; State-War-Navy Coordinating Committee (SWNCC), 122; U.S. military aid program for Indochina, 190; U.S. sanctions vs. U.S.S.R., 463–64, 466; U.S.'s economic superiority, 7, 143–44, 524; U.S. State Department on Europe's postwar economic recovery, 121–22. See also Military expenditures

Ecuador, 403

EDC (European Defense Community), 203, 221

Eden, Anthony: Allied Control Commission for Bulgaria, 46–47; Bermuda summit meeting, 217; Churchill's note to regarding Soviet advance to the Balkans, 43; containment policy, 217; Declaration of Four Nations, 33; on dismemberment of Germany, 52; European Defense Community (EDC), 221;

on Manhattan Project, 86; photograph, 223; on Poland issue, 39, 67, 68; Roosevelt meeting, 27; Stalin meeting, 21–22, 23–24, 26

EEC (European Economic Community), 275, 475

Egypt: Aswan Dam project, 245; Carter years, 409–13; Egyptian-Israeli agreements, 382–83, 430–31, 457; Reagan years, 455, 457; response to Eisenhower Doctrine on the Middle East, 246; Soviet aid to, 224, 245, 246, 303; Straits of Tiran blockade, 303–5; Suez Canal, 245; United Arab Republic, 246; U.S. economic assistance to, 302; Yom Kippur War, 368. See also Nasser, Gamal Abdel

Eighteen Nation Disarmament Committee (ENDC), 258, 307

Eisenhower, David, 44

Eisenhower, Dwight D., 211–49; Africa, 246; Allied occupation of Berlin, 77; arms control negotiations, 256–57; Atoms for Peace program, 256; Berlin crisis, 229–31, 258; Bermuda summit meeting, 217; China policy, 233–35, 233–38, 236–38; Churchill and, 45–46, 215, 222; containment policy, 217, 314; covert program in East Europe, 580 n.59; Cuba, 259; Defense Reorganization message, 219; definition of policy toward the U.S.S.R., 214–15; domino theory, 12, 240–41; Eisenhower Doctrine, 245–46; farewell address, 248; Formosa Resolution, 235–36; Geneva Conference, 222–23, 223f; on German reunification, 218; Hungarian revolt, 226–28, 506; International Atomic Energy Agency, 256–57; at Italy's surrender ceremony, 29–30; Khrushchev's campaign for summit with Western powers, 228–31; Khrushchev's tour

of the U.S., 230; Korean War, 10–11, 238–40; Laotian crisis, 314; Latin America, 242, 243–44; liberation policies, 212–16, 227–28, 233–34, 238; on Malenkov regime, 215; Middle Eastern policy, 242, 244–46, 300, 303, 305; military expenditures, 218–19; missile gap, 247–48; NATO, 202, 221; New Look doctrine, 219–21; nuclear weapons, 219–21, 236–37, 248, 254–55, 256–57; Open Skies plan, 257; Paris Summit, 231; persistent avoidance of accommodation, 218, 231–33; photographs of, 220, 223; "A Policy of Boldness" (Dulles), 212; Polish uprising, 226; on Potsdam, 214; Project Solarium, 216–17; public perceptions of, 246–47; on Soviet concern for friendly bordering states, 95; on Soviet dominance during WWII, 70; Soviet emphasis on coexistence, 225–26; State of the Union (1953), 214; tour of Europe, Asia, and North Africa, 230; on Turkey, 115; U-2 American spy plane downed by U.S.S.R., 231; Vietnam, 240–42, 317–18; on world Communism, 233, 242; on Yalta Conference, 214
Elegant, Robert, 381, 438
Ellsberg, Daniel, 320, 325
El Salvador, 403, 449–52, 462–63, 471, 473
Elsey, George, 4, 113
Ely, Paul, 240
Elysee Agreements, 159
ENDC (Eighteen Nation Disarmament Committee), 258, 307
England. See Great Britain
Enhanced radiation (ER) weapons, 415
Enola Gay, 88
ER (enhanced radiation) weapons, 415
ERP (European Recovery Program), 130

Erskine, Graves B., 193
Eshkol, Levi, 301
Estonia, 20, 504, 505. See also Baltic states
Ethiopia, 427, 428
Ethridge, Mark, 94
Eurocommunism, 375–78, 415
European Advisory Commission, 52
European Defense Community (EDC), 203, 221
European Economic Community (EEC), 275, 475
European Reconstruction Conference, 126–27
European Recovery Program (ERP), 130
ExComm, 266–70, 271f

Fairbank, John K., 192
Faisal, King, 369
Falin, Valentin, 498
Falk, Richard A., 369
Fall of Communism: Berlin Wall, 499, 511, 526; Bush response to disintegrating Soviet empire, 499–502; communications revolution, 494; critics of Gorbachev's reforms, 506–7; declaration of end of Cold War, 509, 511, 523; deficiencies in the Soviet economy revealed by, 502, 504; economic hardships following, 495–96, 500–501; German reunification, 497–99; Gorbachev's political reforms, 503–4; growing irrelevance of the Soviet political structure prior to, 503; implications, 495–96; nationalist demands for self-determination, 504–6; Paris summit (1990), 511; redefining U.S. policy following, 524–26; U.S. economic assistance to U.S.S.R. following, 500–501; Washington summit (1990), 506–8, 511
Fallows, James, 446
The Fate of the Earth (Schell), 467–68

Faure, Edgar, 223f
Federal Bureau of Investigation (FBI), 208
Federal Civil Defense Administration, 199
Federal Republic of Germany. *See* Germany
Fermi, Enrico, 85
Fighting to the Finish (Sigal), 88
Final Settlement treaty, 499
Finland: Karelian Peninsula, 20, 21; London Foreign Ministers Conference, 93; Soviet influence, 57, 96, 222, 344; U.S. recognition of, 79; WWII treaty negotiations, 79, 93–94, 106–7, 109
Fischer, John, 75
Fitzgerald, Frances, 442
Fitzwater, Marlin, 506
Fontaine, Andre, 463
Foote, Walter A., 174
Ford, Gerald: 1976 Republican presidential primaries, 385, 388; Angola, 389–90; China trip, 392; Eurocommunism, 375–78, 415; Helskinki Final Act, 385–87; Kissinger as secretary of state, 370, 372; photograph, 386; SALT II treaty, 384–85, 386f, 416; Vietnam War, 378–82
Foreign Assistance Acts of 1974 and 1976, 395–96
Foreign Ministers Conference, 128
Formosa (Taiwan): Cairo and Potsdam conferences on, 178; Carter years, 405, 406–8; Eisenhower administration, 234–37; Johnson administration on, 295, 297; Kennedy years, 279; Reagan years, 455; Taiwan Relations Act, 407–8, 455; during Truman administration, 171, 178–80, 190–91, 194, 195–96
Forrestal, James V., 2, 73, 102, 111, 112, 119, 141
Fosdick, Raymond, 160

Foster, John Watson, 210
Four Power Pact, 122
Fowler, Henry, 338f
France, 134–35; Algeria, 274; Bevin's consolidation of Western Europe proposal, 131, 133; Brussels Pact, 133; Communist Party and Communist influences, 6, 96, 116, 121, 141, 375–76, 377, 415; on creation of West German republic, 138; European Defense Community (EDC), 221; Geneva Conference, 223, 223f; on German reunification, 497; on Germany's postwar economic and financial structure, 107, 122–23; Indochina, 155, 155–60, 157–60, 193, 240, 240–41; Indonesia, 174; Iran-Iraq War, 476; Lebanon commitment, 458–59; Maginot line, 484; Marshall Plan, 126; nationalism, 306; during Nixon administration, 354, 355; Normandy invasion, 35, 44; nuclear weapons, 274–75; postwar economic conditions, 124, 126; postwar return to active role in European politics, 61; the Ruhr, Rhineland, and Saar claimed by, 107, 126–27; Southeast Asia policy, 314; Southeast Asia Treaty Organization (SEATO), 241; Suez Canal, 245; Treaty of Dunkirk, 123; U.S. Mutual Defense Assistance Agreement, 204; Vietnam, 189–90, 192–93, 205, 207, 320, 322; on West Germany's NATO status, 202–3; World War II, 45; on Yamal natural gas pipeline, 461–62. *See also specific leaders by name*
Franck, James, 85–86
Franco, Francisco, 375
Franco-German treaty, 276–77
Frankfurter Rundschau, 476
Fraser, Donald, 395
Free global markets, 53

Fulbright, J. William, 197, 253, 262, 282, 286, 302, 372
Fuller, J. F. C., 35
Fulton College speech, 104, 105f

Gaither Commission Report, 247–48
Galacian oil districts, 35
Galbraith, John Kenneth, 253, 322, 336
Galvin, Robert, 306–7
Garthoff, Raymond, 377–78, 424
Gaspari, Elio, 403
Gates, Robert, 387, 487–88, 490, 494, 523
Gates, Tom, 254
Gemayel, Amin, 459–60
Geneva Conference, 222–23, 223f, 240, 257, 315, 316–17
Genscher, Hans-Dietrich, 462, 463, 497
George, Walter, 118
George II, King of Greece, 60
Georgia, 504
Gephardt, Richard, 500, 501
Germany: Allied Control Council, 80–81; Berlin blockade, 6–7, 138–39; Berlin Conference (1954), 218; Berlin crisis, 229–31, 258, 264–65; Berlin Wall, 401, 499, 511, 526; Brandenburg Gate, 264; Brandt's *Ostpolitik*, 348; creation of East German Democratic Republic, 141; creation of Federal Republic of Germany, 7, 138, 139, 141; East German riots (1953), 216; economy, 107–8, 122–23, 494–95, 523; enhanced radiation (ER) weapons, 415; Final Settlement treaty, 499; Four Power Pact, 122; Franco-German treaty, 276–77; human rights in East Germany, 400; Kennedy's visit to West Germany, 277–78; the Marshall Plan, 126–27, 130; nationalism within Western Germany, 306; NATO membership, 202–3, 221–22, 277,

497, 498, 499; Nazi-Soviet Pact (1939), 20, 49, 504; postwar dismemberment of, 52–53, 61, 77, 80–81, 94–95; postwar industrial material and equipment removed by Soviet Union, 80–81, 107; post-WWI German "stab in the back" theory of an undefeated German army, 19; Potsdam on, 80–81; reunification, 218, 497–99, 511; Soviet assault on Berlin during WWII, 70; Soviet-German WWII clash on the Eastern Front, 17, 20, 70, 74; Soviet recognition of West Germany, 222; West Berlin, 229–31; West Germany on nuclear weapons, 467; West Germany on Soviet occupied Afghanistan, 436; West Germany on U.S. sanctions vs. U.S.S.R., 464; WWII cost of war, 145; WWII reparations, 61–62, 80–81, 107, 130, 498; Yalta Conference on, 80; Yamal natural gas pipeline, 460–62. *See also specific leaders by name*; World War II
Ghana, 246
Gidi pass, 382
Gilpatric, Roswell, 267, 268, 308, 330
Ginzburg, Aleksandr, 400–401
Glass, Andrew J., 481
Glazer, Nathan, 421, 422
GLCMs (ground-launched cruise missiles), 468–69
Godoy, Hector Garcia, 294
Goebbels, Joseph, 28–29
Golan Heights, 368–69, 383, 457
Goldberg, Arthur, 296, 400
Goldwater, Barry, 252, 291, 407, 473
Goodpaster, Andrew, 583 n.97
Gorbachev, Mikhail: Afghanistan, 478–79, 485, 490; arms control, 507, 507–10; Brezhnev Doctrine repealed by, 493–94, 496; Bush on Gorbachev's intentions, 488–89; Bush on Reagan-Gorbachev relationship, 489; criticism of, 506–7;

détente reintroduced by, 484–85, 487, 523; determination of, 523; Geneva Summit (1985), 479–81; on German reunification, 497, 497–99; Malta summit (1989), 507, 509f, 510; Moscow Summit (1988), 484–85; myth of Soviet Union's status as a superpower, 464–65; neoconservatives on, 487, 489–90; on nuclear weapons, 479–81; Paris summit (1990), 511; photographs of, 483, 509; Reagan's first meeting with, 443; Reykjavik Summit, 481–82; rise to power and "new thinking," 478–79, 503–6; on Soviet military power and global expansionism (overview), 441–45; UN address, 485; U.S. economic assistance to U.S.S.R. following fall of Communism, 500–501; Washington summit (1987), 482–84; Washington summit (1990), 506–8, 511; withdrawal of Soviet power from East Europe, 493–94. *See also* Fall of Communism

Gorbachev, Raisa, 478, 482

Gottwald, Klement, 132

Graham, Daniel, 243, 443

Graham, Frank, 174

The Grand Alliance, 17–36, 97–114; Allied policy of unconditional surrender, 19, 35; Atlantic Charter, 17–18, 18f, 20–22, 27, 31, 32–33, 49–50; Clifford-Elsey report, 113; Declaration of Four Nations, 32–34, 50; distrust between, 19–20; end of, 97; Greece issue, 111–12; intensely antagonist diplomacy, 109–10; Iran issue, 104, 110–11; London Foreign Ministers Conference, 93–94, 97, 130–31, 138; Long Telegram, 101, 102–3, 113; Normandy invasion, 35; OVERLORD, 29; Paris Foreign Ministers Conference, 97–114; on Polish-Soviet relations, 25–29, 33–

34, 35–36; Quadrant Conference (Quebec), 29, 30, 33; Sicily invasion, 29; Soviet danger defined in ideological terms, 114; Stalin's Moscow address of February 9, 102–3; structuring of a bipolar world, 109, 112–13; summer and autumn of 1946, 109–10; Teheran Conference, 34–36, 38, 44; Trident Conference, 29; Turkish issue, 97, 104–6, 111; UN as successor to, 97

Grass, Gunter, 497

Great Britain: Anglo-Iranian Oil Company, 242; Anglo-Soviet pact (1942), 31; Baghdad Pact, 245; on Bevin's consolidation of Western Europe proposal, 131; Common Market, 275, 276, 277–78; decolonization by, 155; Geneva Conference, 223, 223f; on German reunification, 497; Laotian crisis, 314, 315; Middle East, 104, 245, 476; nuclear weapons, 275–76, 298; Poland's exiled government in London during WWII, 25–28, 33, 37–41, 48, 56–60, 63, 66–67, 534 n.47; postwar economic conditions, 54, 115; postwar reconstruction plans, 22–24, 99–100, 125–26; postwar U.S.-British relations, 32, 74–75, 76, 99, 106; on Reagan-Gorbachev relationship, 481; reliance on U.S. during war, 30–31; Southeast Asia Treaty Organization (SEATO), 241; Suez Canal, 245; termination of financial assistance to Greece, 115; on U.S. defense of Formosa, 574 n.56; on U.S. sanctions vs. U.S.S.R., 464; Yamal natural gas pipeline, 461–62. *See also specific leaders by name*

Great Depression, 143

The Great Globe Itself (Bullitt), 113

Great Mistakes of the War (Baldwin), 90

Great Society program, 333

Greece: civil war, 142–43; Communist

Party and Communist influences, 60–61, 98, 111–12; Cyprus, 302–3, 372–75; Munich syndrome, 5–6; postwar reconstruction (WWII), 43–44, 60–61; potential for postwar British-Soviet clash in, 43–44, 45–46; termination of British financial assistance to, 115; TOLSTOY meeting, 46, 66; U.S. financial and military assistance to, 115, 116, 118, 120, 142; World War II, 42, 43, 45–46

Green, Theodore F., 236

Greenfield, Meg, 402, 465

Grenada, 404, 453–54, 479

Grew, Joseph C., 71, 73, 84

Griffin, Robert Allen, 190

Gromyko, Andrei A.: Afghanistan, 433; arms control negotiations, 137, 281, 350; Big Four Foreign Ministers conference, 229–30; Cuba, 267, 427; denied landing rights by NJ and NY, 466; human rights issues, 399; Poland issue, 38

Ground-launched cruise missiles (GLCMs), 468–69

Groves, Leslie, 84–85

Groza regime, 65, 99

Guatemala, 242, 243, 403, 449, 451

Guidelines for a Cold War Victory (National Strategy Committee), 306–7

Gulf of Tonkin, 326, 327

Habib, Philip C., 457–58, 603 n.107

The Hague Round-Table Conference of August–October 1949, 175

Haig, Alexander M., Jr., 441–42, 444, 446f, 447, 448–49, 451, 455, 457

Hailsham, Lord, 281

Haiphong Harbor, 364

Halberstam, David, 253, 318, 323–24

Halifax, Lord, 43

Halle, Louis J., 290

Halperin, Morton, 346

Harkins, Paul, 323, 324, 325

Harmon, H. R., 137

Harriman, W. Averell: appointment, 32; on China, 86, 280; Economic Cooperation Administration (ECA), 133; Laotian crisis, 316–17; Polish-Soviet relations, 38, 40, 41–42, 47–48, 60, 68, 69; post-Cuban missile crisis relations, 281; on Reagan's ideological crusade vs. Soviet Union, 466–67; on Soviet economic weaknesses, 50; on Soviet emphasis on coexistence, 225; on Soviet occupation of Eastern Europe, 50–51, 61, 66, 70–72, 77, 78, 132; on Stalin-Byrnes meeting, 98, 555 n.7; Teheran Conference, 46, 49; Vietnam War, 337, 338

Hatta, Mohammad, 174

Havel, Vaclav, 501

Hawkins, Robert B., Jr., 503

Hearst, William Randolph, 167

Heath, Edward, 354

Held, Robert, 462–63

Helskinki Final Act, 385–87, 399, 400, 468

Henderson, Loy, 73, 98, 112, 116, 119, 188, 569 n.86

Herter, Christian, 106, 229–30

Hickerson, John D., 58, 61, 95, 121, 132, 134

Hill, Frances R., 601 n.71

Hilldring, John, 122

Hilsman, Roger W., 280, 295

Hiranuma, Kiichiro, 87

Hirohito, Emperor, 83–84, 87, 88, 89. *See also* Japan

Hiroshima, 88, 89–91, 93. *See also* Manhattan Project

Ho Chi Minh, 156–60; Chinese and Soviet recognition of Democratic Republic of Vietnam, 189; France defeated by, 240–41; infinite resiliency and determination of, 332; Nehru on, 176; Rolling Thunder vs., 328–29; socialist doctrine, 155; U.S. support for French policy, 189–90, 192–93, 207. *See also* Indochina; Vietnam/ Vietnam War

Hoffman, Paul G., 133

Hoffmann, Stanley, 465, 526

Hofstadter, Richard, 442

Hogan, Michael J., 133

Honduras, 403, 449, 451, 452, 471, 473

Honshu invasion, 83

Hoopes, Townsend, 337

Hoover, Herbert, 2, 133, 178, 201

Hopkins, Harry, 20, 30, 36, 62, 64, 77–78

Hornbeck, Stanley, 174

Horn of Africa, 427

Houston economic summit, 523–24

Howard, Roy, 167

Howe, Geoffrey, 454

Huang Zhen, 405

Hughes, Thomas L., 286

Hull, Cordell: on Allied policy of unconditional surrender, 35; Declaration of Four Nations, 32–34; on dismemberment of Germany, 52; on economic aid to Britain, 54; on expansionist ambitions of Axis powers, 19; on free global markets, 53; Harrison's warning about Soviets to, 49; on occupation of Rumania and Greece, 43–44; photograph, 39; resignation, 54–55; on U.S. policy of postponing territorial and political decisions until end of WWII, 18, 27; U.S. response to the Soviet Union's territorial ambitions formulated by, 21, 23, 24, 33–34

Human rights, 390–91, 395–401, 403–4, 417, 484

Humphrey, George M., 218, 221

Humphrey, Hubert H., 257, 336, 339

Hungary: Kadar regime, 228; London Foreign Ministers Conference, 93; nationalism, 306; NATO membership status, 497; post-Cold War economy, 495–96; post-WWII Communist party membership, 96; post-WWII economic conditions, 66; Soviet occupation, 35, 61, 65–66, 344; TOLSTOY meeting, 46; uprising during Eisenhower years, 226–28, 506; U.S. recognition of, 79, 94; withdrawal of Soviet power from, 493–94, 496; World War II, 42, 57; WWII treaty negotiations, 79, 93–94, 106–7, 109

Hunter, Holland, 502

Hurley, Patrick J., 161, 162f, 170

Husak, Gustav, 310

Hussein, Saddam, 476

Huston, Cloyce K., 95

Huyser, Robert, 429

Hydrogen bombs, 182–83, 186, 219

Hyland, William, 387

ICBMs, 247–48, 351, 353, 469

Iceland, 135

Ideological expansionism: fear of Soviet military aggression at root of anti-Communist sentiments, 3–5, 114, 514–15; nationalism as universal defense vs. Soviet threat, 514–15; NSC on, 8

Ikle, Fred. C., 443

Il Messaggero, 462

Inchon landing, 196f, 197

Incirlik Air Base, 374

India, 155, 279, 574 n.56. *See also* Nehru, Jawaharlal

Indian Ocean, 436

Indochina: French colonial war, 155–58, 189–90, 192–93, 204–5, 207, 240–41; Geneva Conference on, 240–41; Melby-Erskine mission, 193; U.S. fear of Communist movements under Moscow's command, 9, 10–11; U.S. military aid to, 190, 194, 205. *See also* Ho Chi Minh

Indonesia, 174–75, 227, 296

INF (Intermediate Nuclear Force)
    Treaty, 469, 482–84, 483f
Information barrier, 494
Ingersoll, Robert, 395
Institute of U.S.A. and Canadian
    Studies, 399
Inter-American Commission on
    Human Rights, 397
Inter-American Court of Human
    Rights, 404
Inter-American Development Bank,
    294
Interdivisional Committee on Russia
    and Poland, 50
Intermediate Nuclear Force (INF)
    Treaty, 469, 482–84, 483f
International Atomic Energy Agency,
    256–57
International Monetary Fund, 54, 496
Iran: Azerbaijani settlement, 97–98,
    104, 110–11; Baghdad Pact, 245;
    Carter years, 398, 428; CIA
    authorized by Eisenhower to
    overthrow government, 242;
    Iran-Contra affair, 476–77 (see also
    Nicaragua); Iranian crisis of March
    1946, 104; Iran-Iraq War, 476–77;
    London Foreign Ministers
    Conference on, 97; oil, 110–11;
    postwar reconstruction (WWII), 1,
    2, 97–98, 100–101, 245
Iraq, 245, 430, 455, 476–77
Isaacs, Harold, 153
Isolationism, 120–21, 201
Israel: American Jewish lobby, 304,
    410, 430–31; Carter years, 408–13,
    412f; Egyptian-Israeli agreements,
    382–83, 430–31, 457; Eisenhower
    years, 303, 305; Johnson adminis-
    tration, 300–302, 303–5; Kissing-
    er's shuttle diplomacy, 368–69; the
    Liberty attacked by, 305; nuclear
    weapons, 456; Osirak, 455; Reagan
    years, 455, 457–60; refusal to sup-
    port U.S. Vietnam policies, 303;
    Six-Day War (1967), 304–5, 367;

UN Resolution 242 on, 305, 368,
    409, 411, 431; Western Tripartite
    Declaration, 245; Yom Kippur
    War, 367, 383. *See also* Middle East
Italy: Communist Party, 96, 141–42,
    375–76, 377, 415; economic
    disintegration during Ford years,
    375; Lebanon commitment, 458–
    59; London Foreign Ministers
    Conference, 93; Mussolini
    overthrow, 29; NATO, 135;
    postwar reconstruction (WWII),
    46; potential for postwar British-
    Soviet clash in, 43; Trieste, 107,
    108; World War II, 29–30, 42, 79,
    93–94, 106–7, 108–9; on Yamal
    natural gas pipeline, 461–62
Iwo Jima, 82

Jackson, Henry, 12, 247–48, 335, 353,
    384–85, 387
Japan: China's wartime successes vs.,
    160–61; constitution, 154; Draper
    Committee report, 177; economy
    and trade, 176–77, 523; expanding
    influence during Nixon years,
    358; Indochina's independence
    declared following surrender,
    156–57; Indonesian nationalists
    supported by, 174; Iwo Jima, 82–83;
    Kissinger's diplomacy towards,
    383–84; Manhattan Project, 84–93;
    Potsdam Declaration on, 87–89,
    154; Quadrant Conference, 82; San
    Francisco Conference, 153; U.S.
    bases, 153, 177, 178, 179, 205; U.S.
    peace treaty with (1951), 205; U.S.
    post-surrender policies, 153–54;
    World War II, 82–93. *See also*
    East Asia
Jarring, Gunnar, 305
Javits, Jacob, 400–401
Jebb, Gladwyn, 63
Jenkins, Peter, 383
Jenner, William, 167, 234
Jessup, Philip C., 179, 188

Jewish emigration from the Soviet
Union, 384–85, 387
Jewish lobby, 304, 410, 430–31
Johnson, Louis, 182
Johnson, Lyndon B., 283–311;
Alliance for Progress, 292, 294;
arms control negotiations, 307–10,
350; bipolar East-West arms
buildup, 287–90; bridge building
policy, 306–8; China policy, 295–
98, 299; Cuba, 292–95; détente,
306, 310; Dominican Republic,
310–11; domino theory applied to
Vietnam War by, 12; East Asian
affairs, 295–98; on French declarations of independence, 298, 299–
300; Great Society program, 333;
Guidelines for a Cold War Victory
(National Strategy Committee),
306–7; Kennedy's assassination,
290, 291; Latin America, 292–95;
Middle East, 300–305, 367; on
missile gap (as senator), 247–48;
negotiation from strength concept,
283–84; nuclear weapons, 287–89,
291, 298–99, 306–10; overview of
policies, 290–91; Panamanian challenge, 293; photographs of, 297,
338; Prague Spring, 310; on relationship between domestic and foreign policy, 290; rocking chair
doctrine, 294, 311; space program,
308; State of the Union (1964), 307;
State of the Union (1967), 310
Johnson administration: Vietnam
War, 325–41; antiwar movement,
336, 339; avoidance of defeat
strategy, 332–33; Baltimore
address, 332; Camp David meeting,
331; casualties, 333–34; costs of,
333, 596 n.93; criticism of, 335–37;
Gulf of Tonkin, 326, 327; Hanoi's
goals, 332; increased military
spending, 307–8; international
opinion on, 595 n.87; Johnson as
vice president, 318–19; long, slow

retreat from Southeast Asia, 337–
41; McNaughton memorandum,
334–35; media criticism of, 336–37;
Munich syndrome, 335; Operation
Plan 34A, 325–26; pacification
strategy, 334; Paris negotiations,
338–41; Tet Offensive, 337; U.S.
bombing of the North, 327–29,
333, 337, 338, 339; on U.S. objectives, 332; U.S. public opinion on,
333, 341; Vietnamese political
activity as irrelevant to U.S. policy,
334; White Paper, 329; the Wise
Men, 337, 338f
Joint Chiefs of Staff: creation of, 128;
JCS 1067 directive, 53
Joint Soviet-American Commission
on Korea, 154
Jones, Howard, 559–60 n.9
Jones, Joseph M., 123, 562 n.34
Jordan, 246, 348
Judd, Walter, 167, 197, 234, 235
Jupiter missiles, 269, 270, 281

Kadar, Janos, 228
Kalb, Marvin and Bernard, 347
KAL 007, 465–66
Karelian Peninsula, 20, 21
Kase, Toshikazu, 87
Kato, Masuo, 87
Katyn incident, 27–29
Kaufman, Henry, 500
Keating, Kenneth B., 266
Keegan, George J., 438
Kem, James P., 120
Kennan, George F.: absence of any
perceptible dangers in the U.S.-
Soviet conflict, 522; Alliance for
Progress, 258–59; appointment to
the State Department, 102–3;
Atlantic alliance proposal, 134; on
Bevin's consolidation of Western
Europe proposal, 131; on the
Chinese Civil War, 169; on
Communist threat to East Asia,
176; on fall of Czech government,

132; on Indochina, 192–93; on Indonesia, 175; on Japan's postwar economy, 177; Long Telegram, 3–4, 101, 102–3, 113; the Marshall Plan, 124, 130, 562 n.37; on North Korean invasion of South Korea, 197; *The Nuclear Delusion*, 467–68; on nuclear war, 183, 288–89; on Okinawa, 176; Peace Corps, 255–56, 256f; persistent rejection of Kennan's views on both NATO and Germany, 150; photograph, 271; Policy Planning Staff (PPS), 123, 124, 124–25, 134, 139; on Polish-Soviet relations, 56; on postwar Germany, 139; postwar reconstruction role, 52, 53, 150, 151; Project Solarium, 216; on Reagan's ideological crusade vs. Soviet Union, 464; on recognizing the Soviet sphere, 58; Reith Lectures, 231–32; on solidarity of Communist movements, 48, 285; on Soviet behavior in Eastern Europe, 51, 75, 537 n.13; on Soviet expansionism in Southeast Asia, 164, 173–74; on Soviet threat during Carter years, 424–25; on Stalin-Byrnes meeting, 99, 555 n.4; on the Truman Doctrine, 119; on Vietnam War, 336; "X" article, 128–30

Kennedy, Edward M., 505–6
Kennedy, John F., 251–82; advisors, 253, 260–61; Alliance for Progress, 291–92; ambivalence on foreign affairs, 251–52; arms control negotiations, 256–58, 307; assassination, 290, 291–92, 324; Bay of Pigs, 260–61, 272; Berlin question, 264–65; Captive Nations Week, 264; China policy, 278–80; Cuba, 259–62, 265–72, 281, 292, 294–95, 348, 354, 427; de Gaulle's anti-Anglo-Saxon crusade, 276–78; domino theory applied to Vietnam

War by, 12; ExComm, 266–70, 271f; final speeches, 282, 283; on Formosa, 279; Grand Design for Europe, 272–78; inaugural address, 251, 262; Khrushchev meeting, 262–64, 491; Khrushchev's correspondence with, 269–70, 280; Laotian crisis, 314–17; Latin America, 258–59; Middle East, 301; military expenditures, 254–55, 264; on missile gap, 254–55; negotiation from strength concept, 283; nuclear weapons, 272–78, 275–76, 287–88, 298; Panamanian challenge, 293; Peace Corps, 259; photographs of, 256, 263; post-Cuban missile crisis relations with Soviets, 280–82; during presidential campaign, 252, 254; State of the Union (1961), 252; State of the Union (1963), 323; U.S. as "watchmen on the walls of world freedom," 282; Vietnam War, 313, 317–25, 382; in West Germany, 277–78

Kennedy, Robert, 261, 268, 269, 270
Keynesian economics, 53–54, 185
Keyserling, Leon, 185
Khan, Yahya, 356
Khanh, Nguyen, 325–26, 327, 328
Khmer Rouge, 366
Khomeini, Ruhollah, 429–30, 431–32
Khrushchev, Nikita S.: arms control negotiations, 258, 281; arrogance, 225–26; Berlin crisis, 229–31, 258, 264–65; campaign for summit with Western powers, 228–31; on Churchill's Fulton College speech, 104; Cuba, 265–72, 348; Cyprus crisis, 303; economic program, 224, 580 n.53; emphasis on coexistence, 225–26; Kennedy meeting, 262–64, 491; Kennedy's correspondence with, 269–70, 280; the Kitchen Debate, 230; on nuclear war, 288; Paris Summit, 231; perceptions of successful Communist rule, 224;

photograph, 263; Poznan riots, 226; Sino-Soviet alliance, 238; Soviet grip eased by, 223–24; support for wars of national liberation, 285–86; tirade vs. Stalin, 224, 238; U.S. tour, 230; on Vietnam War, 322; Western Sovietology on, 420

The Kiel Canal, 100

Kim Il Sung, 195. *See also* North Korea

King, Ernest J., 83

Kirchwey, Freda, 214

Kirkpatrick, Jeane, 421, 443–44, 449, 454, 476

Kissinger, Henry A., 343–70; Carter policies criticized by, 438; criticism of, 370–74, 380, 383, 390, 391–92; Eurocommunism, 375–78, 415; Ford administration, 370, 372; on global environment at start of Nixon presidency, 343; on Gorbachev's policies, 490; Greek-Turkish confrontation over Cyprus, 372–75; Helskinki Final Act, 385–87; on human rights, 395–96, 398; INF pact criticized by, 483; Iran hostage crisis, 431; on legitimacy, 347–48; linkage policy, 346, 348; Middle East diplomacy, 368–69, 382–83, 391; Moscow Summit (1974), 384–85; Nixon-Kissinger relationship, 347; Nobel Peace Prize, 366; on nuclear weapons, 424; overview of détente policies, 343–49, 388–90; photographs, 345, 386; popularity of, 367, 369–70, 391; on post-Cuban missile crisis strategic requirements, 354; as Reagan advisor, 471–72; request for FBI surveillance of associates, 370; SALT treaties, 350–51, 384, 386f, 416; on Soviet or Cuban involvement in Africa, 428; Trilateral Commission on, 393–95; U.S. -China relations, 356; Vietnam War, 358–61, 364–66, 378–82;

"The Year of Europe" speech, 354–55, 383

Kistiakowsky, G. B., 330, 424

The Kitchen Debate, 230

Knowland, William F., 167, 178, 190, 221, 234, 235, 568 n.58

Koen, Ross Y., 167

Kohak, Erazim, 495

Kohl, Helmut, 480, 497–98

Kohlberg, Alfred, 167, 189

Kohler, Foy, 422–23

Koje Island, 239

Kolakowski, Leszek, 224

Komer, Robert W., 301, 334

Konoye, Fumimaro, 88

Korea/Korean War: costs of Korean War to U.S., 596 n.93; during Eisenhower years, 238–40; Joint Soviet-American Commission on Korea, 154; Moscow Conference, 154; prisoner of war issue, 239; Soviet establishment of Communist regime in the north, 154, 195, 207; 38th parallel line, 154, 197–98; World War II, 88

Kosygin, Alexei, 305, 308, 309

Kozlov, Frol R., 230

Kraft, Joseph, 367, 432, 437

Krauthammer, Charles, 474

Kristol, Irving, 421, 422, 523

Krul, Nicolas, 436

Krulac, Victor, 324, 325

Kuriles, 86, 88

Kuznetsov, Vasily V., 272

Ky, Nguyen Cao, 328–29, 330–31, 340, 361

Kyushu invasion, 83, 86

Laird, Melvin, 360

Lane, Arthur Bliss, 51

Lansdale, Edward, 260, 261, 318

Lansing, Robert, 210

Laos, 159, 204, 240, 314–17, 363, 381–82

Laqueur, Walter, 421, 422

Larson, Arthur, 330, 583 n.97

Laski, Harold J., 143

Las Villas Province (Bay of Pigs), 260–61, 272

Latin America: Act of Bogota, 258–59; Alliance for Progress, 258–59, 291–92, 294; Carter years, 403; Eisenhower's policies, 242, 243–44; human rights issues, 403–4; Johnson administration, 292–95; Kennedy's assassination, 291–92; Organization of American States (OAS), 244, 261–62, 268–69, 294; Panama/Panama Canal, 293, 403, 425–26; Pentagon's School for the Americas, 403; Rio Pact, 243. *See also specific countries by name*

Lattimore, Owen, 169, 191

Latvia, 20, 504. *See also* Baltic states

Law, Richard, 75

Lawrence, David, 90, 214, 577 n.10

Lawrence, Ernest O., 85, 183

League of Nations, 55

League of Vietnam Independence (Vietminh), 156–57. *See also* Vietnam/Vietnam War

Leahy, William D., 48, 71, 73, 80, 83, 101, 118

Lebanon, 246, 454, 457–60

Le Duc Tho, 364–65

Lefever, Ernest W., 443–44

Leffler, Melvyn P., 558 n.45

Le Figaro, 480

Legvold, Robert, 424

Leighton, John, 164

LeMay, Curtis, 82–83, 91–92

Lend-Lease agreements, 31–32, 54, 99–100

Lewis, Anthony, 401

Lewy, Guenter, 380

Liberation policies, 212–16, 227, 233–34, 238

The *Liberty*, 305

Libya, 448

Life magazine, 3, 54–55, 129, 167, 252

Lilienthal, David E., 136–37

Linebacker I, 364–65

Linebacker II, 365

Linkage policy, 346, 348, 351–52, 403

Lin Piao, 296–97

Lippmann, Walter: on absence of evidence that Soviets were catalyst in Asia's political upheaval, 191; on Anglo-American alliance vs. Soviets, 76; Byrnes criticized by, 108; on China policy, 188, 235, 357; on coexistence of Communism and democracy, 112; on Dumbarton Oaks formula, 73; on Germany's division, 549 n.55; on Kennan's "X" article, 129–30; on limited spheres of influence, 75; on price of postponement, 58; on Red Scare, 2; on Soviet concern for friendly bordering states, 95; on the Truman Doctrine, 119; on U.S. expansion into worldwide power vacuum, 144

Lithuania, 20, 504–6. *See also* Baltic states

Litvinov, Maxim, 542 n.73

Lloyd, Selwyn, 237

Lodge, Henry Cabot, 226, 228

Lodge, Henry Cabot, Jr., 324, 326, 359

Lodge, John Davies, 170

London Declaration, 511

London Foreign Ministers Conference, 93–94, 97, 130–31, 138

London Observer, 94, 109

Long, Robert L., 455

Long Telegram (Kennan), 4, 101, 102–3, 113

Lovett, Robert A., 131, 134, 174–75, 201–2, 268, 338f

Low, Richard, 54

Lublin Poles, 40–41, 47–48, 56–59, 63, 66–67, 68–69, 71–73, 78

Luce, Henry R., 129, 167, 233–34

Lukacs, John A., 35

Lundestad, Geir, 208

Luttwak, Edward, 422

Lwow, Poland, 35, 38, 40

MacArthur, Douglas: on Chinese-Soviet relations, 199; domino theory applied to Vietnam War by, 12; on Formosa, 191; Inchon landing, 196f, 197; on Japan, 83, 177; on North Korean invasion, 196; on Okinawa, 176; photograph, 196; as supreme commander of the Allied Powers (SCAP), 154

Macdonald, Dwight, 90

Macedonia, Greece, 42, 45

MacLeish, Archibald, 76

MacMillan, Harold, 231, 275–76, 279

Maginot line, 484

Maisky, Ivan, 23–24, 43

Makarios, Archbishop, 302–3, 372–74

The Making of a Quagmire (Halberstam), 324

Malayan model of counterinsurgency, 321–22

Malenkov, Georgi, 215–16, 222, 224

Malik, Jacob, 83, 198f

Malta summit (1989), 507, 509f, 510

Manchester Guardian, 63, 107

Manchester Guardian Weekly, 169, 191, 213

Manchuria, 62, 88, 153, 162, 187

Mandelbaum, Michael, 524

Maneuverable reentry vehicle (MARV), 385

Manhattan Project, 84–93. *See also* Atomic weapons

Mann, Thomas C., 292, 293

The Mann doctrine, 292

Mansfield, Mike, 293, 324–25, 328, 331, 383, 597 n.112

Mao Zedong: Carter years, 406; Chinese Civil War, 160–71, 178; international recognition of Communist-led government, 168–71, 176; "lean to one side" speech, 170–71; People's Republic of China established by, 171; photograph, 162; power based on ideology and

coercion, 192; presumed Soviet influence over, 10; response to the White Paper, 169; Sino-Soviet pact, 187–88; socialist doctrine, 155; WWII, 160–61. *See also* China

Marchais, Georges, 375

Marin, Peter, 438–39

Mark, Louis, Jr., 545 n.4

Markey, Edward J., 469

Marshall, Charles Burton, 387, 423–24

Marshall, George C.: on Atlantic security pact, 134; on Bevin's consolidation of Western Europe proposal, 131, 133; Chinese Civil War, 161–62, 163, 164–65, 166; on Europe's damaged economy, 123–25; on Greece and Turkey, 116; on Ho Chi Minh, 157–58; on Italy, 141–42; on Japan, 83; on Mediterranean operations, 29; Moscow Foreign Ministers Conference, 123; OVERLORD, 34; photograph, 165; on Soviet behavior in Eastern Europe, 72, 75; on the Truman Doctrine, 118

Marshall Plan, 6, 124–27, 130–31, 132, 133

Martin, Edwin M., 259, 269, 292

Martin, Graham, 379

Martin, Joseph, 170

MARV (maneuverable reentry vehicle), 385

Marxists and Marxism, 4, 289–90, 449–52

Masaryk, Jan, 132

Matlock, Jack, 492–93

Matsu, 235–37

Matthews, H. Freeman, 4, 73, 101, 102, 106, 112, 126

McCarran, Pat, 167, 199

McCarthy/McCarthyism, 3, 188, 188–89, 579 n.47

McCloy, John J., 139, 202, 258, 272, 330, 338f

McConaughy, Walter P., 237

McCone, John, 265, 268, 295, 329
McCormick, Anne O'Hare, 33, 48, 103
McCormick, Robert, 167
McFarlane, Robert, 478
McGeehan, Robert, 398
McGhee, George, 119
McGovern, George, 421
McKellar, Kenneth, 120
McNamara, Robert: on Arab-Israeli conflict, 304; China policy, 295–96; on Cuba, 267, 271; as Kennedy's secretary of defense, 253; on nuclear weapons, 254–55, 273, 309, 468, 520; photograph, 297, 338; on SEATO, 316; on U.S. policy following fall of Communism, 524–25; Vietnam War, 320–21, 323, 324, 325–26, 327, 329–31, 334, 336
McNaughton, John T., 330, 334–35
Meese, Ed, 446f
Meir, Golda, 301, 368
Melby, John, 193
Merchant, Livingston T., 178, 189
Messianic ideology, 14
Michael I, King of the Rumanians, 65, 66
Michel, Robert, 470
Middle East: American Jewish lobby, 304, 410, 430–31; Arab nationalism, 224, 245–46; Baghdad Pact, 245; Camp David accords, 411–13, 412f; Carter years, 408–13, 412f, 428–32; Egypt, 382–83, 455, 457; Eisenhower years, 244–46, 300; Israeli-Egyptian peace treaty, 430–31; Johnson administration, 300–305; Kennedy administration, 301; Kissinger's shuttle diplomacy, 368–69, 382–83, 391; oil and sea lines, 99, 428–29, 459, 461; Reagan administration, 455–56, 457–60; Six-Day War, 304–5, 367; Soviet postwar expansion plans, 98, 302, 430; Suez Canal, 245; Truman administration, 111; UN

Resolution 242, 305, 368, 409, 411, 431; Western Tripartite Declaration on Arab-Israeli arms, 245; Yom Kippur War, 367, 383. See also specific nations by name
Mikolajczyk, Stanislaw, 37, 38–41, 47–48, 56, 78
Mikoyan, Anastas, 171, 230, 266, 271
Military expenditures: under Brezhnev, 420; Carter years, 420; Eisenhower years, 218–19; Kennedy years, 254–55, 264; Reagan administration, 445–47; Truman's defense program, 182, 184–85, 193–94, 200–201, 206
Miller, Norman C., 432
Millis, Walter, 581 n.70
Minh, Duong Van, 325
MIRVs (multiple independently reentry vehicles), 351, 353, 384–85, 417, 419, 510
Missile gap, 247–48, 254–55
Mitla pass, 382
Mitterand, Francois, 375, 463
MLF (Multilateral Defense Force), 276, 298–99, 308
Moffat, Abbot Low, 158
Mohammad Reza Pahlavi, Shah of Iran, 398, 428–30
Molotov, Vyacheslav M.: Churchill meeting, 222; Churchill-Stalin agreements on spheres of influence, 46; on German reparations, 130; London Foreign Ministers Conference, 93–94; the Marshall Plan, 125–26, 130; Moscow Foreign Ministers Conference, 122–23; Paris Foreign Ministers Conference, 106–7, 108; Poland issue, 40, 41, 47–48, 60, 68; Potsdam, 80; on second front, 23–24; Truman meeting to discuss Lublin Poles, 71–73; war with Japan, 88
Mondale, Walter, 385, 395, 414–15
Monnet, Jean, 124, 127

Montreux Convention, 47, 98, 111, 119
Moore, John Norton, 476
Moran, Lord, 63
Morgenthau, Hans J., 188, 288–89, 595 n.76
Morgenthau, Henry, 52–54
Morgenthau Plan, 52–53
Moro, Aldo, 375
Moron Air Base, 377
Morse, Wayne, 246
Moscoso, Teodoro, 292
Moscow Conference (1943), 33, 43, 62, 99
Moscow Conference (1945), 136, 154
Moscow Conference (1947), 122–23
Moscow Olympics (1980), 434
Moscow Summit (1972), 351–53, 372
Moscow Summit (1974), 384–85
Moss, Robert, 427
Mossadeq, Muhammad, 242
Mouvement Republicain Populaire, 121
Moynihan, Daniel Patrick, 421, 428, 472, 503, 525
MPLA (Popular Movement for the Liberation of Angola). See Angola
Multilateral Defense Force (MLF), 276, 298–99, 308
Multiple independently reentry vehicles (MIRVs), 351, 353, 384–85, 417, 419, 510
Munich syndrome, 5–6, 10–12, 67, 117–18, 335
Murphy, Robert, 68
Muskie, Edmund S., 364, 436–37
Mussolini, Benito, 29
Mutual Defense Assistance Act (1949), 138
Mutual Defense Assistance Agreement (1950), 204
Mutual Security Act (1951), 201

Nagasaki, 88, 91. See also Manhattan Project

Nasser, Gamal Abdel, 245, 302. See also Egypt
National Association of Manufacturers, 462
Nationalism: Asian, 154–55, 157–58, 174–76, 191–92; described, 150; Eisenhower on, 233, 242; during Johnson administration, 306; liberation ideology vs., 150; Marxists on, 289–90; of Middle Eastern states, 224, 245–46; nationalist demands for self-determination within Soviet Union, 493–94, 504–6; Nixon on, 346; Soviet appeal to, 203; as universal defense vs. Soviet expansionism, 4, 285–86, 289–90, 514–15
Nationalists (China). See Chiang Kai-shek
National Liberation Front (NLF), 339–40
National Security Council (NSC): ExComm, 266–70, 271f; on Italy, 142; Kremlin's challenge defined by, 8–9; National Security Act, 127–28; NSC 7 study on Soviet ideological expansionism, 8, 147–48; NSC 20/1 on Soviet influence, 148–49; NSC 20/4 on Soviet influence, 8, 149; NSC 34 on Soviet influence in China, 164; NSC 48/1 on Soviet conquest of China, 10, 172; NSC 48/2 on U.S. policy in Asia, 179–80; NSC 48/5 on China's close attachment to the U.S.S.R., 203–4; NSC 58 on Soviet influence in Eastern Europe, 148; NSC 68 on Truman's national defense policy, 8–9, 184–87, 200, 206; NSC 149/1 review of size and structure of the military during Eisenhower years, 219; NSC 162 on nuclear strategy, 219–20; Project Democracy, 452; Project Solarium, 216–17; United States Objectives and Courses of Action

with Respect to Southeast Asia,
205–6

National Security Resources Board,
128

National Strategy Committee, 306–7

NATO (North Atlantic Treaty
Organization): Able Archer, 466–
67; Acheson on, 137–38, 232;
antinuclear protesters, 468–69;
Berlin crisis, 264–65; Carter's
European policy, 414–15; challenge
to allied unity, 300; costs to U.S.
to defend, 500; creation of, 7, 135–
36; Cyprus crisis, 303, 372–75;
during Eisenhower administration,
221; Eisenhower as supreme
commander, 202; Eurocommunism, 375–78, 415; European
Defense Community (EDC), 203,
221; France's withdrawal from, 298,
299–300; Germany's membership,
202–3, 221–22, 277, 497, 498, 499;
Helskinki Final Act, 385–87;
Mediterranean front, 372–76; MLF
(Multilateral Defense Force), 276,
298–99, 308; Multilateral Defense
Force (MLF), 276; Mutual Defense
Assistance Act, 138; nuclear
weapons, 272–74, 276, 291, 298–99,
420, 466–67; as postwar stabilizing
force, 284–85; as "shield against
aggression" (Truman), 300;
supreme command posts, 299;
Turkey as member, 245; Warsaw
Pact members invited to, 511;
Yamal natural gas pipeline, 461–62

Natural gas, 460–62

Nazi-Soviet Pact (1939), 20, 49, 504

Negotiation from strength concept,
186, 214–15, 283, 519

Negroponte, John D., 452

Nehru, Jawaharlal, 175–76, 188, 227.
See also India

Neoconservatives, 421–23, 431, 443–
44, 487, 489–90

Nessen, Ronald, 380

The Netherlands, 96, 174–75. See also
Benelux countries

Neutron bombs, 415

New Deal, 133

New Look doctrine, 219–21

New Republic, 75–76, 103, 153

Newsweek, 63

New York Council on Foreign
Relations, 209

New York Daily News, 447

New Yorker, 524

New York Herald-Tribune, 64

New York Times: on arms limitations,
418; on Carter Doctrine, 435;
Committee on the Present Danger,
202; on Indochina, 204–5; on
Kissinger's bipartisan commission
report on U.S. policy, 472; on
Schultz, 458; on Soviet expansionism, 11, 132, 198–99; on U.S. Indochina policy, 190; on Vietnam War,
323–24; on Yalta Conference, 64

New Zealand, 67, 205, 241, 279, 314

Ngo Dinh Nhu, 321–22, 324

Nguyen Thi Binh, 340

Nicaragua, 403–4, 426, 449–52, 462–
63, 471, 473–77, 479

Niebuhr, Rheinhold, 108

Nielsen, Waldemar A., 580 n.53

Nimitz, Chester, 90

1967 War (Six-Day War), 304–5, 367

Nitze, Paul H.: arms control
negotiations, 353, 521; on collapse
of Soviet influence in Eastern
Europe, 501–2; Committee on the
Present Danger (CPD), 423–24; on
Cuba, 260, 268; on détente, 387;
Gaither Commission Report, 247;
NSC 68, 184–87, 206; on nuclear
threats to U.S., 199; Team B report,
422–23

Nixon, Richard M., 343–92; on Africa
(as vice president), 246; China
policy, 298, 355–58, 371–72, 405;
détente, 371–72, 388–90; Greek-
Turkish confrontation over Cyprus,

372–75; on human rights, 395–96; INF pact criticized by, 483; the Kitchen Debate, 230; on Korean War (as vice president), 240; Latin American tour as vice president, 244; linkage policy, 346, 348, 351–52, 403; Middle Eastern policy, 368, 368–69; Nixon-Kissinger approach to the Soviet Union, described, 343–49; Nixon-Kissinger relationship, 347; nuclear weapons, 310; Panama Canal, 425; photographs of, 345, 352, 357; retrenchment, 391, 461; Strategic Arms Limitation Talks (SALT), 350–51, 384; U.S.-Soviet relations at start of term, 350–53; Vietnam War, 339–40, 346, 358–67, 362–65, 367, 372, 378, 382; Washington summit (1973), 353; Watergate scandal, 369, 370; on weapons of mass destruction, 349; "The Year of Europe" declared by, 354–55, 383

NLF (National Liberation Front), 339–40

Nolting, Frederick E., Jr., 323, 324, 325

Normandy invasion, 35, 44. *See also* OVERLORD

North, Oliver, 477

North Atlantic Treaty Organization. *See* NATO

Northern Bukovina, 20

North Korea: costs of Korean War to U.S., 596 n.93; during Eisenhower years, 238–40; Joint Soviet-American Commission on Korea, 154; Moscow Conference, 154; prisoner of war issue, 239; South Korea invaded by, 10–11, 194–98, 200, 202, 204; Soviet establishment of Communist regime in the north, 154, 195, 207; 38th parallel line, 154, 197–98

Norway, 135

Novotny, Antonin, 310

NSC. *See* National Security Council

The Nuclear Delusion (Kennan), 467–68

Nuclear Non-Proliferation Treaty (1968), 308, 456, 468

The Nuclear Taboo (Tannenwald), 520

Nuclear weapons: Atomic Energy Act, 274; Carter years, 416–20; China, 295–96, 308; Cold War, overview, 519–21; de Gaulle on, 274–75, 276; deterrent capability, 183; Dulles proposal vs. Chinese invasion of offshore islands, 236–37; Eisenhower years, 219–21, 236–37, 248, 256–57; Geneva Conference on, 223, 257; Germany's acquisition of, 499; hydrogen bombs, 182–83, 186, 219; Intermediate Nuclear Force (INF) Treaty, 482–84, 483f; International Atomic Energy Agency, 136–37, 183, 256–57, 307; Israel, 456; Johnson administration, 287–89, 291, 298–99, 306–10; Jupiter missiles, 269, 270, 281; Kennedy administration, 272–75, 272–78, 275–76, 287–88, 298; Kissinger, Henry A. on, 349, 424; McNamara, Robert on, 254–55; Multilateral Defense Force (MLF), 276, 308; NATO, 291, 298–99, 420, 466–67; New Look doctrine, 219–21; Nixon administration, 310, 349; Nuclear Non-Proliferation Treaty (1968), 456; Osirak, 455; Outer Space Treaty, 308; Rapacki Plan for a nuclear-free zone, 232–33; Reagan administration, 445–46; Single Integrated Operational Plan (SIOP-62), 254–55; South Africa, 456–57; Soviet production, 288, 299, 306–10, 479–81, 514; Truman administration, 199, 206; United Nations on, 308. *See also* Arms control and disarmament; Atomic weapons

Nunn, Sam, 419

Nutter, Warren, 374, 387–88
Nye, Joseph S., Jr., 526

OAS (Organization of American
    States), 244, 261–62, 268–69, 294,
    404
O'Connor, Raymond G., 530 n.5
Octagon Conference, 52
O'Daniel, Lee, 120
Oder-Neisse line, 56, 59, 81, 497–99
O'Donnell, Kenneth, 324–25
Ogburn, Charlton, 160, 174
Oil: Angola's off shore oil fields, 456;
    Arab oil sold to Israel, 413; Carter
    years, 436–37; Iran, 110–11, 242,
    398; Johnson years, 300; OPEC,
    428–29, 461; Soviet production,
    503; Soviet threat to oil and sea
    lines of the Middle East, 99, 434
Okinawa, Japan, 82–83, 84, 153, 176,
    178, 179, 191
OLYMPIC invasion, 83
Olympics (Moscow), 434
O'Neill, Thomas, 401, 473
OPEC, 428–29, 461
Open Skies plan, 257
Operation Bagration, 44
Operation Breakfast, 360
Operation Mongoose, 261, 272
Operation Plan 34A, 325–26
Operation Urgent Fury, 453–54
Oppenheimer, Robert, 85, 86, 89–90,
    553 n.100
Organization of American States
    (OAS), 244, 261–62, 268–69, 294,
    404
Osirak, 455
OSS (U.S. Office of Strategic
    Services), 156, 157
Ostpolitik, 348
O'Sullivan, James L., 158
Ottawa Foreign Ministers
    Conference, 497–98
Outer Mongolia, 62
Outer Space Treaty, 308
OVERLORD, 29, 34–35, 44

Overseas Press Club, 103

Pachter, Henry, 267
Pacific Northwest skiers, 199
Paine, Christopher, 447
Pakistan: Baghdad Pact, 245;
    independence from Great Britain,
    155; Reagan years, 455, 457;
    SEATO membership, 241, 245;
    Soviet expansionism, 224, 245, 434
Palach, Jan, 493
Palestine Liberation Organization
    (PLO), 301, 368, 382, 408–11, 430–
    31, 457–60
Panama/Panama Canal, 293, 403,
    425–26
Pan-Arab movement, 245–46
Panikkar, K. M., 197
Paraguay, 403
The paranoid spokesman, 442
Paris Club, 494
Paris Foreign Ministers Conference,
    7, 106–7, 108, 139, 151–52
Paris summit (1990), 511
Paterson, Thomas G., 556 n.21
The Pathet Lao, 317
Patriotism. See Nationalism
Patterson, Robert, 2, 111
Pauley, Edwin, 80
Payne, Robert, 143–44
PCI (Italian Communist Party),
    141–42
Peace Corps, 255–56, 256f, 259
Peaceful Nuclear Explosions Treaty,
    508
Peffer, Nathaniel, 192
Pentagon Papers, 320
Peoples Republic of China. See China
Pepper, Claude, 120–21
Pershing IIs, 420, 469
Persian Gulf, 430
Peru, 259, 403
The Pescadores, 178
Pfaff, William, 357–58
Philippines: independence granted
    to, 176; on recognition of China,

168; Southeast Asia Treaty
Organization (SEATO), 241; U.S.
commitment to, 178, 179, 194, 205,
398; vulnerable to attack from
Formosa, 191
Phillips, Howard, 483
Phnom Penh, 366
Ping-pong diplomacy, 356–58
Pipes, Richard, 387, 422–23, 424, 435,
443, 461
Pisar, Samuel, 397
PLO (Palestine Liberation
Organization), 301, 368, 382, 408–
11, 430–31, 457–60
Podhoretz, Norman, 421, 422, 454
Poindexter, John, 477
Poland: Churchill on Soviet
domination, 67, 68; Curzon line,
21, 26, 33, 35, 37–38, 47–48, 59;
December 1981 unrest, 463–64;
economy and trade, 494, 495–96;
exiled government, 25–28, 33, 37–
41, 48, 56 60, 63, 66–67, 534 n.47;
German reunification, 497–99;
implications of democracy, 495–96;
as litmus test of post-War East-
West cooperation, 56; Lublin
Poles, 40–41, 47–48, 56–59, 63, 66–
67, 68–69, 71–73, 78; NATO
membership status, 497; Oder-
Neisse line, 56, 59, 81, 498–99;
Polish forced labor during WWII,
498; Polish language press campaign vs. Soviets, 28; Polish-Soviet
relations during WWII, 37–40, 47–
48, 56–57; Polish-Soviet Treaty of
Riga (1921), 26, 28, 33, 38; Poznan
riots, 226; Roosevelt on, 67; Solidarity movement, 463–64, 493–94;
Soviet invasion of, 20, 37–38, 57,
344; Teheran Conference, 47–48;
Truman administration on, 77–78;
Warsaw uprising, 41–42, 49; withdrawal of Soviet power from, 493–
94, 496; Yalta Conference on, 57,
59, 66–67, 68–69, 71–72

Polaris submarine missile, 275–76,
298
"A Policy of Boldness" (Dulles), 212
Policy Planning Staff (PPS): on
Atlantic security pact, 134; on
atomic weapons, 137; creation of,
123; on Cuba, 270; on demilitarized
Germany, 139; initial report
prepared by, 123, 124–25; Nitze as
director, 184–87; NSC 68 on
Truman's national defense policy,
193; on program to contract Soviet
power and influence, 148; on Soviet
expansionism in Southeast Asia,
164, 173–74
Polish-American Congress, 63
Polish-American Democratic Organi-
zation of Chicago, 57
Polish-Communist Committee of
National Liberation, 40. See also
Lublin Poles
Pompidou, Georges, 299
Popular Movement for the Liberation
of Angola (MPLA). See Angola
Portugal, 135, 376–77
Postwar reconstruction (WWII),
17–24; Allied interventions in
Northern Russia, the Crimea, and
Siberia, 2; Atlantic Charter, 17–18,
18f, 20–22, 27, 31, 32–33, 49–50,
55; Bretton Woods Conference,
53–54; Declaration on Liberated
Europe, 61; dismemberment of
Germany, 24, 52–53, 61, 94–95;
early predictions of Soviet
expansionism, 1–5; European
Advisory Commission, 52; London
Foreign Ministers Conference,
93–94, 130–31; Morgenthau Plan,
52–53; Munich syndrome, 5–6;
overview, 517–18; Poland as litmus
test of East-West cooperation, 56;
Potsdam, 78–82, 86–89; reconstitution of Versailles following, 17–18,
19; reparations, 61–62, 80–81, 107,
130, 498; Roosevelt's Grand Design

for the postwar world, 52; Roosevelt's United Nations Organization proposal, 55–56; Soviet plans for, 19–20, 65–66; Soviet weaknesses, 144–46; U.S.-British relations, 76; U.S. expansion into worldwide power vacuum, 144; U.S. policy of postponing territorial and political decisions until end of WWII, 18, 27; U.S. postwar economic superiority, 143–44; Yalta Conference, 59–69, 71–72, 73, 80, 86, 156, 214, 474. *See also* Stabilization of Europe

Potsdam, 78–82, 86–89; on Chinese-Soviet relations, 86–87; Dulles on, 212; Eisenhower on, 214; on Formosa, 178; Four Power Pact, 122; on German reparations, 107; on Indochina, 156; on Japan, 154, 177; Lend-Lease agreements, 99; photograph, 79; on Polish-German border, 497–98; postponed by Truman until Manhattan Project successful, 92; Yalta Conference vs., 80

Powell, Colin L., 485
Power, Thomas S., 255
Powers, Thomas, 515
Poznan riots, 226
PPS. *See* Policy Planning Staff
Prague Spring, 310, 344, 350, 377
Project Democracy, 451–52, 477
Project Solarium, 216–17

Qavam, Ahmad, 110–11
Quadrant Conference (Quebec), 29, 30, 33, 52, 82
Quemoy, 235–37, 238
Quirino, Elpidio, 168

Rabin, Yitzhak, 409, 460
Radescu, General, 65, 93
Radford, Arthur W., 219, 235, 236, 240
Radio Free Europe, 417
Radio Liberty, 417

Ramadier, Paul, 121, 141
Rankin, Karl Lott, 171, 233, 238
Rapacki, Adam, 232–33
Reagan, Ronald, 441–85; advisors, 443–44, 448–49, 485; Africa, 455, 456–57; "allergy to detail," 469; anti-Communist rhetoric, 442–43, 448–49, 465, 484, 487, 489; anxieties of antinuclear movements, 467–70; arms control negotiations, 469–70, 480, 481–82, 484, 507, 509–10, 523; assessments of the Soviet armed forces, 447; Bush on Reagan-Gorbachev relationship, 489; Carter Doctrine endorsed by, 455; Central America, 449–52, 461–63, 471–77, 479; Cold War fears revived by, 522–23; criticism from the right, 484–85; détente reintroduced by, 484–85, 487, 523; European alliances, 461–64; "evil empire" speech, 443; Geneva Summit (1985), 479–81; Grenada invasion, 453–54, 479; Haig's resignation, 457–58; on human rights, 443–44; ideological crusade vs. Soviet Union, 464–67; on improving U.S.-Soviet relations, 477–78; Iran hostage crisis, 432, 441; Iran-Iraq War, 476–77; Kissinger's bipartisan commission report on U.S. policy, 471–72; Libya, 448; Middle East, 455–56, 457–60; military expenditures, 445–47; Moscow Summit (1988), 484–85; myth of Soviet Union's status as a superpower, 464–65; NATO's command post exercise (1983), 466–67; neoconservatives on, 443–44, 487, 489–90; oil issues, 459; photographs of, 446, 483; Poland's December 1981 unrest, 463–64; as presidential candidate, 385, 387, 468; Reagan Doctrine, 473–76, 525; revisionist expectations, 447–48; Reykjavik Summit, 481–82; Sandinistas, 449–

52, 462–64, 473, 476–77; Soviet
intervention in Afghanistan, 441,
448, 455; on Soviet military power
and global expansionism, 441–45;
Taiwan, 455; transition to Bush
administration, 487–93; on Viet-
nam War, 441–42; Washington
summit (1987), 482–84; on Yalta
Conference, 474; Yamal natural gas
pipeline, 460–62
Red Scare (1919–1920), 2–3, 513
Red Scare (1950–1954), 3–5. *See also*
McCarthy/McCarthyism
Reed, Charles S., 158, 160
Reed, Thomas C., 467
Reischauer, Edwin O., 404
Report of the Committee on the
National Security Organization
(Eberstadt Committee), 182
Republic of Indonesia, 174–75, 227,
296
Reston, James, 58, 106, 270–71, 289,
327, 371, 373, 481
Retrenchment, 461
Reykjavik Summit, 481–82
Rhee, Syngman, 154, 194, 197, 239.
See also South Korea
The Rhine-Danube, 100
Rhineland, 107
Rice, Condoleezza, 492
Ridgway, Matthew B., 220, 238, 438
Rieber, Alfred J., 561 n.21
Rio Pact, 243
Robertson, Walter S., 237–38
Robinson, Geroid T., 101–2
Rockefeller, David, 393–95, 431
Rockefeller, Nelson A., 378
Rocking chair doctrine, 294
Rogers, William P., 367, 371
Rohrabacher, Dana, 506
Rolling Thunder vs., 328–29
Romulo, Carlos, 191
Roosevelt, Franklin D.: on Allied
policy of unconditional surrender,
19, 35; Atlantic Charter, 17–18, 18f,
20–22, 27, 31, 49–50; on Baltic

States, 36, 46; on Bern meeting, 69;
on Bulgaria, 42; Casablanca
Conference, 19; on Chiang
Kai-shek, 161; Churchill's relationship with, 31, 32, 34, 49, 51; confrontations with Soviets avoided by,
49, 51, 65, 66, 67–68; death and
succession, 70–71; on dismemberment of Germany, 52–53; economic
aid to Britain, 54; on German reparations, 80; Grand Design for the
postwar world, 52; on Indochina,
155–56; on Japan's acceptance of
total defeat, 84; Latin America, 426;
Manhattan Project, 84; military
collaboration with Soviet Union vs.
Germany, 25; on occupation of
Rumania and Greece, 43–44; photographs of, 18, 39, 60; on Poland,
28, 33, 35–36, 37–39, 41–42, 47–48,
56–57, 67–69; on Soviet dominance
during WWII, 30, 51, 70; Stalin on
U.S.S.R.'s exclusion from Allied
Control Commission for Italy, 29;
Stalin's relationship with, 31–32,
34–36, 38–39, 53, 63, 69–70;
Teheran Conference, 34–36, 38,
47–48; United Nations Organiza-
tion proposal, 55–56; on U.S. policy
of postponing territorial and politi-
cal decisions until end of WWII,
27; Yalta Conference, 59–69
Rosenthal, Benjamin S., 373
Rostow, Eugene, 423–24, 431
Rostow, Walt, 253, 270, 301, 303,
318–19, 327, 336–37, 467
Roundtree, William M., 246
Roxas, Manuel, 176
Rozmarek, Charles, 63
The Ruhr, 107, 126–27, 130, 138
Ruina, Jack P., 502–3
Rumania: London Foreign Ministers
Conference, 93; nationalism within,
306; postwar reconstruction
(WWII), 42–43; Soviet occupation,
20, 45, 57, 61, 65, 344;

Stalin-Byrnes meeting, 98–99;
TOLSTOY meeting, 46, 66; U.S.
refusal to recognize following
WWII, 79, 93–94, 95, 98–99, 100;
WWII treaty negotiations, 79, 93–
94, 106–7, 109
Rumsfeld, Donald, 476
Rusk, Dean: on arms control deliberations, 520–21; on China policy,
278–79, 280, 295–97; Committee
on the Present Danger (CPD), 423–
24; Cuba, 260, 261–62, 267, 269; on
Egypt, 303; European-centered
issues, 291; on Formosa, 190–91; on
Indochina, 189–90; as Kennedy's
secretary of state, 253; Laotian crisis, 314–16; the Marshall Plan, 124;
on Munich syndrome, 12; on need
for Communist leaders to abandon
goal of world revolution, 283, 284;
negotiation from strength concept,
283; on new dimensions of the Cold
War in 1950, 199; on North Korean invasion, 197; on nuclear
weapons, 288, 299; photographs of,
297, 338; Six-Day War (1967), 305;
on Soviet expansionism, 203, 204;
on the Truman Doctrine, 119–20;
on U.S.-Soviet relations during
Nixon administration, 349; Vietnam War, 323, 324, 329, 335, 338
Russell, Bertrand, 287
Russia, the Atom, and the West
(Kennan), 231–32

Saar, 107
Sabra Palestinian refugee camp,
458–59
SAC (Strategic Air Command), 255
El-Sadat, Anwar, 368, 409–13, 412f
Safire, William, 347, 364, 422
Sagdeyev, Roald Z., 484
Sakhalin, 86, 88
Sakharov, Andrei, 484
Salisbury, Harrison E., 579 n.49
Salisbury, Lord, 217

SALT I treaty, 468
SALT II, 350–51, 384–85, 386f, 416–
20, 468, 480, 481
Sandinistas, 426, 449–52, 462–63,
462–64, 473, 476–77
San Francisco Conference, 68, 73–74,
153
Santo Domingo, 293–94
Santos, Eduarto, 243–44
Sarit Thanarat, 314–16
Sarnoff, David, 252
Sato, Naotake, 84, 88
Saudi Arabia, 302, 430, 455, 457
Savimbi, Jonas, 475
Sazonov, Sergei, 207
SCAP (supreme commander of the
Allied Powers), 154
Schell, Jonathan, 467–68, 596 n.99
Schlesinger, Arthur, Jr., 318, 320
Schlesinger, James R., 368, 430
Schmidt, Helmut, 415, 436, 462, 468
Schneider, Mark L., 401
School of the Americas (SOA), 403
Schroeder, Gerhard, 306
Schuman, Robert, 159
Schwartz, Thomas A., 290, 298
Scowcroft, Brent, 487, 488f, 489–90,
491–92, 507, 509, 510
SDI (Strategic Defense Initiative),
470, 480, 481–82, 523
Sea-launched cruise missiles
(SLCMs), 510
Sea lines, 99
SEATO (Southeast Asia Treaty
Organization), 241, 242, 245, 314–
17, 401
Sebald, William J., 237
Self-determination, 4
Service, John Stewart, 161
Shales, Tom, 482
Shanghai Communiqué, 405, 406–7
Shaplen, Robert, 323
Sharon, Ariel, 458, 460
Shatila Palestinian refugee camp,
458–59
Shazar, Zalman, 301

Shcharansky, Anatoli B., 400–401
Sheehan, Neil, 323–24, 325
Sherman, Forrest P., 194
Sherwin, Martin, 87
Sherwood, Robert, 52
Shevardnadze, Eduard, 487, 498
Shoup, David, 255
Shulman, Marshall D., 288–89, 399–400, 416
Shultz, George P., 457–58, 469–70, 474, 477–78, 482, 485, 487
Sidey, Hugh, 434
Sigal, Leon V., 88
Sikorski, Wladyslaw, 26, 27–28, 37, 532 nn.23, 25
Simpson, Alan K., 501
Simpson, William H., 70
Singapore, 155
Single Integrated Operational Plan (SIOP-62), 254–55
Sino-Soviet Treaty of Friendship and Alliance, 88, 187
Six-Day War (1967), 304–5, 367
Sjahrir, 174
Skates, John Ray, 551 n.84
Skybolt project, 275–76, 298
SLCMs (sea-launched cruise missiles), 510
Smith, Gerard, 468
Smith, Walter Bedell, 45, 123
Smuts, Jan, 55
SOA (School for the Americas), 403
Somalia, 427
Somoza, Anastasio, 404, 426, 449, 452
Soong, T. V., 86–87
Sorensen, Theodore C., 260, 268, 270
South Africa, 431, 456–57
Southeast Asia Collective Defense Treaty, 326
Southeast Asia Treaty Organization (SEATO), 241, 242, 245, 314–17, 401
South Korea: Carter years, 398, 405; costs of Korean War to U.S., 596 n.93; during Eisenhower years,

238–40; Joint Soviet-American Commission on Korea, 154; KAL 007 commercial airliner, 465–66; Moscow Conference, 154; North Korea invasion, 10–11, 194–98, 200, 202, 204; prisoner of war issue, 239; 38th parallel line, 154, 197–98; U.S. commitment to defense of, 177–78, 180, 194
South Vietnamese (ARVN) forces, 323–24. See also Vietnam/Vietnam War
Southwest Africa People's Organization (SWAPO), 456
Souvanna Phouma, 314, 316
Soviet Union. See Cold War, overview; Communism, overview; Fall of Communism; specific leaders, events, policies, and regional issues by name
Spaak, Paul-Henri, 232–33
Spaatz, Carl A., 88
Space programs, 281, 308
Spain, 375, 377, 415
Spellman, Cardinal, 30
Sputnik I, 247
SS-20s, 468, 469, 481
Stabilization of Europe, 115–52; Berlin blockade, 138–39; Britain replaced by U.S. as key defender of Europe and eastern Mediterranean, 118; Brussels Pact, 133; Cold War as justification for totalitarianism, 145–46; Czech coup, 132–34; European Recovery Program (ERP), 130; Europe's damaged economy, 122–25, 122–26; Federal Republic of Germany, 139, 141; France's postwar vulnerability to Communist encroachment, 121, 141; Greece and Turkey, 115–21, 142–43; Kennan's "X" article, 128–30; Marshall Plan, 6, 124–27, 130–31, 132, 133; military preparedness vs. Soviet expansionism, 136; National Security Act (U.S.), 127–

28; NATO, 135–36, 137, 150; Paris Foreign Ministers Conference, 7, 106–7, 108, 139, 151–52; Soviet ideological expansionism, 127, 146–50; Soviet weaknesses, 144–46; Soviet-Yugoslav relations, 6, 47, 142–43, 148, 149–50, 172–73; U.S. expansion into worldwide power vacuum, 144; U.S. postwar economic superiority, 143–44. *See also* Postwar reconstruction (WWII)

Stalin, Joseph: on Allied policy of unconditional surrender, 35; on Baltic States, 36; Berlin blockade, 6–7, 138–39; Bern meeting, 69; Byrnes meeting, 98–99, 100–101; Churchill and, 46–47, 49, 51, 66, 74, 104; Cold War as justification for totalitarianism, 145–46; on continuing hostility between the Communist and capitalist worlds, 101; death, 215, 239, 256, 257; dismemberment of Germany, 52–53, 141; excluded from Allied Control Commission for Italy, 29; on German reparations, 61–62, 80–81; Hopkins and, 77–78; human rights, 400; industrial material and equipment removed from Germany by, 80–81, 107; Japan, 62; on Mao, 171; Montreux Convention revisions, 47; Moscow address, 101; motives and intentions, 14; on nationalism, 289–90; North Korean invasion approved by, 195; photographs of, 60, 79; postwar reconstruction plans, 20, 21–24; Potsdam, 78–82, 86; pro-Soviet government for Poland established by, 28, 40–41; Roosevelt's relationship with, 31–32, 34–36, 38–39, 53, 63, 69–70; on Roosevelt's United Nations Organization proposal, 55; on second front, 24–25; Sino-Soviet pact, 187–88; Stalin cult of leadership denounced by Khrushchev,

224, 238; Stalinization of Eastern Europe, 1–2, 127; Teheran Conference, 34–36, 38, 44, 47–48; TOLSTOY meeting, 46, 50–51, 66; Truman on, 72–73, 81–82; Yalta Conference, 60–69

Standing Group on Cuba, 292

Standley, William, 26, 31–32

Stanton, Edwin F., 10, 171

START (Strategic Arms Reduction Talks), 469, 484, 508–10

Star Wars (SDI/Strategic Defense Initiative), 470, 480, 481–82, 523

Stassen, Harold E., 257

State-War-Navy Coordinating Committee (SWNCC), 122, 124–25

Stettinius, Edward R., 38, 39, 58, 62, 63, 70–71, 72

Stevenson, Adlai, 253, 268, 269, 278

Stimson, Henry L., 52, 72, 84–85, 86, 89–90, 91, 92, 95

Stockholm Agreement, 498

Stone, Marvin, 432, 434

Stone, Richard, 426

Straits of Tiran, 303–5

Strategic Air Command (SAC), 255

Strategic Arms Limitation Talks (SALT), 350–51, 384–85, 386f, 416–20, 468, 480, 481

Strategic Arms Reductions Treaty (START I), 469, 484, 508–10

Strategic Defense Initiative (SDI/Star Wars), 470, 480, 481–82, 523

Strauss, Lewis L., 183, 257

Strausz-Hupé, Robert, 514

Stuart, John, 165

Suez Canal, 245, 428

Suharto, 296

Sukarno, 174, 296. *See also* Indonesia

Sulzberger, C. L., 119

Summary Report (U.S. Strategic Bombing Survey), 90

Summer, William Graham, 516

Sunday Times, 463

Sununu, John, 488f

Super-bomb. *See* Hydrogen bombs

Supreme commander of the Allied
  Powers (SCAP), 154
Suzuki, Kantaro, 84, 87, 88
SWAPO (Southwest Africa People's
  Organization), 456
Swing, Raymond Gram, 76
SWNCC (State-War-Navy Coordi-
  nating Committee), 122, 124–25
Symington, W. Stuart, 182, 199
Syria, 246, 303, 348, 368, 430, 455,
  457, 459–60
Szilard, Leo, 85, 91

Taft, Robert A., 201, 578 n.34
Taiwan. See Formosa
Talbott, Strobe, 484, 487, 509, 514
Tannenwald, Nina, 520
Taraki, Mohammed, 433
Taylor, Maxwell, 268, 319–20, 327,
  328, 329, 333
Team B report, 423, 424, 443–44
Technological superiority, 7
Teheran Conference, 34–36, 38, 44,
  47–48, 55, 62, 212
Telemetry encryption, 419
Teller, Edward, 183, 281, 306–7, 553
  n.100
Tenth Inter-American Conference,
  243
Test Ban pact, 468
Tet Offensive, 337
Thailand, 241, 314–16
Thanat Khoman, 315
Thatscher, Margaret, 478, 482, 492
Thieu, Nguyen Van, 328–29, 330–31,
  339, 340, 360, 365, 378. See also
  Vietnam/Vietnam War
Thompson, Kenneth, 474
Thompson, Llewellyn, 267, 268,
  270
Thomson, James C., Jr., 332
Thrace, Greece, 42, 45
Threshold Test Ban Treaty, 508
Thurman, Strom, 514
Time (magazine), 101
Times (London), 462, 480–81

Tito, Marshal, 6, 47, 142–43, 148,
  149–50, 172–73
Togliatti, Palmiro, 141
Togo, Shigenori, 83, 87
TOLSTOY meeting, 46, 50–51, 66
Toon, Malcolm, 464
Torrejon base, 377
Tower, John, 487
Trade. See Economy and trade
Tran Van Do, 339
Treaty of Dunkirk, 123, 131
Treaty of Riga, 26, 28, 33, 38
Treaty of Versailles, 17–18, 19, 132
Treaty on Conventional Forces in
  Europe (CFE), 508–9
Tri, Nguyen Bao, 328
Trident Conference, 29
Trieste, 106–7, 108
Trilateral Commission, 393–95, 414
Trinity, 86, 92
Truman, Harry S.: anti-Soviet
  attitudes, 72–73, 103–4; atomic
  weapons, 181, 199; on Britain's
  economic welfare and role in world
  affairs, 99–100; China policy, 11,
  161–71, 178, 189, 198–200, 203;
  Churchill's Fulton College speech,
  105f; Clifford-Elsey report, 113,
  119; containment policy, 206–7,
  209–11, 215; elections of 1948,
  134–35; European Recovery Program (ERP), 130; Federal Civil
  Defense Administration, 199; Formosa, 178–80, 190–91; Greece and
  Turkey, 5–6, 111, 115–21, 142; on
  Indochina, 156, 190, 192–93; on
  Iran, 100; on Italy, 141–42; on
  Japan, 84, 205; Kennan's Long
  Telegram, 4, 101, 102–3, 113; Korean War, 10, 194–98, 200, 202,
  238–39; on Lublin Poles, 71–73;
  McCarthy's Communist conspiracy
  in Washington, 188–89; military
  expenditures, 182, 193–94, 200–
  201, 206; Munich syndrome, 5–6;
  national state of emergency

declared vs. Soviet threat, 199; on
NATO, 300; Navy Day speech, 95;
negotiation from strength concept,
214–15; on NSC 68 on Truman's
national defense policy, 184–87,
193, 206; nuclear weapons, 84–93,
136–37, 183, 199, 206; photographs
of, 79, 105, 117, 165; on Polish-
Soviet relations, 81; on postwar
peace treaties, 109; Potsdam, 78–
82, 86; on Soviet expansionism, 11,
14, 75–77, 93–96, 98, 132–33, 198–
200; on Stalin, 81–82, 100–101;
Truman Doctrine, 5–6, 117–21,
117f, 119–21, 136, 165, 474, 562
n.45; U.S.-Soviet relations at start
of term, 70–73; Vandenberg Resolution, 134
Tucker, Robert W., 422, 443, 455,
474
Tudeh Party, 110–11
Tulchin, Joseph S., 292, 295
Turchin, Valentin, 400
Turkey: Baghdad Pact, 245; Cyprus
crisis, 302–3, 372–75; Montreux
Convention, 47, 119; Munich
syndrome, 5–6; as NATO member,
245; postwar reconstruction
(WWII), 98; Soviet expansionism,
1–2, 97, 104–6, 111, 115–16, 115–
21, 143, 245; transportation routes,
115; U.S. bases in, 374; U.S.
financial and military assistance to,
118, 120, 372–74; U.S. Jupiter
missiles, 269, 270, 281; World
War II, 45–46
Turner, Stansfield, 426

Uganda, 421–22
Ugarte, Augusto Pinochet, 391
The Ukraine, 62, 504
Ulam, Adam B., 341
UN. See United Nations
Union of Polish Patriots, 534 n.47
United Arab Republic, 246
United Fruit Company, 243

United Nations (UN): Afghanistan,
456; arms control negotiations, 281;
arms embargo vs. South Africa,
456–57; on Atlantic Charter, 21;
China not recognized by, 204;
China's membership status, 200,
279, 356–57; creation of, 33, 55, 62,
73–74; Gorbachev's 1988 address
before, 485; Gromyko denied
landing rights by NJ and NY, 466;
Iranian crisis of March 1946, 104;
Korean War, 194, 197, 204, 239;
limitations of, 74; NATO created
to fulfill intentions of UN Charter,
135; Nicaragua, 475–76; on nuclear
weapons, 136–37, 308; Potsdam on,
80; Resolution 242 on the Six-Day
War (1967), 305, 368, 409, 411,
431; Roosevelt's proposal, 55–56;
San Francisco Conference, 73–74;
as successor to the Grand Alliance,
97; Suez crises, 245; U.S. blockade
vs. Cuba, 268–69; U.S. nonrecognition policy, 278–79; U.S.S.R.
attack on Hungary, 227–28; Viet-
nam as member, 405; Yalta
Conference on, 80
United States. See specific leaders,
events, policies, and regional issues by
name
United States Objectives and Courses
of Action with Respect to Southeast
Asia (NSC), 205–6
University of Chicago's Metallurgical
Laboratory, 85–86
Uruguay, 403
U.S. Arms Control and Disarmament
Agency, 258, 307
U.S. Democratic Party, 421
U.S. Department of Defense, 208
U.S. Department of State, 188–89,
204, 208, 396, 492
U.S. News on Hiroshima, 90
U.S. Office of Strategic Services
(OSS), 156, 157
U.S. Republican Party, 103–4, 388

U.S. Senate Internal Security
  Subcommittee, 199
U.S. Strategic Bombing Survey, 90
Ustinov, Dmitri, 433
U-2 American spy plane downed by
  U.S.S.R., 231

Valenti, Jack, 294
Vance, Cyrus: on Carter Doctrine,
  435; China policy, 406, 408; on
  European issues, 414, 415; on
  human rights, 398–99; Iran hostage
  crisis, 432; Middle East diplomacy,
  408–9, 413, 431; Moscow Olympics, 434; on nuclear weapons, 416–
  18; photograph, 394; on Soviet/
  Cuban involvement in Africa, 427–
  28; on Vietnam War, 416
Van Cleave, William, 422–23, 443,
  445
Vandenberg, Arthur H.: on Bevin's
  consolidation of Western Europe
  proposal, 131; on Chinese Civil
  War, 166, 170; on Europe's
  damaged economy, 125; on Greece
  and Turkey, 116; on Lend-Lease
  agreements, 99; on the Marshall
  Plan, 131; Paris Foreign Ministers
  Conference, 106; photograph, 165;
  on Polish-Soviet relations, 57; on
  Truman's anti-Soviet policies, 73,
  118, 120; on U.S. assistance to
  Britain, 106; Vandenberg Resolution, 134; verbal assault on the
  Kremlin, 103–4
Van Fleet, James, 238–39
Vann, John Paul, 324
Versailles Conference, 155
Vienna Summit, 262–64, 263f
Vietnam/Vietnam War, 313–41;
  Americans missing in action
  (MIAs), 405; antiwar movement,
  336, 339, 361–62; Ap Bac, 323–24;
  avoidance of defeat strategy, 332–
  33; Bao Dai government, 159–60,
  189–90; Camp David meeting, 331;
  Carter years, 404–5; casualties,
  333–34, 366; China's invasion of,
  408; Chinese and Soviet recognition of Democratic Republic of
  Vietnam, 189; costs of, 333, 596
  n.93; counterinsurgency program,
  321–23; coup vs. Diem, 324;
  criticism of, 335–37; détente, 372;
  Diem's behavior toward the
  Buddhists, 324; domino theory
  applied to, 11–13, 313, 318, 331–
  32, 335, 341, 381–82, 416; Dulles
  on internationalization of war, 240;
  Easter offensive, 364; Eisenhower
  years, 317–18; Elysee Agreements,
  159; end of, 367; Ford years, 378–
  82; France defeated by, 189, 320,
  322; Gulf of Tonkin, 326, 327;
  Hanoi's goals, 332; increased
  military spending, 307–8; independence granted to by Geneva
  Conference, 240–42; international
  opinion on, 595 n.87; Israeli refusal
  to support U.S. Vietnam policies,
  303; Johnson administration, 325–
  41; Johnson's advise to Kennedy,
  318–19; Johnson's Baltimore
  address, 332; Kennedy years, 313,
  317–25, 382; Lansdale's memorandum, 318; Laotian crisis, 314–17;
  Linebacker I, 364–65; Linebacker
  II, 365; McNaughton memorandum, 334–35; media criticism of,
  336–37; Munich syndrome, 11–13,
  335; Nixon years, 339, 340, 346,
  358–67, 378, 382; North on, 477;
  Operation Breakfast, 360; Operation Plan 34A, 325–26; pacification
  strategy, 334; Paris negotiations,
  338–41, 359, 362–63, 365; Pentagon Papers, 320; Reagan on,
  441–42; reports from foreign
  correspondents, 323–24; Tet
  Offensive, 337; UN membership,
  405; U.S. bombing of the North,
  327–29, 333, 337, 338, 339; U.S.

Mutual Defense Assistance
Agreement (1950) with, 204; U.S.
public opinion on, 333, 341;
Vietnamese political activity as
irrelevant to U.S. policy, 334; Viet
Nam Syndrome, 428, 438, 439,
441, 472–73; warnings ignored by
Kennedy and advisors, 322, 324–25;
White Paper, 329; the Wise Men,
337, 338f
Viguerie, Richard, 483
Vilna, Poland, 38, 40
Vinson, Carl, 182
Vinson, Fred M., 100
Vladivostok agreement, 384–85, 386f,
416–18
Vyshinski, Andrei, 41, 65, 71

Walesa, Lech, 463–64, 493–94
Wallace, Henry A., 76, 108, 120–21
Wall Street Journal, 63, 419, 437–38
Walsh, Edmund A., 199
Walters, Barbara, 380
Ward, Barbara, 580 n.53
Warnke, Paul C., 402, 414, 416, 417,
418, 424
Warsaw Pact, 222; Helskinki Final
Act, 385–87; London Declaration
on, 511; termination of, 496, 498,
508
Warsaw uprising, 41–42, 49
Washington Post, 63–64, 138, 182, 507
Washington summit (1973), 353
Washington summit (1987), 482–84
Washington summit (1990), 506–8,
511
Watergate scandal, 369, 370
Weapons of mass destruction
(WMD), 349, 415, 499, 508. *See also*
Nuclear weapons
Wedemeyer, Albert C., 161, 163
*Wehrmacht*at Stanlingrad, 30
Weinberger, Caspar W.: on
Afghanistan, 445; on Central
America, 452; on end of Cold War,
523; Iran-Contra affair, 477; on

Lebanon, 460; military expendi-
tures, 447; on nuclear weapons,
445, 467, 469–70, 480; photograph,
446; on Reykjavik Summit, 482;
Shultz vs., 458; on Yamal natural
gas pipeline, 461
Welles, Sumner, 73
Western Tripartite Declaration, 245
West Germany. *See* Germany
Westmoreland, William, 328, 329,
330–31, 333, 334, 336, 337
Wheeler, Earle, 304
Wherry, Kenneth, 167, 170
White House Years (Kissinger), 359
Whitney, Thomas P., 222
Will, George, 422, 432, 484–85, 523
Wilson, Woodrow, 55, 391
Winant, John G., 23, 52
WMD (weapons of mass destruction),
349, 415, 499, 508. *See also* Nuclear
weapons
Wolff, Karl, 69
Woodcock, Leonard, 405, 407
World Bank, 54
World Court, 475–76
World Jewish Congress, 410
A World Restored (Kissinger), 347
World War I, 19, 55, 98
World War II: Allied plans for
reconstitution of Versailles
following, 17–18, 19; Allied policy
of unconditional surrender, 19, 35,
52; Anglo-Soviet pact (1942), 31;
Balkan states as Axis power, 42;
Bern meeting, 70; closing days, 51–
52; death tolls, 13, 145; fall of Berlin, 70, 74; Hitler's invasion of the
Soviet Union, 20; Japan, 62, 82–93;
Maginot line, 484; Mediterranean
operations, 29; military aid provided to Soviet Union by Allies, 24–
25; Munich syndrome, 5–6, 10–12,
67, 117–18, 335; Nazi-Soviet Pact
of August 1939, 20, 49, 504; Normandy invasion, 35, 44; Operation
Bagration, 44; OVERLORD, 29,

34–35; Polish-Soviet relations during, 25–29, 33–34, 35–36, 37–40, 47–48, 56–57; second front, 17, 24–25, 44, 70; Sino-Soviet Treaty of Friendship and Alliance, 88; Soviet annexation of Baltic states, 20, 21–22, 27; Soviet motives and intentions during, 14–15; Soviet price of war, 145, 146; Soviet's heavy contribution and subsequent expansion of power, 48–49, 57–58, 65; Teheran Conference, 34–36, 38, 44; treaty negotiations, 79, 93–94, 106–7, 108–9; U.S. on expansionist ambitions of Axis powers, 18–19; Warsaw uprising, 41–42, 49; *Wehrmacht* at Stanlingrad, 30. *See also* Postwar reconstruction (WWII); the Grand Alliance

"X" article (Kennan), 128–30
Xuan Thuy, 338, 340, 361

Yalta Conference, 59–69; China, 86, 88; Declaration on Liberated Europe, 61; Dulles on, 212; Eisenhower on, 214; on Germany, 80; photograph, 60; Poland issue, 57, 59, 66–67, 68–69, 71–72; postwar dismemberment of Germany, 61; Potsdam vs., 80; purpose of, 59; Reagan on, 474; reparations, 61–62; Roosevelt on colonial rule, 156; on UN Charter, 73; Western reaction to, 63–64
Yamal natural gas pipeline, 460–62
Yarmolinsky, Adam, 267
Yeh, George, 237
Yeltsin, Boris, 504
Yemen, 302, 430
Yom Kippur War, 367, 383
Yost, Charles W., 189
Young, Andrew, 431
Young, Kenneth T., 317, 319
Yugoslavia: break with the Kremlin, 6, 142–43, 148, 149–50, 173; Chinese Titoism, 172–73; Communist forces in Greece aided by, 112; Communist Party, 415; Dulles on, 213; potential for postwar British-Soviet clash in, 43–44, 47; TOLSTOY meeting, 46; Trieste, 107, 108; World War II, 45, 57

Zaire, 427
Zhdanov, Andrei, 146–47
Zorin-McCloy agreement, 258
Zukov, Georgy, 44
Zumwalt, Elmo R., 438

About the Authors

NORMAN A. GRAEBNER, Randolph P. Compton Professor of History and Public Affairs, Emeritus, the University of Virginia and recipient of the University's highest honor, the Thomas Jefferson Award, is an internationally acknowledged authority on U.S. international affairs. He is a leading exponent of the realist school in the study of American diplomacy. Widely acclaimed as an outstanding speaker, Professor Graebner has received many high awards, including honorary degrees from more than a half-dozen other universities. He also was a Harold Vyvyan Harmsworth Professor of American History at Oxford University and a Thomas Jefferson Visiting Scholar at Downing College, Cambridge. Professor Graebner is the author, coauthor, or editor of more than thirty books and some 130 articles, essays, and book chapters. Included among his most influential works are *Empire on the Pacific: A Study in American Continental Expansion* (1955, 1983); *Ideas and Diplomacy: Readings in the Intellectual Tradition of American Foreign Policy*, with commentary (1964); *Foundations of American Foreign Policy: A Realist Appraisal from Franklin to McKinley* (1985); and *America as a World Power: A Realist Appraisal from Wilson to Reagan* (1984). He published his memoirs in 2002 titled *A Twentieth-Century Odyssey: Memoir of a Life in Academe*.

RICHARD DEAN BURNS is Professor Emeritus and former chair of the History Department at California State University, Los

Angeles. He has authored and edited more than a dozen books and two-dozen in-depth articles covering arms control, diplomatic history, international law, and American foreign policy. He most recently authored *The Evolution of Arms Control* (2009). A bibliographer, essayist, and editor, Burns has long been involved in preparing reference books such as the internationally recognized *A Guide to American Foreign Relations Since 1770* (1983) and the critically acclaimed twentieth-century presidential bibliography series. Dr. Burns designed and edited a three-volume *Encyclopedia of Arms Control and Disarmament* (1993) that also received two national awards; coedited the three-volume *Encyclopedia of American Foreign Policy*, second edition (2002); and edited a three-volume *Chronological History of United States Foreign Relations* (2002) and a *Cold War Chronology, 1917–1992* (2005).

JOSEPH M. SIRACUSA is Professor of International Diplomacy and Head of Global, Language, and Justice Studies at the Royal Melbourne Institute of Technology, where he is a specialist in nuclear politics and global security. A native of Chicago and longtime resident of Australia, he is internationally known for his writings on nuclear history, diplomacy, and presidential politics. He has worked with Merrill Lynch in Boston, the University of Queensland, and for three years served as senior visiting fellow in the Key Centre for Ethics, Law, Justice and Governance at Griffith University. Among his numerous books are *A History of United States Foreign Policy* (1980), with Julius W. Pratt and Vincent DeSantis; *Depression to Cold War: A History of America from Herbert Hoover to Ronald Reagan* (2002), with David G. Coleman; *Presidential Profiles: The Kennedy Years* (2004); *Real-World Nuclear Deterrence: The Making of International Strategy* (2006), with David G. Coleman; *Nuclear Weapons: A Very Short Introduction* (2008); and *Reagan, Bush, Gorbachev: Revisiting the End of the Cold War* (2008) with Norman A. Graebner and Richard Dean Burns.